the Rational Public

Fifty Years

of Trends

in Americans'

Policy

Preferences

Benjamin I. Page & Robert Y. Shapiro

☑ THE RATIONAL PUBLIC

AMERICAN POLITICS AND POLITICAL ECONOMY SERIES
Edited by Benjamin I. Page

Benjamin I. Page and
Robert Y. Shapiro

☑ THE RATIONAL PUBLIC
Fifty Years of Trends in
Americans' Policy Preferences

The University of Chicago Press
Chicago and London

BENJAMIN I. PAGE, who is the Gordon Scott Fulcher Professor of Decision Making at Northwestern University, has written several books, including *Who Gets What from Government*. ROBERT Y. SHAPIRO is associate professor of political science at Columbia University.

The University of Chicago Press gratefully acknowledges the assistance of the Gordon Scott Fulcher Fund for Research on Decision Making, Northwestern University, in the publication of this book.

The University of Chicago Press, Chicago 60637
The University of Chicago Press, Ltd., London
© *1992 by The University of Chicago*
All rights reserved. Published 1992
Printed in the United States of America
00 99 98 97 96 95 94 93 92   5 4 3 2 1

Library of Congress Cataloging-in-Publication Data

Page, Benjamin I.
  The rational public : fifty years of trends in Americans' policy preferences / Benjamin I. Page and Robert Y. Shapiro.
     p.   cm. — (American politics and political economy series)
  Includes bibliographical references and index.
  ISBN 0-226-64477-4 (cloth). — ISBN 0-226-64478-2 (pbk.)
  1. Public opinion—United States—History—20th century.
  I. Shapiro, Robert Y., 1953–   II. Title.   III. Series: American politics and political economy.
HN90.P8P34   1992
303.3'8'0973—dc20   91-15590
                                                           CIP

Contents

N 90
28
34
992
op. 2

Tables and Figures

Preface

☑ This book has two related objectives: first, to show that public opinion is "rational," in a specific sense of that term; and, second, to describe what kinds of government policies the American public favors in the early 1990s and how and why its preferences have changed over the years. Besides making a general argument, then, the book offers a concise but fairly thorough history of Americans' policy preferences from the 1930s to the beginning of the 1990s.

Both objectives are related to the authors' commitment to democracy: their conviction that ordinary citizens are not to be feared, that governments should respond to their wishes, and that the politically active should learn more about what the public wants.

The book is intended for a broad audience. The text and the graphs should be understood easily by anyone interested in the subject, whether citizen, student, policymaker, or scholar.

The main argument is that the collective policy preferences of the American public are predominantly *rational,* in the sense that they are *real*—not meaningless, random "nonattitudes"; that they are generally *stable,* seldom changing by large amounts and rarely fluctuating back and forth; that they form *coherent* and mutually consistent (not self-contradictory) patterns, involving meaningful distinctions; that these patterns *make sense* in terms of underlying values and available information; that, when collective policy preferences change, they almost always do so in *understandable* and, indeed, *predictable* ways, reacting in consistent fashion to international events and social and economic changes as reported by the mass media; and, finally, that opinion changes generally constitute *sensible* adjustments to the new conditions and new information that are communicated to the public.

In order to back up these sweeping claims we have gathered together an enormous amount of data, drawn from hundreds of opinion surveys of the American public that were conducted over a period of more than fifty years. Some of the data were found in obscure places and had barely seen the light of day; others are more familiar, at least to specialists.

Besides the unique comprehensiveness of this collection of data, what makes it unusual is the focus on *collective* policy preferences. We are interested in what proportion of the public favored a given policy at a particular moment, how that level of support related to opinion about other policies, and how and why it changed or remained the same over time. This contrasts with many survey researchers' focus on how and why the attitudes and actions of different individuals differ from each other. (To be sure, we do deal with group differences, especially in Chap. 7, but chiefly in order to understand trends in the collective preferences of the American citizenry as a whole.) We are more concerned with patterns and trends among the general public than with individual differences.

Some parts of our argument are supported by fairly simple quantitative data analyses. In Chapter 2, for example, we use aggregate data from about 1,000 repeated survey questions to show that most observed opinion changes have been small or insignificant and that fluctuations are quite rare. In Chapter 7 we tabulate similarities and differences in many opinion trends for population subgroups in order to demonstrate that they have mostly moved in parallel. Chapter 8 uses eighty cases in which survey questions were repeated at short intervals to show that what has been reported on network TV news has helped determine how public opinion has changed. At various points we report statistics on social and economic trends, occasionally using regression analyses to relate collective opinion changes to changes in society and the economy.

Much of our argument, however, requires evidence of a more qualitative and descriptive sort. In order to assess the coherence and consistency of collective public opinion, the extent to which clear distinctions are made and opinions fall into meaningful patterns related to underlying values, it is necessary to look closely at the public's preferences concerning a wide range of different policies. Beyond counting and correlating, we have to discuss what the patterns are and what they mean. This takes up a substantial part of this book, especially in the chapters concerning various specific aspects of foreign and domestic policy.

Moreover, in order to judge whether or not changes in collective opinion are understandable and sensible we have to put them into historical context. We need to look closely at opinion changes and figure out how they relate to international events, social and economic and demographic changes, and the like. This often requires historical investigation, with close attention to the precise dates of opinion surveys and to what was going on in the world at the time. (We also want to know about any divergences between what was happening and what the American public was told was happening.) Thus the policy-specific chapters include a lot of descriptive historical material.

In order to support our argument about the rational public, therefore, we were compelled to present a great deal of historical description of Americans' policy preferences and of the national and international events that shaped them. Once this was begun we decided to follow through with a reasonably complete history, as being valuable in itself even if some parts were less crucial than others to the rationality argument.

This means that we have ended up with a large book, not all of which will be essential to the needs of all readers. A few readers may find most of what they want in a single chapter: policy analysts, for example, may want to turn immediately to their areas of specialty, such as questions of economic regulation and social welfare (Chap. 4) or recent foreign policy issues (Chap. 6). Historians may care most about the description and interpretation of opinion trends in Chapters 3–6. Those most interested in our theoretical argument about the rational public may want to concentrate on Chapters 1, 2, 8, 9, and 10, skimming one or more of Chapters 3–6 in order to note some of the qualitative and quantitative evidence concerning specific areas of public policy. Some political psychologists and sociologists and others concerned with the behavior of individuals and social groups may want to look most closely at Chapters 1, 2, and 7. We hope, of course, that many readers will find the whole book valuable.

This book has been long in the making. We owe large debts to many institutions and individuals, not all of whom our fallible records and memories can recall; we ask indulgence from those inadvertently omitted.

First, we want to thank those who have conducted opinion surveys and helped make the results available for research. Many survey organizations, including NORC (University of Chicago), the University of Michigan's Survey Research Center, Gallup, Harris, Roper, and others are cited throughout the book. For helping us assemble data which these organizations originally collected, we thank the following data archives and their staffs: NORC, and especially its librarian, Patrick Bova, and Tom W. Smith and James Davis, codirectors of the General Social Survey; the Roper Center for Public Opinion Research (University of Connecticut), with assistance from Everett Ladd, William Gammell, Marilyn Potter, and Lois Timms-Ferrara; the Inter-university Consortium for Political and Social Research, University of Michigan; and the Louis Harris Data Center (Institute for Research in Social Science, University of North Carolina), with assistance from Diana McDuffee, the late Frank Munger, Jr., and Stanley Presser (Humphrey Taylor and David Neft at the Harris organization provided additional information about Harris surveys). Kathleen Frankovic at CBS News Surveys, Adam Clymer and Barbara Farah at the

New York Times, Douglas Schoen of Penn + Schoen Associates, and Market Opinion Research (Detroit) also provided data; Cambridge Reports, Inc., kindly permitted Shapiro to report a few of its past survey results in his earlier articles which we have used and cited here.

We owe particular thanks to the institutions that have housed our research operations and data: the political science departments at the University of Chicago (with special help from Lorraine Dwelle), the University of Texas at Austin, Northwestern University, and Columbia University; NORC, under its directors Kenneth Prewitt, Norman Bradburn, and Robert Michael, and with valuable administrative assistance from Julie Antelman, Alicia Evans, and Aurora Punzalen; and Columbia University's Center for the Social Sciences, under its directors Jonathan Cole and Harrison White, associate director Pnina Grinberg, and assistant director Walter Bourne.

We are grateful for research support from several organizations: from the National Science Foundation, for early help in assembling our survey data archive under grant no. SES-7912969 and for later assistance with the media impact research under NSF grant SES83-08767; the Social Science Research Council, with special help and encouragement from Robert Pearson; from the Frank C. Erwin Chair in Government at the University of Texas; the Columbia University Council for Research in Social Sciences and the faculty development program; the Spencer Foundation, through Columbia University Teachers College; the Ford Foundation Project on Social Welfare and the American Future; and the Gordon S. Fulcher Fund for Research on Decision Making, Northwestern University.

We are especially indebted to the large number of people who helped assemble the evidence for this book and provided intellectual advice and guidance, often well beyond the call of duty or friendship. We once again thank those who were cited in related articles—most notably in Page and Shapiro (1983) and Page, Shapiro, and Dempsey (1987)—who are not listed below.

John Gillroy, Glenn Dempsey, and Sasha Heid were major collaborators: John is a coauthor of Chapters 5 and 6, and for a period he helped oversee the survey archive at NORC; Glenn helped supervise and collaborated on the media research cited in Chapter 8; Sasha assembled much of the remaining data for this book and various articles before the archive was moved to Columbia.

In sorting and tabulating survey trend data and other evidence, we benefited from the capable assistance of Suzanne Klein, Michael Galati, Susan Karplus, Leah Knowlton, Jae Choi, Kathleen Bawn, Eric Schmaler, Susan Brooks, Joe Torres, Jeff Trapp, Charles Mull, John Treantaffelas,

John Kendzior, Paul Gronke, Ted Zang, Robert Rosenberg, Theodore Rueter, Marjorie Nicol, Mary Preston, Kurt Veith, and Daniel Gehn. In the course of collaborating on the data analysis for parts of this book and other projects with Shapiro at Columbia, ever-encouraging suggestions and commentary were provided by Harpreet Mahajan, Kelly Patterson, John Young, Steve Farkas, Sara Offenhartz, Lawrence Jacobs, Brigitte Nacos, Judith Russell, and Ted Tsekerides. We are indebted to Harpreet Mahajan and especially to Sara Offenhartz for their computer wizardry and their extensive help in doing statistical analyses and producing the many graphs so important to this book.

We profited from colleagues' comments at conferences and talks at many places around the country, including the University of California at Irvine, Stanford University, the Midwest Political Science Association, the American Association for Public Opinion Research, the American Political Science Association, the University of Chicago, Williams College, the Massachusetts Institute of Technology, and Harvard University.

Many colleagues have made valuable suggestions relevant to particular chapters or to the book as a whole. In an order roughly corresponding to the sequence of chapters and the chronology of contributions, they include, but are by no means limited to, the following:

(Chaps. 1, 2, and 10) Mathew McCubbins, Bernard Grofman, Peter Ordeshook, Mark Petracca, David Prindle, Donald Wittman, Tom Ferguson; Joseph Bessette, Jeffrey Tulis, Tom Schwartz, Gavan Duffy, Melvin Hinich, John Zaller, Tom W. Smith, Robert Erikson, Ira Katznelson, Kenneth Janda, Christopher Achen, Larry Bartels, Robert Axelrod, Dennis Chong, Henry Brady; Tom Graham, George Marcus, Benjamin Barber, Jane Mansbridge, Donald Kinder, Virginia Sapiro, Jennifer Hochschild, Richard Nelson, Demetrios Caraley, Ester Fuchs, Robert Jervis, Richard Briffault, Charles Cameron, Howard Schuman, Charles Sabel, Paul Peterson, Morris Fiorina, and Sidney Verba.

(Chaps. 3, 4, and 7) D. Garth Taylor, Tom W. Smith, Tom Ferguson, Dennis Chong, Jane Mansbridge, Charles Hamilton, Christopher Jencks, Fay L. Cook, Ester Fuchs, Demetrios Caraley, Hilary Silver, Paul Peterson, Sunita Parikh, Lawrence Bobo, Ethel Klein, and John Williams.

(Chaps. 5 and 6) Marjorie Nicol, Tom Ferguson, Peter Trubowitz, Eugene Wittkopf, Deborah Larson, Richard Sobel, Tom Graham, Bruce Russett, Daniel Chomsky, Robert Jervis, Jack Snyder, Brian D'Agostino, and Alvin Richman.

(Chaps. 8 and 9) Gavan Duffy, Lucig Danelian, D. Garth Taylor, Alexander Hicks, Murray Edelman, Charles Lindblom, Phillip Schrodt, David Fan, Michael Margolis, Gary Mauser, Ben Ginsberg, Lance Bennett, Herbert Gans, Ora Simcha-Fagan, Tom McCarthy, Todd Gitlin, Daniel Hallin, Michael MacKuen, Lutz Erbring, Jim Kuklinski, and Noam Chomsky, and Donald Saari.

We are also grateful for discussions with and ideas from Allen Barton, Richard Pious, Dennis Quinn, Eric Smith, Eleanor Singer, Michael Delli Carpini, Nathaniel Leff, Alan Westin, Lewis Edinger, Mildred Schwartz, Phil Davison, Al Gollin, Russell Neuman, Allan Silver, Thomas Cook, Darrell West, Jim Stimson, James Gibson, Kathryn Yatrakis, Judith Mack, Douglas Chalmers, Philip Oldenburg, Thomas Bernstein, Roger Hilsman, Steven Cohen, Harold Watts, and Alfred Stepan.

Some of our ideas can be traced back to Page's work with Richard Brody at Stanford University. More recently, we are also particularly grateful to Tom Ferguson, who made numerous suggestions about elite influences upon public opinion, and to Tom Graham, who insisted upon the autonomous force of public opinion and the importance of genuine party competition. Neither of us was fortunate enough to meet V. O. Key, Jr., but the spirit of his work was important in shaping ours.

Our deepest personal thanks go to our families, including helpers Eleanor, Tim, Alex, and Benjamin, and especially to Mary De Florio and Mary Page, who endured—for longer than they or we care to remember—all the absences, tensions, and travails inherent in such a project, and who supported us in many important ways.

Despite these many debts we are, of course, entirely responsible for the analyses, interpretations, and arguments in the book, some of which may provoke controversy.

Benjamin I. Page
Robert Y. Shapiro

Evanston and New York
December 1991

1 Rational Public Opinion

☑ We propose to show in this book that the American public, as a collectivity, holds a number of real, stable, and sensible opinions about public policy and that these opinions develop and change in a reasonable fashion, responding to changing circumstances and to new information. Our evidence comes from many hundreds of opinion surveys conducted between 1935 and 1990.

Our theme of a rational public flies in the face of a great deal of conventional wisdom and scholarly commentary. It is common to express skepticism about, even disdain for, the knowledge and the reasoning capacity of the public. We will argue that such skepticism and disdain are not well founded.

The most persuasive evidence that is usually brought forth to support a negative view of public opinion—namely, survey research findings concerning the political ignorance and inattentiveness of individual citizens and the changeability of their expressed policy preferences—does not actually speak to the question of public opinion as a whole. As will be shown here, *collective* public opinion has properties quite different from those of the opinions of individual citizens, taken one at a time.

It makes a great deal of difference to political theory and political life whether or not public opinion behaves in a rational fashion. According to a central strand of democratic theory, the policy preferences of ordinary citizens are supposed to form the foundation for government decision making.

The past several centuries of Western political thought and practice have brought increases in popular participation and political equality. The American political system, already founded on the principle of government by the consent of the governed, rapidly evolved toward a more democratic polity with a broader franchise, more direct election of officials, and closer communication between politicians and public. The Founders' wary republicanism gave way to Lincoln's government "of the people, by the people, and for the people," and to Woodrow Wilson's direct leadership of, and responsiveness to, public opinion. Now most

Americans take for granted that citizens' preferences should be the chief determinant of policy-making.

During the twentieth century, in fact, democratic ideals—if not always democratic practices—have swept much of the globe. In the 1980s a new wave of democratization began to transform Latin America, and there were powerful stirrings in China. At the end of that decade the people of Eastern Europe and the Soviet Union demanded (and, to an amazing extent, received) the right to vote in free elections. The "populistic" democratic ideal of directly representing the public's preferences, and weighting all citizens equally, has reached a high point of worldwide esteem.

There are reasons to believe that, in countries like the United States with open political competition, citizens' policy preferences have a substantial impact on what governments do. Some economics-style theorizing suggests that they are a major influence on policy-making (see, e.g., Downs 1957; O. Davis, Hinich, and Ordeshook 1970; Enelow and Hinich 1984; McKelvey and Ordeshook 1986). And some empirical evidence supports the idea. On issues salient enough to be included in national opinion surveys, public policy in the United States apparently corresponds to majority preferences about two-thirds of the time (A. Monroe 1979, 1983). Significant *changes* in the public's preferences are followed by congruent changes in policy also about two-thirds of the time (Page and Shapiro 1983). The liberalism or conservatism of citizens in the different states strongly affects whether states enact liberal or conservative policies (G. Wright, Erikson, and McIver 1987; Erikson, Wright, and McIver 1989). (For a review of studies concerning relationships between public opinion and policy, see Shapiro and Jacobs 1989.)

How can the powerful trend toward expanded participation in governance, and the widely accepted arguments that public opinion should and does influence policy, be reconciled with a picture of ordinary citizens as ignorant and capricious in their policy preferences? If the public is ill-informed or unreliable, it would seem foolish, even dangerous, for policy-makers to pay any attention to it. Are all the theories and practices in which citizens' policy preferences hold a high place inconsistent with the true nature of public opinion?

We think not. We reject the notion of the 1970s that deficiencies of the public may make democracies "ungovernable" (Crozier, Huntington, and Watanuki 1975) and the canard of the 1980s that the American people are incapable of grasping budgetary or other problems.

It is not our intention to argue that democracy works perfectly in America or to claim that the public is always right. In fact, public opinion is sometimes ignored, and we will show that it is also sometimes manipulated or deceived. Our point, instead, is that the public as a collective body is capable of holding sensible opinions and processing the information made available to it. The chief cure for the ills of American democracy is to be found not in less but in more democracy; not in thwarting the public's desires but in providing it with good political information and heeding its wishes.

The Uninformed Citizen

James Madison, Alexander Hamilton, and other founders of the national government feared the "passions" of the public and the "fluctuations," "violent movements," and "temporary errors and delusions" of opinion. It was for this reason that they devised a variety of hedges and limits around popular sovereignty. As Madison declared in Federalist Paper no. 63, arguing in favor of the proposed U.S. Senate:

> I shall not scruple to add that such an institution may sometimes be necessary as a defense to the people against their own temporary errors and delusions. . . . (T)here are particular moments in public affairs when the people, stimulated by some irregular passion, or some illicit advantage, or misled by the artful misrepresentations of interested men, may call for measures which they themselves will afterwards be the most ready to lament and condemn. (Hamilton, Madison, and Jay 1961 [1787–1788], p. 384; see also nos. 49, 62)

Or Hamilton in Federalist Paper no. 71, advocating an energetic and independent executive:

> The republican principle . . . does not require an unqualified complaisance to every sudden breeze of passion, or to every transient impulse which the people may receive from the arts of men, who flatter their prejudices to betray their interests. . . . (T)hey sometimes err. (Hamilton, et al. 1961 [1787–1788], p. 432. see also Federalist Paper no. 68; and Page and Shapiro 1989b)

With the success of the relatively populistic Jefferson and Jackson, American politicians began to shy away from such rhetoric, but some important thinkers continued to hold skeptical views of public opinion even as the political system became more democratic. In the mid-nineteenth century, the aristocratic observer Alexis de Tocqueville lamented the tendency of public majorities to tyrannize over minorities, and he deplored the conformist pressures of opinion (de Tocqueville 1945 [1835,

1840]; see also Noelle-Neumann 1979, 1984). (Toward the end of the nineteenth century, however, another eminent foreign visitor, Lord Bryce, declared public opinion to be the ultimate force behind American government and judged it to be "on the whole wholesome and upright"; he saw the tyranny of the majority as "no longer a blemish on the American system," if it had previously been [Bryce 1897, pp. 238, 343].)

Perhaps the most harsh modern critic of public opinion has been Walter Lippmann. Writing just after World War I, disillusioned with the unjust Versailles peace and the failure of the League of Nations and of Wilsonian progressivism (Steel 1980, pp. 171, 214–216), Lippmann blamed the American public. In *Public Opinion* (1965 [1922]), he asserted that objective reality differs sharply from the "pictures in our heads," which "often mislead(s) men in their dealings with the world outside" (p. 18). Many barriers limit peoples' access to the facts; they must rely upon culturally and personally grounded "stereotypes" to organize their thinking, but those stereotypes lead to blind spots and errors and contradictions. Lippmann quoted Sir Robert Peel on "that great compound of folly, weakness, prejudice, wrong feeling, right feeling, obstinacy and newspaper paragraphs which is called public opinion" (p. 127), and declared that only the use of vague, emotion-engaging symbols by hierarchical authorities produces a common will.

Shortly thereafter, in *The Phantom Public*, Lippmann went even further. He declared it a "false ideal" to imagine that the voters were "inherently competent" to direct public affairs. "If the voter cannot grasp the details of the problems of the day because he has not the time, the interest or the knowledge, he will not have a better public opinion because he is asked to express his opinion more often" (1925, pp. 20, 36–37).

Early Survey Evidence

Lippmann's work was not based on systematic data from opinion surveys (or any other systematic data, for that matter), but others' studies of individuals' beliefs and attitudes soon seemed to support his bleak assessment. After modern-day survey research got under way in the 1930s (for a history, see J. Converse 1987), scholars found many Americans to be ignorant of basic political facts, inattentive to and uninterested in politics, and apparently voting—if they troubled to do so at all—on the basis of rigid socioeconomic characteristics or habitual party attachments or ephemeral candidate images rather than reasoned deliberation about public policy. Some survey researchers ultimately concluded that (on certain issues, at least) policy preferences scarcely exist in the mass public: surveys elicit "nonattitudes" or doorstep opinions that fluctuate randomly and are based on the barest wisps of information.

In their 1940 Erie County election study, for example, Lazarsfeld, Berelson, and Gaudet (1968 [1944]) found that demographic characteristics and interpersonal influences were highly related to voting choices (especially highly in that election, as it turned out) and that most people made up their minds long before the election—findings that were taken, not necessarily correctly, to be inconsistent with well-informed, issue-oriented voting. The Columbia sociologists' 1948 Elmira study demonstrated that few citizens paid much attention to politics, even in a presidential campaign; that many people were confused about candidates' stands on such major issues as the Taft-Hartley Act (they were not helped, to be sure, by candidate Dewey's ambiguous position); and that demography and personal influences once again seemed more powerful than issues in voting decisions. People were seldom converted by new information during the campaign; instead, their predispositions were reactivated or reinforced (Berelson, Lazarsfeld, and McPhee 1954).

The University of Michigan scholars whose national surveys and social-psychological orientation came to dominate the study of citizen politics in the 1950s and 1960s painted a somewhat different, but no more attractive, picture of voters. Party loyalty replaced demographic characteristics and personal influences as the prime mover of political behavior; citizens continued to look poorly informed, and their policy preferences seemed only weakly related to voting decisions. A crucial chapter of *The American Voter* indicated that even on such important issues as government help with jobs, aid to education, or the stationing of American troops abroad, large proportions of the public did not know what the government was currently doing, where the opposing parties stood, or even what they themselves wanted the government to do (Campbell et al. 1960, chap. 8).

Panel studies—repeated interviews with the same individuals—cast still further doubt on the meaningfulness of ordinary citizens' policy opinions. In his influential article, "The Nature of Belief Systems in Mass Publics," Philip Converse (1964) reported that, when the same people were asked the same questions about public policy repeatedly (in 1956, 1958, and 1960), their answers varied from one survey to the next without predictable patterns. Converse said that the weak relationships between a respondent's answers at one time and those at another—especially on the issue of the government's role in electric power and housing—tended to fit a model in which significant proportions of people "offer meaningless opinions that vary randomly in direction during repeated trials over time" and respond to surveys "as though flipping a coin." Converse concluded that "large portions of an electorate do not have meaningful beliefs, even on issues that have formed the basis for intense controversy among elites for substantial periods of time" (pp. 243–245). He also found that well-organized liberal-conservative belief systems, common among political elites, were rare in the mass public.

The finding of instability in individuals' responses about public policy proved pivotal in cementing a bleak picture of public opinion. Discussing the same panel data a few years later, Converse (1970) coined the term "nonattitudes." He attributed the apparently random responses to people having "no real attitudes" on the matter in question but feeling obliged to give a response. Converse estimated that something less than 20% of the total sample had "real and stable" attitudes on the electric power and housing item (pp. 175–176). Later still, Converse and Markus (1979) found much the same sort of response instability in the 1972–1974–1976 National Election Studies (NES) panel surveys.

Some data on changes in individuals' responses from one survey to the next are given in table 1.1. People who favored or opposed public ownership of power and housing in 1956, for example, frequently switched their stands in 1958 and often did so again in 1960; only 24% of all respondents consistently answered "agree" or consistently answered "disagree" in all three surveys (60% avoided taking sides in at least one interview). On other issues, the amount of fluctuation was less but still substantial. Only 37% of all respondents took the same stand on school segregation in all three surveys, while 38% failed to offer an opinion at least once.

Substantial response instability can also be found in reinterviews of respondents after only a few weeks or months, as the 1984 preelection and postelection data in table 1.1 show. Nearly half (46%) of all respondents gave different answers to the job guarantee question when they were asked twice.

Several scholars have argued, however, that much of this response instability may have resulted from measurement error rather than actual fluctuations in citizen's opinions. Many imperfections and limitations of survey research—from errors in recording or keypunching responses to ambiguities in question wording, the artificiality of forced-choice answers, and pressures of the interviewing situation—could lead survey data to misrepresent what people really think and cause variations (perhaps random variations) in reported responses.

TABLE 1.1 Instability of Individuals' Expressed Preferences

A. Distribution of Responses to Questions Asked in the 1956–1960 Panel

			Power and Housing "The government should leave things like electric power and housing for private businessmen to handle." (%)	School Segregation "The government in Washington should stay out of the question whether white and colored children go to the same school." (%)
1956	1958	1960		
Agree	Agree	Agree	19	19
Inconsistent responses			16	25
Disagree	Disagree	Disagree	5	18
(Avoided taking sides in at least one interview)			60	38
Total cases			(1,130)	(1,130)

B. Preference Instability in Preelection and Postelection Responses

	Preelection Response, 1984		
Postelection Response, 1984	Government Should Guarantee Job and Good Standard of Living (%)	In Between/ No Opinion (%)	Government Should Let Each Person Get Ahead on His Own (%)
Government should guarantee job and good standard of living	*14*	9	4
In between/no opinion	8	*14*	7
Government should let each person get ahead on his own	6	12	*26*

Source: Survey Research Center 1956–1960 panel data; National Election Studies 1984 election data; Erikson, Luttberg, and Tedin 1988, pp. 45, 47.
Note: Cell entries represent percentage of the entire sample.

When these scholars have analyzed panel data using models explicitly allowing for measurement error, they have found indications that, on most issues, most Americans have "true" underlying attitudes that are quite stable, despite survey responses that vary with a random component (Achen 1975; Erikson 1979; Jackson 1979, 1983; Feldman 1990; see also Kinder and Sears 1985). Currently some promising theorizing and research suggests that longer questions, which contain opposing viewpoints or "frames," can reduce measurement error substantially (Zaller and Feldman 1988, 1989; Nelson and Kinder 1989).

This point about measurement error is very important for our own analysis, because it suggests that the typical citizen may have a number of real policy preferences, even though it may be hard to learn about them through one-shot survey questions. While it has proven very difficult to ascertain exactly how much response variability is attributable to measurement problems, and how much to true opinion changes or to the expression of ambivalence due to conflicting considerations (see Achen 1983; Zaller and Feldman 1988), it will be seen that several of these factors could lead to unstable responses by individuals even while the same surveys were accurately measuring real and stable *collective* public opinion.

During and after the 1960s, a number of researchers joined V. O. Key, Jr. (1966), in challenging various aspects of the early voting research and championing the position that ordinary Americans are "responsible" or "rational." They showed that citizens' perceptions of the policy stands of parties and candidates were considerably more clear and accurate when the stands themselves were more distinct: in the highly ideological presidential election of 1964, for example, as opposed to that of 1956, or in the primaries rather than the general election of 1968 (Pomper 1972; Page and Brody 1972; Page 1978). In elections with sharper contrasts between candidates, voters also seemed to pay more attention to issues when they cast their ballots, and to have more highly structured liberal-conservative belief systems (Nie, Verba, and Petrocik 1979).[1]

In addition, the use of more sophisticated analytical methods involving perceived issue distances between candidates and voters seemed to reveal more issue voting in general than had previously been discovered (Page and Jones 1979; though a somewhat differently specified model maintained the primacy of party affiliations: Markus and Converse 1979). Citizens were also found to take account of issues retrospectively, and party loyalty itself was shown to be partly issue based (Fiorina 1981). Even the once-maligned tendency of voters to focus on personal traits of candidates was reinterpreted as sensible, given the importance in the

United States of individual leaders—especially presidents (Popkin et al. 1976). Research in the 1980s upheld most of these findings (see Popkin 1991; also Aldrich, Sullivan, and Borgida 1989, who show that candidates even have to reckon with voters' opinions toward foreign affairs).

The research on voting did not always speak directly to the topic of this book—which does not concern voting behavior but rather *the nature of citizens' policy preferences*—but it was highly suggestive. It indicated that the more conflictual political environment of the 1964–1972 period, with Goldwater's conservative candidacy, the Vietnam War, racial unrest, and McGovern's distinctly liberal campaign—along, perhaps, with the expanded national and local television news coverage that made political information more accessible than before—had produced a more politically attuned American voter, more prone to use ideological labels, more attentive to politics. Or, more precisely, the stimuli of the 1960s and 1970s and 1980s revealed capacities for perception and choice that the voters had presumably had all along, but that were partly obscured by the blandness of the political environment and the indistinctness of alternatives. As V. O. Key, Jr., expressed it:

> The voice of the people is but an echo. The output of an echo
> chamber bears an inevitable and invariable relation to the
> input. . . . voters are not fools. . . . the electorate behaves about
> as rationally and responsibly as we should expect, given the
> clarity of the alternatives presented to it and the character of the
> information available to it. (1966, pp. 2, 7)

The Extent of Political Knowledge

Still, all this scholarly revisionism about capabilities of the citizens scarcely touched the well-established finding that most peoples' knowledge of politics is quite meager. Survey research has continued to confirm that Americans, who have a great deal of formal education by world standards, do not know very much about politics. Various surveys in the 1970s, for example, indicated that only 52% of American adults knew that there were two U.S. senators from their state; only 46% could name their representative in Congress; and only 30% knew that the term of a U.S. House member is two years. As few as 23% at one point knew which two nations were involved in the SALT talks (Strategic Arms Limitation Talks between the United States and the Soviet Union). Perhaps most striking of all, in 1964 only 38% knew that the Soviet Union was not a member of NATO, the alliance of Western European and North American countries directed against the Soviets (see table 1.2).

Similarly, in the summer of 1987, at the height of the Reagan

TABLE 1.2 Political Information among American Adults

Percentage(s)	Year(s) (Respectively)	Survey Organization(s)
94 know the capital city of the U.S.	1945	Gallup
92, 96 know the length of the president's term	1947, 1989	Gallup, SRLVCU
77, 89 know meaning of "veto" (presidential)	1947, 1989	Gallup, SRLVCU
79, 89, 79, 74 identified governor of home state	1945, 1973, 1987, 1989	Gallup, Harris, NORC-GSS, SRLVCU
82 identified countries occupying Germany	1950	Gallup
67, 79, 74 identified current vice-president	1952, 1978, 1989	Gallup, NORC, SRLVCU
74 know meaning of the term "wiretapping"	1969	Gallup
72 know Margaret Thatcher is head of state	1984	Roper
68 understand Nixon's Economic Plan	1971	Gallup
68 know President limited to two terms	1970	SRC
63, 69, 68 know which party has most members in U.S. House of Representatives	1947, 1978, 1989	Gallup, NORC, SRLVCU
63 know China to be Communist	1972	SRC
62 can explain United Nations organization	1951	Gallup
61, 55 understand Lindberg's views on WWII	1941	Gallup
56, 55 know which party has most members in U.S. Senate	1947, 1989	Gallup, SRLVCU
56 correctly identify term "fallout"	1961	Gallup
53 understand term "Fifth Column"	1940	Gallup
52, 43 identified Marshal Tito	1949, 1951	Gallup
52 know that there are two U.S. senators from each state	1978	NORC
51, 57 know what a business (economic) recession is	1947, 1989	Gallup, SRLVCU
51 know that Warren Burger is Supreme Court justice	1984	Roper
48 understand proposed national service law	1944	Gallup
47, 30 know term of U.S. House member is two years	1946, 1978	Gallup, NORC
41, 50 know what the Fifth Amendment is	1957, 1989	Gallup, SRLVCU
43 could describe SDI	1985	M&K
40 able to locate Iran	1951	Gallup

(*continued*)

TABLE 1.2 (Continued)

Percentage(s)	Year(s) (Respectively)	Survey Organization(s)
35 39, 25 identified both U.S. senators of home state	1945, 1973, 1989	Gallup, Harris, SRLVCU
38 know Russia is not a NATO member	1964	Gallup
38, 46, 37, 29 identified U.S. congressman from home district	1947, 1973, 1987, 1989	Gallup, Harris, NORC-GSS, SRLVCU
34 can name the current secretary of state	1978	NORC
31, 46 know first 10 amendments are the Bill of Rights	1954, 1989	Gallup, SRLVCU
31 identified head of local school system	1987	NORC-GSS
29 can explain Supreme Court's obscenity ruling	1973	Gallup
24 can explain First Amendment	1979	Gallup
23, 38 identified 2 nations involved in SALT	1979	CBS/NYT
15 can explain McCarran Act	1955	Gallup
12 identified Bretton Woods Plan	1945	Gallup

Source: Data compiled by the authors and taken from Erikson et al. (1988, p. 42), Graham (1988, p. 331), and Delli Carpini and Keeter (1991, table 1).
Note: M&K refers to Marttila & Kiley; SRLVCU refers to the Survey Research Laboratory, Virginia Commonwealth University; see Chapter 2 for a listing of the other survey organizations.

administration's Iran-Contra scandal—when Oliver North and John Poindexter and others had testified extensively in televised hearings—the ABC News/*Washington Post* poll found that barely half of the public (54% in August, not appreciably more than the 52% a few months earlier) knew that the United States was supporting the rebels rather than the government in Nicaragua. In July 1987, according to a CBS News/*New York Times* survey, only about one-third could correctly locate Nicaragua as being in Central or Latin America; another 21% said South America (see Morin 1987).

Moreover, in June 1987, only 8% of Americans could name the chief justice of the U.S. Supreme Court, William Rehnquist, and only 7% could name Alan Greenspan as being the replacement for Paul Volcker as chairman of the Federal Reserve Board. In contrast, 30% named media starlet Fawn Hall as Lt. Col. North's secretary (Morin 1987).

Nor does the available evidence indicate any great increase over the last forty years in the public's level of political knowledge, which may have increased or decreased a bit but remains low and largely unchanged

(Delli Carpini and Keeter 1991; S. Bennett 1989; Neuman 1986, pp. 14–17; E. Smith 1989; Graham 1988).

Such findings often startle those who encounter them for the first time. To the political cognoscente, these survey results seem to demonstrate abysmal public ignorance. Upon reflection, though, they do not really provide unequivocal grounds for holding the American citizenry in contempt.

Some of the political information questions in surveys amount to little more than trivia quizzes. Others put a heavy premium upon knowledge of numbers and proper names that are of questionable value to ordinary citizens. Does it really matter whether people can name political figures, so long as they can find or recognize their names when needed and know something about the main candidates on the ballot? How important was it to be able to identify SALT or NATO or other acronyms, so long as people knew the United States belonged to an anti-Soviet military alliance and had talked about arms control with the USSR? Is it really necessary to know the length of terms of office? Elections come when they come, regardless. Perhaps it was not essential in the 1980s for citizens to keep the confusing situations in El Salvador and Nicaragua straight, so long as they understood that the United States had been trying to overthrow a leftist government south of the border and to defend other governments against leftist insurgencies.

There would be more reason to be discouraged if it could be shown that the public failed to understand more critical matters; or that it acquired blatantly incorrect information when routinely offered the correct facts; or that the public had no capacity to learn over time as particular issues and political figures became more prominent and important. But this is not the case.

Familiarity with political matters is strongly related to the amount and duration of attention that particular issues and political figures receive in the mass media. Table 1.3 shows how the public's ability to distinguish official friend from foe in Nicaragua increased over time as the issue received more press attention. (Very likely a still larger percentage would have noted Reagan's support for the "Contras," had this term been used in the question.) Similarly, as table 1.2 indicated, there are noteworthy and explicable variations in knowledge across different issues.

The public gradually learns more and more about competitive political candidates for national office when their campaigns are publicized, as is shown in figure 1.1 (see Keeter and Zukin 1983; Bartels 1988). Early in the 1987–1988 electoral season, Democratic presidential candidate Michael Dukakis was unfamiliar to 70% of American voters; this shrank

TABLE 1.3 Change over Time in Public Knowledge about Which Side
the United States Was Supporting in Nicaragua, 1983–1987

	7/83 (%)	11/83 (%)	3/85 (%)	6/85 (%)	3/86 (%)	5/87 (%)	8/87 (%)
Rebels	29	26	37	46	59	52	54
Government	24	24	23	20	13	21	20
Neither	1	a	1	1	1	1	1
No opinion	47	50	39	34	27	26	24
(N)	(1,505)	(1,505)	(1,506)	(1,506)	(1,148)	(1,509)	(1,205)

Source: Sobel (1989, p. 120). ABC News/*Washington Post* surveys. Question: "Do you happen to know which side the U.S. is backing in Nicaragua, the rebels or the government?"
aLess than .5%.

almost to nothing (2%–8%, based on different samples) by election day. Vice-presidential candidates Lloyd Bentsen and Daniel Quayle were unknown to many people even after they were nominated, but they soon became familiar figures.

Furthermore, there is evidence that most Americans do grasp the essentials of major issues like nuclear weapons and arms control (Graham 1988), even if they do not know a lot of specific details.

Still, it is undeniable that most Americans are, at best, fuzzy about the details of government structure and policy. They do not know with

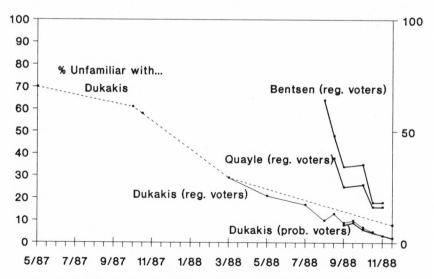

FIG. 1.1   Decline in percentage of public *unfamiliar* with new presidential and vice-presidential candidates, 1987–1988. See Appendix for further description of figures.

any precision how much money is being spent on the military, foreign aid, education, or food stamps. They have only a dim idea of what is going on in foreign countries or (in many cases) even where those countries are. They do not know much about monetary policy or economic regulation or labor relations or civil rights. Thus it would be unrealistic to expect the average American to hold well-worked-out, firmly based preferences about a wide range of public policies. Surely this is one reason that responses to survey questions often change from one interview to the next. And surely Lippmann was right to deride the myth of the omnicompetent citizen.

We take little comfort from the fact that this political ignorance is generally "rational" in the economist's sense of that term. As Anthony Downs (1957, chaps. 11–13) long ago pointed out, rational decision making (i.e., decision making that tries to maximize happiness or utility) leads ordinary citizens *not* to gather a great deal of political information. People have other things to do and to think about: work, family, friends, recreation. To gather and analyze political information is costly in time and foregone opportunities. It requires energy and thought and sometimes money. The benefits are not great; usually they are not worth much investment except by those who happen to enjoy watching the political fray. A single individual cannot hope to wield any appreciable influence through his or her vote, so there is not much point to studying hard in order to vote right. Widespread political ignorance, therefore, and attention only to whatever bits of information come easily to hand, follows from rational self-interested behavior.

Our own argument, however, does not stop with this rather weak assertion about individual rationality, which makes public ignorance seem natural and inevitable. Our claim is a very different one. While we grant the rational ignorance of most individuals,[2] and the possibility that their policy preferences are shallow and unstable, we maintain that public opinion as a *collective* phenomenon is nonetheless stable (though not immovable), meaningful, and indeed rational in a higher, if somewhat looser, sense: it is able to make distinctions; it is organized in coherent patterns; it is reasonable, based on the best available information; and it is adaptive to new information or changed circumstances, responding in similar ways to similar stimuli.[3] Moreover, while we grant that recorded responses of individuals to survey questions vary from one interview to another, we maintain that surveys accurately measure this stable, meaningful, and reasonable collective public opinion.

How is this possible? By what magic can it occur? The answer has to do with the statistical aggregation process, in which the expressed opinions of many individuals are summed or combined into a collective whole, and with social processes in which many people receive communications and think and talk with each other. These processes give collective public opinion and collective survey responses certain properties ("emergent" properties) that are not shared by the individual opinions and responses that make them up (see Schelling 1978). The simple process of adding together or averaging many individuals' survey responses, for example, tends to cancel out the distorting effects of random errors in the measurement of individuals' opinions. Similarly, statistical aggregation tends to eliminate the effects of real but effectively random (i.e., offsetting) opinion changes by individuals. And social processes involving division of labor and collective deliberation mean that collective opinion responds—more fully and attentively than most individuals can hope to do—to new events and new information and arguments.

In order to see how this can occur, it is necessary to examine the nature of individual and collective policy preferences and the relationship between them.

From Individual Ignorance to Collective Wisdom

A typical individual's policy preferences, it seems fair to assume, are neither perfectly informed and fixed nor totally uninformed and random. Instead, they are based on some fundamental needs and values that are relatively enduring (see Feldman 1988); on some uncertain beliefs concerning how public policies relate to those needs and values; and on some incomplete fragments of information that tend on the whole—though not, perhaps, with total consistency—to support those beliefs.

If this is so—if citizens' preferences are dependent upon uncertain beliefs, bolstered by incomplete bits of information—then new information or arguments that bear upon beliefs about policy alternatives can change people's policy preferences. (Mass media stories bearing on who is responsible for a problem, for example, may affect citizens' attributions of responsibility, thereby altering their preferences: see Iyengar 1991; Entman 1989; Krosnick and Kinder 1990.)

Thus pieces of new information, some enduring but some transient and quickly contradicted, may push an individual's preferences back and forth in a seemingly random fashion, so that he or she may give fluctuating survey responses of the sort that have been interpreted as revealing "nonattitudes." Similar fluctuations in expressed opinions can result if an individual is ambivalent about a given policy and entertains a set of conflicting considerations (Hochschild 1981), perhaps randomly choosing one, in "top of the head" fashion, under the pressure of the interview situation (Zaller and Feldman 1988). Shifting responses can also result from various sources of measurement error.

Yet it is also consistent with this picture that at any given moment an individual has real policy preferences, based on underlying needs and values and on the beliefs held at that moment. Furthermore, over a period of time, each individual has a central tendency of opinion, which might be called a "true" or *long-term preference*, and which can be ascertained by averaging the opinions expressed by the *same individual* at several different times. If the individual's opinions fluctuate randomly around the same central tendency for a sustained period of time, his or her true long-term preferences will be stable and ascertainable, despite observed momentary fluctuations in opinion.[4]

If this picture of individuals' opinions is correct, then at any given moment the public as a whole also has real *collective* policy preferences, as defined by any of various aggregation rules: majority-preferred policy choices (if such exist), or average positions on attitude scales, or proportions of the public choosing particular policy alternatives over others. (In this book we will be particularly concerned with what proportion of the public favors one policy or another.)

Moreover—and this is the key point—at any given moment, the random deviations of individuals from their long-term opinions may well cancel out over a large sample, so that a poll or survey can accurately measure collective preferences as defined in terms of the true or long-term preferences of many individual citizens. As a result, the measurement of collective public opinion is largely free of the random error associated with individual attitudes. Further, if the true (long-term) opinions of individuals remain fairly stable over a lengthy period of time—or if they change in offsetting ways—collective public opinion as measured by surveys will be stable, quite unlike the fluctuating individual opinions and responses that make it up.

More generally, if individuals' real opinions, or measurements of those opinions, are subject to *any* sort of random variation—whether from transient scraps of information that temporarily change beliefs and preferences, or from question ambiguity or interviewing mistakes or keypunch errors, or from "top of the head" sampling of conflicting considerations, or from mood swings, or any other factor that is independent from one citizen to another—then simple statistical reasoning indicates that those errors will tend to cancel each other out when the opinions of individuals are aggregated. Collective measurements—averages (means or medians), majority or plurality choices, marginal frequencies of responses—will tend accurately to reflect the "true" underlying or long-term opinions of the individuals.

That is to say, even if individual opinions or survey responses are ill-informed, shallow, and fluctuating, collective opinion can be real, highly stable, and, as we will see, based on all the available information; and it can be measured with considerable accuracy by standard survey techniques. *If* the available information is accurate and helpful (which depends upon the nature of a society's information system), collective opinion can even be wise.

These assertions about the stability and meaningfulness and measurability of collective public opinion are very general; they do not depend upon any particular theory of exactly how individuals form and change opinions, process information, or give survey responses. They are consistent with a wide variety of psychological and measurement theories.

Similarly, there are many ways in which individual (and collective) opinion could respond to new, policy-relevant information, which we see as a central aspect of collective rationality. It is possible—though we doubt it often happens—that individuals make elaborate cost-benefit calculations on their own each time new information is available. More likely, responsiveness to new information results from individuals using cognitive shortcuts or rules of thumb, such as reliance upon trusted delegates or reference figures (friends, interest groups, experts, political leaders) to do political reasoning for them and to provide guidance. If such cue givers are available and reliable, people may be able to form or adjust their opinions sensibly without elaborate instrumental calculations.

For the sake of illustration, let us consider individual and collective public opinion concerning a specific policy issue that arose during the early 1980s: namely, how many—if any—MX multiple-warhead nuclear missiles the United States should produce.

The MX Missile Example

The MX issue is just the sort of complicated technical matter, involving an obscure acronym, about which it would be foolish to expect many people to have detailed information or to hold carefully worked-out opinions. (In fact, at the beginning of 1983, when the policy debate was fairly far advanced, the Roper organization found that 55% of Americans admitted they knew "very little" about the MX; 31% claimed they knew "something"; and only 7% said "a lot.") Thus the MX would seem a prime suspect to be the object of "nonattitudes." If real, stable, measurable public opinion existed on this issue, presumably it could exist on almost any issue.

Many complicated matters were relevant to judgments about the MX: estimates of its dollar cost (including possible overruns), its range and accuracy, the cost and feasibility of various basing modes, the environmental impact of rail or "racetrack" basing, whether deep burrowing or ground mobility or airplane launching would work, how vulnerable existing silos would be if hardened, and the like. Other factors included the current strength of U.S. strategic forces, assessments of Soviet strength and intentions, and general beliefs or theories about arms races and strategic deterrence. Would MX deployment signal a drive for first strike capability, encouraging the Soviets to attack preemptively? Would such a new weapon system serve as a "bargaining chip" for negotiated disarmament, or would it just provoke faster armament?

It would be pure fantasy to imagine that the average American had carefully worked out what he or she thought about all this. Yet ordinary citizens had some useful materials to work with in forming opinions about the MX, starting with basic values and beliefs related to international peace and security issues (including whether the United States or the USSR was "ahead" in strategic weaponry, and how much of a threat the Soviets posed), and related to domestic problems that were competing for scarce budgetary resources. Moreover, members of the public could, without a great deal of effort, obtain many cues about the MX from more or less trusted sources. President Reagan, a popular leader, repeatedly supported the missile (which he called the "Peacekeeper") as necessary to deterrence and useful for negotiating arms reductions. Several leading congressional Democrats opposed the MX as expensive and destabilizing. Scientists and defense officials and politicians (including some Westerners who did not want mobile missiles running around large areas of their states) debated basing modes. The Scowcroft Commission, while laying groundwork for the less vulnerable "Midgetman" missile, backed the MX as strategically desirable and asserted that the hardened silo-basing mode would work. The TV news featured experts debating production costs and the likely effects on deterrence and the arms race.

Our point is not that everyone followed all this with avid attention; of course not. But many people were exposed to bits and pieces of expertise and advocacy. A rational citizen could use these scraps of readily available information to form a tentative opinion about the missile. When a survey interviewer came to the door, the respondent could offer that tentative opinion, as 42% did in November 1981, when NBC asked whether or not the MX should be deployed. Or, if uncertainty remained too great, he or she could say "don't know" or "no opinion," as 58% did at that early date. It follows from our argument that even "don't know" or "no opinion" responses—responses that were exceptionally frequent in this case—need not indicate total lack of opinion; they can instead signify a sensible lack of certainty about which alternative to pick, and are sometimes given by highly educated and well-informed respondents (Brady and Ansolabehere 1989; Tom Smith 1982a).

Some of the information and cues that individuals received about the MX probably tended to push their opinions back and forth from one day to another: news stories about wasteful military spending (outlandishly expensive Air Force coffee makers and toilet seats were featured in the media); films on the horrors of nuclear war; reports of Soviet blustering or aggressiveness; comments by Reagan, congressional Democrats, or others mentioned above. Given the complexities and uncertainties of the issue, it is easy to see how an individual's opinion might have fluctuated back and forth, in "nonattitude" fashion, depending upon the most recent input of information.

Yet it is also easy to see how an individual could develop a central tendency of opinion, or long-term policy preference, either based upon accumulated specific beliefs about the MX or deferring to the judgment of others—like the Republican president, or trusted Democratic leaders, or a TV commentator. And if the individual's day-to-day views fluctuated randomly around this central tendency, then repeated survey questions could be used to measure it. There would be random changes from one interview to the next, but over a series of interviews the individual's average response would tend to approximate his or her true long-term opinion. One could compute the average response and calculate a confidence interval around it based on the variance in responses.

This phenomenon is illustrated in figure 1.2. A hypothetical individual's expressions of opinion at various times about how many missiles to produce are shown as distributed according to a more or less normal curve. This hypothetical person (in hypothetical repeated surveys) sometimes favored very few missiles, and sometimes a substantial number, but the responses clustered fairly closely and symmetrically around a point in the range of approximately twenty missiles: just enough (he or she may have thought) to demonstrate U.S. capability and to provide a bargaining chip, but not enough to be immensely costly or to upset the stability of deterrence. If this individual's responses to repeated surveys were averaged,

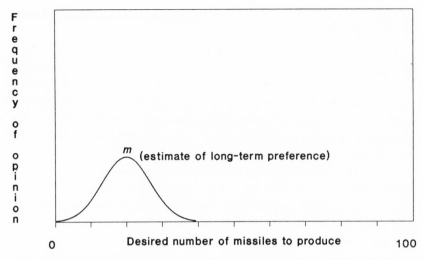

FIG. 1.2   Distribution over time of a hypothetical individual's opinions about production of the MX nuclear missile.

the average would tend to produce a fairly reliable estimate of the individual's long-term preference—namely, favoring production of some twenty or twenty-five missiles.[5]

The idea is not that all Americans held opinions like those shown in figure 1.2. Most individuals' response distributions concerning the MX were probably less smoothly shaped and more widely dispersed, and some people were too uncertain to venture answers, but the same scattering of responses around a long-term central tendency would probably occur for all individuals offering answers.

For our purposes, however, the most important implication is that the logic of averaging out random fluctuations in order to find a stable central tendency applies even better to *collective* than to individual opinion. It might be intrusive and impractical to interview one citizen a dozen or more times in order to get an accurate estimate of his or her true long-term preferences; and who cares, anyhow? But it is commonplace to interview some 1,500 Americans at about the same time by means of a sample survey. So long as the measurement errors in different individuals' opinions are not systematically related to each other, such a survey can produce a highly reliable estimate of collective preferences, as of the moment of interviewing. And so long as the bits of information temporarily affecting different individuals at the time of their interviews are also random, then these will also be reliable estimates of stable *long-term collective preferences:* col-

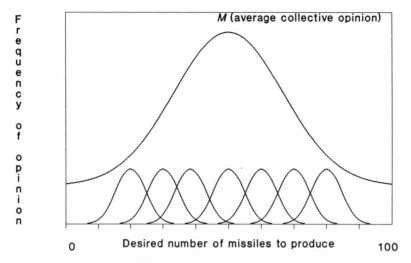

FIG. 1.3   Hypothetical distribution of collective public opinion on production of the MX nuclear missile.

lective preferences as defined in terms of the individual's long-term preferences.

Figure 1.3 illustrates this point with a hypothetical distribution of several individuals' opinions concerning how many MX missiles should be produced. Each individual has a distribution of tentative, changing responses around his or her stable long-term preference, just as in figure 1.2. The central tendencies of different individuals' responses, in turn, form a frequency distribution which is shown in the figure as a larger, higher curve. Long-term collective public opinion can be characterized by an aggregation (an average, say) of the individuals' true long-term preferences. In figure 1.3, the average long-term most preferred policy—represented by point "M"—is for about fifty missiles to be produced. This would closely correspond to the average response in a large survey.

Thus the accurate measurement of real and stable collective public opinion involves no magic tricks, just a simple application of the law of large numbers. (See Feller 1950, on laws of large numbers and related limit theorems.) At any given moment, everyone's survey response may differ from his or her long-term preference. But if the differences are random, and if many people are sampled, then it is possible to get good estimates of the true distribution of long-term public opinion by aggregating the measured individual opinions of the moment into averages or (more typically) into percentages giving each different response. The more people are surveyed, and the more tightly each individual's own (hypothetical) variable responses cluster around their central tendency, the more accurately we can ascertain the state of public opinion. On a relatively important and familiar issue, with carefully worded questions, the usual national survey of 1,500 or so respondents can reveal the true state of collective policy preferences quite closely, with a small (and knowable) degree of error.[6]

It may surprise the reader (as, in fact, it surprised us) to learn that the rather skimpy available data concerning opinions about the MX actually tend to fit the theoretical picture we have sketched. Despite the complexity and relatively low visibility of the issue, and the frequent "don't know" responses and admissions of ignorance, the data suggest that collective public opinion concerning the MX was real, measurable, stable, and (given the information that was made available) rather reasonable. Moreover, it seems to have adjusted to new information.

In the November 1981 NBC survey that had 58% "no opinion" responses, for example, 55% of those who expressed opinions said they favored "President Reagan's plans to deploy MX missiles"; 45% opposed. In the Roper survey conducted in January 1983, where many admitted knowing very little about the MX, those who offered opinions arrayed themselves along a continuum of support: 14% of them favored going ahead as Reagan wanted and basing MXs in hardened silos—the "Dense Pack" mode; 59% thought Congress was right to hold up the MX until a better basing system could be ("is") found; and 27% felt the United States should not make the MX at all. (Roper reported that the same general patterns of attitudes existed among people with all three different stated levels of knowledge.)

The apparent shift in the center of gravity of collective opinion between these two surveys is of interest. In 1981, when the Reagan administration was warning of a "window of vulnerability" and pushing hard for its military buildup, a plurality of Americans backed the president on the MX; but two years of debate and congressional action seem to have made a significant difference. In 1983 a large plurality favored the slowdown to reconsider basing modes. (Indeed, as we saw, more people [27%] wanted no MX at all than [14%] backed the president's Dense Pack plan.) We hesitate to infer anything definite about opinion change from these quite different survey questions, but they do suggest that a shift may have occurred.

Equally interesting, however, is the *stability* of collective public opinion after the early 1983 Roper survey. In June 1984, when Harris asked whether people favored or opposed various bills that had been passed by the House of Representatives with Speaker O'Neill taking a leadership posi-

TABLE 1.4 Collective Opinion Stability on the MX Missile Issue, 1985

"Recently, President Reagan has had some serious disagreements with Congress. Now who do you think was more right—Reagan or Congress—in their differences over . . . cutting back on the MX missile, which is favored by Congress and opposed by Reagan?"

	5–6/85 (%)	7/85 (%)
Reagan	41	41
Congress	59	59

Source: Harris surveys. "Not sure" responses (omitted in this table for clarity about the balance of opinion among those with opinions) were 7% in the first survey and 6% in the second. "Both" or "neither" responses were less than .5% each time.

tion, 64% of those with opinions said they favored delaying the spending of funds for the future development of MX missiles until April 1985. In May to June 1985, a very similar 59% of those with opinions said Congress was "more right" than President Reagan in cutting back on the MX missile. Most striking is the finding displayed in table 1.4: in July 1985, responding to the identical (May/June) Harris question, a virtually identical 59% again favored cutting back on the MX missile, as favored by Congress and opposed by President Reagan. This stability in collective public opinion is impressive.[7]

"Nonattitudes" Revisited

The MX example was deliberately chosen as an extreme case. If meaningful public opinion existed on such an issue, with its technical complexity, low levels of information, high uncertainty, and frequent "don't know" responses, then it very likely exists on simpler and more salient issues closer to everyday experience.

In fact, the very survey questions from the Michigan panel studies that are said to reveal "nonattitudes" among individual citizens give quite a different impression when we look at them for evidence about collective public opinion. In table 1.5 we return to the 1956–1960 issues of school segregation and the government role in electric power and housing, but this time we examine *collective* opinion: the proportions of the public (among those expressing opinions) that took one position or another in each survey. In each case the public's aggregate level of support—and even its degree of enthusiasm—for each policy remained remarkably stable over all three surveys in the four-year period. Even on the famous

Table 1.5 Stability of Collective Opinion on Various Issues

A. Distribution of Responses to Questions Asked in the 1956–1960 Panel

	1956 (%)	1958 (%)	1960 (%)
"The government should leave things like electric power and housing for private businessmen to handle":			
Agree strongly	43%	43%	47%
Agree	16	17	16
Not sure, it depends[a]	10	9	8
Disagree	11	11	9
Disagree strongly	21	20	20
(N)	(1,249)	(1,323)	(1,476)
"The government in Washington should stay out of the question of whether white and colored children should go to the same school":			
Agree strongly	40	40	38
Agree	9	9	7
Not sure, it depends[a]	7	6	8
Disagree	11	8	9
Disagree strongly	33	38	38
(N)	(1,550)	(1,625)	(1,672)

B. Preference Stability in Preelection and Postelection Responses

	1984 Preelection (%)	1984 Postelection (%)
1 Government should guarantee job and good standard of living	12	10
2	8	7
3	13	12
4	23	23
5	19	23
6	15	15
7 Government should let each person get ahead on his own	10	11
(N)[b]	(1,918)	(879)

Source: American National Election Studies, University of Michigan, Codebooks for 1956, 1958, and 1960 surveys; tabulations from 1984 American National Election Study data. We owe special thanks to Kelly Patterson for help in examining these and other panel data.

[a] This category was coded separately from "don't knows" and "no opinions," which together averaged approximately 500 cases for the power and housing question, and 200 for the school segregation item.

[b] The N's reported here exclude the "don't knows" and "not ascertained" responses (including those who "haven't thought much about this").

power and housing item, none of the observed changes were big enough to distinguish from chance variation due to the vagaries of sampling. The same striking stability is found, over the course of the 1984 election year, for each category of the seven-point item concerning whether the government should guarantee a good job and standard of living. In Chapter 2 we will see that this sort of stability is typical of collective public opinion.

To be sure, totally random, equiprobable responses by individuals could, in theory, produce stable patterns of collective opinion in successive surveys. If respondents flipped coins to decide between two policy alternatives, for example, about half of them would pick a given policy each time a survey was conducted. But the stability we have observed cannot be accounted for in this way. The actual response frequencies differ markedly from the levels that random equiprobable choice would yield: it is not the case that 50% favor each of two alternatives, 33% favor each of three, and so forth. (In the power and housing case, for example, about twice as many people agreed as disagreed with leaving things to private businessmen.) It will be shown in later chapters that aggregate survey responses to questions with two or three alternatives come in every imaginable frequency, not just 50% or 33%.

Moreover, we will see that the responses reveal coherent patterns across many related issues, and that (when they change) they generally reflect predictable and reasonable reactions to new information and changed circumstances. All these characteristics are inconsistent with purely random or artifactual responses. ("Response sets," for example, cannot account for the changes in response to identical items.)

The data in table 1.5 on the "electric power and housing" question are especially notable. Responses to this item have been offered as exhibit number one in the case for nonattitudes, since there was such a high degree of instability in the expressed opinions of individuals. (Much of this instability may reflect measurement error; the survey question jumbled together two substantially different issues and did not clearly delineate the policy alternatives.) Even in this case, however, where—as table 1.1 showed—many individuals' responses fluctuated back and forth during the four-year panel, collective public opinion stayed very much the same from one survey to the next. And collective opinion was not haphazard; it reflected Americans' predominant beliefs and values, particularly their support for private enterprise and limited government (see Chap. 4).

Thus there need be no conflict between the bleak survey findings about individuals and our much more benign view of collective public opinion. Even though individuals may often hold only weak and poorly informed opinions, subject to measurement error and random change due to new information, there can still exist a stable, meaningful public opinion based on the underlying central tendencies of individuals' opinions. And sample surveys eliciting the expressed opinions of many individuals at a given moment may quite accurately reveal what collective public opinion looks like. It is aggregate data from such surveys that we will discuss in the bulk of this book.

More than that, we will see that collective public opinion as measured in surveys tends to be based on, and responsive to, all available information. The idea, again, is that individuals, exposed to random bits of information, may err or be misled about an issue and may form policy preferences not well suited to their needs and values; but the public as a whole, so long as these errors are randomly distributed, will make use of all available information and choose the appropriate policies.

One way this can work is indicated by Condorcet jury theorems, which show that, if individuals have even a modest tendency to be correct, a collective decision by those individuals can have a very high likelihood of being right. More than two centuries ago, Condorcet demonstrated mathematically that if a number of individuals independently try to answer a question of fact, and if each has the same fairly good (better than fifty-fifty) chance of being correct, then a collective decision by majority vote will have a much higher probability of being correct. The jury as a collective body does much better than a single juror could do alone (Condorcet 1785; see Grofman and Owen 1986, esp. pp. 93–102). Nicholas Miller (1986) has applied similar reasoning to the analysis of public opinion and majority rule: if each citizen acts independently, with a reasonable chance of being correct about his or her true interests (defined as the preferences he our she would hold if completely informed), a majority vote or majority preference among many citizens will have a very high chance of correctly reflecting majority interests.

Of course, the conditions under which such theorems hold are not always met in the real world. Neither jurors nor members of the public really act independently of each other. (This can hurt, if they are swayed by plausible but false arguments from fellow citizens. On the other hand, personal interaction can help, if collective deliberation enables people to work together in sorting out the true from the false.) Also, much of the force of the Condorcet analysis depends upon what quality of information is available and how information is distributed. Just as juries can be moved by deceptive advocates or by perjured testimony, the public can be deceived by propaganda. We will have more to say about this subject. Still, this kind of analysis does point out a way in which collective public opinion can be wiser than the individual opinions that make it up (see Wittman 1989).

Can Surveys be Trusted?

The serious study of public opinion has to depend on opinion surveys. But can they be trusted? Our answer is *yes,* if they are used with care.

We have already seen that surveys can successfully measure collective public opinion in spite of random measurement errors or fluctuations in the responses of individuals. Such random errors, like the more familiar sampling errors, lower the reliability of measurements but do not bias them. Large, representative samples generally take care of the matter. Several other kinds of measurement issues, however, need to be addressed.

Unidimensionality

Our graphs of hypothetical opinions about MX missile production were artificial, and should not be taken to imply that we are making wild assumptions about the nature or measurement of policy preferences. The unidimensionality we tacitly assumed, for example, in dealing with an individual's average responses (the assumption that each individual favored an ideal number of missiles to produce and was less and less happy with each additional missile added to or subtracted from the ideal), was purely a convenience. In the remainder of this book we assume little or nothing about the structure of individuals' policy preferences, except in order to make sense of responses to seven-point scales (which do presume unidimensionality) and in alluding to the Arrow problem in connection with the discussion of democracy in Chapter 10. To a large extent we will be concerned with simple, dichotomous choice data—for example, percentages of the public that "favor" or "oppose" a particular policy alternative—which assume nothing at all about the full structure of preferences.

Cardinality

By the same token, the precise, cardinally measured policy alternatives in the MX example (the numbers of missiles desired), designed to permit estimation of mean (average) numbers of missiles preferred, are not typically asked about in survey questions. It is assumed, probably correctly, that most people would not be comfortable trying to specify exact numbers. But we do not need to estimate or compute averages. Most of the theoretical arguments we made about means apply just as well to *percentages* of choices among two or three broadly worded policy alternatives, the kind of data we will generally be dealing with.

Normality

Similarly, the neat normal distributions for hypothetical individuals in figures 1.2 and 1.3 were prompted by aesthetics, not necessity. Central tendencies—means and proportions—can be calculated for any shape of distribution, so we need not assume anything at all about how an individual's or the population's responses are distributed. Confidence levels are not terribly sensitive to distributional assumptions, either.

Separability

In order fully to interpret collective responses to survey questions, however, it *is* sometimes necessary to make certain assumptions about the interrelationships among different issues in people's minds. Relationships involving complementarity or substitutability of policies can enormously complicate the measurement of individuals' preferences. For example, a citizen might have wanted to cut MX missile production if and only if the money saved went for Trident submarine-launched missiles, or if and only if it went to antipoverty programs, but this would be very hard to find out. Survey researchers rarely try to do so. Thus it is usual to study one issue at a time, assuming separability of preferences or ceteris paribus logic or some similar justification for ignoring related issues. The best we can do is to use the available data, nearly all of which deal with a single issue at a time, and stay alert for any conspicuous signs of complementarity or substitutability or other interrelationships.

Sincerity

In order to make use of survey data to measure collective policy preferences, it is also necessary to assume that responses are honest and sincere, or at least not systematically dishonest. (Some proportion of flippant, nonserious responses need not be a problem, so long as they are scattered randomly across the population.) Fortunately, people do seem generally to give honest answers. Obvious exceptions, like reluctance to reveal personal use of cocaine to an interviewer, will seldom cause difficulty; we are more interested in less sensitive matters like preferred penalties for drug offenses. The strategic responses foreseen in some rational choice theories—according to which, for example, a respondent might offer an opinion more extreme than she or he really favored in order to move measured collective opinion closer to his own preference, hoping for vote-seeking politicians to enact policies accordingly—do not seem to be given with any frequency in surveys of the mass public, either because people haven't figured out how to give them or because they think it wrong to do so.

In any case, the study of *changes* in collective preferences using repetitions of identical questions (our central focus) should be largely immune to distortion from social desirability effects, strategic responses, or any other source of dishonesty, so long as those misrepresentations stay fairly constant over time.

Random Error

One measurement assumption that we have alluded to requires special attention here because we will discuss important situations in which it fails: namely, the idea that errors or temporary changes in different individuals' opinions are independent of each other. In a society with extensive communications media the same information may reach many people at once, so that temporary fluctuations can occur in collective as well as individual opinion. This will be of particular interest when we discuss the mass media and causes of collective opinion change, and it bears also upon the possibility of manipulating collective public opinion. We will note situations in which errors or changes are random and situations where they are not.

Question Wording

A related problem is that a poorly worded survey question, offering a one-sided dose of policy-relevant information (e.g., "Do you support President Reagan's policy of aiding the Nicaraguan Freedom Fighters in order to stop Communism in Central America?"), may deflect respondents from their long-term preferences and cause a temporary change in measured collective public opinion. This is one bothersome sort of "question wording effect"—a loose term that covers a multitude of sins along with the innocent observation that people tend to give different answers to different questions. Obviously, one must set aside or discount biased questions when one is trying to gauge *levels* of public support for particular policies (see Payne 1951; Schuman and Presser 1981). Also, small differences in question wording (e.g., "dealing with drug addiction" vs. promoting "drug rehabilitation") can change what policy is being asked about (Rasinski 1989).

Fortunately, decades of experience with survey research have enabled most pollsters to field well-designed, balanced questions, which continue to improve. In any case, however, concerns about question wording are largely irrelevant to our analysis of *changes* in collective preferences, since we use repetitions of identically worded questions. Observed changes in responses cannot be attributed to question wording that does not change (see Schuman and Scott 1989). (Effects of a more subtle sort, resulting from culturally defined changes in the meaning of identical words, must be watched for and noted, but they seldom cause much difficulty.) When we have compared levels of support for different policies, we have paid careful attention to question wordings, and where possible have relied on those with identical formats.

Context Effects

One potentially troubling problem is that responses to a given question may vary depending upon the context of other survey questions in which it is embedded (Schuman and Presser 1981). Respondents may tend to favor a lower level of military spending, for example, when they are thinking about domestic spending priorities than when they have just been asked about a series of foreign policy problems. Or they may be more willing to pay taxes after voicing support for various spending measures. Changes in the context of an identical question from one survey to the next could, therefore, lead to a change in responses. When we know about such changed contexts we can and do take them into account and alert the reader to them. With some surveys (e.g., those for which we have been unable to obtain full questionnaires), however, the context is difficult or impossible to ascertain; the best that can be said is that we have found very few anomalous or inexplicable opinion changes (beyond what might be expected due to sampling error) in examining responses to thousands of survey questions, so the problem is probably not very serious in our data.

Taking everything into account, we believe that the available survey data are generally reliable and appropriate for our purposes. We see survey research as a remarkably effective research tool, particularly in recent years when practitioners have been able to take advantage of long experience. Carefully worked out sampling schemes permit confident inferences abut the opinions of millions of Americans, based on interviews with a few hundreds of them. Modern instrument design and interviewing techniques, combining art and science, elicit meaningful responses. Aggregate results of the sort we are concerned with (percentages of respondents giving particular answers) tend to average out individual-level errors and fluctuations. And our focus on changes over time in responses to identical questions overcomes most of the usual travails associated with imperfect question wording.

Throughout the book we will deal with various problems related to opinion measurement as they come up, and we will make occasional caustic comments about particular survey questions or survey organizations. All in all, however, we believe that the survey data we will be using generally succeed in accurately measuring collective policy preferences, and especially in assessing the nature and extent of collective opinion change.

How Does Collective Opinion Change?

In the course of explaining how collective public opinion can be meaningful and measurable, we have also given reasons to expect it to be stable and have offered a few illustrations of its stability. But sometimes, of course, collective opinion does change—occasionally by a lot. Indeed, the extent, nature, and causes of changes in Americans' collective policy preferences are major subjects of this book.

Such changes can occur, as we will see, in a variety of ways (gradually or abruptly, temporarily or for the long term), and for a variety of reasons, depending upon how individuals' opinions—or the composition of the population—change, and how those changes cumulate. In later chapters we will explore what factors have actually caused U.S. public opinion to alter. Here we will simply outline some possible processes of change.

Gradual, long-term changes in public opinion can, of course, occur when individuals' opinions stay the same but the composition of the population changes. Members of older generations die and are succeeded by new generations with different characteristics and different experiences and perhaps different political needs, values, and beliefs. Birth and death rates may vary among ethnic, religious, economic, or other groups with distinctive opinions. Or young people in general may differ from the old people they replace, reflecting recent events and ideas that gave the new cohort distinct formative experiences. There may also be differential immigration or emigration of people with differing opinions.

More important, as we will see, collective opinion change also occurs when many individuals change opinions in the same direction at the same time. This can be gradual or sudden; it can follow from shared personal experiences or from shared information about events.

Gradual changes may occur, for example, when many individuals slowly undergo changes in experiences and life circumstances. The mix of occupations may alter (perhaps away from farming, then away from manufacturing and toward service industries); incomes may rise with economic growth or fall with recessions; people may move from the country to cities or suburbs; they may get more years of formal education; minority groups may work toward equal treatment; alternative life-styles may come and go, gain and lose currency. As a result, the needs and values, as well as the beliefs, of many citizens may change and bring about corresponding changes in policy preferences. Changes of this sort are especially important with respect to opinions concerning domestic policy.

Similarly, the political world may change in ways that alter the perceived costs and benefits of policy alternatives for many citizens at once. New technology may produce new possibilities or new problems. International trade and investment may prosper or decline or shift focus. Foreign countries may change economically, socially, or politically (with revolutions, new alliances, famines, economic expansion), creating problems or opportunities. Crises or wars may occur. Some of these events— especially those involving foreign policy—may be sudden, leading to abrupt changes in collective public opinion.

Some kinds of individually based opinion changes operate through individuals' personal experiences: their own upbringing, jobs, daily lives. But most matters that bear on foreign policy—and many domestic matters as well—are known to citizens only indirectly, through information received from the mass media.

When an individual has new experiences or receives a flow of news over a period of time, the various bits of new information do not always randomly counteract each other in the fashion we discussed earlier; instead, they may cumulate and alter the individual's beliefs in a systematic way that produces a real long-term change in policy preferences. To return to the MX missile example, an individual might—over a period of weeks or months or years—be exposed to many comments and news stories with a similar thrust. Various credible sources might argue, for example (as they did between 1981 and 1983), that the "window of vulnerability" was never going to open, after all; that the United States was plenty strong militarily but needed domestic programs; that the underground silos in which the MX missiles were to be based were vulnerable to a preemptive first strike and would therefore invite such an attack. As information of this sort accumulated, the individual might well change his or her beliefs about the missile's value and become less favorable toward producing it. If this individual were repeatedly interviewed by survey researchers, his or her answers about the missile might still vary, with an element of randomness due to the chance character of the latest inputs of information, but they would also show a shift in central tendency, signaling a genuine change in long-term opinion.

Sometimes the opinions of many individuals may undergo changes in offsetting directions, so that collective public opinion is not affected. But other times, many individuals receive the same new information at about the same time and change their beliefs and preferences in similar ways. Then collective public opinion changes accordingly.

Parallel opinion change by many individuals at once is especially likely in an advanced industrial society like that of the United States, in which the media of communications are pervasive and highly centralized. Each day's news, from various sources, is collected and disseminated across the country by the Associated Press and other wire services. Much the same events, statements, and actions are reported on television network news programs and in local newspapers throughout the nation. Sooner or later, directly or secondhand from friends and acquaintances, most Americans are exposed to the same news—at least the same big news. If a space shuttle explodes just after launch, millions of viewers see the disaster on TV. Or, if a presidential commission reports that underground missile silos are vulnerable and that smaller, mobile missiles would be superior, the word is echoed by reporters, commentators, and politicians, and it gets out to many Americans. If the Soviets propose a sweeping new arms control treaty, lots of people hear about it. In each of these latter cases, collective public opinion (about the MX missile between 1981 and 1983, for example), may well change.

The centralized nature of the information system has a number of important consequences. For one thing, some long-term opinion changes by individuals are likely to be aggregated into enduring collective opinion changes. We want to know how often this has happened, what has caused it, and for which policy issues it has occurred.

For another thing, public opinion can change temporarily, as a result of temporary opinion shifts by many individuals at the same time. A dramatic one-shot event can impress millions of people at once and cause a sudden blip in public opinion before it fades from memory or is counteracted by other information. A persuasive speech by a popular president (even a misleading speech) might have a significant effect before being contradicted by events or by opposition political leaders. Temporary changes in collective public opinion, as well as long-term changes, could therefore be picked up by sample surveys.

It is this possibility of temporary, short-term shifts in public opinion that might provide a modern basis for Madison's and Hamilton's concerns about "fluctuations," "violent movements," and "temporary errors and delusions" in opinion, in contradiction to our rationality argument. We will want to assess arguments about the capricious, whimsical, or misguided nature of public opinion by examining how frequently and how abruptly opinion does in fact change; how large and how long lasting the opinion changes are; and what causes them.

For a full assessment of the role of public opinion in democratic politics, the quality of information the public receives matters, too. It is important to judge, as best we can, whether the information that produces opinion changes is generally true or false, enlightening or misleading. We need to know whether the contents of the mass media do in fact have significant effects on public opinion, and, if so, what is the quality (and what are the sources) of what appears in the press and on TV. A centralized information system could suffer from biases or distortions in the information conveyed through the media: biases or distortions which might deflect public opinion away from what it would be if fully and accurately informed. Democracy has little meaning if public opinion is manipulated.

By the same token, however, centralized and pervasive media can make possible genuine collective deliberation, in which the public learns, discusses, listens to policy debates, and is educated. Experts, foundations, think tanks, commentators, and the media themselves might all play a part in deliberative processes, helping citizens understand how their needs and values bear upon public policy, and thus helping them form policy preferences intelligently. This could contribute to the rational character of collective public opinion.

The Plan of the Book

In the following chapters we analyze patterns, and especially trends, in the collective policy preferences of the American public over a period of fifty years or more, using a large collection of polls and surveys conducted between 1935 and 1990. We also examine various influences on public opinion, the quality of the information provided to the public, and implications for the working of democracy.

Chapter 2 concerns the extent of stability in collective public opinion and the size and frequency of opinion changes. It also discusses the *form* of changes, especially the frequency of abrupt shifts or fluctuations. This bears upon the question whether or not public opinion moves erratically and capriciously, and thus irrationally.

Chapters 3 and 4 deal in considerable detail with patterns and trends in opinion about domestic policies. We describe the major opinion changes that have occurred and indicate how they have related to underlying social and economic trends as well as to particular events and new information. Chapter 3 concerns social issues, including civil rights and racial equality; civil liberties; crime and law enforcement; women's rights; and matters of life-style. On several of these issues, public opinion moved gradually but strongly in a liberal direction during the 1950s and 1960s. It then leveled off and in some cases retraced a step or two in a conservative direction in the late 1970s and early 1980s, before stabilizing or resuming a liberal trend. In only a few but important cases did conservative movement continue.

In Chapter 4 we turn to domestic economic issues: social welfare policies (federal help with jobs, income assistance, education, medical care, housing, and the like); labor-management relations; economic regulation; energy; and the environment. Public opinion remained rather steady on most of these issues, except for shifts reflecting the current strength or weakness of the U.S. economy, or responding to unusual events. Coherent patterns of opinion, linked to Americans' basic beliefs and values, are of particular interest.

Chapters 5 and 6 concern foreign policy. They are organized according to historical periods, types of policy, and the specific countries or geographical areas to which policies applied. Chapter 5 begins with an overview of long-term trends in internationalist (as versus isolationist) attitudes. It then examines, in a chronological fashion, Americans' attitudes toward Hitler's Germany and World War II; the Soviet Union and related issues of the postwar and early Cold War years; the Korean War; and the United Nations and arms control.

Chapter 6 takes up the relatively quiet decade after the Korean War; subsequent changes in public opinion related to the new U.S. foreign policy activism of the 1960s (especially the Vietnam War); relations with China; conflicts in the Middle East; and the periods of détente, renewed tension with the USSR, and once again détente. Whereas the domestic policy chapters focus on how public opinion responded to gradual trends in U.S. society and the economy, the foreign policy chapters emphasize the role of international events—sometimes abrupt events—and the part played by the media-reported statements and actions of presidents and other opinion leaders.

Chapter 7 deals with opinion trends among particular subgroups in the population: that is, trends among Americans grouped according to age, sex, race, region of the country, educational level, income, and the like. It shows that (with certain important exceptions) opinions of different groups have tended to move in parallel, all going in the same direction at the same time.

Chapter 8 examines the causes of opinion change. It generalizes about the effects of societal trends and international events as described in Chapters 3–6, and goes on to show that the proximate cause of most opinion changes has been information transmitted through the mass media, particularly news and interpretations from certain credible sources.

Chapter 9 explores aspects of the quality of information that is conveyed to the public. It discusses ways in which public opinion is both educated and manipulated: how collective deliberation occurs, but certain kinds of misinformation tend to be provided to the public.

Finally, Chapter 10 summarizes and evaluates our evidence concerning the rationality of the general public: the extent to which collective public opinion is real, meaningful, and coherent, reflecting underlying values and beliefs; the extent to which it fluctuates or is stable; whether it changes capriciously or through reasonable and consistent responses to information and events. The chapter also appraises the place of public opinion in democratic policy-making.

2 The Myth of Capricious Change

☑ It is widely believed that the American public's policy preferences shift frequently, rapidly, and arbitrarily. This supposed capriciousness is sometimes invoked as an argument against unrestrained democracy: as a reason to limit the working of the popular will and to leave decision making to the wise and able.

Such antidemocratic views have an impressive pedigree. In the debate over ratification of the U.S. Constitution, for example, Federalist Paper no. 63 argued that a "select and stable" U.S. Senate would serve, like senates elsewhere, as "an anchor against popular fluctuations" and as a defense to the people against their own "temporary errors and delusions." Even the extensive American states, it said, were not immune to infection from "violent passions" (Hamilton et al. 1961, pp. 382, 384–385). James Madison objected, in Federalist Paper no. 49, to Jefferson's proposal that Virginia should allow for popular conventions to alter its constitution or correct breaches in it. Madison alluded to the "danger of disturbing the public tranquility by interesting too strongly the public passions" (p. 315).

Similarly, Hamilton in Federalist Paper no. 68 advocated indirect election of the president on the grounds that it would permit judicious deliberation, and not afford opportunity for "tumult and disorder" or "convulse the community with any extraordinary or violent movements." Separate assembly of the electors in the states where they were chosen would expose them much less to "heats and ferments" (p. 412). Hamilton also—in Federalist Paper no. 71, arguing for an energetic and independent executive—declared that the republican principle does not require an unqualified complaisance to every "sudden breeze of passion" or to every "transient impulse" of the public. The people sometimes err; it is the duty of the guardians of their interests to withstand any "temporary delusion" in order to given them time for more cool and sedate reflection (p. 432).

Thus one important element in the Founders' suspicion of public opinion was a belief that it was subject to rapid and extreme change. This notion has retained currency up to the present day, particularly with respect to foreign policy.

In the early Cold War years, Gabriel Almond (1960 [1950]) declared

37

that on questions of foreign policy Americans tend to react with "formless and plastic moods which undergo frequent alteration in response to changes in events"; even the reaction to crises is "a mood, a superficial and fluctuating response" (p. 53). In a chapter on "The Instability of Mood," Almond noted the hypothesis that

> foreign policy attitudes among most Americans lack intellectual structure and factual content. Such superficial psychic states are bound to be unstable since they are not anchored in a set of explicit value and means calculations or traditional compulsions. (p. 69)

Presenting data based on responses to Gallup's "most important problem" question, Almond maintained that under normal circumstances the American public tended to be indifferent to matters of foreign policy because of their remoteness from everyday interests and activities. He argued that only immediate threats break into the focus of attention, and that the moment the pressure is reduced there is a "swift withdrawal, like the snapping back of a strained elastic" (p. 76).

Almond referred to most Americans' "quite casual and external acquaintance with the facts of world affairs" (p. 81), giving some survey evidence. He went on, in a chapter on "Changes in the Foreign Policy Mood," to discuss rapid changes between 1945 and 1948 in expectations of a new war and postwar alterations in attitudes toward Russia, the United Nations, and nuclear weapons.

Almond's "mood theory" has not escaped criticism (see, most notably, Caspary 1970). Almond himself, in his revised (1960) introduction to the book, spoke of the "maturation" of mass opinion since 1948 and of a "real stabilization of foreign policy awareness and attention," a "real moderation in the fluctuation of American moods" (p. xxii). Yet the mood theory persists, in the form of a widespread scholarly and popular image of changeable, fickle public opinion. For example, it underlies the foreign policy "realist" view that public opinion is "a barrier to coherent efforts to promote the national interests that transcend the moods and passions of the moment" (Holsti 1987, p. 23; see also the literature reviews in Wittkopf 1990, and in Russett 1990).

Curiously, concrete evidence to support the image of volatile opinion—whether in Almond's early Cold War period or later—is quite scanty. Much of that image apparently reflects confusion about how to interpret survey data.

Some careless observers, noticing many three- or four-percentage-point differences between polls taken a few days or weeks apart, have jumped to the conclusion that public opinion frequently changes within short periods of time. But, of course, such small variations should be expected as a normal result of sampling error. When different samples of people are interviewed, small differences in the results do not necessarily indicate any real change at all in the opinions of the population.

A surprising number of opinion watchers, including respectable journalists, pollsters, and scholars, have made another elementary mistake: they have drawn inferences about opinion change from the public's answers at different times to different survey questions. But question wording matters. What may seem to be very slight shifts in wording (*"a* league of nations," versus *"the* League of Nations"; emphasis added) can alter people's interpretations of what a question means, and thereby alter their responses even while their opinions stay constant. This can lead to exaggerated impressions of opinion change (see Schuman and Presser 1981; Lipset 1976).

Roshco (1978) and Ted Smith and Hogan (1985, 1987) have noted how various conflicting "trends" of increasing or decreasing public support for the Panama Canal treaties in 1977–1978 were inferred from comparisons among many polls fielded by several different survey organizations. But few of the questions were actually repeated in the same form. Some differed markedly in wording and in the responses they elicited. The rather bald item, for example, featured in an early Opinion Research Corporation (ORC) study funded by a conservative group, which asked about "turning ownership and control of the Panama Canal over to the Republic of Panama," produced many more negative responses than did the Gallup and Harris survey questions specifying that the United States would retain defense and/or transit rights. After carefully examining the data, Roshco concluded that the apparent trends were probably artifacts of question wording; a *steady* ratio of about five to three Americans opposed the treaties throughout the period, although more support was found when respondents were specifically assured about the reservation of U.S. rights. In addition to emphasizing this substantial stability of opinion, Smith and Hogan blamed the press and pollsters for errors of interpretation and for deficiencies in reporting the actual survey questions and data.

The only safe way to identify opinion change, then, is to compare answers to *identical survey questions,* as we do in this book.[1]

A different—and somewhat more subtle—source of confusion about opinion volatility is a failure to distinguish between policy preferences and other kinds of public opinion. Most of the credible evidence of rapidly changing public opinion does not involve policy preferences at all. Rather it concerns beliefs or attitudes about objects that themselves change, or about which information alters rapidly.

Almond's most striking data on "mood" changes, for example, concerned sharp fluctuations in the percentages of Americans who, in Gallup surveys, mentioned a foreign policy issue as "the most important problem facing this country today." Almond reported (1960, p. 73) that the proportion mentioning foreign policy rose by an enormous forty percentage points between February and April 1948, and then dropped 23% between April and June of that year. (Hereafter, we will often use this convenient shorthand—"23%" for "twenty-three percentage points.") Likewise, it rose 32% between December 1946 and March 1947 and then fell 26% by September.

But the "most important problem" question measures salience or intensity or attention, not preference. Responses to it naturally jump around as dramatic events occur and as the media devote coverage to one issue and then another. To take Almond's example, the early postwar years were particularly eventful in American and world politics. The year 1947 brought the announcement of the Truman Doctrine, the Taft-Hartley Act, and the Marshall Plan; in 1948 came the Czechoslovakian coup, the Berlin blockade, and civil rights and other domestic issues that enlivened the presidential election year. In fact, Almond's 32% rise in foreign policy mentions during early 1947 came just after the March 12 Truman Doctrine speech that raised alarms about alleged Communist aggression in Greece and set a whole new course for U.S. foreign policy; the huge 40% jump in the spring of 1948 followed the Czech coup of February and the April 1 beginning of the Berlin blockade, which was seen as possibly sparking war with the USSR. After these cataclysmic events, it was certainly reasonable for more Americans to name foreign policy problems as "most important"; and, when these crises cooled down and other matters occupied the newspaper headlines, it is not surprising that fewer cited foreign affairs.[2]

Fluctuations in salience do not, however, necessarily imply anything about changes in policy preferences—which, as we will see, are quite stable. Indeed, Caspary (1970) has shown that during the very period that Almond studied, Americans' preferences for taking an "active part" in world affairs remained virtually constant, at a high level.

Similarly, images of volatile public opinion may arise from "fever charts" that track the popularity of presidents. Presidential popularity rises and falls markedly in response to events and to news reports about presidential performance (see, e.g., Mueller 1970; Brody and Page 1975; Kernell 1978; MacKuen 1983). But here, too, the attitudes in question concern a very changeable object: the president's "handling" of his job, which may be outstanding one week and abysmal the next. It is not surprising that people tend to alter their assessments of presidential performance after triumphs or disasters occur. Again, this need have little or nothing to do with changes in policy preferences.

Perhaps casual observers of public opinion have been led furthest astray by data concerning the standing of presidential candidates, based on popularity or "trial heat" polls conducted early in presidential election campaigns. These are notoriously volatile, especially during the primaries and caucuses before the major parties hold their national nominating conventions. In 1975 and 1976, Jimmy Carter rose quickly from having less than 1% support to become the leading candidate and eventually the Democratic nominee for president. Michael Dukakis did much the same thing in 1987 and 1988. Other candidates like Gary Hart in 1984 have come from nowhere, enjoyed a massive surge in popularity, and then trailed off or suddenly faded. Early front-runners like George Romney in 1968, Edmund Muskie in 1976, and Gary Hart in 1988 have dropped precipitously for various reasons (see Aldrich 1981; Bartels 1988; Shapiro et al. 1990a, 1990b).

The causes of this volatility are not hard to find. The average citizen starts an election year with very little knowledge of most nonincumbent candidates. Early polls reflect little more than the extent of name recognition, which (as we saw in the last chapter) can change quickly. New information—concerning a surprising primary victory, for example, or a scandal like Hart's amorous adventures, or a miscue like Romney's Vietnam "brainwashing" remark or Muskie's alleged tears—is interpreted and magnified in the media and broadcast to millions of people at once. In the absence of other information, such material can have an overwhelming effect upon judgments about the personal character and attractiveness of candidates.

Public policies, on the other hand, are ordinarily less subject to concentrated media attention. Even when the spotlight is on, they are inherently less subject to startling revelations. Policies, unlike candidates, don't weep or stumble or philander. Citizens probably also have an easier time linking long-debated policies—as opposed to previously unknown or vaguely known candidates—to general attitudes and stable beliefs about government. Consequently, new, discrepant information more often suddenly alters peoples' judgments of politicians' personalities and skills and styles than changes their assessments of the costs and benefits of alternative government policies.

Fluctuations in what Americans see as the "most important problem" or in the popularity of candidates or presidents, then, do not necessarily tell us anything, one way or the other, about the stability or instability of policy preferences.

Not much direct evidence has been produced concerning the stability of policy preferences themselves. Over the years, in fact, a number of students of public opinion have expressed skepticism about claims of capricious change and have observed that collective public opinion about policy is ordinarily quite stable (e.g., Key 1961; Erikson and Luttbeg 1973; A. Monroe 1975; Ladd 1983; Erikson, Luttbeg, and Tedin 1988; Sussman 1988). Even de Tocqueville (1945 [1835, 1840]) and Lippmann (1956), while criticizing public opinion on other grounds, characterized it as stable—as perhaps all too slow to change. According to Lippmann (p. 23), the public tends to say simply "No" to any change in course on momentous matters of war and peace, vetoing the judgments of informed and responsible officials. De Tocqueville (1945 [1835, 1840]) declared, "When once an opinion has spread over the country and struck root there, it would seem that no power on earth is strong enough to eradicate it" (2:271). But such judgments have been based on general impressions and distillations of experience rather than systematic data analysis, so that we cannot be sure whether or not they are correct.

There do exist some good collections and reports of trend data using identical survey questions: Cantril with Strunk 1951; J. Davis and Smith 1990; Tom Smith and Rich 1980; W. Miller, A. Miller, and Schneider 1980; W. Miller and Traugott 1989; Niemi, Mueller, and Smith 1989; "Poll Trends"—formerly "The Polls" and, much earlier, "The Quarterly Polls"—articles in *Public Opinion Quarterly; The Gallup Poll Monthly* (formerly *The Gallup Report* and the *Gallup Opinion Index*); the poll sections of *Public Opinion* magazine (no longer in publication—similar sections appear in *The American Enterprise* and in the Roper Center for Public Opinion Research's *The Public Perspective*); and various private and proprietary reports (e.g., the original sources for Cambridge Reports, Inc., 1985). But these are, individually, limited in scope—often to a single topic or a single survey organization—and they have not, to date, been fully used to assess the general extent of stability and change in policy preferences. (Important exceptions are Simon 1974; Mayer 1990; and, using mainly NORC-GSS data, J. Davis 1980, Tom Smith and Rich 1980, and Tom Smith 1982b, 1989.) Accordingly, we assembled our own comprehensive collection of data.[3]

Our Data

Over the course of ten years we have systematically gathered aggregate data ("marginal frequencies" of responses: i.e., the percentages of respondents giving various answers to survey questions) from many national surveys—in fact, from *all* published or otherwise available surveys of the American public's policy preferences that we could find, beginning with the first Gallup and Roper polls of 1935 and continuing into 1990.[4]

This collection includes data from many thousands of questions asked in many hundreds (into the thousands) of surveys conducted by prominent organizations like the American Institute of Public Opinion (AIPO or Gallup, founded by George Gallup); Louis Harris and Associates; the Survey Research Center/Center for Political Studies (SRC/CPS) at the University of Michigan, which conducts the American National Election Studies (NES), and which we will usually refer to as SRC/CPS; NORC (formerly the National Opinion Research Center) at the University of Chicago, which conducts the General Social Survey (NORC-GSS); Hadley Cantril's old Office of Public Opinion Research (OPOR) at Princeton; the Roper Organization, founded by Elmo Roper; the television networks and major newspapers (CBS News/*The New York Times*, ABC News/*The Washington Post*, NBC News/Associated Press, and the *Los Angeles Times, LAT*); TRENDEX, Inc. (for the General Electric Quarterly Index of Company Relations: see J. Black 1983); Yankelovich, Skelly, and White; Penn + Schoen Associates; Cambridge Reports, Inc. (CRI); and the Opinion Research Corporation (ORC). In addition, with help from a mail questionnaire sent to a broad list of survey organizations, market research firms, and members of the American Association for Public Opinion Research (AAPOR), we uncovered many polls done by smaller market research or political consultant firms (see Shapiro and Dempsey 1982).

We cannot hope to have found everything, but we believe we have gathered the largest and most comprehensive set of information about Americans' policy preferences ever assembled.[5]

Given our interest in opinion stability and change, it was essential to find questions that were asked more than once with identical wording. For this book we sorted through more than 10,000 policy preference questions, seeking those that were repeated in identical form. For the period of more than fifty years we found well over one thousand such questions,[6] covering a broad range of policies. Somewhat more than half concern domestic policy and somewhat less than half concern foreign policy. They deal with government spending, taxes, laws, regulations, court decisions, and officials' actions. They concern executive, legislative, and judicial policies at all levels of government—particularly policy at the national level, but also including many state and local issues. They touch upon all sorts of policy areas, ranging from nuclear weapons and military alliances and foreign aid for various countries, to spending on education and health and highways, to the rights of the accused, school desegregation, and abortion.

While these repeated questions do not represent a random sample of all policy issues or of all hypothetically possible survey questions—one can hardly imagine how such a sample could be drawn—they are extraordinarily diverse and are, in a broad sense, representative. And, of course, they constitute very nearly the universe of actual repeated questions. The data from these repeated survey questions (supplemented, upon occasion, by particularly illuminating one-shot surveys and by questions asked with slight and carefully noted wording variations) provide the main data for this book, much of which concerns the instances of statistically significant change in public opinion.

The present chapter draws upon a large subset of these data, for which we have been able to calculate precise measures of opinion stability and change: namely, data from 1,128 survey questions that were asked with identical wording at two or more time points by five survey organizations—NORC, Gallup, SRC/CPS, Harris, or OPOR. The 1,128 were assembled by sorting through more than 6,000 survey questions. They constitute a vast and fully representative majority of the repeated items in our entire collection to date. They, too, are quite diverse, addressing all types of policy activity by all levels and branches of government, covering a wide variety of foreign (38%) and domestic (62%) policy issues. They provide an exceptionally good opportunity to examine whether American public opinion about policy has in fact behaved in a volatile or capricious manner.[7]

Using this set of 1,128 repeated survey questions, we made several calculations. First, for each question we ascertained whether or not any statistically significant change in opinion occurred, taking a movement of six percentage points (excluding "don't know," "no opinion," or "not sure" responses)[8] to constitute a significant change. In most of our surveys, a 6% change is statistically significant at better than the .05 level. That is to say, there is less than one chance in twenty that the observed change in responses could have resulted from random sampling error when there was no real opinion change in the population. Thus a change from 61% to 67% of the public supporting federal aid to education would be counted as significant, but a change from 61% to 66% would not.[9]

Next, whenever significant changes occurred—whether only once, or more than once if a single question was repeated several times—we classified each as a separate *instance* of change, to be used as a unit of analysis for investigating the magnitude and rapidity of opinion changes that did occur.[10]

Finally, for a limited subset of 173 questions that were repeated often enough, we calculated whether or not opinion *fluctuated:* that is, whether or not it changed significantly back and forth within a short time.

The Stability of Collective Public Opinion

Our data reveal a remarkable degree of stability in Americans' collective policy preferences, clearly contradicting any claim of frequent changes or wild fluctuations in public opinion.

The most striking finding is that more than half—58%—of the 1,128 repeated policy questions showed no significant opinion change at all: that is, no change of 6% or more.[11] Domestic policy opinions (63% of them having no significant changes) were somewhat more stable than foreign policy opinions (51%), but it is interesting that even in the realm of foreign policy, the home of the "mood theory," half our repeated questions showed no significant opinion change (see table 2.1).[12] That is to say, on many issues, both domestic and foreign, Americans' collective opinions remained very nearly the same on survey questions that were repeated a number of months or years after they were first asked.

To be sure, this does not prove that opinion about those policies did not change while no surveys were in the field. But data on frequently repeated survey questions, discussed below, cast doubt on the likelihood of unobserved changes. And pollsters and scholars have incentives to find opinion changes so that they can write interesting columns and articles; hence available poll data are more likely to overstate than to understate the frequency of change.

Moreover, even most of the significant changes we found were not very large. When we examined all 556 significant changes in collective

TABLE 2.1 Frequency of Significant Changes in Collective Opinion on Repeated Policy Questions

	No Change		Change		Total Questions	
	%	(*N*)	%	(*N*)	%	(*N*)
All issues	58	(655)	42	(473)	100	(1,128)
Domestic policy	63	(440)	37	(263)	62	(703)
Foreign and defense policy	51	(215)	49	(210)	38	(425)

Note: Entries refer to the proportion of repeated survey questions upon which collective public opinion changed significantly (by 6 percentage points or more). Gamma = Yule's q = −.24; $p < .05$.

TABLE 2.2 Magnitude of Significant Changes in Collective Policy Preferences

	6%–7%		8%–9%		10%–14%		15%–19%		20%–29%		30%+		Total	
	%	(N)	%	(N)	%	(N)	%	(N)	%	(N)	%	(N)	%	(N)
All issues	22	(125)	21	(117)	29	(162)	14	(79)	10	(53)	4	(20)	100	(556)
Foreign and defense policy	21	(54)	22	(55)	28	(71)	15	(38)	12	(30)	3	(7)	46	(255)
Domestic policy	24	(71)	21	(62)	30	(91)	14	(41)	8	(23)	4	(13)	54	(301)

Note: Gamma = −.05 (n.s.).

preferences (which occurred in response to the 473 questions with one or more opinion changes), it became clear that many of these were rather modest. Nearly half of them (242, or 44%) were less than ten percentage points. Most of those involved changes of 6% or 7%—statistically significant but hardly startling (see table 2.2).

Contrary to what one might expect, foreign and defense opinion changes were not appreciably larger than domestic.[13] There were, however, some variations among specific types of foreign and domestic issues, as shown in the first column of table 2.3, below. Certain issues on which there have been sweeping, long-term opinion trends (China, communism, civil liberties, abortion, crime) or big events (Nixon and Watergate) naturally involved instances of change that were, on the average, larger.

Thus when we analyzed the public's responses to more than 1,000 policy preference questions, each repeated over fairly long time intervals, we found, for most of them, little or no change in public opinion. Often a question produced about the same answers when it was first asked as when it was asked again a year or two, or even several years, later.

It is worth repeating that foreign policy items did not differ much from domestic ones in this respect. As tables 2.1 and 2.2 make clear, significant opinion changes were only moderately more frequent on foreign than domestic policy, and the magnitude of those changes was not noticeably greater. The public's "moods," as reflected in policy preferences, apparently do not change on foreign policy much more frequently or by any greater amount than on domestic policy.

In order to illustrate the stability of collective public opinion (and to introduce the kind of graph that will be prominent throughout the book), we display in figure 2.1 the trend in responses to a survey question about whether or not the United States should take an "active part" in world affairs. This is the same general foreign policy issue examined in Caspary (1970), but we have included identical items from both Gallup and NORC and have excluded "don't know" and "no opinion" responses from the calculation of percentages. Every one of the eighteen times this question was asked between 1945 and 1956[14]—during the tumultuous early years of the Cold War—about 70%–80% of Americans with opinions said they wanted the United States to take an "active part" in world affairs. Such flat trend lines are not universal, but they are not uncommon, either, as we will see in later chapters.

One technical aspect of figure 2.1 should be pointed out. This graph, like all others in the book, leaves room on the vertical axis for the *full range* of proportions of the public that might take a particular stand—

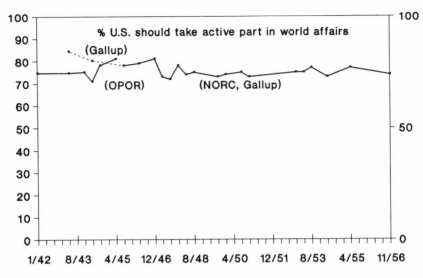

FIG. 2.1   Opinion stability: foreign policy activism, 1942–1956.

from 0% to 100%—even when all the actual proportions fall into a very small part of the range. Only in this way can we easily see the extent of stability or change in opinion, relative to the full possibilities of change that could have occurred. Only in this way, too, can we see at a glance— by the height of the line on the graph—how favorable or unfavorable public opinion was toward the policy.[15]

Odd as it may seem, few journalists or scholars have presented graphs in this way. Most graphs of public opinion in newspapers and magazines and books are displayed with chopped off tops, or chopped off bottoms, or both, so that only part of the 0%–100% range is shown. This has the advantage of not "wasting" blank space where no data points appear, but it has the much more serious disadvantage of conveying a misleading impression: an impression of more change than actually occurs. Even a 5% change in public opinion looks enormous on a graph that allows for a range of only ten percentage points, because the change takes up half the available space. Many published graphs magnify changes in this rather blatant fashion, presenting jagged lines that leap up and down as they run across the page but actually cover only small opinion changes that may have occurred over a relatively long period (see Tufte 1983 for an excellent discussion of various types of distortion in the visual display of data).

An uncharitable interpretation of the practice of chopping off graphs would be that it is a conscious or unconscious way to "lie with statis-

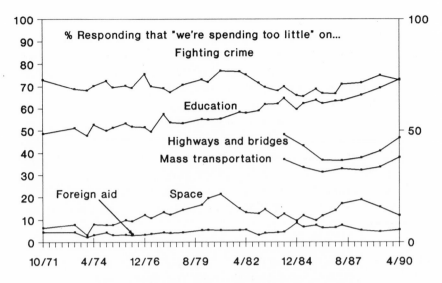

FIG. 2.2   Stable spending preferences, 1971–1990.

tics"—to convey, visually, a point the author wants to make that is not really supported by the quantitative data (see Huff 1954). Whatever the motivation, the effect is definitely misleading. This practice has undoubtedly contributed to the widespread impression that collective public opinion about policy is volatile. In this book we present only graphs that cover the full range of possible responses, in order to present an accurate picture of trends in collective public opinion.[16]

Further examples of opinion stability, concerning both domestic and foreign policy spending issues, are given in figure 2.2. In many surveys throughout the 1970s and 1980s, Roper and the NORC General Social Survey repeatedly found that about 65% to 75% of Americans with opinions thought that we were spending "too little" on "halting the rising crime rate"; only 4%–8% said "too much," and the rest said "about right." Similarly, a fairly steady (though slowly growing) 55%–65% of the public said we were spending "too little" on improving the nation's education system, while a small and declining 12%–3% said "too much." An equally stable but far lower 5% or so said "too little" was being spent on foreign aid, with a steady 70%–80% saying "too much."

Similar decades-long stability or gradual change of collective opinion is characteristic of most other Roper/NORC-GSS spending items with the very striking exception of the 1979–1980 jump and 1980–1981 reversal in desires for increased military spending, which we will examine in Chapter 6. Throughout the 1970s and 1980s, about 60%–70% said "too little" was being spent on "dealing with drug addiction"; 50%–70% said "too little" was spent on "improving and protecting the environment" (as we will see in Chap. 4, the figure dipped to the bottom of that range in 1980 and then recovered reaching 75% in 1990); and 55%–70% on improving and protecting the nation's health. By contrast, only 8%–20% said "too little" was being spent on space exploration (more said so in the 1980s than the 1970s), with fully 40%–60% saying "too much."

The persistently high levels of support for a wide range of social spending programs are especially noteworthy given the supposed "right turn" in public opinion in the late 1970s and early 1980s. They suggest that Reagan administration policy moved more in a conservative direction than ordinary Americans' opinions did (see Chap. 4, below; and Ferguson and Rogers 1986).

In addition, the sharp differentiation of the public's reactions to different programs that is apparent in figure 2.2 and related data—the very high support for spending on crime and drugs, for example, and nearly as high on education, the environment, and health, but very low support for space exploration and even lower for foreign aid—supports a central argument of the following chapters: that collective public opinion makes meaningful distinctions. It is hard to see how such big differences could be artifacts of the question format (which was kept identical across issues) or could result from purely random, equiprobable "doorstep opinions." The data indicate that people have genuinely different opinions about different government programs.

The finding of collective opinion stability is an important piece of evidence about the rationality of public opinion; it provides a fundamental background for the rest of our research. But stability is dull. Once this basic tendency has been established, there isn't a lot more to say about stability per se, except to provide periodic examples and reminders of it. Moreover, stability forms only one element in our overall conception of opinion rationality.

Much of our attention from here on, therefore, will be devoted to the more interesting topic of opinion change: when, how, and why, over a fifty-year period, Americans' policy preferences have altered, and how those changes fit our argument about the rational public.

Large Opinion Changes

To return to table 2.2 once again, our data indicate that very large opinion changes, of twenty percentage points or more, are quite uncommon. They constitute only 13% of our 556 instances of significant change. Changes of thirty percentage points or more constitute only a tiny

4%. Or, to put it another way, in the 1,128 cases of repeated items we examined—many of which were repeated several times over long periods, so that there were plenty of chances to detect opinion change—we found a total of only seventy-three cases in which opinion changed by more than twenty percentage points. In only twenty cases did opinion change by more than thirty percentage points. It is very hard to reconcile this with the notion that public opinion is labile or volatile or moves violently.

At the same time, however, the large opinion changes—while few in number—have had great political importance. Some of them signaled extraordinary transformations of American politics. For that reason, even though they are atypical, they deserve close attention in later chapters and a brief mention here.

In domestic affairs, for example, there were large increases from the 1950s to the 1970s in support of civil liberties for Communists, Socialists, and atheists. Opinion also became much more favorable toward abortion, interracial marriage, desegration of housing, and desegregation of schools. It moved against—and later for—capital punishment. After the 1960s, large numbers of Americans turned toward favoring greater strictness by the criminal courts, and during the unraveling of the Watergate scandal there was a strong swing toward favoring the impeachment of President Nixon. Less familiar large changes include a twenty-eight percentage point drop between 1942 and 1977 in support for the idea of national identification cards, and a steep (32%) increase between 1949 and 1974 in approval for employing epileptics.

One of the most impressive opinion changes we have encountered (though it is not included in any of our tabulations because it does not explicitly concern public policy) is the remarkable forty-eight percentage point increase that Gallup found between 1938 and 1975 (NORC-GSS tracked further changes) in public approval "of a married woman earning money in business or industry if she has a husband capable of supporting her" (see Chap. 3).

Most of these large opinion changes came very gradually, as part of glacial movements in Americans' beliefs and life circumstances. They certainly do not constitute evidence of capricious changes in public opinion.

With respect to foreign policy, there have been substantial changes in preferences concerning defense spending, size of the army and navy, stationing troops abroad, and giving military aid. Feelings about postwar policy toward Germany became markedly more harsh in the course of World War II. Attitudes toward China and the Soviet Union mellowed considerably during and after the 1950s. There were greatly increased desires for de-escalation as the wars in Korea and Vietnam dragged on. Support for the SALT II treaty dropped markedly during the ratification debate. Support for increased military spending jumped up temporarily at the close of the 1970s and fell again in the early 1980s. One of the largest changes in foreign policy preferences was a drop of thirty-seven percentage points, between 1935 and 1973, in support for the idea of requiring a popular referendum before declaring war.

There was nothing capricious about these changes, as we will see by examining them in historical context. And we want to emphasize once more that their size is exceptional. Opinion changes of substantial magnitude are uncommon.

The Shape of Opinion Change

As we have seen, then, in the middle and late twentieth century, the period for which survey data exist, it is simply not true that collective policy preferences have changed frequently or by great amounts. Perhaps Madison and Hamilton were right about the volatility of American public opinion two centuries ago; we have no way to check.[17] But in modern times, at least, references to "transient impulses" or "violent passions" give an incorrect impression (see Page and Shapiro 1989b).

The general pattern of stable collective survey responses is consistent with our argument in Chapter 1 that the measured attitudes of individuals have a random component (whether resulting from measurement error or random inputs of information or both) which is largely cancelled out in the aggregation process, so that only people's more real and enduring preferences are reflected in survey evidence about collective public opinion. That is, our findings so far are consistent with one important aspect of the idea of a rational public.

The fact of stability alone, however, cannot conclusively establish either the reality or the rationality of collective opinion. Collective stability could, in theory, arise from purely random survey responses: as we noted in Chapter 1, if survey interviewees flipped mental coins, a nearly equal (and, therefore, nearly constant) proportion of them would pick each available response alternative each time a question was asked. Or stable responses could reflect rigid, uninformed habits, or deeply embedded unconscious urges, or reflex responses to irrelevant symbols. For further evidence about collective rationality, we must consider in detail how public opinion is distributed (i.e., how many Americans say they favor or oppose various policies), how preferences concerning different issues relate to each other, and how and why collective opinion changes.

Much of our argument, therefore, depends upon the detailed analysis, in Chapters 3–6, of opinion distributions and opinion changes in historical context. That analysis will make clear, as figure 2.2 already indicated, that aggregate survey responses do not generally divide fifty-fifty or in other arbitrary ways as they would if respondents were flipping mental coins. Instead, the collective responses to different questions vary widely and form coherent patterns across issues. We will see also that collective opinion changes do not move in helter-skelter fashion but instead respond sensibly to changes in information and changes in reality.

In this chapter we can only offer a few hints about that kind of evidence. Here we will focus upon data concerning the form, shape, and rate of opinion changes, which also bear, in a significant though more limited way, upon the rationality question. In particular, we will distinguish among three different types of opinion changes. All 556 instances of significant opinion change were classified according to whether they were *gradual* or *abrupt*, and whether or not they constituted part of a *fluctuation*.

We called a change "abrupt" if it occurred at a rate of ten percentage points or more per year. (The rate of change was calculated simply by dividing the magnitude of change by the time interval over which it occurred; see below.) This rather generous criterion was chosen to make sure we did not understate the amount of abrupt change; it includes as abrupt any significant (six percentage points or more) change occurring within approximately seven months, along with bigger shifts that took longer.

A "fluctuation" involves reversals in the direction of opinion change within a given time interval. We specified, as the criterion for a fluctuation, two or more significant changes in opposite directions within two years, or three or more within four years. In principle a fluctuation might or might not include one or more abrupt changes; in practice most of them do. We strictly required that fluctuations be based on statistically significant changes in order to avoid giving false substantive interpretations to random sampling error. By the same token, of course, we may have missed some small opinion fluctuations that were real though not big enough to pass the significance test. But any such miniature fluctuations would not be of much interest; they would not constitute evidence of capricious changes or volatility in opinion.

"Gradual" changes are defined as any significant shifts in opinion that are neither abrupt nor part of fluctuations. Thus the typology is exhaustive, and gradual changes are exclusive of the others, but abrupt changes and fluctuations (which involve different research questions and different units of analysis) tend to overlap.

Abrupt Changes in Preferences

Many critics of public opinion have implied that public opinion changes quickly. Madison and Hamilton did so when they wrote of "sudden breeze(s)" of passion, or "impulse(s)," or "violent passions" among the public. Almond's "mood theory," too, refers to sudden, as well as frequent and large, opinion changes. Our computation of rates of change for each instance of significant opinion change, with a rate of ten percentage points or more per year defined as "abrupt," permits us to judge just how frequently U.S. public opinion has undergone rapid change.

Despite the general prevalence of stability or gradual change, abrupt opinion changes are in fact rather frequent. Fully 229, or 41%, of our 556 significant change cases (from the 473 questions showing at least one change) met the criterion of abruptness. This is not an enormous number relative to the 1,128 repeated questions we examined, nor relative to the much larger number of pairs of time points—over 4,000—we compared. (Many questions were repeated several times.)[18] Still, the rapidity of change in a number of cases was quite striking, especially with respect to foreign policy.

We calculated the annual rate of opinion change for each of our instances of significant change simply by dividing the number of percentage points of observed change by the number of years (or fraction of a year) within which the change took place.[19] There is a strong contrast in rates between foreign and domestic issues. The average (mean) rate of change for all our foreign policy instances of change was thirty-one percentage points per year, compared to only twelve percentage points for domestic cases. (The medians were twelve and four percentage points, respectively.) That is, foreign policy opinion changes were nearly three times as rapid as domestic, on the average, presumably because circumstances tend to change more quickly in international affairs.

A similar contrast appears when comparing the frequency of abrupt changes on foreign and domestic issues. The second column of table 2.3 indicates the proportion of our significant change cases, within various policy areas, that occurred at a rate of ten percentage points per year or faster. Only 27% of the domestic policy cases, but 58% of the foreign policy cases, were abrupt according to this criterion. Opinions on many foreign policy issues related to World War II, the Korean War, the Vietnam War, foreign aid, defense policy, and the Middle East changed at rapid rates. In the domestic realm, comparable frequencies of abrupt

TABLE 2.3 Magnitudes and Rates of Opinion Change for Different Types of Issues

	Average Magnitudes of Opinion Change (Percentage Points)	Percentage of Opinion Changes 10 Percentage Points or More per Year	(N)
All issues	12.5	41	(556)
Foreign/defense policies:[a]	12.6	58	(255)
World War II	12.0	100	(24)
Korean War	11.5	88	(8)
Vietnam War	10.0	79	(28)
Middle East	13.6	68	(18)
Foreign aid	11.3	65	(26)
National defense	14.0	61	(23)
Soviet Union	12.2	44	(27)
International organization	10.4	41	(22)
Draft	10.2	40	(5)
China	17.2	37	(19)
Fight communism	15.5	32	(22)
Other foreign	12.1	48	(23)
Other foreign-domestic, mixed[a]	9.9	33	(21)
Domestic policies:[a]	12.4	27	(301)
Nixon/Watergate	16.6	100	(10)
Economic issues	11.8	65	(43)
Labor	11.9	44	(18)
Civil rights	12.5	28	(25)
Social welfare	9.6	20	(15)
Big government	10.8	15	(20)
Political reform	12.3	13	(23)
Abortion	18.2	8	(13)
Crime	15.1	6	(16)
Social-style issues	12.6	4	(27)
Gun control	9.8	0	(9)
Education	10.5	0	(6)
Civil liberties	18.0	0	(24)
Other domestic	10.0	32	(41)

[a]The other foreign/domestic, mixed items were reclassified as foreign or domestic, depending upon their substantive content, in calculating the total foreign vs. domestic magnitudes of opinion change and rates of change (as a result the N's for specific policies do not sum directly to 255 for foreign and defense, and 301 for domestic, but they do so when the 21 foreign-domestic cases are reclassified).

change occurred only on issues related to the economy and to Nixon and Watergate. In all these cases, sudden changes in events and circumstances led to correspondingly quick changes in public opinion, but such changes are more common in the realm of foreign policy.

One complication in interpreting the foreign/domestic contrast is that survey organizations have tended to repeat foreign policy questions at much shorter time intervals than domestic. (Based on the 473 questions showing change in table 2.1, an average of seventy-six days elapsed between surveys for foreign policy questions as opposed to 145 days for domestic.) Abrupt changes are more likely to be detected when questions are asked frequently, so our data may overstate the rapidity of foreign as opposed to domestic changes. Comparing foreign and domestic policy questions that were asked equally often, however, we still found more rapid changes in responses to the former. Survey organizations no doubt choose to repeat foreign affairs questions at shorter intervals precisely because they expect to find—and do find—quicker opinion changes.

On the face of it, the substantial number of abrupt opinion changes, especially on foreign policy, might seem to confirm the "mood theory." But three considerations work against this conclusion. First, collective opinion on most of our repeated opinion questions (including foreign policy issues) did not undergo any significant changes at all, and when it did the changes were not usually very large; even the cases we have classified as "abrupt" were mostly quick but relatively small (six or seven percentage points, for example, within seven or eight months). There is little evidence of violent movement in opinion. Second, as we will see below, when preferences about foreign policy change rapidly in response to events they seldom "snap back"—fluctuations are rare.

Third, just as collective opinion stability is not sufficient evidence of rationality, rapidity of opinion change is not enough in itself to constitute evidence of capriciousness. One must go on to inquire into the patterns and the causes of change. We will do so in later chapters, finding sensible reasons for most abrupt opinion changes. Virtually all cases of abrupt opinion change have been related to significant events that rational citizens would take into account. In particular, most abrupt foreign policy opinion changes have followed wars, confrontations, or crises, in which major changes in the actions of the United States or other nations have understandably affected calculations about the costs and benefits of alternative policies.

One illustration of abrupt opinion change involves the impact of the Tet offensive during the Vietnam War. At the end of January 1968, the

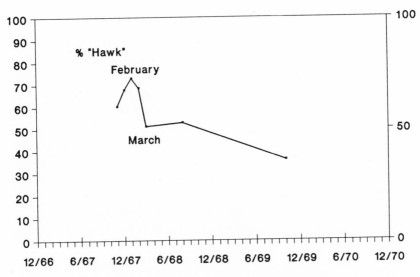

FIG. 2.3   Abrupt opinion change: the Vietnam War.

North Vietnamese and the National Liberation Front (NLF) launched sudden, coordinated attacks all over South Vietnam, causing considerable destruction and even bringing the fighting to the courtyard of the U.S. embassy in Saigon. Between early February and early April, as many leaders and commentators interpreted the offensive as a disaster for the United States that cast doubt on chances of victory, considerably (22%) fewer Americans described themselves as "hawks" about the war; more called themselves "doves" and wanted to reduce the military effort—a change that proceeded at an extremely rapid rate (see figure 2.3). We will have more to say about this case in Chapter 6. For the present, it stands as an example of abrupt, but certainly not capricious or inexplicable, change in collective policy preferences.

Of all the domestic policy preferences we have examined, opinions about Richard Nixon and the Watergate break-in and cover up showed the most dramatic rapid change: a rise of thirty-four percentage points in desires to impeach Nixon and compel him to leave office, in less than one year—between June 1973 and May 1974—as evidence of his misdeeds accumulated (culminating in the tape recording of the president saying "Do it.") Other survey questions repeated at somewhat different times also showed rapid increases in support for bringing Nixon to trial and for removing him from office (see Chap. 8). Again, there was nothing inexplicable about this.

Fluctuations

One of the principal indictments against public opinion has been that it fluctuates or vacillates; that it changes back and forth rapidly, in different directions, for little or no good reason. The Federalist Papers, for example, spoke of "popular fluctuations," "temporary" errors and delusions, and "transient" impulses. The elastic band metaphor of the mood theory suggests much the same thing.

The notion that public opinion fluctuates has retained some currency in recent times, perhaps because of the instability of individuals' responses in panel data and because surveys have revealed rapid back-and-forth movements in aggregate responses about "most important problems," presidential popularity, the standing of political candidates, and the like. But, as we will see, such movements are not at all characteristic of collective policy preferences.

In order to assess the extent of fluctuations, it is necessary to examine data from policy questions that were repeated several times at short intervals. We operationally defined a fluctuation as consisting of two or more significant opinion changes in opposite directions within two years, or three or more changes back and forth within four years, and we found 173 different survey questions that were asked frequently enough to detect such fluctuations if they occurred.

In only 18% of the cases—thirty-one out of the 173—did the collective opinions of Americans actually fluctuate. There was little difference in this respect between foreign and domestic issues: 21% (nineteen of eighty-nine) foreign questions, versus 14% (twelve of eighty-four) of the domestic, involved fluctuations. This certainly does not suggest that the public's preferences are volatile or vacillate wildly, even with respect to foreign policy.

These proportions might possibly be understated if our statistical criteria were too strict—which hardly seems to be the case—or if some fluctuations occurred undetected between opinion measurements. But it seems just as plausible that the proportion of fluctuations may be *overstated* because of the tendency of polling organizations to repeat questions that show opinion changes and to drop those that do not. As we pointed out earlier, pollsters, journalists, and scholars have incentives to find opinion changes. Even so, rather few opinion fluctuations have turned up in fifty years of surveying policy preferences.

Moreover, the fluctuations we did find did not represent unpredictable or irrational changes. Several of them involved *shifting referents:* that is, survey questions in which the wording stayed the same but referred to a shifting reality. Domestic examples include whether taxes were "too high," whether or not President Kennedy's policies should "move to the left," and whether or not President Johnson was pushing racial integration "too fast." Each of these questions invited reference to current government policy at the moment of the interview. Policy can change from one survey to the next, eliciting altered responses from people with unchanged preferences. (When taxes go up, more people are likely to call them "too high.") Questions with shifting referents are naturally more apt to produce fluctuating responses than are questions asking about specific policy alternatives that retain a fixed meaning, yet such fluctuations do not necessarily signify any real changes in collective policy preferences.

The same point applies to such foreign policy questions as those asking whether the United States had gone "too far" concerning involvement in world affairs, whether or not people were making "too many" sacrifices for national defense, and whether the United States should "be firmer" with Russia. Responses favoring a more firm or less firm policy depended partly upon changing realities: whether government policy at the moment was relatively tough or conciliatory. In this respect, they resemble the fluctuating levels of approval of a president's handling of his job, which depend upon how things have gone recently.

When we set aside questions with shifting referents, very few examples of fluctuating public opinion remain. One of those unusual cases is illustrated in figure 2.4, which shows how support for continuing Marshall

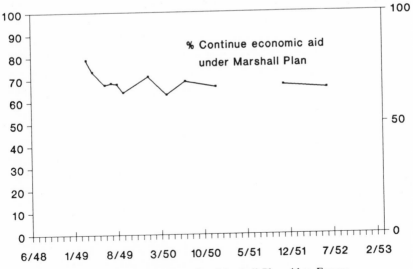

FIG. 2.4   Opinion fluctuation: Marshall Plan aid to Europe.

Plan aid to Europe fell significantly, rose, and fell once again during 1949 and 1950. This was a time of turbulent international events, including Soviet nuclear weapons testing and the onset of the Korean War; it is not surprising that many Americans would recalculate the need for aid to Europe on the large scale of the Marshall Plan, though a majority continued to support it throughout the period. (We will discuss this case further in Chap. 5.)

In the few cases of true fluctuations in policy preferences, changing realities and new information that was provided to the public render those fluctuations understandable. We have found no appreciable evidence of capricious, whimsical, or incomprehensible back-and-forth movements of public opinion.[20]

Gradual Shifts of Opinion

Most of the changes in policy preferences we have observed involved gradual trends or small incremental movements of opinion. More than half—59%—of our 556 instances of significant change, for example, were neither abrupt nor part of fluctuations. The point becomes still more clear if we remember that more than half of our 1,128 repeated policy questions showed no significant change at all; some portion of them (perhaps as many as two or three hundred) presumably underwent real but very small changes which, if added to the larger gradual changes, would indicate that some two-thirds or three-quarters of all observed opinion changes were gradual.

This two-thirds or three-quarters proportion of gradual changes would be still higher if the calculation were based on comparisons of all adjacent pairs of identical survey questions, which are more numerous than the questions themselves. From any particular moment when a given survey question was asked, to the next time it was asked, the odds are very good—in fact, overwhelming—that public opinion remained about the same or changed only gradually.

To be sure, one might argue that the available data overstate the gradualness of opinion change because we cannot tell what was going on while no surveys were in the field. Many (232, or 49%) of the 473 questions with significant changes were asked at only two time points, so they could not reveal any fluctuations in opinion; some were repeated with long time intervals between surveys, so that any abrupt changes would not be likely to show up either.

We can address this objection by further examination of the subset of 173 policy questions (involving 246 instances of opinion change) that were repeated often enough, and closely enough together, so that fluctua-

TABLE 2.4 Frequency of Gradual Changes in Collective Policy
Preferences (among Responses to 173 Questions Asked Frequently
Enough to Detect Fluctuations)

	Gradual		Not Gradual		Total Changes	
	%	(N)	%	(N)	%	(N)
All issues	43	(107)	57	(139)	100	(246)
Domestic policy	62	(69)	38	(42)	45	(111)
Foreign and defense policy	28	(38)	72	(97)	55	(135)

Note: Gamma = Yule's q = .61 ($p < .05$).

tions could be revealed if they occurred. Among those 246 instances of
change, 43% (107) were gradual—neither abrupt nor part of a fluctuation
(see table 2.4, which highlights the big difference between foreign and
domestic issues). Again, gradualness would appear still more prevalent if
the 139 abrupt or fluctuating changes were contrasted with the 2,663 pairs
of time points at which these identical questions were asked.

Another way of looking at this is to note that as a proportion of the
173 different *questions* that were frequently repeated, nearly half (78, or
45%) involved only gradual changes—not abrupt changes or fluctuations—despite the many possible chances for opinion change.

To focus on these 173 often-repeated questions probably understates
the frequency of gradual opinion change. As we have already noted, these
questions are not likely to be representative of survey questions generally.
Many of them involve shifting referents, and many were no doubt repeated a number of times precisely because pollsters expected—and found—
fluctuations or abrupt changes, which are considered more newsworthy
than stability or gradual changes.

By regarding our calculations as suggesting upper and lower
bounds, it seems reasonable to estimate that about one-half to three-
quarters of all measured opinion changes—including a very high proportion of those concerning domestic policy but a lower proportion of
foreign—are gradual; and that the proportion is much higher if it is
thought of in terms of pairs of repeated survey questions.

A way of combining our findings of stability and gradual change in
policy preferences is to say that public opinion about policy tends to be
highly autocorrelated. That is, the level of public support for a particular
policy in one survey is a very strong predictor of the level of support in a
subsequent survey.

We were able to calculate the extent of this incremental movement in a precise way, while statistically controlling for many other influences on opinion, by using a special data set: collective responses to a sample of eighty survey questions that were asked twice within fairly short intervals (averaging two or three months). These are the data which will also be used in Chapter 8 to investigate the impact of TV news on public opinion. They are broadly representative of all available policy questions that have been repeated at short intervals, without regard to whether opinion changed a lot, a little, or not at all.

According to these data, the inertia of public opinion is very powerful indeed. Across the eighty cases, the unstandardized regression coefficient for the level of opinion at time 2 as a function of opinion at time 1 was a remarkable .97. Opinion at t_1, alone, accounted for more than 85% of the variance in opinion at t_2. This is a very high degree of stability (see Page, Shapiro, and Dempsey 1987, pp. 28 and 30; and Chap. 8, below).

We have confirmed this finding by doing a similar analysis (but without controlling for TV news variables) of this chapter's 556 cases of significant opinion change, regressing the level of opinion at the end of each instance upon the level at the beginning. The regression coefficient was a high .76, and opinion at t_1 accounted for 58% of the variance at t_2, even though this set of cases is biased against stability: the average time intervals are long, the cases of no change or insignificant change are excluded, and the instances were defined so as to maximize the amount of observed change.

Much the same pattern is apparent in long time series of opinions that are available on particular issues. When a policy preference question is repeated many times, the level of opinion in one survey tends to persist to the next survey; the level at the second survey tends to persist until the third; and so forth. Opinion change, if any, is incremental. Our graphs of hundreds of significant opinion changes (a number of which are presented in later chapters) make this visually clear.

Figure 2.5 gives an important example: the very large, but long and slow, rise between 1942 and 1985 in the proportion of white Americans saying that white and Negro or black students should go to "the same schools" rather than different schools. There was a huge increase of sixty-one percentage points in "same schools" responses, among those with opinions; yet—as best we can tell—this change took place in a smooth, nearly linear fashion over the forty-three year period,[21] averaging only 1.4 percentage points of opinion change per year. This and a number of

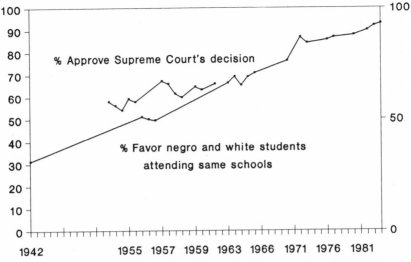

FIG. 2.5   Large, gradual opinion change: school desegregation, 1942–1985.

other large, gradual liberalizing opinion trends concerning civil rights will be examined further in Chapter 3.

Similarly, large and gradual opinion changes occurred from the 1960s through the 1980s on issues of birth control (e.g., the availability of birth control information) and abortion. Four NORC and NORC-GSS items asking whether it should be "possible for a pregnant woman to obtain a legal abortion" under various circumstances—danger to the mother's health, birth defects, poverty, desire to have no more children— are graphed in figure 2.6. All showed roughly thirty percentage point increases in approval of abortion between 1965 and the mid-1970s, with a small drop-off afterward and a small but discernible resumption of liberalization by 1989. We cannot be sure that opinion changed gradually between 1965 and 1972 (though collateral evidence from Gallup polls strongly suggests it did); but it is clear that during the 1970s and 1980s opinion changed only in relatively small and gradual ways.

Figure 2.6 again illustrates that collective public opinion is capable of sharp distinctions. In every survey, very large majorities thought "it should be possible for a pregnant woman to obtain a legal abortion . . . if the woman's own health is seriously endangered by the pregnancy," and nearly as many did so "if there is a strong chance of serious defect in the baby"; but much fewer thought abortion should be legal "if the family has a very low income and cannot afford any more children," and still

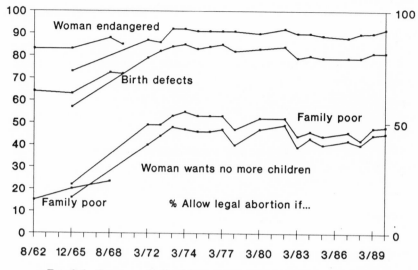

Fɪɢ. 2.6   Large, gradual opinion change: legal abortion, 1962–1990.

fewer thought so if the woman "is married and does not want any more children." One may or may not like the way in which the public makes these distinctions, but they are certainly meaningful, coherent, and consistent over time. These aggregate trends can hardly be the result of random responses. (Opinions about abortion will be examined further in Chap. 3.)

On a number of other social issues, including civil liberties, legalization of marijuana, capital punishment, and the courts' treatment of criminals, Americans' policy preferences have changed substantially but gradually since the 1950s and 1960s (see Chap. 3). On many of these issues, survey questions have been asked at fairly frequent intervals. By the 1970s, the survey research business was booming, and (thanks to George Gallup and especially to the NORC General Social Survey, under the leadership of James A. Davis and Tom W. Smith) the careful repetition of identical questions was becoming common. Since there are few major gaps in these time series in recent years, we can be especially confident that nothing very dramatic happened between surveys and that the opinion changes were really gradual.

During the 1970s and 1980s, frequently repeated survey questions also tracked gradual opinion changes on such matters as government spending on social welfare, health, the cities, drug addiction, and government provision of jobs or a decent standard of living. (These issues will be dealt with further in Chap. 4.) For some policy issues and some periods—such as the World War II and early postwar years that were heavily surveyed by Gallup, OPOR, and NORC—time series are available on foreign policy issues, which reveal gradual trends in opinion on such matters as foreign policy activism, foreign aid, the United Nations, admission of China to the United Nations, and spending on defense—though, as table 2.4 showed, gradual changes have been much less common on foreign and defense policy than on domestic issues (see Chaps. 5 and 6).

As will be shown in more detail later, most gradual opinion changes are understandable in terms of underlying transformations in American society and in the world.

Conclusion

Our evidence indicates that the collective policy preferences of Americans have been quite stable. Public opinion about policy does not by any means undergo incessant change. Roughly half our repeated survey questions, including many that were repeated several times over substantial numbers of months and years, showed no significant changes at all. The figure would be much higher if it were based upon the number of question repetitions rather than the number of different questions asked.

Furthermore, when opinion change does occur, it is usually modest in magnitude. Many instances of change have involved shifts of only six or seven or eight percentage points: enough to reach statistical significance but not enormous substantive significance. This should not be forgotten in later chapters when we devote special attention to a few exceptional cases of large change.

Fluctuations of opinion, movements back and forth in different directions, are very unusual. We found fluctuations in fewer than one-fifth of the frequently repeated survey questions we examined, even though there is reason to believe that those questions were repeated precisely because pollsters expected to find changes. Moreover, most of the fluctuations we found involved survey questions with "shifting referents," in which the reality being referred to, rather than the preferences of the public, may have changed.

Collective public opinion on a given issue at one moment in time is a very strong predictor of opinion on that same issue at a later time.

The one finding that may seem discordant with this picture of stability is that, when public opinion moves at all, it sometimes moves abruptly, especially with respect to foreign policy. But this usually does not involve very large changes, and it certainly does not mean that public opinion moves capriciously. Most abrupt opinion changes represent understandable responses to sudden events, especially in international affairs.

Our data on the frequency and size and rate of opinion changes, therefore, do not offer much support for the notion that there are sudden breezes or fluctuations or transient impulses in public opinion. They go a long way toward refuting the myth of capricious opinion change.

In order to move further with our argument, to show that Americans' collective policy preferences are coherent and reflect underlying values and that they generally change—when they do so at all—in reasonable ways, we need additional kinds of evidence. We must examine more closely what kinds of distinctions the public makes, what patterns of policy preferences exist, and how collective preferences relate to each other across issues. We also need to analyze the instances of significant opinion change in their historical context and to explore their causes. These are the subjects of the four chapters that follow (Chaps. 3–6)—which are organized according to types of policy and historical periods—and also of Chapter 8, which concerns general patterns of opinion change.

3 Opinions about Social Issues

☑ We begin our detailed examination of Americans' collective policy preferences by considering public opinion on what can be called "social issues." Separate sections of the chapter are devoted to domestic policies concerning such matters as civil rights, civil liberties, crime and punishment, women's and minorities' rights, abortion, and life-styles.

The survey data on these issues—like those treated in later chapters—help fill out our picture of rational public opinion. They show that the public's preferences form coherent patterns and make sharp distinctions among different policy alternatives. When preferences have changed they have done so in understandable and sensible ways, reacting to changes in objective circumstances or available information.

In one important respect, however, public opinion on social issues has differed from that concerning other kinds of policies. The data reveal a number of exceptionally large opinion changes, some amounting to as much as twenty or thirty percentage points or more. As we saw in Chapter 2 (tables 2.2 and 2.3), opinion shifts of such magnitude are not at all common. Because of their inherent interest and their great political significance we will give them special attention, even at the risk of losing sight of the more general phenomenon of opinion stability.

Several of these large changes, especially those monitored by NORC's General Social Survey (GSS), have been well documented in the scholarly literature (e.g., J. Davis 1980; Tom Smith 1982b; see Tom Smith and Arnold 1990), while others will be new to nearly all readers. Most have involved movement in a liberalizing, more tolerant, or more egalitarian direction. Most of them occurred gradually over many years.

Some of the opinion shifts resulted from fundamental technological and economic and social changes, along with increasing levels of formal education and the replacement of older, more conservative members of the population by new, more liberal cohorts. In several cases new information and political events, such as those related to the Cold War and the civil rights movement, also played an important part. These sweeping changes in public opinion (accompanied or followed, in many cases, by major changes in discourse and in public policy) have established a new social environment in the United States, quite unlike that of decades past.

Civil Rights and Racial Equality

The expressed attitudes of white Americans toward black Americans have undergone a great transformation over the last forty or fifty years, a change greater than on any other issue. On a wide range of policies related to public accommodations, employment, schools, neighborhoods and housing, and intermarriage, whites moved from advocating total separation and an inferior status for blacks to favoring legal equality and substantial desegregation.

This is not by any means to say that racism, hostility, or even racial violence has been eliminated; much less is it true that harmonious racial integration has been achieved in the United States. Most whites at the beginning of the 1990s still said they disliked the idea of living in predominately black neighborhoods or sending their children to predominately black schools, and large majorities opposed policies like school busing that could bring about such results. But the principle of desegregation was almost universally accepted, and substantial majorities favored government policies to enforce legal equality and to bring about certain kinds and degrees of desegregation.

At the beginning of the 1940s this was certainly not the case. A 1942 NORC survey which provides a major baseline for measuring trends found that only 31% of white Americans thought black and white children should go to the same schools; 69% thought they should go to separate schools.[1] Only 46% of those with opinions opposed "separate sections for Negroes" on streetcars and buses, and only 36% said it would make no difference to them if a Negro with the same income and education as they had moved into their block. Fully 86% said Negroes should have separate sections in towns and cities while 72% favored separate restaurants. Moreover, only 50% of the public thought that "*some* restaurants in this town should serve both Negro and white people."

The 1942 survey did reveal certain limited egalitarian sentiments within this context of separation and segregation: an overwhelming majority (91%) thought "Negroes should have the same chance as white people to get a good education," and 90% favored equal pay for equal work by blacks. But the "equal" in "separate but equal" only went so far. In 1944 NORC found that only 45% said "Negroes should have as good a chance as white people to get any kind of job"; the majority thought white people should get the "first chance" at jobs.

In the early and middle 1940s, then, large majorities of whites took for granted that blacks should be consigned to separate public accommodations, separate schools, and separate neighborhoods. Few favored government action to desegregate or to prevent job discrimination. Underlying these policy preferences were widespread beliefs that blacks were genetically inferior. In 1939, for example, 76% of the respondents to a Roper poll said Negroes had generally "lower" intelligence than white people. Upon further probing, most explicitly said that this was partly because Negroes were *born* less intelligent. In 1942, a majority (53%) of white respondents told NORC "no" when asked whether Negroes are "as intelligent" as whites—"that is, can they learn things just as well if they are given the same education and training?"

Already by the late 1950s, however, many of these beliefs and preferences had changed markedly. By the late 1960s and early 1970s they had completely turned around.

Changes in attitudes of whites about school segregation are particularly striking. The mere 31% that favored black and white children going to the same schools in 1942 grew to 50% in 1956, 66% in 1963, 71% in 1965, 76% in 1970, an overwhelming 88% in 1980, and 93% in 1985. This change of more than sixty percentage points is the largest for any policy preference question of any kind among the thousands we have examined.[2] We saw it dramatically illustrated in figure 2.5 of Chapter 2.

This "same schools" time series indicates that attitudes about school desegregation continued to liberalize even through the supposedly conservative 1980s. Likewise, from 1982 to 1984, public opposition to "the federal government giving tax exemptions to schools that segregate whites and blacks" grew from an already high 75% to a full 86% (Harris).

The available data on public accommodations and employment indicate similar trends. As reported by Schuman, Steeh, and Bobo (1985), the 46% of whites that in 1942 opposed separate sections for Negroes on streetcars and buses grew to 62% in 1956, 79% in 1963, and a weighty 88% in 1970. The 45% in 1944 who said Negroes should have as good a chance as white people to get a job grew slightly in two years, and then (after a multiyear gap in which the question was not asked) reached 85% in 1963, 89% in 1966, and a remarkable 97% in 1972. (Some of the early opinion changes, and some data that are no longer available, are discussed in Hyman and Sheatsley [1953, 1956]; Sheatsley [1966]; and M. Schwartz [1967]. See also Schuman et al. [1985]; Taylor, Sheatsley, and Greeley [1978]; Tom Smith and Sheatsley [1984]).

Unfortunately, few survey questions were repeated with identical wording starting in the 1940s, so that on some aspects of civil rights we cannot be certain exactly when opinions began to change or how far they

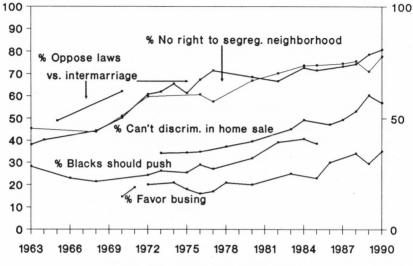

FIG. 3.1   Racial issues, 1963–1990.

moved. Repeated questions about housing segregation, for example, began only in the 1960s. The opinion that "black people have a right to live
wherever they can afford to, just like anybody else" (as opposed to white
people having "a right to keep black people out of their neighborhoods")
rose by twenty-two percentage points, from 69% to 91% (from 65% to
88% among whites) between 1964 and 1976, according to an SRC/CPS
question with a slight variation in wording. According to a repeated
NORC-GSS item, disagreement (either "slightly" or "strongly") with
the sentiment that "white people have a right to keep blacks out of their
neighborhoods and blacks should respect that right" rose dramatically, by
twenty-five percentage points, between 1963 and 1982. (See figure 3.1,
which includes several civil rights items from the 1960s and subsequent
years.)

By 1963, 73% of whites said that Negroes should have the right to
"use the same parks, restaurants, and hotels as white people," a proportion that grew to 88% in 1970. Approval of "strict segregation," as a
general principle, stood at only 25% in 1964; it dropped further to 14% in
1972 and to a tiny 5% in 1978. (It should be noted, however, that
responses in the ambiguous "something in between" category increased
more than responses favoring desegregation. Moreover, Schuman et al.
[1985, pp. 74–77] suggest that answers to this vague question are heavily
dependent upon which specific policy questions immediately precede it
on a survey questionnaire.)

One of the most striking changes, because it involves a highly personal and emotional matter, is the big growth in acceptance of racial intermarriage. In late 1963, only 38% of white Americans opposed "laws against marriages between blacks and whites" (NORC). As shown in figure 3.1, this proportion rose to 45% in 1968, 50% in 1970, 61% in 1972, 67% in 1976, and 72% in 1977, before leveling off, even dipping a bit, and then rising to 79% in 1990. The proportion of all respondents that Gallup found disapproving of state "laws making it a crime for a white person and a Negro person to marry" rose in similar fashion, from 49% in early 1965 to 62% in 1970.[3]

In this connection, Gallup found a 36% (again, we will often use this shorthand of "36%" for "thirty-six percentage point") rise among whites, between 1958 and 1983, in general "approv(al)" of "marriage between whites and nonwhites." But it is important to note that this level of approval—increasing from a minuscule 4% to a still low 40%—remained considerably *lower* than opposition to miscegenation laws. That is, the public's policy preferences concerning government action can be quite different from its general attitudes about groups or behavior. This point is often ignored in the interpretation of survey data; we will see, for example, that opposition to homosexuality and abortion has sometimes been confused with support for laws forbidding them. Evidence that the collective public distinguishes between disapproval and the imposition of legal sanctions contributes to our picture of rational public opinion.

Limits to Integrationist Sentiment

Some of the leading accounts of these liberalizing trends (e.g., Sheatsley [1966]; Greeley and Sheatsley [1971]; Taylor et al. [1978]; Tom Smith and Sheatsley [1984]) have been criticized as exaggerating the importance of the changes. It is said that they put too much faith in verbal responses to rather generally worded questions, ignoring the persistence of racism and segregation and the failure of white Americans to support concrete policy measures that would bring about integration (M. Jackman 1978; Sears, Hensler, and Speer 1979).

We disagree with this objection, at least in its extreme form. More than lip service is involved; the public's preferences have really shifted away from legally enforced segregation, and the alteration in verbally expressed norms and principles has been accompanied by important changes in behavior and in public policy. Nonetheless, it is true that the United States continues to be a highly segregated society and that racism is far from extinct. To understand how this can be so, and why at the same time the changes in public opinion are real and important, it is necessary to look more closely at exactly what kinds of opinions have changed.

As Schuman et al. (1985) point out, there are limits in the extent to which white Americans favor concrete policies *implementing* the principle of desegregation. Indeed, there are severe limits to the kind of desegregation that is accepted even in principle. When it comes to schools, for example, the same public that overwhelmingly says it thinks white and black students should go to "the same schools" rather than "separate schools" has been divided over the question of *how many* black children should go to *which* formerly all-white schools, and what (if anything) the government should do about it. According to Gallup, a majority (56% in June 1954, rising to 67% by December 1956: see figure 2.5) has long approved the Supreme Court's *Brown v. Bd. of Education* decision of 1954, which declared legally enforced school segregation to be unconstitutional. But this does not necessarily imply support for full-scale integration: it may mean no more than allowing black children who happen to live in predominately white attendance districts to go to their local schools if they wish, or forbidding school authorities to draw attendance lines deliberately in order to segregate.

When Americans are asked whether "the government in Washington should see to it that white and black children are allowed to go to the same schools," only a minority says the government should see to it—and a markedly declining minority, at that, if one takes account of the rising "no interest" responses. Only 42% of all white respondents (including in the calculation those with "no interest") favored government action in 1964, 36% in 1968, 31% in 1974, and 25% in 1978 (Schuman et al. 1985, pp. 88–89). Even when the phrase *"allowed* to go" was repeated at the end of this NES question in 1966 and 1970, presumably in order to counteract any implication of compulsory integration, a higher but still only minority 48% and 46% said the government should see to it.

The point comes out even more clearly when school busing is mentioned. There has been a modest trend toward more acceptance of busing in the 1970s and 1980s: an 8% drop in opposition between March 1970 and October 1971 (Gallup), and—according to a different SRC/CPS question that contrasts neighborhood schools—a 6% decline between autumn 1972 and autumn 1976. More important, as shown in figure 3.1, NORC-GSS found a 19% drop in opposition to "the busing of (Negro/Black) and white school children from one district to another," between 1976 and 1990, with most of the change occurring in the middle 1980s. This declining opposition has several explanations: many families, especially in the suburbs, now know they don't face any prospect of busing; in practice busing generally works out much better than people fear (see Hochschild 1984); magnet schools and the like reduce some of the negative aspects. (In a 1981 Harris survey, a substantial 55% of white parents—not far below the 74% of blacks—reported that school busing was a "very satisfactory" experience.)

But the overwhelming fact is that large majorities of Americans have opposed busing virtually everytime they have been asked about it. In 1976, NORC found only 16% in favor and 84% opposed. Even in 1990, after several years of change in a probusing direction, only 35% favored busing and 65% opposed it. NBC, CBS, Harris, and other organizations that have asked differently worded busing questions have consistently come up with similar results: decreasing, but still majority, opposition. An NBC survey in May 1981 showed 81% opposed to busing, and the figure was 78% in 1982; a CBS survey in June 1981 found 83% against. More recently, Harris reported that white opposition to busing dropped from 78% in 1967 but remained at 57% in 1988.

In recent years, a substantial proportion of blacks—close to half— have opposed busing, presumably because the hassle and disruption (if only as a result of white opposition) are seen to outweigh the benefits. For example, NBC found 52%, and CBS 45%, of blacks opposed to busing in mid-1981. Similarly, the NORC-GSS data from 1972 through 1989 reveal an average black opposition of 45%, with a 46% reading in 1989 and 37% (within sampling error of 46%) in 1990.

Desegregation of public accommodations, which entails only the most casual and transient contact between races and is not seen as infringing on anyone's "liberty," has evoked much more enthusiasm than school desegregation. Support for a public accommodations law rose by 12%— to a solid 66%—between June 1963 and January 1964 (Gallup), after the March on Washington and President Kennedy's death and President Johnson's advocacy of quick action on civil rights, before the passage of the 1964 Civil Rights Act. (According to Harris surveys in November 1963—before Kennedy's death—and March 1964, voters' support for "civil rights legislation to strengthen the rights of Negroes and other minority groups" increased from 64% to 70%.) The opinion among whites that the government in Washington should "support the right of black people to go to any hotel or restaurant they can afford" grew from 44% in late 1964 to 50% in 1968, 60% in 1970, and 66% in 1974, even when the slightly growing "no interest" responses are included.[4] Sentiment that the government should "stay out" of desegregating public accommodations fell by 11%—to 28%—between autumn 1968 and late 1970, according to SRC/CPS (Schuman et al. 1985, pp. 88–90).

Policies that might involve wholesale integration at close quarters, however, or interference with individual choices, compensatory discrimination, or significant costs for the white majority—whether in schools, housing, jobs, or spending programs—have met very substantial (though declining) resistance.

The increasing sentiment that blacks "have a right to live wherever they can afford to" (shown in figure 3.1), for example, was accompanied by a large rise from 1973 to 1989 in the proportion of whites favoring a law that a homeowner "cannot refuse to sell to someone because of their race or color" (NORC-GSS), from 34% to 57% pro open housing (53% in 1990). But a rather substantial 45% in 1990 still favored allowing homeowners to decide for themselves whom to sell to, even if they preferred not to sell to blacks. And personal reactions to housing integration depend on how many and what sort of black neighbors are envisioned. A strong majority of whites by 1978—86%, up thirty-one percentage points since 1963, according to Gallup—said they would not move "if black people came to live next door" (Schuman et al. 1985, pp. 106–107); and in 1972 85%, dramatically up from 35% in 1942 and 53% in 1956 (Sheatsley 1966, p. 222), told NORC it would not make "any difference" if "a Negro with the same income and education as you have, moved into your block." But only a minority of whites in a 1978 Gallup survey (46%, up from 20% in 1958 and 23% in 1963) said they would definitely not move "if black people came to live in great numbers in your neighborhood" (Schuman et al. 1985, pp. 106–107). As with schools, most whites prefer neighborhoods with a clear white majority.[5]

Similarly, support for equal employment opportunities has never extended to affirmative action that involves quotas or active federal involvement. In 1978, for example, a CBS survey found 60% opposed to hiring quotas, up fractionally from the previous year. Indeed, only a medium-sized minority (36%) of all white SRC/CPS respondents in 1974 said that the government in Washington should "see to it that black people get fair treatment in jobs." Many chose the alternative response that these matters should be left "to the states and local communities," and a rising proportion (24% in 1974 vs. 13% ten years earlier) expressed "no interest," so that support for equal employment legislation actually showed no tendency at all to increase between 1964 and 1974 (Schuman et al. 1985, p. 88). When Gallup asked in five surveys between 1977 and 1989 whether "ability as determined by test scores" or preferential treatment "to make up for past discrimination" should be the main consideration for jobs and places in college, fully 88%–89% responded test score ability.

To round out the picture, support for increased spending to help blacks and other minorities has always been modest and, in fact, dropped from 1973 to 1978. The proportion responding to NORC-GSS that "too little" was being spent on blacks stood at 35% in 1973—strikingly lower than for anticrime, antidrug, medical, and education programs—and it dropped to 26% by 1978 (staying there in 1980) as the U.S. economy worsened. It bounced back a bit by 1982, but only to 30%, and then edged up to a high of 38% in 1987 and 40% in 1990. SRC/CPS found that responses favoring government efforts to "improve the social and economic position of blacks and other minority groups" (response categories 1–3) stood at only 31% in 1970 and 30% in 1988, with some shifting in between (see Shapiro et al. 1987a).

From a moral standpoint, one might celebrate the sweeping trend of opinion against legal segregation while lamenting the aversion of many white Americans to concrete measures that would undo segregation's effects. From the standpoint of our argument about rationality, however, the public's distinctions among policies—for better or worse—do form a coherent pattern of collective opinion. The pattern involves a selfish but natural reluctance by contemporary whites to pay fully for the consequences of the past enslavement of blacks. Such reluctance fits well with prevailing American values, particularly with a pervasive individualism that insists upon individual rather than group responsibility, with ideas about liberty, and with a somewhat legalistic notion of equality of opportunity that focuses on raising formal barriers so that energetic and talented individuals can get ahead (Sniderman and Hagen 1985; McClosky and Zaller 1984; Hochschild 1981; see Hartz 1955). (See also Roth 1990, Sears et al. 1980, and Bobo 1988, among others, concerning the current debate on the social psychology of racial attitudes involving values versus "symbolic racism" versus "group conflict.") The public resistance to strong integrationist policies may be regrettable, but it is not irrational or inconsistent.

Causes of Change

Not only is the pattern of Americans' opinions about civil rights differentiated and coherent when observed at one moment in time, but changes in collective opinion have reflected sensible reactions to changes in information and in objective circumstances.

The heart of the opinion change, the sweeping liberal trend encompassing many specific issues, is difficult to account for with precision because early survey data are sparse and because the movement of public opinion has generally been so slow and steady. Unlike some foreign policy cases discussed in later chapters, there is little evidence of sharp changes in civil rights opinions that can be associated with specific events. Instead, we must mainly look to broad historical developments.

One popular interpretation is that "the Supreme Court did it." Undeniably, the *Brown v. Bd. of Education* school desegregation decision of 1954, which declared that separate schools were inherently unequal and violated the equal protection clause of the Fourteenth Amendment, laid the legal groundwork for overturning state action that enforced segregation of any kind. It would seem quite plausible, on the face of things, that *Brown* and later Court decisions played the major role in leading and shaping public opinion. As best we can determine, however, this was not, in fact, the case.

The absence of any survey question asked just before and just after the *Brown* decision makes it impossible to measure its immediate impact with precision; for example, we cannot tell how much, if any, of the big jump in opinion favoring school desegregation between 1942 and 1956 (see figure 2.5) should be attributed to the Court. But the slow, steady shifts in opinion that continued long after *Brown* (especially in the South) suggest that something other than a one-shot Court decision was at work; at best, the Court's impact would seem to be diffuse, indirect, and delayed. More tellingly, the available—though fragmentary—evidence indicates that public opinion on related issues moved in an antisegregation direction well before the 1954 decision. These data are displayed in figure 3.2. As the graph shows, opinions and attitudes on a variety of matters moved together, establishing a strong pattern of change from 1940 to 1948 concerning social, economic, and political equality for blacks. Data reported by Mildred Schwartz (1967, p. 131) concerning attitudes toward Negroes' intelligence from 1944 to 1946 reveal that much attitude change occurred in the North, mainly among people with high school or less education.[6]

The existence of a steady trend both before and after 1954 suggests that broader social forces were at work and that the Court itself may have responded to (rather than created) a changed climate of opinion. At least one major analysis argues that the Supreme Court had little or no impact at all upon public opinion (or, indeed, on public policy, since segregation did not markedly diminish until after the Civil Rights Act of 1964), not even by a "trickle down" effect through activists (Rosenberg 1991).

What, then, *did* energize the pro–civil rights opinion trend? A good many events of the late 1950s and early 1960s, heavily covered by the mass media, surely played a part. They include the 1956 Montgomery bus boycott, President Eisenhower's reluctant dispatch of federal troops to enforce desegregation of the Little Rock schools in 1957, the de-

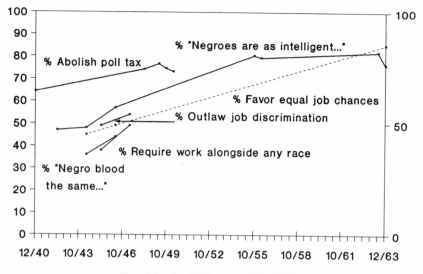

FIG. 3.2   Racial issues, 1940–1963.

colonization of Africa and the emergence of new states whose diplomats protested U.S. segregation, the lunch counter sit-ins of 1960, the "freedom rides" of 1961, the 1962 confrontation over desegregating the University of Mississippi, the 1963 March on Washington and Martin Luther King's inspirational address, John Kennedy's 1960 campaign phone call to Rev. King's wife when King was in jail, Kennedy's 1963 proposal of legislation and his assassination later that year, the bombing that killed four black children in a Birmingham church, President Johnson's passionate advocacy of civil rights, and the passage of the 1964 Civil Rights Act.

These, however, were not isolated events. Many of them were manifestations of a powerful social movement that ultimately raised white as well as black Americans' consciousness of the mistreatment suffered by black people and undermined support for or acquiescence in the most oppressive and arbitrary forms of discrimination. Despite the general hostility of Americans to protests and demonstrations, televised images of Southern policemen beating peaceful black demonstrators and setting dogs upon them galvanized the nation. There can be little doubt that the civil rights movement and Southern whites' highly visible "massive resistance" to it had a major impact on public opinion (see Branch 1988; Garrow 1978; Chong 1991; Burstein 1979).

Still, the fact that the pro–civil rights opinion trends began at least as early as the 1940s and persisted over so many years indicates that

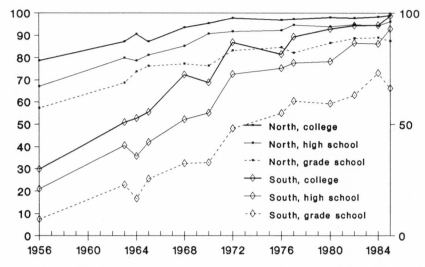

FIG. 3.3   Responses favoring school desegregation by education and region, 1956–1985.

something more long-lasting and fundamental was occurring than any series of particular events or even the organized civil rights movement, which did not get under way with any vigor until the late 1950s and then faded after the 1960s.

A little can be added to the explanation by examining opinion trends among different subgroups of the population. Responses by educational and regional subgroups to the "same schools" question (which is typical of most civil rights items in this respect) are graphed in figure 3.3. At each point in time, in both the North and the South, those with higher levels of formal education tended to be more favorable to school desegregation, although there was, of course, convergence as support for desegration neared unanimity. This difference reflects a real effect that persists after very extensive multivariate statistical controls (see Chap. 7). Over a period of years, therefore, the gradual rise of educational levels among Americans presumably contributed to the prointegration trend—though this contribution turns out to have been very small (see A. Smith 1982).

North-South differences were even greater than education differences, especially in the early years. Among Southern whites in 1956, only a very small minority favored black and white children going to the same schools. Much of the opinion trend, therefore, was concentrated in the South. Southerners of all education levels moved fastest and farthest, gradually converging with Northerners, so that by the mid to late 1970s strong majorities in both regions favored blacks attending the same schools as whites.

Rising educational levels and the South's catching up with the North tell only part of the story, however (Mayer 1990). As figure 3.3 makes clear, the various educational and regional groupings also moved in parallel over time, all of them increasingly favoring school desegregation. Much the same thing is true of groups distinguished by age, urban/rural residence, occupation, gender, or religion. Americans of all sorts tended to turn against segregation. This parallel movement of subgroups in the population—which, as we will see in Chapter 7, is characteristic of opinion trends on most issues—indicates once again that something fundamental was occurring throughout the nation among all strata of society.

We believe that the trend is best understood within a broad historical context. For two centuries or more, the world has seen a slow and sporadic, but apparently inexorable, breakdown in status inequalities based on ascribed characteristics: inherited social class or caste, nationality, religion, race, or gender. The revolutions in France, the American colonies, Russia, and China, as well as anticolonial and national independence movements around the world—most recently in Eastern Europe—all exemplify this change. Virtually everywhere, ascribed inequalities have lost ground in the legal, political, economic, and social spheres.

The specific case of American blacks is, in large part, a manifestation of this worldwide tendency. It also has some unique features. In particular, the middle and late twentieth-century shift in U.S. public opinion abut civil rights seems to have resulted from the dissemination through the population of particular kinds of new information and interpretations, based on demographic changes and new experiences.

The abolition of slavery after the Civil War did not mean that whites had abandoned their beliefs in blacks' inherent inferiority or in the desirability of racial separation. Few Americans in the nineteenth-century challenged the basic tenets of racism. But around the turn of the century the emerging school of American anthropologists, under the leadership of Franz Boas, began to stake out the position that big differences in human behavior could be attributed to culture and environment rather than heredity. Then the northward migration of many blacks, and their adaptation to sophisticated urban life (most notably in the post–World War I Harlem Renaissance), helped convince anthropologists and sociologists at Columbia University and elsewhere that blacks were not, in fact, inherently unequal (Young 1979; see also Franklin and Moss 1988).

As Young has shown, during the 1920s and 1930s the belief in the equality of blacks spread among social scientists and elites and then the general public, including blacks themselves—many of whom had previously taken their low status for granted. It was reinforced by revulsion against Hitler's racism and by the service of blacks in World War II, which was followed by President Truman's order desegregating the armed forces and (in 1948) by his civil rights proposals. Extensive postwar black migration to northern cities led to further highly visible successes in the arts and entertainment and business. Formal legal equality in that region ensured that the growing black population attained substantial political power. (John Kennedy's election victory in 1960, for example, arguably depended upon black votes in key cities.)

The achievements of blacks in the North undermined old stereotypes of inferiority. The mere 47% of whites that said blacks are "as intelligent" as whites in 1942, for example, jumped to 80% in 1956 (NORC). Psychological research began to suggest that prejudice and bigotry reflected unpleasant personality traits. Taken together with fundamental American ideas about equality (see Myrdal 1944), the increasingly widespread belief that blacks were not inherently different from other human beings led logically (if not smoothly or quickly) to the conclusion that they should not be treated differently, separated, or discriminated against. This opinion activated blacks and converted whites. At the same time, increasing black political power in the North gave white politicians— especially Democrats—extra reason to go along, and eventually produced a realignment of the parties in which the Democrats replaced the party of Lincoln as the chief defenders of civil rights for blacks (see Carmines and Stimson 1989; Petrocik 1981).

If this account is correct—and, of course, historical explanation is seldom certain—then any opinion-leading roles of the Supreme Court and President Johnson and other political figures were quite secondary, reacting to change, helping mainly to legitimate the evolving egalitarian beliefs and to spell out policy implications. The civil rights movement was more important, forcing attention on the issue and dramatizing the realities of racial oppression, especially in the South. Foundation money from the Rockefellers and others helped to energize civil rights research, publicity, and activism. But the fundamental source of change was demographic, the northward migration which led to blacks' achievements in northern urban environments and whites' recognition of those achievements.

Northern whites, for reasons dating back to abolitionism and the Civil War, were relatively quick to sympathize with the plight of blacks in the South and to apply Northern principles of legal equality to the Southern situation. (To be sure, the implementation of full social and economic equality in the North has been another matter.) Whites in the South were slower to accept the idea of black legal equality but eventually caught up, for the most part, under the influence of Northern pressure and the "new" South's own modernization, urbanization, rising education levels, generational replacement, and—probably to a lesser extent—immigration from the North (see Firebaugh and Davis 1988; Mayer 1990; Carmines and Stimson 1989, chap. 8, offers some evidence that fits well with our rationality argument).

The effects spilled over into other areas of public policy. As the civil rights movement won legislative victories in the mid-1960s, it became apparent that the same principles could apply to other groups in society. If discrimination against blacks was wrong, people came to think, so was discrimination in general. Women, who constituted a majority but a disadvantaged majority of Americans, increasingly asserted their rights to equal treatment. So did various minorities. We will see in a later section of this chapter that public opinion moved toward favoring equal rights for women, the elderly, Latinos, the disabled, and gays as well, following dynamics partly unique to particular groups and partly conforming to the general egalitarian trend.

Civil Liberties

Between the 1950s and the 1970s, more and more Americans came to favor protection of civil liberties for people with certain unpopular views: particularly the rights of free speech, a free press, and freedom of association for Communists, Socialists, and atheists.

In 1954 Samuel Stouffer conducted an important study that showed what many took to be an alarming lack of support for civil liberties by the public. Although a solid majority (66%) of those with opinions favored allowing a Socialist ("a person who favored government ownership of all the railroads and all big industries") to give speeches in their community, only small minorities of the public would allow an "antireligionist" (38%) or a "Communist" (28%) to do the same. Substantial majorities wanted to remove antireligious books (63%) and especially Communist books (71%) from public libraries; 40% would even remove a Socialist's book. Likewise, 62% opposed allowing a Socialist to teach in college; an overwhelming 88% opposed allowing antireligionist teachers; and a nearly unanimous 94% wanted to fire Communist teachers (see Stouffer 1955).

We do not agree with the assertion that such opinions were not "consistent" with the public's embrace, in the abstract, of democratic

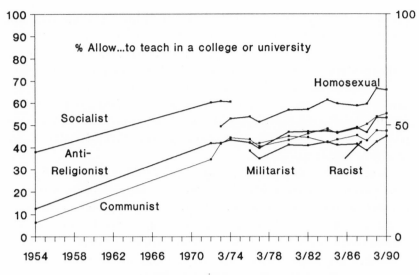

FIG. 3.4   Civil liberties, college teachers, 1954–1990.

values like free speech (Prothro and Grigg 1960; McClosky 1964); as Justice Holmes among others has made clear, one may favor freedom of expression and at the same time wish to restrict certain kinds of speech on the grounds that they harm or endanger society. Still, most Americans in the middle 1950s undeniably had rather narrow conceptions of what sorts of liberties should be protected for whom.

When the NORC General Social Survey (beginning in 1972) repeated a number of Stouffer's questions, however, it found very large changes in the responses.[7] As can be seen in figure 3.4, which presents trends for the representative case of college teachers, the public gave much more libertarian answers to these questions. A majority now favored civil liberties under nearly all the circumstances mentioned. The change was particularly great with respect to Communists. By the spring of 1973, 33% more people than in 1954—a total of 61%—favored allowing Communist speakers; this leveled off but then rose a bit more to 66% in 1989 and 1990. By 1978, 35% more, for a total of 64%, opposed removing Communist books. By 1974, 38% more (though still only 44%) opposed firing Communist teachers; this reached 55% in 1990.

A similar, though slightly weaker, trend applied to the rights of antireligionists. By 1972, 29% more Americans, for a total of 67%, favored allowing antireligious speeches; 26% more (63%) opposed removing antireligious books; and 30% more (though still only 42%) wanted to allow antireligious teachers. (This figure reached 53% by 1989 and 1990.) Similarly, by the spring of 1972, 15% more Americans (for a total of 81%) favored permitting Socialist speakers, 22% more (60%) wanted to allow Socialist teachers, and 13% more (73%) opposed removing Socialist books from local libraries.

Shorter NORC-GSS time series (with new items, not drawn from Stouffer) indicate that support of freedom to speak, put books in libraries, and teach college rose substantially between 1973 and 1989 for homosexuals; between 1976 and 1990 it stayed at a high but only slightly increasing level for racists and militarists, although there was markedly less support for allowing racists and militarists to teach college.

Because of the long period before 1972 during which none of these civil liberties questions was asked, we cannot be sure of the precise timing of the main changes. Graphs like figure 3.4 that connect the dots between far-apart surveys may give a misleading impression of gradual change. We cannot rule out the possibility that opinions changed suddenly, right after 1954 or just before 1972, or that fluctuations back and forth (perhaps including a temporary decline during the period of the Vietnam War and urban unrest) interrupted the general trend. But the finding of only gradual and generally liberalizing changes in opinions in the NORC-GSS surveys of the early 1970s suggests, at least, that something similar was happening earlier. More direct evidence comes from a closely related opinion trend. The proportion of Americans telling NORC that members of the Communist party should not be allowed to speak on the radio dropped six percentage points (from 77% to 71%) between 1957 and 1963, indicating that opinions were beginning to liberalize by the early 1960s (see figure 3.5, below).[8]

The overall changes in civil liberties opinions from 1954 to the 1970s are comparable in magnitude to the opinion changes on civil rights. They, too, are among the largest we have found among the thousands of policy questions examined. And they, too, occurred for reasons consistent with our picture of a rational public.

The changes are sometimes attributed to rising educational levels. Stouffer pointed out in the 1950s that Americans with more formal education tended to be much more protective of the civil liberties he studied than others were. He found, for example, that 66% of the college graduates, but only 16% of those with no more than a grade school education, fell into the "more tolerant" category on a summary scale (Stouffer 1955, p. 90). Stouffer's elite sample of "community leaders," too, gave more libertarian responses than average citizens—an identical 66% were "more tolerant" (Stouffer 1955, pp. 50–51).

Both these findings have generally continued to hold up in later years:

the highly educated and various elites—delegates to political conventions, community leaders, lawyers—still tend to be more supportive than the general public of civil liberties (McClosky 1964; Nunn, Crockett, and Williams 1978; McClosky and Brill 1983). This has led some observers to argue that the proper working of American democracy depends heavily upon a relatively small elite rather than on the beliefs, values, and opinions of the mass public (see Neuman 1986; we are skeptical and will have more to say about this below).

The reason commonly given for these differences is that formal education exposes people to diverse ideas and emphasizes rational discourse, leading to greater tolerance of dissent and more valuing of the right to propagate ideas of all sorts, even offensive ones (Hyman and Wright 1979). But any such effects probably depend, in part, upon the predominant ideas in the society and the educational system at the time, especially on the interests and values of influentials. It is not clear that more education in Nazi Germany or Stalinist Russia invariably led to more tolerance.

In the context of the relatively liberal American educational system of the mid-twentieth century, it is certainly plausible that the increases in average levels of education between the 1950s and the 1970s contributed to the rising support for civil liberties. According to J. Davis (1975), in fact, increased schooling could account for about one-third of the trend. But this was certainly not the whole story. Opinions changed in a parallel fashion among all the education groups of the population. And new cohorts of Americans reaching adulthood in the 1960s and 1970s were even more liberal than their increased formal education would lead one to expect.

Moreover, the meaning of "tolerance" and the precise role of education in affecting these opinions is very much open to question. Sullivan, Piereson, and Marcus (1982) have argued that tolerance, as a general orientation, should be measured in relation to people and ideas that are considered dangerous or offensive. The Stouffer and early NORC-GSS questions measured tolerance only toward certain left-wing groups, which may have varied in perceived offensiveness over time, and which may have been perceived differently by people of different educational levels. The objects of tolerance need to be taken into account.

Very likely the main targets of intolerance have changed since the 1950s. In 1978, when people were asked by NORC to pick from a list the group they "like(d) the least," they chose not only Communists (29%) and atheists (8%) but the Ku Klux Klan (24%), the "new left" Symbionese Liberation Army (8%), and Black Panthers (6%), and a scattering of other groups (Sullivan, Piereson, and Marcus 1982, p. 86). Most people were quite intolerant of their least-liked group, saying that members should not be allowed to hold public rallies (66%), should be "outlawed" (71%), should not be allowed to teach in public schools (81%), and should be banned from being president of the United States (84%) (Sullivan et al. 1982, p. 67). According to a *multivariate* model using this kind of "content-controlled" measure of tolerance, the differences between highly educated people and others (taking effect through a sense of psychological security, ideological liberalism, and general democratic norms) were not as strong as other studies have indicated (Sullivan et al. 1982, pp. 114, 225).

Thus Stouffer's and other education findings were probably inflated: not only was it bivariate but it specifically applied to the Communist, Socialist, and atheist target groups, which in 1954 were most disliked by respondents of lower education. In addition, Schuman and Presser (1977, p. 167) have shown that some of the Stouffer/GSS question wording, which makes antilibertarian responses particularly easy ("Somebody in your community suggests the book should be removed from the library. Would you favor removing the book, or not?"), leads to bigger education differences than more balanced items do.

Using indirect evidence, one recent study indicates that education's effect on tolerance is mediated by cognitive sophistication (Bobo and Licari 1989). This makes sense, to the extent that there are constitutionally or otherwise legally protected rights that the cognitively sophisticated know about and want to safeguard. Constitutional provisions and Court decisions are undoubtedly better known by the sophisticated. The role of cognitive sophistication is more complicated, however, if the threat posed by a particular group is perceived differently by those of differing sophistication.

Historical Events and Circumstances

In any case, opinions about various aspects of civil liberties have not all moved in lockstep, simply and solely reflecting education levels or some sort of generalized "tolerance" or intolerance. As we have seen, such opinions have varied markedly with respect to different policies (college teaching is much more sensitive than speeches or books) and different ideas or groups (fewer Americans have wanted to protect liberties for Communists than for Socialists or atheists). An important source of this differentiation is varying perceptions of the threat or danger or offensiveness of different groups (Sullivan et al. 1982, pp. 186, 225)—which is also a major source of opinion change over time, as the public's views of various groups have changed.

Willingness to let antireligionists speak and write and teach, for example, has risen partly because Americans' religious beliefs have weakened. Between 1964 and 1973, NORC surveys found a drop of more than 15% in the proportion of respondents attending religious services once a week or more. Atheists seem less offensive to those unsure of their own faith. There is now less disapproval of interfaith marriages; greater willingness to vote for political candidates regardless of their religious or atheistic backgrounds (about 25% more willingness to vote for atheists in 1978 than 1958, according to Gallup); and greater acceptance of the separation of church and state.

Likewise, the especially large increase in support for the civil liberties of Communists resulted partly from the fact that Stouffer asked his questions in the depths of the Cold War, when many Americans believed what their leaders told them: that domestic Communists posed a serious threat of espionage or even revolution. During the 1970s and 1980s, by contrast, such concerns would have seemed fanciful—though worries about the radical right, the New Left, racists, terrorists, and others partly may have taken their place. (In the late 1980s the NORC-GSS consistently found people less protective of the liberties of militarists than of others mentioned.) Little wonder that more people were willing to tolerate Communist speakers, writers, and teachers when communism presented no credible threat.

Survey data collected prior to 1954 provide additional evidence that changing circumstances have in fact affected opinions about civil liberties (see figure 3.5). They do not reveal uniform, mechanical increases in tolerance as education levels rose but rather changes of different magnitudes and in different directions—sometimes growing *less* tolerant—depending upon world and national events. Between 1938 and 1942, for example, as the United States entered World War II and national security became a primary concern, a Gallup and OPOR question revealed a drop of 9% in the proportion of Americans that favored "allowing 'radicals' to hold meetings and express their views."[9] Data reported by Hyman and Sheatsley (1953, p. 15) show a similar change, with 8% more of the public in favor of restricting freedom of speech "with respect to certain times, subjects, and groups," in January 1941 than in February 1940 (OPOR). But between July 1942 and February 1945, after the USSR had fought as a United States ally through most of the war and the struggle with Germany was nearing an end, giving less reason to fear internal subversion from Communists or Nazis, there was a 16% rise (to 47%) in the proportion that favored permitting radical meetings.[10]

Similarly, majorities of Americans throughout the 1940s thought that membership in the Communist party should be forbidden by law, but the size of the majority dropped substantially from 76% in May 1941 (when prewar anticommunism and anger at the nonaggression pact be-

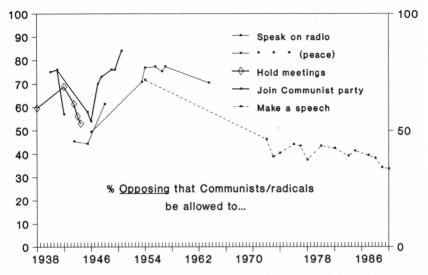

FIG. 3.5   Free speech and assembly for Communists, radicals, 1938–1990.

tween the Soviet Union and Germany ran high), to 54% in June 1946, when wartime cooperation between the United States and the USSR had not yet completely broken down. (The initial drop occurred between May 1941 and June 1942, in response to the Nazis attacking Russia and the United States entering the war.) The proportion of Americans wanting to outlaw the Communist party then rose again to 76% by March 1949 as the Cold War worsened, and to 84% by the end of 1950 during the Korean War (Gallup).

During the early years of the Cold War, when the Truman administration's "loyalty-security" program and the House Un-American Activities Committee and Senator Joseph McCarthy and others were arousing fears of domestic communism (Freeland 1972), the public expressed less willingness to allow newspapers to "criticize our form of government" (a 9% rise in opposition, to 36%, between April 1948 and May 1953: NORC). Gallup surveys in May 1948 and April 1953 revealed a 10% rise, to a near unanimous 93%, in support for "requiring all members of the Communist party in this country to register with the Justice Department in Washington." As McCarthyism flourished, NORC found more people wanting to "find out all the Communists in the country, even if some innocent people are accused": 68% favored this in January 1956, up 8% since May 1953. (Nunn et al. 1978, p. 37, report a big drop from 64% to 25% between 1954 and 1973, according to a slightly different trend item.)

Most striking is the NORC item we have already mentioned concerning Communists on the radio. Between early 1946 and the beginning of 1954 there was a dramatic 28% drop, to the very low level of 23%, in the proportion of Americans thinking that members of the Communist party should be allowed to speak on the radio. Most of this change, 22%, occurred by November 1953. (See figure 3.5, which graphs the corresponding rise in percent opposed.) This, and the items showing increased opposition to critical newspapers and more eagerness to "find out" all the Communists, demonstrate beyond doubt that as the Cold War developed and McCarthy-style anti-Communist fervor increased, acceptance of civil liberties for Communists fell markedly.

The postwar decline in favoring civil liberties for Communists is important for several reasons. For one thing, it drastically affects how one should interpret the trend between 1954 and the 1970s. Libertarianism does not simply increase automatically as time passes and educational levels rise. Stouffer's 1954 survey, the usual baseline, is a misleading starting point for analysis because it came at a very atypical time; it happened to record anti-Communist attitudes very nearly at their peak. The post-1954 increase in support for civil liberties, in fact, formed something like a mirror image of the earlier Cold War decline. Here we basically agree with Mueller's (1988) conclusions with respect to public tolerance of Communists, but we offer more evidence at the far ends of the trends pieced together in figure 3.5. Anticommunism stood near a peak as World War II began and Russia reached a temporary modus vivendi with Hitler; it dropped to a historic low as Hitler attacked Russia and U.S.-Soviet cooperation blossomed during the war; it rose to prewar or higher levels during the Cold War; it then declined and by 1990 probably reached an all-time low, given perceptions of warm Gorbachev-era U.S.-Soviet relations (see Chaps. 5 and 6).

By the same token, the argument that elites are more tolerant than the masses and must be relied upon to preserve democracy requires considerable qualification in light of the early postwar data. The fact is that, while a few elites spoke up for civil liberties, many—not just Dies and McCarthy but leaders of both parties from Presidents Truman and Eisenhower on down to the state and local level—deliberately contributed to anti-Communist fervor (see Gibson 1988). Often they did so by means of false or misleading information and interpretations, a matter to be discussed further in Chapter 9. With very few exceptions, the press was slow to provide space for critical appraisals (see Bayley 1981). But our main point here is that, given the information that was made available, the public reacted in understandable and indeed fairly sensible ways to what they could reasonably see as varying levels of threat to U.S. society.

We would not want to argue that the American public is highly tolerant of dissent. In fact, Americans have regularly been hostile to virtually all protest groups or social movements in their early stages: even civil rights protests, anti–Vietnam War demonstrations, and the women's rights movement, whose positions ultimately gained substantial support and helped bring about important changes in pubic opinion and in policy (see Chap. 8). As McClosky and Brill eloquently point out (1983, chap. 1), tolerance is unnatural, difficult, an acquired taste. The most natural thing in the world is to want to silence people who are offensive or dangerous, especially in times of peril. Much of the American public has succumbed to that impulse when the world has looked threatening and when elites and the press have egged them on.

Still, there can be little doubt that the predominant opinion trend of the last fifty years or so has been toward more tolerance for at least certain kinds of dissent, and less demand for government interference with individuals' liberties. A further illustration of that trend, and of the importance of circumstances and events, comes from public reactions to a Gallup question about whether everyone in the United States "should be required to carry an identification card containing, among other things, his picture and his fingerprints."

In the midst of World War II, identification cards were apparently considered a reasonable national security precaution, and increasing proportions of Americans supported requiring everyone to carry such a card: 77% did so in July 1942. Thirty-five years later, however, in 1977—a year that was relatively calm and tranquil—only 47% favored such identification cards. This drop of 30% is among the largest in our data. The opposition to identification cards (in contrast to routine European practice) exemplifies the U.S. public's strong concern for the privacy of individuals.

It is also noteworthy, given our claims about rational public opinion, that the public makes a number of distinctions among different kinds of threats to privacy. Support varies with the degree of intrusiveness and with other possible costs and benefits. Simple extension of the use of Social Security cards, for example, is considerably more acceptable than the issuance of new identification cards with photographs and fingerprints. In each of four surveys between 1977 and 1984, about two-thirds of the public told Gallup that everyone should be required to carry "an identification card such as a Social Security card."

Concern about privacy has also manifested itself in opposition to

computerized data banks on citizens, and—especially after Watergate—
in overwhelming opposition to government wiretapping of citizens. (See
Katz and Tassone [1990] and Louis Harris and Associates and Westin
[1990], which summarize the available trend data on privacy and show
how the public has rationally distinguished the costs and benefits of data,
banks.) We will discuss this further in connection with crime policy.

Crime, Punishment, and Gun Control

With respect to crime and punishment, like the other topics we have
discussed, the public has exhibited rational opinions, differentiating clearly among alternative policies and reacting to changing realities. But (for
good reasons) the opinion trends have differed in certain respects from
those on the civil liberties discussed above. Public opinion concerning
criminal justice and the rights of the accused moved in a liberal direction
from the 1950s to the 1960s (and in some cases the mid-1970s), but then
increasing concerns about crime led to more desire for stringent punishment and less support for procedural safeguards. Opinion about gun
control has followed a special dynamic of its own.

In the middle 1950s, at the same time that Stouffer and others were
finding rather low public support for freedom of speech and the press, most
Americans expressed somewhat cavalier attitudes about the rights of
people accused of crimes. The Fifth Amendment protection against self-
incrimination (which was then being invoked in congressional hearings by
those accused of Communist associations) was scorned by some elites who
referred to "Fifth Amendment Communists" and was held in low repute by
the public. Majorities of Americans favored rather stringent treatment of
criminals. The Warren Court decisions protecting the rights of the accused
were quite unpopular.

Unfortunately, we have found very few repeated survey questions to
establish precise trends on these matters up to the 1960s. The best trend
data are those documenting a strong 26% decline in support for capital
punishment for murderers, between 1953 and 1966, which we will discuss
below. But a great deal of circumstantial evidence based on one-time survey items suggests that there was a general libertarian trend. It seems safe
to assume, for example, that fewer Americans in the early 1960s would
have supported "sterilization of habitual criminals and the hopelessly in-
sane" than the 84% who did so in 1937. (Indeed, the Gallup organization
might well have shrunk from repeating that question if asked to do so.)

Based on the circumstantial evidence, we think it probable that the
public became substantially more solicitous about procedural rights and
due process of law in the early 1960s than it had been in the 1950s or ear-

lier. Very likely the same factors affecting attitudes about freedom of speech and the press—namely, the decline of the Cold War, increasing domestic tranquility, and rising educational levels—led Americans to shift emphasis somewhat away from punishing the guilty and toward protecting the innocent.

Around the middle of the 1960s, however, the tide turned. Urban riots by blacks, and then protests and demonstrations against the Vietnam War by students and others, together with increased media reports of violent crimes (the reports apparently being more important than crime rates themselves: see Funkhauser 1973a and 1973b) led to increased desires for "law and order." This was reflected in, and perhaps accentuated by, George Wallace's and Richard Nixon's 1968 presidential campaign attacks on the Warren Court and on Ramsey Clark's Justice Department (Nixon declared that "(t)oday all across the land guilty men walk free from hundreds of courtrooms. Something has gone terribly wrong in America": R. Harris 1970, p. 23), and in the strong rhetoric of Vice-President Agnew and Attorney General Mitchell during the Nixon administration.

Between April 1965 and January 1969, for example, there was a very substantial 26% rise, to 83%, in the proportion of the public who believed that the courts were "not harsh enough" in their treatment of criminals (Gallup) (see figure 3.6). Responses to a slightly different Harris survey question showed a big 33% increase between October 1967 and 1978 in the feeling that courts were "too lenient," with more than half (twenty percentage points) of the increase occurring by 1970. According to NORC-GSS, using the Gallup question, this trend continued into the 1970s, with a 15% increase in "not harsh enough" responses between early 1972 and spring 1978. The Harris question showed a 16% rise in "too lenient" responses between August 1973 and March 1982.

The perceived purpose of punishment also changed. Between 1970 and 1982, according to slightly varying Harris items, the 78% who said the "main emphasis" in most prisons should be on rehabilitation rather than punishing the individual or protecting society from future crimes fell to 46%. Likewise, Gallup found that the 17% in July 1955 who thought it was more important to "punish them [those in prison] for their crimes" rather than "get them started 'on the right road,' " rose to 34% by 1982 and 44% in June 1989.

The same increased desire to punish criminals was reflected in an August 1970 Harris poll, when 73% of those queried said that "a person who commits a horrible crime should be compelled to answer questions about it during a trial." This rejection of the Constitutional protection against self incrimination rose a further 11% over the next three years. Likewise in au-

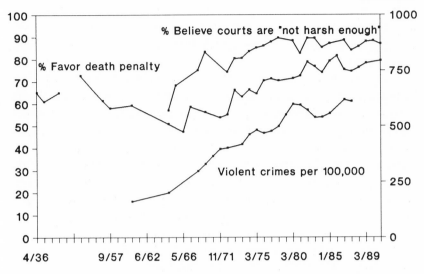

Fig. 3.6   Capital punishment and courts' treatment of criminals, 1936–1990.

tumn 1970, 49% located themselves on the "stop criminal activity" (as opposed to 34% on the "protect the legal rights of those accused") side of an SRC/CPS seven-point scale.

The trend toward punitiveness was not mechanical or inexorable, however; opinions reacted to information and events, moving in different directions at different times and distinguishing among different types of criminal justice policies. A sharp rise in demand for harsher treatment of criminals, for example, can be bracketed between April and September 1965, after the rioting in Watts in mid-August and an upsurge in the reporting of crime. (Stinchcombe et al. 1980, pp. 67–68, show that desires for harsher courts were related particularly strongly to fear of crime in 1965, more so than in later years.) On the other hand, with the end of urban unrest and the decline of antiwar demonstrations after about 1970, concern over law and order eased somewhat. Between autumn 1970 and the beginning of 1975, the SRC/CPS "stop criminal activity" self-ratings dropped 7%. Between autumn 1970 and the end of 1972, 11% fewer people (though still a total of 55%) indicated on another CPS seven-point scale that they wanted to "use police and the national guard" to stop disturbances in colleges and high schools.

Similarly, the Watergate scandals seem to have moderated opinions on certain criminal justice issues. From Vietnam-obsessed 1969 to Watergate-era 1974, for example, Gallup and NORC-GSS found more than a

30% rise, from 50% to 83%, in opposition to wiretapping. (This heavy opposition subsequently declined a bit, as concerns about fighting crime rose.) Between autumn 1972 and August 1978, support for requiring newspaper reporters to reveal the names of their sources in court dropped 12%, to only 25% in favor (Gallup), largely, it would appear, because of the roles of journalists in exposing government misconduct in the Watergate affair: half the change had occurred by October 1973. Similarly, between March 1974 and the beginning of 1976, public endorsement of having FBI computer files on individuals dropped 7%, to only 25% in favor (Harris), probably responding to post-Watergate revelations of abuses of power by the CIA and other government agencies.

Still, as figure 3.6 shows, desires for more strict court treatment of criminals continued to rise through most of the 1970s. And between autumn 1974 and the beginning of 1979 there was a reversal in the trend of opinion concerning rights of the accused, with 12% more locating themselves on the "stop criminal activity" side of the seven-point CPS scale. Throughout the 1970s and 1980s, as we saw in figure 2.2, sentiment that "too little" money was being spent to stop crime remained extremely high: 73% in 1971, 72% in 1982, 75% in 1989, and 73% in 1990, according to Roper and NORC surveys. It eased off a bit during the 1979–1982 recessions but remained as high or higher than for any other issue surveyed.

Capital Punishment

Several of the main trends we have discussed are apparent in responses to the frequently repeated Gallup, NORC, and Harris questions concerning capital punishment for persons convicted of murder. Support for capital punishment declined rather gradually and steadily from the mid-1950s to the mid-1960s, but then jumped up in 1966–1967 and, after a pause, rose gradually through the 1970s and 1980s (see figure 3.6).

According to Gallup, for example, in November 1953 a solid 73% of Americans favored capital punishment for murderers. This support gradually declined twenty-six percentage points—to just 47% in favor— by May 1966, in harmony with the general libertarian movement of opinion at that time. Then, however, it rose a marked 12% in one year (by June 1967), in response to riots in black ghettos and increased reports of crime, including the highly publicized murder of eight nurses by Richard Speck. After a pause, the figure increased by 16% between October 1971 and April 1976, reaching 70% in favor of capital punishment for murderers. The upward trend continued, regaining the 1953 figure of 73% in favor in 1981 and going on to 78% in 1985, where opinion leveled off through 1990.

Similarly, the Harris organization found a 28% rise between 1965 (45%) and 1977 (73%) in the proportion of Americans favoring the death penalty, with 72% still in favor at the beginning of 1983. NORC-GSS surveys show that support rose 6% between early 1972 and spring 1973 and (according to a slightly different time series) 7% between 1975 and 1977, with a 79% reading in 1990.

Furthermore, according to Harris, between 1973 and 1977 there were 8% and 13% rises in support for the death penalty for all killers of policemen and for all first degree murderers, respectively. (Here, too, the public drew some clear distinctions in levels of support.) During the same 1973–1977 interval Harris also found a 12% increase, to a level of 54%, in support of capital punishment "even if it could be proved . . . that the death penalty was not more effective than long prison sentences" as a deterrent. Clearly, much of the pubic accepted retribution, the expression of community outrage, or incapacitation as sufficient justification for capital punishment; some data suggest a focus on incapacitation.

The rise in support for capital punishment is consistent with the public's loss of faith in the idea of rehabilitation, as noted above: perhaps not an altogether unreasonable judgment, given the state of prisons and the criminal justice system in the United States.

Gun Control

This is obviously connected with issues of crime and punishment, but the relationship is not as straightforward as one might think. The survey data indicate that Americans make a number of distinctions among policies concerning firearms. Most people at most times have favored regulation but not prohibition of most kinds of weapons, with opinion varying according to weapon type; many cherish the right to bear arms for self-defense and (particularly in the West and South) for hunting and target shooting. Events involving crime and assassinations and the like have affected attitudes about gun control in understandable ways that are different from their effects on opinions about other crime-related policies.

Rather than displaying nonattitudes, or reacting automatically and emotionally to the mention of guns, the American public distinguishes fairly sharply among types of weapons (long guns, handguns, cheap "Saturday night special" handguns, assault rifles, automatic weapons), among different types of policy measures (prohibitions, permits, registration), and among types of possible gun owners (ordinary citizens, the young, felons). These distinctions have sometimes eluded academics and pollsters, but they are critical to understanding the coherent pattern of public attitudes and the reasonable ways in which opinions have changed.

There is little evidence of majority support for laws totally *banning* the main categories of firearms. "Saturday night specials" and assault rifles, yes, but certainly not long guns, and probably not handguns. Practically the only scrap of evidence in favor of a handgun ban comes from a 1959 Gallup survey, taken at a high point of procontrol sentiment, when 63% said they thought there should be a law which would "forbid the possession" of pistols and revolvers "except by the police or other authorized persons." But the ambiguous phrase "authorized persons," conceivably encompassing ordinary citizens with permits, probably inflated support for prohibition.

The same 1959 Gallup survey is more useful for pointing out several clear distinctions in the public's thinking. For example, 57% said they thought it should be illegal for private citizens to have loaded weapons in their homes. But only 35% favored completely forbidding "the use of guns" (presumably including long guns) by persons under age eighteen, while 53% wanted strict regulations on their use versus only 12% that wanted to continue with few regulations.

Opposition to banning guns (particularly long guns) altogether has been especially strong among white Protestant males in the South and West—members of what Stinchcombe et al. (1980) call the "hunting culture." Support for prohibiting the use or ownership of firearms continues to come mostly from women and from urban areas, where guns are more a source of danger than of entertainment. But even this support has apparently diminished somewhat because of the double-edged character of guns in urban settings: they are seen as a means of protection as well as a source of threat.

As reported crime rates and fear of urban crime increased in the mid-1960s, support for relatively stringent forms of gun control dropped markedly. By the beginning of 1965, according to Gallup, 9% fewer people than in 1959—just 48%—favored outlawing loaded weapons in the home, and 10% fewer (53%) favored forbidding possession of pistols. By August 1966, 7% fewer—only 28%—favored forbidding guns to people under eighteen years old. Some of this erosion of support occurred in the urban population, which increasingly was purchasing handguns with the idea that they would be useful in self-defense. The mainly rural owners of long guns reacted to increased crime rates by buying pistols, not by favoring gun control. Sentiment for outright bans has mostly focused on cheap "Saturday night specials" and, in the late 1980s (responding to spectacular killings on the streets and even in schools) on assault rifles.

On the other hand, large majorities of Americans have always favored certain fairly limited kinds of *regulations* and restrictions upon gun ownership and use. They continue to do so, with variations in the level of support depending upon events and circumstances. According to a Gallup question, a policy of requiring police *permits* for guns was endorsed by 82% in December 1963, shortly after President John Kennedy's assassination. There were 70% (down 12%) who favored permits even at the extreme low point of support in August 1966, and 75% did so in 1972. According to the NORC-GSS, which asked the same question, public backing for gun permits stayed around 75% through the 1970s (see Tom Smith 1980b) and the early 1980s, with only a slight upward blip in response to the assassination attempt on President Reagan—who continued to oppose gun control even after his narrow escape. Support for gun permits stood at 76% in 1974 and 1975 and 71% in 1980, rising again to 80% in 1990 but producing the predominately flat trend line shown in figure 3.7.

Opinion on the milder but more inclusive step of *registering* guns has been similar to that on permits: highly supportive. In June 1968 (shortly after the assassinations of Robert Kennedy and Martin Luther King, Jr.), Harris found that 84% favored registering all guns; 73% still favored registration in June 1979. Harris data also show that the majority favoring registration of handguns rose by 11% (to an overwhelming 80%) between 1971 and 1975, and that support for requiring permits for rifles increased by 7% (to 75%) between 1975 and 1978. Curiously, the proportion of citizens favoring handgun registration dropped sharply, by 14%, between 1978 and 1980 (Harris), and the majority favoring stricter laws on handgun sales dropped 10%, to 63% in favor, between May 1975 and January 1980 (Gallup). We are not sure how to account for these changes except perhaps in terms of foreign policy tensions and the Reaganite movement to "get government off our backs." Roper found steady support for banning guns between 1975 and 1978; NBC found a bit of increase in support for gun permits between December 1979 and April 1981.

Backing for gun regulation has generally been strongest among the same demographic groups that tend to favor outright bans, namely, women and urban residents. (For a thorough discussion see Stinchcombe et al. 1980, chap. 5.) As the above examples indicate, it has tended to rise when traumatic events like political assassinations involving mail order rifles or cheap handguns have highlighted the possible benefits of controls, and then has fallen back as tranquility has returned and as hunters and the National Rifle Association and its weapon-manufacturing backers have lobbied against legislation and influenced public debate. Support for

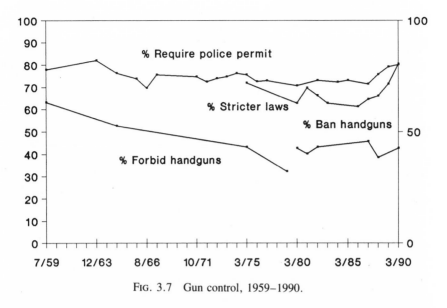

FIG. 3.7   Gun control, 1959–1990.

restrictions, like bans, also eroded somewhat as urban dwellers with rising fears of crime moved to purchase guns for self-defense.

Women's and Minorities' Rights

In the next three sections we will discuss a variety of interrelated social issues involving the rights of women and minorities, birth control, abortion, human life, and styles of living. The connections and distinctions that the public has drawn among these issues suggest a considerable degree of collective sophistication, as do the patterns of opinion change over time.

During the 1960s and 1970s, public opinion moved strongly in a liberal direction on most of these matters. But several of the liberalizing trends hit a plateau in the 1980s. New information and new social problems in the 1980s brought certain reversals, particularly with respect to drugs and sexual behavior.

Just as the public increasingly favored civil rights and legal equality for black Americans, it came to approve of equal treatment for various other groups, including women, Latinos and other minorities, "senior citizens" or the elderly, "gays" or homosexuals (these changing labels themselves reflected and perhaps affected attitude changes), and the disabled and handicapped. Even "affirmative action programs in *industry*" ("provided there are no rigid quotas") for women, for "Spanish-Ameri-

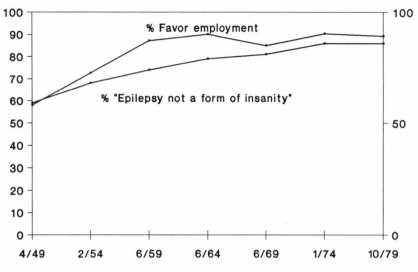

FIG. 3.8   Attitudes about epileptics, 1949–1979.

cans," blacks, Vietnam veterans, and especially the physically handicapped, each won 72% support or more among those with opinions, according to Harris surveys in 1978 and 1982; support for "affirmative action programs in *higher education*" was usually even a bit stronger. (The physically handicapped received the most support [over 90%], followed by Vietnam veterans [80% or more] with respect to both jobs and education.) Further data on some of these groups are scanty but show similar tendencies.

To take a little-noticed but important sign of changing attitudes, between 1949 and 1974 Gallup found a remarkable thirty-two point rise in the percentage of Americans who said that epileptics should "be employed in jobs like other people." Among those who said they had read or heard about epilepsy, the proportion approving equal employment rose from 58% to 90%. As figure 3.8 shows, this trend was paralleled by increasing knowledge that epilepsy (which can now be controlled and goes unnoticed in the vast majority of sufferers) is not a form of insanity. The same trend appears in responses to a question about willingness to allow one's children to play with epileptics. Increased knowledge of social—and, in the case of epilepsy, medical—realities, transmitted through the mass media and popular culture, have increased understanding, tolerance, sympathy, and support for legal protection of many sorts of people who are "different."

The case of homosexuals is especially interesting because of the extremely widespread (and even increasing) public distaste for the idea of

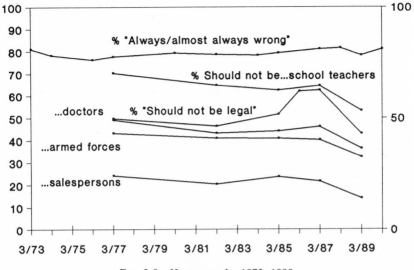

FIG. 3.9   Homosexuals, 1973–1990.

homosexuality, which, throughout the 1970s and 1980s, about 80% of the public called "always" or "almost always wrong." Yet, as figure 3.9 shows, far fewer people wanted homosexual relations to be *illegal,* another example of the public's capacity to make distinctions. With the outbreak of the AIDS (Acquired Immune Deficiency Syndrome) epidemic in the early 1980s and the attribution of its spread to homosexual activity, the proportion of Americans saying homosexual relations should not be legal rose temporarily. (Even in this conservative environment, NBC surveys found a strikingly liberal trend: support for legal restrictions on the sexual activities of AIDS carriers dropped 10% between 1985 and 1986.)

Soon, however, as heterosexuals' fears that they themselves would get AIDS diminished, and as drug-needle-sharing emerged as a more serious source of disease transmission, the tide turned. The NORC-GSS found that public support for protection of Stouffer-type civil liberties for homosexuals, always at high levels, continued to rise. By 1989, the idea that homosexual relations between consenting adults should be legal rebounded sharply (by 19%), from 38% to 57%, according to Gallup (Kagay 1989, p. 13; we have excluded "don't knows" in figure 3.9). At the same time, especially between 1987 and 1989, support for equal job opportunities for homosexuals grew as well, but with continuing marked distinctions among different occupations: overwhelming majorities approved homosexuals in sales work, but fewer approved them in the military or as doctors, and still fewer as high school teachers, members of the clergy, or elementary school teachers (who could influence children). While tolerating homosexuality, most Americans did not want to encourage it.

Women

Equality for women, who have been the subject of many more surveys than most other groups, has enjoyed an especially strong long-term trend of increased support. In 1972, for example, 49% of the SRC/CPS respondents located themselves on the side of a seven-point scale that favored giving women an "equal role with men in running business, industry, and government," while only 31% took the "women's place is in the home" side. Support for an "equal role" then rose by 11%—to 60%—at the beginning of 1979, and to 62% by December 1980. Similarly, between 1970 and 1975, Harris surveys showed a 21% increase in the proportion of Americans saying that the status of women should be strengthened, and between 1981 and January 1985 ABC found an 8% increase, from 71% to 79%.

The most sweeping and dramatic evidence of changed attitudes concerns the *employment* of women, as exemplified by a Gallup question that was asked in 1937 and repeated by Gallup in 1975. In 1937, with jobs scarce in the midst of the Great Depression, only 18% of Americans said they approved of a woman "earning money in business or industry" if she had a "husband capable of supporting her." (According to Gallup's 1939 variations on this question, Illinois and Massachusetts were actually considering legal restrictions on the employment of women.) In 1975, however—itself a time of some economic stringency—fully 71% approved of married women earning money in business or industry, an enormous rise of 53%. According to NORC-GSS—asking the same question—the figure rose even further to 86%, in 1985; it slipped a bit, to 79%, in 1989 but edged back to 82% in 1990.[11] These data are presented in figure 3.10.

Various recent survey questions capture related trends concerning women and jobs. Between 1970 and 1975, for example, there was a 9% rise—to 73%—in the proportion of the public generally favoring more day-care facilities (Harris). Between 1972 and 1977 there was an 8% drop in the proportion saying that female employees whose husbands have jobs should be laid off first (SRC/CPS); in 1977 only 39% of Americans expressed that view. And after a 1977 NORC-GSS survey there was a 17% drop in agreement with the sentiment that women should "take care of running their homes and leave running the country to men," with only 21% agreeing in 1988 and a further drop to 18% in 1990.

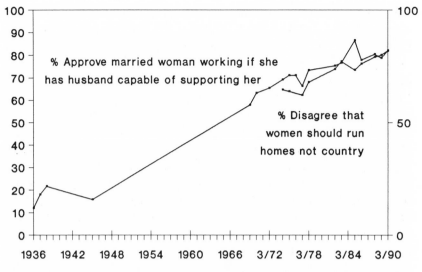

Fig. 3.10   Women working outside the home, 1936–1990.

The shift in favor of equal employment opportunities for women seems, like the similar movement with respect to blacks, to have followed naturally from basic American values of individualism and equal opportunity, once old, firmly rooted habits of mind were vigorously shaken and attention was focused on the issue. Just as blacks had to overcome beliefs that they were somehow inferior and not worthy of equal treatment, women had to overcome the widespread view that they were weak and helpless and were needed at home for housekeeping and child raising—a conception that crumbled in the face of changes in the labor market (growing demand for female workers and growing need for the money, both by two-paycheck and by female-headed families), the increased availability of birth control devices, and preferences for smaller families. We will say more about these matters below and in Chapter 8.

The opinion shift occurred in a more or less parallel fashion across virtually all segments of society: men and women, young and old, urban and rural. Contrary to a widespread assumption, at any given moment in time men tended to endorse female equality about as much as women did, though fundamentalist Protestants, churchgoers, those with many children, older people, and those from rural areas and the South all tended to oppose egalitarian measures like the ERA in somewhat higher proportions than others. Among women, those in the labor force (especially young, highly educated, and professional women) were most supportive of women's liberation; lower-income women mostly worked out of necessity rather than for self-fulfillment, and many homemakers objected to any implication that their focus on family was not worthwhile (see Mansbridge 1986, pp. 213, 216, 106; Sapiro 1984; Klein 1984). Gradually, however, all groups moved in the direction of accepting various aspects of gender equality, including the idea that women should be allowed freely to work outside the home if they wanted or needed to.

On the ERA—the Equal Rights Amendment to the Constitution, which Congress approved and submitted to the states for ratification in 1972 but which was approved by only thirty-five of the necessary thirty-eight states before time ran out in 1982—there was no discernible change in public opinion at all. Virtually all polls showed solid majority support throughout the decade. In September 1970, for example, CBS found that 60% of those with opinions favored "an 'Equal Rights' amendment" that would "guarantee that women would have all the rights that men have." In October 1974, Gallup found 78% support in response to a complicated question about voting on an equal rights proposition. In March 1975, Gallup asked whether respondents favored or opposed "the Equal Rights Amendment . . . which would give women equal rights and responsibilities" and found 65% of those with opinions favored ERA. The proportion stayed very nearly the same all thirteen times this question was asked by NBC and Gallup from 1975 through 1981 (see the very useful table in Mansbridge 1986, pp. 206–209).[12] Some of these trends are displayed in figure 3.11; our figures, as usual, exclude "don't knows."

Likewise, a different NBC question about "the Equal Rights Amendment . . . often referred to as the ERA" (not further characterized) elicited about 60% support each of the eleven times it was asked from 1980 to 1982, as did a similar CBS question asked ten times in those same years. Support for ERA was also usually close to 60% in response to a Harris question asked eight times between 1975 and 1981, even though this balanced item mentioned the opposition argument that women "need to be protected" by special laws. Support for ERA was found to be substantially higher—77%—in April 1982, when Harris interviewers read the actual (attractive but presumably unfamiliar) text of the amendment to respondents.

In May 1982, Harris columns in newspapers around the country declared "ERA Support Soars as Deadline Nears," and reported that the 50% (with "don't knows" included in the base) that favored ERA on the "need to be protected" question in January 1982 had jumped to 63% in April (from 52% to 65%, excluding "not sure" responses). As Mansbridge (1986, pp. 16–18, 211) points out, however, this was an artifact of

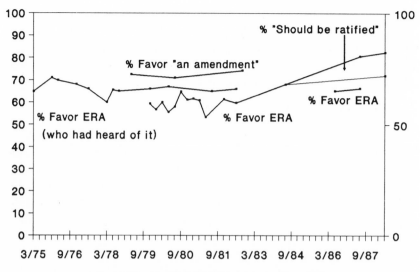

FIG. 3.11   Equal rights for women, 1975–1988.

questionnaire context—or, more precisely, of information provided to respondents in the survey process. In the April survey, Harris first asked the question in which the actual text of ERA was read ("Equality of rights under the law shall not be denied or abridged by the United States or by any State on account of sex"); this elicited more approval than simple references to ERA. Harris then immediately asked the "need to be protected" question and a third question that cited various economics-oriented pro and con arguments. With the wording of the proposed amendment freshly in mind, more respondents approved it when they answered the other two questions than had previously done so. The Harris organization's failure to mention this questionnaire effect created a misleading impression of opinion change at a crucial moment in the ratification process and raised question about the researchers' motivations.

Thus the strong campaign for ERA led by the National Organization for Women and the "STOP ERA" campaign headed by Phyllis Schlafly—funded by fundamentalist Protestant churches and other social conservatives as well as by some business interests concerned that women's wages might rise—had no net effect upon the general public. The Schlafly campaign, however—with some unwitting assistance from pro-ERA enthusiasts—made wildly exaggerated charges about the possible effects of ERA (mandating unisex bathrooms, legalizing homosexual marriages, requiring abortion funding, breaking down families, and the like) that raised enough doubts in Illinois and other pivotal states to prevent ratification; Constitutional amendments, of course, require super-majority approval (Mansbridge 1986). After the battle was over, polls showed somewhat increased support for an ERA.

Birth Control, Abortion, and Human Life

Birth control and abortion are closely related to other issues of women's rights, both because they touch upon females' autonomy and privacy and because birth control can spare women from unwanted preg-nancies and free them for employment outside the home. Indeed, the technological development of highly effective birth control pills and de-vices may have been a crucial factor in the greatly increased work force participation by women, which in turn fueled demands for equal treat-ment in the workplace and elsewhere.

Even as early as the 1930s, the level of public approval of birth control was already high. Although long gaps between surveys and changes in question wording prevent precise measurement of the magni-tude or timing of opinion changes during the late 1940s and the 1950s, there seems to have been a substantial increase in support in those years.

In May 1936, 70% of Americans with opinions told Gallup that "the distribution of information on birth control [should] be made legal." In 1938 and again in 1939, 72% favored making birth control information available to married people. (At that time and until the 1965 Supreme Court decision in *Griswold v. Connecticut* it was illegal in some states to disseminate birth control information or devices.) Variant Gallup items concerning birth control information for married people in 1940, 1943, 1945, and 1947 all indicated 73%–77% approval.

By 1959 the public went further. In response to a different Gallup item, fully 84% said they thought birth control information should be available to "anyone who wants it." Support for this position fell off a bit in 1962 but rose to 92% in a 1974 NORC-GSS survey—staying at vir-tually the same level in 1975, 1977, 1982, and 1983, after which the question was no longer considered worth asking. Paralleling this was an 8% increase in support for making birth control information available to teenagers. The steady high levels of support for birth control and sex education in the 1970s and 1980s are shown in figure 3.12. As the figure also indicates, however, Harris surveys from 1982 to 1985 found a stable, substantial (45% or 50%) level of support for the idea that teens should be required to have parental permission in order to get assistance from fami-

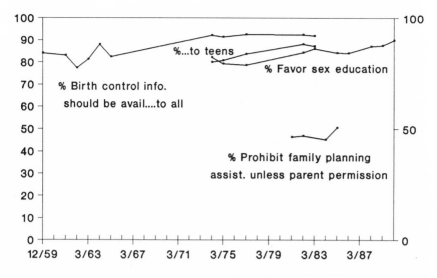

FIG. 3.12   Sex education and birth control, 1959–1990.

ly planning clinics—another instance of the public's distinctions among related policies.

Abortion

Abortion is not generally viewed by Americans as just another method of birth control, since it raises a tangle of questions involving a woman's right to control her body (e.g., after rape or incest), the proper treatment of fetuses with genetic defects, and the sanctity of human life—along with the question of when human life begins. Most Americans dislike the idea of abortion, considering it a painful last resort at best; but most have come to accept the idea of permitting it under a variety of circumstances.

As we saw in Chapter 2 (figure 2.6), the public distinguishes sharply among different circumstances under which it should be possible for a woman to obtain a legal abortion. Many more people express approval of permitting abortion in cases involving danger to the mother's health, or birth defects, or rape, than when childbirth is simply undesired or is inconvenient due to poverty or single-parent status. Still, from the mid-1960s to the mid-1970s there was a strong, parallel growth in public acceptance of a woman's right to have an abortion under any or all of these circumstances.

Between the end of 1965 and spring 1974, according to a number of NORC questions repeated by NORC-GSS, there was a 27% increase (to

86%) in the proportion of Americans arguing that it should be possible for a pregnant woman to obtain a legal abortion in the case of rape, 28% (to 85%) in the case of birth defects, 33% (to 55%) in the case of poverty, and 32% (to 50%) in the case of a single parent. Between 1965 and 1973 there was a 19% rise in approval of abortion (to a full 92% approval) when the mother's life was endangered, and a 32% rise (to 48%) when no more children were wanted. Very similar Gallup questions in 1962, 1965, 1968, and 1969, concerning the birth defect and poverty circumstances, indicate that the trends began in the middle 1960s and proceeded gradually until the early 1970s.

In the middle-to-late 1970s, however, support for abortion diminished slightly; it then rose and fell a bit in the early Reagan years. A CBS/NYT item showed a 6% drop between 1977 and 1979 in the proportion saying a woman and her doctor should decide. NORC-GSS found a 7% decline by 1978 in support for permitting abortion in the cases of poverty or wanting no more children, and 9% in the case of a single parent. Then, for about the next ten years, support for abortion remained fairly steady under most of the circumstances the NORC-GSS mentioned, except poverty, where support continued to decline a bit—perhaps because of Reagan-era suspicion that both poverty and pregnancy are voluntary.

Nonetheless, public support for the right to have an abortion remained high. In 1979, 71% still thought that a woman and her doctor should decide (CBS/NYT). In 1990, the NORC-GSS found that 92% approved of permitting abortion when the mother's health was endangered, 85% in case of rape, and 81% in case of birth defects; although only 48% in case of poverty, 45% when no more children were wanted, and 45% when the mother was single and did not want to marry.

Of course, there is reason to doubt the feasibility of actually enforcing laws based upon such distinctions among women's motivations. Some respondents to the slightly ambiguous GSS question ("Please tell me whether or not *you* think it should be possible to obtain a legal abortion if . . .") may have focused more on the word "possible" than the word "legal" and expressed feelings about what a woman *ought* to do rather than what she should be legally permitted to do.

Some evidence for this interpretation comes from an April 1989 CBS/NYT survey, in which a solid 71% of those with opinions said it should not be possible for a woman to obtain a legal abortion if the pregnancy "interfered with work or education"—a selfish-sounding formulation. But when forced to take a stand without reference to circumstances, given the three choices of keeping abortion "legal as it is now," or making it "legal only in such cases as rape, incest, or to save the life of the mother," or deciding that it "not be permitted at all," a majority of those with opinions—51%—favored "legal as . . . now." Only 9% wanted to forbid abortion altogether. According to various SRC/CPS surveys, typically no more than 10%–15% of Americans would not permit abortions under any circumstances. Between 1976 and 1984 Harris found about 70% opposed to a Constitutional amendment prohibiting abortions. Large majorities regularly affirm that the decision about an abortion should be left to a woman and her doctor; in the April 1989 CBS/*NYT* survey, 72% of those with opinions said that "if a woman wants to have an abortion and her doctor agrees to it," she should be allowed to have an abortion (Dionne 1989).

As of late 1989 and early 1990—after the Supreme Court decision in *Webster v. Reproductive Services,* which permitted more state restrictions on abortion—most Americans appeared to favor keeping government mostly out of abortion choices, though they favored various regulations (requiring teenagers to inform at least one parent and perhaps to get parental consent, and requiring tests for fetal viability before late abortions: see Apple 1989).

One might well imagine that the Supreme Court decision in *Roe v. Wade,* which struck down state bans on abortion, played a major part in liberalizing public attitudes on the subject, but this seems not in fact to have been the case. The NORC-GSS abortion questions asked in March 1972 and March 1973, before and after the January 1973 *Roe* decision, permit us to see that very little, if any, of the collective opinion change occurred just after the Court decision. The naked eye can observe a small (6%) rise in the proportion approving abortion in the case of birth defects between 1972 and 1973 and a similar 6% rise for the poverty case between 1972 and 1974, but not much else. A sophisticated analysis by Franklin and Kosaki (1989) indicates that the Court in fact produced a very small rise in support for abortion in the three most clearly health-related circumstances. For the three more discretionary circumstances, however, it polarized opinion—stimulating group activity on both sides, so that non-whites and Catholics (especially those who frequently attended church) moved against discretionary abortion, while others moved more in favor. Thus the net direct impact of the Court decision upon collective public opinion as a whole was negligible.

There had already been substantial movement in public opinion long before the Court spoke, including 9% rises in approval of abortion in the poverty and birth defect cases from 1962 and 1965, respectively, to 1969, according to Gallup items.

The bulk of movement on the defects question—fully twenty-one percentage points according to NORC—occurred between 1965 and 1972, before *Roe v. Wade*. And if we are willing to overlook minor variations in wording between Gallup and NORC-GSS questions (variations that produced little difference in responses when the two versions were asked at the same time by NORC and Gallup in December 1965), most of the change on the poverty question—a big thirty-two percentage points—occurred between 1962 (Gallup) and 1972 (NORC), before the Court's decision.

It seems even more certain in the abortion case than in the case of civil rights that public opinion mostly changed first. Court action was quite possibly a consequence of the opinion change but not much of a cause. This inference is further supported by the fact that a number of state legislatures liberalized their abortion laws in the 1966–1972 period, before the Supreme Court decision but after the movement of public opinion began (Luker 1984; Tatalovich 1988). (Similarly, the anti-abortion *Webster* case followed a mild conservative drift in opinion and indications in 1982 and 1984 that abortion opponents held their views more strongly than supporters; Scott and Schuman 1988.)

Of course, it is hard to rule out various kinds of diffuse, indirect, or lagged effects (see Rosenberg 1991). But it is possible that the effects of *Roe* (and *Webster* as well) upon public opinion were largely neutralized by each decision's mobilization of its opponents.

Much of the change in public opinion about abortion seems to have resulted, ultimately, from objective material factors: changes in the social and economic environment and changes in technology that preceded action by politicians or organized political groups. In 1962 and 1964–1965, for example, the drug thalidomide and a rubella epidemic led to large numbers of very distressing, highly publicized birth defects and to much public discussion of abortion as a way to cope with high-risk pregnancies. Counts of articles on abortion in the *Readers Guide* and the *New York Times* Index show sharp rises in the 1960s and early 1970s. *Life* and *Time* and other periodicals featured interviews with anguished women and with medical experts. [13]

During about the same period, the development and diffusion of the contraceptive pill and the increasing employment of women in the work force were making birth control even more universally acceptable, despite the continued opposition of the Roman Catholic Church, and abortion was increasingly regarded as a birth control technique of last resort. In addition, sexual activity and premarital pregnancies among young people were increasing (premarital conception among white teenagers rose from 29% of first births in 1955–1958, to 52% in 1967–1970: O'Connell and Moore 1980, p. 18). Furthermore, and perhaps most important of all, the technology of abortion itself changed. A new and much safer surgical procedure (vacuum aspiration) was developed, so that patients' death rates plummeted after about 1966. Horror stories subsided, and the atmosphere of guilt and fear surrounding abortions diminished somewhat. Since many abortions were being performed regardless of what the law said, it was widely argued that they should be made legal so that they would be available to all and carried out under medically approved conditions.

As a general matter, social change often may arise fundamentally from the working of impersonal forces of the sort just mentioned—technological and demographic changes and the like—which we will discuss further in Chapter 8. But often particular people and organizations and institutions articulate and manifest those forces in the political process. In the case of abortion, like civil rights, there can be little doubt that individuals and organized interest groups played important roles in reflecting, interpreting, transmitting, amplifying—and sometimes resisting—the effects of changes in objective circumstances.

The AMA and other groups of medical professionals, for example, reacted to the measles and thalidomide episodes and to changes in abortion techniques by holding a number of conferences in the early 1960s that endorsed abortion reform. Beginning in the mid-1960s, several new pro-abortion organizations were formed. The Association for the Study of Abortion (1964), the National Family Planning Council (1968), and the National Abortion Rights Action League (1969) joined established groups like Planned Parenthood in publicizing and lobbying for pro-abortion changes and promoting the concept of "choice." More broadly, much of the women's movement took up the right to abortion as a key element in a broader program of giving women more control over their lives.

State legislatures and then the Supreme Court increasingly granted legal recognition and legitimacy to abortion, so that members of the public could approve of a legally sanctioned right to choose abortion without necessarily feeling any personal enthusiasm for abortion itself.

Similarly, the later (and smaller) turn in public opinion away from legal abortion undoubtedly reflected, at least in part, organized "right to life" campaigns. Beginning in the late 1960s, and gathering momentum with the formation of the National Right to Life Committee in reaction to *Roe* in 1973, many new anti-abortion or "prolife" organizations (often linked to the religious Right or, especially, to the Roman Catholic Church) sprang up. They publicized arguments about the sanctity of human life (stressing adoption as the alternative to abortion), displayed gruesome pictures of aborted fetuses, picketed clinics, and—with considerable success—lobbied for restrictions on state and national funding of abortions. Single-issue groups like the Legal Defense Fund for Unborn Children and Americans United for Life filed many amicus briefs with the Supreme Court from 1973 to 1986 (Tatalovich 1988, pp. 191–192).

Anti-abortion activity continued into the 1980s, distributing the emotionally potent film "Silent Scream" and picketing (even bombing) abortion clinics; but the movement lost some impetus as the Reagan administration, despite its talk about "family values," failed to give the anti-abortion cause much concrete support. Then the feared consequences of the 1989 *Webster* case galvanized abortion supporters. At the beginning of the 1990s, the predominant fact remained the strongly pro-abortion shift in public opinion since the 1960s.

Life

Concern about human life enters, in a variety of complicated ways, into several social issues besides abortion and capital punishment. Euthanasia or mercy killing, for example, also raises difficult questions about the value of life and who (if anyone) is entitled to terminate it. In 1947, only 41% of those with opinions answered "yes" to the Gallup question, "When a person has a disease that cannot be cured, do you think doctors should be allowed by law to end the patient's life by some painless means if the patient and his family request it?" In 1973, by contrast, 56% said "yes"—an increase of fifteen percentage points. NORC-GSS repetitions of the same question showed further increases to 62% in 1977, 69% in 1988, and 72% in 1990. A related Harris item showed an 18% increase between 1973 and 1985 in support for the idea that a patient with a terminal disease ought to be able to "tell his doctor to let him die." These and a related NORC trend concerning the "right" of a person with an incurable disease "to end his or her own life" are shown in figure 3.13.

The substantial differences in responses to the three questions graphed in figure 3.13 are of the sort sometimes trivialized as "question wording effects." We see them quite differently, however: they once again illustrate the public's capacity to make distinctions. The questions mean different things. Support for euthanasia was highest in response to the Harris item, which offered a long argument in favor of it (none against), spoke in terms of "terminal" (not just "incurable") disease, and put the decision firmly in the hands of the patient who would "tell" his doctor to "let him die." The Gallup/NORC-GSS reference to "a disease that cannot be cured" (not at all the same thing as a terminal illness) and to

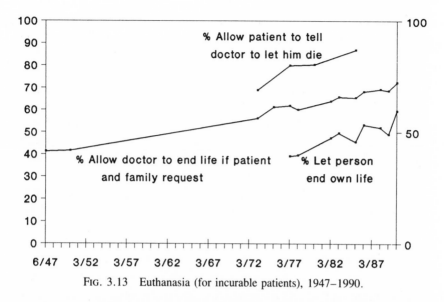

Fig. 3.13   Euthanasia (for incurable patients), 1947–1990.

doctors being "allowed" to "end the patient's life" (not just let him die) if requested, naturally won less support from those protective of life. And the NORC-GSS "right to end his or her own life" in case of "incurable disease" (not necessarily life threatening) understandably garnered the least support of all these items.[14] Question wording matters because people pay attention to the precise language of survey questions and react to it in reasonable ways.

More generally, we can see from the capital punishment, abortion, and euthanasia examples that an important feature of collective public opinion concerning life and death issues has been a high degree of *differentiation*. There is a rejection of absolute prohibitions against causing death, and a willingness to distinguish among lives of different kinds and qualities (defective or healthy fetuses at various stages of development, terminally or incurably ill patients, criminals, victims) and among possible life takers (doctors, patients themselves; those seeking abortion because of rape, birth defects, or birth control). Whatever one's own views may be of the moral and other issues involved, this kind of differentiation fits well with our view of collective public opinion as coherent and sophisticated.

Life-Styles and Traditional Values

Issues of life-style involve considerably less profound, but still significant, matters like the regulation of sexual behavior, the use of alcohol and marijuana, and gambling. In most of these areas the public, even if it did not exactly embrace a "greening of America" during the 1960s (Reich 1971), nevertheless increasingly tolerated deviation from established middle-class norms—before retreating slightly toward orthodoxy.

In the sexual realm we have already mentioned the high and stable or rising approval of contraception and abortion, and the increasing opposition to discrimination against homosexuals. Americans in the 1960s and 1970s also seem to have become increasingly tolerant of premarital sex and adultery, though it is difficult to find repeated survey questions concerning public policy on these topics. As we have seen, growing proportions of the public also approved of sex education in the schools.

Pornography is a different matter. True, between August 1970 and August 1973 there was a 10% drop, to just 28%, in the proportion of the public agreeing that "no one should be allowed to have pornographic [material] in his possession" (Harris). But this shift proved to be short-lived; it was reversed, in part, during a period of unusual agreement among traditionalists and feminists, the latter concerned with sexual exploitation. There has been and remains little support for unrestricted pornography, as indicated by the stable, near unanimous approval for restrictions—either in general or at least for persons under eighteen—shown in figure 3.14. (For a status report on the "sexual revolution," see Tom Smith 1990c.)

Similarly strong—and related—traditional values are apparent in the continually high support for prayer in the schools, also shown in figure 3.14, although this support has waned a bit with rising acceptance of church/state separation. Yet another bulwark of traditional sentiment is loyalty to the American flag, which large majorities want to protect. In May 1990, for example, CBS/NYT found that 86% of those with opinions wanted "burning or destroying the American flag as a form of political protest" to be "against the law"; 75% favored a Constitutional amendment, if that were the only way to make it illegal (New York Times 1990). Patriotism, out of fashion among cosmopolitan elites, is very much alive among the citizenry.

More clearly illustrative of liberalizing trends is the case of alcoholic beverages. Most Americans long ago rejected legal prohibitions against the use of alcohol. In 1941, for example, only 41% of the surveyed public told Gallup they would vote "dry" if the question of national prohibition should come up again. (This proportion dropped a bit, to 37% in 1944, even under wartime discipline and with many men unsurveyed overseas; it dipped a bit more after the war and then regained the 1941 level in 1948.) According to a more specific and inclusive

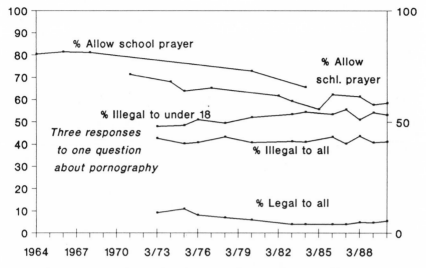

FIG. 3.14 Traditional values: pornography, school prayer, 1964–1990.

Gallup item graphed in figure 3.15, in 1942 only 32% favored "a law forbidding the sale of all beer, wine, and liquor throughout the nation." After dropping and then rebounding by 1956 (a movement for which we have no explanation), this limited support fell substantially to 19% in 1977 and leveled off at 18% in 1984, with most of the decline occurring by 1966 (see figure 3.15).

Similarly, when many young people in the late 1960s and middle 1970s began to use marijuana as a recreational drug, and it became apparent that the available medical evidence gave little reason to fear "reefer madness," the public tended to move in a liberalizing direction.

Gallup data show a 17% rise (to 30%) in the proportion favoring legalizing the use of marijuana between 1969 and 1977; NORC-GSS data show a 12% rise between 1973 and 1978; and Harris data indicate that there was a 7% increase in backing for legalization between early 1974 and mid-1977. Between 1972 and the beginning of 1977 SRC/CPS found a 12% drop (to 56%) in the proportion of respondents putting themselves on the higher-penalties side—as opposed to the make-use-of-marijuana legal side—of a seven-point scale. (To be sure, only 27% located themselves on the make-use-of-marijuana legal side of the midpoint.)

Even at the end of the 1970s, large majorities still opposed legalization of marijuana: 70% opposed it in 1978, according to NORC-GSS. But many Americans came to favor lighter penalties or "decriminalization." In 1977, for example, a majority of those with opinions—56%—told

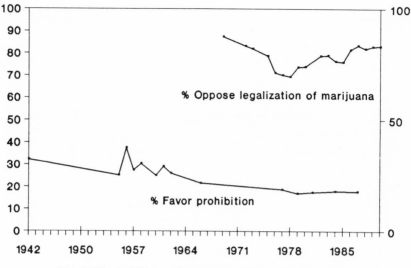

FIG. 3.15   Prohibition of alcohol and marijuana, 1942–1990.

Gallup that possession of small amounts of marijuana should not be treated as a criminal offense.

In the late 1970s and early 1980s, however, public opinion began to move in the opposite direction. In 1982 Gallup found 79% opposed to legalization of marijuana, up substantially from the 70% of 1977. The 1978 NORC-GSS figure of 70% against legalization rose to 83% by 1987, where it remained in 1990 (see figure 3.15). The 56% who had told Gallup in 1977 that possession of small amounts of marijuana should not be treated as a criminal offense fell by 8% to a minority—48%—in May 1985. The 1980s saw a general reaction against drug abuse, which was increasingly perceived as an important cause of violent crime in the cities, impinging upon many middle-class lives. Drug problems received especially high public attention after 1985, when the *New York Times* and other media featured stories about an epidemic of "crack" cocaine use. Similarly, with leadership from MADD (Mothers Against Drunk Driving) and other groups, the public moved toward favoring harsher penalties for driving while intoxicated.

The increased tolerance in the 1960s and 1970s for formerly outlawed behavior with respect to sex and drugs could be characterized as an increased reluctance to prosecute "victimless crimes" as well as a desire to expand the scope of individual choices. Much the same trend seems to have applied to gambling, where it was accelerated by revenue-hungry state governments that established official lotteries. Harris data (marred, however, by variations in the populations sampled) indicate a substantial increase between 1972 and 1975 in the proportion of the public that favored legalization of off-track betting on horses, and smaller increases in the proportions that favored legalizing bets on boxing, auto racing, professional tennis, and professional hockey.

The subsequent decline in tolerance for unconventional practices and life-styles reflected a growing public belief that certain "victimless" crimes did, after all, have victims. Drunk drivers killed people. Marijuana, according to newer medical evidence, created "psychological dependency" and had at least as serious health effects as tobacco. Cigarette smoking in public was reported to harm those who involuntarily inhaled the smoke. Drug addition caused people to commit crimes in order to finance their habits. As we have seen, when alarm grew concerning the spread of the deadly AIDS disease, some came to see sexual promiscuity—especially among homosexuals—as a threat to everyone's safety. (Later, when the threat of homosexual transmission was seen to be less, concern decreased.) In the middle and later 1980s, aspiring public figures like Gary Hart, Douglas Ginsberg, and John Tower were held to stricter public standards regarding sexual and alcohol- or drug-related behavior.

It is important, however, not to exaggerate the Puritanism of the 1980s, which, after all, coexisted with a great deal of pleasure seeking and self-indulgence. The reversals of liberalizing trends were mostly limited in magnitude and focused upon certain health- and safety-related policies about which people quite reasonably changed their calculations of costs and benefits in the light of new information. Despite the conservative policy climate of the Reagan years, and agitation by Jesse Helms's Moral Majority and other elements of the religious Right, Americans maintained or increased the liberal tendency of their opinions on many important social issues.

While one should not forget the continued conservatism of Americans on certain questions involving law and order (e.g., drugs and capital punishment), school prayer, pornography, the flag, and other matters, the great story about social issues in the mid–twentieth-century United States remains the gradual, sweeping liberalization that occurred over several decades: the strong trends toward increased support for civil rights, civil liberties, women's rights, and the legal tolerance of diversity. Again, the public's policy preferences are often more tolerant than personal social attitudes are.

Social Rationality

Many social issues are highly controversial and arouse strong feelings. It is hard to discuss them without reference to what is right and wrong. From our own value perspectives, for example, it would be tempting to rejoice in the liberalizing trends on civil rights, civil liberties, and women's rights, while at the same time regretting that there remains substantial public opposition to certain specific freedoms of speech and the press, rights of the accused, racial equality, and strict gun control. But we do not wish to engage in disputes over the pros and cons of alternative policies. Much less do we want to argue that the public is always right.

Our argument for a rational public does not include a claim that the voice of the people is the voice of God. Nor do we maintain that public opinion is always based upon factually correct premises; in fact we have suggested at various points, and will argue further in Chapter 9, that opinion sometimes reflects errors and misrepresentations and biases in the available information. (We will see, however, that this is a greater problem with respect to foreign policy than domestic, and that the public is remarkably resistant to hokum; in any case, it makes no sense to blame the public for tending to believe the information provided to it.)

What we maintain, instead, is that collective public opinion is real; that it forms coherent patterns and makes reasonable distinctions among policies, in accordance with the underlying values of Americans and the information that is made available to them; and that public opinion reacts to new information and events in ways that are generally understandable and sensible. This chapter has shown that this is true of Americans' opinions about social issues. The following chapters will show that it is also true about matters of economic welfare and foreign policy.

4 Economic Welfare

☑ In this chapter we will examine collective public opinion concerning economics-related domestic issues. Sections of the chapter deal with social welfare policies, including Social Security, help with jobs, income maintenance, redistribution of wealth and income, medical care, education, and urban problems; labor-management relations, unions and strikes; economic regulation, inflation, energy, and the environment; and taxes.

Here, as in Chapter 3, are concrete examples of how public opinion meets our criteria for rationality. In each of these policy areas, the public has made clear distinctions among policy alternatives, has exhibited coherent patterns of preferences that reflect underlying beliefs and values, and has shown understandable, and generally sensible, reactions to changing circumstances and to the information that is presented in the mass media. We will, however, note some important cases in which the information presented to the public may have been misleading, and we will begin to explore what that implies for the conception of a rational public.

One difference from the previous chapter will become apparent. Opinions about matters of economic welfare have not changed as much as those concerning social issues. Nothing comparable to the enormous opinion shifts on civil rights, civil liberties, or women's rights can be found here. To be sure, the trend data are not as complete as would be desired, but they are sufficient to indicate that Americans' opinions about economic matters have been generally stable since the New Deal years of the 1930s, despite alternations in Republican and Democratic control of government and despite some drastic changes in the policy climate in Washington.

Even in the late 1970s and early 1980s, for example, when conservative rhetoric and conservative policy initiatives abounded, little evidence of anything more than a minor and temporary "right turn" in public opinion can be found (see Ferguson and Rogers 1986). Throughout that period the public consistently favored more spending on the environment, education, medical care, the cities, and other matters, and it never accepted the full Reagan agenda of "deregulation."

Because of the stability of public opinion, we will in this chapter be somewhat less concerned with cases of opinion change and more attentive to *patterns* of collective preferences. We will focus on how the public distinguishes among policies, accepting some and rejecting others, in ways that reflect a coherent view of public policy: a view that the reader may or may not share, but one that makes sense in terms of Americans' basic values and the information available to them about how the world works.

Since the first surveys of the 1930s, most Americans have said they favor a number of policies that fit together into a substantial, though bounded, welfare state: Social Security; certain kinds of help with jobs, education, income support, medical care, and urban problems; recognition of labor unions and a qualified right to strike; macroeconomics policies to counteract high unemployment or inflation; and regulation of business practices, working conditions, and, more recently, consumer safety and the environment. Americans have been no more eager than people elsewhere to pay taxes, but—contrary to a great deal of fashionable public bashing—they have generally been willing to come up with revenue to pay for the policies they favor.

This configuration of preferences reflects a fundamental individualism that esteems individual responsibility and individual initiative, and relies primarily upon free enterprise capitalism for economic production and distribution. Yet it also reflects a sense of societal obligation, a strong commitment to government action in order to smooth capitalism's rough edges, to regulate its excesses, to protect the helpless, and to provide a substantial degree of equal opportunity for all.

Social Welfare Policies
Social Security

The Social Security system of retirement, survivors, and disability insurance has always been extremely popular, one of America's great political successes. In December 1935, 89% of the public told Gallup interviewers that they favored "government old age pensions for needy persons";[1] 90%–94% favored such pensions according to two different Gallup questions asked in 1938, 1939, and 1941. In February 1937, after the 1935 Social Security Act had gone into operation, 78% of those answering a Roper question approved "the United States old-age pension law," while only 22% disapproved. In July 1938, Gallup found 89% approving "the present Social Security laws which provide old-age pensions and unemployment insurance" (see Schiltz 1970).

Given these overwhelming levels of support for Social Security in the early years, pollsters have not bothered to ask about it regularly, so we lack good time series data. But in two 1952 Roper surveys, 92% of Americans replied that passing "Social Security laws . . . that give pensions to people over 65" was a "good thing to do" rather than a "mistake."

Amidst the financial stringency of the 1970s and early 1980s, as experts warned that the demographic "bulge" of baby boomers would eventually retire and want Social Security benefits while relatively few workers would be around to pay the payroll taxes that would finance them, there was much publicity about enormous future deficits in Social Security. The *Wall Street Journal* sounded alarms over possible multi-trillion dollar shortfalls and the impending "bankruptcy" of the system unless benefits were cut and taxes raised (Schwarz 1988).

The public reacted (reasonably enough) by expressing some pessimism about the future of Social Security (Penner 1982), but *policy preferences* were generally quite resistant to such scare talk. Substantial majorities, ranging from 54% to 68% according to different questions, still opposed "gradually increasing" the retirement age or raising it from sixty-five to sixty-eight, according to 1977–1983 polls by Gallup, Yankelovich, Harris, the *Los Angeles Times*, CBS/*New York Times*, and Audits & Surveys. Similar majorities opposed cutting benefits for early retirees. Large majorities continued (as in various surveys since 1952) to favor removing earnings limits for those receiving benefits. Most Americans—from 62% to 83%, according to several questions asked between 1978 and 1983—wanted to expand Social Security coverage to include government and nonprofit workers. Most found Social Security taxes "about right"; there was some "too low" sentiment but not a lot.

Except for a degree of receptivity to delays in cost-of-living adjustments and to taxing the benefits of the wealthy (Shapiro and Smith 1985), then, there is little evidence of public support for the Social Security benefit cuts and large payroll tax increases enacted with bipartisan elite support in 1983. (By the end of the 1980s it had become clear that these "reforms" had produced big surpluses in the Social Security fund which were being used to offset the overall government budget deficit rather than to provide for future retirement benefits. Taken together, the 1981 income tax cuts and 1983 payroll tax increases simply shifted revenue extraction from progressive to regressive taxes.)

In fact, according to the responses to some four dozen surveys by various organizations between 1961 and 1989, many more people always wanted to *increase* than wanted to decrease Social Security spending. Very large majorities, on the order of 80%–90%, have opposed cuts; majorities (not just pluralities) said "spend more" rather than the same amount or less, or said "too little" was being spent, or said the government should "do more" to improve Social Security benefits. In most of

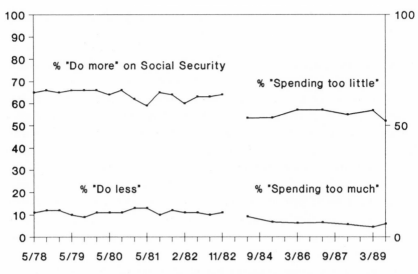

FIG. 4.1   Social Security, 1978–1990.

the sixteen Trendex surveys[2] between 1978 and 1982, for example (shown in figure 4.1 along with responses to a later NORC-GSS question), about two-thirds of the public said "do more" rather than do less or do about the same. The "do more" figure dropped as low as 59% only once, in May 1981, at the height of Reagan administration budget cutting. This certainly did not amount to much of a "right turn" in public opinion on this issue, despite the major public relations efforts to drum up support for cutting the program.

The extent of public support for Social Security is particularly well documented by a 1986 survey conducted by Northwestern University in which 57% of respondents with opinions said they wanted to increase benefit levels, while only 3% wanted to decrease them. (Of six other social welfare programs inquired about, only Medicare won substantially stronger support.) Eighty-two percent said they were "satisfied" that "a part of every working person's income goes to support the Social Security program." Of those, 90% said they would be opposed to spending cutbacks, and 71% said that in order to prevent cuts they would be willing to have people pay more Social Security taxes (Cook and Barrett 1988, pp. 345–347).

The secret of Social Security's immense popularity seems to be threefold. First, the program is designed to benefit large numbers of recipients, actually or potentially including most of the population. Second, benefits are targeted to people in circumstances under which they have little or no control and which particularly evoke a sense of societal obligation (Bobo 1991): the elderly, disabled, widowed. It is hard to argue that Social Security encourages dependency by providing incentives to become old, disabled, or widowed. (To be sure, the effects of the program upon private savings and on work by the elderly have been subjects of controversy.) Third, Social Security was designed to be seen, and is seen, primarily as a compulsory insurance program in which wage earners are forced to put aside some current income to provide for future disability or retirement. Even though most workers now realize that the taxes they pay are not really saved but are spent on those currently retired, and that an intergenerational transfer of income takes place (Yankelovich, Skelly, and White 1985), there remains a connection between what they pay in and what they expect to get out. This system of aiding broad categories of the "truly needy," under a logic of self-insurance, seems to fit well the American conception of fairness (see Cook 1979; Hochschild 1981).

A multivariate analysis of the sources of individuals' support for Social Security (using the Northwestern data) tends to confirm this explanation. Especially important are beliefs that the program benefits society as a whole, that people who get Social Security have no other source of income, and (less crucially) that it helps beneficiaries become more independent (Cook and Barrett 1988, pp. 349–352).

Employment

Most Americans have also favored government action to help provide work. In three SRC/CPS surveys done in 1956, 1958, and 1960, for example, more than two-thirds of those with opinions (67%, 69%, and 72%) said that the government in Washington ought to "see to it that everybody who wants to work can find a job." In seven CBS/*NYT* surveys between 1976 and 1978, slightly rising proportions—ranging from 71% to 77%—answered the same question the same way. Three Yankelovich, Skelly, and White surveys in 1976 and 1977 found slightly increasing majorities of 60%–66% favoring "the passage of a full employment bill in which the government guarantees a job to everyone who wants to work." As shown in figure 4.2, in response to every one of forty-six Trendex surveys between 1966 and 1982, substantial majorities—all larger than 60%—said they would like the government to "do more" (rather than do less or do about the same) on "expanding employment."

With each recession, public support for general government action to help with jobs has tended to increase, especially in contrast to support for "welfare" or "relief" (see Shapiro, Patterson, Russell, and Young 1987a, 1987b). The sensitivity of policy preferences to real world condi-

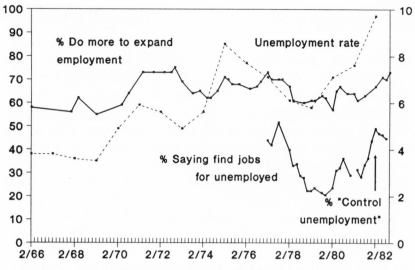

FIG. 4.2   Employment, 1966–1982.

tions can be seen in figure 4.2; backing for the government to "do more" on "expanding employment" has tended to rise and fall along with the actual unemployment rate. The correlation ($r = .64$, $p < .01$, for sixteen yearly time points from 1967 through 1982) is not perfect, of course, in part because of measurement error and because of variations in the way information about the economy is provided to the public (during this period public tolerance for unemployment gradually rose as leaders and the media emphasized inflation as a problem); but it is quite substantial. Figure 4.2 also indicates that objective circumstances affected what policy focus the public wanted as between inflation and unemployment. Mentions of employment or jobs as the most important economic problem for government remained high after the 1973–1974 recession, declined substantially amidst alarms about inflation during the Carter years, rose with the 1979–1980 recession, dipped a bit, and then rose substantially during the 1981–1982 recession.

The question, of course, is *exactly what* the government should do about employment. Here the public has been cautious and has made some clear distinctions.

Support for direct government employment has mostly been limited to special situations, particularly involving young people. During the Great Depression, for example, the Civilian Conservation Corps had very strong public support: 82% "in favor of CCC camps" in 1936, and 78% in 1938 who thought the camps "should be made permanent" (Gallup).

Echoing this experience, in four Gallup surveys of 1961, 1962, 1963, and 1976, well over 80% of the public said it was a "good idea" for the federal government to "set up youth camps—such as the CCC camps of the 1930s—for young men who want to learn a trade and earn a little money by outdoor work." Somewhat smaller majorities in several Gallup polls (dropping by 7% between 1964 and 1971, however) also favored *requiring* all out-of-work young men between the ages of sixteen and twenty-two to join a youth conservation corps. "Job Corps" training and employment for young adults remained a popular part of the Great Society after other programs fell from favor.

Certain other specific, but limited, job-related programs also have won public backing. In two 1972 surveys, Harris found overwhelming majorities of 92% and 93% personally favoring a federal program to "give productive jobs to the unemployed." SRC surveys from 1961 and Roper surveys from 1981, 1982, and 1983 revealed more people saying "too little" than saying "too much" was being spent on unemployment insurance benefits, with 40% or more saying "about right." The idea of retraining programs provided by private firms (as opposed to government) has been quite popular; so, especially since the 1980s, have been day-care facilities and unpaid parental leaves—though paid leaves and job sharing had not, by the end of the decade, caught on. And Roper surveys of 1976 and 1982 revealed considerable support (rising from 57% to 66%) for tax breaks or other incentives to encourage businesses to expand or "hire people they wouldn't otherwise take on."

All of the programs we have mentioned, however, assume that private enterprise is the chief source of jobs and that government simply facilitates and moderates the effects of the labor market.

Income Maintenance

The idea of a guaranteed income has been considerably less popular than help with employment. This clear difference again illustrates the public's capacity to make distinctions. It reflects Americans' concern with productivity, work incentives, and individual responsibility.

In the 1970s and 1980s, for example, when SRC/CPS changed its old job question and used a seven-point scale asking whether the government in Washington should "see to it that every person has a job and a good standard of living" (thus inviting confusion between welfare and work), only 30%–32% of the public located themselves on the "see to it" side of the midpoint. More felt government should "just let each person get ahead on his own." Indeed, support for a guaranteed job and standard of living dropped abruptly to 22%—for reasons that are not clear to us—

in the postelection survey of 1976; it stayed about the same in 1978 and then recovered to 31% in late 1980, hovering around the 30% level in 1982, 1984, 1986, and 1988.

Income guarantee proposals without a strong employment require-ment have had comparatively little support (see Shapiro, Patterson, et al. 1987a, pp. 127–128). Even at the height of the Great Society period there was little public enthusiasm for a general guaranteed income program, or for a "guaranteed wage," or even for a negative income tax, as described in various ways by Harris questions.[3]

In principle, large majorities favor government support for the needy. Various questions asked in the 1930s and 1940s, for example, found high agreement—in the 65% to 81% range—with the proposition that government should "provide for all people who have no other means of obtaining a living," or who "have no other means of subsistence" (Roper). In 1976 and 1977, Harris found overwhelming (96%) agreement that "(i)t's not right to let people who need welfare go hungry." In 1983, 88% of those with opinions told the *Los Angeles Times* that they favored the government "helping people who are unable to support themselves."

The idea of preventing hunger has particularly great appeal. Gallup surveys from such diverse time points as 1939 and 1969 reveal strong support—on the order of 70% in both years—for a Food Stamps program for people on relief or with low incomes. To be sure, CBS/*NYT*, *L.A. Times,* and ABC/*WP* surveys at the beginning of the 1980s (when Presi-dent Reagan and others were telling stories about the use of food stamps to buy junk food and gin) showed majorities favoring cutbacks in the Food Stamps program, but ABC/*WP* found a strong reversal in this view during the middle and late 1980s, with the 51% that favored a decrease in spending in 1981 dropping to 33% in 1986 and 28% in 1989, while (in 1989) 21% wanted to increase Food Stamp spending and 50% wanted to leave it about the same.

Along with general sentiment in favor of helping the needy, however, there is doubt about some income maintenance programs, especially about "welfare," which for some people (particularly after the antiwelfare pub-licity of the 1970s and early 1980s) has conjured up images of laziness and dependency and of black welfare mothers giving birth to illegitimate chil-dren. In the Harris surveys of 1976 and 1977, at the same time that large majorities were agreeing that it is not right to let people who need welfare go hungry and that government has a "deep" or "basic" responsibility for seeing to it that the poor are taken care of (71% and 78% agreeing, respec-tively), 93% and 94% of Americans said that "(t)oo many people on welfare could be working"; and 91% and 94% said "(t)oo many people on welfare cheat by getting money they are not entitled to." Of course, such beliefs are not inconsistent with wanting to help the poor, and may in fact have been correct; the system virtually forces recipients to "cheat" (i.e., earn unreported income) in order to survive (Jencks and Edin 1990).

In 1976, 55% of respondents strongly agreed with a Yankelovich statement that "there is more concern for" the "welfare bum" than the hard worker. Similarly, in 1980 a majority (57%) told CBS/*NYT* that "most people who receive money from welfare could get along without it if they tried" rather than really needing help. And only about a third of respondents with opinions told CBS/*NYT* in 1978 (34%) and 1980 (35%) that they thought government programs of the 1960s to improve the conditions of poor people had "generally made things better"; most thought they didn't have much impact or actually made things worse. (The "made things better" response did increase markedly to 47% in 1984, however—and remained at 41% in 1986—after high unemployment and economic hardship in the 1979–1982 recessions overcame early Reagan-era concern about "fraud, waste, and abuse.")

According to Gallup polls, majorities of Americans have long favored excluding recent arrivals from welfare payments (82% felt that way in 1961); using the courts to pursue unwed fathers (82% in 1961, 73% in 1965); and giving local communities more say about who gets how much relief (65% in 1961, 73% in 1979). "Workfare" is especially popular: in two 1972 surveys, 94% told Harris they would personally favor "making people on welfare go to work," and surveys by NBC in 1977, Roper in 1976 and 1977, Gallup in 1979 and 1985, and ABC/*WP* in 1985 yielded much the same results. (Exact percentages vary because of substantial differences in question wordings. See Shapiro, Patterson, et al. 1987b, pp. 279–280.)

The balance of opinion has generally favored cutting back on "welfare" spending (when that term is explicitly used), especially during the middle and late 1970s, when inflation was seen as overshadowing unemployment as a major economic problem. Between February 1974 and April 1976, for example, according to NORC-GSS surveys, the proportion of people saying we were spending "too much" on "welfare" rose by 19%, to a total of 63% saying "too much"; only 14% said "too little," and the rest said spending was "about right." The balance of opinion became considerably less negative in the early 1980s, with "too much" responses dropping twenty-two percentage points, to 41%, in 1984 and staying stable afterward; but even then they outweighed the 25% saying "too little." More people continued to favor cutting welfare spending than wanted to increase it all the way to the end of the 1980s. Roper, using the same question, found

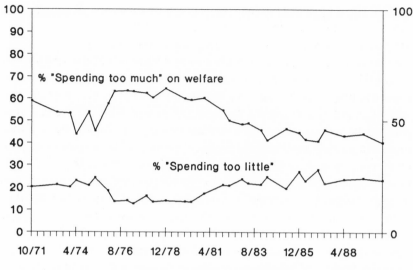

FIG. 4.3   Welfare, 1971–1990.

much the same trend of increased opposition to welfare spending between 1973 and 1976 and a decline in opposition—though it remained substantial—in the early 1980s. These trends in opinion toward welfare are presented in figure 4.3, which combines NORC-GSS and Roper surveys.

As the above examples indicate, survey measures of public support for social welfare programs and spending are highly sensitive to exactly how policies are described. Different questions elicit different answers. Questions about programs for "the poor," for example, often get a remarkable thirty or forty percentage points more support than similar questions about "welfare" that are asked at the same time (Tom Smith 1987; Shapiro and Patterson 1986). Some observers (e.g., Opinion Roundup 1988) have attributed this to the public being "ambivalent" about government.

Ambivalent, perhaps: Americans want people to help themselves when they can but want government to help those who cannot. We would emphasize that these attitudes are not inconsistent with each other. The "welfare"/"poverty" difference, in particular, represents something other than a capricious "question wording effect"; it captures exactly this distinction. Most Americans don't like the idea of welfare programs that give cash payments to people, some of whom may not be truly helpless and may thereby be discouraged from helping themselves. (Politicians have probably tended to exaggerate the number of welfare recipients who could support themselves and, paradoxically, have created work disincentives by refusing to subsidize the working poor.) But most Americans want to give jobs to everyone who can work; to provide basics like food and medical care to those who cannot otherwise afford them; and to take care of people in categories that clearly cannot help their condition: the blind, disabled, aged, and the like. And, indeed, a large majority wants to increase benefits under SSI, while more want to increase than want to decrease AFDC (see Cook 1979; Cook and Barrett 1988, p. 345).

Again, we do not mean to say that the American public is perfectly informed about poverty or is as humane and farsighted as one might want; our point is that these views are consistent with one another, form a coherent pattern, reflect the information made available to the public, and fit with Americans' underlying values—which combine generosity with individualism.

Figure 4.3 does show a "right turn" in public opinion with respect to welfare, which occurred *before* Ronald Reagan was elected president. These and other data also show that the right turn ended shortly after Reagan took office. In six CRI surveys, majorities agreed that President Reagan's budget reductions were "cutting too deeply into social programs that help poor and disadvantaged people": the 53% agreement of early and middle 1981 grew to 60% at the end of that year and stayed at 60% or 61% in 1982, 1983, and 1984. Thus the right turn was followed quickly by a liberal rebound, a pattern found in other countries as well (Shapiro and Young 1989).

Redistribution

Surveys since the 1930s have shown that the explicit idea of income redistribution elicits very limited enthusiasm among the American public, with the level of support varying somewhat according to economic conditions. Seldom have more than half of Americans backed the principle of reducing economic differences between the rich and poor. Only about half the respondents (49% and 50%) told Trendex in two 1982 surveys, for example, that "the difference between the income of the rich and the poor in this country is much too great." A majority of 60% located themselves on the "reduce income differences between the rich and poor" (through taxes or income assistance) side of an NORC-GSS seven-point scale in 1973; but—in another example of a right turn—this fell substantially to 43% by 1980, when the U.S. economy was weaker and conservative rhetoric filled the media; it then recovered only to 49% in 1984, which is about where it remained through the 1980s—reaching 52% in 1990. There has also usually been less than majority support for limiting busi-

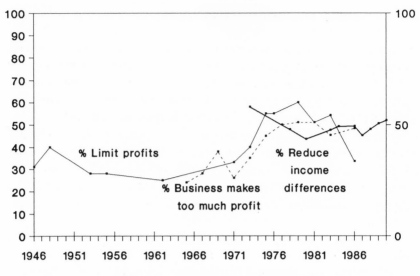

Fig. 4.4   Redistribution, 1946–1990.

ness profits, with a marked increase in the 1970s (perhaps because of high oil company profits after the sudden OPEC price rises) and a dropoff thereafter (see figure 4.4).

These data clearly indicate that extensive income redistribution, which does not fit at all well with individualism and Lockean liberalism, is not popular (see Hochschild 1981; Shapiro, Patterson et al. 1987a, 1987b). The same thing is evident in the lack of support for highly progressive taxes, as we will see below. Redistributive fervor was not much apparent even in depression-era 1939. When Roper asked, "Do you think our government should or should not redistribute wealth by heavy taxes on the rich? Confiscate all wealth over and above what people actually need to live on decently, and use it for public good?" 61% said the government should not redistribute wealth, and 83% said it should not confiscate wealth. Most Americans are content with the distributional effects of private markets.

As one would expect, support for employment and income maintenance and other redistributive programs varies significantly according to income level. Those with relatively low incomes, who would benefit the most, tend to be most favorable. It might be thought that such differences were largest in the 1930s and 1940s, when class cleavages over politics were more prominent than in recent years and when the political parties were perceived as far apart on these issues. But, in fact, there is little evidence of such a change. Class differences in preferences about re-distributive policies have long been substantial and remain so.

For the 1939 Roper items on redistributing or confiscating wealth, for example, there were 34% and 22% differences between the opinions of respondents classified as "prosperous" and those classified as "poor," with "upper-middle" and "lower-middle" opinions falling in between. In 1944, 49% of those with low incomes favored government public works programs, while only 27% of those with high incomes did: a 22% difference. In the 1970s and 1980s, generally comparable differences (though, of course, item wordings and income groupings vary) can be found between the opinions of high- and low-income groups. In 1977, for example, a CBS poll showed a 21% difference in opinion concerning a $2,000 guaranteed income, between respondents with less than an $8,000 income and those with $12,000–20,000 (see also Shapiro and Patterson 1986).

We will see in Chapter 7 that these income differences are genuine; they mostly persist when one controls statistically for other variables. We will also see, however, as the above examples imply, that opinion *trends* among high- and low-income people have been much the same; the substantial differences between them have tended to remain fairly constant. Because the processes of preference change are mostly society-wide, cutting across all groups in the population, we are able to analyze opinion changes as if the public were homogeneous.

Medical Care

Most Americans favor certain kinds of government help with medical care, especially health insurance, medical care for the needy, and promotion of medical research. In fact, assistance with medical care has come to be viewed as an entitlement, with popularity comparable to that of Social Security. In 1960, 1962, and 1978 (according to slightly variant SRC/CPS and CBS/NYT questions), large majorities of 75%–85% said that government ought to "help people to get doctors and hospital care at low cost." At least since the enactment in 1965 of Medicare for the aged and Medicaid for the needy, large majorities of the public have seen medical care as a "right" to which all citizens are entitled: NORC found 87% so responding in 1968, and Roper, asking a slightly different question, found 78% in 1975 and 81% in 1979 (see Shapiro and Young 1986).

Numerous NORC-GSS and Roper surveys over many years have revealed persistent and large majorities saying that the government is spending "too little" on medical care; never more than 8% (only 3% in

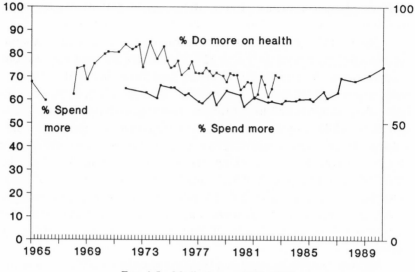

FIG. 4.5   Medical care, 1965–1990.

1990) have said "too much." By the same token, in forty-nine Trendex surveys from 1965 to 1982, never fewer than 60% responded that the government should "do more" on "health measures"; never more than 14% said "do less" (see figure 4.5).

In a March 1949 Gallup survey, half (50%) of those with opinions favored President Truman's national health insurance plan, but support dipped abruptly—by 8%, according to a December survey—after fierce opposition and charges of "socialized medicine" from the American Medical Association and Republican congressmen (see D. Truman 1971, pp. 227, 231). In recent years, many survey questions have indicated that large majorities favor a "national health insurance" system that would cover everyone. Based on various different question wordings, Yankelovich found 73% support for NHI in 1976 and 70% in 1977; NBC found 67% support in 1978 and 66% in 1979; and ABC found 75% in 1984.

But this does not necessarily mean that people want the federal government to provide it. When NHI was contrasted with "the present system of private insurance and health plans" in nine Roper surveys from 1973 through 1983, opinion was much more evenly split, with support dropping to the 43%–53% range.[4] Much the same is true of the seven-point scale used by SRC/CPS and Market Opinion Research, which compared support for a "government health insurance plan" with expenses "paid by individuals and through private insurance like Blue Cross." When the government or taxes are explicitly mentioned, support is generally lower, though it usually still outweighs the opposition by a bit. On a five-point NORC-GSS scale, only 50% of respondents in 1975 put themselves on the side of the "government in Washington" helping people pay medical bills, in contrast to people taking care of themselves. This dropped to 44% in 1984 but then rebounded and grew to 57% in 1990.

This pattern of differentiated responses makes sense, if most Americans want a mixed public and private system with some variety and choice, in which private insurance is available but the government oversees, regulates, and perhaps subsidizes or acts as a provider of last resort (see Shapiro and Young 1986; Erskine 1975b; and—especially on NHI— Payne 1946).

Already in the 1930s and 1940s, large majorities of Americans favored government sponsorship of medical research. In 1939, 90% of a Gallup sample favored a proposal "that the federal government spend three million dollars for clinics to fight cancer." In 1946 Gallup found 91% approval of having government spend $100 million to find ways of preventing or curing cancer, and 73% of the approvers were willing to pay more taxes to provide the money; this rose to 83% in 1954. A similar Gallup question about heart disease won 85% approval in 1948, with 85% of those people willing to pay more taxes. (Approval of heart disease spending stayed steady in 1954, but willingness to pay more taxes dropped 6%.)

Cancer and heart disease, not surprisingly, continued to be considered among the "most serious diseases or medical problems facing the country today," on through the 1980s. According to 1985 and 1986 CBS/*NYT* surveys, however, AIDS ranked as an even more serious national problem than heart disease, reflecting the threatening new AIDS epidemic and the increasing attention devoted to it in the mass media (see Singer, Rogers and Corcoran 1987, pp. 584–585). In 1985 CBS/*NYT* also found 61% responding that "too little" was being spent on AIDS research (only 6% said "too much"), and 60% said the government should help AIDS patients with medical costs more than it helps people with other medical problems.

In recent years, general support for government spending on medical care has tended to rise and fall somewhat with the strength of the economy and the perceived urgency of medical costs and problems, but it has always been quite high. As figure 4.5 shows, desires for increased spending or more government action dropped from the mid-1970s to 1982, when inflation and medical costs soared and conservative rhetoric dominated public discourse. Still, support stayed quite high, around the 60% level. It then increased further as the continuing recession threatened jobs and medical coverage and as people's out-of-pocket medical expenses increased with rising deductibles and co-payments.[5] Again, if there was a "right turn" it was a mild one, it preceded Reagan, and it was quickly reversed after he took office.

In 1978, for example, the proportion of the public telling NORC-GSS interviewers that "too little" was being spent on "improving and protecting the nation's health" was down 10% from the 1974 peak, but even then it remained at a very high 57%, compared to only 7% saying "too much." This 57% "too little" figure edged back up to 60% by 1984 and then reached its highest point ever, 74%, by 1990.[6] The Trendex item in figure 4.5 shows an even higher level of support but also somewhat more of a drop than Roper/NORC-GSS, perhaps because of its explicit mention of government in the context of the antigovernment sentiment of the late 1970s, and for sampling reasons.[7] The lengthy Trendex time series shows very strong majorities saying that the government should "do more" (rather than less or the same amount) on "health measures." The "do more" responses rose above 80% in the early 1970s but then dropped by nearly 25%, according to surveys in 1981 and 1982. (The Trendex surveys stopped before there was much chance to detect a liberal rebound.) Still, even at the early 1980s low point, support remained high. Taking all these data together, the most important point is that the proportion of the public wanting the government to help with medical care is quite high and increased a bit further in the 1980s, despite—or because of—the Reagan administration.

Education

An overwhelming public consensus favors government action on education. Education is seen as a key ingredient in equality of opportunity and as a public good, not just a benefit for individual citizens. The history of educational assistance, however, has been complicated by questions involving the separation of church and state, civil rights, and federal-local relations.

During the 1950s, substantial majorities favored federal aid for elementary and secondary education. In December 1955, for example, Gallup found that 74% of those with opinions favored "federal aid to help build new public schools," and this rose to 80% by January 1957. But support then dropped a hefty 16% by February 1961, perhaps in reaction to controversies over school desegregation and the Powell amendment that tied education aid to civil rights progress and over the question of aid to Catholic parochial schools (see figure 4.6).

Both before and after the passage of the 1965 Elementary and Sec-

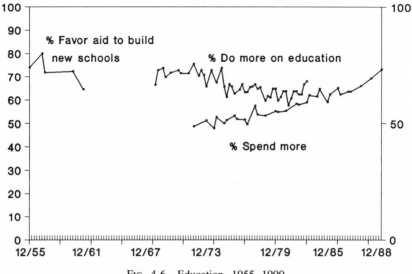

FIG. 4.6   Education, 1955–1990.

ondary Education Act, many Americans have expressed skepticism about the role in education of "the government in Washington" as opposed to "states and local communities." In SRC/CPS surveys of 1964 and 1968, 60% and 63%, respectively (excluding 5%–6% "depends" responses), said that "education for grade and high school children . . . should be handled by the states and local communities." But, of course, local "handling" does not preclude federal aid.

In fact, education has long been an area in which most Americans want government to spend more money. Even at the end of recession-ridden 1982, according to a Chicago Council on Foreign Relations survey fielded by Gallup, 61% said they wanted to expand spending on education while only 7% wanted to cut it back. Similarly, as we saw in Chapter 2 (figure 2.2), NORC-GSS surveys from 1973 through 1990 found much greater support for spending more than for spending less, with education given high priority along with the very popular programs of crime control, health, combating drug addiction, and protecting the environment.

There was little evidence of any significant "right turn" in opinion on education matters during the Reagan era. True, support for doing "more" according to the Trendex series shown in figure 4.6 was a bit lower in 1978–1981 than it had been earlier, but the series ended with a slight upward shift—as did a follow-up question (not shown) concerning support for a tax increase to fund this increased activity. (In 1982, 74% of those who wanted to do more supported a tax increase.) Moreover, the Roper and NORC-GSS series about spending (figures 2.2 and 4.6) revealed steadily increasing support after 1977, if not earlier, with a reading in 1989—at about the time President Bush declared his intention to confront urgent problems in education and to be the "education president"—of a new high of 69% wanting to spend more on education. This grew further, to an all-time high of 73% in 1990.

Many Americans at various times have also favored nonspending measures to improve the quality of public education. Gallup surveys in 1958 and 1959, for example, showed majorities for establishing a national high school examination and increasing the amount of grade school and high school homework. Backing for more homework dropped in the 1960s (down 6% for grade schools by 1961 and 15% for high schools by 1965, leaving only 45% in favor of each). But support for the national examination rose by 12% between late 1958 and early 1976, reaching a level of 68% in that year and then 73% in 1981, as local schools received lower "grades" from the general public. (See Elam 1978; *Gallup Report* no. 252 [September 1986], p. 14, and *Gallup Report* no. 288 [September 1989], p. 39, which show the drop in grades occurring after 1974. This trend was reversed later in the 1980s, but the public's grades did not return to their 1974 level.)

Cities and Race

Toward the end of the 1960s, the War on Poverty emphasized the "urban crisis": the poverty and decay of inner cities, which came to be associated with the poor conditions under which blacks and other minorities lived. President Lyndon Johnson's actions and rhetoric, coupled with the urban unrest of the period, apparently influenced opinion on these issues. Support for urban programs did not diminish much, if at all, during the Nixon years, but it dropped by the mid- to late 1970s. Some trend data are shown in figure 4.7.

Between December 1968 and October 1971—perhaps in reaction against the Nixon administration's "benign neglect" of urban problems—Harris found a 13% rise, to a very substantial 51%, in the proportion of Americans saying more money should be spent "to help the cities"; 38% said "the same amount" and only 10% said "less." The long Trendex series in figure 4.7 shows that, in most of forty-seven surveys between 1968 and 1982, those wanting the government to "do more" on urban renewal outnumbered those wanting it to do less by about two to one. (As previously noted, some of the minor ups and downs in Trendex trend lines presumably reflect sampling errors; the jump in "do more" responses in April–May 1968 probably indicates heightened concern about urban un-

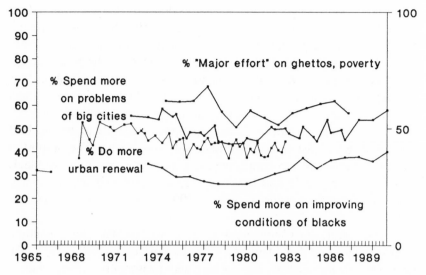

FIG. 4.7   Cities and race, 1965–1990.

rest after the Martin Luther King assassination.) Support for doing more about urban renewal tended to be a bit lower, but only a bit, at the end of the period than at the beginning. Responses to the Trendex item concerning support for "helping minority groups" shows a similar trend, suggesting that attitudes about race and the cities were related (see Wright 1977).

As the Roper and NORC-GSS item graphed in figure 4.7 shows, the proportion of Americans saying we were spending "too little" on "solving the problems of big cities" also strongly outweighed the proportion saying "too much," throughout the 1970s and 1980s; it declined a bit around 1975–1976, bottoming out during 1978–1980, but recovered to a consistently better than a two-to-one ratio over "too much" by about 1982.[8] Still, preferences concerning the cities did not recover as thoroughly from their right turn as did other attitudes (they took until 1988–1990 to return to their 1973–1975 level); the public tended to favor placing greater policy burdens on state and local governments without greater federal revenue or assistance (see Caraley 1986, 1991; Fuchs 1991; Shapiro and Patterson 1986).

According to Roper, there was a very high level of support in the early 1970s for government making "a major effort . . . now" to "solve the problems caused by ghettos, race, and poverty," with more than 60% saying "major effort," about 30% saying "some effort," and less than 10% saying these problems were "not needing any particular government effort now." But "major effort" responses declined sharply, from 68% to 51%, between 1977 and 1979, recovering to 59% by 1984. Explicitly race-focused policies may have suffered more of a right turn in opinion than other policies did. Consistent with this pattern, the proportion of Americans telling NORC-GSS that "too little" was being spent on "improving the conditions of blacks" never got as high as the comparable cities and urban renewal responses—only 35% said "too little" in 1973, with 23% saying "too much"—and it dropped gradually to 26% in 1978 and 1980, when just as many people said "too much." The proportion saying that too little was being spent to improve the conditions of blacks slowly recovered to 31% in 1982, and a new high of 37% in 1984, where it leveled off before rising to 40% in 1990, when only 16% said "too much."

In general, our examination of social welfare and other economic issues reveals a mild and temporary "right turn" on several of them. The economic stringencies of the 1970s, and conservative interpretations thereof, caused a dip in desires for government spending on welfare, redistribution, medical care, the cities, and minorities—though not (appreciably) on education or social security. Later, when the economy entered and then recovered from the 1981–1982 recession and the Reagan administration was seen as cutting appropriations to the bone, public sentiment for more spending rebounded. Although it is difficult to be precise about the matter, there are indications of a differentiated public reaction to particular kinds of economic distress and particular kinds of programs. Inflation curtailed spending desires more than unemployment did, and support for redistributive programs and for relatively discretionary programs like space exploration dropped most, while backing for basic middle-class benefits held steady and support for help with jobs actually increased.

Labor-Management Relations

By the time the Wagner Act was passed in 1935, most Americans probably (data are scanty) favored government protection of the right of workers to organize and bargain collectively through unions. In 1936, Gallup found 76% saying they "favor(ed)" unions. General support for unionization, within a private enterprise economic system, has persisted ever since. But this support has been qualified by backing for various regulations and restrictions on union activity and especially on strikes. Moreover, support for unions has varied with war and peace and with changing economic conditions. It has apparently waned over time, as the hard-fought struggle for labor gains and the unequivocally positive image of the labor movement passed into history, and especially as the unionized portion of the work force has shrunk in the face of a sustained employer offensive and foreign economic competition (see Goldfield 1988; Lipset and Schneider 1983, chap. 7).[9]

Working conditions have long been a concern. In April 1936 Gallup found that a solid majority of the public, 61%, favored a constitutional amendment to ban child labor. (The Supreme Court had earlier declared statutory regulations of child labor to be unconstitutional.) This support jumped up an additional 15% by February of the following year, as such an amendment was being considered seriously by several state legislatures.

The main aims of the Wagner Act were presumably also popular, given the high general approval of labor unions in 1936, but there was evidently disappointment with the particulars of the act. Judging by open-ended responses, disappointment came from both ends of the political spectrum, but it was particularly stimulated by the National Association of Manufacturers and U.S. Chamber of Commerce propaganda drive against the act, assisted by the press's focus on a few highly aggressive labor leaders (Lee 1980 [1966], pp. 10–12). By April 1938, most Americans told Gallup they wanted to revise or even repeal the Act; only 38% favored keeping it unchanged, and this dropped further to about 30% over the next year until opinion returned to an even split by the end of 1939 and 1940, according to separate repeated questions by Roper and Gallup. But sentiment for a complete repeal always remained quite low—between 10% and 19%. By 1946, amidst a wave of postwar strikes, there was an increase in dissatisfaction with the Wagner Act; only 29% wanted to leave it as it stood. (The Taft-Hartley amendments were passed in 1947.)

The high level of approval of unions was always accompanied by a desire to regulate them strictly, and World War II increased this. The proportion of the public who said that "the government's attitude toward labor unions" was "not strict enough" increased by 16% from 52% in 1942 to 68% in mid-1943, according to NORC surveys, before dropping off slightly (see figure 4.8, below).

During World War II, people were also willing to sacrifice certain employment protections and benefits for the sake of the war effort. In October 1941, with tensions high just before U.S. entry into the war, Gallup found that 76% favored forbidding strikes in defense industries, and by the next month, as the U.S. relations with Japan and Germany worsened, this policy received 6% more support. Two Roper surveys reveal that the Japanese attack on Pearl Harbor added only a little to the already strong sentiment: a December poll before Pearl Harbor found

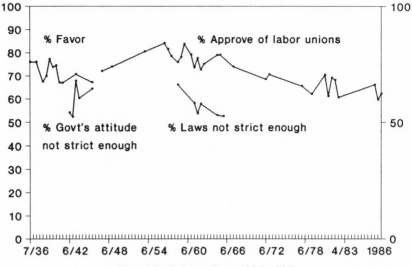

FIG. 4.8   Labor unions, 1936–1986.

88% supporting a law forbidding defense strikes during "the emergency," which rose to 93% after the attack. According to Gallup, in February 1942 91% favored a law forbidding such strikes, although this dropped slightly by May 1943 as the war effort began to bear fruit. Various survey questions show opposition to strikes at close to the 80% level throughout the war.

Similarly, in March 1942, with the United States at war, 67% favored a long work week without special overtime pay—either no overtime pay at all, or overtime only after forty-eight or more regular hours—in defense industries (Gallup). This policy lost 8% of its support by October 1942, perhaps because the immediate threat of defeat had diminished or because of the passage of a wage stabilization policy and a big tax increase that month. As the war came to an end, support for sacrifices understandably decreased. Backing for Truman's proposal to draft and send back to work strikers in essential industries, for example, dropped 6% between the May and June 1946 Gallup polls, though it remained at a substantial 52%.

After the war, as we have seen, there was much dissatisfaction with the Wagner Act and substantial sentiment for stricter regulation of unions. When the restrictive Taft-Hartley Act was passed in 1947 over President Truman's veto, however, Gallup found that, among those who had heard of Taft-Hartley, somewhat more disapproved it (54%) than approved it (46%). In July 1947, most of those with opinions wanted to revise or repeal Taft-Hartley; only 29% wanted to leave it unchanged. With businessmen and congressional Republicans defending the act, the proportion of the public who wanted to leave it unchanged surged upward 19% by January 1948, but as Truman intensified his own campaign against the "slave labor law" in election-year 1948, the "unchanged" proportion dropped again, by 16% between January and May of that year—only to rebound 10% by August. Such unusual volatility on a major domestic issue (even taking into account the small and imperfectly designed samples in these early surveys) undoubtedly reflected the public's confusion about the technical features of the act: confusion that was abetted by heated political rhetoric, propaganda, and misinterpretation (see Berelson et al. 1954, pp. 217–233; Ross 1968; Lee 1980 [1966]).

In any case, according to another Gallup item, in April 1949 only 27% of those with opinions favored outright repeal of the Taft-Hartley Act. This dropped a bit by June 1949 and fell to a tiny 9% in October 1953, when the Eisenhower presidency brought a considerably less pro-union attitude to the federal government. Indeed, by the end of the 1950s, after congressional investigations revealed corruption and racketeering in the Teamsters and other unions, much of the public was receptive to yet more restrictive regulation of organized labor. In January 1959, 65% of those with opinions told Gallup that the laws regulating labor unions were "not strict enough." This figure dropped to 54% by September 1961 after the restrictive Landrum-Griffith Act of 1959 had been enacted, and stayed at about the same point during three surveys in 1962, 1965, and 1966.

All in all, the substantial public support for unionization has been qualified by suspicion about various union practices. As the items graphed in figure 4.8 and others indicate, there has been strong support for regulation of unions, along with concern about such matters as closed shops, featherbedding, and misuse of union funds. Some of this may be attributable to information presented in the mass media, which (as we will discuss further in Chap. 9 below) have not always been kind to the American labor movement.

During the 1950s, as incomes rose, Americans began to contemplate—though not always to accept—the possibility of increased leisure time. Toward the end of 1953, a solid 78% in a Gallup poll said the workweek in most industries should *not* be reduced from forty hours to thirty-five hours, but this opposition dropped to 64% at the end of 1964 (rebounding to 70% according to a survey at the beginning of 1966). One factor contributing to the opposition was pure economic rationality—unwillingness to give up cash: in 1953, 41% told Gallup that, if the workweek were cut, workers should get the same pay they had received for forty hours of work, and this rose to 52% support at the beginning of 1955.

Strikes

As we have noted, most Americans dislike dissident movements, protests, or demonstrations of almost any sort (see also Chap. 8). Those involving organized labor are no exception; labor's most potent weapon, the strike, is quite unpopular. Beginning with the earliest surveys, most Americans have expressed distaste for strikes, which involve obvious economic and social costs and are often portrayed by the mass media as violent and unjustified. (The media are themselves business enterprises that profit when workers are docile; most newspapers opposed prolabor legislation during and after the New Deal and strongly supported Taft-Hartley: see Lee 1980 [1966]; Parenti 1986, chap. 5.) Gallup found in 1937, for example, that 67% favored making sit-down strikes illegal in their states. A similar attitude was suggested—though, of course, the circumstances were special—in the big majorities that favored forbidding strikes in defense industries during World War II.

Aversion to strikes is especially clear in the widespread support for compulsory arbitration. In 1965, 57% of those with opinions endorsed a Gallup suggestion that no strike be permitted to go on for more than seven days; after that time the union and employer would be compelled to accept terms set by a government-appointed committee. Support for this idea rose 10% further by January 1966, after strikes by airline machinists, New York City transit workers, and railway firemen, but fell back 7% by August after labor peace returned. As we noted in Chapter 2, such abrupt changes in opinions are generally associated with major events—in this case strikes.

Intermittent data from the 1960s to the 1980s also indicate widespread opposition to strikes by public employees, especially those with sensitive jobs. According to Gallup surveys, about half the public approved of strikes by sanitation workers and teachers, but solid majorities opposed strikes by policemen or firemen (see figure 4.9). There has been general support for allowing all these employees to join unions but not to disrupt services by strikes. Again, the collective public is able to make a number of sharp distinctions in its policy preferences.

Opposition to strikes has varied with the political environment and economic conditions as well as publicity about work stoppages and other events. Between late 1967 and 1970, for example, Harris found 7% more approved permitting school teachers to strike, and approval rose 10% further by August 1974, reaching 61%, after the Vietnam War protests

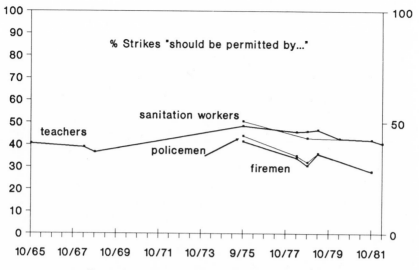

FIG. 4.9   Strikes by public employees, 1965–1982.

were over (and during the especially liberal climate surrounding Nixon's resignation). The similar Gallup question displayed in figure 4.9 showed a 10% rise in approval between February 1968 and September 1975. Between 1970 and 1974 there were 7% and 12% rises in the proportion approving strikes by hospital and newspaper workers, respectively. Toward the end of the 1970s, however, in economically harder times with pressures on local governments to retrench, Gallup surveys (in 1975 and 1978) found 11%, 12%, and 7% drops in the proportions of Americans who favored permitting firemen, policemen, and sanitation workers to strike. Harris and Roper surveys registered similar, though smaller, declines.

Despite its reservations about strikes, the public generally approves of unions in their role as protectors of workers. Similar support for worker protection over the years has been evident in attitudes concerning the forty-hour workweek, minimum wages, and safety conditions. Some backing for unions results from suspicion about the motives and activities of business—especially big business—suspicion that also affects opinions concerning economic regulation.

Economic Regulation
Private Property and Capitalism

Large majorities of Americans accept capitalism and reject socialism as a general way of organizing the economy. On the increasingly rare occasions when pollsters have asked about public ownership of means of production, the idea has generated little enthusiasm outside specific areas like utilities.

True, in 1936, in the midst of the Depression, a Roper-*Fortune* poll found majorities favoring public ownership of various utilities: electric lights, gas, telephones, water, trolleys, and buses. (This despite an intensive covert propaganda campaign during the 1920s by the National Electric Light Association, which FTC investigations revealed to have substantial impact on the content of school and college textbooks: see D. Truman 1971, pp. 233, 238, 243.) Similarly, in January 1937, according to Gallup, 67% favored public rather than private ownership of electric power companies. A July 1937 Gallup survey even found a bare majority (53%, up from 39% in late 1936) for government ownership of banks, and in 1939 Roper-*Fortune* found large majorities favoring government-owned hospitals and medical service (80%) and national resources (63%).

But in the same 1939 Roper-*Fortune* survey, only minorities favored government ownership of some or all railroads or insurance companies, and only 24% wanted nationalization of factories that produce "the essentials of life." All the Gallup and Roper questions about government ownership of the electric power industry, banks, and railroads asked *since 1945* have produced responses of 70% or more opposed (see Shapiro and Gillroy 1984a, 1984b, pp. 674–677). Support for government ownership has virtually vanished.

Moreover, even in 1942—during wartime, with depression memories fresh—only 38% of those with opinions said that "some form of socialism would be a good thing . . . for the country as a whole," while 62% called it a bad thing. Similar (unfortunately not identical) recent questions suggest that this minority support for socialism has declined still further. In 1976, only 14% told Cambridge Reports they would favor "introducing socialism into the United States," while 86% opposed it. In 1981 Civic Service repeated this question and found no change: 14% of those with opinions were in favor, 86% opposed (see Lipset and Schneider 1983, pp. 282–283).

In recent years overwhelming majorities of Americans have expressed approval of a private enterprise, capitalist economic system. In 1981, for example, Civic Service found that 90% of those with opinions agreed with the statement, "The private business system in the United States works better than any other system yet designed for industrial countries," while only 10% disagreed. In 1974, a solid majority (60%) in a Roper survey cited "our free enterprise system" as one of the "major causes of United States greatness" (Lipset and Schneider 1983, p. 285).

In 1975 and 1976, Harris found very large majorities agreeing with statements that "the American economic system," or "free enterprise for business," provides the highest living standards in the world; means freedom for the individual; produces advanced technology; and is the most efficient the world has known (see Lipset and Schneider 1983, chap. 9; McClosky and Zaller 1984; Chong, McClosky, and Zaller 1983).

American public opinion—even among those who consider themselves liberals—seems unusually procapitalist compared with opinion in much of the world, including the social democracies of Europe (see Verba and Orren 1985). Americans are exposed to many messages about the virtues of free enterprise in their schools and universities and churches, and in mass media advertisements, editorial commentary, and statements by public officials, civic leaders, and experts. In the United States the Left has an unusually weak voice.

To explain this procapitalist thrust of opinion and information is not easy; a full account would require untangling the complicated historical roots of American exceptionalism. One major factor, no doubt, is simply the great objective success of the American economy, which has produced enormous (if unequally distributed) abundance, especially compared with noncapitalist countries. Other factors have to do with the balance of political forces in the United States, particularly the weakness of organized labor, which in turn may reflect such historical elements as the presence of a Western frontier, ethnic divisions among immigrant workers and former slaves, and the absence of a full-fledged feudal system at the country's origins. Without a strong labor movement the corporate-owned mass media tend toward "centrist" but clearly procapitalist coverage and interpretations, and corporations heavily influence teaching, research, politics, and indeed every phase of American society affecting the flow of information to the citizenry (see Miliband 1969, chaps. 7, 8; Parenti 1986, chaps. 1–4, 6). This is not shocking; practically every society tends to reproduce its own social and economic structure.

In any case, however, public support of capitalism does not mean that Americans oppose government regulation of the economy. Quite the contrary. The devastating experience of the Great Depression apparently convinced most Americans once and for all that uncontrolled private enterprise, left to itself, could not be trusted to produce steady prosperity or to protect workers and consumers. During the depression the public's chief concerns were jobs and economic relief. But the sparse survey data of the time indicate that majorities also sought regulation of wages and hours and working conditions, and approved of the New Deal (and older)

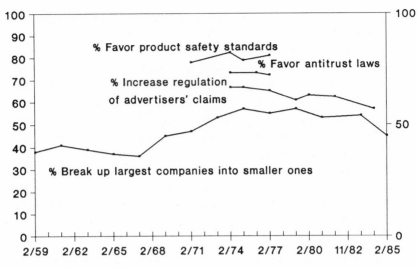

FIG. 4.10   Regulation against big business and industry.

regulatory agencies dealing with transportation, communications, securities markets, labor disputes, and the like.

These and other proregulation opinions persist. In addition to collective bargaining and social insurance and minimum wages, most Americans have also favored price controls during inflationary periods; regulation of advertising and competitive practices; and—especially in the last two or three decades—regulation of workplace and product safety, product quality, and the environment. The strong and generally stable support for certain kinds of regulation is shown in figure 4.10. We will also note some variations over time based on the state of the economy and the country's experience with particular kinds of controls.

Many citizens are especially suspicious of *big* business, which is seen as a source of high prices and profits and excessive power. Thus majorities have favored government fostering of competition through antitrust laws and the breakup of big firms, contrary to the long-term trend toward increasing corporate concentration. The majority support (even when "don't knows" are included) for the proposition that "many of our largest companies ought to be broken up into smaller companies" (shown in figure 4.10) is very striking during the middle and late 1970s, when international oil firms were seen as profiting from an oligopoly position. Harris in 1974, 1976, and 1977 found strong majorities opposed to eliminating the antitrust laws even if in some industries it were found to be "more efficient to have a few big companies instead of a lot of small ones."

Inflation and Price Controls

An area in which regulation has generally been popular, but with unusually great fluctuations over time, is that of price inflation.

When World War II brought full employment, and pent-up civilian demand chased supplies of goods that were limited by the war effort, attention turned to the problem of inflation—a topic about which many years of repeated survey questions exist.[10] During the war, the public generally favored strict government controls. In December 1943, for example—with the Office of Price Administration (OPA) in operation—when NORC asked whether the government "should be trying to keep prices from going higher than they are now," 96% of those with opinions said "yes." Among those people, 63% said "all" prices should be kept where they were, as opposed to allowing some to go higher. At the same time, a somewhat lower though still hefty 84% favored keeping *wages and salaries* from going higher, but most of them—74%—thought "some" wages and salaries (perhaps including their own) should be allowed to rise. Willingness to have government "freeze your own income where it is now" barely reached 50% at its peak. Once again a coherent set of distinctions, in this case based on simple self-interest.

By March 1945, after further experience with the inflationary pressures of the wartime economy, 16% more in NORC surveys favored keeping all wages as they were, and 16% more wanted all prices frozen. In three surveys during 1943 and 1944, OPOR found majorities of more than 80% wanting to "keep price ceilings a while after the war," or some

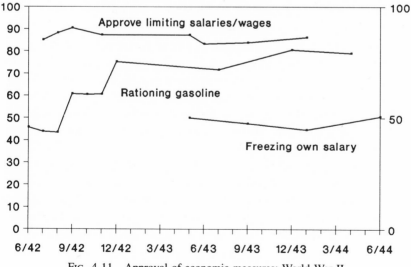

FIG. 4.11   Approval of economic measures: World War II.

variant of that sentiment. Figure 4.11 summarizes the differentiated but high—and, in the case of gas rationing, sharply increasing—support for controls during World War II.

Since World War II, public attitudes concerning anti-inflation policies have varied with the state of international relations and with economic conditions and experiences. Wars and high inflation rates (not altogether independent of each other) have generally led to increased backing for controls, "freezes," or rationing; but changes in circumstances, declines in inflationary pressures, and unhappy experiences with the effects of controls—economic distortions, shortages, and the like—have eroded that support. Thus opinions about inflation have fluctuated more than those concerning most other domestic policy areas.

In October 1950, for example, during the tense early months of the Korean War, 68% told Gallup that a wage and price freeze would be a "good idea" (as vs. a "fair" or "poor" idea); but this dropped to 58% a year later when the war was stalemated. At the very end of 1965, when the Vietnam War buildup was well underway, 52% (according to Gallup) favored a wage and price freeze for the duration of the war. This support dropped to 39% by October 1966, as President Johnson and other leaders argued against it, but then—as the inflationary effects of financing the war started to become apparent and were much publicized—support for a freeze rose again, reaching 55% (according to a variant item not mentioning Vietnam) by May 1970. Figure 4.12 displays these fluctuations, which contrast with the high stable support for controls during most of World War II shown in figure 4.11. As can be seen in figure 4.12, support for controls tends to reflect actual changes in the inflation rate ($r = .7$, based on roughly concurrent inflation rates).

At the outset of the 1970s, public enthusiasm for price controls was undimmed by any recent experience with them. In November 1971, after President Nixon's tentative "Phase One" imposition of some controls, 42% said wage and price controls should be "more strict" (only 17% said "less strict"), and this figure rose 16%—to a level of 58%—by March 1972, with Republicans changing opinion more than Democrats. (See also McClosky and Zaller 1984, pp. 152, 329n. 29. This sort of differential partisan change will be dealt with in Chap. 7; to one degree or another partisanship probably conditions most of the opinion leadership by popular presidents that is discussed in Chap. 8.) In the fall of 1970 and again in autumn 1972, fully 47% of Americans located themselves at the extreme point ("total government action against inflation") of a Michigan seven-point scale.

But the erratic series of Nixon (and, later, Ford) price control

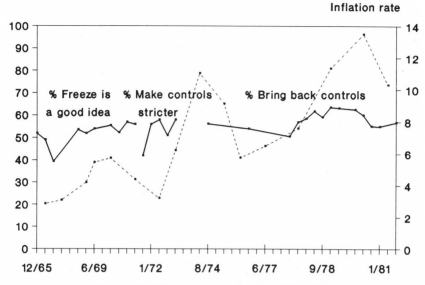

FIG. 4.12   Wage and price controls, 1965–1981.

"phases," together with changes in inflation rates and other economic events, led to a complicated set of fluctuations in public opinion. During late 1972, Harris found large drops in the proportions of people saying that too many big price increases were being allowed, or wanting to be tougher on pay increases, or wanting a "freeze" rather than the current system of controls; but also an 8% increase in the proportion wanting to be tougher on electric and gas companies. (Energy prices were only rising a bit faster than others in 1971 and 1972, but the public was especially suspicious of these big businesses.) At about the same time, the proportion of Americans placing themselves at the "total government action" extreme of the Michigan seven-point scale suddenly dropped ten percentage points in the postelection survey at the end of 1972. But Harris found that the proportion favoring a "freeze" versus the current system soared 26% in the first six months of 1973, as inflationary pressures, and especially food prices, increased.

In September 1973, according to Harris, only 39% favored removing controls altogether (in November 37% favored removing all except in industries with shortages). These proportions dropped 17% and 11%, respectively, by the end of the year, when the effects of the OPEC oil boycott began to be felt and fuel prices started to rise. In 1974, in 1976, and four times during 1978, Gallup found majority support (among those with opinions) for the idea of "having the government bring back wage and price controls"; and as the inflation rates rose sharply and the second round of OPEC's oil price rises took effect in 1979, 64% favored bringing back wage and price controls, up 13% from February 1978. On into the beginning of the 1980s, when the Consumer Price Index was rising more than 10% per year, majorities continued to favor price controls; support rose as inflation did. (The exception is President Carter's last year in office, 1980, when support for price controls diminished, presumably because of the Republicans' election-year assault on regulation and because of public skepticism about the administration's competence.)

Balanced Budget

The overwhelming majority of Americans has long favored a balanced government budget, though the meaning of the term is subject to interpretation and the notion of balance may have more symbolic than concrete importance (see Savage 1988). Keynesian arguments for stimulative deficits—and attacks on the family budget analogy as misleading—seem to have made little headway with the public, except perhaps for short periods during major recessions. Especially in the 1970s and 1980s, budget balancing was taken as gospel, as a crucial means for fighting inflation.

In early 1973, for example, 65% told Gallup that balancing the federal budget was "very important," and this sentiment rose 7% by early 1976. Gallup polls in 1976, 1978, and 1979 showed very heavy support for a constitutional amendment requiring a balanced federal budget: in each poll, 85% to 88% of those with opinions favored the amendment. Later Gallup and NBC questions with different wordings show support at moderately lower but then largely restored levels from 1978 to 1987. NBC, for example, found 85% favoring "a constitutional amendment which would require the Federal Government to balance its budget" in December 1978. This figure dropped steadily to 72% in August 1982, as unemployment worsened and inflation decreased—and the Reagan administration took no steps to enact such an amendment; but then, as the economy improved while the Reagan tax cuts and military spending buildup produced enormous deficits, and financial interests again sounded inflation alarms that reverberated in the media, it increased to 81% in April 1986. When Gallup in 1987 described the details of a proposed amendment to a well informed subsample, 70% favored it, up from 64% in 1985.

Renewed public backing for balanced budgets also took the form of support for the Gramm-Rudman legislation that mandated spending cuts: 59% in favor at the end of 1985, according to ABC/*WP*. (According to

Gallup and others, however, there has been strong [as high as 80%] opposition to raising income taxes in order to reduce the deficit—an opinion encouraged by the rhetoric, if not the actions, of the Reagan and Bush administrations.)

Much of the anti-inflation and antideficit sentiment of the 1970s and 1980s was very likely influenced by a massive and misleading public relations campaign energized by banks, holders of bonds and other debt instruments, insurance and real estate firms, and others whose assets or profits were threatened by rapid inflation and high interest rates. The campaign was joined by conservative politicians and economists (some of them subsidized by, or dependent upon, prodeflation economic interests), who portrayed "inflation" as a monstrous evil, caused by government profligacy, that pushed ordinary people into higher tax brackets and eroded their savings and pensions (see Ferguson and Rogers 1986, chaps. 3–4).

This rhetoric ignored the role of the relative jump in energy prices, as opposed to a general price rise; when overall prices doubled from 1971 to 1980, the price of fuel oil and other household fuel commodities increased nearly *fivefold* (excluding gas and electricity, which nearly tripled: Stanley and Niemi 1990, p. 384; U.S., President 1989, pp. 373–376). It blamed "vast increases" in government spending, when spending as a percentage of GNP was stable and low relative to that of other industrial countries; it oversimplified the relationship between deficits and inflation (ignoring the key issue of monetization); and it greatly exaggerated the harm to taxpayers—the federal income tax was in effect indexed by periodic rate cuts—and to pensioners, many of whose benefits were, in fact, overindexed so that real payments *rose* with inflation.

On inflation-related issues, then, it seems possible that citizens' opinions may have been manipulated against their own interests, to favor holding down wages and cutting government programs that benefited them. This (along with labor relations) is one of the first instances of likely opinion manipulation we have encountered so far; others will come up in this and the following chapters.

Energy

The "energy crisis" of the 1970s persuaded many Americans to support a variety of measures designed to keep prices down and/or to increase supplies of energy. In September 1973, declining U.S. oil reserves and production and increasing reliance on imported oil led large proportions of the public to tell Harris interviewers that they favored a major federal role in solving the energy shortage (83%), developing new oil sources without delay (76%), and getting foreign governments to help out (60%). (Few, however—only 36%—wanted to tax car owners more for larger cars.)

The world energy picture was profoundly affected by the Arab-Israeli war of October 1973. Protesting the U.S. supply of military equipment to Israel, the Organization of Petroleum Exporting Countries (OPEC) cut production and banned exports to the United States. At the end of November, President Nixon announced "Project Independence," supposedly designed to end reliance on foreign energy sources by 1980. Shortly thereafter, in December 1973, a Roper survey found 79% saying that we were spending "too little" on "increasing the nation's energy supply." After the OPEC boycott ended in March 1974, however, the price of crude oil stood at four times its 1973 level, and U.S. gasoline and heating oil prices had doubled, with drastic effects on the U.S. economy.

It is difficult to track public reactions to these events with precision, since Harris repeated its September 1973 (preboycott) questions only in late March 1974, just after the boycott ended. Certain specific proposals had lost appeal: support for more "supervision" of "the production and use of oil, gas and electricity" and for leasing federally owned land to oil companies both dropped 7%; opposition to delaying new oil sources fell 6%; and support for taxing large cars fell even lower, by a substantial 11%. One survey question did pinpoint the effect of the boycott's end: between February and March 1974 there was a sharp (19%) drop in support for rationing gasoline.

After the boycott, however, when oil prices—bolstered by new OPEC production quotas—stabilized at much higher than preboycott levels, there was some recognition of a permanently changed energy picture. The March 1974 Harris survey indicated that desire for a major federal role in energy had risen 6% since September; tolerance for allowing higher prices fell 8% (to 20%); and the pious hope for help from foreign governments had jumped 16%. As the lessons of the oil price shock sank in, overwhelming majorities favored the government making a "major effort" to develop and conserve energy: Roper found 80% or more in favor of such an effort every year from 1975 through 1981, with a peak of 89% in 1977 (see figure 4.13). More Americans favored raising gasoline taxes to conserve fuel: 54% favored a contingent $0.10 per gallon tax in January 1975, up 9% from October 1974 (Harris). As of March 1975, Harris found that many Americans favored such policies as using naval oil reserves (52%) and allowing issuance of tax-free bonds for power plants (65%), though only 29% wanted to slow down pollution cleanups. These reactions to events seem generally sensible.

Support for some of these policies declined, naturally, as the urgency

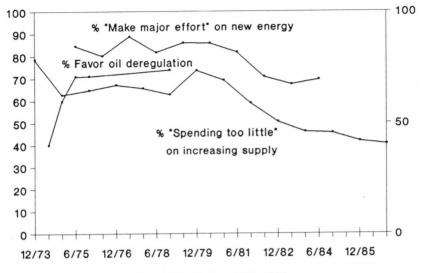

FIG. 4.13   Energy, 1973–1986.

of 1973–1974 faded. By March 1976, support for power bonds had dropped 8% since 1975, and by July support for using oil reserves and slowing cleanups had fallen by 11% and 7%, respectively. Between March 1975 and July 1976, Harris also found that the proportion of Americans that favored creating a government-owned oil corporation and taking over troubled electric utilities—ideas highly repugnant to private businessmen—dropped by 7% and 9%, respectively. (Desires to "break up" major oil companies did remain high, however, and even rose during 1977.)[11]

The policy alternative that really caught on in the later 1970s was the one most favored by oil companies: deregulating oil prices in order to encourage production (at the same time, of course, increasing profits). As shown in figure 4.13, support for deregulation rose from 40% in July 1974 all the way to 74% in December 1978.

Throughout the middle and late 1970s, the major multinational oil companies waged an active public relations campaign to rehabilitate their tarnished images and avoid costly government restrictions. Mobil, the leader in this respect, spent many millions of dollars for advocacy ads on television and on newspaper editorial pages and columns in Sunday supplements. It closely monitored the media and attacked the press for "gossip" and "sensationalism" in publicizing oil company windfall profits, low tax payments, and environmental abuses; argued for higher profits to help capital formation and for energy independence through decontrolling natural gas prices and opening up offshore drilling; and criticized taxes and government regulations of the environment and energy, sometimes hiring ostensibly objective journalists like Martin Agronsky to deliver the pitch from a fake television newsroom. Mobil and other companies also subsidized pro-oil editorial cartoonists as well as academic researchers and experts (Berkman and Kitch 1986, pp. 279–288; Bagdikian 1987 [1983], pp. 61–68).

As our survey data indicate, however, this PR campaign had mixed results. The public was highly resistant on some energy-related issues. The oil companies did not achieve their maximum objectives. Still, they very likely did succeed to a substantial extent in moderating what they saw as hostile public attitudes.

One great success of the oil industry, as we have seen, involved opinion about "deregulation" of oil prices (a somewhat murky concept that implies a reference to rationing or direct price controls; windfall profits taxes were the bigger issue during most of the period). In four-and-a-half years from 1974 to 1978, a 40% proderegulation minority became a solid 74% majority. Similarly, from 1973 through 1980, seven Roper surveys found increasing support for the idea that environmental protection laws had gone "too far"—an energy-related view we will discuss further below. When people were asked whether "producing energy or protecting the environment" was "more important," pro-energy responses rose from 37% to 49% between 1977 and 1979.

On the other hand, during the late 1970s opposition to taxing large cars eroded somewhat; Roper found a big (14%) drop in resistance between 1977 and the second oil price shock of 1979. In August 1979, with long lines at gas stations, Gallup found that 55% of the public favored giving the president standby authority to ration gasoline, up from 47% the previous May.

Later, however, when energy prices stabilized once again and then fell—an "oil glut" was proclaimed in the early 1980s—and when other economic problems took center stage, poll questions about energy policies were asked less frequently, and (sensibly) public support for government action on energy declined; policy actions followed suit (Ahrari 1987). The 89% that in 1977 favored Roper's "major effort" by government to develop and conserve energy fell just below 70% in the 1982–1984 period. Roper also found a large, steady 28% drop between 1979 and 1983 in the proportion saying we were spending "too little" on energy (see figure 4.13). Similarly, the Roper trend toward thinking that environmental protection laws had gone "too far" was reversed after 1980. But the Iraq-Kuwait crisis that began in 1990 brought signs of renewed public support for energy conservation and regulation.

The chief lesson of two decades worth of energy-related polls would seem to be that the public adjusted its preferences in reasonable fashion to changing events.

Nuclear Power

In the mid-1970s, nuclear power appeared to offer an attractive alternative to high-priced, foreign-controlled oil. In 1975, several Harris poll questions indicated strong public support for encouraging the development of nuclear power: 80% or more of the public said nuclear plants were "worth the risk" if various safety and environmental measures were taken (88% said so under the condition that they would "not pollute"); a large minority (46%) even favored nuclear plants in their own areas despite hypothetical state government opposition. (About half of Roper's respondents [49%] at the beginning of October 1975 said it would be "safe" to have an atomic energy plant "somewhere near here.") In general terms, 77% of Americans in 1975 (74% in July 1976) told Harris they favored "the building of more nuclear power plants in the United States." Still larger majorities said they favored nuclear power if it would lead to lower utility rates.

Support for nuclear energy slipped gradually starting around the third quarter of 1976, however, as the urgency of the energy crisis abated, the costs of nuclear plants rose, and experts and environmental groups raised questions about pollution, waste disposal, and safety. In July 1976, for example (and even more so in October–November, according to ABC News–Harris press releases), Harris found support down by six to nine percentage points when it repeated the 1975 survey items. According to Roper, responses favoring an "expanded program to develop atomic energy" declined from 67% in 1974 and 66% in 1975, to 60% in 1976 and 1978. Harris reported further gradual declines during 1978 (well *before* the Three Mile Island accident), with 69% for building more nuclear power plants in March and 65% in October.

A large, sharp drop in public backing for nuclear power followed the accident at Three Mile Island in March 1979, when a reactor cooling system failed and some radioactive material was discharged into the atmosphere. Intense press coverage galvanized public fears about nuclear safety. Between October 1978 and mid-April 1979, Harris polls revealed a sudden, nearly 15% decline (to 50%) in the proportion of the public favoring "building more nuclear power plants," for a total decline over

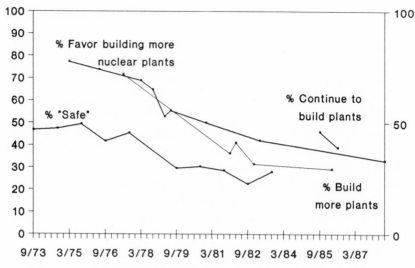

FIG. 4.14   Nuclear power, 1973–1986.

the four years since 1975 of a full 25% (see figure 4.14). CBS/*NYT* found a similar (24%) drop in support for nuclear power between July 1977 and April 1979. Roper's "safe . . . someplace near here" responses, 45% even in September 1977, fell steeply to 30% in September 1979.

The news media have been criticized for allegedly sensational coverage of TMI, and it is true that many members of the public developed fears of nuclear explosions or other catastrophes of kinds discounted by most scientists (Rothman and Lichter 1982, 1987). But people's concerns over possible meltdowns and large-scale releases of radioactivity were not necessarily exaggerated: the Kemeny Commission later reported that a meltdown had in fact been a real possibility after the cooling failure at TMI. If anything, over the years public opinion may have been misled or manipulated in a *pro*nuclear direction. The Atomic Energy Commission had for a long time suppressed reports questioning plant safety (Ford 1984), and "experts" dependent on the nuclear industry sometimes stretched the truth in order to discredit the objections of the antinuclear movement. The secrecy and government control of information in this highly technical area resembled some of the foreign policy cases we will discuss in Chapters 5 and 6, and probably permitted similar kinds of manipulation of opinion.

The TMI accident was a watershed event. After the accident, a CBS/*NYT* survey found that 60% of Americans disapproved having a nuclear power plant in their own communities, way up from 38% in 1977.

Similarly, NBC found 46% of those with opinions agreeing that "all nu-clear plants" should be "closed down" until questions about safety were answered. Backing for this position dipped slightly in 1981 and 1982, but continued to come from nearly half the population. After 1983, according to Cambridge Reports surveys, opposition to building more nuclear plants remained at the 65% level or above, and it increased once again in 1986 after the Chernobyl accident. (This despite the blizzard of propaganda from the U.S. government and the nuclear industry that the Chernobyl di-saster did not imply dangers for the United States, on the false grounds that the plant design was different and Soviet safety standards were far in-ferior: Luke 1990.) Later in the 1980s, pronuclear opinion was further eroded when (after years of reassurances and secrecy) environmental and safety scandals emerged at military nuclear weapons plants. Again, in our judgment, the public reacted reasonably and responsibly to events and new information (see Freudenburg and Rosa 1984).

The Environment, Health, and Safety

Beginning in the 1960s, undoubtedly spurred on by the early writings of Rachel Carson, Ralph Nader, and others, and by the activities of en-vironmentalist and consumerist movements, the public came to favor a variety of new regulations to protect consumers and workers and the en-vironment.

Between 1961 and 1965, for example, Gallup found a 13% in-crease—to the high level of 79%—in the proportion of Americans that favored requiring safety belts in automobiles. Between March 1965 and four years later, Harris found that a very substantial 21% more—for a total of 89%—came to favor the already popular requirement of health warnings on cigarette packages. From September 1967 to June 1971 there was a 19% rise in the proportion willing to pay $15 "more in taxes" to combat pollu-tion.

Several aspects of environmental protection already enjoyed high lev-els of support in the middle 1960s. That support rose further and peaked in the early 1970s, well after the first "Earth Day" in 1970. It declined some-what during the late 1970s (never, however, getting very low), and then recovered to very high levels by the end of the 1980s. At the early peak, in January–February 1972, Trendex found 93% saying they would "like to see something done" in their community or part of the country about "con-trolling water pollution." The figure for "controlling air pollution" was only a little lower, at 88%, and for "increas(ing) national parks and wilder-ness areas" it was about 79%. These different levels of opinion concerning

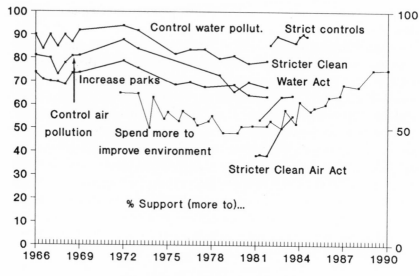

FIG. 4.15   Environment, 1966–1990.

different aspects of the environment—water, air, and parks—again exemplify a differentiated public opinion (see figure 4.15).

Sentiment in favor of certain health and safety regulations continued to grow during the mid-1970s. In a March 1975 Harris poll, 10% more than in February 1974 said the government should be allowed to ban products without prior disclosure. A large majority preferred "health warnings" rather than bans as "(the) way to solve the product safety problem," but that dropped 6% (to 71%) between March 1975 and the beginning of 1977 (Harris). Over the same period, according to Harris, 10% more came to favor making manufacturers liable for product-related injuries even if a product is "obviously misused" (even though 90% agreed it was "unfair" to put all the safety blame on manufacturers). Other Harris and Roper surveys from 1971 to 1982 show high and stable support for regulation of product safety (at the 80% level) and regulation of misleading advertising (65%).

Deregulation

During the same period, however, economic stringency and increased concern about efficiency, along with businessmen's aversion to costly EPA and OSHA regulations, led to a movement toward deregulation. Certain aspects of this movement won substantial public support, for good reasons. The argument made by George Stigler and other conservative economists, that old-style regulation (e.g., through licensing, the ICC, the CAB) was generally inefficient and mostly benefited the regulated, were highly publicized and became widely accepted—even by liberals like Senator Edward Kennedy who favored deregulation of the airlines and other transportation industries.

But by using the broad symbol of "deregulation," business (especially environment-threatening oil, steel, and chemical firms, and small businesses worried about OSHA) succeeded to some extent in deflecting criticism onto the new consumer-, environmental-, and worker-oriented regulation, for which the politics and economics were very different. Murray Weidenbaum's estimate that regulation of business cost the economy more than $65 billion in 1976, growing to $100 billion in 1979 (a figure that was almost certainly exaggerated and took no account of the corresponding benefits; Schwarz 1988 [1983] pp. 98–107) was widely quoted. Subsidized antiregulation studies proliferated. The Advertising Council—funded and directed by corporations and using some Commerce Department money—distributed thirteen million booklets attacking the evils of inflation and listing government regulation as the primary cause (see Parenti 1986, pp. 72–79).

Americans' latent skepticism of big government, red tape, and bureaucracy was activated. In an autumn 1973 Harris survey, while only 36% of the public went so far as to agree that "the best government is government that governs the least," 88% accepted the proposition that "the elected officials have lost control of the bureaucrats who really run things"; these proportions rose 8% and 9%, respectively, by March 1976. Between the election period of 1974 and the beginning of 1977, SRC/CPS found a large 22% increase in the proportion on the side of a seven-point scale saying that the "federal government in Washington" should have less "influence and power." In June 1978, 47% told ORC there should be "less government regulation of business," with only 27% saying there should be more and 25% saying the present amount was about right; the proportion favoring "less . . . regulation" rose to 50% in August 1979 and 59% in December 1980, when it far outweighed the 21% for more regulation. A similar CRI question produced very nearly the same trend over the same years (see Shapiro and Gillroy 1984a, 1984b).

The public's move toward deregulation extended to some opinions concerning health, safety, and, as indicated in figure 4.15, the environment. Between mid-1973 and late 1977, for example, Gallup surveys showed a 7% decline in the already small (24%) proportion of the public that favored a $25 fine for not wearing seatbelts; such a drop was especially notable in a period of high inflation when the burden represented by the hypothetical $25.00 amount was decreasing. (This trend later reversed, as seat-belt laws were passed by a number of states, public education campaigns began to work, and seat-belt use increased.)

In late 1973, Roper found a 15% decline in the proportion saying "too little" money was being spent to improve and protect the environment, compared with a survey done two years earlier. Similarly, over the four years from spring 1973 to spring 1977, NORC-GSS found a 14% drop (from 65% to 51%) in the proportion thinking we were spending too little money to improve and protect the environment. Roper found a drop of 6% between the end of 1977 and the end of 1978. Throughout the 1970s and 1980s, however, "too little" responses always outnumbered "too much"; opinion never tilted toward actually cutting environmental spending. The spending items graphed in figure 4.15, above, generally show declines in the early-to-middle 1970s that stabilized by about 1979 and then began to rise again (see Gillroy and Shapiro 1986).

Nonspending environmental policies were also affected. Between 1976 and 1979—an oil crisis year—Harris discovered a 10% rise (to 66%) in support for slowing down pollution cleanups in order to solve energy problems. The Trendex items displayed in figure 4.15 show that desires to "see something done in your community" about water pollution, air pollution, and increasing national parks and wilderness areas all gradually declined from 1972 to 1980 and 1981. Again, however, very substantial majorities continued to favor action on all these matters in all years, and the public continued to make the same distinctions among different environmental problems and policies.

A minor casualty of the deregulation movement seems to have been the tentative effort to get the United States to join most of the world in the use of the metric system of measurement. Businessmen, concerned about conversion costs, resisted; educational efforts in the schools and elsewhere faltered; and Gallup found a large drop in public support for metric conversion between 1971 and 1977, from 50% to 35% among those who knew what the metric system was.

As we have seen, the general trend toward deregulation joined with slackened concern over energy supplies (after the 1973–1974 crisis passed and before that of 1979 arrived) to weaken support for various measures of energy regulation in the middle 1970s. The trend also affected antitrust policy. In November 1975, 64% of Americans told Harris interviewers that big companies ought to be allowed to get together for joint planning in the public interest, a rise of 11% since July 1974. However, Harris's battery of questions about *eliminating* antitrust laws "if . . . " (e.g., if having only a few big companies were more efficient) actually showed *drops* in support for eliminating the laws, from 1974 to 1976 and 1977. Large majorities opposed elimination under all circumstances in every year. The public's receptiveness to deregulation, then, had definite limits. Support for deregulation in the abstract never penetrated a number of specific areas.

The deregulation movement culminated, in a sense, with the end of the Carter years and the election in 1980 of President Reagan, who spoke vigorously of cutting government "interference" with the economy and made antiregulatory appointments to the Interior Department, EPA, OSHA, and elsewhere.

Re-regulation

What is most striking about public opinion on these matters, however, is how small the deregulatory "right turn" was, how quickly and thoroughly proregulation opinion recovered during Reagan's first term, and how favorable most Americans were to environmental and other regulations at the end of the 1980s (e.g., Dunlap 1985).

The outcry against prodevelopment Secretary James Watt at the Interior Department and the scandal over bungled toxic waste cleanups at EPA undoubtedly hastened the recovery of proenvironmental opinion. So did periodic oil spills and mounting evidence about acid rain, nuclear waste, and other environmental contamination that threatened the air, soil, water, and climate. By 1990, global warming and depletion of the ozone layer had become major concerns. Figure 4.15, above, shows the sweeping rise from about 1980 onward in the proportions of Americans saying that "too little" was being spent on the environment. By 1990, 75% said "too little," far outnumbering the 5% who said "too much" (NORC-GSS).

A Media General/Associated Press poll in May 1989 found majority backing for a wide variety of environmental measures including mandatory trash recycling, a ban on household aerosols, strict emissions controls at power plants, urgent action (no matter what the cost) to clean toxic waste and protect drinking water, new safety rules and emergency cleanup teams at all major oil facilities (even if that would raise the price of oil and gasoline), strict smokestack controls at oil- and coal-burning power plants (even if electricity prices would rise), and a ban on new oil drilling in the Arctic Wildlife Refuge in Alaska or (by a smaller margin) off the shores of California and Florida. At the beginning of the 1990s it was clear that the overwhelming majority of Americans was committed to government protection of consumers and the environment.

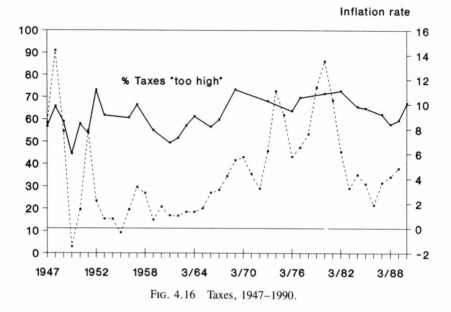

FIG. 4.16   Taxes, 1947–1990.

Taxes

The polls confirm, to no one's surprise, that most Americans are not keen to pay taxes. Over the years Gallup and NORC-GSS have repeatedly asked whether people consider the amount of federal income taxes that they themselves have to pay "too high" or "too low" or "about right." With few exceptions (in only two of twenty Gallup surveys conducted between 1947 and 1973, and none of the ten NORC-GSS surveys from 1976 to 1990), a majority of those with opinions has always said "too high." No more than 2% have ever felt sufficiently public spirited or guilty to say "too low" (see figure 4.16).

Of course, the Gallup/NORC-GSS "too high" tax item refers to respondents' *own* taxes. These figures probably overstate opposition to income tax *rates* in general, since many people oppose loopholes by which others—especially the wealthy—benefit; people can reasonably favor increased tax revenues while wanting to lower their own payments. Indeed, we will see below (in the section on progressive taxation) that most Americans, when asked, have wanted to set tax rates at about their current effective levels. Still, it is true that proposals for tax increases often meet substantial disapproval from the public, even (as noted above) at times of strong concern about budget deficits.

This may seem to threaten our picture of rational public opinion. V. O. Key (1961, pp. 165–168) long ago observed that many citizens' inclination to support spending on a variety of programs, while comprehensible in terms of self-interest, was not "consistent" with their resistance to taxes. Our graphs on taxes and spending programs might suggest the same thing. At the beginning of the 1990s, politicians and pundits frequently bemoaned the public's unwillingness to bite the bullet of increasing taxes in order to reduce federal budget deficits. A *New York Times* analysis of a CBS/*NYT* poll in May 1990, for example, spoke of "deeply ambivalent" and "contradictory" public views that acknowledged the deficit as a very serious problem calling for immediate action, yet strongly opposed reducing spending on education or Social Security or the environment, and rejected as "unacceptable" political elites' proposals for creating a (regressive) federal sales tax or raising the tax on gasoline (Oreskes 1990, pp. 1, 13).

Can we defend the rational public against charges of fiscal profligacy?

Yes. The 1990 CBS/*NYT* data themselves suggest how. Majorities of the public were, in fact, willing to cut certain programs (foreign aid, overwhelmingly; military spending, by more than a two to one margin) and to raise some taxes (on beer and liquor, and on incomes over $200,000, both by overwhelming margins),[12] which could have reduced or eliminated the deficit—but not in the way the elites apparently had in mind. (The same issue of the *Times* carried an editorial opposing tax increases on high incomes.) It is difficult to perceive any inconsistency in the public's preferences in these data, or indeed in other data we are aware of. Surveys are usually too incomplete to cover the full range of tax and spending and overall budget policies or to explore *tradeoffs*.[13]

The truth of the matter seems to be that most people oppose large parts of the federal budget that have been identified as "wasteful"—most important, in the 1980s and early 1990s, military spending. People oppose general tax rises that would be spent on things they don't want. Again and again survey questions, several of which we have mentioned, report that majorities of Americans say they are willing to pay more taxes for specific purposes like medical care and research, Social Security, education, and the environment. Indeed, support for such public goods is highly price inelastic compared with private consumer goods (Green 1990). It is not inconsistent for Americans to want to limit taxation to what is needed for programs they want funded.

Although the Gallup/NORC-GSS "too high" tax question is of limited use in understanding what fiscal policies Americans favor at one moment in time, it provides a long time series of responses that is useful for illuminating opinion dynamics. As figure 4.16 (above) and the Appendix show, the proportion saying "too high" has fluctuated up and down over the years—much more so than opinion on most issues—because of such factors as changes in tax levels and real after-tax incomes and the way tax money has been spent, which in turn have varied with the state of the economy and with U.S. fortunes in peace and war. (It correlates rather highly, as expected, with inflation rates, which can account for 40% or more of the variance in "too high" responses according to various regression models we estimated. See also Hansen 1983.) We view these opinion changes as generally sensible and understandable, and (like those concerning inflation and unemployment) as consistently related to objective circumstances.

In March 1947, for example, Gallup found 57% saying that their income taxes were too high. This figure rose to 66% by the end of the year, but then dropped a full 22%, to an all-time low of 44% saying "too high," in March 1949. The "too high" proportion then rose sharply during the unpopular Korean War, with its wage and price controls and high military spending, reaching a peak of 73% in February 1952. It fell back to 62% by February 1953, as President Eisenhower took office undertaking to end the war.

After a fairly steady decline until the end of the 1950s (under what was seen as a tight-budget Eisenhower administration), "too high" responses dropped still further, to 49%, in February 1961, when the public was apparently willing to pay to meet what President Kennedy portrayed as the Soviet challenge in space and in developing countries and elsewhere—while at the same time (as 1961–1963 Gallup and SRC/Consumer Finance surveys show) strongly favoring Kennedy's "economic growth" tax cuts. But 12% more said their taxes were too high in March 1964, as Social Security taxes rose and Great Society spending programs were being proposed. There was a further rise (again reaching a peak of 73% saying "too high") by March 1969, as people became disillusioned with paying for the expensive and unsuccessful Vietnam War along with Great Society domestic spending. (In 1969, Harris found fully 82% agreeing that "too much tax money is going into wars and defense." This figure dropped a large 19%—to a still high level of 63%—by early 1977, after the Vietnam War and during publicity about the alleged Soviet arms buildup.)

After Vietnam there followed a slight peacetime relaxation of concern about taxes when taxpayers were no longer footing a large bill for an unpopular war. Consistent with post-Vietnam Gallup data, Harris found that between May 1974 and January 1975 the view that *sales* taxes were too high dropped 7%, to 54%; that airline taxes were too high dropped

8%, to 51%; that taxes on liquor were too high dropped a substantial 14%, to 34%; and that cigarette taxes were too high dropped 11%, to 44%. Yet, over the same period, 6% fewer Americans (33%) wanted to raise companies' taxes, and 9% more (70%) thought an income tax cut would be "worthwhile"; 9% and 10% fewer, respectively, wanted to eliminate the oil depletion allowance (49%) or housing incentives (41%).[14] Harris surveys also indicate that there was a rise in the effective tax rates desired between January and October 1975 (a year in which mild tax reforms were passed), when 8% more wanted to eliminate housing incentives and 7% more (51%) wanted to eliminate cattle raising deductions.

There followed, however, another rise in NORC-GSS "too high" responses during the late 1970s, as one of the more pronounced elements in the temporary general increase in opposition to various aspects of government taxing and spending. The federal income tax was increasingly seen as the "worst" or "least fair" tax (see below). On taxes there was a significant right turn. Many people perceived that inflation was driving down real incomes and pushing people into higher income tax brackets—though average taxes as a percentage of income did not in fact rise (see Schwarz 1988 [1983], pp. 83–93).

Sentiment that taxes were "too high" dropped markedly, however, after the big 1981 tax cut, as one would expect they would. (Similarly, NBC found an 80% combined "too high" and "much too high" response in June 1978, which dipped to 73% by May 1981, presumably in anticipation of the Reagan cuts.)

Objections to taxes as too high continued to decline with the 1982 tax reforms and increasing rhetoric about the importance of reducing budget deficits; many people preferred more taxes to cuts in popular domestic programs. According to ABC surveys there was an 8%–10% increase in support for a tax increase to reduce the budget deficit (though still only to the 31% or 37% level) during the 1982–1984 period, based on a sample of voters. This temporarily reversed after the 1984 campaign year, when President Reagan and other Republicans fiercely attacked Walter Mondale's proposal to raise taxes, but from March 1985 to February 1986 support for a tax increase (as measured by a differently worded question) rose again from 22% to 30%.[15] Likewise, NORC-GSS "too high" responses once again declined (figure 4.16).

Progressive Taxation

The American public has not expressed much support for the kind of progressive taxation that would be required to redistribute incomes substantially. In fact, the best available evidence indicates the public has favored effective tax rates at approximately the levels existing at the time poll questions have been asked.

At scattered intervals in the past, Gallup asked respondents to imagine they were members of Congress setting personal income tax rates, and inquired how much should be paid by families of four with varying amounts of income: $3,000 per year, $5,000, $10,000, or $50,000. If the aggregate responses (which Gallup confusingly referred to as the "median average[s]") are expressed as percentages of those hypothetical family incomes, the results—in 1961, for example, the last time these questions were asked—come rather close to the actual effective rates of the income tax at those income levels, as calculated by Pechman and Okner (1970; see Page 1979). (The Gallup organization itself apparently did not realize this; it contrasted the public's desires with its own oversimplified calculations of actual tax rates.)

The most interesting feature of these Gallup findings is that neither the tax rates chosen by the public, nor the quite similar actual effective tax rates, were very progressive. High-income people were not asked to pay a much higher percentage of their income than were low-income people. The very highly progressive rates formerly published in IRS rate tables, which at one time ranged up to 90% on top incomes, were always eroded by exemptions and deductions and exclusions, so that (as of the middle 1960s) no income group paid more than about 17% on the average (Pechman and Okner 1970). Most Americans did not seem to object seriously. In fact, in 1952, 73% of Americans (up 8% from 1951) told Gallup they favored a 25% top limit on income taxes in peacetime—this at the time of a 90% top statutory rate.

True, the U.S. public has sometimes expressed a desire that "those with higher incomes should pay even more of their income into taxes than they do now"—as nearly half did, according to self-placement on that side of SRC/CPS seven-point scales in 1972 (46%) and 1976 (40%). The middle 1970s probably represented a high point of sentiment for loophole closing and progressive reforms. Between 1969 and 1973, Harris found a modest 7% rise (to 34%) in the proportion saying corporate taxes were too low. Harris also found in May 1974 that 58% wanted to eliminate the oil depletion allowance (falling to 49% in January 1975) and, in October 1975, that 51% (up 7% from January) wanted to eliminate cattle raising deductions. (Some mildly progressive tax changes were in fact enacted in 1974, 1975, and 1976, before the push for "capital formation" and the highly regressive changes of 1978 and 1981.)

At times, many Americans have also said they favored "a higher tax rate for wealthier people," as 69% or 70% did according to *Los Angeles Times* surveys in August 1981 and in 1982 after the 1981 Reagan tax cuts were strongly criticized for mostly benefiting the wealthy. But not *much* higher, apparently. The abandonment of even nominally progressive rates begun in 1981 (when the top rate was cut from 70% to 50%) was virtually completed in 1986 (the top tax rate dropped to 28%). This was a highly regressive change, helping high-income people much more than low or middle, but it did not produce much public outrage; just a sense that things had gone a bit too far, manifested, for example, in the 1990 support (mentioned above) for increasing taxes on incomes over $200,000.

The public's preferred levels of taxes for Gallup's hypothetical families varied somewhat over the years, but not according to any pattern of desiring greater or lesser redistribution. Instead, they all tended to go up or down in accord with general attitudes about levels of taxing and spending. Between 1941 and 1951, for example, after the great World War II expansion of government and the onset of the Korean War, people came to favor higher taxes at all income levels; and between 1951 and 1956, when the Korean War had ended, they wanted lower taxes.[16]

Lack of interest in tax progressivity has been evident, not only in opinions about income tax rates but also in attitudes concerning the relative merits of various different kinds of taxes. Many ORC and Gallup surveys for the Advisory Commission on Intergovernmental Relations (ACIR), and two CRI surveys in 1977 and 1984, have shown that the public has generally tended to call the progressive federal income tax and local property taxes the "worst" or "least fair" taxes, as contrasted with the regressive state sales taxes and Social Security payroll taxes which take high proportions of revenue from working-class people.

The public's preference for excise taxes on luxuries, and perhaps those for "sin taxes" on alcohol and tobacco (despite their regressivity), are understandable; sales taxes may be favored because they are easy to pay; and Social Security taxes have recently met some resistance as they have bitten deeper (CRI found the substantial majority that saw them as more fair than the income tax vanished between 1977 and 1984). But the relative receptivity to regressive taxes raises the general question why low-income majorities are willing to tax themselves more than people of higher income.

Depending upon one's values and one's economic theory, it is possible either to admire the rational public's farsighted devotion to economic growth (favoring a tax structure that neoclassical economics says provides strong incentives to work and save and invest), or to lament widespread public misunderstanding of how taxes work, a misunderstanding which leads to mistaken preferences. In our own view, tax policy—like monetary policy—is a highly technical realm that is ripe for concealment and mystification. In the making of tax laws, the "scope of conflict" (Schattschneider 1960) is often exceptionally narrow; when loopholes are legislated in closed committee meetings, many citizens do not know what is going on. Moreover, vast resources have been spent for propaganda campaigns in favor of "supply side" regressive tax cuts, low taxes on capital gains, encouragement of "capital formation," and the like (Martin 1991). Public opinion may have been manipulated (see Page 1979; and 1983, chap. 2). The Gallup and other data showing opposition to progressive tax rates suggest that something more than simple misunderstanding of tax incidence is going on; Americans seem to be—or to have been made— genuinely unenthusiastic about income redistribution.

Other Domestic Issues
Political Institutions and Processes

In order to spare the reader's patience and pocketbook, we will refrain from discussing our full collection of opinion data about political reforms and certain domestic issues connected with foreign policy. We will only sketch the outlines of the data and indicate how they fit our arguments about the rational public.

Americans' opinions concerning political institutions form a coherent pattern, one that is highly patriotic (in the sense of approving the U.S. Constitution and existing institutions) but also highly prodemocratic, willing to entertain reforms seen as increasing the power of ordinary citizens.

Large majorities have opposed major constitutional amendments or overhauls of the system. Even in the dark days of 1974, when President Nixon was about to resign in disgrace, 52% told Roper that the political system was "basically sound"; that figure rose to the 70% level in 1977, 1981, and 1983. But majorities ranging from 73% to 86% have wanted to do away with the electoral college and elect the president by popular vote. Some 70%–80% of Americans have favored choosing presidential candidates in a nationwide primary rather than through party conventions. Before the 1971 ratification of the Twenty-sixth Amendment, 60%–70% favored granting the vote to eighteen-year-olds.

The same prodemocratic theme connects preferences for limiting private campaign contributions (70%–80% in favor) and limiting campaign spending. It underlies the strong (70%–80%) rejection of a six-year term for presidents, that perennial elite proposal to insulate the executive from popular control. By the same token, the public has supported majority-vote cloture of Senate filibusters. In our data, only the public's divided feelings about an election day holiday (which would broaden participation), and perhaps its opposition to public financing of congressional campaigns, seem discordant with the clear pattern of favoring increased democracy.

Opinion changes concerning political reform issues—like the issues discussed elsewhere in the book—have represented reasonable responses to circumstances and events. The view that the system is "basically sound" was depressed during Watergate and rose afterward. Desires to abolish the electoral college were high in the tricky third-party years 1948 and 1968. Backing for a nationwide primary was especially strong in 1952 and 1968, when popular candidates (Dwight Eisenhower, Eugene McCarthy, Robert Kennedy) were being resisted by party regulars. The eighteen-year-old vote was most popular in wartime, when voteless young people were fighting for their country. Backing for campaign reforms increased after the Watergate scandals. Attitudes toward two-term limits, a six-year presidential term, and whether the president should have "less power" have all varied with the performance of incumbent presidents. Support for Senate cloture was highest when civil rights bills were being filibustered; limits on congressional terms were most favored when Congress was seen as performing poorly; and the minority view that the Supreme Court should have less influence grew after unpopular decisions.

The most spectacular opinion changes on political matters involve Nixon and Watergate: a 32% increase in the proportion saying Nixon should resign (Harris), and a 36% rise in responses that he should be "impeached and compelled to leave the presidency" (Gallup), both responding in 1973–1974 to gradual revelations of information about the Watergate break-in and coverup (see Chap. 8, below, and Lang and Lang 1983).

The Domestic Side of Foreign Policy

Several domestic issues, including the draft, the space program, tariffs and trade, immigration, and the admission of new states, are closely intertwined with foreign policy. They will come up from time to time in the foreign policy chapters (5 and 6) but deserve brief mention here as well. Each of them fits our argument that the rational public makes coherent distinctions among policies and circumstances.

Public opinion about the military *draft* and alternative nonmilitary service, for example, has generally reflected the realities of international relations, with support naturally highest when war was threatened or under way. At the end of the Vietnam War there was strong (76%) support for the new all-volunteer army. This fell steadily in the 1970s, to a low of 32% in 1980, as alarms about Soviet power and the Iranian hostages provoked majority support for a "return to the draft." But the Reagan arms buildup and resumption of foreign policy tranquility eliminated most prodraft sentiment by 1985, when ABC found only 26% in favor (see Tom Smith 1990b, for a recent summary of opinions about national service).

Support for the *space program* (intimately connected with the development of military missiles) has also, quite reasonably, followed trends related to military and foreign policy as well as economic trends and events involving space exploration itself. President Kennedy's "man on the moon" program caught the popular imagination, but Vietnam and Great Society expenses dampened funding enthusiasm. Especially after the 1969 moon landing excitement, through the middle 1970s, large majorities (61%–63%, according to NORC-GSS) said "too much" was being spent on space exploration, with only 8% or 9% saying "too little." Support for the space program grew along with desires for a military buildup in the late 1970s; it then leveled off in the 1980s, with about 40% saying "too much" and only 12%–19% saying too little (see Chap. 2, figure 2.2). Unlike opinion about defense spending, support for the space program did not actually decline in the 1980s; instead, a growing proportion of the public said its primary emphasis should be on scientific exploration rather than national defense. Large majorities continued to call the space shuttle a "good investment" even right after the Challenger disaster (J. Miller 1987). But space has remained considerably less popular than major social programs, with more people wanting to cut the program than to increase it.

Most Americans like the idea of free *trade* (and cheap imports) in principle, but over many years (especially the economically pressured 1970s and 1980s) large majorities have favored some measure of protectionism to safeguard American jobs. Roper in the 1970s found about 70% saying the United States should "place restrictions" on imports; in 1973 and 1978 Harris found 63% and 65% for "more" restrictions. But the aim is reciprocity: a different Harris question in 1983 and 1985 showed high (72%–76%) support for a system under which "more American goods and services would be allowed into Japan and Western Europe" and more of their goods would be allowed into the United States.

Americans, though mostly descended from immigrants, tend to resist further *immigration,* particularly of sorts that entail assimilation problems or supporting impoverished newcomers or labor competition that could drive down the wages of American workers. A number of Roper, Gallup, and Harris questions from 1939, 1946, 1965, and later years show strikingly large majorities against opening the doors to European refugees, against "more" immigrants, or (especially in the 1970s and 1980s) against letting in more immigrants from Mexico. In 1980, 1983, and 1984, about 80% favored punishing the employment of undocumented workers (Gallup). These attitudes may be selfish and perhaps short-sighted, but they cannot be called irrational; ordinary Americans have more to lose and less to gain than do the employers who are glad to hire cheap new labor.[17]

Conclusion

The detailed discussions in Chapters 3 and 4 of preferences concerning domestic issues have helped fill in our portrait of rational public opinion. The patterns of opinion on social issues in Chapter 3, often including sharp distinctions among alternative policies, made sense. The opinion changes, some of them quite large (on civil rights, civil liberties, women's rights and the like), could be understood as reasonable responses to a changing world.

On the economic issues discussed in this chapter, opinion changes have mostly been smaller and less prominent, but these changes, too, have represented comprehensible and generally reasonable reactions to events and circumstances and new information. Opinions about employment, inflation, taxes, and energy, for example, reacted in systematic and consistent ways to objective trends in prices and unemployment rates. Because of the predominant stability of opinions, we concentrated a good deal on *patterns* of preferences within and across issues, showing that the American public makes coherent distinctions among policies and holds opinions that fit together into backing for individualism and a limited, but substantial, welfare state.

The high and generally stable public support for government action on Social Security, education, jobs, medical care, the cities, the environment, consumer safety, and the like—and willingness to pay taxes for these purposes—is especially striking. We noted a number of dips during the late 1970s in support for taxes, regulation, and social spending (especially on welfare, redistribution, minorities, and medical care), but in nearly every case this "right turn" of opinion was small and temporary; opinion never altered much and soon rebounded in a liberal direction, usually by the early 1980s. In other cases (e.g., spending on Social Security and education), there was hardly any change at all or even a continued movement in a liberal direction. Ferguson and Rogers (1986) are correct, therefore, in arguing that the policy right turn of the Reagan years cannot be accounted for as a response to public demands. Throughout the Reagan years and on into the Bush years, Americans favored *more,* not less, spending and action on virtually all these economic welfare programs. As we saw in Chapter 3, much the same thing was true of most social issues (see also Mayer 1990).

In the course of explaining stability and change in opinions, however, one troubling issue has come up. We alluded to several cases in which the public may have been subjected to incorrect or misleading information (e.g., concerning labor unions, welfare, inflation, nuclear energy, regulation, and perhaps taxes); we have acknowledged that in some cases this may have had an effect, and public opinion may have been manipulated. Does such a possibility contradict our arguments about a rational public?

No, it does not. In the first place, most of our arguments have to do with the collective *capacity* of the public: its capacity to hold coherent, consistent, stable, real preferences that react in understandable and sensible ways to changing circumstances and new information. All this is based on whatever information and interpretations the public receives. None of it conflicts with the possibility that the public, if bombarded with misinformation, can be fooled. To the extent that misleading or incorrect information is provided, the finger of blame ought to point not at the public but at the providers of information.

But, second, we can go somewhat beyond these capacity arguments and maintain that actual public opinion, at least on most of the domestic matters we have discussed, is in fact highly resistant to manipulation, and should be taken seriously as an authentic input into democratic policy-making. We have seen many cases, including several instances of barely discernible shifts to the right, in which a great deal of what might be called heavy-handed propaganda has had very little effect on opinion.

Most Americans, as a collectivity, know rather clearly what they want, especially concerning jobs and health and education and other matters of daily experience. It is particularly difficult to confuse people about such things when a measure of political pluralism provides at least some vestigial segment of elites who champion the public's long-standing wishes—roughly the situation that existed in the 1980s. Most of the time, collective deliberation works fairly well.

When it comes to foreign policy, however, or to special domestic matters like nuclear energy or repression of dissidents which involve foreign-policy-like secrecy and national security concerns, the situation may sometimes be different. In national security matters, especially international crises, government officials sometimes hold monopoly or near-monopoly control of information; no significant elite opposition speaks out; and the public can be deceived. We will encounter several such cases in Chapters 5 and 6. We will grapple further with what they mean for the rational public there and also in Chapters 8, 9, and 10.

The next two chapters are organized largely in a historical fashion (with some topical sections as well), locating opinion trends in the context of American and world history. Much of our attention will return to issues of opinion *change*. We will see that many changes in the public's foreign policy preferences have been rapid and abrupt, reacting to sudden and even cataclysmic international events like wars and crises. We will see also that the public's reactions have generally been understandable and sensible, given the information that is made available.

5 Foreign Policy: World War II and the Cold War

(Coauthored by John M. Gillroy)

☑ When it comes to foreign policy, our main theme is the same as in previous chapters: that collective public opinion is *rational,* in the sense we have defined the term—real, stable, differentiated, consistent, coherent; reflective of basic values and beliefs; and responsive (in predictable and reasonable ways) to new information and changing circumstances.

Our assertion of public rationality is even more controversial with respect to foreign than domestic matters, because elites have held public opinion concerning foreign policy in especially low esteem. As we noted in Chapters 1 and 2, a number of scholars and observers have argued that ordinary Americans have little interest in or information about foreign affairs; that the opinions they hold, if any, are poorly grounded and unstable; and that collective public opinion vacillates capriciously according to "moods" (e.g., Lippmann 1922; Almond 1960 [1950]).

Many foreign policy analysts and policymakers probably continue to believe some version of a "mood theory," and in any case are not much interested in responding to public opinion. Bernard Cohen found, for example, that government officials and staff members at the State Department's Bureau of Public Affairs believed the public had little capacity to contribute substantively to dialogue about foreign policy; they shared the view, "To hell with public opinion. . . . We should lead, and not follow" (B. Cohen 1973, p. 62).[1]

We have already seen that some of these common notions about foreign policy opinions are incorrect. To be sure, overall information levels concerning foreign affairs are indeed rather low, though they are not so abysmal as is often assumed and may have risen in recent years.[2] But, as we argued in Chapter 1, the logic of "information pooling" and the mutually offsetting nature of random errors, together with processes of collective deliberation, make it possible for collective public opinion to be meaningful and stable even when individuals' opinions are based on limited information and have large elements of randomness. The data in Chapter 2 demonstrated that, in fact, collective public opinion about foreign policy tends to be rather stable, seldom changing by large amounts and rarely fluctuating (though it often changes abruptly when it does change).

Now we must show that foreign policy opinions have further attributes of rationality: that collective preferences are meaningful, not merely the result of coin tosses or doorstep opinions; that they form differentiated and coherent and consistent patterns; that they relate to underlying values; and that preferences change in sensible and predictable ways in response to events and new information.

We can do this only by examining the public's preferences and preference changes in specific detail. In the course of discussing most major aspects of foreign policy and most of the significant opinion changes in our data, we will see that our criteria for rationality have generally been met. Virtually all collective preferences form differentiated, coherent, consistent patterns within and across issues. Further, the instances of opinion change generally represent understandable and reasonable responses to international events, as reported and interpreted in the U.S. mass media and by elites.

Since public opinion tends to change more abruptly on foreign policy than on domestic matters, we can often bracket opinion changes within narrow segments of time and can, with a fair degree of confidence, identify events that caused them. In fact, a large part of these chapters will be devoted to showing that—with a few exceptions which we will note—opinion changes have been explicable and reasonable.

Even more than in the last chapter, the issue of *manipulation* of opinion will rise to haunt us. We certainly do not claim that the public has always correctly judged the best foreign policy interests of Americans or of humankind. Nor would we assert that political leaders and the media have always reported truthfully or interpreted events correctly. Indeed, we will discuss some conspicuous cases in which the public has been given deceptive or misleading information about world affairs.

We therefore repeat that our central arguments have to do with the *capacity* of the public to form rational opinions, *given the information available*. On most domestic matters, about which elites often compete and provide multiple sources of information, the public can use its capacities to form opinions that are not only rational in our sense but also "authentic," consistent with "true interests"—that is, opinions that approximate fully and correctly informed preferences. In foreign affairs, on the other hand, government monopolies of information (and consensus among elites) may sometimes lead the public astray from preferences it would hold if fully informed. This raises troubling questions that we will discuss further. We will see, however, that even in foreign affairs public opinion often resists elite persuasion and reacts more or less independently to the logic of world events.

In this and the following chapter, we will describe chronologically a number of trends in public opinion, discussing World War II, the origins of the Cold War, the Korean conflict, Vietnam, détente, the new Cold War, and renewed détente with the Soviet Union. Most of the major foreign policy issues are so closely tied to U.S. relations with principal adversaries (Nazi Germany and Japan, and then the Soviet Union), and so much affected by the ups and downs in those relationships, that the best way to organize the discussion is historically. But it is also useful to devote separate sections to certain special topics: the general issue of isolationism and interventionism, the United Nations, U.S. relations with China, and the Middle East.

Isolationism and Internationalism

Perhaps the most fundamental issue for a nation's foreign policy concerns how actively that nation will attempt to influence events in the international arena. Almond, Lippmann and others have found the American public particularly deficient on that score: unconcerned about foreign affairs and reluctant to take up the burdens of world responsibility.

The fact is, however, that for about fifty years—beginning even before direct U.S. involvement in World War II—the great majority of Americans has recognized the inevitability of involvement in world affairs and has favored an active role for the United States. The proportion favoring an active role has stayed high and rather stable, not fluctuating much; when it has changed it has done so in reasonable response to changing circumstances.

This is evident in figure 5.1, which graphs the extent of internationalist responses to some relevant survey questions from the 1940s through the 1980s. Different wordings have been used by different survey organizations (not all are included in figure 5.1). One wording has referred to taking "an active part in world affairs" (NORC, OPOR, Gallup), others to "concern(ing) ourselves with problems in other parts of the world" (NORC, SRC/CPS), and still others to whether the United States should "mind its own business internationally," (Gallup) or whether it was "better for the United States to work closely with other nations" (Gallup).

According to all these items, a substantial majority of Americans clearly rejected isolationism as a general proposition; they embraced internationism to meet the challenges of World War II in the 1940s and

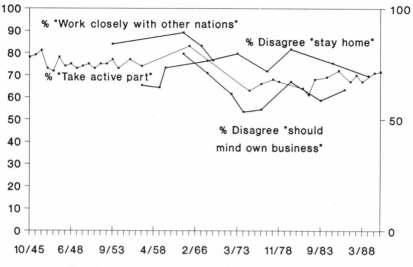

(after a slight postwar drop) during the Cold War. Throughout the 1950s there was fairly steady support for an "active part"—by more than 70% of those with opinions[3] in NORC surveys. (We used this same item to illustrate opinion stability in figure 2.1.) Support rose to a peak of 83% at the beginning of the Vietnam War in 1965; it fell somewhat, though not enormously, as the war went badly, and later showed signs of an upswing after the war ended. The other items shown in figure 5.1 reflect comparable levels and similar trends.

Of course, we are talking about a rather general sort of internationalism. Support for an active U.S. role does not necessary mean supporting particular policies like foreign aid or the use of U.S. troops abroad, which have often been quite unpopular. (Nor, contrary to some assertions, is there anything at all contradictory about holding different views on different specific policies.) Indeed, the concept of foreign policy activism lumps together many different sorts of possible policies— hawkish and dovish, uncooperative and accommodating, multilateralist and unilateralist, anti-Communist and antiauthoritarian or anti-Fascist. The meaning of internationalism varies among individuals (see Wittkopf 1990) and has undoubtedly varied over time as well.

Still, the data certainly refute the notion that Americans are isolationist. Moreover, they indicate (as Chap. 2 demonstrated more systematically) that the foreign policy attitudes of the collective public are generally quite stable.

A closer look at the moderate rises and falls in the extent of internationalist responses indicates that they have followed world events in understandable and reasonable ways.

In 1935, when the Gallup organization began its national polling, Americans were wary of foreign entanglements. Most were concerned about the depressed U.S. economy and were disillusioned with the failure of peace after the "war to end all wars," World War I. Unfortunately, we cannot tell exactly how people would have answered the "active part" question in the 1930s, because it was not asked until 1942. But collateral evidence is consistent with the impression that isolationism predominated. In a September 1935 Gallup survey, for example, fully 75% favored a "national vote" before any declaration of war. (This proportion stayed much the same in 1936 and 1937 before apparently starting to drop to the 50% level in 1938 and especially in 1939 [according to slightly different questions asked by Gallup and Roper] when the danger of sudden war increased.) As late as February 1939—again according to Gallup—barely half of the American public favored selling war materials to England and France. In October 1939 (i.e., even after the invasion of Poland), only 29% wanted to declare war on Germany.

As the war in Europe went badly for the allies, however, even before the United States entered combat, most Americans acknowledged that the United States would have to play "a larger part" in world affairs after the war than it did before. This attitude long preceded the Cold War agitation to which it is sometimes attributed, and even preceded direct U.S. involvement in World War II. In an October 1941 Roper survey, 61% said they favored a larger postwar role. (A 67% figure is reported for December 1941. Since the exact interviewing dates are unavailable, we cannot tell whether or not it was affected by Pearl Harbor.) War involvement apparently added to the internationalist sentiment; by June 1943, after a year and a half of U.S. participation in the war, fully 83% responded "a larger part" to a very similar Roper question (see Cantril 1951, p. 1055).

In January 1942, when OPOR first asked an "active part" question, 75% of those with opinions declared that "when the war is over" the United States should "take an active part in world affairs" (Cantril 1951, p. 1055). Support for that position stood at 71% in April 1944 and increased near the war's end, rising to 81% in March 1945. When the Gallup organization began to ask an "active part" question without mention of the war being over, it received internationalist responses from 84% of the public in March 1943, 80% in May 1944, 78% in October 1945, 79% in February 1946, and 81% in November 1946, with a slight dropoff (to 78%) as of early September 1947. Again, these strongly internationalist opinions long preceded the Cold War.

NORC asked a virtually identical "active part" question[4] in March 1947 and found internationalist sentiment at 73%: lower than Gallup's 81% figure of the previous fall, perhaps because of postwar fatigue and a desire for return to normalcy. The total apparent drop from 81% (Gallup, November 1946) to 72% (NORC, June 1947) looks substantial and statistically significant—about twice the size of the drop to the next Gallup survey, in September—but given possible differences in the early interviewing and sampling methods of the organizations we cannot be sure that all of it represents real opinion change.[5]

In any case, throughout the early Cold War period, roughly 75% of Americans with opinions, according to our figures, continued to favor an active U.S. role in the world. The figure rose as high as 83% in a 1965 NORC survey, then fell markedly—to 63% by early 1975—reflecting an understandable post-Vietnam disillusionment and desire for foreign policy restraint. (The SRC/CPS "just stayed home" item showed a similar temporary drop in "disagree" responses between late 1972 and late 1976, though a large majority (72%) continued to be internationalist.) Then support for an active role grew as part of a general resurgence of international activism—now more unilateralist than multilateralist—in the late 1970s, rising to 72% in early 1985 and standing at 71% in 1990 (see Rielly 1987).

These changes make sense. It is hardly surprising that many Americans responded to Hitler, even before Pearl Harbor, by endorsing an active foreign policy role; or that the war itself increased internationalist feelings; or that the end of World War II, the onset of the Cold War, and the painful experience of Vietnam all affected attitudes somewhat. None of these moderate opinion changes supports the implication of the "mood theory" that the public is fickle and undependable (see Caspary 1970; and Chap. 2, above; cf. Almond 1960 [1950]).

Subgroups, Internationalism, and the Attentive Public

Here, as in previous chapters, we have mostly been speaking of the U.S. public as if it were a homogeneous whole. But does everyone think about and react to foreign policy in the same way, or think about it at all? What of different subgroups in the population: men, women, the young, the old, Northerners, Southerners? In particular, what about the highly educated as opposed to those with less formal education? This has been a classic concern for scholars (see Hughes 1978; Key 1961). Many analysts of foreign policy have argued that Americans who are "attentive" or have a great deal of education tend to have opinions that are different from (and perhaps superior to) the opinions of other people, that their opinions move differently, and that they tend to influence others (see Almond 1960 [1950]; Rosenau 1961; J. Miller 1983; Neuman 1986).

We will address differences among population groupings more fully in Chapter 7, but their special importance with respect to foreign policy justifies a brief digression here.

As noted in Chapter 7 (analyzing several thousand subgroup time series), *trends* in attitudes toward foreign policies—just like those concerning domestic policies—do not usually differ much from one subgroup of the population to another. Different groups of Americans, whether classified according to sex, age, region, formal education, or other criteria, usually move in parallel. Most trends apply across the board, and any differences are generally too small to detect or to be certain about; they are seldom of great substantive importance.

At first, this may seem puzzling or counterintuitive. We might well expect some types of people to be much more sensitive than others to events, changing conditions, and new information—either generally, or on matters of special concern to them. This would seem to be especially pertinent in the case of foreign policy, where opinions sometimes change abruptly and where world events are crucial. For example, one might assume that the foreign policy opinions of the less well educated would be the most volatile, since their lack of prior knowledge and limited cognitive capacities might allow them to be pushed easily in any direction.

The evidence suggests, however, that—if anything—this is the opposite of the truth. The better educated, in fact, show somewhat *more* variability in opinions over time (see Richman 1972; P. Smith 1961; Mueller 1979; MacKuen 1984), apparently because—while they are more resistant to opinion change due to their prior knowledge and sophistication—they are also much more exposed to new information and better able to take it into account. But the balance between these exposure and acceptance effects may vary by issue. On many issues there are no educational differences at all—or only short-lived differences—in opinion trends. To get at the subtleties of these opinion dynamics requires careful theorizing about cognition and about the interaction between individuals' exposure to and their acceptance of new information (see Zaller 1987, 1990b; MacKuen 1984; Geddes and Zaller 1989).

For us the main point is that the broadest and most persistent pattern in the trend data is one of *parallel publics*. When aggregate preferences change, especially when they do so over a lengthy period, all segments of the public generally move in the same direction, and usually at about the same rate. Apparently—given our pervasive system of mass communications—important new information usually reaches most groups about equally well, is accepted as about equally credible, is processed with about equal success, and engages common values, thus leading to similar opinion changes.

This point about parallel movement of opinion, however, must be sharply distinguished from the issue of the *levels* of opinion among subgroups at a given time. The opinions of different population groups sometimes differ quite markedly, beginning at the moment opinions are first formed or expressed, reflecting different values and interests and circumstances. Differences by education and region, for example, played an important part in our discussion of opinions concerning civil liberties, civil rights, and related social issues in Chapter 3. Some notable subgroup differences have also occurred in foreign affairs.

We have alluded to one of the biggest differences of this sort, which has stimulated a lot of scholarly writing: the contrast between the foreign policy opinions of Americans with a high level of formal education and those with less education. In the postwar years, scholars have generally found that highly educated people tended to be much more internationalist (see, among others, Scott and Withey 1958; P. Smith 1961; Hero 1966; Richman 1972; Mueller 1973). This is evident in figure 5.2, which shows the proportion of "active part" responses among three educational subgroups: those with only a grade school education, those with at least some high school, and those with some college. In the 1940s and at the beginning of the Cold War the differences were remarkably great. In July 1948, for example, an overwhelming 92% of the college educated favored an active role, in contrast to only 59% of those with grade school education.

As figure 5.2 indicates, these educational differences persisted through the 1950s and remained strong through the 1970s and 1980s, decreasing only very slightly if at all. In March 1988, for example, 81% of respondents with some college favored an "active part," compared with only 50% of those who had not finished high school (NORC–GSS). By the same token, when the different education groups changed opinion, they did so in very similar ways. Both parallel movement and sharp differences in opinion levels can be seen in the graph.

What should we make of these big opinion differences among educational groups? During the early Cold War period, Gabriel Almond (1960 [1950]), and then other scholars like James Rosenau (1961), argued that only the "attentive" public (presumably the highly educated public) paid attention to leaders, knew what was going on in the world, and

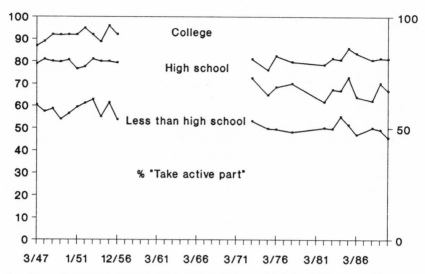

FIG. 5.2   Proportions favoring U.S. involvement in world affairs, by level of education, 1947–1990.

therefore supported—as these scholars did—a strong anti-Communist U.S. role in international affairs. The inattentive were simply ignorant.

This argument may have exaggerated both the magnitude and the implications of public ignorance, with the effect (conceivably also the purpose) of explaining away the unpopularity of certain official policies. To the extent that most Americans did know little about foreign affairs in the 1950s, this was probably less true by the 1980s (see Chap. 1). Not only did average educational levels rise, but foreign affairs became more obviously important to people's daily lives, and improved communications (especially television news) brought more foreign policy information to everyone, including those with little formal education. In any case, however, we have pointed out that people can arrive at sensible opinions by attending to trusted cuegivers and their own life experiences, without needing to amass a great body of information.

Furthermore, as we suggested in Chapter 3 when discussing civil liberties, the precise significance of education-related differences in opinions is not entirely clear. The Almond-Rosenau argument emphasized cognitive aspects of education, especially skills at obtaining and comprehending political information. These are definitely important dimensions of education. But formal education is also related to people's economic position in society, since those with more education tend to earn high incomes and those with higher incomes (or wealthier parents) tend to get more schooling. Thus people of low education tend also to be poorer, and their lower incomes as well as their lack of schooling may have some effect on their attitudes about foreign policy. Lower-income people have good reason to be more concerned about getting dinner on the table than giving out foreign aid; arguably they have less stake in protecting investments abroad or in arming against communism than high-income people do. Thus isolationism among low-income people should not be dismissed as wholly due to ignorance; it may also reflect objective self-interest. (The self-interested dimension of opinion, which is by no means universal, is discussed further in Chap. 7.)

But beyond this socioeconomic complication, the educational process itself has had strong effects on certain opinions, including internationalism. When income is statistically controlled, high-education people have still expressed more internationalist opinions and supported more activist policies (see Chap. 7, below; and Mueller 1973). These true effects of education are not, however, unambiguous in origin. They may, for example, reflect exposure in college to elite norms or propaganda rather than to information per se. Those with a lot of formal schooling tend to receive a strong dose of whatever beliefs and values are propagated by the institutions of their society—including, in the postwar United States, the Cold War anti-Communist consensus.

When levels of opinion differ according to educational experience, one should not jump to the conclusion that the highly educated are always right.[6]

Party Leadership

As we have indicated, the foreign policy opinions of most population subgroups, even those that differ substantially in level of opinion, have generally moved in parallel over time. One significant exception—worth a further brief digression—involves partisan subgroups: people who identify with different political parties. Republicans and Democrats have sometimes changed policy preferences differentially, in response to opinion leadership by presidents and party officials. Communications from elite partisan figures apparently have the most credibility among citizens who are fellow partisans.

During the 1930s, for example, Republicans tended to be more isolationist than Democrats. This was true both at the elite level, where the nationalistic, labor-intensive firms that backed the Republicans tended to favor protective tariffs and aloofness from Europe (Ferguson 1983), and at the mass level, where elite persuasion (with Republican figures opposing President Roosevelt) was reinforced by the ethnic backgrounds and social positions of Republicans that tended to produce less hostile feelings toward Germany. For example, in response to a June 1937 Gallup question, 70% of Democrats versus 56% of Republicans favored a "world disarmament conference."

World War II and the Cold War muted this party difference. The whole country fought Hitler, and afterward many Republicans, every bit as anti-Communist as the Democrats, grudgingly came to accept an active anti-Soviet foreign policy. But the leadership of the internationalist war hero (and Republican) President Eisenhower appears to have been particularly important in effecting opinion change among Republicans. After the four years of Eisenhower's first administration, 1953–1956, fewer strong Republicans (43%) than strong Democrats (49%) said that "this country has gone too far in concerning itself with problems in other parts of the world"; between 1952 and 1954, this proportion of strong Republicans had dropped sharply—by approximately 30%—whereas strong Democrats did not change at all (Campbell and Cooper 1956, pp. 88–90; Key 1961, pp. 450–452; see also Belknap and Campbell 1951–1952). Such partisan opinion leadership may be a widespread phenomenon (see Chap. 7 for further discussion).

Hitler's Germany and World War II

When we turn from general questions of isolationism and internationalism to look historically at trends in specific policy preferences, we can more clearly see certain features of collective opinion rationality. The specific preferences form coherent patterns, and they change in understandable and sensible ways. This is evident, early on, in the shifting preferences concerning preparedness and war against Nazi Germany and Japan, when events unfolded in Europe and Asia and when the Roosevelt administration (quite mindful of public opinion) reacted to them.

As we have noted, most Americans tended to be rather isolationist during the 1930s. They wanted to rebuild the depressed U.S. economy and attain social justice at home, not become embroiled in what they considered (with some cause) to be messy and distant power struggles in Europe and Asia. Internationalism may have been strong among certain elites but was weak among the general public.

This is not to say that Americans did not care about nor take positions concerning matters abroad. Many did care and did take positions, if only because they feared that the United States could easily be drawn against her will into a European or world conflict. People tended to blame Germany, Italy, and Japan for aggressiveness and sympathized with the victims of aggression. According to an August 1937 Gallup survey, for example, most Americans (73%) thought there would be another world war, and when they were asked what nation would be responsible for starting it their main responses were Germany (30%), Italy (27%), and Japan (19%), with 11% saying Russia, and only 13% offering the names of other countries. Most were also pessimistic about whether the United States could stay clear of involvement in such a war.

When Japan invaded Manchuria in 1937, the lines of opinion sharpened. In September of that year, Gallup found that the sympathies of Americans in China's struggle with Japan ran 43% to 2% in favor of China, with 55% responding "neither." The 43% figure jumped up to 59% in October, after the Japanese seized most of China's best cities and farmlands (attracting much U.S. press coverage), and after Roosevelt gave his "quarantine the aggressor" speech on October 5. Sympathy with China continued rising to a weighty 74% in June 1939, with only 2% supporting Japan. Similarly, from February 1937 to February 1938, as the Spanish Civil War became part of a larger struggle against fascism and as Franco's rebel Falangists engaged in strategic bombing of their countrymen, sympathy for the anti-Franco Loyalists rose from 65% to 75% (Gallup). It remained at the same level or higher through 1938.

Still, feelings ran high against any U.S. involvement in such escalating conflicts. In November 1936, fully 95% of the public responded to Gallup that the United States should not take part again if another war like the (first) World War developed in Europe. In an October 1937 Gallup survey, 69% preferred having Congress pass strict neutrality laws as opposed to "leaving the job up to the President." And despite the public's sympathy with China, in October 1937 63% said they would not "join a movement to stop buying" goods made in Japan. In January 1938, 70% said they wanted the United States to withdraw its troops and warn its citizens to leave China. According to a February 1938 Gallup survey, 64% thought that the United States should not "allow shipment of arms and ammunition from this country to China." (Results from some of the Gallup surveys discussed in this and the previous paragraphs are readily available only in Gallup and Robinson 1938, esp. pp. 388–389.)

But the public responded to changing information and changing realities. Toward the end of the 1930s, as Hitler's Germany aggressively expanded its influence and territory in Europe, annexing Austria (1938), occupying Czechoslovakia (1938–1939), and finally precipitating war with Britain and France by invading Poland (September 1, 1939), the American public began to move toward favoring preparedness and aid to the Allies. The precise ways in which this happened deserve detailed attention, particularly because the interplay of events, the media, and political leadership raise questions about opinion manipulation.

During this period, President Franklin Roosevelt—whose party coalition included some important multinational firms as well as Anglophiles and anti-Nazis—certainly opposed German expansionism and favored the Allied cause. At certain moments in the late 1930s he spoke out for military preparedness: at the beginning of 1938, for example, he called for a "big battleship" navy and an increase in appropriations (Beard 1946, p. 212). As we will see, however, most of Roosevelt's prewar rhetoric was actually rather timid; he contributed to opinion change in other ways, mainly through encouragement of public relations efforts by nominally nongovernmental interventionist groups, through his interpretation of events, and especially through his control of policy (see White 1979; R. Steele, 1985a, 1985b; Winfield 1984; Jacobs 1991). Only in 1941 did Roosevelt turn to active manipulation of events and management of information; by then the administration had purposeful activity to publicize through the network of interventionist organizations (Steele 1985b, pp. 68–69).

The American public largely changed opinion in response to international events, as those events were reported in the media and interpreted by opinion leaders—in a fashion that was anti-German and evoked support for Germany's opponents. People continued to want to avoid war, but, as reports of German aggression piled up, more and more Americans favored building up United States military strength, helping Britain and France, and being ready for war if necessary.

From a rather early point, most Americans favored military preparedness. In both September and November 1938, for example, when Germany demanded and received at Munich the Sudentenland of Czechoslovakia, a steady and substantial majority (more than 70%) favored building a larger navy. Between February and March 1939, as Hitler (in mid-March) took the rest of Czechoslovakia, support for selling war materials to England and France in case of war rose sharply, by fourteen percentage points, to 66%. During the same period sentiment for selling food to the allies, already embraced by a substantial 76% majority, rose another notch to 82%.

As Cantril (1940, 1947, 1951, 1967) has documented, none of this represented war fever. In a February 1940 Gallup poll, after several months of "sitzkrieg" lull, only 23% of Americans actually favored declaring war on Germany—6% fewer than had done so in October 1939, just after the invasion of Poland. According to a different question asked three times by OPOR between December 1940 and April 1941 (a period during which Lend Lease was passed and Germany took Yugoslavia and Greece), the proportion favoring a declaration of war and sending the army and navy to Europe increased by only 6%, to a tiny 9% of the public. (This question, like others, offered the attractive alternative, "do everything possible to help England except go to war"; see below.) But in July 1940, OPOR found fully 79% willing to pay "considerably more taxes now" to meet the cost of national defense—another example of public willingness to pay for desired programs.

Throughout this period, public opinion moved further toward active opposition against Germany. In eight surveys between May 1940 and April 1941, large majorities of about 70%–75% told Gallup and OPOR that the United States should "do everything possible" to help England (and, in the case of Gallup, France) "except go to war." As figure 5.3 makes clear, smaller but substantial and growing majorities of 60% and more told OPOR that it was "more important" to defeat Germany (or to "help England win"—Gallup) than to stay out of war. The public's desire to help without fighting if possible, but to fight if necessary, seems altogether reasonable; it is important to observe that this resolution was formed well before Pearl Harbor.

The war went badly for the Western allies during 1940 and 1941. The Low Countries and Scandinavia fell in April and May 1940, and France surrendered in June. ("Do everything" responses jumped up 8% between May and early June, before dipping a bit in late June and recovering by September.) Britain did win the air war over its skies in the fall of 1940, probably preventing a German invasion of the British isles and winning considerable sympathy from Americans (see Cantril 1967, p. 47); but Yugoslavia and Greece fell in April 1941, and Germany invaded Russia that June. During this period both the administration and organized groups pushed harder for aid to Britain, and Americans expressed increasing willingness to help out by methods short of involvement in combat.

Roosevelt and his public relations apparatus were skillful in the use of personal appeals, in getting onto page one of the papers, and especially in using radio and news films. Roosevelt himself was cagey, ducking complex or specific discussions with the press. In foreign (unlike domestic) policy he did not face hostile newspaper editors and publishers, especially with respect to Japan, though he did carry on some debates with reporters (White 1979; Steele 1985b).

Early in 1941, President Roosevelt campaigned hard for his Lend Lease program of aid to the allies, giving a major speech on January 6 and

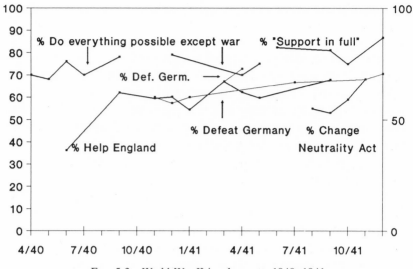

Fig. 5.3   World War II involvement, 1940–1941.

orchestrating testimony to Congress by many administration officials; the bill passed and was signed on March 11. Between January (survey interviews from January 2–7) and March (March 9–14),[7] Gallup found that 7% more, for a total of 67%, favored helping England win "even at the risk of getting into the war," indicating a modest but significant degree of opinion leadership. From April (April 10–15) to May (May 22–27), when Roosevelt declared that the United States was operating a "neutrality patrol" in the Atlantic and various shooting incidents were reported, there was an abrupt shift of 11% in the proportion of Americans favoring the use of the U.S. navy to guard ships going to Britain. (On May 27—right at the end of Gallup's second interview period and too late to affect these results—the president proclaimed a national emergency; he declared that the delivery of supplies to Britain was "imperative," and announced that the U.S. "patrol" against "attacking raiders" was being extended. Beard 1948, pp. 103–104; see also Dallek 1979; Heinrichs 1988. We will see that these events raise issues about opinion leadership or manipulation.)

From September (interviews September 19–24) to October (October 24–29) 1941, as the U.S. media reported German submarine attacks on American destroyers and Roosevelt sought authority to arm merchant ships, Gallup polls showed a sharp 13% increase—from 55% to 68%—in the proportion of the public saying that the United States should permit shipment of war materials to Britain. (It eventually became known that both the September 4 attack on the *Greer* and the October 17 attack on the

Kearney had, in fact, been provoked by the U.S. ships tracking and announcing the positions of German submarines in the Western Atlantic; indeed the *Kearney* apparently depth charged the sub before it was attacked.)

Similarly, opposition of Americans to Japan heightened. By January 1940, 75% of a Gallup sample wanted to forbid the sale of war materials to Japan, and this rose to an overwhelming 90% in October of that year, after the July U.S. boycott on strategic products and the September embargo on scrap iron.

Events and Mediation

The logic of world events, as objective phenomena, played a major part in these opinion shifts toward preparedness and involvement in war. Many Americans were predisposed to favor the Allies because of strong cultural and economic ties with Britain and because of revulsion at Hitler's totalitarian government and its aggressive foreign policy. Given this predisposition, bad war news like the German conquests of Denmark, Norway, Belgium, Holland, and France—and the evacuation of British troops at Dunkirk—in the spring of 1940 made it increasingly appear that U.S. help would be required if Britain were to prevail; indeed, it looked as if the United States had better get ready to defend itself. The public's reaction seems reasonable.

But the American public was not reacting solely to unmediated events; specific leaders and groups reported what was going on, drew attention to it, and offered interpretations that were important in changing opinions. From our vantage point it is easy to forget how deeply entrenched was the American public's opposition to any new involvement in a foreign war. The U.S. Congress had passed strict Neutrality Acts in 1935 and 1937. "Entangling alliances" were in disrepute. Opinion supportive of large-scale U.S. aid to the Allies grew only after a vigorous campaign against isolationism, aided by Winston Churchill's eloquence (especially his "blood, sweat, and tears" speech on May 14, 1940, and his moving accounts of the air war over Britain the following fall), and led in America by people with political and cultural affinities to Britain, with economic interests in protecting American markets and investments abroad, and (in some cases) with the aim of substituting American influence for that of England in a dismembered British empire (Shoup and Minter 1977, chap. 4, highlight these latter motives in analyzing early Council on Foreign Relations planning for a postwar world).

Groups like the Century Club (an offshoot of the Council on Foreign Relations), the Free Trade Committee, and William Allen White's Committee to Defend America by Aiding the Allies—some of these funded and inspired by internationally oriented investment bankers like J. P. Morgan and the Chase Manhattan—organized a massive public relations campaign. White's effort was particularly important because of his base in Kansas at the heart of Midwestern isolationism (Johnson 1944 gives a glowing account).

White's committee, founded in April 1940, reacted to the German invasion of the Low Countries with an "emergency telegram" that favored arming the United States and aiding the allies, and it stimulated the growth of some 300 local chapters by the beginning of July. Working closely with President Roosevelt and his administration, the committee sponsored a full-page "Stop Hitler Now" newspaper ad on June 10, and it worked through the summer to build support for sending destroyers to Britain, with rallies, radio talks (e.g., by General Pershing, August 4), more newspaper ads ("Between Us and Hitler Stands the *British* Fleet," July 30), and reprints.

After the destroyers-for-bases deal was announced on September 3, 1940, White's committee emphasized Britain's need for airplanes—featuring a letter by General MacArthur warning against being "too late"—and argued against Charles Lindbergh's new America First Committee.

White himself opposed repealing the neutrality laws or using the navy to convoy aid to Britain—and, in fact, resigned his chairmanship over these issues at the beginning of January 1941—but in January and February 1941 the committee vigorously supported the Lend Lease bill with mass mailings, pamphlets, and even a movie ("It Can Happen Here") that generated a flood of mail to Congress. The Chicago chapter alone mailed out some 100,000 letters and passed out 30,000 handbills at factories. After White's resignation, the committee advocated U.S. convoying of aid and (late in June) active participation in the battle for the Atlantic, moving closer to the position of the New York–based Century Club and the Fight for Freedom Committee.

President Roosevelt's Role

In the process of moving public opinion, President Roosevelt and his multinational wing of the Democratic Party played a part that was crucial but largely indirect. As we will see in Chapter 8, popular presidents who speak out strongly in favor of a policy can expect to increase public support for it by a modest amount—perhaps five or ten percentage points—within a few months. Roosevelt took some advantage of this (limited) power to lead opinion, as our examples have indicated, but he did so very cautiously; his rhetoric never got too far out in front of the public. He noted his alarm at events but always reiterated his commitment to peace (Steele 1985a, 1985b; Dallek 1979). Instead of persuasion through speech making, Roosevelt exerted most of his influence through the private preparedness groups and through the control of events.

The president had stuck mainly to domestic concerns through the middle of the 1930s. Upon signing the Neutrality Act in 1935, he complained of its inflexibility but committed the government to the "avoidance of any entanglements which would lead us into conflict" (Beard 1946, p. 165). In 1936, he warned about the perils of war in light of the ominous events in the Rhineland and Spain and the formation of the Berlin-Rome Axis, but he continued to emphasize American nonentanglement, neutrality, and nonintervention. His May 1937 speech urging a "concerted effort" by peace-loving nations was exceptional, and when it raised a furor he backed off a bit and fell silent (Beard 1946, pp. 184–187; Beard closely and very critically examined Roosevelt's foreign policy statements from 1932 through 1940; Dallek 1979 and Heinrichs 1988 are far more sympathetic to Roosevelt but agree on most basic facts).

Roosevelt's calls for increased naval arms at the beginning of 1938—and indeed his espousal of rearmament generally—was cast in terms of American defense only, not collective security; afterward he again fell silent, reacting to the Czechoslovakian crisis with no more than an appeal for a peaceful solution and a reiteration of no U.S. political entanglements. In the fateful year 1939, too, even when Roosevelt warned of the perils of war and aggression (and persuaded Congress to modify the arms embargo provisions of the Neutrality Act after the invasion of Poland), he continued to speak out against entanglements and denied that American boys would be sent abroad.

During the 1940 election year Roosevelt dealt with the catastrophic European events in a restrained way. He specifically endorsed the Democratic platform pledge that the United States would not participate in foreign wars "except in case of attack," and (with no more accuracy than that of several other presidents before and since) flatly said, "Your boys are not going to be sent into any foreign wars." He treated the September 1940 provision of destroyers to Britain as a canny "deal" in which the United States gained bases. Even Roosevelt's "arsenal of democracy" speech of December 1940, which contributed to a temporary 8% rise in the proportion of the public that favored aid (see Cantril 1947, p. 227), emphasized avoiding combat (" . . . the whole purpose of your President is to keep you now, and your children later . . . out of a last ditch war") while "sending every ounce and every ton of munitions and supplies that we can possibly spare to help the defenders who are in the front lines" (Roosevelt 1940, pp. 633, 641).

During 1941 Roosevelt's actions steadily moved the United States into involvement in the war, but his rhetoric tended to conceal this reality. His push for Lend Lease early in the year dealt with U.S. aid, not combat. After the passage of Lend Lease, Roosevelt denied that the United States would "convoy" foreign ships carrying U.S. arms to the allies, but very soon (in April), under the rubric of the "neutrality patrol," U.S. destroyers in the Western Atlantic were trailing German submarines and broadcasting their locations to the British, who then attacked them. With little public notice, the policy evolved into convoying U.S. ships to Iceland (in July), and (September 3) destroying surface "raiders" that entered the "general area" of the sea lanes to Iceland. Then, later in September, the convoy system was broadened to include non–U.S. ships that joined the run to Iceland. Finally, effective October 11, the U.S. navy was directed to protect "all merchant ships" and to destroy any German or Italian forces encountered. (Beard 1948 critically analyzed Roosevelt's 1941 rhetoric and actions in great detail; his account is generally confirmed—though, again, with much more sympathy toward Roosevelt—by Dallek 1979, and Heinrichs 1988.)

Thus by the time of the allegedly unprovoked attacks on the U.S.S. *Greer* (September 4) and especially that on the *Kearney* (October 17), which Roosevelt so vehemently denounced and used to move public opinion, the United States was actively protecting British shipping, pursuing German submarines, radioing their positions to British warships, and (in at least one case) dropping depth charges.

Roosevelt also misrepresented the nature of the Atlantic Conference with Churchill in August 1941. He heralded the idealistic "Atlantic Charter," which called for no aggrandizement or territorial changes against the will of the people concerned, the right of all peoples to choose their form of government, free trade, economic collaboration, freedom from fear and want, freedom of the seas, and abandonment of the use of force; all highly popular objectives. But Roosevelt claimed that he had made "no new commitments" and that the United States was "no closer to war," not mentioning the agreements on escorting British convoys and on parallel action against Japan, or his expressed intention of provoking an incident with Japan that would result in war. (According to Churchill's account, "[FDR said] he would become more and more provocative. . . . The President . . . made it clear that he would look for an 'incident' which would justify him in opening hostilities": Dallek 1979, p. 285.)

Most important, Roosevelt misled the public about U.S. moves that contributed to tense relations with Japan. Throughout the autumn of 1941—while denouncing Japanese expansionism in Indochina and elsewhere in the Far East—he indicated that the United States and Japan were at peace and were negotiating their differences.[8] On and after November 27, official statements indicated that tensions were rising but that the United States was awaiting Japan's response to the latest American proposal. Even on December 2, Roosevelt said that the United States was at peace with Japan and "perfectly friendly, too." Roosevelt characterized the December 7 assault on Pearl Harbor, the day after it happened, as a "surprise offensive," an "unprovoked and dastardly attack." In his December 15 message to Congress, the president said the U.S. government had on November 26 presented a "clear-cut plan for a broad but simple settlement," and that, "determined . . . to exhaust every conceivable effort for peace," Roosevelt on December 6 had sent a personal message to the Emperor of Japan.

What Roosevelt concealed, however, was that the U.S. "proposal" of November 26 was in effect an ultimatum, known at the time to be virtually certain to provoke action by Japan, because it insisted on a rollback of Japanese influence from China and Indochina. Ever since the freezing of Japanese assets and the cutting off of trade on July 25, 1941, which sharply reduced Japan's access to oil (a move preceded by the embargo on strategic products on July 5, 1940, and the embargo on scrap iron September 25 of that year), Japan had complained about being "encircled."

In accord with the Atlantic Conference agreement with Churchill, Roosevelt on August 17, 1941 told the Japanese ambassador that, if Japan took further steps of military domination of neighboring countries, the United States would be compelled to "take immediately any and all steps" necessary to safeguard its interests. For the next two months the United States hedged and evaded a proposal for a Pacific Conference by the moderate Konoye government, which eventually fell from power largely because of its failure to take strong action against the United States. The United States then rejected the new Tojo government's proposal of a "modus vivendi" (November 20), even though secret decoded Japanese messages had indicated that there was a serious desire for settlement and that this was the last chance for peace.

At this time large majorities of Americans favored peace with Germany on a status quo basis (according to OPOR, for example, three-quarters of those with opinions in late November 1941 favored a peace that would leave Germany holding the countries she had conquered so far), and it is plausible that the same applied to Japan—though the public favored resisting any further Japanese moves. (Gallup found a bare majority in March 1941 willing to "risk war" to keep Japan from the Dutch East Indies and Singapore. As of November 1941, 72% told Gallup the United States should "take steps now to prevent Japan from becoming more powerful, even if this means risking war with Japan.") Conflict with Japan provided the key for Roosevelt to win popular backing for U.S. entry into the war with Germany.

At the American "war cabinet" meeting of November 25, 1941, according to Secretary Stimson's notes, Roosevelt said the United States was likely to be attacked as soon as the next Monday, and the question was how to maneuver the Japanese into firing the first shot without too much danger. Military commanders were then warned (inadequately) of the danger, and Secretary Hull prepared the critical November 26 memo, after which he told Stimson he had broken off the talks and washed his hands of the matter; it was now in the hands of the military.

Japan's December 7, 1941, attack on U.S. forces, a shocking surprise to the American people, was therefore not by any means a complete surprise to top government officials, except in its targeting of Pearl Harbor rather than (say) the Philippines. It represented a predictable result of Japanese and U.S. policies.

Thus Roosevelt's leadership of the United States into war involved only limited direct persuasion of the public. In fact (as we have noted and as Cantril [1967, pp. 44–50] points out), the president balanced his overt statements and actions rather carefully so as not to offend prevailing opinions, to stay only one step ahead. Roosevelt showed great skill (with Cantril's assistance) at interpreting foreign policy polls and at tailoring his political strategy and his messages accordingly; he is probably the most skillful president at this we have had, at least until Reagan (see Graham 1989b).

Roosevelt's opinion leadership was mostly indirect. It depended heavily on taking actions that shaped events—some of which actions were concealed from or misrepresented to the public—as well as supporting publicity campaigns by people outside government.

Americans are so used to crediting Roosevelt with a great feat of statesmanship in resisting the Axis, that little attention has been paid to his manipulation of public opinion or to the troubling questions it raises. Of course, defenders of FDR might argue that he engaged in deception for the sake of a higher truth: that Americans would have agreed with him if they had been fully informed. (If so, why not just tell the truth?) Alternatively, defenders might maintain that, whatever a hypothetical informed public might think, Roosevelt was right. But one should be very cautious about accepting such arguments because they rest on untested (perhaps untestable) assumptions and pose obvious dangers for democracy. Justifications of this sort cannot easily be confined to such noble goals as defeating fascism; they could be used to rationalize practically any action by political leaders. A strategy of deception—as opposed to trying to persuade the public, or even openly defying it—has the pernicious effect of rendering citizens unable to hold their leaders to account for their actions.

We have presented the case of preparedness and entry into World War II in detail because it teaches several important lessons. One is that the public reacted in quite reasonable fashion to world events, as those events were reported and interpreted. A natural and understandable reluctance to fight a war gave way, in the face of increasing reports of danger to friendly countries and to the United States itself, to a growing public desire to prepare militarily, to aid Britain and France, and to accept the risks of direct involvement.

But a second lesson is that events were mediated through the activities of individuals and groups, including political leaders. Moreover, the information provided to the public was sometimes false or misleading—especially during the final maneuvering that led the United States into war with Japan and Germany, when President Roosevelt closely controlled events and managed information about them. It is possible, then, for the rational public to be misled, especially on matters of national security and foreign policy. We will return to this subject.

Wartime and Postwar Opinion

President Roosevelt's maneuvers against Japan were particularly important because of the profound effect that the Pearl Harbor "surprise" attack—as it was portrayed and explained to the public—had upon policy and opinions about the war. Congress quickly declared that a state of war existed with Japan. Shortly thereafter (December 11), Germany and Italy, in accord with their treaties, declared war on the United States, and the United States was engaged in war on a worldwide scale.

The dramatic impact that Pearl Harbor had upon public opinion toward foreign affairs is indicated by responses to two similar—unfortunately not identical—questions about peace based on the status quo, which were asked just before and just after the Japanese attack. In mid-November 1941, three-quarters of the public (76% of the respondents who offered opinions) told OPOR that they favored peace "today" on the basis of Britain "keeping the British empire as it now stands" and Germany "holding the countries she has conquered so far." In the middle of December, however, just after the Pearl Harbor attack and the declarations of war, only 10% of those with opinions told OPOR that they would favor peace "now" if Hitler offered peace to all countries "on the basis of not going farther, but of leaving matters as they are now." Fully 90% opposed such a status quo peace, suggesting a complete and enduring reversal of opinion. In February and again in March 1942, 92% took the same position (see Cantril 1947, p. 249).

In February 1942 Gallup also found that a solid majority, 66%, favored total mobilization. (Within eight months the proportion favoring mobilization dropped by 6%. Such a "falling off" of opinion often occurs after intense news ends, as the temporary portion of its effect fades.)

Once the United States was at war, opinions about certain policies fluctuated with events at home and on the battlefield. These included opinions toward "sacrifices" for defense, the military draft, and wartime information policies. Willingness to talk peace—as opposed to insistence on a harsh and total victory—also varied with the extent of U.S. sacrifices and with military success or failure (see figure 5.4). Again the opinion changes represent reasonable responses to reported events.

Responses to an OPOR question whether the United States should accept a peace offer *from the German army* if Hitler were out of the way, for example (graphed in figure 5.4), shifted back and forth markedly, depending upon how feasible a complete victory seemed. The proportion favoring a negotiated peace fell from 36% in June 1942 to 23% in August 1943, after the tide began to turn the allies' way with successes at Midway (June 3–6, 1942), in North Africa (October 1942–March 1943), Stalingrad (November 1942), Guadalcanal (February 1942), and Sicily (July 1943). (Cantril [1967, p. 176] particularly emphasizes the "amazing" rise from 36% to 81% in the proportion of the public that was optimistic that the allies were winning, immediately after the October 1942 invasion of North Africa.)

Support for a peace negotiated with the German army (assuming Hitler out of the way) rose again, however, to 40% in April 1944, as the war effort progressed slowly without any opening of a Western front. It then dropped to 29% in August 1944, after the Normandy invasion (June) and the Russian offensive into Eastern Europe (taking Warsaw in August) brought total victory closer. It rose once more, to 37% in February 1945, with the German counteroffensive in Belgium while the allies were bogged down in the West, and finally dropped to 24% in April 1945, as the allies triumphantly moved toward Berlin from both East and West. We

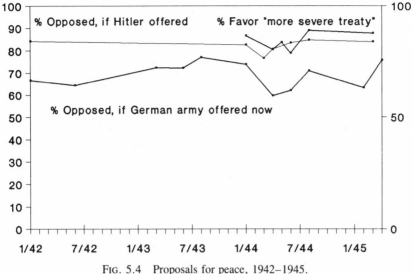

FIG. 5.4   Proposals for peace, 1942–1945.

have seen how unusual such opinion fluctuations are, but they make sense in reaction to the weighty and rapidly changing events of wartime.

OPOR surveys showed that the proportion of Americans that favored discussing peace *with Hitler*—obviously a less desirable outcome—was never as high; only 17% favored that idea in January 1944, for example. Support for negotiating with Hitler did not change as much as support for negotiating with the German army (see figure 5.4), but it followed the same principles when it did. The figure rose 6% by March 1944, for example, as allied progress bogged down, and then dropped to a 15% level in August after the invasion of France. Likewise, insistence on a "more severe" peace than that "at the end of the last war" (OPOR)—while staying high throughout 1944 and 1945—dropped from 87% to 79% in the frustrating period between January and June 1944 (the reported survey date is June 20, just after Normandy D-Day), but then rose 10% by August, in response to the breakthrough in France and the Russian offensive.

By 1945, many Americans had escalated their war aims. Between the beginning of 1943 and August 1945 NORC found a very large (21%) increase, to 60%, in the proportion wanting the United States to obtain new bases at the end of the war. (By November 1943 the Joint Chiefs of Staff were in fact planning for a postwar ring of bases that would ensure U.S. hegemony over the Atlantic and Pacific oceans: Lefler 1984, p. 350.) Between November 1943 and October 1944, according to Gallup,

21% fewer Americans chose relatively mild postwar policies—to "strictly supervise" or to "rehabilitate" Germany or to "do nothing"; a substantial 44% (up from 23%) wanted to "destroy Germany completely." (This 44% figure dipped only slightly, to 39%, as the war wound to a close in May 1945.) In April 1945, 86% of Americans told Gallup they favored using German men to "rebuild cities in Russia which they have destroyed," up 15% since July 1944.[9]

Soon after World War II, however, the Cold War—especially the Berlin blockade and the fighting in Korea—quite reasonably changed Americans' perception of (West) Germany from enemy to ally. During 1948 and 1949, large majorities (86% in June 1948, as the blockade was completed, and 88% in January 1949, according to NORC) wanted to keep U.S. occupation troops in Germany, presumably because of the Soviet threat; this dipped to 81% the following June after the lifting of the blockade. With the outbreak of the Korean War at the end of June 1950, NORC surveys found a sharp upsurge of sentiment for building up the German army: a jump of 18% (to 62%) between mid-June and July. (Indeed, some U.S. leaders and analysts argued that Korea was a diversion to cover aggression in Europe.) Similarly, according to NORC, substantial majorities came to favor integrating German troops into the defense of Europe; 64% did so in February 1952, up from 57% in October 1951. Sixty-two percent of Americans continued to favor integration of German troops in September 1954.

The Korean War also naturally caused more Americans to think of Japan as an ally rather than an adversary. NORC found a 9% rise, to a weighty 87%, in opinion favoring trade with Japan between December 1946 and October 1951, with support staying at about the same level in 1955. At the beginning of August 1950, during the dark early days of the Korean War, fully 81% (Gallup) favored building up a Japanese army. This edged up to 84% in January 1951, after the Chinese intervention; it declined to a still high 78% in September 1953, as the Korean conflict wound down.

Thus, when the American people learned that the world had changed, when postwar events (as interpreted by the media and their political leaders) kept telling them that former enemies were now needed to counter the Soviet Union, they understandably embraced policies of rearmament, trade, and alliance with Germany and Japan.

The Soviet Union and the Early Cold War

The American public's specific attitudes toward the Soviet Union and communism further illustrate rational reactions to reported circumstances and events. They also once again raise questions about the quality of information that was provided to the public, and about the possible manipulating or misleading of opinion.

Public attitudes toward the Soviets have varied significantly with historical events, but a basic suspicion and dislike that manifested itself in some of the earliest opinion surveys mostly endured for decades afterward. In 1937, for example, Gallup found 59% of the public saying that, if forced to choose, it would rather live under the kind of government in (Nazi) Germany than under the kind in Russia. Germany was viewed, however, as a much greater strategic threat to Europe and hence to the United States; in 1938, 82% of those taking sides told Gallup they would rather see Russia than Germany win a hypothetical war between the two (see Levering 1976, p. 17). The public was prepared to draw important distinctions about the Soviets depending upon events and the political context.

The German-Soviet nonaggression pact of August 1939—by means of which the Soviets purchased temporary security for themselves at the cost of protecting Hitler's eastern flank and enabling him to take half of Poland and attack the West—virtually eliminated (for a time) any remaining American sympathy for the Soviets, even on the Left; "popular front" movements collapsed. The subsequent Russian attack on "poor little Finland" in November 1939, in order to secure the North against temporary ally Hitler, provoked nearly universal media condemnation of the USSR, with emphasis on Finland's helplessness, its unique repayment of U.S. war debts, and its allegedly democratic government. The public was outraged: in December 1939 Gallup found Americans sympathizing with Finland and against Russia at a remarkable 99% to 1% ratio. In January 1940, Stalin appeared on *Time* magazine's cover as "Man of the Year," with the caption "Ivan the Terrible was right" (Levering 1976 provides an excellent account of the interplay among opinion leaders, the media, and public opinion concerning wartime U.S.-USSR relations).

Again, however, new circumstances led to new attitudes. After Hitler invaded Russia in June 1941, Winston Churchill and others sparked a major change in U.S. opinion. In July, Gallup found that 77% would like to see Russia win the "present war" with Germany; only 4% favored Germany. As war news filled the papers and the airwaves, portraying valiant Russian resistance, even the American Legion came to favor intervention, and in October 1941 Lend Lease was extended to Russia without controversy. Many Americans suspended their fear of communism—foreign and domestic—for the sake of stopping the Nazis. The less hostile trends in opinions toward "radicals" and Communists have already been described in Chapter 3 (see figure 3.5).

Especially after the United States entered the war on the allied side, opinion about the USSR shifted strongly. Roper polls for *Fortune* magazine, conducted in October 1941 and February 1942 (before and after Pearl Harbor and the Declaration of the United Nations), show a very sharp 24% jump, from 22% to 46%, in the proportion saying Russia should be treated as a "full partner" along with Britain in the fight against the Axis. Many came to realize that the Russians were making enormous sacrifices on the eastern front, which in fact became the only scene of major combat between German and allied troops. By the end of 1941 Germany had reached the fringes of Moscow and controlled an area of Russia larger than Germany itself. (The failure of the West to open an early second front became a major source of Soviet mistrust that later contributed to the Cold War.)

As the United States went to war and sought to build up allied strength, fewer Americans (though still 73% of them, comparable to the 75% for Great Britain) expressed the opinion that Russia should have to pay for Lend Lease aid. The 9% decrease in the proportion favoring Russian repayment between the February and March 1942 NORC surveys, however, was a bit less than the parallel 12% drop (to just 54%) with respect to beleaguered and resource-poor Nationalist China. At that time Japan was rapidly seizing control of Southeast Asia.

Again, events did not act alone; they were interpreted by leaders and the mass media. The years 1942 and 1943 brought intense pro-Russian media news and commentary. Henry Luce's internationalist publications glorified the courageous Russian defenders. The National Congress of Soviet-American Friendship, with high-level sponsors including Vice-President Wallace, held large rallies. *Time* magazine once again featured Stalin as "Man of the Year," in January 1943—but this time a courageous, Nazi-fighting Stalin (Levering 1976, p. 105). Wendell Willkie's best-selling *One World* portrayed the Soviets as vital, dynamic postwar partners. In March 1943, an impressive photo of Stalin graced the cover of a special *Life* magazine issue filled with praise for the USSR. The pilot hero Eddie Rickenbacker brought back word of Russian movement toward capitalism and democracy.

During the war, some twenty-five major films and documentaries depicted modern Russia favorably, including the slick documentary *Moscow Strikes Back* (1942); the army's powerful orientation film *The Battle of Russia* (1943), which was shown to all recruits and then released commercially; and the major motion pictures *Mission to Moscow, The North Star,* and *Song of Russia,* which offered positive images of the Russian people (featuring stars like Walter Brennan, Robert Taylor, Walter Huston, and Gregory Peck) against a bestial enemy (Small 1974, p. 461; Levering 1976, Chap. 5).

Even at its peak, Soviet-American wartime cooperation never meant that the underlying suspicion was gone. But during most of the war substantial majorities of Americans with opinions said Russia could be trusted to cooperate with us. Trust reached a high point around 70% of those with opinions (NORC, 71%; OPOR, 68%; Gallup, 64%) in November 1943, just after the optimistic Moscow foreign ministers' meeting of October.

The tide of pro-Russian publicity ebbed in 1944, rose as the allies closed in on Berlin and joined forces, and then ebbed again after Germany surrendered. By 1944, allied victories were raising questions about the shape of the postwar world and particularly about the Soviet Union's establishment of a sphere of influence in Eastern Europe. Once again led by media commentary, Americans' fear of and hostility to the Soviets began to grow once more.

The public reacted negatively to the setting up (July 1944) and the Russian recognition (January 1945) of the pro-Communist Lublin government for Poland, and was only temporarily reassured by the excessively rosy interpretations (from President Roosevelt and others) of the February 1945 Yalta agreement to "reorganize" it; later events seemed to constitute a Russian betrayal. Americans disliked the early 1945 installation of a Communist regime in Rumania; the power struggle over (and secret U.S. agreement to) multiple Russian votes in the U.N. General Assembly; the Soviet army's "race" to Berlin; the brief Soviet refusal to leave northern Iran in 1946—reversed under U.S. pressure; and what Churchill in March 1946 called an "iron curtain" falling over Eastern Europe.

Leftist (ostensibly coalitional) regimes were established under the protection of Soviet troops in Hungary (June 1947) and Czechoslovakia (February 1948). In March 1947 the Truman Doctrine on aid to Greece and Turkey was enunciated; in June the coup in Hungary occurred; in July the Soviets had pulled out of the Marshall Plan conference of European nations, and Kennan's doctrine of "containment" was articulated. By July 1947, U.S.-Soviet relations were quite hostile and the American public shared that hostility. (A useful overview of events is LaFeber 1985.)

The deteriorating public perception of Russia is apparent in figure 5.5, which shows the percentage of Americans at various times who said Russia could be trusted to "cooperate with us" or could be counted on to "meet us halfway" in working out problems together. Optimism decreased rapidly. The post-Yalta March and April 1945 figures of 64%

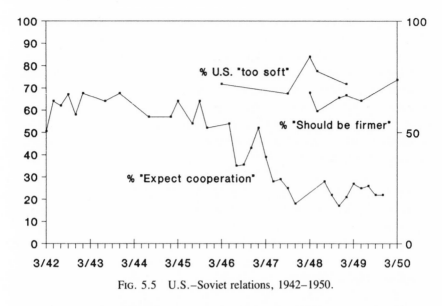

FIG. 5.5   U.S.–Soviet relations, 1942–1950.

(Gallup) and 69% (OPOR) trusting the Russians dropped significantly by May. They then fell precipitously, all the way to a meager 18% (according to the NORC "halfway" wording) in late 1947.

The account of these trends in Caspary (1968) glosses over some differences in survey organizations and question wording,[10] but it does clearly establish that opinion changes were strongly related to incidents of "refractory" Soviet behavior as reported in the U.S. media. Using an exponential time decay model with an impact half-life of six months, a cumulative measure of "refractory" and "conciliatory" Soviet behavior correlated rather highly ($r = .50$) with expectations of cooperation (Caspary 1968, p. 42). The correlation would presumably be even higher except that the variant question wordings introduced measurement error, and certain kinds of "general" Soviet behavior and official U.S. characterizations of the Soviets were excluded from the media content measure (Caspary 1968, pp. 43–44).

The same events that affected these general perceptions of Soviet cooperativeness also influenced Americans' policy preferences. Between October 1947 and March 1948, for example (just after the February coup in Czechoslovakia), the proportion of the public who felt the United States was being "too soft" toward Russia increased by 17%, reaching a very high level of 84% (Gallup). Only 3% thought the United States was being "too tough." Increasing numbers said we should "stop any attempt by Russia to control the countries near her in Europe and Asia"—58% in an April 1947 NORC survey (just after the Truman Doctrine speech of

March), up from 51% in October 1946. Support for universal military training rose by 10% between the end of 1947 and March 1948 (just after the Czech coup), according to Gallup, and at the beginning of 1949 big majorities—though not quite so close to unanimity as in 1939—favored increasing the size of the air force, the navy, and the army. Judging by our data, the overthrow of the democratic regime in Czechoslovakia may have been particularly critical to U.S. public opinion.

Responses to a NORC question about whether we should compromise or "be firmer" with Russia also shifted with events. Support for firmer policies stood at 68% in April 1948, shortly after the Czech coup; it dropped to 60% in June, and rose to 74% in March 1950 after the crucial 1949 events of the Soviet nuclear test and the Communist victory in China. By April 1950, 89% of Americans, up 6% from NORC surveys three months earlier, said they considered "stopping the world spread of communism" to be "very important." (The "be firmer" response fell again to 65% in November 1953, after Stalin's death and the end of the Korean War.)

Cold War events affected attitudes toward a variety of policies concerning foreign aid and relations with Europe. By March 1949, for example, NORC found solid support for military aid to Europe (60% approving), for continuing the Marshall Plan (79%), and for maintaining or increasing the level of recovery spending (60%). Yet, as we saw in figure 2.4 of Chapter 2, support for the Marshall Plan fluctuated through 1949 and 1950, dropping 14% by September 1949 after the Berlin blockade ended in April, the NATO treaty was ratified in July, and Mao's advances drew attention to China. Support for the Marshall Plan regained 7% by January 1950 but lost 8% again by April 1950, for reasons that are not clear to us. In that month, 61% of Americans told NORC that "too much" was being spent on "our program for European recovery," up a very large 21% since March 1949.

Opinion about the military side of relations with Europe followed a somewhat different path from that of the economic side. As figure 5.6 indicates, for example, backing for military aid fluctuated somewhat, then rose steadily and settled at a high level. In NORC surveys, advocacy of "sending military supplies to the countries of western Europe" dropped abruptly, by a dramatic 12% (to 48%) between March and April 1949, when the Soviets agreed to lift the Berlin blockade, Mao crossed the Yangtze, and Truman moved to stop aiding the Nationalists. But it then recovered 8% by June as Senate hearings supported the NATO treaty. Approval of military aid continued to rise after it was announced that the Soviets exploded an atomic bomb (in September 1949) and the

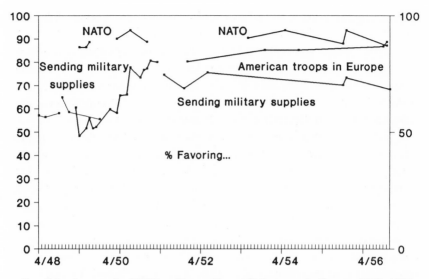

FIG. 5.6   Support for NATO, military aid, and U.S. troops in Europe, 1948–1956.

Chinese People's Republic was formally proclaimed (in October). Support rose 6% from January to mid-June 1950, and a quick additional 12% (from 66% to 78%) between mid-June and the end of July—after North Korea invaded the South—reaching 80% in favor of military supplies to Europe by March 1951. According to a slightly different question, it stayed in the 70% range from May 1951 through November 1956.

As figure 5.6 also makes clear, large majorities of Americans—around 90%—favored "the North Atlantic treaty," or the U.S. "agreement with the countries of Western Europe, to defend each other against any attack," in every one of eleven surveys between June 1949 and November 1956. Similarly, at least 80% of Americans in each of five surveys, from November 1953 through December 1956, said that the number of American troops stationed in Europe was "about right" or that "more" should be sent; only a gradually declining 11%–20% said we had too many troops there. This certainly does not look like isolationism. The U.S. public accepted the logic of the Cold War and favored appropriate policies to carry it out.

The Attentive Public, Revisited

Here we return briefly to the topic of an attentive public (earlier touched upon in connection with internationalism), and deal with three interrelated matters: to what extent people of high education differ in opinions from others, lead others' opinions, or react differently to events and the media.

In the case of the Cold War rise in suspicions of Russia and desires to contain communism, certain alleged processes of opinion leadership through an attentive public do not hold up well under careful scrutiny. In considering the decline in perceptions of Soviet cooperativeness displayed in figure 5.5, for example, one might assume that the change was led by the most highly educated members of society—those with the greatest cognitive skills, the best access to information, and the biggest stake in U.S. foreign policy—who might be expected to react most quickly to news reports of Soviet aggressiveness and to change their policy preference right away, persuading the less educated and less attentive to catch up later. Such a pattern is implied in various ideas about a foreign policy "attentive public" and "two-step flows" of communication (Katz and Lazarsfeld 1965), or about the attitudes of core versus peripheral members of society (see Galtung 1965; Gamson and Modigliani 1966). (On the other hand, as we have mentioned, the well educated—with more fully developed, firmer opinions—might have been expected to be less susceptible to the influence of events or public information campaigns designed to alter opinions.)

When we examine the actual trends in perceptions and opinions by Americans with different levels of education, however, a picture emerges that is more complicated than either of these notions. When we look closely at Caspary's (1968, p. 29) data, for example, we find that the highly educated did indeed move a bit more quickly toward increasing their doubts of Soviet intentions;[11] but for two reasons they can hardly be said to have "led" the opinions of the less educated. First, and most important, all groups generally moved in parallel, at the same time; any prior movement by the well educated is minimal. Second, a larger proportion of the less educated had in fact already arrived where the more educated were headed (see figure 5.7). Even in March 1945, near the height of the wartime alliance, when 62% of Americans with a college education thought we could trust the Russians to cooperate, only 51% of the grade school educated thought so. As the Cold War worsened, an important component of opinion change was the shift by the higher educated toward mistrust, the same position that more of the low educated had held all along. Mueller (1973, 1979) reports similar findings from various periods concerning expectations of war and other issues.

The significance of this fact is not completely clear. It does not actually contradict the idea that those with more education are quicker to

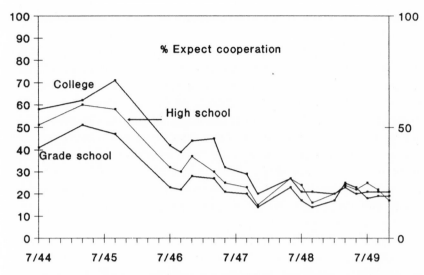

FIG. 5.7   Expectations of Soviet cooperation, by education level, 1944–1949.

react to events and new information; in a number of cases they seem to do so. Caspary (1968) points out, for example, that Americans with little formal education may have been very slow to change opinions previously as well, preserving initial hostility toward Russia even when wartime events seemed to make it inappropriate. On the other hand, in other cases, those who are most attentive may have the greatest mass of preexisting information and may, therefore, be highly resistant to change. Perhaps an important variable distinguishing these opposite outcomes is the novelty of the new information and how far-reaching it is.

Nor, of course, does the finding of preexisting anti-Soviet attitudes among those with little education demonstrate that superior wisdom or foresight is generally found among the unschooled. It does, however, force us to be wary of any claim that the well educated always lead public opinion. It also points up the hazard of inferring that a population sub-group that happens to hold a particular opinion before other subgroups do (or even one that moves more quickly to a particular opinion) necessarily exerts leadership when others catch up. If we were to accept such inferences in general, we would have to concede that those with little formal education led their highly educated fellow citizens into Cold War attitudes.

Setting aside this difficult question of leadership, the hypothesis that the highly educated often move *first* is supported with respect to a number of policy preferences. At the beginning of the Cold War period, Americans of little formal education, who tended to be lukewarm about the United States taking an "active part" in the world (see figure 5.2), also tended to be much less supportive than the college educated of such policies as increasing defense spending, giving military aid to Europe, aiding European recovery with the Marshall Plan, and the like. Gradually, however, citizens with less education came to support such policies, moving in the direction of the better educated and in some cases closing the gap. Through the beginning of the Vietnam War, at least, better educated people generally tended to react more positively and more quickly to most new U.S. foreign policy initiatives, whether peaceful or belligerent (see Mueller 1973).

We will return to a more systematic discussion of opinion trends among educational and other subgroups in Chapter 7.

Media and Elite Opinion Leadership

Our skepticism about the leadership role of the well educated does not mean we reject the idea of elite influence upon mass opinion. Quite the contrary. Especially in the realm of foreign policy, where information can be centrally controlled, it seems especially likely that public opinion is often led—not by the "well educated" as a group, who may in fact be particularly exposed to influence—but by public officials and other influential groups and individuals, through complex processes involving objective events, official accounts and media reports of events, and interpretations by politicians, commentators, and experts. In some cases, officials and influentials may manipulate opinion through incomplete or misleading or false information.

In his analysis demonstrating the impact upon public opinion of Cold War events, Caspary (1968) was careful to refer to *reported* events, reserving for separate research the question of possible biases in news reporting or errors in interpretations by news sources. Two important questions were left open: (1) Did U.S. presidents or other American leaders, rather than the events themselves, influence public opinion? And (2) were there any systematic biases in the reporting of events or in the arguments and interpretations that influenced the public?

President Truman and Secretary of State Marshall and others certainly did attempt to lead public opinion; there can be no doubt of that. In his March 12, 1947, Truman Doctrine speech, for example, the president set forth broad new principles for worldwide intervention: alluding to the Greek civil war ("The very existence of the Greek state is today threatened by the terrorist activities of several thousand armed men, led by Communists"), he declared that the United States should "help free peoples to maintain their free institutions and their national integrity against aggressive movements that seek to impose on them totalitarian regimes." Truman said the United States should "support free peoples who are resisting attempted subjugation by armed minorities or outside pressures," without mentioning any geographic limitations (H. Truman 1947, pp. 526, 527).

In his Harvard speech in June of the same year, Secretary Marshall focused on the "dislocation of the entire fabric of European economy" and Europe's need for foreign food and other essential products, declaring it was "logical that the United States should do whatever it is able to do to assist in the return of normal economic health in the world" for the sake of political stability and peace (Marshall 1947, p. 533). But in selling the aid program to Congress and the public, the Truman administration depicted it as a program to stop aggressively advancing communism. George Kennan's famous "X" article in July 1947 declared that "(t)he main element of any United States policy toward the Soviet Union must be that of a long-term, patient but firm and vigilant containment of Russian expansive tendencies" (Kennan 1947, p. 575)—"containment" that was soon defined chiefly in military terms. Thus the rhetoric of 1947 laid the foundations for an intense, protracted campaign to convince Congress and the American public that the United States should take active economic and, especially later, military measures to support anti-Communist regimes around the world.

Systematic quantitative evidence indicates that the reported statements and actions of experts and commentators and popular presidents do indeed tend to have substantial effects upon Americans' policy preferences (see Chap. 8, below; and Page et al. 1987). In the specific case of the Truman Doctrine speech, Kernell (1976) has argued that President Truman had little immediate impact on the public's broad anti-Soviet opinions or overall anticommunism, though Truman did greatly increase the salience of foreign policy problems and did gain support for his proposal of $400 million in military assistance to Greece and Turkey. The better educated and fellow partisans, in particular, were most receptive to leadership. There can be little doubt, however, that cumulatively, over time, the president and other officials and "experts" like the anonymous "X" played a vital part in arousing anticommunism and mobilizing public support for Cold War policies (see Leigh 1976; Foster 1983). Not international events alone, but also the *interpretation* of events by American elites, and the *reporting* of events and interpretations by the U.S. media, led to changes in public opinion.[12]

Opinion Manipulation?

The role of elites and the media is of real significance, however, only if they act as something other than simple transmission belts that convey objective facts to the public. Our second question is the crucial one: Were the reports and interpretations biased or false or misleading? It is important to make judgments about such matters, even at the risk of entering a thicket of historical controversies in which it is not always easy to disentangle truth from falsehood.

With the clarity of hindsight, it is now apparent that many interpretations of Soviet behavior offered in the American media and by U.S. leaders were, if not deliberately deceptive, at least misleading and only loosely connected with objective events. Indeed, American leaders and the mass media seemed to have an uncanny ability to turn on or turn off the anti-Communist spigot from one year to the next, as it served what they considered U.S. national interests. Surely Joseph Stalin did not magically switch from despotic villain in 1940, to benevolent father of his people in 1942, to villain again in 1947, as U.S. publicity implied (see Kriesberg 1946–1947; Walsh 1947; Small 1974; Levering 1976); what changed was the relation of the Soviet Union to official U.S. foreign policy.

The most important case in point, with enormous long-term consequences, is the postwar arousal of anti-Soviet sentiments. Outrage at the closing of an "iron curtain" in Eastern Europe—that is, at Soviet imposition of influence through its occupation forces and local Communist parties—involved, to some extent, a misreading or misrepresentation of history. To the Russians, who had been invaded from the West by Napoleon, the Kaiser, and Hitler, and who had just lost more than twenty million lives fighting Germany (about forty times the American losses against both Germany and Japan), the issue was not so much communizing Eastern Europe as it was establishing a secure buffer. Western leaders recognized Soviet fears of a future German resurgence, and at the Moscow and Yalta conferences of October 1944 and February 1945—having little choice in the matter—the allies effectively conceded that only a Soviet sphere of influence in Eastern Europe and much of Germany could guarantee security. (Truman essentially ratified this understanding at Potsdam in July 1945, but then concealed it from the public.) Americans' hopes for capitalist democracies in East Germany and in Poland and the rest of Eastern Europe, where they would threaten the USSR, were rather naive. Official encouragement of such hopes by Roosevelt and

Truman and others was misleading. Similarly, in selling the Marshall Plan and NATO, the Soviet threat to Western Europe was greatly overstated (Gaddis 1982, Lefler 1984, and others show that U.S. leaders were aware of Soviet weaknesses and moderation).

Moreover, the U.S. press and political leaders intentionally or unintentionally misinterpreted a number of specific events, casting Soviet actions in an excessively bad light. Soviet troops occupying a revolt-torn section of Iran, bordering the USSR, were portrayed as aggressors; their withdrawal in May 1946 was not granted its full conciliatory significance (see Kuniholm 1980). Yugoslav (not Russian) support for the Communist-led National Liberation Front in Greece, which had constituted the core of the anti-Nazi resistance in that country during World War II and enjoyed substantial popular support, was characterized as Soviet or "outside" pressure—for example, in the key Truman Doctrine speech, which also omitted to mention the reactionary and repressive nature of the "free" Greek government, the fact that the United States was replacing neocolonial British influence, and the crucial role of U.S. economic interests in markets and Middle Eastern oil. (Wittner [1982, Chap. 3] tells how Truman and Acheson followed Senator Vandenberg's advice to "scare hell out of the country": the "urgent appeal" from the Greek government for aid was initiated and written by the United States [p. 73], and an elaborate public relations campaign laid the groundwork for Truman's speech.)

In interpreting the politics of Poland and Rumania and the coups in Hungary and Czechoslovakia, American leaders tended to ignore Soviet security interests and to overstate the chances for genuine democracy or representative government in countries whose recent histories had been dominated by feudalism and fascism. The Berlin blockade of 1948–1949, portrayed as the Russian bully's attack upon an isolated bastion of freedom, was seldom put into the broader context of Western moves that the Soviets saw as threatening—especially the merger of the Western world economy through currency changes and other measures. (As early as 1946, George Kennan was arguing that the western zones of Germany should be walled off against eastern penetration and integrated into Western Europe: Gaddis 1972, p. 828).

The point here is not to apologize for postwar Soviet foreign policy or to argue that the United States could or should quietly have acquiesced to it. Many Soviet actions were clearly harmful to the people of Eastern Europe, who were quick to seize independence when they finally had a chance in 1989. In any case, rivalry between superpowers whose spheres of influence bump into each other may well be inevitable—regardless of ideology—because of differing economic and strategic interests. But the ideological fervor of the U.S. crusade to "contain communism," which crystallized largely *after* specific military, economic, and political anti-Communist policies were first decided upon and put into effect (Larson 1985), was whipped up partly on the basis of misinformation and mis-leading interpretations of events. Thus during the early Cold War, U.S. public opinion can be said, to a significant extent, to have been manipulated.[13]

How should one judge manipulation of public opinion in the Cold War context? Those enthusiastic about the idea of rebuilding Western Europe, expanding American power, and counteracting Soviet influence after World War II tend to be tolerant of what they see as justifiable exaggerations in a good cause, just as opponents of fascism praise Roosevelt for maneuvering the United States into the war. But again, such a posture raises classic questions about ends and means. In a democracy, where policy is supposed to rest ultimately upon citizens' preferences, any misinformation that alters those preferences must be regarded with special concern.

The Korean War

The war in Korea (or, as the Truman administration preferred to call it, the Korean "conflict" or the United Nations "police action") further illustrates how the American public has reacted rationally to events, as those events have been reported to it; but also how the information provided has sometimes been misleading.

In Korea, American soldiers for the first time engaged in combat against Communist opponents. The war itself—and the dramatic policy changes and expanded Cold War rhetoric for which it became an occasion—solidified public opinion in favor of a number of anti-Communist policies in Europe as well as Asia. As was the case during World War II, battlefield successes and reversals of fortune brought corresponding rises and falls in public support for various specific policies.

On June 25, 1950, after a series of incidents and mutual provocations, North Korean forces crossed the Thirty-eighth Parallel (the line demarcating the "temporary" Soviet and American occupation zones) into the South, seeking to overthrow the shaky minority regime of Syngman Rhee and to reunify the country by force. President Truman quickly decided to give military assistance and then to commit U.S. troops, which were legitimated by the United Nations Security Council as part—actually the bulk—of a nominally international force. While the North

Koreans rapidly pushed far south to the Pusan perimeter, the United States began a spectacular summer and autumn of policy changes that included commitments to Formosa and French Indochina, a proposal to rearm Germany, a tripling of defense spending, and an invasion of North Korea (Cumings [1981b, 1990] analyzes the background of the Korean War, emphasizing civil conflict and South Korean provocations; Rees 1964 describes the war itself; LaFeber 1985, chap. 5, discusses its ramifications.)

The outbreak of war naturally led the U.S. public to focus on Asia. In an August 1950 Gallup poll, 55% of Americans said it was equally important to "stop Russia" in Asia as it was in Europe. By this time, after initial hesitation, the Truman administration was blaming the Soviets for the invasion: Acheson said the Russians had "presented a check" which was drawn on the bank account of collective security. In October, 69% told NORC they favored military aid to Asia. (Both the "stop Russia" and the aid figures dropped a bit in subsequent months as the news from Korea became less intense.)

But this focus on Asia did not at all imply that the public wanted to neglect Europe. As we noted earlier, one result of the war was a big jump from 44% to 62% (NORC) between June and July 1950 in the proportion of Americans wanting to build up a new German army in the parts of Germany occupied by the United States, Britain, and France. This occurred well before September, when the Truman administration decided to push for German rearmament and proposed it at a Foreign Ministers meeting in New York. Public support for using German troops in Europe's defense later fell off a bit but then rose from 57% in October 1951 to 64% in February 1952.

The Truman administration followed its July 1950 requests for an enlarged military budget with an announcement in September that there would be "substantial increases" in the number of U.S. troops in Europe. But the proportion of Americans that favored sending large numbers of U.S. troops to Europe dropped a remarkable twenty-three percentage points (to 39%) between September and December 1950 (NORC), as congressional Republicans objected and as the victorious Inchon landing and the U.S. drive through North Korea to the Yalu River—the border with China—provoked full-scale Chinese intervention in November which forced U.S. and South Korean troops back south across the Thirty-eighth Parallel. The Korean War seemed to demand higher priority. (Support for sending troops to Europe regained a bit, 6%, by late January 1951, as the threat to South Korea eased.)

The administration promised more American money—as well as

soldiers—to Europe, partly in order to quiet French and British fears of German rearmament. As we indicated earlier, public support for military aid to Europe rose a very large 22% (to 80% in favor; NORC) between prewar March 1950 and March 1951. According to another repeated NORC question, support for military aid then fluctuated somewhat, at a high level, from 74% in May 1951 to 69% in November and back to 76% in June 1952.

The unfolding logic of the Korean War brought about some of these opinion changes without much explicit guidance from the administration. The idea of rearming Germany, for example, was not publicly broached by U.S. officials until well after public opinion had shifted to embrace that and a variety of other ways to resist perceived Communist threats. Many opinion changes, however, resulted from conscious decisions to use the Korean War to justify new policies elsewhere, such as the immediate protection (by the U.S. seventh fleet) of Chiang Kai-Shek's Chinese Nationalist remnants on Taiwan, and the quick increase in military support for the French in Indochina. "NSC-68," Paul Nitze's secret strategy review circulated at the end of March 1950, had already presented an exaggerated picture of Soviet expansionism (overruling Russia experts Kennan and Bohlen) and argued for a major anti-Communist military buildup; the Korean War was a convenient occasion to carry out its recommendations (see Wells 1979).

The impact of the Korean War extended over a broad range of foreign policy issues. NORC surveys found high support for economic aid to "friendly countries in Asia," rising from 69% in July 1950 to 77% in April 1951. Subsequently, the proportion thinking it a "good idea" to send military supplies "to help build up the armies of countries friendly to us" rose from an already high 71% in June 1951 to 79% in May 1953. Similarly, Gallup surveys indicated that more Americans wanted to spend more money on propaganda; according to NORC, more citizens said government officials were "telling the people all they should" about foreign policy; and, as we have seen, backing for military aid to Europe and for the rearming of Germany and Japan rose.

The urgency and high costs of fighting in Korea also led the public to make some clear distinctions in its reactions. In contrast to increased sentiment for military aid, for example, fewer Americans wanted to provide aid to help the standard of living in what a NORC survey question indelicately called "backward countries in the world": there was a 12% drop in support between November 1949 (79%) and November a year later (67%), with nearly all the decline coming after April 1950.

As the war ebbed and flowed, opinions on certain matters fluctuated. Support for the proposition that we were making "too many

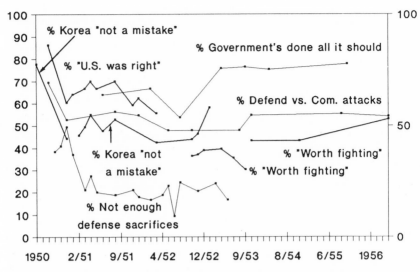

FIG. 5.8   Korean War, stopping communism, 1950–1956.

sacrifices" (vs. "not enough" or the "right amount") for defense, for example, dropped 11% between March and April 1951 (when MacArthur was urging new efforts for victory), rose 9% by August, and dropped 9% between November 1951 and April 1952. Looking at it the other way around, responses of "not enough" dropped 14% between May and June 1952, and rose 15% again by August (see figure 5.8). As we have seen, this sort of rapid fluctuation in opinions is unusual. It reflected the shifting referent inherent in the question (different actual "sacrifices" were being made at different times) and the changing prospects for peace, as well as changes in prices, taxes, the draft, rationing, and real disposable incomes.

Similarly, attitudes concerning whether Secretary of State Acheson should be kept in his cabinet position rose and fell with the course of the war and other events at home and abroad. Acheson had been widely blamed for the "fall" of China, for his support of Alger Hiss, and for declaring Korea to be outside the U.S. defense perimeter in January 1950. Sentiment for firing Acheson varied as his performance (or at least the perceived results of his performance) changed.

After the dramatic see-saw events of 1950 that ended with the Chinese reversal of the U.S. push into North Korea, and Truman's refusal to let MacArthur bomb China, the Korean War settled in January 1951 into a stalemate roughly along the lines of the Thirty-eighth Parallel, the prewar boundary. In April, General MacArthur's frustrated public demands for "victory" led President Truman to fire him, an unpopular move that was followed by MacArthur's triumphant homecoming and congressional hearings.

Then, on June 23, 1951, the Soviet U.N. representative, Jacob Malik, made a dramatic speech proposing truce talks, which the United States quickly accepted. As it happens, the University of Michigan's Survey Research Center was conducting interviews at that time. James Davies (1952) observes that the public reacted "meaningfully, sensibly, rationally" (p. 777): the 21% of those with definite opinions who (just before the speech) had expected "in the next few months our relations with Russia" would get better, jumped up to 40% ten days after Malik spoke. People of varying income, education, and occupations reacted to about the same extent, but those living in large metropolitan areas (for whom, Davies suggests, the threat of nuclear war was greatest and any relaxation of tensions most relevant—and who, we would add, may have been most fully exposed to the news) showed by far the greatest increases in optimism (pp. 784–787.)[14]

During the summer of 1951, however, the truce talks made little progress. Once the war had been stalemated along prewar lines and did not end quickly, the U.S. public became less and less happy about it. The proportion of people calling U.S. involvement a "mistake" or "wrong" grew, corresponding to the cumulative magnitude of U.S. casualties (Mueller 1971, 1973). Opinion favoring a pullout of U.S. troops rose 13%, to a substantial level of 30% (NORC), between December 1951 and February 1952, as the truce talks dragged on. In other respects, however, frustration led to belligerence. The rather alarming 64% (NORC) of Americans who in August 1951, as the Communists broke off the truce talks, favored allowing U.S. planes to cross the "border now and bomb supply bases inside China" rose a further 9% by October. (Support for bombing China fell back to its previous level by March 1952, however, as the stalled talks resumed.)

An increasing majority—rising 13%, to a level of 65%, between March and June 1952 (NORC)—opposed repatriating North Korean and Chinese prisoners of war, who were portrayed by U.S. officials and media as reluctant to go home. (Some did later refuse repatriation.) But during the period of stalemate the public's desire to attack in the event peace talks broke down dropped sharply, by 15% (from just over 47% to just under 33%), between June and October 1952 (NORC)—rebounding more than halfway (9%), however, over the next month, a change for which we have no explanation.[15]

The favorite policy option of many Americans was one that foreshadowed the popularity of "Vietnamization" in a different war fifteen years later. A large majority came to agree with the presidential candidate Dwight Eisenhower that the South Korean ("ROK") army should be trained and equipped to take the places of American soldiers, a move with obvious advantages to the United States: continued military strength with reduced risk to American lives. The proportion of the public favoring this policy, according to Gallup, grew by a solid 20% during 1952, from 67% in February to 87% in November, perhaps because of Eisenhower's campaign. Similarly, between April 1951 and December 1952, NORC surveys found that 15% fewer Americans (dropping from 48% to 33%) wanted the United States to spend more on its rearmament program.

After Eisenhower's election to the presidency and Stalin's death (March 1953), the Korean truce talks got serious. An agreement was finally signed in July 1953; prisoners were exchanged, and most American troops came home. The public relaxed some of its concern about communism in Asia. According to NORC, 48% of Americans put a higher priority on stopping communism in Europe than in Asia in mid-May 1953, 10% more than had done so in April 1951. Gallup found that 7% fewer Americans (though still 78% of them) wanted the United States to build up Japan's army in September 1953 than had expressed that desire in January 1951.

The sentiment in favor of "stopping Russia" in Europe rather than Asia had already risen rapidly, by 21% (from 37% to 58%) between August 1950 and January 1951 (Gallup), when—after the U.S. counterattack and the Chinese intervention—the war settled back to the thirty-eighth Parallel. Europe-centered opinions dropped back only partway (12%) between January and December 1952. (We are not sure why.) Willingness to give aid to repair war damage in South Korea, which was already high, rose another 6% between April 1952 and June 1953, reaching 69% in favor (NORC), as the official state of war neared its end and attention could turn to postwar rebuilding.

The Korean War case, much like World War II, shows an American public that reacted sensibly to the onset of the war, to successes and failures in the fighting, and to the end of hostilities—as those events were reported to it. Again, however, political leaders created or used or interpreted some events (especially the origins and implications of the war) in ways that probably misled the public. Our foreign policy data include a complex mixture of cases in which opinion was led, or was manipulated, or moved independently of (sometimes in opposition to) efforts at persuasion.

The end of the Korean War opened a relatively quiet decade of American foreign policy, in which relations with the Soviet Union calmed somewhat. There were relatively few crises, compared with the early Cold War, and the United States concentrated on questions related to the United Nations and the emerging countries of the Third World, many of them asserting neutrality in the East-West struggle.

The United Nations

Since the 1940s the American public's attitudes toward the United Nations have been very positive, based upon strong desires for international peace and cooperation. Initial high hopes dimmed somewhat (reasonably enough) when Cold War conflicts and changing U.N. membership raised skepticism about the organization's effectiveness and its usefulness to U.S. foreign policy. Despite increasing official U.S. disdain for the United Nations, however, the public remained remarkably supportive of the organization.

In the middle and late 1930s, as the League of Nations proved impotent against the expansion of Hitler and Mussolini, the American public expressed little enthusiasm for Woodrow Wilson's dream of peacekeeping through world organization. In 1935, for example, even in response to a pleasantly worded Roper question ("If war in Europe is averted through the League of Nations, do you believe the United States should join the League?"), two-thirds of the public—66%—said "no."[16] According to a different (Gallup) question, about the same proportion of Americans, 67%, opposed joining the League of Nations in October 1937, after Hitler had remilitarized the Rhineland (March 1936) and after Mussolini had conquered Ethiopia (May 1936) despite Hailie Selassie's appeals to the League. In June 1938, after the German army occupied Austria and Hitler proclaimed the Austrian-German union, Gallup found, not surprisingly, that only 48% of Americans thought the time was ripe for the leading nations to hold a disarmament conference, down 8% since June 1937.

When World War II actually began, however, support for world organization began to increase, presumably because people saw the lack of effective organization in the 1930s as a cause of the war. In May 1941, Americans divided about evenly over whether or not they would like to see the United States join "a" league of nations after the war was over, and in July they split 50-50 over whether the United States should have joined the League of Nations after the last war.

The U.S. entry into the war accentuated desires for a new world order, and wartime cooperation with the British and Soviets and others encouraged hopes for it. According to Gallup, high percentages of Americans (84% in January 1942, for example) favored taking an "active part" in world affairs "when the war is over." Support for joining "a league of nations" after the war jumped up 22% (to 73%) in Gallup surveys between May 1941 and June 1942, after twenty-six nations including the United States signed the United Nations Declaration in January 1942.

(Notice that this increasing support long preceded any official campaign for a postwar U.N.) According to OPOR, in April 1944 public sentiment for joining a league reached a very high 84%—quite a reversal from the 1930s—as FDR campaigned strongly in favor of a world organization (concerning this campaign, see Hero 1966; Foster 1983; Leigh 1976; Scott and Withey 1958). Similarly, three OPOR surveys in 1943 and 1944 revealed steady support of 85% or more for an "international police force" after the war to keep peace around the world.

During the war the allies were sometimes referred to as the "united nations." By the time the United Nations Organization was chartered at San Francisco in April 1945, an overwhelming majority of the public (91% in April and 93% in May, according to OPOR) favored U.S. membership, despite doubts about the Security Council veto, multiple Soviet membership, and the trusteeship system. In the early postwar years, majorities told NORC they favored United Nations "inspectors to see if each country is living up to its agreements" on nuclear plants (78% in February 1947, up another 7% by October) and favored international control of atomic energy (64% in October 1947) (see Graham 1989b, which shows how the Truman administration designed the "Baruch Plan" to defuse popular support for internationalization of nuclear energy).

The Cold War, however, dampened hopes for cooperation. Already in August 1946, 55% of Americans said we should rely on our own defenses, not the United Nations—up 8% from February (NORC). By June 1948, support for international control of atomic energy had dropped fourteen percentage points from the October 1947 level, to 57% in favor. While a strong majority (75% as late as October 1949, according to Gallup) still said the United Nations had done a good job rather than a poor job in trying to settle world problems, large percentages (66% in April 1947 and 72% in May 1948, up from only 46% at the beginning of 1947, according to Gallup) began to express dissatisfaction with the progress the United Nations had made to date. In June 1949, 60% of the public (up 8% from April 1948) told NORC that making the United Nations into a world government was not a good idea.

The fact that a U.N. Security Council resolution and a nominally multinational force under the U.N. flag served as the rubric for American troops to fight in Korea apparently increased the U.S. public's regard for the organization. According to NORC, for example, between November 1949 and the Korea successes of October 1950, approval of the idea of setting up a single world government that would control the armed forces of all countries rose 13%. To be sure, the U.N. involvement in Korea also made attitudes about the United Nations vulnerable to frustrations with the war. Opinion that the United Nations had done a "good job . . . in trying to solve the problems it has had to face" (Gallup) dipped[17] to 61% by January 1951, after the Chinese had intervened and routed U.S. and South Korean forces from North Korea. But "good job" responses increased markedly to 75% by September 1953, after peace was achieved. They kept rising to a peak of 89% in October 1955 and remained near that very high level on into the early 1960s.

Support for continuing U.S. membership in the United Nations, too, rose and fell somewhat during the Korean war: rapidly, but not by very much, as figure 5.9 makes clear. According to NORC, promembership sentiment increased 7% between January 1951 and May 1952, dropped 8% by November 1953, and rose 10% again by August 1955. (The sharpest opinion changes came in 1953, as prospects for peace in Korea fluctuated.) It is noteworthy, however, that during this period public support for continued U.S. membership in the United Nations never fell below the 85% of late November 1953. In fact, Gallup found that over the entire decade between November 1951 and January 1962, advocacy of giving up U.N. membership actually dropped by a net eight percentage points (see figure 5.9 and the discussion in Hero 1966). The positive impact of the Korean war suggests that an important factor in pro-U.N. sentiment was the perception that the United Nations—then heavily dominated by the West—was serving U.S. national interests. But continuing high levels of support over several decades also indicate a deeply rooted and genuine desire for international peace and cooperation.

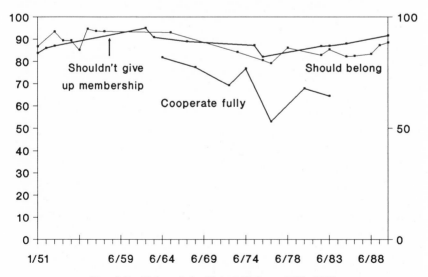

FIG. 5.9   U.S. and the United Nations, 1951–1990.

During the middle 1950s, presumably because of peace in Korea and the replacement of Stalin by more conciliatory Soviet leaders pursuing "peaceful coexistence," there was also increasing public support for the idea that the Soviet Union should remain in the United Nations (up 14% to 74% between December 1952 and November 1956, according to NORC), and substantial support for building up the U.N. emergency forces by adding U.S. and Russian troops. Sixty-eight percent favored this in a February 1958 Gallup poll; support dropped 13%, however, by January 1961, perhaps because of the movement of the United Nations away from complete agreement with U.S. foreign policy (as noted below) and because of bilateral tensions related to Berlin in 1959 and 1960, the U-2 downing and abortive summit conference of May 1960, and the debate over a "missile gap."

At the end of the 1950s the character of the U.N. General Assembly changed dramatically, as many newly independent nations joined the organization. In 1960 alone, seventeen new members—sixteen of them African—entered the United Nations. These countries, just liberated from Western colonialism, were strongly anticolonialist and anti-imperialist and tended to profess nonalignment in the East-West struggle.

As the power of the nonaligned countries in the United Nations grew, Americans soon found the General Assembly adopting resolutions contrary to what U.S. officials defined as our national interests. At the beginning of the 1960s, for example, in the formerly Belgian Congo (now Zaire), the United Nations and Secretary General Hammarskjold tended to support the volatile leftist Premier Patrice Lumumba and to oppose the secession of the right-wing Moise Tschombe's mineral-rich Katanga province, which was coveted by Belgian and U.S. mineral companies. (It was later revealed that the CIA had laid plans to assassinate Lumumba: U.S. Senate 1975. Gibbs 1991 documents some little-known connections between American business interests and U.S. policy in the Congo.)

Eventually nationalism proved stronger than pro-U.N. internationalism for some Americans. True, as Hero (1966) points out, public support for the United Nations remained generally high into the early 1960s; but it began to drop a bit as movements to "get the U.N. out of the U.S. and the U.S. out of the U.N." sprang up with backing from Barry Goldwater and other conservative Republicans, and as U.N. peacekeeping operations bore questionable fruit. Between July 1960 and April 1964, for example, Gallup found that 9% fewer Americans (a drop from 86% to 77%) said it was a "good idea" to build up the emergency force so that it could deal with small ("brush fire") wars throughout the world.

Even basic support for U.S. membership in the United Nations began to decline somewhat in the middle 1960s, according to the Gallup and NORC surveys shown in figure 5.9. This was accentuated in the late 1960s and the 1970s, as many nations opposed U.S. actions in Vietnam and as Arab and other Third World countries pursued a campaign against Israel and Zionism. United Nations support among liberal American Jews ebbed. United States ambassadors to the United Nations, like Daniel Patrick Moynihan and (later) Jeanne Kirkpatrick, as well as Presidents Nixon and Reagan and other political figures, increasingly criticized the organization; Jimmy Carter's Third World–oriented Ambassador Andrew Young represented only a brief pro-U.N. interlude. The proportion of Americans saying the United States should "cooperate fully" with the United Nations declined from 82% in 1964, to 53% in 1976, according to Gallup (recovering somewhat, to 64%, by 1983). In the twenty years between two NORC surveys in 1956 and 1976, 14% fewer Americans said they wanted the United States to stay in the United Nations. Between January 1962 and November 1975, Gallup found that 13% more wanted the United States to give up membership (see figure 5.9).

Thus public backing for the United Nations reacted in an understandable fashion to events. Still, figure 5.9 makes clear that support always stayed high. Even at the relative low point of 1976, a majority (53%) wanted to "cooperate fully" with the United Nations. Throughout the nearly four decades from 1951 through 1990, support for continued membership in the United Nations remained at the 80% level or better; it stood at 89% or better in 1990.

In the late 1980s and beginning of the 1990s, when the Soviet Union endorsed cooperative peacekeeping moves in various parts of the world and Soviet President Gorbachev emphasized the importance of international law and the United Nations as instruments of world peace, there were signs of a further upswing of pro-U.N. attitudes among the American public, reinforced by U.S.-U.N. success in the Gulf war.

The data suggest that for some time the American public has generally felt more enthusiasm for the United Nations than have foreign policy officials. Like the steady public backing for Social Security and other social programs in the 1980s, this continued high support for the United Nations indicates that public opinion can sometimes be quite resistant to elite persuasion.

In discussing the attitudes of Americans toward the United Nations, we have outrun our chronological treatment of other issues in U.S. foreign policy. In the next chapter we return to the relatively quiet foreign policy decade from 1953 to the early 1960s, and then deal with the Vietnam War, China, the Middle East, and the post-Vietnam course of U.S.-Soviet relations. We will see further examples of coherent preferences and rational reactions to reported events, along with cases of misleading information that has sometimes succeeded and sometimes failed to manipulate public opinion.

6 Vietnam, Détente, and the New Cold War

(Coauthored by John M. Gillroy)

☑ For about ten years after the Korean War, the international scene was relatively quiet, and Americans' opinions concerning foreign policy issues were correspondingly stable. Important international events occurred, to be sure, but this period was much calmer than that of the early Cold War or the fighting in Korea. Then the turbulence of the Vietnam War brought large opinion changes. There followed a series of shifting events and opinions: détente with the Soviet Union, a new Cold War, and—after the middle 1980s—renewed détente of a potentially far-reaching sort. We will deal with these matters mainly in chronological order, devoting separate sections to China and to the Middle East.

Throughout the more than thirty-five years of American history discussed in this chapter, however, the nature and dynamics of public opinion remained fundamentally the same. While new events and circumstances gave rise to new issues, and while a number of Americans' policy preferences changed, the basic characteristics of public opinion and the basic processes of opinion change were much the same as described in the previous chapter.

Once again, Americans' collective preferences about foreign policy generally formed coherent patterns that were related in sensible ways to underlying beliefs and values. Opinions were mostly stable; when they changed they did so in response to new information about world events, as reported in the media and as interpreted by political leaders and commentators. Collective public opinion generally reacted in a reasonable fashion to the available information.

Here, too, we will note several cases in which the public received misleading information or in which government officials were deliberately deceptive. There were also, however, important instances in which public opinion moved relatively autonomously and proved quite resistant to manipulation or persuasion.

The Peaceful Eisenhower Decade

From the end of the Korean War in 1953 to the Cuban missile crisis of 1962—a period that mostly coincided with the two presidential terms of Dwight Eisenhower—American foreign policy enjoyed relative peace.

Certain crises did, of course, capture national attention and in some cases lead to abrupt opinion changes: the 1954 fall of the French in Indochina, for example; the Quemoy and Matsu crises of 1954–1955 and 1958; the British-French-Israeli invasion of Egypt in 1956; the Soviet repression of the Hungarian revolt that same year; and disputes over Berlin culminating in the building of the wall between East and West in 1961. But U.S. troops did not fight anywhere in the world. No regular American forces came very close to combat, except perhaps for those in the Formosa straits and the marines sent to Lebanon in 1958. Tensions with the Soviet Union were lower. Much of U.S. foreign policy involved "force without war," relying on military aid and small-scale interventions along with covert actions that did not gain public attention until much later.

The effects of this relative tranquility are evident in our opinion data. Changes in public opinion about foreign and defense policies were a bit smaller during this period (averaging 11.2 percentage points) than over the whole range of our study (12.6 percentage points). More important, the 1953–1962 opinion changes were much less *abrupt*. Over the entire period of our study reported in Chapter 2, fully 58% of the 255 instances of foreign and defense opinion change met our criterion for abruptness (change at a rate of ten percentage points or more per year). But only *24%* of the forty-five foreign policy changes that ended during the 1952–1962 period were abrupt, about the same proportion as we found for domestic opinion changes (27%) in the whole data set. Abrupt opinion changes occur most often in times of war or international turmoil, not in times of peace.[1]

Early in the 1950s, tension in Europe eased with the establishment of clear East-West boundaries, including the tightening of the East German border and establishment of a buffer zone in May 1952. The Nineteenth Congress of the Communist party of the USSR, in October 1952, emphasized "peaceful coexistence" between socialist and capitalist states. Once Stalin died and the Korean War ended in 1953, U.S. relations with the Soviets improved considerably.

The public reacted appropriately to these new circumstances, with considerably more peace-oriented attitudes, especially on the use of nuclear weapons. The proportion of Americans wanting "war now" with the Soviet Union, according to NORC surveys, dropped 10% between November 1951 and September 1954, to a very low level of 7%. NORC also found a drop from 74% to 61% between May 1952 and April 1954 in the proportion of the public saying the United States should use the A-bomb right away if there were "a big war with Russia"; in 1954, 61% still favored doing so, but in January 1955 only 50% did, according to a similar but not identical question. Likewise, NORC found a drop of 8% (to just 47%) between April 1954 and January 1955 in the proportion wanting to use the H-bomb right away if Russia attacked a European ally, with the figure staying about the same in November 1955. By the middle 1950s, then, there was considerable opposition to the use of nuclear weapons, including majority rejection of the Dulles doctrine of "massive retaliation" in Europe (see Graham 1989b).

International cooperation looked more feasible. Large and growing majorities of the public favored various kinds of peaceful relations with the Soviet Union. Between August 1953 and May 1956, Gallup found a 12% increase, to 57%, in the proportion that favored "working out a business arrangement to buy and sell goods" with the USSR. (A slightly variant question referring to "an arrangement" rather than a "business arrangement" elicited an even higher 65% favorable response in June 1955.) Between October 1952 and April 1957, according to NORC, the proportion of Americans wanting to continue diplomatic relations with the Soviets rose by 15%, to a solid 80%. In April 1956, 67% wanted Eisenhower to extend invitations to top Soviet leaders to visit the United States (NORC), and in November 1956, 80% favored exchanging musicians and athletes. (These figures dropped 6% and 12%, respectively, by December 1956 and March 1957, presumably reflecting the full effect of Russian suppression of the Hungarian revolt in the first week of November 1956, but they remained well above the 50% level.)

There can be little doubt that opinion leadership by President Eisenhower played an important part in this rise of cooperative sentiment. Eisenhower, evoking his background as chief military orchestrator of the World War II victory in Europe, harkened back to wartime collaboration with the Soviets, especially with General Zhukov. Setting aside earlier advocacy of "rolling back" the Iron Curtain and threats of "massive retaliation" for any Soviet aggression, Eisenhower and Secretary of State Dulles called for summit meetings, exchanges, and peaceful relations with the Soviets, even while taking a hard anti-Communist line in the Third (or, as it was then called, the "underdeveloped") World. As we already noted (in Chap. 5), members of Eisenhower's own Republican party showed substantial movement between 1952 and 1954 in an internationalist direction; they also became somewhat less hostile toward the USSR and more receptive to peaceful coexistence.

The thaw in U.S.-Soviet relations did not mean the public abandoned anti-Communist policies; support (especially for NATO) remained generally stable, but it did ease off a little. For reasons that are not clear, the proportion of Americans wanting to "cut back aid to Europe's armed strength against communism" actually dropped, according to Roper, between October 1952 and September 1956; support for the proposition that we should "keep on trying to build up the armed strength of countries of Western Europe to resist communism like we've been doing" rose from 32% to 41% (still only a minority). A different question asked in June 1952 and November 1956 by NORC, however, showed that support for explicitly military aid to Europe declined by 7%, despite the Soviet repression in Hungary just before the second survey. Support for the defense "agreement with the countries of Western Europe, to defend each other against attack" peaked at an overwhelming 94% in November 1955, according to NORC, and dropped a bit (to a still extremely high 87%) one year later. And, after the Korea-related 8% rise from June 1951 to May 1953, there was a 9% decline (to 70%) in backing for military aid to "help build up the armies of countries that are friendly to us" between May 1953 and April 1956 (NORC).

With military pressures reduced, support for economic aid increased. Between November 1950 (in the depths of the Korean War) and relatively peaceful March 1955 there was a solid 15% rise (to 81%), according to NORC, in support for economic aid to improve the living standards of "backward" countries. NORC also found that increasing numbers of Americans—19% more in November 1954 (60%) than in June 1953 (41%)—thought we should pay more attention to Latin America. (This may have been related to U.S. government alarms about communism in the region, manifested in the March 1954 Caracas resolution and the CIA-backed June 1954 coup against Guatemala's Arbenz regime.) Between September 1956 and December 1958, the SRC/CPS election studies found that support for economic aid to poor countries rose 10% (to 61%). Such aid was being strongly advocated by the Council on Foreign Relations (with leadership from David Rockefeller), the newly founded Atlantic Council, and others.

The post-Korea shift in public support from military to economic aid is made especially clear by survey questions that *explicitly posed a trade-off* between the two. Between wartime August 1952 and more tranquil June 1956 there was a great upsurge of 26% (to 81%), according to NORC, in the proportion favoring economic as against military aid to U.S. allies. Support for economic aid versus military supplies to Asia "to keep communism from spreading" (NORC) rose by 9% (to 86%) between September 1954 and November 1955. Economic aid may have reached a peak of popularity sometime around—or shortly before—the

November–December 1958 SRC/CPS survey, when 61% agreed that the United States "should give economic help to the poorer countries of the world even if they can't pay for it."

Already in the middle and late 1950s there were some signs of decreases in support for foreign aid, however: a drop of 9% (to a still very high 83%) in endorsement of economic aid "to countries that have agreed to stand with us against Communist aggression" between November 1956 and April 1957 (NORC); and an overall decline of 14% (from 57% to 43%) in support for economic aid to nonallies "like India" between January 1956 and April 1957 (also NORC), although between September and December 1956 there was a temporary 8% rise to 55%, reflecting the impact of events in Eastern Europe.[2] Enthusiasm for aid to Eastern Europe in the wake of the Hungarian revolt—58% favored aid in mid-November 1956, according to NORC—proved to be temporary, dropping 10% by April 1957.

One threat to the peacefulness of the 1950s was the struggle in Indochina between the French colonialists and Ho Chi Minh's Nationalist and Communist Viet Minh movement. As we have mentioned, the United States took the beginning of the Korean War in June 1950 as an occasion for a number of military moves throughout Asia, including the interposition of the Seventh Fleet between Taiwan and the Chinese mainland (preventing Mao's Communists from completing their conquest of Chiang Kai-shek's Kuomintang) and the sending of large amounts of military assistance to the French in Indochina—ultimately taking over nearly the entire financial burden of the war.

As the French position in Indochina worsened, there was serious discussion of the United States using force—even perhaps the A-bomb—to bail them out. Support among the American public for sending U.S. soldiers rose by a substantial 15% between August 1953 and May 1954, according to Gallup, but it remained extremely low: only 24% in favor (21% in late May; 20% in mid-June).[3] Reluctance to commit American troops, short of a major crisis directly involving the United States (or a cheap, quick victory), has been a strong and persistent pattern in U.S. public opinion. Responding to pressure from the British and from U.S. congressional leaders, President Eisenhower decided against the use of U.S. air power in April 1954 (C. Roberts 1954; Herring 1979, pp. 30–37).

The fall of Dien Bien Phu in May 1954, followed by the Geneva peace agreements, foreclosed the possibility of immediate U.S. military involvement in Indochina. The United States soon began to build up the Diem regime in South Vietnam instead, thwarting the Geneva provisions for reunification and setting the stage for the next phase of the struggle. Welch (1972) presents evidence of tensions between press coverage and administration positions toward Vietnam between 1950 and 1956, but ultimately the press's dependence on official sources led to full publicity for the administration's messages to the public, and—time and again— press support for administration policies, culminating in backing for Diem (see also Aronson 1973 [1970]).

During the 1950s, the United States engaged in several covert military operations around the world, including those in Iran (overthrowing the Mussadiq government in 1953), Guatemala (overturning Arbenz in 1954), and Indonesia (aiding the rebels against Sukarno in 1958). But these actions were by their nature virtually invisible to the general public and were not widely known even among the highly attentive, until exposés by Wise and Ross (1964) and others were published in the 1960s. For the most part—as best the public could tell—the war hero Eisenhower presided over a peaceful period in U.S. foreign policy. Public opinion changed little.

The Vietnam War

By the late 1950s, many Americans came to feel uneasy about gains by the Soviet Union in rocketry (exemplified by the testing of the world's first ICBM in August 1957 and by the dramatic launching of the Sputnik space satellite in October of that year) and about leftist or Communist advances in Cuba (where Castro's revolution took power in January 1959), in Laos, and elsewhere.

Political and business leaders (e.g., in the Gaither and the Rockefeller Brothers reports) began to talk of a Communist tide in world affairs and of a need for the United States to respond with more armaments and more rapid economic growth to meet the challenge. They maintained that the United States was "falling behind" the Soviet Union in many areas, including science education and the production of strategic nuclear missiles.

An alleged "missile gap," which turned out (and was known by some at the time) to be illusory, and which in any case would not have substantially affected U.S. deterrent power (Kaplan 1983; Bottome 1971; see Chap. 9, below), was postulated by certain journalists and politicians who supported the air force. John F. Kennedy took up this theme of potential strategic vulnerability in his 1960 presidential campaign; he deplored the "missile gap" and also emphasized Soviet progress in the "underdeveloped" world, arguing that the United States should greatly increase its military spending and its limited war capabilities. He said we should be willing to "bear any burden, pay any price" for the sake of freedom around the world, and he promised to "get America moving again" (Kennedy's militant 1960 speeches make sober reading today: see U.S. Congress 1961).

No doubt the alarmist rhetoric of Kennedy and others contributed to changes in public opinion that pointed toward more anti-Communist activism abroad. The unpleasant Korean experience was also receding into the past. A steadily increasing proportion of Americans, according to SRC/CPS, agreed strongly that "(t)he United States should keep soldiers overseas where they can help countries that are against communism": 49% in autumn 1956, 55% in 1958, and 63% in autumn 1960.[4]

The public apparently favored the peaceful side of the Kennedy program, including the proposed nuclear test ban treaty (see Rosi 1965; Terchek 1970; Childs 1965; Graham 1989a, 1989b). Little specific survey evidence is available about public preferences concerning the new Kennedy policies of strategic arms buildup, "flexible response," counterinsurgency forces, and the like; the public generally supported building (though not using) nuclear weapons, but there are certainly no indications that Americans were demanding U.S. involvement in Vietnam or elsewhere. Still, such active anti-Communist moves as the unsuccessful Bay of Pigs invasion of Cuba in April 1961 and the confrontation over Soviet missiles on that island in autumn 1962 won broad public acceptance, judging by short-term jumps in Kennedy's approval ratings; they foreshadowed at least a climate of acquiescence in the growing deployment of U.S. combat "advisors" in Vietnam after November 1961 and in the escalation of Vietnam involvement in 1964 and 1965.

The Gulf of Tonkin and Escalation

Now that more of the facts are publicly available, the Tonkin Gulf incident of August 1964—the key event used to justify overt U.S. military involvement in Vietnam—looks like a classic case of opinion manipulation. President Johnson and the Department of Defense denounced two "unprovoked attacks" upon U.S. destroyers off the coast of North Vietnam as "open aggression on the high seas"; Johnson ordered a "retaliatory" air strike on North Vietnamese installations and rushed through Congress the Tonkin Resolution that authorized "all necessary measures" to "prevent further aggression." The U.S. media (with the then-obscure exception of I. F. Stone's *Weekly*) mostly reported the official account without question. Only much later did Americans learn that the first attack—on the USS *Maddox*—caused no damage or casualties and that the alleged second attack, on the *Turner Joy,* probably never occurred at all: a nervous and inexperienced sonar man apparently picked up false signals in the stormy seas. Johnson had known before his speech that there was grave doubt about the occurrence of any attack (see Goulden 1969; Windchy 1971; D. Wise 1973; Gravel 1971, vol. 3; *New York Times* 1971).

Far from being an innocent victim, the *Maddox* had been probing North Vietnamese radar defenses by electronically simulating U.S. attacks, near where U.S.-directed South Vietnamese forces were raiding the North (as part of ongoing harassment and sabotage under Operation Plan 34A) at about the same time. Indeed, the circumstances suggest— though the Pentagon historian denies—that one purpose of missions like the *Maddox*'s may actually have been to provoke an incident. The administration had made contingency plans for striking at North Vietnam and had prepared a draft congressional resolution for introduction at the appropriate moment (*New York Times* 1971, pp. 234–306).

The Tonkin incident, like Pearl Harbor, the Truman Doctrine, and the start of the Korean War, proved to be a crucial event for opinion and for policy. After Tonkin, the administration quietly prepared for sustained air attacks on North Vietnam but delayed action until President Johnson had been reelected. In February 1965, it seized upon guerrilla attacks on the U.S. bases at Pleiku and Qui Nhon as occasions for "retaliatory" air strikes on the North, which were quickly transformed into operation Rolling Thunder, the multiyear, massive strategic bombing program (*New York Times,* 1971, pp. 307–381; Herring 1979, pp. 128–130, 133. One administration official is said to have remarked that "Pleiku's are like streetcars"—pretexts for escalation come by all the time). The State Department issued a "white paper" that used flimsy evidence to argue that the "Viet Cong" (National Liberation Front) movement in South Vietnam represented "aggression" from the North, ignoring the NLF's indigenous support and the temporary nature of the North-South border under the Geneva accords. Gradually, with little publicity, U.S. ground troops were sent to Vietnam in growing numbers and with increasingly active missions (Herring 1979 gives a good basic history of the war).

Some opposition arose in the Senate; Lippmann and Reston and a few other commentators complained; the first protest "teach-ins" were held; and after President Johnson told wild stories to justify U.S. intervention in the Dominican Republic in April 1965, reporters began to write of a "credibility gap" (Wise 1973, pp. 32, 59–61), with increasing reference to Vietnam. But for the most part the mass media and the American public accepted the official argument that communism would have to be stopped in Vietnam or dominoes would fall throughout Southeast Asia and perhaps beyond. Indeed, Joseph Alsop and *Time* magazine and other voices urged stronger action. (See Hallin 1986, a thorough study analyzing 1961–1965 *New York Times* coverage and 1965–1973 TV news, which largely confirms the early work of Lawrence Lichty and refutes the myth of "oppositional media" with respect to Vietnam.)

In an April 7, 1965, speech at Johns Hopkins, President Johnson (without acknowledging the extent of U.S. escalation) tried to account for what was happening: North Vietnam, urged on by "the deepening shadow of Communist China," had "attacked the independent nation of South Viet Nam"; the United States had to resist because "the appetite of aggression is never satisfied." But he said he "remain(ed)" ready for "unconditional discussions" and would provide a billion dollars for Southeast Asian economic development. News reports and editorials were heavily favorable. (See Turner 1985, pp. 111–133. Turner's account of Johnson's unhappy relations with the press, while straining to sympathize with the president and the war, documents many instances of secretiveness and deception.)

Johnson had substantial success at winning public support for the war. Just before the Johns Hopkins speech (interviews April 2–7), Gallup found that 42% of the public favored stepping up the U.S. military effort or going "all out" in Vietnam; only 23% wanted to withdraw completely. (19% favored what was described as the present policy, military action plus readiness to negotiate.) The next month, after Johnson's speech—and after other events including decisions to send 40,000 ground troops to "enclaves," congressional authorization of $700 million to support them, and a five-day "pause" in bombing North Vietnam—the 42% pro-escalation figure declined sharply, to 30%, with 10% more supporting the present policy—a crucial part of which was taken to be pursuit of negotiations.[5] After still another month, when no peace talks occurred (the NLF called the bombing pause a "worn out trick of deceit and threat": Herring 1979, p. 135), pro-escalation opinion rose 7%. In July, Johnson made the fateful decision to send 50,000 more troops to Vietnam immediately, with 50,000 more to go by the end of the year, and an implicit open-ended commitment of whatever troop levels it would take in the future (Herring 1979, p. 139).

The first negative TV news and documentaries on Vietnam (most notably CBS's August 5, 1965, film of marines using cigarette lighters to set fire to Cam Ne village) were a drop in the bucket; from 1965 into 1967 and even later, most TV news stories praised the difficult, courageous work of "American boys" in action, brave ground troops and hotshot jet pilots combating the "Reds" who were guilty of "terrorism" and "irrational murder" (Hallin 1986, pp. 114–158). Opinion moved in a hawkish direction. Between August and October/November (conflicting dates are given)

1965, Gallup polls found a 13% increase, to 60%, in the proportion of the public "inclined" to vote for a congressional candidate who "advocated sending a great many more men" to Vietnam. Gallup also reported an increase in the already solid majority agreeing that we should have "become involved with our military forces in Southeast Asia": the 64% of January 1965 edged up to 67% by April and reached a full 75% in October 1965.

Nor did Senator Fulbright's early 1966 Vietnam hearings turn the public (or the Senate) around. The thirty-seven day bombing pause and "peace offensive" that began on Christmas Eve 1965, with American officials touring the capitals of the world professing U.S. eagerness for peace—a tactic at least partly designed to prepare the public for further escalation (Herring 1986, pp. 165–166)—played well at home; it was presented on TV as a morality play in which "our" peace seekers were willing to "negotiate anything" (not mentioning the crucial exception, political control of Vietnam), but were thwarted by the "stubborn defiance" of the North Vietnamese. The hawkish opinion movement continued. Between December 1965 and April 1966, 15% more Americans in Harris surveys, for a weighty total of 75%, said they thought the administration was "wrong" in *not* blockading North Vietnamese ports. There were increases between 1966 and 1967 in the proportion of the public that wanted to "win" in Vietnam (a 6% rise to just over 45%, as vs. the total of 55% favoring three more pacific options: Harris), and in the proportion willing to reduce programs at home in order to pay for the war (a 7% rise, to 44%: also Harris). (The latter figure dropped substantially, to 27%, by January 1968. At no time did a majority of Americans favor making big domestic sacrifices for the war in Vietnam.) In May 1967, according to Harris, 59% supported invading North Vietnam.

By the time the war was in full swing, then, with several hundred thousand American troops committed in 1966 and 1967, large portions of the public favored forceful policies. This represented a rational response to reported events (some staged or exploited by the administration, to be sure) and to the prevailing interpretations given by officials and the media: that the "free" South Vietnamese were under attack by North Vietnamese Communists, who refused to talk peace and threatened to conquer all Southeast Asia. At the same time, the public made a number of reasonable distinctions: most Americans favored the use of U.S. money and weapons rather than troops, when possible; the vast majority rejected facile use of nuclear weapons (in 1965 and 1966 Harris surveys only 17% said the administration was wrong not to use such weapons); large majorities insisted on efforts to negotiate a settlement; and few thought the war worth major domestic sacrifices.

Disillusionment

Gradually it became apparent that victory would not be cheap or easy, and the public reacted accordingly. The U.S. casualties mounted until as many as 100 men a week were being killed, with casualty counts displayed on TV news every Thursday along with pictures of dead American soldiers going home in body bags. There were occasional scenes of the burning and maiming of Vietnamese civilians and the destruction of their villages. Harrison Salisbury's reports from Hanoi at the beginning of 1967 highlighted civilian casualties in bombing the North. Reports of political turmoil and corruption in South Vietnam soured many Americans' views of their allies. The NLF and the North Vietnamese did not give up despite frequent announcements of progress at the "five o'clock follies," the Saigon news briefings.

Antiwar protests were usually portrayed in the media as extreme, violent, and deviant—Gitlin (1980) shows how protesters adapted to the fact that only dramatic actions got any attention—and as giving aid and comfort to the enemy. Chet Huntley alluded to Hanoi's "paroxysms of joy" about demonstrations. Reports of protests made the public angry, but they also drew attention to Vietnam and raised the domestic costs of the war. Later portrayals of protesters "working within the system," like the "earnest, clean-shaven" youths campaigning for Eugene McCarthy in the 1968 New Hampshire primary, may even have won a measure of legitimacy for dissent.

More and more Americans began to see the war as a "mistake" in which the United States should never have gotten involved (see figure 6.1). As with Korea some fifteen years before, the proportion of "mistake" responses rose fairly regularly in proportion to the cumulative magnitude of U.S. casualties (Mueller 1973) as well as the increasing dollar costs and disruptive demonstrations at home. The popularity of President Johnson dropped calamitously, largely in response to bad news from Vietnam (Brody and Page 1975).

By no means, however, did all opposition to the war take the form of favoring immediate withdrawal. A large portion of the public wanted to "win the war in Vietnam pretty soon or get out": 65% in July 1966, according to Harris, dipping to 59% in September 1966 and edging back to 64% in October. Many were willing to use maximum force to gain victory; about one quarter favored nuclear weapons (see Simon 1974, p. 181). (As figure 6.1 indicates, even in 1969–1971, when sentiment for withdrawal had risen markedly, the public distinguished sharply between "immediate" withdrawal—favored by only a minority—and "continu-

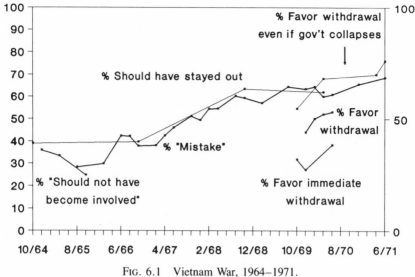

FIG. 6.1   Vietnam War, 1964–1971.

ing" troop withdrawals even if the South Vietnamese government collapsed—which large majorities favored.)

Around the middle of 1967, the public began to get a few hints of disagreements within the administration. Secretary of Defense Mac-Namara was becoming skeptical about the war and resisting General Westmoreland's requests for more troops. Some businessmen and bankers and elite publications began to have doubts. In October and November 1967, as large North Vietnamese forces began to fight fixed battles with U.S. soldiers at Con Thien and Dak To and then (in January 1968) at Khe Sanh, American casualties mounted and troop morale dropped. Reporters and weary soldiers began to ask whether it was worth the cost (Hallin 1986, pp. 159–210).

Such sentiments were reflected in Harris surveys of May 1967 and March 1968 that showed only between 21% and 24% wanting to fight on to an eventual total victory, and in surveys showing a 9% increase, from May to August (mostly after July) 1967, in the proportion wanting to try to "end the war and get out as quickly as possible," which reached 36% in August. (It climbed further to 43% by March 1968, after the Tet offensive.) Some of these poll results were featured in the *Washington Post* on August 28 and November 13, 1967, under the headlines "Public Support for War Decreases," and "Public Confidence in President Plunges to All-Time Low of 23%."

Then the Tet offensive, which began at the very end of January 1968 with coordinated NLF and North Vietnamese attacks throughout South

Vietnam and even an assault on the U.S. embassy in Saigon, deeply shocked the American public. Televised scenes of urban destruction and bloody corpses, of U.S. soldiers destroying Ben Tre village "in order to save it," of General Loan on a Saigon street shooting a helpless prisoner in the head, of marines bogged down fighting through the rubble of Hue, and of the seventy-seven day siege of Khe Sanh, where CBS reported "no end in sight," and reporters invoked Dien Bien Phu analogies; all this helped transform the public's view of the war. True, as Braestrup (1976) exhaustively argues, the purely military outcome was not the complete disaster that some media reports implied; North Vietnamese casualties were heavy, and NLF cadres were devastated. (There are, however, many errors and exaggerations in Braestrup, and a marked divergence between the generalizations and the specific documentation: Chomsky 1978; Herman and Chomsky 1988, pp. 211–228 and appendix 3.) But the unmistakable lesson of Tet came through: a U.S. victory, if possible at all, was going to be very costly. Claims of steady progress, based partly on inflated body counts, seemed ridiculous. The "light at the end of the tunnel" looked very dim.

The public's initial reaction to the Tet offensive was, understandably, belligerent, but—upon reflection—opinion moved against the war. The proportion of Americans labeling themselves "hawks" in Gallup polls rose 13% between December 1967 and early February 1968. As the offensive went on through February and the news about it was digested, however, and as commentators and politicians and government officials began to suggest the war should be ended, the proportion of self-declared hawks dropped sharply, down 5% by late February and down a total of 22% (from the early February high) in April, to a bare majority 51%. It dropped a further 15%, to only 36%, by the end of 1969. This Tet-induced drop in the proportion of hawks, as we saw earlier (Chap. 2, figure 2.3), is one of the largest, most abrupt opinion changes in our data.

Many businessmen and bankers and professionals, and several elite publications like the *New York Times* and the *Wall Street Journal,* turned against the war as hopeless, too costly, disruptive, and a cause of inflation and gold outflows. Walter Cronkite returned from Vietnam and declared on TV (February 27) that we were "mired in stalemate"; only serious negotiations could end the war. Eugene McCarthy and then (after McCarthy's strong showing March 12 in New Hampshire) Robert Kennedy challenged Johnson for the presidency on an antiwar platform. The administration itself was in disarray. Defense Secretary Clifford, like McNamara before him, turned skeptical about the war and resisted the military's request for 206,000 more troops; the committee of "Wise

Men" (headed by Dean Acheson and heavily representative of past foreign policy officials, investment bankers, and lawyers) concluded the war wasn't worth the cost. March 31, on live nationwide television, President Johnson declared a partial bombing halt, called for negotiations, and withdrew as a candidate for reelection. Suddenly all the talk was of peace, not victory. As we noted above, the proportion of the public wanting the United States to "get out as quickly as possible" from Vietnam rose from 36% to 43% between May 1967 and March 1968 (Harris). Between February and June 1968, ORC surveys found a sharp drop (from 40% to 20%) in support for increasing U.S. troop commitments in Vietnam. (Related data are reported in Brody, Page, Verba, and Laulicht 1969.)

Predominant opinion, however, still opposed immediate withdrawal. Most Americans, along with the newly antiwar businessmen and media, favored policies something like the Johnson administration's partial halt to bombing North Vietnam—while still heavily bombing the South—in April 1968, the more complete halt in bombing the North in November, and the gradual troop withdrawals by the new Nixon administration beginning in mid-1969 (see Page and Brody 1972). Even long before Tet there had been very strong support for "Vietnamization," replacing U.S. troops with South Vietnamese. In a November 1966 Gallup poll, 71% favored training ARVN troops and withdrawing American soldiers; this rose to 73% for Vietnamization in early April 1967 and 77% in late February 1968.

Withdrawal

The Nixon administration pursued a two-track policy on the war, with a public track and a private one. Early in 1969 it secretly ordered heavy B-52 carpet bombing of Cambodia and increased the bombardment of and raids into Laos. Later in the year it began secret peace talks, but—frustrated by North Vietnam's refusal to negotiate withdrawal from the South—it planned, as a threat, Operation Duck Hook, a "savage, decisive blow" that would include bombing Hanoi and Haiphong, destroying dikes and harbors and rail lines, and invading the North (Hersh 1983, chaps. 4, 5, 10; Shawcross 1979). Meanwhile, in public, the administration pursued open but fruitless peace negotiations, reduced U.S. troop activity (after taking heavy casualties in battles like that for "Hamburger Hill" in May 1969), and—in June, under the rubric of "Vietnamization"—announced the first unilateral withdrawals of U.S. troops, which were continued in September and in subsequent months and years.

As the war dragged on, however, with slow troop withdrawals and no peace agreement, pressure grew to end the fighting quickly. Antiwar demonstrations resumed in the autumn of 1969. Congressmen criticized the secret new B-52 bombings of Laos that were revealed in February 1970. The U.S. "incursion" into Cambodia at the end of April led to angry protests on college campuses (with demonstrators killed at Kent State and Jackson State) and to various antiwar moves, including the Cooper-Church amendment and the McGovern-Hatfield proposal, in Congress. From Tet on, media reports about drugs, racial conflicts, and disobedience among American soldiers (even "fraggings"—killings of officers with fragmentation grenades) increased, and stories about atrocities by U.S. troops (most notably those at My Lai, first reported in November 1969) began to appear. The South Vietnamese were increasingly depicted in the media as taking over the burden of the war but also as incompetent, corrupt, and divided among themselves (Hallin 1986, pp. 159–210).

Given the dismal state of the war, many Americans came to favor rapid troop withdrawals. Between the SRC/CPS preelection survey of autumn 1968 and the postelection survey of 1970 (completed in January 1971, before the disastrous February "Lam Son 719" South Vietnamese invasion of Laos), there was a 15% increase, to 37%, in the proportion wanting to pull out entirely from Vietnam. Between the *post*election 1968 (interviews November 6–February 24, 1969)[6] and postelection 1970 SRC/CPS surveys, the proportion of people locating themselves at the extreme "immediate withdrawal" end of a seven-point scale rose by 8%. Between November 1969 and the beginning of February 1970—that is, between a poll following a successful Nixon speech and then one taken during congressional protests against the B-52 bombings of Laos—Gallup found a dramatic 14% rise, from 22% to 36%, in the proportion favoring the position of some senators "that we should withdraw all our troops from Vietnam immediately." And the proportion of people choosing withdrawal (immediately or by a varying deadline approximately one year away) from among four Vietnam policy options went up 8%, to 52%, between the Gallup polls of December 1969 and May 1970, during the Cambodia incursion. (It stayed at 53% in August 1970.)

Similarly, according to Harris, the proportion of Americans that favored continuing U.S. withdrawal, even if the South Vietnamese government collapsed, rose 13% (to a full 67%) between October 1969 and April 1970, and continued rising to 70% by April 1971 and to 76% by July 1971 (see figure 6.1). Approval of heavy bombing dropped 12% between the beginning of September and October 1972, to a meager majority of 51% (Harris), perhaps in reaction to George McGovern's antiwar presidential campaign, to protests against the current bombing of North Vietnam, and to Kissinger's indications that peace was "at hand." At the same time, though, the idea of a coalition government that would include the Communists never gained much popularity; as late as July 1969, 65% opposed it, although this dropped to a still high 59% by October (Harris). At the end of 1969 most people (57% in December, according to Harris, up 7% since October) still wanted to "keep communism from dominating Southeast Asia."

Substantial and growing majorities favored continuing troop withdrawals—59% in October 1969, according to a different Harris item than mentioned above, rising to 71% in July 1970. Still, not even half (49% in October 1969, and 43% in December: Harris) thought we should get out because the war was "wrong." Only with hindsight (and on into the 1980s and 1990s) did large majorities come to believe the war had been morally wrong, not just a "mistake." (At the end of 1986, for example, 71% of ordinary Americans with opinions—as contrasted with only 43% of a sample of foreign policy leaders—agreed that the war was "fundamentally wrong and immoral": Rielley 1987, p. 37. In the 1990 CCFR survey, 74% of those with opinions agreed.)

These opinion changes again related to events, but they did not necessarily represent unmediated responses to the war itself; various persuasive influences were at work. While Nixon and Kissinger were arguing that only an "honorable" end to the war (preserving the Thieu regime) would be acceptable, many commentators and political figures (as well as internationally oriented businessmen who were worried about the declining gold stock and pressure on the dollar—especially after summer 1971) urged faster withdrawals regardless of Thieu's fate. Dissent, within certain limits, was treated as legitimate.

The effects of demonstrations are a more complicated matter. Our analysis of media impact on policy preferences, in Chapter 8, indicates that protestors—who were usually portrayed unfavorably in the media and were very unpopular with the public (Robinson 1970)—did not have an immediately positive impact on opinion; they probably had a negative effect in the short run. Thus Harris found a significant 6% *drop* in the proportion of the public that said the war was "morally wrong" and that we should get out (as many protestors asserted), between October and December 1969, after the massive October 15 "Moratorium" (which Cronkite called "dignified" and "responsible"), and after Nixon's November 3 "silent majority" speech and Vice-President Agnew's assault on the press. But the protests apparently had a direct effect on policy, aborting the "Duck Hook" escalation plan in the fall of 1969 and forcing reliance on Vietnamization, for example, and cutting short the Cambodia incursion in June 1970 (Hersh 1983, chaps. 10, 16). And, as we have noted, the indirect and long-term effects of protests were to maintain the salience of the war and to raise doubts and increase its domestic costs, helping to move opinion against the war (see Burstein and Freudenburg 1978). Moreover, some young antiwar protestors undoubtedly influenced their parents, including certain key journalists and policymakers.

Public Opinion and Policy

On the issue of U.S. troop withdrawals from Vietnam we have been able to do a statistical study exploring reciprocal relationships, over time, between public opinion and public policy, in order to discover whether and how opinion and policy affected each other. The results, consistent with findings on many other issues reported elsewhere (Page and Shapiro 1983; Farkas, Shapiro, and Page 1990), indicate that public opinion had a substantial impact on the rate of troop withdrawals. Actual withdrawal rates, in turn, may have affected opinion.

Beginning in April 1969, the Nixon administration withdrew troops from Vietnam at an average rate of about 13,000 per month: exactly the right pace, if continued steadily, so that the last U.S. troops would leave in March 1973, shortly after the 1972 election. (Conceivably, this was the "secret plan" to which Nixon alluded in his 1968 campaign—to complete the withdrawal and let the South Vietnamese government collapse only after he was safely reelected. Or perhaps Nixon originally hoped to emulate Eisenhower's quick ending of the Korean War by making nuclear threats or by applying pressure through the Soviet Union and China, and only later settled for unilateral withdrawal with a last-minute face-saving agreement.) But, in any case, the administration never publicized a comprehensive withdrawal timetable; in fact, Nixon obscured it by announcing large troop withdrawals at irregular intervals, covering several months at a time. The actual rate of withdrawal also varied considerably from month to month.

During Nixon's first term, many survey questions were asked about whether troop withdrawals were proceeding too fast or too slowly or about right. As one would expect of reactions to such questions with shifting referents (i.e., to questions which at different times implicitly referred to different current rates of withdrawal), there were some rapid changes in expressed opinions when the current situation changed. These changes were superimposed on a general trend toward favoring faster withdrawals. Harris surveys indicated, for example, 6% fewer saying

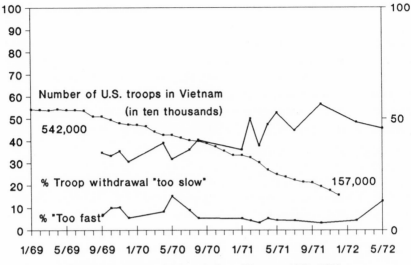

FIG. 6.2   Troop withdrawals from Vietnam, 1969–1972.

withdrawals were "too fast" in July than in May 1970; 10% more saying "too slow" in April than in March 1971; 6% more saying "too slow" (for a total of 56%) in October than in February 1971; but 9% more saying "too fast" in May than in February 1972 (see figure 6.2).

The opinion changes mentioned above are based on repeated questions with identical wording. Unfortunately, however (and contrary to the implication of two misleading press releases dated November 8, 1971, and March 13, 1972), not all of Harris's survey questions about troop withdrawals were identical. They differed in wording in at least ten minor but annoying ways, sometimes referring to "the President," for example, and sometimes to "Nixon"; sometimes mentioning "from Vietnam" and sometimes not; sometimes switching the order of response options. Indeed, despite our best efforts, we may not have spotted all the variations. Still, these slightly varying Harris questions, asked at some seventeen different times (in twelve separate months), are numerous enough and similar enough to produce meaningful results from a time series analysis.[7]

Using an official source on the once secret monthly levels of U.S. troops in Vietnam (U.S. Department of Defense 1972), we calculated the monthly *changes* in troop levels, from October 1969 through December 1971, and regressed them on public opinion variables, using various time lags. The proportion of respondents saying that withdrawals were "too slow" at a given time proved to be a moderately strong predictor of the actual withdrawal rate one month later. That is, an additional 1% of people saying withdrawal was "too slow" tended to be followed one month later by withdrawal of about 488 extra men for the month ($b= -.488$, $r= -.43$, $p < .20$). Thus changes in public opinion apparently had a distinct impact on policy, in this as in many other cases based on similar time series data (see Farkas et al. 1990; see also Page and Shapiro 1983).

Of course, one should be cautious about interpreting this connection between opinion and policy as exemplifying democratic control of government, not only because the coefficient is only moderately large and only marginally significant but also because a growing preponderance of the public throughout this period favored withdrawing troops faster than was actually being done. By late October 1971, in fact, Harris found that fully 53% more Americans said the pace was "too slow" (56%) than said it was "too fast" (3%). In Achen's (1978) term, there may have been policy "responsiveness" to changes in public opinion, without much representation in the sense of congruence or correspondence between policy and the *level* of preferences.

There are also indications of a reciprocal relationship. Public opinion appears to have reacted somewhat—though much less strongly—to the actual rates of troop withdrawal. The more troops were withdrawn in a given month, the fewer "too slow" responses the public gave the next month. To put it more precisely, our data indicate that "too slow" responses declined by about one-quarter of 1% for every 1,000 additional troops withdrawn the previous month ($b= .234$; $r=.24$ n.s.). This estimated effect is very small and not statistically significant, however, perhaps partly for methodological reasons (question wording variations and the usual sampling errors in the survey-measured dependent variable as well as the paucity of cases), but mostly for reasons of substance. Since withdrawal figures were not announced regularly, the public could not easily tell exactly how many troops came out in a given month. Citizens can hardly be expected to react with precision to events that are kept secret. Nonetheless, enough cues about rates of change in troop levels were apparently available so that public opinion could respond somewhat—in a quite reasonable fashion—to the objective magnitude of troop withdrawals. The faster troops came out of Vietnam, the less urgency was felt to speed up the rate of withdrawal (see Weissberg 1976, Chap. 5).

Effects of Vietnam

After last-minute hitches in the peace talks and a final fierce Christmas bombing of North Vietnam, the Paris peace agreement of January 27, 1973, provided for a ceasefire. The collapse of Saigon was delayed for a "decent interval" (Snepp 1977), until 1975. But the agonizing experience of the Vietnam war, including the indelible final scene of South Vietnamese fighting to climb aboard departing U.S. helicopters, left its mark on a wide range of public attitudes about foreign policy. Ordinary Americans were not eager for further adventures abroad. They, like businessmen preoccupied with the strength of the dollar and with deficits and inflation, turned away from interventionist foreign policies, at least for a few years.

The balance of opinion strongly favored spending less on the military, for example. In wartime July 1969, according to Gallup, 57% of the public said we were spending "too much" on defense, far more than the 9% saying "too little." In February 1973, responding to a different NORC-GSS question, 40% said we were spending too much, with only 12% saying too little. (As we will see, this opposition to defense spending decreased once the Vietnam war receded into history and a new Cold War began.)

Moreover, opposition to spending money on foreign aid—now linked in people's minds with the danger of Vietnam-style entanglements—stood at a very high level. This is true in absolute terms and also as compared with the support for the Marshall Plan after World War II and even for aid to "backward" countries in the 1950s. An October 1971 Roper survey found that a heavy majority, 80%, said the United States was spending too much on foreign aid, a majority that edged up even a bit more by December 1973 (see also Chap. 2 and figure 2.2.)

Similarly, between the 1969–1970 period and February 1973, the proportions of Americans willing to use U.S. troops to defend against a hypothetical "danger of Communist takeover" in various places around the world—including West Berlin, Brazil, Thailand, and Japan—dropped by as much as twenty to thirty percentage points in Harris surveys. (Only support for defending Israel did not decline, but it already stood at a low 35% level in 1970.) The impact of Vietnam is evident in the fact that the sharpest drops concerned Asia (Japan and Thailand, above) and that the biggest of all was a 37% decline—to 30%—in willingness to defend South Korea. Of Harris's whole list of fifteen places, a majority in 1973 favored defending only Canada, England, and the Panama Canal Zone (see table 6.1). Clear distinctions based on cultural and geographical proximity and perceived interests are evident in the table. These multiple questions, asked at the same time with an identical format (like the spending and abortion questions graphed in Chap. 2), permit an unusually full display of the public's capacity to make distinctions among related policies.

The survey that Harris conducted for the Chicago Council on For-

TABLE 6.1 Willingness to Send U.S. Troops to Fight Abroad,
1969–1973

"Suppose there were a danger of a Communist takeover of —————, would you favor
or oppose U.S. military involvement, including the use of U.S. troops?"

	1969 (%)	1970 (%)	1973 (%)	Change (%)
Canada		87	73	−14
Panama Canal Zone			66	
England			60	
Western Europe		60	49	−11
Australia		58	46	−12
West Berlin	66		46	−20
Brazil	63		40	−23
Japan	65		37	−28
Israel		36	37	+2
Formosa (Taiwan)	51		33	−18
Greece			32	
South Korea	67		30	−37
Iran			29	
Thailand	51		28	−23
India	40		27	−13

Source: Data reported in *The Harris Survey*, Release, March 26, 1973, and *The Harris Survey
Yearbook* (1973, p. 241).

eign Relations at the end of 1974 likewise revealed broad public
opposition to using U.S. troops abroad. Not only did large majorities of
those with opinions oppose military responses to hypothetical threats
involving Vietnam, Yugoslavia, Formosa, Japan, India, and South Korea,
but they resisted intervention if Israel were being defeated by the Arabs,
if Cuba invaded the Dominican Republic, and even if the Russians took
over West Berlin or (by a narrower margin) if Western Europe were
invaded. In this survey, only a hypothetical invasion of Canada elicited
majority public support for U.S. military action (see Rielly 1975, p. 18).[8]

Some have charged that the public's increased resistance to military
intervention represented a craven "neo-isolationism," an overreaction to
Vietnam. We are more inclined to see it as a sensible response to disaster
and as a reasonable note of caution, particularly when one remembers that
the public would have a second chance to react after any real threat
occurred; answers to these hypothetical survey questions warned politicians not to stir up trouble abroad, but did not necessarily reflect a fixed
determination never again to fight outside North America. In any case,

the general trend of opinion is well summarized by the solid 16% increase from 17% to 37%, between June 1965 and April 1975 NORC surveys, in the proportion of Americans saying we should stay out of world affairs rather than "take an active part" (see figure 5.1). The 8% rise in antiactivist responses between the 1972 and 1976 SRC/CPS election studies also captures a part of the same movement.

The Vietnam case illustrates a number of points about public opinion. We have described numerous rational public reactions to reported events, for example. Some of those events (especially the Tonkin incident) involved official deception and manipulation of opinion. But opinion also moved slowly and powerfully against the war, in response to rising costs and failed objectives, despite official optimism; and the public drew enduring lessons from Vietnam quite at variance with what official Washington wished. Furthermore, the impact of public opinion upon troop withdrawal rates—and very likely upon the decision to end the war itself—was striking. The evidence suggests that public opinion was sometimes manipulated but sometimes relatively autonomous; sometimes led by the government but sometimes influential in affecting government policy.

The strong post-Vietnam shift against military and other involvement abroad was reversed only after a lengthy and intense publicity campaign alleging that the Soviet Union was engaged in a massive arms buildup and aggressive foreign policy actions. We will discuss that reversal after first turning to opinion trends concerning China and then the Middle East.

China

The case of U.S. relations with the People's Republic of China (PRC) offers further examples of how public opinion reacts to international events and how elites' interpretations can affect the public's reactions. But it is most notable for a gradual, inexorable, more than two-decade-long movement of public opinion toward favoring more friendly relations; a movement that proceeded with considerable independence from government policy and that apparently had an important impact on policy.

The huge and mysterious Middle Kingdom, China, has long fascinated Americans and won a warm but ill-informed (and, therefore, fragile) measure of friendship. United States "open door" diplomacy at the end of the nineteenth century was designed to gain access to the enormous Chinese markets, especially for textile manufacturers. American businesses, including Standard Oil, supported the Nationalist revolution of Sun Yat Sen and Chiang Kai-shek (Schirmer 1972). The Nationalists strengthened their U.S. ties through American missionaries and their children (including Walter Judd), through favorable publicity from such Sinophiles as Henry Luce, and through the formal World War II alliance against Japan.

Before and during the war, Mao Zedong's Communist cadres won some favorable U.S. attention as "agrarian reformers" (a misleading label, evocative of American Populists), as opponents of what came to be seen as Chiang's corrupt and repressive regime, and (unlike Chiang) as stout fighters against the Japanese occupation. After the war, however, when the Communists pursued their revolution and fought against Chiang, Cold War anti-Communist attitudes were eventually brought to bear on them as part of what the U.S. government and media portrayed as a monolithic international Communist conspiracy.

By 1948 the American public had little faith in Chiang and little desire to help him. A February 1948 NORC survey, for example, found that only 35% of Americans favored sending military supplies to the Nationalist government. This figure temporarily jumped 12% higher the next month, after the coup in Czechoslovakia and the death of Masaryk heightened Americans' concerns about communism. Over the next few months, however, the Nationalists' cause collapsed; they lost nearly half their troops through defection, and most (about 80%) of their American equipment was captured. The Communists emerged victorious, taking Peking in January 1949 and Shanghai in May. According to a different NORC item, Americans' support for sending military supplies to the Nationalists dropped sharply—by 18%—between April 1948 and June 1949, as Truman moved to terminate aid (see Kusnitz 1984, pp. 153–156).

Despite the U.S. "White Paper" of August 1949 that blamed the Nationalists' defeat on their own inherent weaknesses, and President Truman's January 1950 statement of disengagement from Formosa, China-oriented Republican politicians like Senator William Knowland charged that the Democrats had "lost" China, and continued to push for aid to Chiang's remnants on Taiwan. After Chinese Communist overtures to the United States were rejected, the American consulate in Peking was attacked (January 14, 1950) and the PRC signed a treaty with the Soviet Union (February 1950). The administration spoke out harshly against the People's Republic: Secretary of State Dean Acheson declared in one speech that the Communist leaders were "completely subservient" to Stalin's every whim, and, in another, that China was becoming a "mere dependency" in the Soviet orbit. This misleading rhetoric was apparently intended to goad the Chinese into greater independence (Kusnitz 1984, p. 26), but its chief effect—when taken up and amplified by numerous editors and commentators—was to increase Americans' hostility toward the PRC.

The Korean War, understandably, played a crucial part in solidifying public opposition to the Chinese Communists and reviving support for the Nationalists. As part of its response to the North Korean attack on the South in June 1950, the Truman administration interposed the U.S. Seventh Fleet between Taiwan and mainland China—effectively protecting the Nationalists—and slowly moved toward resuming military aid to Chiang. The massive Chinese intervention in Korea in November 1950, after U.S. troops neared China's Yalu River border, brought U.S. and Chinese soldiers into combat against each other. President Truman raised the possibility of using atomic weapons. The *New York Times* commented that the Chinese could hardly expect to "shoot their way into" the United Nations, a phrase that echoed through the 1950s. As the war continued, Dean Rusk spoke of the Chinese as Soviet puppets; John Foster Dulles called Mao's regime "a creature of the Moscow Politburo"; and Truman referred to the capture of the Chinese people by a "clique of ruthless Communist fanatics" (Kusnitz 1984, p. 53). Others outside the administration were even more vitriolic. The U.S. media followed suit.

Given these interpretations and the fact of war, the public reacted in a reasonable fashion by favoring aid to Chiang and action against the Peoples Republic. In April 1951, NORC found that a large majority of Americans—69% of those with opinions—favored "giving the Chinese Nationalist government under Chaing Kai-shek all the help it needs to attack the Communists on the mainland of China." This support remained strikingly stable over the next year: 67% in May 1951; 71% in August; and 67% in March 1952. During the Korean War, as we have seen, large numbers of Americans (urged on by Senator Knowland, General MacArthur, and others) also favored bombing supply bases in China: 64% did so in August 1951 and 9% more in October, according to NORC. The proportion in favor of bombing dropped 11% by August 1952, however, as the war continued to be stalemated around the 38th Parallel, the prewar boundary.

Shortly after the Korean armistice in 1953, when one might have expected relations with China to begin to thaw, Representative Walter Judd's Committee for (later "of") One Million against the Admission of Communist China to the United Nations got organized, apparently in a closed session of Judd's congressional subcommittee on the Far East. It became a major factor in policy-making, though its effects on public opinion are considerably less clear. The committee, with close ties to Chiang's diplomats in Washington, boasting bipartisan congressional support (notably including liberal Democratic Senator Paul Douglas), and energized by the hyperkinetic PR man Marvin Liebman, circulated petitions and claimed one million signatures by July 1954 (Bachrack 1976; Koen 1974 [1960]).

The Committee of One Million stimulated letters and speeches and testimony arguing that China should not be allowed to "shoot its way into the U.N." or to gain recognition or trade from the United States. Each autumn, before the U.N. General Assembly met in New York, the committee would publish a full-page newspaper advertisement "declaration" against the admission of China, endorsed by a majority of members of the U.S. Congress. Other committee ads characterized China as an "aggressor" nation and opposed "appeasement" (April 1955), accused Peking of involvement in international narcotics smuggling (August 1955), and appealed for "No Trade with the Enemy" (June 1957) (Bachrack 1976, pp. 110, 121, 136).

Neither U.N. admission nor U.S. recognition of China had been favored by the public before the Korean War; both were very unpopular after it. According to one July 1954 Gallup survey, for example, an overwhelming 92% of Americans opposed admission to the United Nations. In August 1955, Gallup found a solid 63% saying the United States should not "go along" with a decision to admit China even if a majority of U.N. members was willing. (According to a March 1954 NORC survey, however, only 25% explicitly advocated U.S. withdrawal from the organization if China were admitted.) The Korean War, with tales of mass attacks by allegedly doped-up Chinese troops firing automatic weapons and blowing bugles, had left bitter memories.

The Eisenhower administration moved in small ways toward accommodation with China but kept up the hostile rhetoric. Secretary of State Dulles, for example, in March and April 1954, alluded to the "incompetence and heartlessness and ruthlessness" of the Chinese government that was going to cause "millions" to die of starvation, and charged that it had stepped up its support of "aggression" in Indochina by its "puppet" Ho Chi Minh. In March 1955 Dulles compared the "aggressive fanaticism" of the Chinese leaders to that of Hitler (Kusnitz 1984, pp. 65, 89).

Toward Accommodation

Despite the hostile talk from the Eisenhower administration and the Committee of One Million, however, the American public very gradually moved toward accommodation and reconciliation with the People's Re-

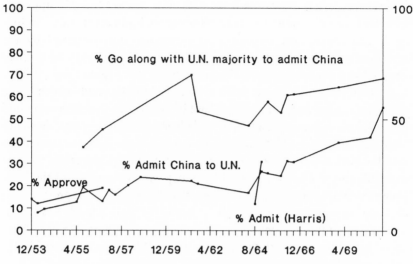

FIG. 6.3   Admission of China to the United Nations, 1953–1971.

public of China. From the mid-1950s onward until the end of the 1980s, the main trend in public preferences about U.S.-Chinese relations was a slow, uneven, but inexorable increase in desires for rapprochement.

There were ups and downs: rises with the Chinese "peace offensive" and the Geneva conference of 1954 and with the Bandung conference of 1955; setbacks with the offshore islands crises of 1954–1955 and 1958, the Kennedy administration's hostility, and the 1966–1969 Cultural Revolution; and a sharp jump with China's 1964 emergence as a nuclear power. But long *before* Richard Nixon's 1971–1972 opening to China, the U.S. public had moved quite a way toward friendliness. The effects of some specific events and also the long-term cumulative trend from 1953 to 1971 are clear in figure 6.3, which charts responses to survey questions concerning admission of China to the United Nations.

This graph makes clear that a much higher (about 30% higher) proportion of the public consistently favored "going along" with a decision to admit China than thought China "should" be admitted or "approv(ed)" admission. This is a sensible distinction. Many people who supported the United Nations, but preferred to keep China out, were presumably unwilling to engage in a divisive battle over the issue or to quit the organization if China entered.

Some of the opinion changes on this issue were large. As we noted above, for example, in July 1954, even after the Geneva conference, only 8% of Americans told Gallup that China should be admitted to the United

Nations; by August 1958 this had risen to 24%. Support for admission rose by 16% between February 1957 and March 1966—with a small intervening drop of 7% between August 1958 and January 1964, presumably due to Cold War tensions and Kennedy administration opposition. Opinion in favor of admission increased by a remarkable 38% between the first week of February 1964 (17% in favor) and May 1971 (55%). Within this same period, Harris surveys pinpointed an abrupt 19% jump between June and November 1964, after the mid-October Chinese atomic bomb test; Gallup registered a 10% rise between February and November. By May 1971, amid publicity about "ping-pong diplomacy" and Nixon's and Kissinger's China opening, Gallup found that more Americans favored U.N. admission than opposed it, by 55% to 45%: a striking turnaround from 1954.[9]

Similarly, Gallup polls in August 1955 and February 1961 revealed a very big 33% increase in the proportion of Americans willing to "go along" if the United Nations admitted China. This figure, too, showed a large but relatively short-lived drop—of 17%—by September 1961, after troubles in Laos (blamed on China by President Kennedy), the Bay of Pigs invasion of Cuba, and tensions in Europe that culminated in the erection of the Berlin Wall and Soviet resumption of atmospheric nuclear testing; it dropped an additional 6% by February 1964, before resuming the upward trend when China demonstrated nuclear capability.

Opinion Leadership and Opinion Autonomy

Certain kinds of opinion leadership—or at least the presence of competing elites—played a part in these changes. By the middle to late 1950s, for example, a number of owners and managers of multinational corporations (including Henry Ford II) and many members of the Council on Foreign Relations came to favor friendly relations with China and access to its markets. Scholars like John King Fairbank and Doak Barnett spoke up for rapproachement and, by 1957, were echoed in the press. Early stirrings also included the Conlon Report to the Senate Foreign Relations Committee in autumn 1959, which advocated a step-by-step "exploration and negotiation" of peaceful relations with China. As late as 1960 the China lobby was still strong enough to suppress a critique of itself: all but 800 copies of the original 1960 edition of Koen (1974) were destroyed by the publisher, and many of the rest were stolen from libraries (see the introduction to the 1974 edition). The existence of pro-China opinion among a faction of elites in this and later periods, however, undoubtedly helped facilitate changes in public opinion.

There were a few sounds about flexibility toward China from such

Kennedy administration figures as Chester Bowles and Roger Hilsman, but the administration essentially squelched the early accommodationist stirrings. (Figure 6.3 shows no pro-China opinion movement at all during the Kennedy years.) Kennedy himself denounced the idea of U.N. membership for the PRC in October 1961. He encouraged the idea that China was a troublemaker in Laos and on the Indian border and was perhaps a greater threat than the Soviet Union. The Johnson administration generally continued this line, especially once the Vietnam War was under way. Still, after the Chinese nuclear weapon test of 1964, public opinion resumed its movement in the direction of supporting U.N. admission.

Between 1962 and 1966 a major Council on Foreign Relations study group explored—and gained some legitimacy for—ideas about better relations with China, taking funds from the Ford Foundation and scholarly guidance from Doak Barnett and Lucian Pye (Shoup and Minter 1977, pp. 207–212). In 1966 many things came together. The CFR sponsored a book (Steele 1966) that used survey data to argue that the American public was more open to friendly relations with the PRC than had previously been thought: an interesting use of public opinion to lead elites. Senator Fulbright held hearings that pointed toward policy changes, and President Johnson relaxed travel regulations for scholars and writers to visit China. The *New York Times* in March reported that "198 experts" favored U.N. seating and recognition of China. (Seven months later the Committee of One Million countered with "114 Liberals" urging the United Nations to bar Peking.) The *New York Times* in November editorialized in favor of a "two-China" policy, and several liberals (Ribicoff, Javits, and—most important—Douglas) resigned from the Committee of One Million.

This campaign did not get very far, however, at least among government officials, because of the Vietnam War and perhaps also the Cultural Revolution. Reports—including one TV special called "Roots of Madness"—about the turmoil of the Cultural Revolution, which began in June 1966 and lasted some three years, no doubt repelled many Americans. More clearly, the deepening Vietnam War set back any changes in China policy. It was often asserted, and perhaps believed, that the United States was fighting Vietnamese proxies of the Chinese. Vice-president Hubert Humphrey, for example, spoke misleadingly of "militant communist aggression, with its headquarters in Peking, China," and we noted LBJ's reference to "the deepening shadow of Communist China" in Vietnam. Yet it is striking that public opinion nonetheless continued to move in favor of U.N. admission of China between 1966 and 1968 (though there was a temporary dip in support for U.S. diplomatic recognition); by

1968, a substantial base of popular support favored a new China policy. Thus public opinion moved before U.S. policy and seems, in fact, to have affected policy.

As the Vietnam War wound down, President Nixon began to follow through on the hints dropped in his CFR-influenced 1967 *Foreign Affairs* article and, with Henry Kissinger's help, played the "China card," forming a strategic alliance against the Soviet Union (see Cumings 1981a). Early in 1969 he dispatched Kissinger to reconnoiter; then travel and trade restrictions were eased in July and December. Fairly soon (at the beginning of April 1971) the U.S. ping-pong team was invited to visit Peking, and millions of Americans suddenly saw friendly scenes of China on their TV screens. In July 1971 Nixon's own trip to China was announced, and in October the People's Republic was admitted to the United Nations.

During these years public opinion became still more favorable to China, at least partly because of the Nixon administration's leadership. Between late 1968 and May 1971 (after the ping-pong but before Nixon's trip), according to Harris, approval of U.N. membership for China rose a remarkable 27%. Support for "two Chinas" at the United Nations apparently increased by about 18% between the same two surveys, although we cannot be certain since the question wording varied slightly. Approval of Nixon's visit was high, never dropping below 72% in favor (Harris), though it fluctuated somewhat from late 1971 to early 1972.

Certain later changes in opinion about China seem on their face to owe something to the presidency of Jimmy Carter (who extended the Nixon-Kissinger liberalization policy), and possibly also to the activities of the Trilateral Commission. According to Harris surveys, support for U.S. diplomatic recognition of China apparently rose a dramatic total of 31% from its temporary (Vietnam War and Cultural Revolution) low point of 47% in late 1968, to 78% in September 1977, shortly before Carter extended recognition. (Much of the change, however, occurred by 1971, as is shown in figure 6.4.) Support for retaining recognition of the Nationalists on Taiwan dropped 7% (to 78%) between September 1977 and June 1978 (Harris), and sentiment for keeping the U.S. alliance with the Nationalists fell 14% (to 77%) between some time in 1976 and June 1978 (Harris).[10] (At all times, many more Americans favored recognition of the PRC than wanted to sever relations with Nationalist China or end the alliance: a reasonable distinction, if hard to implement given the PRC's insistence on "one China.")

Thus the Carter administration may have contributed to the public reconciliation with China; the Nixon administration certainly did so; the

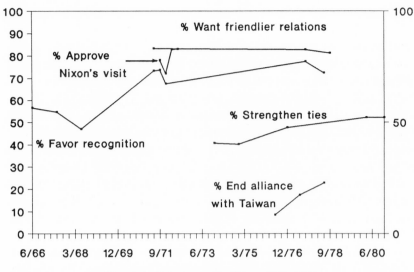

FIG. 6.4   Relations with China, 1966–1981.

CFR and several China scholars probably helped. On the other side, the Committee of One Million and the Kennedy administration very likely played a part in slowing things down for a while, though it is hard to be sure.

Still, the role of opinion leaders—including Presidents Nixon and Carter—should not be exaggerated. For example, public backing for stronger ties with China rose significantly (by 7%) between early 1975 and January 1977 (to 48% in favor of strengthening and only 18% for lessening commitments, according to Roper), before Carter took office, and increased only a bit more thereafter. More important, it is clear from figure 6.3 that a substantial part of the warming trend in public opinion occurred well before Nixon and Kissinger began their spadework. Indeed, a significant part of it seems to have come before the Council on Foreign Relations' campaign of the 1960s.

Once the impassable barrier of the Korean hostilities came down, increasing numbers of Americans may simply have made up their minds that a major power like China had to be dealt with and brought into the international system, no matter what the U.S. government or the Committee of One Million might be saying. China's diplomatic initiatives and especially her development of nuclear weapons bolstered such logic; the 1964 nuclear test clearly had a big effect. Setbacks in the process, too, were mostly related to real-world events. This appears to be another case—like the public's disillusionment with the Vietnam War—in which changes in the opinions of ordinary Americans preceded the actions and rhetoric of most "leaders." Elite influence upon opinion, while important, was not by any means the whole story. (For further discussion of the complexities of opinion leadership and followership in the China case, see Kusnitz 1984.)

The Middle East

United States public opinion about the Middle East has followed a generally stable pattern of support for Israel but reluctance to get directly involved in conflict. Within this basic framework, opinions have changed somewhat in response to major events like wars and peacemaking attempts and the Palestinian uprising.

As Jewish settlers took political power in Palestine and declared Israel an independent state in 1948, most Americans came to feel a cultural and political identification with that largely European, democratic, and capitalist outpost of Western values—an identification undoubtedly accentuated by the efforts of American Jews, most of whom have strongly supported the Jewish state, and some of whom have been prominent in American media, education, and politics. Perhaps most important, many Americans came to see Israel as a strong ally against common foes (communism and radical Arab nationalism) in the Middle East (see Organski 1990).

In disputes between Israel and Arab countries or Arab nationalist movements, large majorities of Americans who have taken a side have generally favored the Israelis. But levels of support for Israel have varied with circumstances and events; support declined somewhat in the 1980s, for example, after Israel's invasion of Lebanon and especially after the Iran-Contra affair and the onset of the Palestinian Intifada. (For survey data though the middle 1980s, see Gilboa 1987. His presentation of data is careful and comprehensive, though the treatment of historical context is sometimes partisan.)

The first available NORC survey on the subject, in December 1944, revealed that a majority of Americans with opinions (53%) thought the British should "set up a Jewish state" in Palestine. (Because of low salience or high ambivalence, however, a large 32% of all respondents said "don't know.") The majority for a Jewish state grew to 61% by November 1945, after the full extent of the Nazi killings of Jews in Europe became widely known. Several polls in 1945 and 1946 showed that large majorities favored the immigration of Jewish refugees to Palestine—though not to the United States. (As we noted in Chap. 4, the American public has tended to resist immigration in general.)

In 1947 and 1948, majorities of those with opinions also favored the U.S.-backed U.N. plan for partition of Palestine, giving part of it to the Jews, though support may have dropped somewhat by April 1948 after the U.S. delegate to the United Nations gave a speech indicating that partition might not be viable after all (Gilboa 1987, pp. 18, 21). In March, according to NORC, a substantial majority (62%) said that "if the Jews in Palestine go ahead on their own and set up a Jewish state anyhow," the United States should "encourage them."

Thus there was broad support, among Americans with opinions, for President Truman's immediate de facto recognition of the newly proclaimed State of Israel on May 14, 1948, as the British departed and Arabs and Jews continued fighting for the land (Grose 1983 discusses the background to recognition). Expressions of general sympathy were high and remained so. Three early NORC surveys, for example, in June and October 1948 and March 1949, found that 71%–75% of those who took a side "sympathize(d)" with the Jews as against the Arabs. (These figures ignore the many respondents who said "don't know" or "both" or "neither"; when they are included, only about 32%–34% of all respondents expressed sympathy with the Jews and 11%–13% with the Arabs.)

But sympathy for the Jews did not mean that the American public advocated U.S. involvement. In July 1948 only 27% told Gallup that they favored selling arms and other war materials to the Jews in Palestine, and indeed Truman imposed an embargo (often honored in the breach) from the end of 1947 until August 1949. As late as November 1955, in fact, even with the stimulus of the Egyptian purchase of Czechoslovakian weapons, only 32% (NORC) favored supplying arms to Israel; the Eisenhower administration shared this reluctance, and no weapons were officially supplied by the United States until 1962. Still fewer Americans were willing to send U.S. troops to Palestine: no more than 22% were, according to three Gallup and NORC surveys conducted during 1946 and 1948, though slight majorities approved having American soldiers take part in a U.N. police force, according to three NORC surveys in 1948 (see Gilboa 1987, p. 23).

In the early 1950s, sympathy for strictly pro-Israel policies was probably dampened somewhat by Eisenhower administration efforts to get along with neutral "underdeveloped" countries, including Nasser's populous and strategically placed Egypt and other Arab oil producers. There was a 9% decline (to just 23%) in support for supplying arms to Israel, for example, between NORC surveys in November 1955—shortly after Nasser arranged to buy Czech weapons—and April 1956 (after the United States had offered to help Egypt with the Aswan Dam and Secretary of

State Dulles had testified against arms aid for Israel, but before the military alliance of Egypt, Syria, Yemen and Saudi Arabia was aimed at Israel).

The Israeli-British-French invasion of Egypt and seizure of the Suez Canal in October–November 1956 was opposed by the United States and by most other governments around the world. President Eisenhower declared that "(t)here can be no peace without law" and that the same code applied to friends as well as opponents. Most Americans disapproved of the invasion; the small proportion saying Israel was "more to blame" in the Middle East dispute rose markedly from 19% in September 1955 to 31% in November 1956. But a larger fraction of the public (47%, up from 38% in 1955) still blamed Egypt. After the initial anti-Israel shift, the blame ratio tilted even further against Egypt when the United States and the Soviet Union forced a cease fire and a British-French withdrawal and when Israel withdrew from Sinai; in April 1957, 57% said Egypt was more to blame (see Gilboa 1987, pp. 28–31).[11]

Ten years later, in May 1967, Nasser's Egypt moved troops into the Sinai peninsula and, occupying Sharm el Sheikh, threatened to close the Gulf of Aqaba to Israeli shipping—a move President Johnson denounced as "illegal and potentially disastrous to the cause of peace." After Jordan signed a mutual defense treaty and put its forces under Egyptian command, apparently preparing for war, the Israelis suddenly attacked on June 5, quickly overrunning and occupying the West Bank of the Jordan River, the Gaza Strip, and the Golan Heights. The U.S. media mostly sided with "brave" Israel and its "strong" and "decisive" leaders (Gilboa 1987, p. 45), emphasizing Israel's underdog status, Arab instigation of the war, and U.S.-Soviet competition in the region.

Many polls on Middle East issues followed. Large majorities of the 80%–90% or more of the public who had "heard or read about the situation in the Middle East" said they sympathized more with Israel than with the Arab nations: 66% with Israel compared to 6% with the Arabs in June 1967, according to Gallup; and a remarkable 46%–1% ("[i]n the latest war between Israel and the Arab states"), according to Harris.[12] We cannot be sure exactly when these high levels of sympathy with Israel began, or why, because of lack of survey data between the Gallup, NORC, and Roper questions of 1947–1949 and 1956–1957, which showed roughly 2:1 ratios of sympathy for Jews versus Arabs, and the differently worded Gallup, Harris, Roper, Yankelovich, and other items from June 1967 onward with much higher pro-Israel responses (see figure 6.5). Very likely, however, the 1967 war—as interpreted by U.S. officials and the media—was a watershed in solidifying sympathy for Israel.

Even in 1967, however, Americans had no interest in direct involve-

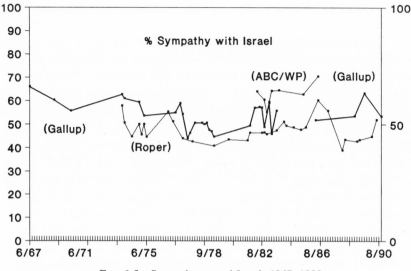

Fɪɢ. 6.5   Sympathy toward Israel, 1967–1990.

ment. The galvanizing impact of the Six Day War was followed by a rise in the already prevailing sentiment that the United States should stay out of the Middle East conflict: up 8%, to a level of 64%, between the first week of June 1967 (at the start of the war) and January 1969, according to an open-ended Gallup question. The majority against involvement grew much further, to 72% in September 1969, and then leveled off at 69% in March 1970 and 67% that September. (Here again our percentages, based on unweighted data to make the surveys comparable, differ slightly from weighted versions.)

After the June 1967 fighting there followed a war of attrition over the occupied territories and lengthy fruitless negotiations. Then, on October 6, 1973, Egypt and Syria started the Yom Kippur War. Their surprise attack was initially successful, but the Israelis beat it back and pushed into Egypt. After matching a Soviet airlift of weapons, the United States (facing the possibility of direct Soviet intervention), forced Israel to cease fire and to resupply the surrounded Egyptian forces. The Organization of Petroleum Exporting Countries (OPEC) protested against U.S. military aid and support for Israel by boycotting the United States, and it sharply raised world oil prices, leading to gasoline shortages in the United States and a deep economic recession.

The American public maintained high levels of sympathy for Israel and rejected the proposition, suggestive of blackmail, that the United States ("we") would have to "find ways to get along with the Arabs, even if that means supporting Israel less": 66% told Harris they disagreed in October 1973, and even more (77%) did so a year later, in December 1974. But eventually the war and the oil crunch, on their own and as interpreted by American leaders and commentators, apparently convinced many Americans that the Arab countries of the Middle East would have to be dealt with; disagreement with the "find ways" statement fell off somewhat. Also, Roper found that the 58% level of "sympathy" for Israel in November 1973 declined substantially, to 45%, by June 1974, as the Yom Kippur War receded into the past and the oil-driven recession worsened. (This drop mainly reflected increases in sympathy with "both" or "neither" side—given by 16% and 25%, respectively, in 1974—not increases in pro-Arab responses, which still amounted to only 7%.)

The oil price rises meant that hundreds of billions of dollars flowed to Arab oil-producing countries. Saudi Arabia alone, for example, earned some $660 billion between 1973 and 1984. Billions of these "petrodollars," in turn, were "recycled" for purchases or investments in the United States, where they created new pro-Arab economic interests. The Aramco oil companies (Exxon, Socal, Mobil, and Texaco) were joined by construction giants like Bechtel and Parsons, which won multibillion-dollar Saudi contracts to build airports and whole cities; by arms suppliers like FMC, Litton, and Raytheon; by the sellers of everything from autos and hotels to news services and waste management; and by U.S. firms with new Arab owners. These firms and Arab governments gradually created a web of American lobbyists and political consultants (including prominent former U.S. government officials), scholars, Middle East Studies centers, and journalists, who tried to counteract the well-established pro-Israel forces in American society and promote more "evenhanded" policies in the Middle East. Their efforts culminated in the successful 1981 campaign to sell AWACS planes to Saudi Arabia (with Boeing and UTC playing key roles), but they began to affect the U.S. climate of opinion earlier than that—for example, through Mobil's advocacy advertisements in leading newspapers (Emerson 1985 provides abundant details on these matters).

The U.S. government also shifted its position somewhat. Henry Kissinger's shuttle diplomacy produced a Suez disengagement in January 1974 and the restoration of full U.S. relations with Egypt; the United States pressured Israel to give up some of its war gains, particularly by means of the March 1975 "reassessment" of U.S. policy which led to the September 1 Egyptian-Israeli interim agreement. Press treatment of Arabs became less negative than it had been (Belkaoui 1978). The relative frequency of pro-Israel or anti-Arab editorials dropped from 40% (10% pro-Arab) in 1974 to 20% (5% pro-Arab) in 1975. In election year 1976, virtually all editorials were neutral; in 1977 they were a little over 10% pro-Israel/anti-Arab, and nearly 30% pro-Arab. (These percentages are estimated from Daugherty and Warden 1979, figure 2, p. 781.)

In the nearly five years between wartime October 1973 (interviews October 19–22) and March 1978 (after Egypt began to make peace with Israel and after the Carter administration proposed to sell F-15s to the Saudis), there was a full 15% rise in the proportion of aware Americans (those who told Gallup they had "heard or read about the Middle East crisis")[13] that favored supplying arms and material to Arab countries, and a 10% drop in the proportion favoring arms for the Israelis. Still, there is little clear evidence of any persistent downward trend in support for Israel before 1977; pro-Israel "sympathy," for example—except for a brief 1975 "reassessment" drop—stayed fairly level (see figure 6.5 and Gilboa 1987, pp. 48, 69).

Anwar Sadat's dramatic November 1977 peacemaking trip to Jerusalem changed many things. The trip was a media spectacular, producing abundant favorable publicity for Sadat's "bold gamble." Much more of the U.S. public than before told Harris that Egypt "really wants just peace," and large majorities saw Sadat as doing an excellent or good job in peace negotiations. "Sympathy" for the Arab nations and for Egypt in particular (volunteered in Roper surveys) went up.

The lengthy ups and downs of negotiations led to some disillusionment—especially with Israel, after the January 18, 1978, breakdown of talks; after Israel's March 11 Litani attack in Lebanon; and after Jimmy Carter's characterization of Menachim Begin as "uncooperative." Following the September 1978 Camp David framework agreement, however, and the March 26, 1979, signing of the peace treaty brokered by Carter, more Americans came to favor friendly policies toward both Egypt and Israel—though not necessarily toward Arab nations generally or the PLO, which rejected the accords as selling out the Palestinians. Between March 1978 and August 1980 (reflecting the Iran hostage crisis as well as the Egyptian-Israel peace), the proportion of the public favoring arms sales to Israel rose from 44% to 58%, and the proportion favoring arms sales to Egypt nearly doubled, from 30% to 56% (Roper)—a remarkable change, especially given the public's general resistance to the sale of weapons abroad. The figure for Saudi Arabia grew by somewhat less (10%), to 34% in favor.

Between July 1978 and February 1980 Roper found that public support for using U.S. troops if Arabs invaded Israel rose sharply, from 25% to a relatively high 43%—probably because of anti-Moslem and anti-Arab reactions related to the Iran hostage situation. Oil, however, remained a crucial consideration. In the last week of March 1979, after the second sharp OPEC price rise and U.S. allocation rules had led to long gasoline lines, a substantial 41% of Americans said we would have to get along with the Arabs even if that meant less support of Israel (Harris); this was up an abrupt 19% from the previous December. (It then dipped 6% by October 1979.)

Still, the realities of OPEC oil power did not at all mean that the American public in the late 1970s and early 1980s was presented with predominantly pro-Arab or anti-Israel information. Quite the contrary; pro-Israel sentiment remained strong in the American media and in American politics. Media coverage of the Moslem world remained sparse and mostly negative and stereotypical (see Said 1981). Some academic Arabists and Middle East study centers in the United States (at the University of Arizona, e.g.) were harassed. Prominent politicians who criticized Israel—including Senators Adlai Stevenson III, J. William Fulbright, and Charles Percy—found themselves in electoral trouble. Support for Palestinian nationalism was still virtually taboo, as the blacklisted actress Vanessa Redgrave discovered (Findley 1985). In the press and on TV news the word "Arab" was often paired with "terrorist." (Herman 1982 discusses selective uses of the slippery concept of "terrorism"; see also Chomsky 1982, 1986.)

The overthrow of the authoritarian Shah Pahlevi of Iran in February 1979 distressed many Americans. The Shah had been a key aid recipient and military client of the United States, which had put the Pahlevis back in power through the CIA-organized coup against Mussadiq in 1953. The Shah had benefited from large Iranian investments by Chase Manhattan and other U.S. banks and from close personal ties with many U.S. leaders, including the Rockefellers, Henry Kissinger, and politicians from both parties (Bill 1988). Pahlevi—who wined and dined journalists and cultivated elite support in the United States—had also enjoyed extraordinarily friendly treatment by the U.S. media, which portrayed him as a staunch anti-Communist ally and as a stern, strict, but vigorous modernizer, a proponent of industrialization, land reform, freedom for women, and Westernization, ignoring his repressive methods and his policy failures. The broadly based anti-Shah demonstrations beginning in January 1978 were characterized in the American media as rampaging "mobs," engaged in "riots" and "anarchy," led by reactionary "Moslem extremists" or "fanatics" allied with Marxists—not as "freedom fighters," the term sometimes bestowed upon anti-Communist rebels elsewhere (Dorman and Farhang 1987).

Thus the fall of the Shah was a shock, and even more so was the November 3, 1979, seizure of some ninety hostages (and of secret documents which revealed what the Iranians called a "nest of spies") in the U.S. embassy in Teheran, after the Shah had been admitted to the United States for medical treatment. Violently anti–U.S. demonstrations and flag burnings made dramatic visual footage for television; they were given especially long and intensive TV coverage, provoking an angry reaction from the American public.

The initial response was to favor coercive action. At the end of November 1979, 62% of the public told Harris they wanted to block Iranian oil, and 70% favored a naval blockade. But by the end of December passions had cooled somewhat, and these percentages had dropped by 18% and 21%, respectively. [14]

Similarly, the meager 28% of Americans who had favored letting Iran "investigate" the hostages at the beginning of December (Harris) doubled—that is, rose a dramatic 28%—by the end of that month.

As the conflict continued into 1980, however, with no progress on freeing the hostages and with massive TV coverage of Iran (ABC's "Nightline" with Ted Koppel was started for this purpose, and CBS's Walter Cronkite ticked off the days of the hostages' captivity), Americans' patience grew understandably thin. Yankelovich, Skelly, and White surveys found that support for using military force if the hostages were tried rose quite substantially, from 48% in December 1979 to 56% in January 1980 and to a very high 64% in May. By February 1980, 46% (up 11% since July 1978) approved of "using" U.S. troops if the Arabs cut off oil shipments to the United States (Roper); and fully 72% (up a marked 26% from one year earlier) approved of the perhaps slightly milder idea of "sending" troops to protect our oil sources, "(i)f there were a threat to our supply of oil in the Middle East" (CBS/*NYT*).

Between mid-March and late March 1980, the proportion willing to "wait as long as necessary" dipped by 6%, to 69% (Harris). Between late March and early April, again according to Harris, the proportion of Americans favoring use of military force if the hostages were put on trial rose by 8%, to 57% of the public. Similarly, following the pattern of high, lower, then higher tension, opinion fluctuated concerning whether or not the United States should continue selling grain to Iran if the hostages were released: Yankelovich found 57% opposed in December 1979, 38% in January 1980, and 49% in March.

As we will see, the hostage crisis in Iran—together with the Soviet movement of troops into Afghanistan—also strongly affected opinions concerning defense spending and various aspects of U.S.-Soviet relations.

The 1982 Lebanon Invasion

The June 6, 1982, Israeli invasion of Lebanon and the heavy bombardment of Beirut, which produced much dramatic television footage of dead and wounded civilians and destroyed buildings, distressed many Americans. There were some charges of media bias against Israel (see, e.g., Chafetz 1985; Karetzky 1986); the oft-repeated early civilian casualty figures (provided by the Palestine Red Crescent via the International Red Cross) may have been exaggerated, and the media, as usual, focused on exciting battle scenes rather than root causes (see Gilboa 1987, p. 136). Yet it was undeniable that Israel's pursuit of the PLO killed many noncombatant Palestinians and Lebanese and badly damaged Lebanon, leading to the virtual disintegration of that country. To some Americans, embattled Israel seemed suddenly to have become aggressive Israel.

After September 16–17, 1982, when several hundred Palestinian refugees including women and children were massacred in Israeli-controlled Lebanese territory (at the Sabra and Shatila camps) by Israel's Christian Phalangist allies, Americans' sympathy for the Arabs rose markedly. Immediately afterward, in fact, the ABC/*WP* trend data show a 10% jump, from 21% to 31% (between August and September 24–26), in the proportion sympathizing "more with the Arab Nations." Gallup/*Newsweek* found very nearly as much sympathy for Arab nations as for Israel—an unprecedented situation which quickly reverted to a strong pro-Israel balance (see the sharp 1982 opinion change in figure 6.5). (Roper had also found a 6% rise in sympathy for the Arabs between June and September 1982, before the massacre but after the Israelis returned to Lebanon following the assassination of President-elect Bashir Gemayel.)

The events in Lebanon made much of the U.S. public aware for the first time of the plight of the Palestinians. At the end of September 1982, ABC found that 61% of the informed public favored a "Palestinian homeland" on the West Bank, up 6% from the already high figure in a survey conducted just before the Sabra-Shatila massacre. This, however, did not necessarily imply support or an independent Palestinian state; many favored Reagan's September 1, 1982, plan for autonomy and then governance by Jordan, an idea which remained quite popular among Americans on into the middle 1980s (see Rielly 1983, 1987).

A majority of the U.S. public (57% in September 1982) told Gallup/*Newsweek* it approved of President Reagan's August 25 decision to send U.S. marines to Beirut in order to "help keep the peace" and to "encourage a withdrawal of Israeli, Syrian and PLO forces." But Americans gradually reduced their support when Reagan sent back the marines on September 29, 1982, after the PLO evacuation, the Gemayal assassination, and the Sabra-Shatila massacre, for a "limited period of time" that turned into sixteen months.

In October 1982, at the beginning of that sixteen-month period, about half the public (49%) told NBC that they approved of Reagan sending American troops to Lebanon (see Gilboa 1987, p. 151). Then the troops came under fire. The U.S. embassy was bombed on April 18, 1983. More marines were sent at the beginning of September 1983, when the Israelis withdrew south to the Awali River; U.S. marines and naval guns openly took the side of the Christian Phalangists against the Druze and the Shiite Moslems in the civil war, receiving sniper fire in return; and Congress became restive. In September 1983, according to Gallup/*Newsweek*, most Americans (58%) wanted the troops brought home; according to CBS/*NYT*, only 40% of the public approved of sending U.S. troops to Lebanon "as part of an international peace-keeping force."

Gallup/*Newsweek*'s 58% wanting to bring the troops home temporarily fell very sharply to 46% at the end of October 1983—after Congress authorized a longer stay, the Grenada invasion indicated that U.S. interventions could be easy and successful, and the public (urged on by Reagan's October 27 address) reacted defiantly to the October 23 truck bombing that killed 241 marines at the Beirut airport. But the longer-term effect of the truck bombing, as people had time to deliberate and debate about it, was very negative.

Harris found a 13% increase in the proportion favoring a pullout from Lebanon between October (36%) and December (49%) 1983. ABC discovered a corresponding drop between late October and December—from 53% to 42%—in the proportion of Americans that thought "United States troops and Israeli troops (together) should push the Syrians out of Lebanon by force." Opinion continued to move as the media reported commentators and experts and political figures, including Republican Senators Baker and Goldwater and Secretary of Defense Weinberger, speaking out against the Lebanon operation. ABC surveys revealed a sharp increase from 42% favoring removal of U.S. troops in late September 1983 to 60% in mid–January 1984. Gallup data indicated that there was also a last-minute jump in sentiment for withdrawing troops—from 63% in January to 81% in February—after President Reagan, on February 7, carried out a withdrawal, ordering a face-saving "redeployment" offshore for "safety" reasons (see Fan 1988).[15]

The Israeli pullback in Lebanon apparently helped defuse American opposition to Israeli policies. Most Americans remained more sympathetic to Israel than to the Arabs—roughly 60% pro-Israel even in August 1982, 64% in September 1983, up to 71% in June 1986, according to ABC/*WP*. Harris found a record high of 70% pro-Israel sympathy in October 1985, after the intensely publicized Achille Lauro hijacking (including the gruesome murder of a crippled American) again associated Arabs with terrorism. There was also substantial support for the large U.S. military and economic aid program, especially since Israel remained a strong ally against Soviet and Arab threats to U.S. interests. But this support was tempered by new sympathy for the Palestinians, concern over oil supplies, and a more critical view of Israeli foreign policy.

Publicity about naval intelligence analyst Jonathan Pollard who spied on the United States for Israel, and then, beginning in December 1986, revelations of Israeli's central role in the Iran-Contra scandal, tended to diminish pro-Israel attitudes. A Gallup survey for the Chicago Council on Foreign Relations in early November 1986, for example, already found 24% in favor of decreasing military aid and arms sales to Israel or stopping them altogether, with only 11% for increasing aid and most people wanting to keep them the same. But a telephone follow-up in January–February 1987, after Attorney General Meese and others revealed Israel's role in initiating secret arms sales to Iran, indicated that the proportion for cutting or ending aid jumped sharply (by twenty-one percentage points) to 45%, with 9% for increasing aid and a much-reduced group favoring the status quo (see Rielly 1987, p. 28; our figures, as usual, exclude "don't knows").

A further substantial decline in sympathy for Israel occurred later, as months of U.S. television reports showed the Israelis using force to subdue the Palestinian uprising (or "intifada") that began in December 1987 in the occupied territories of the West Bank and Gaza. This is evident in figure 6.5, where pro-Israel responses to Roper's sympathy question show a sharp 17% decline (from 56% to 39%) between February 1987 and February 1988;[16] it is also clear in Richman's (1989) analysis of attitude "scalometer" ratings. Pluralities of Americans thought the Israelis handled the uprising too harshly and were critical in other respects as well. Support for the idea of a Palestinian homeland also appeared to increase after the uprising and into 1990 (see Richman 1989; Public Opinion Report 1990, p. 94). At the beginning of the 1990s, many Americans were apparently troubled by the new Likkud-led government's reluctance to negotiate peace with the Palestinians, while at the same time—because of better U.S.-USSR relations—Israel appeared less important as a strategic bulwark against the Soviet Union.

Détente and the New Cold War

After the Vietnam War, U.S.-Soviet relations first relaxed, then moved to renewed hostility, and then turned to detente once again, with a rapidity reminiscent of World War II and early postwar policy changes. Public opinion responded (sensibly, for the most part) to reports of changing circumstances, but it also resisted, to a surprising extent, manipulation by exaggerated or misleading information. Despite the alarms of the new Cold War, most Americans clung to desires for peaceful international relations.

Détente

The winding down of the Vietnam War logically opened the way to better relations with Communist countries. The Nixon administration acted accordingly, promoting détente with the Soviet Union as well as China. There was much talk about making sales to the Russians of grain, computers, and consumer goods like Pepsi-Cola; offering credit and investments from U.S. banks; and organizing natural gas projects: talk that was promoted by interested firms, academic experts, and media commentators. The Chase Manhattan Bank did open a branch in Moscow and large grain sales were, in fact, completed.

Arms control negotiations also went forward. In February 1971 the United States and the USSR agreed to a multinational treaty banning seabed installation of nuclear weapons, and in October 1972 the Americans and Soviets signed "SALT I" (planned as the first in a series of Strategic Arms Limitations Treaties), limiting the testing and deployment of antiballistic missiles. President Nixon visited Moscow in mid-1972. Secretary Brezhnev traveled to the United States in June 1973 and signed a series of agreements on trade and exchanges.

The American public called for and approved of improvements in U.S.-Soviet relations. Between September 1968 and November 1972 (SRC/CPS), there was a big drop of 19% (to 34%) in opposition to trade with Communist countries. By 1974 and 1975, substantial majorities of Americans favored expanding trade with Russia, exchanging scientists, carrying out joint space projects, and selling wheat (see Rielly 1975, pp. 21–22). In December 1975, 81% (Harris) favored "a new SALT arms (control) agreement," and this already very strong support grew to an overwhelming 91% by May 1977.

A particularly striking manifestation of détente involved Cuba, which had been seen by many as an irritant or threat to the United States ever since Fidel Castro's leftist revolution came to power January 1, 1959, executed some of former dictator Batista's secret police, and nationalized American-owned oil refineries (which had refused to process Soviet crude oil), public utilities, and sugar factories. A CIA-organized exile invasion at the Bay of Pigs attempted to overthrow Castro in April 1961. Cuba formed an alliance with the Soviet Union, culminating in the installation (and then the U.S.-forced removal) of Soviet missiles in 1962 and a decade of hostility from U.S. policymakers and the American public.

As part of the general thaw in U.S.-Communist relations at the beginning of the 1970s, however, the United States and Cuba in February 1973 signed a "memorandum of understanding" to curb hijackings and negotiated about other matters. There was discussion (some of it encouraged by Coca Cola, a major sugar importer) of restoring diplomatic relations and relaxing the U.S. trade embargo. Public sentiment for allowing the importation of Cuban cigars rose a remarkable 27% (to 53%) between January 1971 and October 1974, according to Harris. At the beginning of 1975 Roper actually found that a bare majority—but a majority (53%)—of Americans said the United States should "recognize the government of Cuba and establish trade and diplomatic relations," apparently quite a turnaround from earlier years; 54% still favored recognition in March 1977.[17]

But by the middle of the 1970s much of the elite enthusiasm for friendly relations with the USSR and other Communist countries faded. The economic fruits of détente proved disappointing. Trade in technology was slow and the need of U.S. farmers for grain sales to Russia fell after the 1973–1974 droughts caused a jump in world food prices; the Soviets' appetite for bank credits also turned out to be limited. Congressional restrictions essentially scuttled the trade treaty: a Stevenson amendment sharply limited borrowing from the United States, and the Jackson-Vanik amendment (linking the USSR's most-favored-nation status to emigration of Soviet Jews) meant high tariffs on goods from the USSR. (Passage of the Jackson-Vanik amendment was followed by a tightening rather than loosening of emigration restrictions, and the treatment of Soviet Jews became a highly publicized irritant between the superpowers.) Many U.S. firms were turning for trade and investment to the Third World, where relations with the Soviets were competitive rather than cooperative; they disliked détente and sought increased military spending in order to project U.S. force and protect their markets (see Ferguson and Rogers 1981, pp. 15–19).

A New Cold War

By the middle of the 1970s a number of organized groups, some funded by defense contractors and/or multinational corporations, were proclaiming concern about increased Soviet military power and Soviet influence in the Third World. The anti-Communist and prodefense National Strategy Information Center (incorporated in 1962 by William J. Casey, who was later to become CIA director, and other leading businessmen) enjoyed a great upsurge in funding in the middle 1970s and opened a full-scale Washington office to lobby Congress and the executive and to generate press publicity. The American Security Council flourished; the Georgetown Center for Strategic and International Studies, the Atlantic Council, and (from abroad) the Atlantic Institute and the International Institute for Strategic Studies all, in their different ways, promoted increased U.S. military spending and alarm about the USSR.

Already in 1972 Eugene Rostow and other members of the Coalition for a Democratic Majority, a conservative and prodefense group of Democrats formed in reaction to George McGovern's presidential candidacy, were opposing détente. Claiming that it was "dangerous to lull western public opinion" by proclaiming an end to the Cold War, in 1974 they released a paper arguing that the Soviets were pursuing a "headlong drive for first-strike capability" in both nuclear and conventional arms and were retaining the prerogative of assisting wars of "national liberation." In 1974, Paul Nitze angrily resigned from the SALT negotiating team and testified to the Senate Armed Services Committee that détente was a "myth." Rostow, Nitze, David Packard (chairman of Hewlett-Packard, a major defense contractor), and others began to talk with friends about organizing themselves. In 1976, with financial backing from Packard, the Committee on the Present Danger (CPD) was formed. (Though somewhat strident, Sanders 1983 is a useful source.)

The CPD—with the same name and even some of the same personnel (e.g., Nitze) as the committee set up in 1950 to promote Cold War military containment—conducted an extraordinary campaign through the rest of the 1970s, publicizing the allegedly massive Soviet arms buildup and advocating heavy increases in U.S. military spending and active intervention abroad. Soon, helped by reports about Soviet and Cuban influence in Angola, Ethiopia, and elsewhere, and helped also by the report of the CIA "B" team headed by CPD member Richard Pipes, which estimated Soviet military spending as increasing by 3% or 4% per year (substantially faster than the U.S. rate), the committee and others apparently had some success in overcoming post-Vietnam reluctance and moving public opinion their way. (Yet the impact of the CPD is easily exaggerated; public opinion had begun to move before the committee was formed, and opinion changed most markedly only after the events in Iran and Afghanistan.)[18]

Between 1969 and 1977 there was a very large drop (31%) in the proportion of respondents that told Gallup too much was being spent on the military. A substantial part of this shift took place in the middle to late 1970s: a nearly 25% decline, for example, between the Gallup surveys of September 1974 and July 1977. Likewise, two Harris surveys (the second of which, however, apparently introduced an unacknowledged change in wording to the prologue of the question) indicate that the proportion wanting to increase defense spending rose by a sharp 24% (to 52%) just from December 1976 to November 1978. NORC-GSS and other surveys reveal additional large jumps in opinion after the Iran and Afghanistan crises began late in 1979. These rises in support for military spending are among the biggest and most abrupt of our opinion changes; they are included, with defense spending data from the Vietnam era to 1990, in figure 6.6 (see also Russett and DeLuca 1981).

Apprehension about the Soviet Union carried over into other policy areas as well. The high levels of support that Harris had found in 1974 for trade with the Soviets and exchanges of scientists and joint space projects dropped about 10% each by December 1975, though they remained high (at 68%, 64%, and 57%, respectively). (Sentiment for selling wheat rose

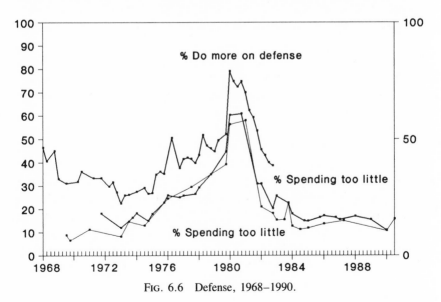

Fig. 6.6   Defense, 1968–1990.

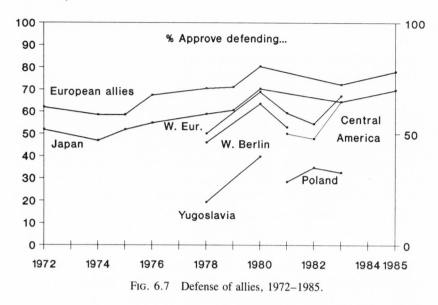

FIG. 6.7   Defense of allies, 1972–1985.

a bit, from 33% to 40% in favor between September and December 1975, for reasons that are not clear.) In the two years following December 1976, there was a rise of 10%—reaching a majority of 58%, according to Gallup—in the proportion of Americans wanting the U.S. to "do more" in the way of spending to protect its people against nuclear attack.

The public's right turn on foreign policy matters, which was much more pronounced than on domestic policy, also extended beyond direct US-USSR relations to encompass interventionism and foreign involvement generally. As figure 6.7 indicates, the post-Vietnam opposition to use of force abroad weakened markedly. The proportion of Americans agreeing with a Gallup statement that the United States should "come to the defense of its major European Allies with military force" if they were attacked by the Soviet Union, rose steadily from the 59% 1975 low point to a hefty 80% by 1980, a very big change. Gallup found comparable changes (though approximately 10% lower levels every year) in support of defending Japan. Asking about the use of U.S. *troops* (a different and significantly less popular idea), Roper found sharp increases, between 1978 and 1980, in willingness to defend Western Europe or West Berlin; rising support between 1981 and 1983 for defending "a Central American country" from a "Communist takeover" by Cuban troops (though less support than for European defense); and much less interest in defending against a Soviet invasion of Poland. (These are reasonable distinctions, one might think, based on geography and perceived importance to the United States.)

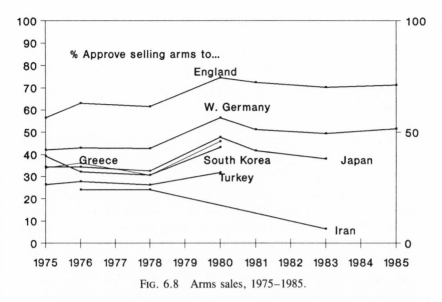

Fig. 6.8   Arms sales, 1975–1985.

Similarly, public opposition to foreign aid and arms sales decreased. Between February 1976 and April 1978, objections that the United States was spending "too much" on foreign aid dropped by 8%, from just over 78% to just under 71%, with still only 4% saying "too little" (NORC-GSS). As figure 6.8 indicates, between 1978 and 1980 (with Iran and Afghanistan again probably playing key roles) substantially higher proportions of Americans—about 12%–15% more—came to think the United States should "sell . . . arms" to a number of allied countries. Figure 6.8 also illustrates sharp distinctions in the public's mind among different countries: a strong majority was always willing to sell arms to England; considerably fewer (never even a majority, until 1980) favored sales to West Germany; still fewer wanted to sell arms to Japan or Greece; and only a very small minority favored selling arms to Iran—as the Reagan administration was reminded, to its sorrow, when the secret sales were disclosed. Arms sales are generally unpopular, presumably because they are seen as risking bloodshed and U.S. entanglement. The public makes cautious distinctions about exceptions.

During this same period there was at least one move toward dovish internationalism: support for the Panama Canal treaties rose 10% between September 1977 and January 1978, to 53% (Gallup), perhaps in response to Jimmy Carter's leadership—with organized help from DuPont's Irving Shapiro and Nelson Rockefeller, among others. As we noted in Chapter 2, however, the administration made exaggerated claims of increased public support based on "trends" in responses to nonidentical survey questions (Roshco 1978; Ted Smith and Hogan 1987). An energetic campaign against "giving away" this vital waterway, by the World Anti-Communist League, the American Security Council, and some Reagan backers from the South and West, left a majority of the public supporting the treaties only if there were strong reservations permitting renewed U.S. intervention in wartime, with little or no overall opinion change during the debate.

One of the most important manifestations of the new Cold War was the erosion of public support for arms control agreements with the Soviets. As early as January 1976, 68% of Americans said it was "dangerous" to cooperate too closely with the USSR and China, up 10% in seven months. Public backing for a "new SALT arms control agreement" had risen 10% (to an overwhelming 90% approving) between the December 1975 and May 1977 Harris surveys, but it dropped back the same 10% by April 1979 (leaving very strong majority support, to be sure), as the Committee on the Present Danger and others charged that such agreements advantaged the USSR. Roper pinpointed a similar 10% drop (to 63%) in support for "a new SALT agreement with Russia" between June and August 1978.[19] Before and after Jimmy Carter Signed SALT II in June 1979, a parade of foreign policy experts and retired military figures testified that verification would be difficult and that the balance of forces would favor the Soviets.

Several different opinion time series from different survey organizations reveal declines in public support for an arms control treaty during 1979. There was a 6% dip between February and March in support for "a new agreement . . . which would limit nuclear weapons," with a further 4% decline during the next month (NBC); a large 19% drop between June and November in the proportion (among the unusually low 36%–45% who said they knew "enough to have an opinion") that favored ratification of SALT II (CBS/*NYT*); and a similar 19% drop in support for the treaty (among those with opinions)[20] between March and October, according to NBC. In the October 1979 survey, NBC found that only 49% of Americans supported ratification. The Senate did not vote approval.

Like the move toward favoring more defense spending, the turning of public opinion against SALT II represented a triumph for advocates of a U.S. military buildup. In retrospect, it is clear that the concerns about verification were exaggerated. Unilateral ("national") techniques, including satellite observation, interception of transmissions, and seismic detection, could provide a great deal of information about Soviet deployments and tests (Talbott 1984). Moreover, the alleged Soviet arms buildup turned out, at least in part, to be an artifact of questionable U.S. accounting methods—which, for example, arrived at mushrooming Soviet budget figures by assuming that a given number of Soviet tanks must cost more and more every year in the same way that U.S. costs were inflating. CIA analysts eventually revised their figures and estimated that Soviet arms expenditures (adjusting more accurately for inflation) had risen only about 2% per year since the mid-1970s, not 3% or 4%, while others questioned whether there had been any increase at all. Most important, the potency of the U.S. deterrent was never in doubt. But Reagan administration officials (who, like John Kennedy's people in 1960, may have believed their alarms before taking office but surely learned the truth when they were running the government) misrepresented the arms balance long enough to take credit for "restoring" U.S. strength (Gervasi 1986; Halloran and Gelb 1983).

One piece of evidence tending to confirm that the arguments against SALT were misleading is the fact that during its first term the strongly anti-Soviet Reagan administration ignored its own campaign rhetoric and, without actually ratifying SALT II, quietly agreed with the Soviets to observe its terms, unworried about any verification or arms imbalance problems.

Tensions Peak: Iran and Afghanistan

Tensions between the United States and the USSR reached a peak with the events of 1979 and 1980 in Iran and Afghanistan. The November 1979 seizure of American hostages from the U.S. embassy in Teheran, as we have already noted, was a shock. For more than a year the hostages were held prisoner while U.S. television reveled in pictures of screaming anti-U.S. crowds, flag burnings, and the like. The American public reacted with rage and frustration.

Compounding Americans' consternation, at the end of December 1979 the Soviet Union sent troops across its southern border into Afghanistan in order to reshuffle and bolster a weak Communist government. The number of Soviet troops in Afghanistan (soon to be bogged down in a nightmarish Vietnam-like struggle against Moslem guerrillas) rose gradually to 85,000 by spring 1980. The U.S. government and media expressed outrage, condemning the move as naked aggression perhaps aimed ultimately at the Persian Gulf—ignoring Russia's border worries, analogous to those the United States would feel about a Communist insurgency in Mexico. The American public responded accordingly.

The cumulative effect of Iran and Afghanistan was devastating to President Carter. After an initial "rally 'round the flag" (a very strong but temporary boost in presidential popularity) which apparently deterred

Edward Kennedy from challenging the incumbent for the upcoming Democratic presidential nomination, Carter's favorable performance rating in the Gallup poll dropped precipitously after early 1980 and the failed hostage rescue attempt (see Brody and Shapiro 1989b). The importance of the events in Iran and Afghanistan was emphasized by Carter's own obsession with the hostages and by heavy media coverage, including much critical commentary from opinion leaders. As Brody (1984) and Brody and Shapiro (1989b) have argued, the "rally" phenomenon works only when U.S. elites are united behind the president; when opinion leaders are divided, events themselves—and their positive or negative results—are more likely to drive public opinion.

Iran and Afghanistan were widely taken as symbols of U.S. impotence and Soviet aggressiveness, and sharply accelerated the public shift away from détente. By the spring of 1980 the proportion of Americans favoring an increase in defense spending had abruptly jumped a remarkable thirty percentage points higher than in the previous (spring 1978) NORC–GSS survey, to fully 60% in favor of more money for the military, while only 12% favored less money and 28% wanted to spend the same amount. This unprecedented jump—about half of which occurred after the Roper survey of December 1979—meant that sentiment for more military spending had risen a total of nearly 50% since the post-Vietnam low of 12% in 1973 (see figure 6.6, above). Likewise, the public's backing for arms sales and for military defense of various countries reached their peaks in 1980 (see figures 6.7 and 6.8).

When the Reagan administration took office in 1981, with many CPD members moving into Defense and State Department positions, it launched a massive military buildup (adding to the already substantial spending increases planned by Carter) that emphasized an expanded navy to project U.S. force in the Third World. The administration aimed hostile rhetoric at the Soviets. In January 1981, for example, Reagan said that the Soviets were willing to "commit any crime, to lie, to cheat" in order to impose a "one-world Socialist or Communist state" over the whole globe. Secretary of State Alexander Haig referred to a network of "international terrorism" directed by the Kremlin, and later accused the communists of "germ warfare" in Afghanistan and Cambodia, a charge that was widely repeated by U.S. officials and the media even after it became evident that the feared "yellow rain" was probably excrement from swarms of bees, containing small amounts of a natural toxin (Wade 1983).

In 1982 and 1983 members of the administration—echoing Claire Sterling, Paul Henze, and Michael Ledeen, whose assertions were given exceptional play by *Readers Digest, TV Guide,* the *New York Times,* and the TV networks—promoted the notion that Ali Agca's attempt to assassinate the Pope in May 1981 had been a Soviet KGB plot, carried out through a Bulgarian connection. These charges, never supported by substantial evidence, may have originated in a disinformation campaign by the Italian SISMI intelligence agency (penetrated by the right wing *Propaganda Due* conspiracy) and in an accidental or deliberate "blowback" to the United States of CIA disinformation spread abroad. Despite the implausibility of the story, it was only belatedly and sheepishly abandoned in the United States after it became obvious that proof was lacking at the trial of the Bulgarians (ending in acquittals in 1986) and after Agca, the main witness, declared himself to be Jesus Christ (Herman and Brodhead 1986 give a fascinating account; see also Herman and Chomsky 1988, chap. 4).

Tensions Ease Once Again

As far as the U.S. public was concerned, however, 1980 was the peak year of new Cold War attitudes; after that they eased. Indeed, a careful look at our data shows that the public never became very belligerent. Most Americans continued throughout this period to oppose most arms sales and most interventions abroad; even the widespread (but temporary) willingness to spend "more" on defense does not tell us how much more, and subsequent events indicate that the Reagan administration went further than the public wanted.

As the military budget grew rapidly under Reagan—while taxes were cut, the government ran up large deficits, the Federal Reserve kept money tight, and the United States slid into recession—both elite and public enthusiasm for further arms spending began to decrease. By spring 1982, only 31% of the public, far below the 60% figure for 1980, favored increased spending on defense, while a trifle more—32%—favored a decrease (NORC-GSS). A Gallup survey for the Chicago Council on Foreign Relations (CCFR) in December 1982 likewise found that more Americans favored cutting back (36%) than wanted to expand (26%) defense spending.[21] According to Roper surveys, the December 1979 balance of opinion—with 45% judging "too little" was spent on defense as opposed to only 18% "too much"—was very nearly reversed in December 1982, when only 20% said "too little" and 40% said "too much." Prodefense opinion continued along a downward trend (see figure 6.6).

In part, this opinion shift reflected concern over domestic policy priorities. To some degree, it simply meant that people thought the arms buildup to date was sufficient; the current policy referred to in the survey questions had shifted. But in part, too, the Reagan administration appears to have produced something of a backlash among the public. People became alarmed over the possibility of nuclear war.

These opinion changes did not proceed entirely without elite influence. For example, real estate interests in urban areas (e.g., Boston-area realty and hotel people, and New York developer Donald Trump) sought a shift to domestic programs like mass transit. Europe-oriented (and often Democratic party–affiliated) multinational corporations worried about Reagan's belligerence and his alienation of European allies, energized the Arms Control Association, and invested money in arms control studies and publicity. Foundation grant programs on "international security and the prevention of nuclear war" (ISPNW) grew spectacularly: a study of seventy-four foundations found that ISPNW grants more than tripled (from $16.5 million to $52 million) from 1982 to 1984, with most of the new money coming from the big, multinationally oriented MacArthur, Carnegie, Ford, Rockefeller, and Alton Jones foundations (Ferguson and Rogers 1986, pp. 146–154).

The "nuclear freeze" movement, which got organized after Randall Forsberg's presentation of the idea to a convention of peace groups in December 1979, struck a popular cord, tapping Americans' basic values and quickly winning strong public support. Large majorities of Americans—79% in April 1982 rising to 84% by April 1984 (ABC)—endorsed a freeze on the building, testing, and deployment of nuclear weapons. Every year from 1981 through 1985 Gallup found a steady 78% to 81% in favor of a bilateral freeze; Harris and CBS/*NYT* found comparably large majorities between 1982 and 1984. In June 1982, in New York City, some 750,000 people—probably constituting the largest political demonstration in U.S. history—came out to support a freeze. A number of freeze proposals won in state and local referenda: in thirty-six of thirty-nine localities (including eight of nine states), for example, in November 1982.

The freeze movement caused confusion and division among elites, and consternation in the Reagan administration. It was joined by more establishment-oriented organizations like the Council for a Livable World, the Union of Concerned Scientists, Physicians for Social Responsibility, and various church and teachers' organizations, and (in February 1982) it was endorsed by Senators Kennedy (D) and Hatfield (R), among others, who won some favorable media attention. *Time* magazine, for example, spoke respectfully (March 29, 1982, p. 10) of the movement's "impeccable Establishment credentials," before dismissing Ground Zero week as "disappointing" (May 3), and virtually ignoring the huge MOBE demonstration in New York in June except to allude to the danger of "radical" or "kooky" elements.[22]

The alarmed Reagan administration considered (but apparently rejected) Eugene Rostow's proposal for a strong PR campaign against the freeze; it tried to discredit freeze leaders with talk of Soviet influence and funding, but then hit on a better plan: to defuse the movement by beginning (though not taking very seriously) "START" arms control talks with the Soviets in July 1982, arguing against anything that would "undercut" the talks. The administration also pushed for more weapons for "modernization" and "bargaining chips"—MX missiles, the B-1 bomber, Pershing and Tomahawk missiles, and (in the following year) the Strategic Defense Initiative (SDI or, as it came to be known, "Star Wars") missile defense.

The freeze movement was eventually endorsed by Democratic party chairman Charles Manatt and other business-oriented Democrats, including some (like Senator Sam Nunn of Georgia) with ties to manufacturers of conventional weaponry who would benefit from a shift away from nuclear spending, and others who for various reasons favored Robert Komer's Europe-oriented "coalition defense" notion emphasizing high-tech land forces rather than Reagan's Third World–oriented buildup that relied heavily on naval aircraft carriers. Various scholars and politicians also tried to transmute nuclear freeze or reduction proposals into "build-down" programs that meant little more than modernizing strategic weapons (Ferguson and Rogers 1986). Between these dilutions and the Reagan counterattack, the freeze idea petered out at the elite level (its last victory was a favorable House resolution in May 1983), despite very strong continued public support.

Public sentiment that U.S. policy should "get tough" toward the Soviets dropped sharply, from 77% in January 1980 to 44% in May 1982 (rising back to 54% in September, however: CBS/*NYT*). As we saw in Chapter 1, the public also expressed considerable doubt about the new multiple warhead MX missile. But again events—carefully managed and interpreted by the administration—proved crucial, at least long enough to save the weapons buildup. The 58% (of those with opinions), who in January 1983 told ABC that the United States should not build the MX, dropped to 49% in June 1983 and to only 43% in September 1984. Similarly, the proportion of the public who said that Reagan was "going too far" in plans to build more nuclear weapons stood at a high 68% in July 1983, but dropped sharply to 47% by November (ABC), after the successful Grenada invasion and after U.S. officials condemned the Soviet's downing of Korean Airlines flight 007 as a deliberate, unprovoked, and

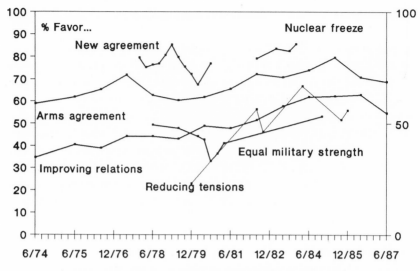

FIG. 6.9   Relations with the Soviet Union, 1974–1987.

barbaric attack on innocent civilians that had revealed the true nature of the USSR. (Hersh 1986 shows that the Soviets actually had good reason to think the airliner was a spy plane; he describes conscious U.S. government misrepresentations of the incident [especially by Secretary Schultz], which was seized upon as a justification for a generally tougher line toward the USSR.)

Thus Reagan used his own actions and official (mis)interpretations of events to counteract dovish public opinion, much as FDR had done before World War II. But the feeling that Reagan was going "too far" on nuclear weapons rose again to 61% by July 1984 (ABC), as the administration seemed to display little interest in arms control agreements, putting its faith in the "Star Wars" missile defense. There were definite limits to the malleability of public opinion. (See figure 6.9 on the public's turn away from the new Cold War, which is also evident in figure 6.6 and—in very muted form—in figures 6.7 and 6.8.) In many areas of foreign policy, including military spending, arms control, military aid and arms sales, and cooperation with the Soviet Union, public opinion by the early 1980s once again heavily favored peaceful policies.

Central America

Central America became increasingly prominent in the Reagan administration's foreign policy and was the subject of an extraordinary number of opinion polls, presumably because of unusually strong and

rather stable public opposition to administration policies. Reagan sometimes moved opinion his way (chiefly by controlling events), but for the
most part he failed to do so. The administration then tried to "marginalize" hostile opinion (W. Lance Bennett, 1989) by discounting its
significance and ignoring it, but ultimately the government had to accommodate the public by changing policy. Like arms control, Central
America demonstrated the limits of persuasion or opinion manipulation—
even at the hands of a "Great Communicator."

To start with President Reagan's clearest success, most Americans—76%, according to an early November 1983 poll by ABC—
approved of the quick, low-cost invasion of Grenada, which the administration explained (based on shaky evidence) in terms of dangers to U.S.
medical students and the construction of an airport that might be used for
military purposes by the Soviets. In this case, quick action and a rapidly
favorable outcome (symbolized by the memorable TV image of returning
medical students kissing American soil), together with tight controls on
the press that kept messy and inconvenient details from the public, enabled the administration to persuade most Americans to back the invasion
and—in its afterglow—to favor other Reagan policies as well.

On the other hand, Reagan administration support for the military-
dominated government of El Salvador (threatened by leftist insurgents)
proved consistently unpopular, particularly when human rights groups
publicized the activities of right wing government-connected "death
squads." Sol Linowitz's "InterAmerican Dialogue," involving much of
the U.S. international business and foreign policy establishment (funded
by the Ford, Rockefeller, and other foundations), urged restraint and
dialogue to achieve stability in Central America, as did the "Miami
Report" and the Council on Foreign Relations (Ferguson and Rogers
1986, pp. 148–149). Any hint of using U.S. forces encountered heavy
public opposition. In March 1982, ABC/*WP* found that 82% opposed
sending U.S. troops; in May 1983, this figure stood at 85%, and 79%
wanted the U.S. to "stay out" of El Salvador. There was also substantial
opposition to military and economic aid: an NBC poll early in 1984
indicated that 71% opposed military aid, while 64% opposed economic
aid to El Salvador.

Figure 6.10 does show significant—about 10%—increases in support for various interventionist measures in El Salvador between February
1983 and February 1984, presumably as a result of Grenada. It also
makes clear that the public distinguished sharply among specific policy
measures. Although Roper's mentions of "leftist guerrillas" generally
elicited higher support than ABC/*WP*'s more neutral questions, when one

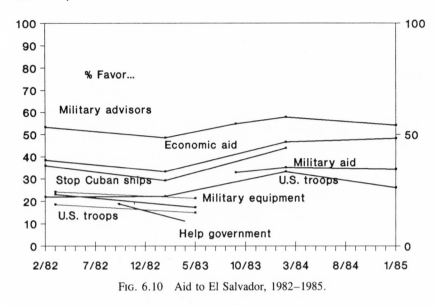

FIG. 6.10   Aid to El Salvador, 1982–1985.

holds organization and question format constant, at each moment in time many more Americans favored keeping "military advisors" in El Salvador "to help train" government troops, than wanted to increase military assistance or—the most distasteful option, favored by only a very small minority—to "send U.S. troops." Even if it was the "only way" to prevent the government from "being overthrown by the leftist guerrillas," at the peak of support in February 1984 no more than 35% of the public favored sending U.S. troops. But again, the main point is the strong continued public opposition to most of these policies, whether sending troops or military aid or even economic aid.

More important, covert operations against the leftist "Sandinista" government of Nicaragua, which began early in the Reagan administration and became one of its major preoccupations, sounded illegitimate (Americans don't like to overthrow governments), elicited fears of Vietnam-like involvement, and provoked broad public opposition. According to CBS/*NYT*, only 30% of Americans favored (as the question prologue put it) "help(ing) people in Nicaragua who are trying to overthrow the pro-Soviet government there" in June 1983, and this figure stayed the same or dropped slightly (to 26%) after Reagan's televised speech following the Grenada invasion and some public talk of invading Nicaragua. Reagan's rhetoric did not produce many instantaneous conversions, in this or other cases.

Cumulatively, the administration's efforts did apparently have some payoff: support for helping overthrow the Nicaraguan government rose significantly, from the 26% of late October 1983 to 33% in April 1984 and 37% in October, where it remained in 1985 (see Sobel 1989, p. 123). But, by the same token, a large majority (62% in May 1985) remained opposed. When it was revealed that U.S. agents had laid mines in Nicaraguan harbors, endangering neutral shipping, the public overwhelmingly disapproved: 84% opposed the mining, according to an April 1984 CBS/*NYT* survey. Most Americans also presumably opposed U.S.-backed distribution of pamphlets that promoted sabotage and assassinations.

Perhaps the most striking feature of the Nicaraguan case, then, is the extent to which the Reagan administration, despite a major effort, failed to persuade the public to back the Contra rebels. Elaborate public relations programs were designed to sell the CIA-organized Contra force (many of whose top military leaders had served the former Somoza dictatorship, and whose operations killed and maimed many civilians) as an indigenous, democratic resistance that cherished human rights. (Chamorro 1987 gives an intriguing inside account of the PR campaign.) Several years of rhetoric from President Reagan and others describing the Contras as "freedom fighters," "the democratic resistance," and "the moral equivalent of the Founding Fathers" failed to produce much movement in public opinion. Undeterred, the administration—as W. Lance Bennett (1989 and 1990) has shown—tried to "marginalize" opinion, ignoring or deprecating it, while secretly carrying out aid policies that were opposed by majorities of the public and (at times) prohibited by Congress (see U.S. Congress 1987).

Figure 6.11 shows the generally stable pattern of public opposition to aiding the Contras in Nicaragua, with only some glacial increase in support after 1983, a modest rise due to the 1986 media blitz, and a temporary Oliver North jump in 1987—to be discussed below. Certain survey questions elicited more support than others, but none (not even Gallup's allusion to helping oppose the "Marxist government in Nicaragua") succeeded in coming up with majority support for administration policy.

The public even more strongly and consistently opposed commitment of U.S. *troops* to Nicaragua, whether for the purpose of aiding the Contras, or for "invading" Nicaragua (Harris), or even in case of a hypothetical Nicaraguan invasion of Honduras, where Gallup/CCFR found 71% opposed to using American troops (Rielly 1987, p. 35). Only in the (highly unlikely) hypothetical event that Soviet missile bases were established in Nicaragua did a bare majority (52% in December 1986) say it favored use of U.S. troops (Rielly 1987, p. 32).

There was some support for economic or "humanitarian" aid to the Contras; some surveys show about 10% more support for "non–military"

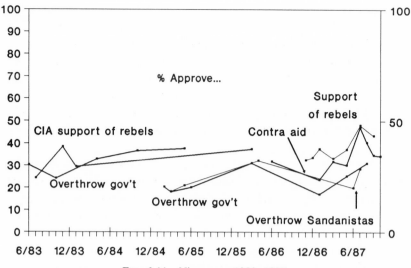

FIG. 6.11   Nicaragua, 1983–1987.

than for "military" aid (see Sobel 1989, p. 124). The administration tried hard in its rhetoric (though apparently not in actual operations) to distinguish between boots and bullets. But military aid was always unpopular, with about two-thirds of the public opposing it through most of the 1980s. Even when the administration convinced Congress to lift the Boland Amendment ban on military aid in the spring of 1986—by mounting an intense campaign that emphasized Nicaraguan leader Daniel Ortega's trip to Moscow and stirred congressmen's fears of seeming to be soft on communism, through such means as "privately" funded TV ads that used Defense Department film footage to attack anti-aid congressmen—and when the *New York Times* and other media subsequently muted their criticism of administration policy (W. Lance Bennett 1989), the public was not swayed much. There was only a modest increase in support for military aid, with a substantial majority still opposed to it.

The colorful, vigorous, and true-believing testimony of Colonel Oliver North before the Iran/Contra congressional investigating committee in the summer of 1987, with North's strong condemnation of Congress's "abandonment" of the "democratic resistance," produced a sharp but temporary upsurge in support for Contra aid: from 32% in favor in January 1987 to 45% in favor in late July, according to CBS/*NYT*. Much of the change was registered during the course of three surveys taken in July: 39% favored Contra aid after the first two days of North's testimony; 41% a week later; and 45% toward the end of the month (*New York Times,* July

24, 1987; we have excluded "don't knows"). ABC/*WP* measured an even sharper jump, from only 30% favoring Contra aid in late May/early June to 49% in mid-July. And *Los Angeles Times* surveys also found a large rise, from 36% in February to 50% in late July 1987.

But even at the peak, there was never a majority supporting aid, and the overwhelming proportion of Americans (85%, according to Gallup) opposed using Iran profits to help the Contras. Moreover, the upsurge in backing for Contra aid itself did not last long. Its transience illustrates some important principles about collective opinion change.

Support for Contra aid rose sharply when the strong, clear message from Colonel North, not significantly challenged or contradicted by other witnesses (an oddity, under the circumstances) or by the mesmerized investigators, dominated the airwaves and was seen by millions of Americans. It dropped again when contrary information began to be aired. In the same way, highly visible international events that are given unified, consensual interpretations by government and other elites (communicated through the mass media) often lead to abrupt opinion changes. But when there is disagreement among commentators and politicians and experts, when media messages are mixed, opinion does not move in such a simple fashion; often it does not move at all.[23] When information is available that can support critical analyses, especially when elites differ, opinion manipulation is very difficult.

Within a week or two after North's testimony ended, a media counterattack began, and public opinion moved back to where it had been. The *New York Times,* for example, featured a story debunking an allegedly great military "victory" by the Contras, which turned out to involve killing a pregnant woman and two small children while achieving no significant military objectives. There were follow-up stories on TV news and a number of critical editorials and comments. A U.S.-sponsored commission reported various human rights abuses by the Contras. Public support for Contra aid fell to only 34% in January 1988, according to CBS/*NYT,* and it remained at about the same low level further into 1988 and 1989, as Congress again restricted the aid program.

When the Arias plan led to negotiations and ultimately a cease fire, Gallup found in October 1987 that 82% of Americans thought the United States should "back the Central American peace plan," and 78% wanted to wait and see whether the plan was successful before continuing aid to the Contras. In time to make things easier for George Bush in the 1988 election, the Reagan administration bowed to public opinion and quietly gave up on what had been the president's pet foreign policy initiative, military aid for the Contras. In 1990, Violeta Chamorro defeated Daniel Ortega in a free election, the Contras were demobilized and resettled, and the Sandinista armed forces and political influence were reduced.

Renewed Détente

Despite all the noise about Central America, the most important subject of foreign policy opinions in the mid-1980s was undoubtedly U.S. relations with the other superpower, the USSR. We have already described how public opinion moved somewhat toward favoring a new Cold War posture in the late 1970s, and then moved quickly away from it. By the middle 1980s, the public overwhelmingly backed measures for a renewed détente. In 1984, for example, Harris found that large majorities of Americans favored new arms limitation agreements with the Soviets (91%) and wanted to resume various friendly activities involving trade, scientific and cultural exchanges (85%), cooperation on energy and in space (72%), and the like. Gallup found similar sentiments in its CCFR survey of December 1986 (Rielly 1987, pp. 14–15). And we have noted the very high backing for a nuclear freeze and the growing desires to cut military spending.

The public's increasing support for détente was eventually helped along somewhat by the Reagan administration's gradual moves in that direction: the summit conferences and agreements of autumn 1985 (Geneva), autumn 1986 (Rekjavik), December 1987 (the Washington summit with Gorbachev at which the Intermediate Nuclear Force agreement was announced), and spring 1988 (Moscow). Much friendlier rhetoric began to displace the earlier denunciations of the "evil empire."

Still, Reagan administration foreign policy had been substantially and unusually far out of harmony with the opinions of the general public (see Rielly 1987, pp. 34–36), and the prodétente opinion changes seem mostly to have preceded rather than followed changes in the administration's line. More important in influencing the public was probably leadership from the freeze movement and from experts and media editorials and commentary, some of it stimulated by foundations and perhaps by those with particular economic interests in reducing military expenditures.

To a large extent, however, the movement in public opinion may have been relatively autonomous, not needing a great deal of leadership—and, indeed, with many "leaders" only falling in line later. To a large extent people reacted to objective events, especially the emergence of a much less threatening Russia that was preoccupied with Gorbachev's "perestroika" and "glasnost" and sought peaceful foreign relations.

Most Americans had always wanted to get along with the Soviet Union. Many, frightened by the alleged "window of vulnerability" and angered by the events in Iran and Afghanistan, had supported the Reagan arms buildup at the beginning of the 1980s. But people became disturbed by the ensuing tensions and harsh rhetoric and sought renewed détente as soon as it seemed possible—a desire to which the Reagan administration eventually responded. Again public opinion seems to have affected policy (see Graham 1989b; Farkas et al. 1990).

The opinion trend in favor of renewed détente continued into the Bush administration, when Gorbachev's spectacular arms control proposals and unilateral force reductions, and his permission (or encouragement) for Eastern Europe to make dramatic moves toward liberalization, democratization, and independence, convinced many Americans that the Cold War could be ended and substantial disarmament achieved. At the beginning of the 1990s the American public's desires for friendly, cooperative relations with the Soviet Union reached an all-time high. Large majorities agreed that the Cold War was "coming to an end" (see Richman 1991), though there were signs of disillusionment early in 1991 as Soviet reforms seemed to falter and Gorbachev pressured the Baltics. Gallup found a high of 53% saying "too much" was being spent on defense in January 1990, before the Iraqi invasion of Kuwait and the dispatch of U.S. troops in August sent pro-military attitudes back up.

Foreign Policy and the Rational Public

The evidence in this and previous chapters simply does not support the notion that collective public opinion concerning foreign policy is random or meaningless or incoherent. We have seen that the American public makes many clear and reasonable distinctions among alternative policies—where to use American troops, for example (table 6.1; figure 6.7), and to whom to sell arms (figure 6.8). Moreover, the public's preferences form coherent patterns that reflect underlying goals and values and beliefs, including strong desires for peace, international cooperation, and reliance on negotiations and agreements; support for military strength, with a willingness to use force when vital U.S. interests appear to be threatened; but great reluctance to intervene in peripheral conflicts abroad with U.S. troops or even with arms sales or military aid. One may agree or disagree with these strands of opinion, but they undeniably fit together into a coherent whole.

Nor does public opinion change in a vacillating, capricious, or whimsical fashion. As we saw in Chapter 2, stability is the rule. To be sure, opinions concerning foreign policy (more often than domestic policy) do sometimes change abruptly. But our close examination of survey data in historical context makes clear that nearly all such changes represent sensible responses to events and to the information that is conveyed to the citizenry.

Little wonder that Hitler's conquests led most Americans to favor aiding Britain and France and then the USSR, or that the apparently sudden and unprovoked Pearl Harbor attack by Japan made the public want to fight back. Nor is it surprising that the outbreak of the Korean war, as described to the public, engendered a willingness to increase defense spending, commit troops, and resist what was perceived as Soviet and Chinese aggression. In the case of these and most other observed opinion changes, it is easy to see how changing circumstances, as reported in the mass media (and interpreted by officials and other opinion leaders) could reasonably alter calculations about the costs and benefits of policy alternatives and thereby cause changes in policy preferences. Moreover, in a number of cases objective events—including war casualties, changes in defense spending, and troop withdrawal rates—have affected opinion in regular and predictable ways.

We are under no illusion that every citizen receives all relevant information and performs careful cost/benefit calculations. Instead, as indicated in Chapter 1 and discussed further in Chapters 8–10, we argue that collective processes of information pooling, cuetaking, and debate and deliberation are fairly efficient, and that individuals' random errors tend to cancel each other out in such a fashion that *collective* public opinion is real and measurable and moves in sensible ways.

The relatively great number of abrupt opinion changes concerning defense and international issues results from certain special features of foreign policy and the world scene. For one, in the international realm objective reality often changes in rapid and fundamental ways. Foreign nations or groups (and the United States itself) often act suddenly and unpredictably, using armed force or diplomacy or economic power in ways that strongly affect the United States—not only through major wars but also by revolutions, hostage takings, boycotts or price rises, minor armed conflicts, and the like. Dramatic events are common in foreign policy.

For another, control of information about foreign affairs tends to be highly centralized, especially in covert actions, crisis situations, and war. Often the U.S. government closely holds the relevant information and can decide what to say; it can present a unified, carefully constructed picture of events to the public, or (with luck) can withhold the facts altogether and prevent the public from knowing about or judging U.S. policy.[24]

Furthermore, in foreign policy the objective or subjective "national interest" of the United States (as a more or less unitary actor on the world stage) is often engaged, in such a way that nearly all Americans agree on the policy implications of a particular event, as that event is communicated to them. Most Americans share common interests or common values, and—as Cantril and Research Associates (1947, p. 213) point out—elites and the media, holding those same values, help provide "common standards" by which to judge an event's policy implications. Most Americans, therefore, react to international affairs in the same way, producing relatively quick net changes in collective public opinion.

These same features of foreign affairs—dramatic events, centralized information, and common values—not only account for abrupt opinion changes by a rational public; they also create opportunities for manipulation of opinion, opportunities that are greater in foreign policy than domestic. To the extent that the federal government—particularly the executive branch—controls information about foreign affairs, it may be tempted to suppress the truth or to disseminate misleading information or falsehoods, albeit in the name of national security and the national interest. We have mentioned some important cases—the onset of World War II, the Truman Doctrine, the "missile gap," the Tonkin Gulf and Vietnam, the Russian scare of the 1970s and early 1980s, KAL007—in which political leaders and others seem to have succumbed to that temptation. In some cases private groups like the Committee on the Present Danger may be able to dominate policy debates in similar ways.

Value consensus, government information control, and also elite-level politics (e.g., the financial dependence of both parties on the same kinds of donors, collusion for bipartisan gain, or simple ineptitude) can sometimes bring it about that political opponents, other elites, and the media do not challenge official interpretations of international reality, even when those interpretations are markedly incorrect. This can be crucial. When political opposition is stifled or silent, the public is much more susceptible to manipulation. (The brief persuasive success of Oliver North illustrates what an unchallenged voice can do.)

Moreover, in addition to controlling information and interpretations, the government can often create or orchestrate events themselves, letting desired opinion changes follow naturally—as FDR did with his Atlantic convoy policies and maneuvering Japan before World War II, and as Reagan did in Grenada and Bush in Panama. As we write, the Iraq war is looking like a similar case. Low-level interventions can create momentum for further actions. Provocative moves like pursuing German submarines or carrying out the Tonkin Gulf raids and patrols can increase the probability of "incidents" that will rally support and justify policies which the executive seeks.

At the same time, however, we have also observed many cases in which attempts at persuasion or opinion manipulation failed: Vietnam (in the long run), China, the UN, arms control and the nuclear freeze, El Salvador and Nicaragua. The public can be remarkably resistant to persuasive attempts by elites and governments, especially when alternative information is available and when some elite faction or factions voice disagreement with the dominant view.

Moreover, public opinion moving as a relatively autonomous force can have a substantial impact upon policy, as it seems to have done in the cases of improved relations with China, opposition to the Vietnam War, and resistance to Contra aid and the Reagan arms buildup, among others. Public opinion concerning foreign policy has to be taken seriously as an influence in democratic policy-making.

We will return to the topic of opinion manipulation in Chapter 9, after examining opinion trends among various subgroups of the population (Chap. 7) and after more systematically appraising the different causes of collective opinion change (Chap. 8).

7 Parallel Publics

☑ For the most part, we have been treating the American public as a homogeneous whole, with collective preferences that move as a unit in response to new information and events in domestic and foreign affairs. Along the way we mentioned a few differences in trends among people of different educational backgrounds and from different regions. But isn't there more to be said about differences among social groups? Shouldn't we pay more attention to opinion trends among people grouped according to such characteristics as gender, race, income, age, religion, and party loyalty?

The stability we found in aggregate public opinion might possibly conceal large, offsetting changes among particular subgroups of the population. The aggregate changes we have described might result from strong opinion movements that were confined to particular groups, while the preferences of the rest of the population stayed constant or even moved in the opposite direction. If different groupings of Americans change their opinions in dramatically different ways, it is misleading to speak of a single "public."

Survey researchers have long been aware that, at a given point in time, different social groups may differ markedly from each other in the *level* of their policy preferences: that is, in the proportions by which they favor or oppose various policies. Group preferences can vary because of differing interests; different social, economic, political, and cultural environments; diverse experiences; or differing positions in society, any one of which can lead to different perceptions, wants, and values.

Black Americans, for example, have special reason to care about civil rights; the elderly about pensions and protection from street crime; young men of draft age about military service. The poor and unemployed tend to favor social welfare programs more than others do. Many American Jews feel a special closeness to Israel. The wealthy are especially averse to redistribution of wealth or income.

We do not wish to overstate the element of self-interest here; scholars, surprisingly, have often failed to find the expected blatant manifestations of self-interest in Americans' policy preferences. True, farmers and labor union members have sometimes been watchful of their economic interests (see Campbell et al. 1960; Hansen 1983); smokers have readily defended their habit and responded to threats to smoking (Green and Gerken 1989). But in study after study, hypotheses involving narrow *personal* self-interest have not been borne out concerning such diverse matters as the Vietnam War and the draft, busing to achieve integration, or the impact of economic conditions (see Sears et al. 1979, 1980; Kinder and Kiewiet 1979, 1981; Citrin and Green 1990 provide a full review). Although people certainly attend to personal interests and concerns close to home, they also draw upon group and societal-wide values and information and take account of the perceived interests of the larger community.

Policy preferences are very often unselfish, then, directed to the common good of the group or nation (see Mansbridge 1990). By the same token, however, opinions based on various sorts of *group* interest seem to be extremely pervasive and important; we will note many examples.

In some cases, such as that of blacks, distinctive group circumstances or interests may lead to—and be reinforced by—a shared group consciousness and solidarity. In addition, some groups (women, e.g.) may not only be concerned with narrow individual or even group self-interest but may have distinctive concerns about issues affecting the citizenry as a whole, such as social equality, peace, control of violence, a clean and safe environment, and other matters involving the common good.

Whatever their basis, group-related differences in political opinions are widespread and have been the subject of a great deal of sociological investigation. We will not attempt to add to that vast literature here; we will only briefly summarize certain important group differences in policy preferences. Our chief concern, instead, is whether groups differ in the way they *change* policy preferences.

There are several persuasive reasons why we might expect that groups would differ in processes of change. If groups tend to differ in their goals and interests, to receive different information, or to undergo different kinds of changes in circumstances, their preferences might change differentially.

Groups that have distinctive values or interests, for example, might be differentially affected by new events or circumstances, so that they change policy preferences in a distinctive fashion.

Or groups that are especially concerned about particular policies that affect them directly might be especially attentive and sensitive to new information or events bearing on them, and might, therefore, be quickest to alter their policy preferences. When crime rates rise or the cost of health care increases, the elderly and the vulnerable might be quick to embrace proposed remedies. When war casualties and draft calls escalate, young men and their families might be the first to turn against war. When recessions hit and unemployment rises, poor and working-class people might be the first and loudest to demand government assistance.

One might also expect certain types of people—particularly those with varying levels of education—to change opinions in different ways because of different levels of exposure and attentiveness to new information, differences in comprehension, and differential openness to persuasion.

People with a lot of formal education tend to read more and learn more about politics, both from the mass media (especially newspapers and magazines) and from well-educated and attentive friends. They tend to be exposed to what various elites and opinion leaders have written and spoken. They have an easier time understanding new ideas and events. They might, therefore, more readily change opinions when events occur or new information is communicated. (We have touched upon some of these ideas in connection with foreign policy attitudes in Chap. 5.) On the other hand, the well educated (and perhaps older citizens as well) may already have a very large stock of experience and information, be convinced that their opinions are well reasoned and correct, and, therefore, be the most resistant to change. Those in the middle ranges of education might combine exposure and openness so as to maximize opinion change (see Converse 1962; Zaller 1987, 1990b).

In addition, as we also noted in discussing foreign policy opinions, it is possible that the pace and timing of opinion change could differ among various groups because of their positions in networks of social communication and opinion influence or leadership. The better educated, for example, might be more likely to act as opinion leaders, not only forming their preferences more quickly than others but also perhaps actively persuading those who are less well informed, or at least passively providing cues and frames of reference for others. Such processes might vary by type of issue, with the most attentive and concerned groups on each issue shifting first and perhaps bringing others along later.

Similarly, if public officials or political parties act as opinion leaders, one would expect citizens with different party loyalties to react differently, paying attention to and following party leaders they trust. Party loyalists are presumably more likely than others to seek out or be exposed to partisan information, to perceive it as credible, and to be persuaded by it, so that opinion dynamics on certain issues might differ among different groups of party identifiers.

On the other hand, any or all of these hypotheses about differential group changes could be incorrect. Public opinion may change in a rather uniform fashion across the whole population, if the national media transmit similar information to all groups and if they receive and process it in similar ways. This is especially likely to be true to the extent that different groups have similar interests or think in terms of *public goods* and the collective or national interest.

As we will see, this latter situation may, in fact, be very common; it turns out that the policy preferences of different social groupings generally move in parallel with each other. But many ideas about differential changes are widely assumed to be true. We need to examine them closely, even if most of them turn out to be incorrect or inapplicable.

To date, empirical evidence about the dynamics of public opinion among population subgroups has been rather limited; it has not yielded any unifying conclusion. Only a small number of policy issues or subgroups have usually been examined at once, and most studies have only covered short time periods (but see Mueller 1973; Davis 1980; Schuman et al. 1985; and esp. Weil's (1985, 1989) and Inglehart's (1990) comparative research). It is difficult to perform complicated multivariate analysis over time, controlling for confounding effects, as is required in order to arrive at firm conclusions about the unique behavior of particular groups. Moreover, scholars have lacked easily available data on groups' responses to a wide range of repeated (identically worded) survey questions. Subgroup trends have not usually been included in the available publications about collective opinion trends but have been published, if at all, only at the same time the aggregate responses to a survey question were initially reported (e.g., in Gallup and Harris and other press releases and in what is currently called the *Gallup Poll Monthly*.)[1] It is difficult to gather together such scattered sources or to obtain the many original data sets needed to tabulate subgroup responses. Accordingly, we once again turn to our own collection of data.

Data and Methods

As part of our data collection effort, we also assembled an unusually large number of subgroup tabulations, drawn mainly from available but dispersed published sources and supplemented by analysis of some full data sets. Using these data we have done several analyses.

One—an early and very general analysis, first reported in Shapiro and Page (1984)—is based on subgroup data concerning 169 repeated policy questions. The 169 items come from four survey organizations: the NORC General Social Surveys (NORC–GSS), 1972–1983; Gallup polls (published in the 1964–1983 volumes of *The Gallup Opinion Index/The Gallup Report*); Louis Harris and Associates (from 1963–1983 press releases and the four existing *Harris Survey Yearbooks* covering 1970–

1973); and the Opinion Research Corporation (surveys done for and reported by the Advisory Commission on Intergovernmental Relations (ACIR), 1973–1982).

These 169 survey questions may not be quite as representative of the whole range of public policy issues as is the larger set of trend items we have examined for the public as a whole; many more concern domestic policy ($n=122$) than foreign policy ($n=47$), for example. But they do include questions about many different sorts of government laws, spending programs, regulations, acts of officials, and outcomes. The responses are broken down according to education, income, occupation, race, age, sex, religion, region, type of rural or urban community, and political partisanship, with the precise variables and categories varying from one opinion question or survey organization to another. There are more than 1,000 sets of short opinion time series, with each set consisting of the trends in responses to one survey question by people in each of the two to six different categories (e.g., Democrats, Republicans, and Independents; men and women) used to group the population according to a particular variable. This adds up to more than 3,000 opinion time series (most of them short: about half based on three or more time points) for particular subgroups of Americans on particular policy issues.

There are several possible ways to compare the behavior of subgroups over time and to estimate whether their trends differ significantly (in a statistical sense) from each other (see, e.g., Taylor 1980; Schuman et al. 1985; Richman 1972; Schwartz 1967). We chose to compare the sizes of *changes* in the opinions of subgroups *between pairs of surveys,* looking at each pair of time points for each time series. That is, we compared and estimated every possible difference in trend between pairs of subgroups, over periods as short or as long in time as happened to be available.[2] We generally inferred (except in cases of small subsamples which required more stringent standards) that movements in subgroups' opinions differed in *substantively* important—not just statistically significant—ways if changes differed by *ten* percentage points or more. As before, these differences were calculated after "don't know," "no opinion," "not sure," and other such responses were excluded and after opinion response categories were dichotomized so as to maximize aggregate opinion change.

For example, if one subgroup's (say college-educated) support for a particular policy increased by ten percentage points between two surveys, whereas another grouping's (say grade-school-educated) support did not change, this difference (10 - 0 = 10 percentage points) would be treated as significant. The same would be true if one group's support increased by five percentage points while another's decreased by the same amount [5-(-5)=10 percentage points], or if one increased by 20% and the other increased by only 10%.

This 10% criterion is a rather conservative one. It justifies a fairly high degree of confidence that each subgroup difference in opinion trend is real and not an artifact of sampling error.[3] By the same token, however, it could mislead us into counting too few differences as meaningful. Observed group trend differences of eight or nine percentage points, for example, are very likely to signal something real even if they do not quite reach standard levels of statistical confidence.[4] Therefore, in a second analysis, using a smaller set of NORC-GSS data on sixty-nine policy issues over a seventeen-year period (1972–1988), we investigated how many subgroup differences in trends reached the level of eight or nine percentage points—reflecting a looser statistical standard.[5] In order to ensure that we were not misled by temporary subgroup divergences due to sampling error or other factors, and to estimate more precisely the relative movement of subgroups over substantial periods of time on issues particularly *relevant* to these groups, we also did a third analysis (again using NORC-GSS data) of relatively long time series on selected issues.

Parallel Opinion Changes by Different Groups

When we examined all 3,000 or so subgroup trends in the large data set and considered the many thousands of differences that could have occurred for various groups between all pairs of time points on each of the many opinion questions, the most striking finding was the lack of group differences. Most of the time, the policy preferences of different subgroups changed (or stayed the same) in similar ways. The trend lines were mostly parallel. When they diverged, they tended later to return to parallel positions.

Table 7.1 presents findings for the entire subgroup data set and for each set of subgroups as defined by a particular population characteristic (gender, race, education, and the like). The table lists each characteristic followed by (1) the total number of potential subgroup differences, based on comparisons of the amount of opinion change between all pairs of subgroup categories (e.g., high, medium, or low education) for all pairs of time points on each opinion item; (2) the number of substantively significant (at least ten percentage points)[6] differences between subgroups that were found; and (3) the number of actual differences as a percentage of the total number of potential differences. The latter figure provides an estimate, based on our 169 repeated survey questions, of how frequently various kinds of differences in subgroup trends occur.

TABLE 7.1 Frequency with Which Subgroup Opinion Movements
Differed Significantly for 169 Repeated Survey Items

Subgroup Variables	Total Pairs of Subgroup Opinion Shifts	Differences among These Pairs	Differences as a Percentage of Total (%)
Sex	1,453	12	0.01
Race	1,435	108	7.5
Education	4,291	209	4.9
Occupation	1,086	65	5.9
Income	7,612	482	6.3
Religion	249	21	8.4
Age	4,881	250	5.1
Partisanship	1,912	83	4.3
Region	5,583	319	5.7
Community	5,782	406	7.0
Total	34,284	1,955	5.7

Source: Shapiro and Page (1984), table 1, p. 36, revised.
Note: Differences in opinion movements of at least 10 percentage points (see text). Not all subgroup tabulations were available for each survey question. The entries above are based on responses to between 90 and 169 questions. Of the 169, 122 were concerned with domestic policies and 47 with foreign and defense issues.

As the table indicates, there were few substantial differences among groups in opinion shifts. They ranged in frequency from a miniscule 0.01% for comparisons between men and women (though, as we will see, this masks some small but persistent differences), to a modest high of 8.4% for people of different religions.[7] When all the comparisons among subgroups are taken together, we find that there were substantial differences in trends less than 6% of the time. That is to say, these differences occurred rather infrequently, only a little more than one-twentieth of the number of times they could have occurred.

The percentages reported in table 7.1 may actually *over*estimate the frequency of group differences in opinion trends. Since we only tried to ensure that each difference be significant at the .05 level (i.e., that we be 95% confident that each true difference was not zero), and since we made thousands of comparisons, many of the differences we found may have occurred by chance. Indeed, if no real subgroup differences at all existed, we would expect to find apparent differences due to sampling error about 5% of the time—very close to the 6% we found. This does not mean that there were actually no real subgroup differences at all (some of those we

TABLE 7.2 Frequency with Which Subgroup Opinion Movements Differed for 69 AA Repeated NORC-GSS Items, 1972–1988

Total Pairs of Subgroup Opinion Shifts	Differences among These Pairs of:					
	8%	9%	10%	11%	12%	13%+
Race: 3,336	160	127	84	94	76	210
	(541 total, 16.2% of 3,336)					(6.3% of 3,336)
	8%	9%				10%+
Sex: 3,374	54	40				64
	(94 total, 2.8% of 3,374)					(1.9% of 3,374)

Note: For sex, all the above differences in opinion movements are statistically signficant at the .05 level or better, assuming simple random sampling. For race, only the differences of at least 13 percentage points are significant at the .05 level (see text). The difference in the total number of pairs for race (3,336) vs. sex (3,374) is attributable to the inclusion of some questions which for a time were not asked of black respondents, so that no comparisons by race could be made.

observed were big enough to be significant at much better than the .05 level), but it does suggest that real differences were quite uncommon.[8]

On the other hand, in counting only differences between groups' changes that were ten percentage points or larger we may have neglected some small, but real, group differences. In order to examine this possibility—and to consider long time periods within which enduring subgroup differences in trends would have plenty of opportunity to unfold—we did a separate, additional analysis using NORC-GSS data on sixty-nine policy preference items for 1972–1988. As table 7.2 indicates, even if we count smaller (8% or more) differences in those data as significant, group differences in trends still appear to be relatively infrequent.

Table 7.2 reports the results of our GSS analysis for gender subgroups, which in our earlier study showed the smallest differences in trends, and for racial subgroups, which earlier showed some of the biggest. For the gender subgroups, which (since there are only two groups, about equal in size) are the largest in these data, 8% differences are statistically significant at the .05 level (assuming simple random sampling). But including them as substantively significant raises the frequency of opinion trends that diverge between men and women to only about 2% of the total, a little more than in the earlier study but slightly less than what we might expect due to chance (cf. table 7.2 with table 7.1).

Similarly, table 7.2 displays the frequency of divergent trends for racial subgroups, using criteria ranging from the 13% differences required for significance at the .05 level, down to 8% (significant at only about the .20 level). In each case, the proportion of subgroup divergences is only a percentage point or two greater than would be expected by chance alone. For example, 11% of the differences amounted to eleven percentage points or more, whereas by chance (assuming no real differences at all) we would expect about 10%. There were differences of eight percentage points or more in not quite 23% of the cases, again about what we would expect by chance.

Still, in order to be completely fair to hypotheses about subgroup opinion chances, we need to search more *purposively* for differences. One step is to examine exclusively cases in which the collective policy preferences of the public as a whole actually changed, to increase the chances of finding differential movement by subgroups. (Presumably one reason for the infrequency of subgroup divergences in tables 7.1 and 7.2 is the inclusion of many short time periods with no aggregate opinion change.)[9] Even more important is to focus on particular issues for which we might expect particular patterns of differential subgroup change. In the case of racial subgroups, for example, it makes sense to take a close look at issues of civil rights and economic welfare.

Accordingly, we examined more closely the NORC-GSS data on opinion changes concerning the same sixty-nine policy issues between 1972 and 1988 (a period long enough to allow differential opinion changes to occur and to reduce distractions from temporary divergences),[10] among subgroups defined according to region, race, education, income (by quartiles), and religion (Jews, and Protestant and Catholic whites). (Gender groups do not require this analysis; the evidence is already overwhelming that they move in parallel.) In each case we confined our attention to issues for which group differences in trends seemed particularly relevant, as indicated by subgroup differences in levels of opinion that persisted when other variables were controlled.[11] The logic here is that genuine differences in subgroups' opinions at one point in time tend to indicate different interests, values, and/or sensitivity that might lead to differential opinion trends.

By this means we selected more than 150 sets of subgroup trends, where there were the largest differences in the levels of subgroups' opinions, for further inspection and time series analysis—comparing different subgroups' opinion movements between individual time points, as we did for tables 7.1 and 7.2, and also comparing rates of opinion change over the full period. A few graphs from these 150-plus comparisons will be presented below, when we discuss particular groups.

There are intriguing variations, but the dominant pattern is once again one of parallel publics. Even on these specially selected cases, the opinions of different subgroups mostly moved in the same directions. This is consistent with our argument about media-transmitted influences to which virtually all Americans are exposed and susceptible. True, there are some patterns of differential change, especially *convergence* of subgroup preferences over time (of the sort we noted in discussing civil rights); and a few interesting phenomena like flip-flopping divergences of opinions that political leaders sometimes engender among party identifiers. We will discuss the exceptions further. But the main pattern, again, is of subgroups changing in the same direction.

Furthermore, the *magnitude,* or the rate, of change by different subgroups tends also to be quite similar. For a selection of our opinion time series involving smooth (more or less linear) trends, we calculated the rate of opinion change for individual subgroups by regressing opinion levels on time. The results indicate some variation, but for the most part different groupings of the population changed their policy preferences during the 1970s and 1980s at about the same speed. (Some of these regression slopes are reported in the Appendix for figures 7.1 through 7.10, and a few are noted in the text below.) Moreover, for nonlinear shifts, visual inspection of graphs generally supports the proposition that opinions changed in tandem and at about the same rate for different subgroups. Some of the graphs displayed below constitute interesting exceptions, since a full display of parallel trends would be boring, but even here the general tendency is apparent.

Most of the time, then, most groupings of Americans change their policy preferences—when they do so at all—in the same direction and to about the same extent. Hence our reference to "parallel publics." Either the many plausible hypotheses concerning divergent changes are incorrect, or—more likely—they are applicable only in a minority of special cases. Most group-based differences in levels of opinion are rather longstanding. They apparently emerge right away when opinions are first formed on new issues, and are faithfully replicated in new cohorts (and with respect to emerging issues) through group-related processes of political learning and shared experiences and circumstances. Thus there can be substantial cross-sectional differences in the policy preferences of different subgroups without many divergent changes over time.

This suggests that, on many issues, most or all subgroups may have sufficiently similar interests (or a common concern for the collective public interest) so as to react to new events and changed circumstances in similar ways. The highly centralized mass media, especially the wire services and television network news, provide much the same information to people all over the country. And, as we noted earlier, the media, political leaders, and other elites often help provide "common standards of judgment" (Cantril and Research Associates 1947) as well. Together, these factors could lead policy preferences of different groups to change in the same ways. And often, of course, subgroups do not differ because nothing much happens and little or no opinion change occurs among any elements of the population: after all, as we saw in Chapter 2, opinion stability is the rule.

Within this context of generally parallel publics, however, there are some important differences among subgroups that deserve discussion. For each of several population characteristics, we will first briefly mention how (if at all) the relevant subgroups tend to differ from each other in *levels* of opinion at any given moment. These could be called "equilibrium" differences in group opinions; they appear in early stages of opinion formation and generally persist over time, as well as holding up when other variables are controlled for statistically. Next we will note some exceptional cases in which the direction or magnitude of opinion *change* differs among groups.

Women and Men

Research has revealed a few large, and many small but consistent and enduring, differences between the policy preferences of men and women, differences which remain after variables other than gender are controlled for.

The largest and most important differences concern violence and the use of force. In practically all realms of foreign and domestic policy, women are less belligerent than men. They are more supportive of arms control and peaceful foreign relations; they are more likely to oppose weapons buildups or the use of force. They much more frequently favor gun control and oppose capital punishment. On these issues, over a twenty-year period, there has been an average opinion difference of about nine percentage points (Tom Smith 1984; Shapiro and Mahajan 1986). Some scholars have suggested that the reasons involve training (and/or even a genetic predisposition) of women to be less aggressive and to act as caretakers and nurturers (see Gilligan 1982; Sapiro 1984).

Gender differences also extend to what might be called "compassion" or "protection" issues involving social welfare assistance to the weak and needy. By a small but persistent average margin of perhaps three or four percentage points, more women than men have favored policies which aid the poor, the unemployed, the sick, and others in need. This kind of difference has also applied to certain policies concerning consumer protection, personal safety, and protection of the environment, with more women than men favoring regulation. Average differences on these regulatory issues increased from about three percentage points in the 1960s to an average of seven percent in the 1977–1983 period (Shapiro and Mahajan 1986, p. 54). (Since then some gender differences have diminished or even vanished, as men moved toward women's positions on old and new issues such as the environment: see Wirls 1986. Gender differences on national defense also decreased in the Gorbachev era, and those on some social welfare issues may have declined as well.)

Furthermore, women have been slightly—and perhaps increasingly—more supportive than men of traditional values involving home, family, sexual mores, life-style, religion, and community. For example, women have been less favorable toward pornography or easy divorce laws.

On specifically feminist political issues like abortion and the Equal Rights Amendment, gender differences have been surprisingly small or nonexistent (Shapiro and Mahajan 1986; see also Mansbridge 1986). At one time men were actually a bit more supportive of abortion than women were, but this difference has virtually disappeared. Women's feminist attitudes, however, appear to be much more rooted in personal experiences, whereas for men these issues are more ideological or symbolic (see Klein 1984). Independent upper-status women, especially in new cohorts, have been particularly supportive of feminism (see Sapiro 1984).

Over the last twenty years, women have apparently become more attentive to and interested in politics. In the 1960s, women tended to give about five percentage points more "don't know" and "no opinion" responses than men to policy preference questions, but the difference has declined to roughly half that (Shapiro and Mahajan 1986, p. 57).

When we turn to differences between men and women in policy preference *trends,* we find remarkably little. In only a tiny proportion (much less than 1%) of hundreds of comparisons did women's and men's policy preferences move in ways that differed by ten percentage points or more. As we saw in table 7.1, this was the smallest of all the subgroup trend differences we examined.

Much the same result appeared when we considered smaller group divergences of 8% or 9% (see table 7.2), or the regression-estimated rates of opinion change. The policy preferences of men and women have almost always moved in parallel.

For illustration, figure 7.1 displays the trends in men's and women's opinions about whether or not police permits should be required before a

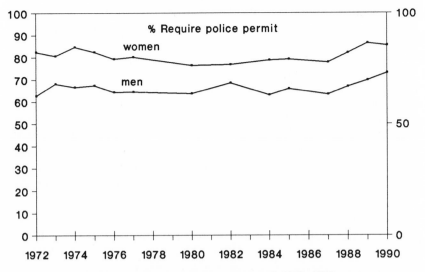

FIG. 7.1   Women and men: gun control, 1972–1990.

person could buy a gun. There obviously have been big gender differences in opinion levels, with women supporting gun control in significantly higher proportions (an average of fifteen percentage points more) than men did. Yet, over the seventeen-year period graphed—except for hints of temporary convergence in 1973 and 1982—the gender difference stayed nearly the same. The two trend lines mostly moved up and down together.

Much the same impression would be conveyed by our graph (not displayed) of men's and women's opinions on capital punishment from 1974 to 1990, which regularly differed by nearly ten percentage points but moved in parallel; or by the graph of opinions on welfare spending (1973–1990), where opinions differed by a smaller three to four percentage points but moved together in even more perfect lockstep; or, indeed, by graphs of any of a host of other issues.

We have found only a few small but interesting exceptions. For example, Shapiro and Mahajan (1986) reported a modest divergence between men and women during the 1970s on the compassion and protection issues, and we have alluded to a convergence on some environmental and defense issues in the 1980s. Other scattered cases of distinctive trends include a sharp drop in women's (but not men's) support for the mining of North Vietnamese harbors between May and October 1972 (Harris), conceivably because of differential receptiveness to the antiwar McGovern campaign, and the slight and temporary convergence on gun control in

1982 shown in figure 7.1. But the far more typical pattern is of that of parallel movement in the opinions of men and women, with certain small but enduring differences in opinion levels.

Blacks and Whites

Black Americans, still emerging from a history of slavery and discrimination, hold a number of quite distinctive policy preferences. By large margins, for example, more blacks than whites—even after taking into account economic status, education, and other personal characteristics—have favored policies of aiding blacks and other minorities and integrating schools, workplaces, housing, public accommodations, and the like.

Based on our analysis of the combined 1972–1988 NORC-GSS surveys (putting together many years to yield a total usable for multivariate analysis of approximately 13,000 respondents, including a substantial number of blacks), an average of 23% more blacks than whites opposed laws against racial intermarriage. After controlling for gender, age, region, community type, income, and education in a linear model, the difference actually *rose* to 27%. (Statistics buffs will appreciate this rare manifestation of a suppressor effect.) Similarly, a remarkable 37% more blacks than whites favored busing for school integration, a figure that stayed at 35% after controlling for the demographic variables.

In somewhat greater numbers than whites, blacks have also tended to favor government spending on welfare and income assistance, education, jobs, medical care, and other redistributive policies. They have been less supportive of foreign involvements and military spending. In addition, more blacks have tended to take certain socially conservative positions, upholding traditional values: opposing abortion, homosexuality, and euthanasia, for example, more than whites do. These differences generally remain substantial after introducing control variables.

As we have already seen, opinion *trends* among blacks and whites have differed more frequently than those for several other subgroups, though still not very often. Differences in trends were substantial enough to meet the criteria of table 7.1, for example, only 7.5% of the time (see also table 7.2).

Some distinct movements of racial groups have occurred on social issues like abortion and euthanasia, about which blacks' opinions have converged somewhat with whites' in recent years (see Wilcox 1990). Conversely, blacks' greater (than whites') disapproval of homosexuality as "wrong" increased a bit further by 1988 (with a tendency to slip back

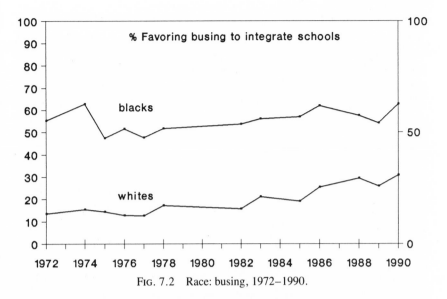

FIG. 7.2   Race: busing, 1972–1990.

in 1989 and 1990), although we have observed no comparable divergence concerning *policies* toward homosexuals' rights and civil liberties.

The most important racial differences in trends concern a wide range of civil rights issues, on which whites—and especially white Southerners—have shown the largest shifts in opinions, tending to catch up with the pro–civil rights attitudes of blacks (see Chap. 3, above, especially figure 3.3; also M. Schwartz 1967; Tom Smith and Sheatsley 1984; Schuman et al. 1985).

More recently, a modest opinion convergence of a similar sort has occurred: over the 1972–1990 period, whites' very limited support of busing for school integration increased somewhat, while support among blacks during the same period dropped a bit and then rose, ending up with little change (see figure 7.2). But by far the more striking feature of figure 7.2 is the very large (nearly 40%), persistent difference between the opinions of blacks and whites; the two trend lines are not far from parallel.[12] A similar overall impression is conveyed by graphs (not displayed) of opinions concerning racial intermarriage, homosexuality, euthanasia, abortion, and other issues: significant racial differences (some large, some small) in levels of opinion but substantial parallelism of movement.

A few other scattered examples of opinion trends that differed by race include a 1980–1981 shift against a balanced-budget constitutional amendment by blacks, whose social programs were being cut by the Reagan administration; distinctively strong reactions by blacks against the Vietnam War (in which black casualties were especially heavy), and, even more than other Democrats, against Nixon in the Watergate scandal; and blacks' lesser increase in opposition to arming Arab nations between 1973 and 1978, conceivably because of declining rapport between blacks and Jews in the United States and more identification by blacks with the Palestinians' cause. Again, however, our main finding is that—even on issues of special concern to blacks—their opinions have tended to move in parallel with the opinions of whites.

The Haves and Have Nots

Although class differences in politics are weaker in the United States than in most of the world (R. Hamilton 1972; Jackman and Jackman 1983), Americans of high and low income—or high and low occupational status, which in the United States amounts to much the same thing—do tend to disagree somewhat about certain public policies that differently affect their material self-interest.

People of lower income, for example, are considerably (often by fifteen to twenty percentage points) more likely to favor social welfare spending programs that promise to help them with jobs, schooling, medical care, and related assistance, particularly when there is an explicit element of redistribution of income or wealth (see Ladd and Hadley 1973). On economic issues, the opinion differences among income groups tend to persist, at about two-thirds or more of their original size, when other factors including education are controlled for. As we saw in Chapter 4, the differences appear to have endured at about the same level since the Depression, although it is difficult to be sure, because the policy context has changed and identical questions with constant meanings have not been asked then and now.

Income-group differences are not nearly as great on tax policy as on social welfare. There is a tendency for those who have a lot of money not to want the government to take it away; high-income people generally oppose progressive income taxes, taxes on capital gains, and other measures aimed at the wealthy. But so do many people of low income—partly, perhaps, because they are confused or misled about complex matters of tax incidence. Lower-income Americans have regularly preferred regressive sales and payroll taxes to the federal income tax (see Chap. 4).

On social issues and most other noneconomic matters, class cleavages are even weaker. Apparent income-related opinion differences mostly disappeared (falling to perhaps one-third of their original size) in our multivariate analyses. Genuinely income-related differences in opinions are confined almost exclusively to economic issues (see Knoke 1979; Himmelstein and McRae 1988).[13]

Regardless of big or little differences in levels of opinion, Americans of different socioeconomic class—like other subgroups—do not differ much in opinion *trends*. They mostly move in parallel. In table 7.1, for example, we saw that important differences between income-group trends occurred only a little more than 6% of the time, and the figure for occupational groups was about the same.

When income-group trends do seem to differ, they sometimes do so because of the different levels of formal education that are closely associated with differences in income and occupation. We will explore such divergences based on differential information and knowledge below. But—based on our multivariate analyses of income effects controlling for education and other factors—there have been a few occasions when opinions of income groups on economic issues diverged in ways apparently linked directly to their positions in society and their material self-interests.

After 1974, for example, when economic stringency and recession hit in the wake of the OPEC oil price rise, the highest income group was apparently first to turn against social welfare spending, and it did so by the largest amount. High-income people's responses that the United States was spending "too much" on "welfare" programs soared to a peak of nearly 75% by 1977 and remained about there in 1978 (look closely at figure 7.3). The antiwelfare opinions of other groups jumped as well but reversed direction by 1978 (especially the lowest-income group), so that

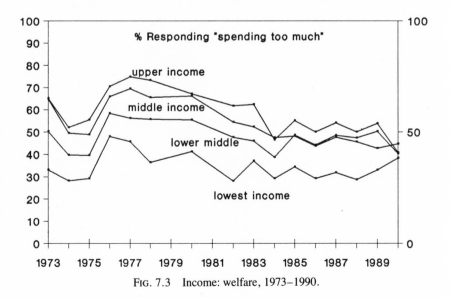

FIG. 7.3   Income: welfare, 1973–1990.

the 1974 opinion gap widened noticeably. It then narrowed again during the middle-to-late 1980s, with an apparent—but we suspect temporary—convergence in 1990.

Similarly, between 1976 and 1982 (when the "supply side" revolt against progressive taxes was at its peak), the proportion of responses among the highest and second highest income quartiles that federal income taxes were "too high" each rose by fourteen percentage points (to 80% and 75%), while those for other income groups increased by only three percentage points.

Again, however, the main tendency is parallel opinion movement by different income groups. Substantial parallelism is evident even in figure 7.3, which was chosen as an example of divergence.

Young and Old

At any moment in history the young and the old may differ from each other for at least two distinct reasons. One involves *"life-cycles"*: age brings with it different economic and social circumstances and physical conditions, so that peoples' attitudes and opinions tend to change as they grow older. The other reason involves *"generations"*: people in different age groups have lived through different experiences—the Great Depression, World War II, Vietnam, periods of economic affluence or stringency—which led them, when they were young and flexible, to form attitudes that they tend to carry through the remainder of their lives.

On the other hand, during a given period all age groups may be influenced by the same events and social and economic conditions, and by the same interpretations offered through the media. When there are no strong generational or life cycle effects, all age groups move about the same way in response to such *"period"* effects.

It is extremely difficult, empirically, to distinguish period, life cycle, and generational effects from each other. There exists no all-purpose method of "cohort analysis" that can be routinely applied to produce reliable and valid estimates of the different kinds of effects. This is a classic identification problem, which requires theoretical specifications and knowledge that go beyond cohort opinion data (Glenn 1989, p. 754–755). Such situationally dependent information is hard to assemble for a collection, like ours, of many separate opinion trends. Still, we think the historical contexts within which we have located our opinion data help us to sort out some of the effects at work (see Glenn 1977, 1989; J. Davis 1975, 1988; Abramson 1983; Delli Carpini 1986; Jennings and Niemi 1981).

Our data indicate that both life cycle and generational differences have sometimes appeared between the opinions of younger and older Americans over the last fifty years. The old have tended, for obvious life-cycle reasons, to be sensitive about threats to their Social Security pensions (proposals to change cost-of-living adjustments, retirement ages, and the like), though in more general terms the youngest age group has actually been just as supportive—if not more so—of government spending on Social Security and Medicare, and the elderly have not sought income transfers to themselves at the expense of transfers to the young (Ponza et al. 1988). Likewise, since the elderly feel more vulnerable to street crime, we would expect them to be somewhat more inclined to favor various types of protection; our multivariate analysis indicates that they have, in fact, been more supportive of gun control than the middle-aged.

For similar reasons, the young would be expected to oppose the military draft, draft registration, and military interventions. As we mentioned at the beginning of this chapter, however, such intuitively appealing expectations are not always borne out. On the one hand, the youngest cohort in the post-Vietnam period has been the most opposed to the draft or national service—by as much as 20% or more. On the other hand, during important periods in recent history, the young were actually the most enthusiastic backers of an activist (even militant) foreign policy. As Mueller (1973, pp. 138–139), M. Rosenberg, Verba, and Converse (1970), and others have shown, the young were the *most* supportive of the Korean War and, contrary to popular belief, of the Vietnam War as well. (The highly visible protesters at elite colleges represented a minority.) Self-interest-based, life-cycle differences in opinions are spotty, at best.

Much more striking are pervasive generational effects. New adult cohorts have typically been the most supportive of the social welfare policies and benefits that were already in place in the society in which they grew up. This has occurred in affluent European welfare states as well as in the U.S. (see Shapiro and Young 1989; Wilensky 1975; McClosky and Zaller 1984). This tendency might be attributed to "socialization," or to "getting used to" existing government programs, but it seems equally consistent with a greater readiness on the part of the young to accept new ideas that work, to embrace programs for which the benefits are seen to exceed the costs.

A generational, as opposed to life-cycle, aspect of age differences is also apparent in the tendency of older Americans to cling more firmly to traditional values. (These differences mostly persist when education and other factors are controlled.) The old, more often than the young, have favored school prayers (a 20% difference in multivariate analysis). The old have tended more than young people do to resist legalizing marijuana (by 24%); to object to pornography, abortions (by about 5%), sex education (by 20%), and birth control information for teenagers (by 23%); to oppose homosexuality, and to resist racial integration (busing by 11%) or civil liberties for deviant groups (Communist books by 24%) (see J. Davis 1975). Such attitudes do not appreciably strengthen with age; they were simply formed long ago and carried through life.

By the same token, newer cohorts—particularly the newest of all—have tended to take the other (the liberal) side on the above issues and also to be more supportive of women's rights, busing, and especially environmental protection (see Inglehart 1990). They have been the most opposed to wiretapping and capital punishment.

Several of the above observations imply that the young may be more receptive to new circumstances and may change opinions at a more rapid rate than the old. There is a small tendency in this direction. In general, however, as with other population groupings, there is little evidence of basically differing patterns of opinion *trends* among different age groups, even when one contrasts the youngest (eighteen to twenty-nine) group with the oldest (over sixty-five) group.

For all age groups, we found mostly common period effects. There were substantial differences between age-subgroup trends in only 5% of the comparisons analyzed in table 7.1. All age groups seem to be affected in roughly the same way by events and new information and changing societal conditions. (The youngest, conceivably because of their higher level of education, do show slightly larger opinion shifts. This may contribute to the development of generational effects: the young, with less experience and less accumulated information—and, in recent decades, the most education—are highly receptive to the latest events in forming their opinions, which they then tend to keep in later years.)

Figure 7.4, on trends in support for the Korean War by different age groups, illustrate this parallelism of age-group trends. In numerous Gallup and NORC surveys between 1950 and 1953 (only some of which are included in the figure), young adults under thirty were less likely than others to say the war was a "mistake" or that the United States was "wrong" in sending troops, but the sharp rises and falls in this sentiment affected each age group in very nearly the same way. Much the same thing has been true of support for the Vietnam War (see Mueller 1973, esp. pp. 138–139, 274–275) and for the vast majority of other issues.

Of the few cases of age-specific differences in opinion changes, most involve opinion *convergence* among age groups. Several examples concern civil liberties and law and order. During the early 1980s, young

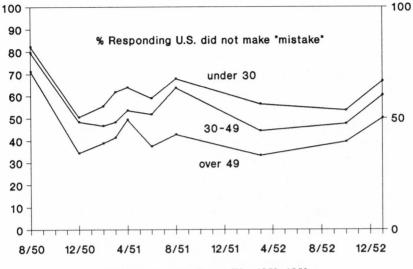

FIG. 7.4   Age: the Korean War, 1950–1953.

people became a bit more conservative and tended to converge toward the position of the older cohorts on capital punishment, treatment of crimi- nals by the courts, legalization of marijuana, general approval of homosexuals, and freedom of speech for Socialists, Communists, and various fringe groups. This presumably reflected the greater receptivity of youth to the conservatizing forces of that era.

No such convergence, however, occurred on economic welfare is- sues. And on certain other issues there was a considerable amount of age convergence of a rather different sort, as older citizens became more liberal on the environment and on sex education, birth control, and some related issues, while the opinions of the young (already at a liberal ceil- ing) hardly moved at all. This greater change by the older age groups is quite unusual; it happened too quickly to be attributable to either life- cycle or generational effects, and may simply be an artifact of survey items that left no room for further changes in young peoples' responses.

Catholics, Jews, and Protestants

Americans of different religions differ in their positions on a number of policy questions. In some cases these differences are related to differ- ing party loyalties, since religion has been one of the enduring bases of party alignments. But many differences follow from distinctive religious and cultural beliefs and experiences.[14]

Throughout the period for which evidence is available, for example,

Jewish Americans have tended to be much more liberal than other groups on a whole range of issues, even after controlling for education, income, and the like. Perhaps because of their own experiences as a persecuted minority, they have extended sympathy and support to other minority groups and have been especially solicitous of civil liberties and civil rights. Jews have overwhelmingly supported freedom of speech, due process of law, and equal rights in employment and education and other realms. Their special concern for the civil rights of blacks largely survived tensions due to competing economic interests and disparate views of the Middle East in the 1970s and 1980s. In the NORC-GSS data for 1973–1990, for example (combined to yield a large sample), 37% of Jews responded that we were spending "too little" to improve conditions of blacks (with only 15% saying "too much"), while a substantially lower 22% of white Protestants and 27% of white Catholics said "too little" (27% and 23%, respectively, said "too much") (see Tom Smith 1990a).

Compared with other groups, Jews are strikingly more supportive of abortion, under practically all the circumstances surveys have asked about. Fully 83% in the NORC-GSS data (1972–1990 combined), for example, favored a right to abortions when a woman simply wants no more children, and an overwhelming 98% favored it in cases of rape or where the health of the mother is endangered.

The relative liberalism of American Jews has also encompassed issues of social welfare, education, and other domestic matters, as well as views toward foreign policy and national defense. (For an early but very thorough historical analysis of religion and opinion toward foreign policy, including evidence on Jews' support for active U.S. involvement in world affairs, see Hero 1973.)

In addition, of course, Jews in the United States and worldwide tend to feel a special affinity for Israel, which stands as a homeland—symbolic or actual—for Jews everywhere. Jewish Americans have overwhelmingly supported military and economic aid to Israel and generally opposed such aid or weapons sales to Arab countries that are not at peace with Israel.

Catholics, who along with Jews and other minorities were part of the New Deal Democratic coalition, have also displayed relatively strong support for social welfare measures, civil liberties, and especially for the encouragement of organized labor, although Catholics' liberalism has never been as strong as that of Jews and has varied more from issue to issue (see Greeley 1989, 1990).

Catholics have also tended to express a number of traditional values related to their faith, especially bearing on the sanctity of marriage and the family and respect for authority. Birth control and abortion are more

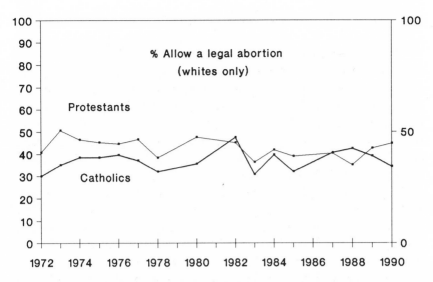

Fig. 7.5   Religion: allow legal abortion if woman wants no more children, 1972–1990.

complicated. Contrary to a widespread impression, ordinary Catholic citizens have been no more opposed than other Americans (taken as a whole) to abortion. Strongly anti-abortion views are confined mainly to church leaders and some of the most religious and active laity (see C. Franklin and Kosaki 1989). There has been only a modest tendency for Catholics to oppose abortion a bit more (about 7% more) than *white* Protestants do, but this difference (much smaller when black Protestants are included) has been diminishing in recent years (see figure 7.5).

When we turn to patterns of opinion *change,* the finding is a familiar one: neither Jews nor Catholics very often differ from Protestants in the direction or magnitude of opinion change. We found noteworthy trend differences among religious groups rather infrequently: just over 8% of the time, according to table 7.1. Many such cases have involved Catholics and Jews, who have predominantly been Democrats, behaving according to party loyalty and diverging from the more Republican Protestants. (The impact of partisanship will be discussed below.)

Another notable set of differences is the generally stable, steadfast Jewish support for pro-Israeli policies, while the opinions of Protestants and Catholics have tended to change more with events and circumstances.

Republicans, Democrats, and Independents

The policy opinions of Republicans and Democrats tend to differ in ways related to the differing economic, ethnic, and religious bases of the two parties as well as to their different receptivity to messages from party leaders.

Since the New Deal—that is, for as long as we have reliable survey data—the Democrats have enjoyed more support among working-class and low-income people, and among Catholics, Jews, blacks, and various white ethnic groups, whereas the Republicans have prevailed among the white and relatively wealthy Anglo-Saxon Protestants. Over this period, white Southerners and some Catholics and ethnics have gradually drifted away from their Democratic loyalty (which suggests why some regional and other opinion differences may have decreased over time), and the large ideological differences of the 1930s and 1940s have diminished. Still, the parties at the beginning of the 1990s continued to differ from each other in similar ways, if not to the same extent, as before (see Ladd and Hadley 1973; Ladd with Hadley 1978; Petrocik 1981; Axelrod 1972, and subsequent communications; Erikson, Lancaster, and Romero, 1989).

In accord with their working-class status and relatively low income, Democrats have tended much more often than Republicans to favor a broad range of government social welfare programs: aid to education, for example, and assistance with medical care, jobs, income, and housing. Democrats have also tended to take the side of labor in labor-management relations, favoring the rights of workers to organize and strike. And, at least since the middle 1960s (as blacks became more important in the party and as white Southerners deserted it), Democrats have tended to be more favorable to civil rights (see Carmines and Stimson 1989).

The differences between party groups vary by issue but are persistent and sometimes large: often ten to fifteen percentage points, but occasionally twice that. To take one example: in 1982, just over one year into President Reagan's first term, 41% of Democrats, but only 15% of Republicans, told NORC-GSS that we were spending "too little" improving the conditions of blacks. This difference dropped a bit but then stayed around twenty percentage points throughout the 1980s. These sorts of opinion differences among party identifiers generally resemble sharper differences at the elite level between activists and money givers and officials of the two parties (McClosky, Hoffman, and O'Hara 1960; Carmines and Stimson 1989).

Once again, however, the differences in opinion levels between population subgroups does not necessarily foreshadow different patterns of opinion *change*. In fact, we found important partisan differences in trends no more frequently than the average for other subgroupings: barely more than 4% of the time, according to the analysis displayed in table 7.1. Republicans, Democrats, and Independents, like other groupings of

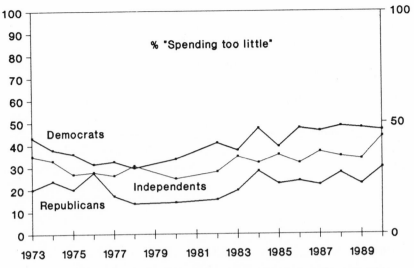

Fig. 7.6   Partisanship: spending to improve the conditions of blacks, 1973–1990.

Americans, generally change opinions—or remain stable—in a parallel fashion.

This is apparent in the graph of opinions about spending to improve the conditions of blacks. (See figure 7.6; Independents, as shown, responded more sluggishly to conditions in the 1970s and 1980s and did not perfectly parallel Republicans and Democrats.) The time-regression slope for Democrats ($b=1.43$), too, was quite similar to that for Republicans ($b=1.06$) and even Independents ($b=.97$; see Appendix).

Still, there have been some important exceptions. In fact, party groups are practically the only ones for which we have regularly found cases of *divergent* movements of opinion, with the opinions of party groups becoming more different from each other over time. Subsequently, these differences are often reduced. Between 1975 and 1983, for example, support among Democrats for the government to help the sick remained the same, while support among Republicans (whose leaders were trying to engineer a "right turn") dropped substantially (NORC-GSS); Republican support then recovered by 1987. Likewise, the proportion of Republicans saying we were spending "too little" on health care dropped from 1974 (62%) to 1977 (46%) but then climbed back (after 1986) under Republican presidents, reaching 68% in George Bush's "kinder, gentler" 1990.

Such divergent partisan trends are undoubtedly related to party leadership of public opinion. As we observed in Chapter 5, two years after the

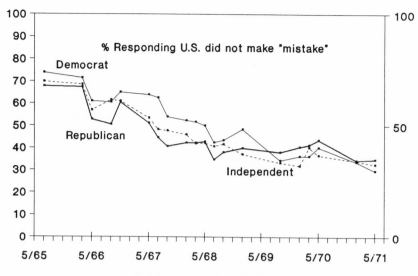

FIG. 7.7   Partisanship: support for the Vietnam War, 1965–1971.

internationalist Republican President Eisenhower took office in 1952, Republican party identifiers had tended to move from their isolationist posture toward favoring active U.S. involvement abroad, while Democrats' opinions stayed much the same (Campbell and Cooper 1956, pp. 88–90). Similarly, John Mueller (1973) has shown that with the 1969 shift from the Democratic Johnson administration to the Republican administration of Richard Nixon, Democrats—formerly more supportive of the Vietnam War—tended to move into relative opposition, while Republicans tended to support the way their president conducted the war (see figure 7.7). (No such switch occurred after the 1952 election; Korea was never seen as Eisenhower's war: see Mueller 1973, p. 118.)

A few similar cases are worth noting. We have already mentioned President Nixon's impact on Republicans' attitudes about wage and price controls, and later party divergences in opinions concerning campaign reforms after Watergate. Further, during the first part of the Carter administration—between 1976 and 1978—Democrats' support for greater U.S. involvement abroad (which had been depressed earlier by disillusionment over Vietnam) increased by five percentage points, while that of Republicans dropped by eight points and Independents stayed the same. In a mirror image pattern, between 1978 and 1983 (presumably because of the change to the Republican Reagan administration) support for more involvement abroad dropped by four percentage points among Democrats and rose by eleven percent among Republicans.

Of course, some of the divergent partisan trends concerning foreign policy activism may have referred to the particular kinds of foreign policies engaged in by particular presidents—Carter's early emphasis on human rights and Reagan's on armed strength, for example—rather than international involvement in the abstract. Alternatively, changes in support for foreign policy activism or in willingness to talk about "mistakes" may simply reflect greater trust for presidents of one's own party, with little policy content.

A broader and more important ambiguity in these nonpanel time series data (which do not involve repeated interviews of the same individuals) is that what appears to be opinion leadership may instead reflect issue-oriented shifts over time in who identifies with one party or the other—internationalists joining the Republican party of Eisenhower after 1952, for example, or civil rights supporters becoming Democrats around 1964 (Carmines and Stimson 1989), or doves becoming Democrats after 1968. After all, people can choose their declared party loyalty more easily than their age or race or gender.[15]

Still, it is quite plausible—especially in foreign affairs, where dependence upon government information is high—that many Americans follow the opinion leadership of their own parties. This is consistent with our view that citizens tend to rely, in forming and changing their policy preferences, upon trusted cuegivers who are thought to share their own values.

Loyalists of the two parties also sometimes react differently to events bearing directly upon party control of government. During the Watergate scandal, for example, Democrats (and, to a lesser extent, Independents) tended to move first and farthest in the direction of favoring Nixon's resignation, while Republican support for Nixon was slower to erode. One of the most important effects of partisanship may be resistance to discordant information that is out of harmony with accumulated beliefs. Yet this very example also illustrates our central argument about parallel publics: despite their slow start, Republicans eventually shifted opinions strongly against Nixon, in the end moving just about as far and at just about as rapid a rate as Democrats.

Northerners and Southerners; City and Country Dwellers

In some cases Americans living in different regions of the country, or in communities of different types (urban, suburban, rural), have differed in their policy preferences. Regional differences tend to be in the middle range—greater than gender differences but less than those by age, for example—while urban-rural and other community differences have mostly been smaller.

White Southerners, with a history of slavery, Jim Crow laws and practices, and fervent support for "states' rights," long took a distinctive stand against civil rights for black people. Southern whites strongly resisted the desegregation of public schools and public accommodations, for example, when most Northerners supported it.

Southerners also have had a long tradition of favoring internationalism—especially free trade—and activism in world affairs, though this changed somewhat by the 1960s as the decline of cotton and the expansion of import-vulnerable low-technology industries undercut free trade sentiment, and the new focus on the developing world encouraged a more militant international posture (Hero 1973, p. 124). Southerners have continued to be especially supportive of the military and defense.

On a variety of social issues, Northeasterners and Westerners (especially those from northern parts of the West) have tended to be liberal and tolerant, whereas Southerners and those from the central Midwest have been much more traditional and conservative.[16] In May 1986, for example, Gallup found that 45% of Southerners explicitly said they had "very traditional and old fashioned values" (placing themselves at positions 1 or 2 on a seven-point scale), compared with only 33% for the rest of the country. In September 1989, Gallup found 59% of Southerners (vs. 45% of Easterners and 44% of Westerners) expressing "a great deal" or "quite a lot" of support for organized religion or the church.

On economic issues the Northeast has also been the most liberal, with the South less so. The South is now more conservative relative to the North than it was in the 1930s and 1940s, in the heyday of Depression-era Southern allegiance to the New Deal Democratic party.

A slow, gradual "nationization" of American politics has diminished some regional differences in policy preferences, but others persist to a substantial extent. Despite extensive interregional migration, influences of the national mass media and the like, the marks of divergent economic and social development remain evident in major regional distinctions, some of which may actually have increased (see Bensel 1984). Our multivariate analyses indicate that regional differences in individuals' policy preferences remain substantial even when a variety of other demographic factors are controlled for; the Northeast and (generally) the West are still most liberal on many issues. In addition, G. Wright et al. (1987), M. Black, Kovenock, and Reynolds (1974), and others have found some striking state-by-state distinctiveness.

On certain issues the regions line up in a slightly different way, with the West looking more like the South than like the Northeast. Westerners and rural dwellers, for example, closer to the nation's frontier heritage and accustomed to open spaces and game hunting, have more heavily opposed gun control than Easterners and urbanites (see Chap. 3, above, and Stinchcombe et al. 1980). The West also more nearly resembles the South than the Northeast in differentially supporting the use of force in international affairs.

Sometimes simple economic self-interest divides regions. In the 1970s, for example, residents of the cold, fuel-oil consuming Northeast favored control of oil prices more than residents of the warm and/or oil producing states of the South did. Similar considerations (supplementing the region's long-standing promilitary and anti-Communist traditions) may have motivated the newly defense-industry-rich South differentially to favor arms buildups in the 1970s and 1980s.

On occasion, regional and community differences have also produced divergent opinion *trends*. In Chapter 3 we discussed the most important example: distinctive regional trends in preferences concerning civil rights for blacks. Beginning at least in the mid-1950s and 1960s, white Southerners moved strongly in a pro–civil rights direction, closing the wide gap between their attitudes and those in the rest of the country, and nearly catching up on many specific matters. The non-South became only a little more liberal or stayed about the same during this period. (See figure 3.3, on school desegregation.) A lesser, but still interesting, example of divergent trends involves indications of differential shifts by different types of communities in opinions about crime and punishment (Stinchcombe et al. 1980).

For the most part, however, the story is a familiar one: regional and community groupings generally move together (or stay the same) in opinion. In table 7.1 we found differential movement in only about 7% of the comparisons among regional groupings, and about the same for various types of communities. Figure 7.8 illustrates the South's distinctively high support for defense spending, but it also shows how all regions of the country participated in the growth in prodefense opinion that culminated in 1980 (after the taking of U.S. hostages in Iran and the Soviet invasion of Afghanistan); people in all regions subsequently moved back toward thinking defense spending was sufficient or too high.

The Schooled and the Unschooled

Educational groupings are of special interest. As we pointed out at the beginning of this chapter, there are several reasons to expect that Americans with different levels of formal education—and with the vary-

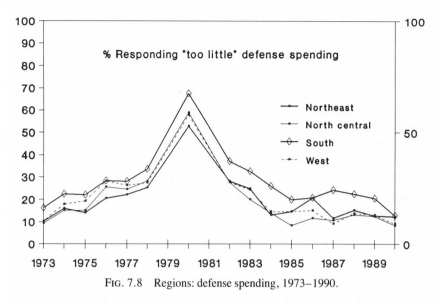

FIG. 7.8   Regions: defense spending, 1973–1990.

ing cognitive skills, amounts of knowledge, and attention to new information that presumably go with education—would react differently to events and would change their opinions in different ways and at different times or at different rates. Moreover, in contrast to other population groups that might be expected to differ only on a few particularly relevant issues, educational groupings might well differ across the board, for reasons that cut across substantive topics.

It is well established that Americans do in fact differ greatly according to educational background in their knowledge and receptivity to new information. Hyman, Wright, and Reed (1975), in a secondary analysis of fifty-four surveys conducted between 1949 and 1971, found significant and often sizable differences in responses to nearly all of 250 survey items testing knowledge; other research shows that increasing the flow of information about a topic boosts knowledge most among the highly educated (Tichenor, Donahue, and Olien 1970). College graduates tend to know more about politics and other matters than do high school or grade school graduates. These differences hold up for every age group and generational cohort, and they persist, weakening only slightly, when one takes into account—that is, statistically controls for—the higher income or occupational status that is associated with the attainment of a higher level of education.[17]

Moreover, people with more education tend to hold certain distinctive values and political attitudes, some related to their generally higher income and social status, but some genuinely transmitted through the schooling process—not necessarily inherent in education per se but following from the particular values that U.S. elites and educational institutions promote.

Thus (as we saw in Chap. 3) well-educated Americans tend, more than the less schooled, to favor civil liberties—freedom of speech and rights of the accused and due process of law—even for unpopular non-conformists or deviant groups. The well educated also tend to favor social and political (though not necessarily economic) equality, including equal rights and integration for blacks. And people with more formal education have tended to support anti-Communist foreign policy activism as well as humanitarian policies abroad, favoring both military and economic aid; they have generally been more receptive to government initiatives of any sort in foreign affairs. (See the discussion of internationalism in Chap. 5.) These educational differences are found in virtually all age and generational subgroups and persist despite statistical controls for income and status and other factors (Hyman and Wright 1979).

In recent years, our data show, people with more education have also tended to be more liberal than others on a wide range of social and life-style issues: more willing to permit abortions, to legalize marijuana, to promote contraception, to ease divorce restrictions, and to allow euthanasia but forbid capital punishment. In our multivariate analysis, the estimates of educational impacts on some of these and other social issues remained quite high (in the 15%–20% range, comparing college graduates with those not completing high school) even when income and other factors were controlled for; the initially substantial relationships with income tended to disappear. (As we reported earlier, just the opposite was true on economic issues.)

To some extent (though, as we will see in Chap. 8, not to a very great extent) the distinctive policy opinions of different educational groups, together with rising average levels of education in the United States, have contributed to certain long-term trends in the policy preferences of the public as a whole: the liberalization of opinion about civil liberties, for example (J. Davis 1975; see also Taylor 1978; Mayer 1990).

It does not follow, however, that there have been noticeably different patterns of opinion *change* by different educational groups. In fact, using the large data set, we found substantial differences in trends in fewer than 5% of our comparisons among education groups (see table 7.1).[18] Given the broad expectations of differences, that is certainly not many. The same thing was true for both foreign and domestic policy issues.

Along with these generally parallel trends, there does seem to be a slight but discernible tendency, as we noted in Chapter 5, for people with the most education—the college educated—to change opinion by the greatest amount (see Richman 1972; Russett and DeLuca 1981; P. Smith 1961; MacKuen 1984). The greater exposure of the highly educated to new information, and their greater ability to process it, does apparently produce a slightly greater propensity to change opinions. But this tendency is small indeed, presumably because it is mostly offset by the larger stock of information that the highly educated possess, which means their opinions are better grounded and more resistant to change (see Converse 1962; Zaller 1987, 1990b).

Thus our data on the legalization of marijuana and (to a lesser extent) capital punishment in the 1970s and 1980s reveal more opinion change by the highly educated. Figure 7.9 shows that college graduates moved somewhat more than other groups, both in a liberal direction (in the 1970s) and in a conservative direction (in the 1980s), in response to changing reports about the medical and social implications of marijuana use. But we also found that on an issue like abortion (see figure 7.10), with strong feelings and well-thought-out opinions—absent any highly relevant new information—college graduates in the 1970s and 1980s were among those *least* likely to change opinion.

Our finding of few differential trends among education groups suggests that individual differences in exposure and acceptance, while theoretically interesting, may not ordinarily play a large part in processes of collective opinion change.[19] Distinctive opinion shifts may be confined to very small groups (e.g., the most highly informed) and particular

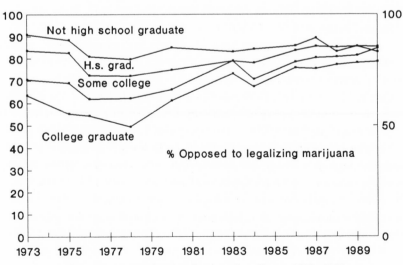

Fig. 7.9   Education: legalization of marijuana, 1973–1990.

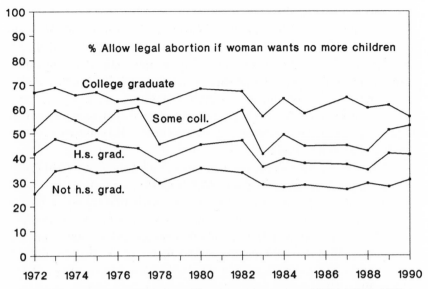

FIG. 7.10   Education: legal abortion if woman wants no more children, 1972–1990.

issues. Our aggregate opinion change data can largely be understood in terms of homogenous movements across the whole population.

Nor can we conclude that the highly educated generally act as opinion leaders, changing their views first and then bringing other members of the population along. True, during the broad liberalizing period of the 1960s, for some issues, the college-educated apparently became more liberal first. People with less education started to catch up later, either because of some delay in information acquisition and processing, or conceivably because of opinion leadership by the educated. Again, during the 1970s and (occasionally) the 1980s, the less educated shifted further in the direction of the liberal attitudes of the better educated on such issues as civil rights, contraception, marijuana, abortion, and euthanasia. This would seem to provide at least some minimal evidence for leadership or some sort of influence by the well educated.

It would be imprudent, however, to leap to that conclusion on the basis of a few plausible examples. In fact, there is comparable—and about equally strong—evidence that would seem to demonstrate just the opposite tendency: leadership of or influence upon the more educated by the *less* educated. We saw in Chapter 5, for example, that the highly educated tended to join their less schooled brethren in increased hostility toward the Soviet Union in the late 1940s. Similarly, in the early 1980s there was a small aggregate decline in support for abortion, which involved the better educated moving in the direction of their fellow citizens with less schooling. The same thing was true of the turn to more conservative positions on capital punishment and divorce laws in the 1970s and 1980s, and (oddly) of temporary increases in opposition to requiring the use of seat belts between 1973 and 1978. It is quite apparent in the trend against legalizing marijuana in the 1980s (see figure 7.9): the well educated moved toward the views of the less educated.

The most definite conclusion we can draw is that such methods of trying to detect opinion leadership are unreliable. It is too easy to mistakenly identify a chance movement of one group's opinions toward those of some other group as a case of influence. Such evidence should probably not be trusted. But if one does take this evidence seriously, it certainly does not indicate any general tendency of the highly educated to lead others in opinion changes. Any elite influence on public opinion apparently proceeds from subgroups of the population that are much smaller, too small to be uncovered in mass survey data (see W. Rogers, Stuhler, and Koenig 1967), and more like the experts and media commentators and political leaders discussed in Chapter 8.

In any case, despite all the interesting hypotheses about differential change, we are left with the conclusion that the opinions of education subgroups—like the other population groupings we have investigated—generally tend to move together along relatively parallel trend lines. Such movement in tandem is evident even in the marijuana and abortion cases graphed in figures 7.9 and 7.10.

Conclusion

The United States is a pluralistic nation of many distinct social groupings, and public opinion is not altogether uniform across groups. On a number of issues the young tend to disagree with the old, the rich with the poor, the college educated with grade school graduates, Southerners with Northeasterners, Republicans with Democrats, and blacks with whites. Differences in people's social and economic surroundings, conditions of life, historical experiences, knowledge, and cognitive abilities give rise to group-related differences in policy preferences.

Still, the bulk of the evidence indicates that different groups do not tend to *change* their preferences very often in very different ways. Among most groupings of Americans, opinions tend to change (or not change) in about the same manner: in the same direction and by about the same amount at about the same time. To put it another way, significant group differences in policy preferences usually either stay constant or alter only very slowly.

There are some important exceptions, as we have seen, and, interestingly, they tend to involve *convergence* of groups toward similar positions. Concerning civil rights, for example, Southerners' opinions moved in a distinctive fashion, catching up to a great extent with the pro–civil rights views of citizens outside the South. Regional and racial groups have converged on certain issues (e.g., euthanasia and abortion, respectively). The young and the better educated at times have tended to be somewhat more susceptible to change, but not inordinately so. Jews have been more steadfast than others on social and economic liberalism and on policies toward Israel. The wealthy and part of the middle class may have been quicker (on occasion) to begin to support major cuts in government spending and income taxes when economic times were tight. And party identifiers have tended to go along with the stands of presidents from their own parties on some issues—most notably foreign policies.

But these are exceptions. For the most part the preferences of the many small publics that make up the general public stay in tandem—moving in parallel or standing still together.

The phenomenon of parallel publics partly reflects the general stability of public opinion. When collective preferences as a whole do not change over a number of years, those of particular groups usually do not do so either. More important for parallelism in opinion *changes,* however, are two key facts about twentieth-century America. The first is that the political information and interpretations conveyed to the public have become highly unified, due to the development of centralized national mass media of communications and (especially in the foreign policy realm) heavy government influence over the flow of political information. Practically all Americans are exposed to the same facts and ideas, through network television news and the wire service reports that dominate daily newspapers and provide the grist for discussion by friends and neighbors.

The second important fact is that people of all sorts, in all walks of life, tend to form their policy preferences not only on the basis of narrow self-interest but in terms of group interests and—especially—the public good, or perceived national interest, taking as their guide common standards of judgment provided by elites through the media (Cantril and Research Associates 1947). Thus a widely publicized event or new idea tends to affect the policy preferences of all groups in about the same way, leading to parallel movement (or, sometimes, convergence) of opinion, even if some groups initially hold—and often continue to hold—preferences that differ somewhat. Quite rare are cases of increasing *divergence* of opinion, in which groups move farther apart, or flip-flops, in which groups switch sides.[20]

Because the policy preferences of all groups generally tend to move in parallel, we can proceed in the next chapter to explore the general causes of opinion change in terms of processes that operate more or less uniformly over the whole population. We can continue to speak of *the* public.

8 The Causes of Collective Opinion Change

☑ The description in Chapters 2–6 of hundreds of significant changes in Americans' collective policy preferences—virtually all the noteworthy changes that were found in our fifty years of survey data[1]—made clear that when public opinion has changed it has not done so wildly or capriciously or randomly; it has generally shifted in comprehensible ways, in response to new information and changing conditions. Indeed, the description of opinion changes in historical context has taken us a long way toward understanding the causes of collective opinion change. Most shifts in Americans' preferences concerning domestic and foreign policy have been associated with certain kinds of major historical events and trends.

In this chapter we will outline the main kinds of trends and events that appear, on the basis of previous chapters, to have affected collective public opinion. Among these are shifting circumstances felt directly by citizens, such as changes in income and educational levels; and events that have been reported to millions of people through the mass media of communications, like wars, international crises, and domestic occurrences. Trends and events of these sorts have often altered peoples' life circumstances, concerns, skills, and resources; in some cases they have actually changed the composition of the population. Many of these developments have also altered peoples' beliefs about possibilities, facts, and causal connections, thereby altering their opinions concerning the feasibility or desirability of alternative public policies. When many people have been affected in the same way at the same time, collective public opinion has changed.

Many events, however—especially distant happenings in foreign affairs—do not directly and immediately affect ordinary citizens and, therefore, do not speak for themselves. These cannot have much impact on public opinion unless they are reported in the mass media, so that people are aware of them. Moreover, their effects depend heavily upon how they are *interpreted:* precisely how they are framed and related to people's beliefs and values and to the costs and benefits of alternative policies. Such interpretations, too, are largely propagated through the mass media. After discussing broad patterns in historical events and trends, therefore, we will turn to a more focused analysis of media effects on the collective public. We will see that the media themselves, and certain news sources whose statements and actions they report, have had strong effects on public opinion.

Gradual Social and Economic Trends

A number of important long-term changes in American public opinion can be understood in terms of gradual social, economic, or political trends (domestic or international) that have altered the composition of the population, life circumstances, and people's understandings of the world. Such trends include enormous economic growth and large rises in income levels; increases in formal education, accompanying economic growth; migration of black Americans from the rural South to the urban North; the entry of more and more women into the paid work force and other changes in their lives; and changes in the economic and political strength of nations and in their alignments with each other.

Since many social and economic changes have occurred in a more or less steady, linear fashion, moving concurrently with each other and with gradual shifts in public opinion, it is difficult to sort out the separate impact of each factor and to be sure what actually caused opinion changes. The up-and-down variations that give bite to time series analyses are not usually present. Nor are the boundedness and time asymmetry that allow one to infer that a particular discrete event, preceding a sudden opinion change, probably caused the opinion change.

Still, we will outline some compelling, broad patterns that generally fit with social theory and with common sense. Sometimes it is possible to rule out plausible but incorrect hypotheses about alternative influences. In some cases cross-sectional variations in opinions (e.g., distinctive policy preferences held by different age or educational groups), together with gradual changes in the makeup of the population (through cohort succession and rises in levels of income and education), help bolster causal inferences based on the broad trends.

Economic Growth

Economic growth has been a fundamental cause, consequence, and manifestation of many slow, cumulative changes in American society. It has involved industrialization; major occupational shifts from farming, to blue-collar industrial labor, and then to white-collar service work; migration from rural areas to cities and then suburbs; large rises in income levels; shorter workweeks and increases in leisure time; increases in consumption of many goods like housing, cars, appliances, and entertainment; and widespread increases in exposure to formal education. Over the course of American history, all these changes no doubt affected public opinion (and, taken together, transformed it); but, during the last fifty years, some evidently have been more important than others.[2]

Some of these changes are captured by the trends in Gross National Product (GNP) and family incomes shown in table 8.1. After the economic decline of the Great Depression, which (as measured by GNP) hit bottom in 1933, the nation's real economic output rose sharply after 1940—spurred by wartime production—and, after a postwar pause, it grew more slowly but fairly steadily until 1973. (The "constant dollar" figures, adjusted for inflation, provide the most meaningful comparisons.) The economy then stagnated for nearly a decade, largely because of sharply rising energy price rises and international competition; it resumed growth after 1982. Similar postwar trends occurred for median family incomes, which ap-

TABLE 8.1 Gross National Product and Family Income, 1930–1988

A. Gross National Product, 1930–1988
(dollars in billions)

Year	Current Dollars	Constant (1982) Dollars
1930	$91.1	$642.8
1933	56.0	498.5
1935	72.8	580.2
1940	100.4	772.9
1945	213.4	1,354.8
1950	288.3	1,203.7
1955	405.9	1,494.9
1960	515.3	1,665.3
1965	705.1	2,087.6
1970	1,015.5	2,416.2
1973	1,359.3	2,744.1
1975	1,598.4	2,695.0
1980	2,732.0	3,187.1
1982	3,166.0	3,166.0
1985	4,014.9	3,618.7
1988	4,864.3	3,996.1

(continued)

TABLE 8.1 (*Continued*)

B. Median Family Income (1939–1988)

Year	Current Dollars	Constant (1982) Dollars
1939	$1,231	$8,860
1945	2,390	13,276
1950	3,216	13,355
1955	4,137	15,444
1960	5,620	20,892
1965	6,957	22,085
1970	9,867	25,430
1973	12,051	27,142
1975	13,719	25,500
1980	21,023	25,513
1985	27,735	25,776
1988	32,191	27,211

GNP Sources: 1929–1987: U.S. Department of Commerce, *Survey of Current Business* (Washington D.C.: Government Printing Office, September 1988), pp. 57, 59; 1988: U.S. Department of Commerce, *News*, "Gross National Product: Fourth Quarter 1988 (Final)," press release, March 23, 1989, pp. 7–8. Income Sources: 1939, 1945, 1950, 1955: Bureau of the Census, *Historical Statistics of the United States, Colonial Times to 1957* (Washington, D.C.: Government Printing Office, Series G 147–168); 1960, 1965, 1970: Bureau of the Census, *Historical Statistics of the United States, Colonial Times to 1970*, U.S. Government Printing Office, Series G 189–204; 1975, 1980, 1985, 1988: Bureau of the Census, *Current Population Reports*, Consumer Income P-60, no. 168, "Money Income and Poverty Status in the United States 1989," table D. Consumer Price Index Sources: 1939–1970: Bureau of the Census, *Historical Statistics of the United States, Colonial Times to 1970*, Washington, D.C.: Government Printing Office, Series E 135–166; 1975–1988: Bureau of the Census, *Statistical Abstract 1990*, Washington, D.C.: Government Printing Office, table 762.

proximately doubled (in constant 1982 dollars) from just over $13,000 in 1950, to $27,000 in 1973, but then dropped until the mid- to late 1980s.

Along with economic growth came many technological innovations that greatly changed peoples' lives. Transportation and communication were still slow and cumbersome in the 1930s, for example. The development of telephone service, radio, air travel, interstate highways, and television—along with the income and wealth so that many could afford to use them—opened up new opportunities for travel and communication; they brought the country and the world closer together, increasing exposure to information about national and world affairs. The shift from agricultural to industrial work and increasing urbanization (as well as the increased number of women working outside the home) tended to break up extended families, weaken family and community ties, and create a new set of urban policy problems; but it also exposed Americans to more diverse people, ideas, and activities.

Such changes have had gradual but profound effects on public opinion, many of them occurring before the period of our study. By the time of the earliest surveys, for example, industrialization had produced public support for government action to protect workers from wage oppression, unemployment, disability, or drastic boom-and-bust business cycles—through unionization, minimum wages, unemployment insurance, Social Security, economic stabilization policies, and the like. Higher incomes freed public resources and willingness to spend on government aid for education, medical care, aid to the poor, and other social programs discussed in Chapter 4. Later (largely during the fifty years we have studied), still higher incomes and steady employment permitted new attention to workplace safety, protection of the natural environment, and other public goods once viewed as luxuries. (We would not go quite so far, however, as to characterize this as "post-materialist" society: Inglehart 1990.)

Similarly, pressures of the agricultural economy (together with availability of resources) led to support for assistance to farmers, but in the last few decades the decrease in farm population has undoubtedly eroded backing for agricultural price support programs. Urbanization and the social problems associated with it (again together with the availability of resources), gave rise to desires to spend money to help the poor and fight crime and drugs, and to have courts punish crime severely. The relative decline in the industrial labor force, in favor of service industries, probably helped dilute support for unionization and strikes.

Formal Education

Rising levels of formal education, associated with economic growth and linked with improved communications and increased leisure time to attend to public affairs, is of particular interest, though education per se turns out not to be of such fundamental importance to opinion trends as one might imagine.

Better educated people acquire knowledge and cognitive skills and habits of learning. They are exposed to diversity, to information about different kinds of people and ideas and life-styles, and especially to prevailing norms and values. As we have seen, the policy preferences of the highly educated often differ from those of the less educated, so that one would expect changing educational levels to produce changing collective opinion.

During the 1950s, 1960s, and 1970s, higher and higher proportions of Americans went to high school and college. As table 8.2 indicates, in 1940 the average (median) American had completed only about nine years of schooling—that is, only a little more than junior high school; but by 1988 the figure was edging close to thirteen years, signifying completion of high school plus a year of college. (By about 1950 most young people were continuing their education through high school, and they gradually replaced their less-educated elders in the population; also, during the five decades covered by table 8.2, black people very nearly caught up with whites in years—if not necessarily quality—of schooling.)

As average education levels increased further after the 1950s, higher proportions of Americans expressed tolerance for allowing dissenters—

TABLE 8.2 Rising Levels of Formal Education, 1940–1988

| | Median Years of School Completed by Age and Race, 1940–1988 | | | |
| | 25 Years and Over | | 25–29 Years | |
Year	All Persons	Black Persons	All Persons	Black Persons
1940	8.6	5.7	10.3	7.0
1947	9.0	6.9	12.0	8.4
1950	9.3	6.8	12.0	8.6
1957	10.6	7.7	12.3	9.9
1960	10.6	8.0	12.3	9.9
1965	12.1	9.8	12.4	12.1
1970	12.1	9.8	12.6	12.1
1975	12.3	10.9	12.8	12.5
1980	12.5	12.0	12.9	12.6
1985	12.6	12.3	12.9	12.7
1988	12.7	12.4	12.8	12.7

Source: 1940, 1950, 1960, 1970, 1980, 1985, 1988: Bureau of the Census, *Statistical Abstract of the United States 1990* (Washington, D.C.: Government Printing Office, table 215); 1975: Bureau of the Census, *Statistical Abstract of the United States 1980* (Washington, D.C.: Government Printing Office, table 236); 1947, 1957, 1965: Bureau of the Census, *Statistical Abstract of the United States 1970*, (Washington, D.C.: Government Printing Office, table 158).

Communists, Socialists, atheists—to give public speeches, have their books in public libraries, and teach in schools. As we noted in Chapter 3, increased education could account for perhaps one-third of this trend (J. Davis 1975). But the decline of the Cold War and the fading of religious commitments were more fundamental causes. People at all educational levels changed opinion, and new cohorts were particularly susceptible to the changed situation, increasing support for civil liberties even beyond what their increased educational attainments could account for. Earlier, in fact, acceptance of civil liberties for Communists did not simply rise mechanically with education levels after 1940 but fell as the Cold War developed.

Migration, Workplace, and Other Factors

The liberalizing movement of public opinion about civil rights, too—with greatly increased acceptance of integration in public accommodations, neighborhoods, schools, jobs, and marriages—resulted in part from rising levels of education among white Americans. But again, education played a smaller part than one might expect; the opinions of the educated and unschooled all changed in similar ways (A. Smith 1982; Firebaugh and Davis 1988), partly because of other sorts of gradual social change. In particular, the participation of black people in the armed forces and especially their migration to the urban North (see table 8.3), where their accomplish-

TABLE 8.3 Black Migration North, 1900–1980

	Percent Black								
	1900	1910	1920	1930	1940	1950	1960	1970	1980
Northeast	1.8	1.9	2.3	3.3	3.8	5.1	6.8	8.9	9.6
Urban Northeast[a]	2.2	2.2	2.7	4.0	4.6	6.2	8.4	11.6	NA
North Central	1.9	1.8	2.3	3.3	3.5	5.0	6.7	8.1	6.2
Urban N.C.[a]	3.2	3.0	3.8	5.4	5.5	7.5	9.6	11.6	NA
South	32.3	29.8	26.9	24.7	23.8	21.7	20.6	19.1	18.6
Urban South[a]	31.0	28.1	24.3	25.7	23.7	21.4	20.8	20.5	NA
West	0.7	0.7	0.9	1.0	1.2	2.8	3.9	4.9	5.2
Urban West[a]	4.1	3.3	3.0	7.7	3.3	5.0	8.0	10.2	NA

Source: Percentages calculated by authors, based on data from (for 1900–1970): U.S. Department of Commerce, Bureau of the Census, *Historical Statistics of the United States: Colonial Times to 1970. Part 1* (Washington, D.C.: Government Printing Office, 1975); and (for 1980): U.S. Department of Commerce, Bureau of the Census, *Statistical Abstract 1981* (Washington, D.C.: Government Printing Office, 1981).
Note: NA = not available.
[a] Percent black and other nonwhite populations.

TABLE 8.4 Women in the Work Force Outside
the Home, 1930–1988

Civilian Labor Force Participation Rate,
Overall and by Sex

Year	Total	Male	Female
1930	53.2	82.1	23.6
1940	55.2	82.5	27.9
1945	61.6	87.6	35.8
1950	59.2	86.4	33.9
1955	59.3	85.4	35.7
1960	59.4	83.3	37.7
1965	58.9	80.7	39.3
1970	60.4	79.7	43.3
1975	61.2	77.9	46.3
1980	63.8	77.4	51.5
1985	64.8	76.3	54.5
1988	65.9	76.2	56.6

Source: U.S. President, *Economic Report of the President, Transmitted to the Congress (1990)* (Washington, D.C.: Government Printing Office, 1990), table C-36; Bureau of the Census, *Historical Statistics of the U.S. Colonial Times to 1970* (Washington, D.C.: Government Printing Office, 1975), Series D 29–41.

ments refuted old racist stereotypes, set in motion a trend toward acceptance of equality that was accentuated by a number of events including the civil rights movement's protests and demonstrations. The powerful trend toward acceptance of equal rights later manifested itself also in more opposition to discrimination against Latinos, the elderly, the disabled, and women.

In the strong shift of public opinion in favor of women's rights and abortion, too, social trends other than (or additional to) rising education played important parts. Gradually, over the decades, more and more American women began to work outside the home—nearly twice as many, for example, in 1988 (57%) as in 1950 (34%) (see table 8.4). Middle and upper-middle-class women, as they struggled to win jobs in business and the professions, articulated their resentment of traditional barriers and formed a women's movement, which affected the opinions of men as well as women. Women's unwillingness to have their work disrupted by involuntary childbirth helped increase acceptance of abortion, which also grew as a result of certain specific events (the well-publicized deformed fetuses caused by rubella epidemics and the drug thalidomide) as well as key technological changes—the invention of an effective birth control pill, which helped popularize and legitimize birth control generally, and the development of safer clinical procedures for abortion that helped take the operation out of back rooms and put it into outpatient hospitals and clinics.

The case of increasingly liberal opinions toward women's rights and abortion, beginning in the 1960s, illustrates well the public's response to a number of changing circumstances, and also the difficulty in separating the effects of each factor and their interactions. As figure 8.1 suggests, the opinion liberalization described in Chapters 2 and 3 occurred as more women entered the labor force, fertility dropped, divorce rates increased, women's education levels rose, and feminist movement activity increased. Comparing these full time series since 1890, Klein (1984) has argued persuasively that the trends after 1960 were unique and that the simultaneous occurrence of several interacting factors was crucial.

In the realm of foreign affairs, the great increase in levels of Americans' formal education—together with the development of air travel and the rise of television coverage of world events—may have helped maintain a high level of support for an active U.S. role in the world during and after World War II, including the establishment of alliances, stationing troops abroad, providing foreign aid, supporting the United Nations, and so forth. When internationalism became the norm at the elite level, the educational system may have contributed to its broad public acceptance as well. But

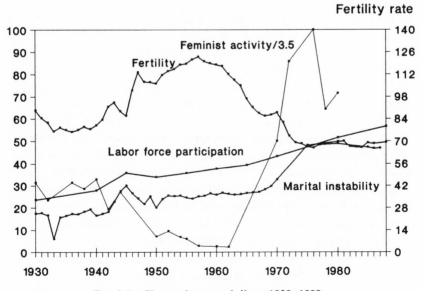

Fig. 8.1   Changes in women's lives, 1930–1988.

worldwide events and trends seem to have been more important: World War II itself, and the emergence of the United States as a world economic and military power, with huge global markets and extensive military bases and alliances, facing perceived threats from the Soviet Union.

In fact, as indicated in Chapter 5, Americans' internationalism reached a high level even before U.S. involvement in World War II. The "active part" question, and other trend items with big education-group differences in opinions, show no particular rise in aggregate internationalism as education levels rose, and new cohorts replaced old ones, in the 1950s and 1960s. With the partial exception of a few cases like admission of China to the United Nations (Glenn 1977), rising levels of education and cohort replacement have had little discernible effect on collective opinion about foreign policy (see Mayer 1990).

Certain other kinds of social changes have affected opinions on various issues. The increasing use of marijuana by young people during the 1960s, at a time when youth was glorified in advertisements and popular culture, apparently led (presumably because the effects of the drug had not been shown to be much worse than those of tobacco or alcohol) to increased sentiment for legalization or reduced penalties. Later, evidence of negative medical and social effects, and increasing problems with "crack" cocaine and other drugs, brought a gradual reversal in public attitudes.

The immigration of many Puerto Ricans to New York City apparently contributed to an increase in the number of Americans favoring statehood or independence for the island. Immigration of large numbers of undocumented Mexican workers, during a period of weakness in the U.S. economy and vulnerability of the American work force, brought more people to favor restrictions on immigration and punishment of employers who hired illegal aliens.

Many of the social and economic trends we have mentioned involved changes in the composition of the American population, or direct and immediate changes in people's circumstances and interests that led naturally and directly to changed policy preferences. When there is more money to spend, or people move from the country to the city and take on new jobs, or when new technologies become available and new social problems arise, it is not surprising if people tend to want their government to do different things. Such trends can be viewed as largely exogenous influences upon public opinion—independent influences subject only minimally, if at all, to elite leadership or preference manipulation.

That is to say, certain social and economic trends produce changes in policy preferences that are in a sense *autonomous*—largely independent of, and resistant to, distortion by the media or special interests. Such opinion changes are presumably just the sort postulated in democratic theory: preferences that accurately reflect citizens' objective needs and circumstances and that can form the bedrock of democratic social choice.[3]

This is particularly true of domestic policies, with which people often have relevant firsthand experience. (Even when they do not, relatively diverse information channels and competing political elites often make it possible for ordinary citizens to figure out what is happening.) But also in the case of foreign policy, as we noted in Chapters 5 and 6, some opinion changes arguably occur relatively directly, in reaction to objective developments that unfold in the international system.

The increasing power and expansionism of Germany and Japan, for example, clearly increased Americans' support for military preparedness and their willingness to aid the allies and (eventually) to get involved in fighting World War II. Likewise, the Soviet Union's Communist ideology and its emergence as a major European power after World War II contributed to Americans' alarm and their competitive reactions. Given Cold War conflicts, the logic of the situation itself appeared to dictate increasing acceptance of Germany and Japan as U.S. allies. Similarly, the increasing importance of the People's Republic of China in world affairs may have mandated U.S. diplomatic recognition and acceptance of U.N. membership. And, understandably, the growth of Third World influence at the United Nations naturally caused some U.S. disenchantment with that organization. Pressures of international economic competition helped undercut Americans' desires for social spending and their support for unions. The Soviet Union's moves toward disarmament and renewed détente in the 1980s almost inescapably encouraged, if they did not require, U.S. reciprocity, and allowed Americans to devote more attention and resources to domestic problems.

Still, the nature and the policy implications of "objective" changes that have affected public opinion are not always so obvious, even in some of the cases we have mentioned. Citizens' assessments of the significance of trends and events—indeed, their very awareness of them—often depend crucially upon information and (especially) interpretations provided by elites, largely through the mass media. (As we have noted, the effects of an "objective" experience like formal education involve not only cognitive training, and conveying information, but also inculcating particular norms and values and providing standards of judgment for interpreting contemporary events.) The dependence of opinion changes upon media interpretations is most obvious in the case of world events, which ordinarily must appear in the mass media if they are to affect public opinion at all, and which are usually reported and interpreted through the media in the context of official U.S. foreign policy. We will return to the subject of media influence after discussing the impact of various kinds of events.

Historical Events

Again and again, in our historical account of foreign policy opinions—and sometimes in the domestic policy chapters as well—we saw that abrupt opinion changes coincided with specific events and conditions, especially wars, international crises, or the state of the economy. Often the available survey data bracketed these events closely enough so that we could be confident that they caused the opinion changes.

War

Our data indicate that the events which have most frequently and most strongly affected American public opinion have involved war or armed conflict. The imminent threat of war has typically increased Americans' support for preparedness, defense spending, alliances, foreign aid, and the like; the actual outbreak of war has mobilized opinion even more sharply. During the fighting, there often has been acceptance of domestic sacrifices and economic controls of a kind that would be resisted in peacetime. Battlefield events and the general progress of a war have affected opinions about economic sacrifices, appropriate terms for peace, and the prosecution of the war itself. The end of war has usually brought desires for return to full peacetime conditions—fewer controls, lower taxes, and reduced armed forces. Outcomes of wars have affected feelings about international involvement, world organization, alliances, foreign aid, the use of military force abroad, and indeed the whole range of foreign policy issues.

During the half-century of American history for which we have survey data, the most pervasive single influence on public opinion was the *Second World War*. In its inception, its prosecution and general course, and its conclusion, World War II transformed American public opinion concerning virtually all aspects of foreign affairs and a number of domestic policies as well.

As Chapter 5 made clear, the beginning of war in Europe led more Americans to favor a larger army and navy, aid for Britain and France, and a military draft; it also increased support for direct U.S. involvement. The Japanese attack on Pearl Harbor inflamed the public and propelled the United States into the war. As the fighting progressed, more Americans were willing to accept wage and price controls, long working days, high taxes, and prohibitions on strikes.

Reports of the prewar pact between Germany and the USSR outraged Americans, but when Germany invaded the USSR and the Russians resisted stoutly, more Americans came to favor aiding and cooperating with the Soviets. (These events affected attitudes about civil liberties for U.S. Communists as well.) Early in the war, when the Axis powers proved hard to defeat, more Americans approved of aid and forgiveness of debts to the Soviets, the Chinese, and other allies. As the tide turned and the allies moved closer to victory, the public began to insist upon harsher peace terms, the pacification of Germany after the war, and the taking of new U.S. military bases abroad. And wartime cooperation among the allies helped build support for a postwar United Nations.

The end of the war brought desires for a return to peacetime conditions: relaxing wage and price controls, permitting strikes, cutting taxes, reducing work hours, and increasing pay. It also encouraged high hopes for lasting peace: support for the United Nations and international control of atomic energy, free trade, and assistance to war victims. These trends were counteracted only by the growth of the Cold War.

The *war in Korea* produced analogous, though more limited, changes in U.S. public opinion. Reports of the North Korean attack of June 1950 and the U.S. government reaction to it crystallized what were already hostile public attitudes toward the Soviet Union and China. More Americans began to favor a military buildup and armed intervention in Korea, military and economic aid to other Asian countries, and the strengthening of the alliance with Western Europe.

During the course of the Korean War, the public again expressed more willingness to make sacrifices in terms of wage and price controls, taxes, desisting from strikes, and the like; support for such policies fluctuated with the fortunes of war. The American public's hostility toward the new Communist government of China reached a high point with China's intervention in Korea; larger majorities rejected U.S. diplomatic recognition or admission of China to the United Nations, and many favored bombing Chinese territory. The end of the Korean War, like the end of World War II, led to wishes for a return to peacetime conditions—ending controls and lowering taxes. It also brought gradual increases in approval for negotiating and trading with the Soviet Union, admitting the People's Republic of China to the United Nations, and aiding developing countries.

The *Vietnam War,* too, and events leading up to it, caused a variety of changes in American public opinion. The Tonkin Gulf incident and other preliminary skirmishes, as they were reported to the public at the time, increased public willingness to fight in Vietnam. The ups and downs of the war, including reported "peace feelers" and South Vietnamese government crises and military engagements, led the public to express more or less support for military measures, peace talks, or withdrawal. As in

Korea, the apparent lack of progress, despite increasing U.S. troop levels and increasing numbers of casualties, eroded support for domestic sacrifices and increased opposition to the war. This was especially so after the 1968 Tet Offensive seemed to show that all the effort had been in vain.

During the Vietnam War, antiwar demonstrations in the United States led to increased desires for "law and order" and some loss of support for civil liberties, although they apparently had no immediate and direct impact on opinion toward the war itself. (See, below, the discussion of public opinion toward protests.) The demonstrations also provoked opposition to the eighteen-year-old vote, support for which had earlier risen in response to young soldiers' sacrifices—just as it had during World War II and the Korean conflict. The financial demands and progress of the Vietnam War led to increasing but then decreasing support for defense spending.

The Vietnam War experience, taken as a whole, provoked a lingering public skepticism about the use of military force abroad, reluctance to spend more money on defense, resistance to foreign aid and foreign involvement generally, distrust of government-provided information, and suspicion of presidential power.

Crises and International Events

Major international crises and events not involving the United States in war (but sometimes entailing a serious danger of war) have also had substantial and often abrupt effects on public opinion.

Before World War II, for example, the German remilitarization of the Rhineland, the Anschluss of Austria, and the dismemberment of Czechoslovakia increased Americans' willingness to rearm.

After World War II, the actions of the Soviet Union (as reported and interpreted in the U.S. media, a point to which we will return), especially Soviet backing of the 1948 coup in Czechoslovakia and the blockade of West Berlin, greatly reduced the number of Americans favoring trade or negotiations or cooperation with the USSR, and cut support for the United Nations and for international control of atomic energy.

With regard to the Middle East, a number of events have affected opinions about policy toward Arab countries and Israel. The 1948 establishment of the State of Israel and quick U.S. recognition; the 1956 Suez invasion, together with the emergence of Arab nationalist regimes in Egypt and elsewhere; the 1967 War and Israeli occupation of the West Bank and Gaza; the 1973 War and subsequent OPEC oil boycott and price rises; the Camp David agreements; all led to ups and downs in support for and sympathy with Israel and the Arabs and (after 1973) in support of various energy conservation and regulatory measures at home. The Israeli invasion of Lebanon in 1982 somewhat undercut the American public's high level of support for Israel. The truck bombing of U.S. marines in Lebanon provoked desires for the United States to remove its forces from that country. The Iran-Contra scandal and the lengthy Palestinian uprising in the West Bank and Gaza reduced public support for aid to Israel. In general, during the post-1948 period, reported threats or dangers to Israel increased Americans' willingness to help protect that country, but the expansion of Israeli influence in the region and reports of harsh treatment of Arab civilians tended to reduce U.S. support.

The general tranquility of the 1950s and Soviet overtures for "peaceful coexistence" produced fewer (and, especially, less abrupt) opinion changes—along with increased public desires for trade and negotiations with the Soviets, and less desire to use nuclear weapons. However the imminent collapse of the French in Indochina in 1954, as reported and interpreted in American press, did provoke some (minority) backing for U.S. assistance or intervention. The same lack of events, no doubt, slightly increased the public's willingness to recognize China and admit her to the United Nations. But this willingness dipped in response to what were seen as aggressive domestic or international actions by China (e.g., the Quemoy and Matsu crises and the Cultural Revolution); it rose markedly when China tested a nuclear device and thereby showed herself a force to be reckoned with.

Although the relatively slow growth in U.S. military spending after the Vietnam War, together with reports of a Soviet arms buildup and Soviet initiatives in Africa and elsewhere, led to gradually increasing support for raising the defense budget, this trend was sharply and strikingly accelerated in 1979 by the Soviet intervention in Afghanistan and by the much-televised seizure of hostages in the American embassy in Iran. The hostage seizure also aroused desires for economic or military action against Iran. Later, the end of the hostage crisis and the implementation of the Reagan arms buildup, together with frightening rhetoric from the administration, revelations that U.S. warnings of the Soviets' own buildup had been exaggerated, and generally conciliatory behavior by the Soviets under Gorbachev (including withdrawal from Afghanistan), caused fewer people to favor U.S. arms increases and more to want a freeze on nuclear weapons, trade and exchanges with the Soviets, and the like. But the Iraqi invasion of Kuwait somewhat restored support for defense spending.

The Ambiguity of "Events" as Causes

There is, however (as we have already indicated at various points), a twofold ambiguity about treating wars, international crises, and other events as causes of opinion change. First, as discussed further below, *interpretations* of events rather than the events themselves may often be crucial; the media and government officials and others who provide interpretations may sometimes be the real movers of public opinion. Second, and equally important, presidents and other officials can sometimes *control events*. When they do so, events are only the proximate causes of opinion change; the real impetus comes from the officials and those who influence them.

In Chapters 5 and 6, we gave several important examples of U.S. government control over events. German U-boat incidents and the Japanese attack at Pearl Harbor, which led directly to U.S. involvement in the war and thoroughly transformed public opinion, did not occur in a vacuum; they resulted, at least in part, from President Roosevelt's maneuvering. The Truman Doctrine crisis, a critical step in the acceleration of the Cold War and the building of anti-Soviet attitudes, was not sprung on a passive United States but resulted from the U.S. decision (after the British withdrawal from Greece) to intervene and sound an alarm based on the manufactured Greek "request" for aid. Likewise, the Tonkin Gulf incident, so pivotal for U.S. involvement in Vietnam, was not only an ambiguous event subjected to deceptive interpretation but resulted, at least in part, from U.S. provocations of North Vietnam. Later examples include U.S. interventions in such places as Grenada and Panama, both undertaken unilaterally.

To be sure, the control that presidents and policymakers exert over events is seldom complete. Nor is it necessarily as secretive or deceptive as some of the above examples suggest. Nixon's visit to China and Carter's mediation in the Middle East fall into the same category: important voluntary actions that changed international circumstances and thereby affected public opinion. In each such case, the event itself can provide, at best, only an incomplete explanation of opinion change; the underlying causes reside with the officials who brought about the event and with those who influenced the officials.

We will discuss this further after dealing with domestic events, over which the executive branch generally has less control.

Domestic Events and Conditions

Although sudden, dramatic events are less common in the domestic sphere than the foreign, certain kinds of unexpected domestic developments have occurred and have led to abrupt changes in public opinion.

The nuclear accident at Three Mile Island in 1979 was of this sort. When the reactor cooling system failed and radiation was released into the

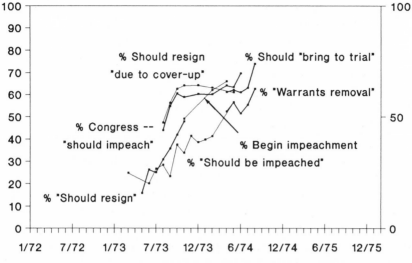

FIG. 8.2   President Nixon and Watergate, 1973–1974.

atmosphere, previous assurances that such accidents would not happen lost credibility. Many Americans concluded that the costs of nuclear power were greater than they had thought, and support for nuclear power, which was already declining, took a sudden drop.

Similarly, the revelations of Watergate-related wrongdoing in the Nixon administration rapidly led many people to conclude that campaign finances needed closer regulation, that President Nixon was personally involved and ought to be impeached, and that the presidency itself should be restrained. As figure 8.2 shows, a variety of poll questions indicate a very strong and rapid rise in the proportions of the public who said Nixon should resign, or be impeached and brought to trial, or be removed from office. Several opinion changes in the graph coincide with specific events, like the trial of the Watergate burglars; John Dean's allegations of White House involvement; the October 1973 "Saturday Night Massacre," in which Nixon fired the attorney general and his deputy because they would not dismiss Special Prosecutor Cox; the impeachment hearings; and the final "smoking gun" tape recording (see Lang and Lang 1983).

Again, the urban riots as well as the antiwar demonstrations of the middle and late 1960s and early 1970s apparently reduced sympathy for minorities and eroded support for spending money on urban problems. Together with reports of street crime and mass murders, they increased public support for capital punishment, conservative appointments to the Supreme Court, and more harsh treatment of criminals. The assassinations of John Kennedy, Robert Kennedy, and Dr. Martin Luther King each led more

Americans to favor gun control. Certain disruptive or inconvenient labor strikes undercut support for the rights to unionize and to strike.

An illustration of the systematic fashion in which public opinion reacts to events and conditions is that the trends in opinion about capital punishment and about harsher court treatment of criminals (described in Chap. 3) both responded rather strongly to actual crime rates. A simple time series analysis of opinion levels and measured crime rates revealed correlations in the very substantial .8 range.[4]

Various political events of a less sensational nature have also affected opinion. Early Senate filibusters against civil rights bills produced support for rules changes. The Third Party efforts of Henry Wallace and George Wallace made more Americans favor abolishing the electoral college and electing the president by popular vote. Revelations of corruption in labor unions contributed to increased support for strict regulation of labor. The Reagan administration's scandals in the Environmental Protection Agency made more Americans favor stronger actions to protect the environment.

Sometimes domestic policy actions by government have affected the public's expressed policy preferences, if only by satisfying people's desires and reducing demands for further action (see Weissberg 1976, chap. 5). After the Senate liberalized its cloture rules and cut off some civil rights filibusters, fewer people sought majority cloture. When President Nixon appointed conservatives to the Supreme Court, the backing for more such appointments was reduced. After the 1974 campaign reform legislation, fewer Americans sought strict regulations. Once the Reagan arms buildup was under way, fewer sought increases in defense spending. When taxes have been cut, fewer people have said the level is "too high"; when taxes have gone up, the opposite change has occurred. But in some such cases, shifting referents in the survey questions can produce altered responses without real preference changes.

The Economy

Many important domestic events have to do with the economy. Depressions, recessions, periods of growth and episodes of inflation have affected opinions about a number of domestic and foreign policies. Some of these events have been gradual and cumulative in nature, so that they contributed to the gradual trends we already discussed; others have been more abrupt.

The Great Depression, which lowered incomes and threw many people out of work, undoubtedly increased support for relief programs, job assistance, social insurance, strict regulation of business, and the like, though we lack pre-Depression surveys to document the extent of change.

Within the period for which we have opinion data, however, ups and downs in the economy have often clearly affected attitudes about taxes and spending policies. This is especially obvious in recent years when survey items have been repeated frequently. High inflation rates, for example (even when accompanied by recession, as in the 1970s), have contributed to significant (though temporary) declines in support for taxes and for spending on medical care, welfare, the cities, foreign aid, and space exploration. When real (and after-tax) incomes have dropped, more people have tended to find the level of taxes too high. Recessions and high unemployment have increased support for domestic welfare spending and the tendency to worry about foreign competition and to back tariffs and other protectionist restrictions on trade. High inflation rates—from the mid-1970s to the early 1980s, for example—have also brought more Americans to favor wage and price controls and balanced government budgets. The OPEC oil boycott and price rises of 1973–1974 and 1979 led many more Americans to favor measures for energy conservation, price controls, rationing, and the breakup of big oil companies as well as favoring aid to and friendly relations with Arab oil producing countries.

Since economic conditions fluctuate from time to time, it has been possible to use time series analysis to show that public opinion varies with such conditions and events in regular, predictable ways. In Chapter 4 we saw that support for doing more about employment has varied systematically, and substantially, with the actual unemployment rate. Similarly, Hibbs (1979) found that the unemployment rate affects the trade-offs that people favor between proemployment and anti-inflation macroeconomic policies. And we offered further examples in Chapter 4: like support for federal income taxes, support for wage and price controls has covaried with the rate of inflation—when inflation is high, more people want controls. (On public sensitivity to economic conditions, see also Shapiro and Conforto 1980.)

Such examples—along with the crime rate case above—are particularly important because they indicate that the public's reactions to particular events are not only explicable, after the fact, but are *predictable;* that is, the public reacts consistently, in the same way, to the same conditions. This regularity of response is an important element in our conception of public rationality.

The Mass Media and News Sources

As we noted in connection with gradual trends, some trends and events have a more or less unmediated impact on the public. Certain objective conditions related to domestic policy, for example, are felt directly by millions of people at once: rising or falling incomes, prices, or taxes; or a greater abundance of consumer goods. But experiences like unemployment, criminal victimization, or being drafted and sent to fight abroad are experienced directly by relatively few. And many sorts of events, especially in foreign policy, are quite remote from the personal experience of most people. They are perceived only indirectly—usually through news reports in the mass media. Most Americans learn about a nuclear power plant accident, a coup in Latin America, or a conflict in the Middle East only by glimpsing a newspaper headline or watching TV news or getting the word from friends who have seen news reports.

Even events that are experienced personally may not be known in their full magnitude or their political significance except through the mass media. An individual laid off from his or her job may think it a purely personal mishap, unless there is news of rising unemployment in the nation as a whole. A wartime injury or death of a family member or friend brings personal grief, but its political meaning becomes apparent only when newspapers or TV report many other casualties. Rising prices are noticed at the gasoline pump or the grocery store, but their nationwide significance may be felt only when the media focus on "inflation" as a nationwide phenomenon.

Thus public opinion often responds not to events or social trends themselves but to *reported events*. It makes a good deal of difference which events are reported, which are emphasized, and which are ignored. It also matters what sorts of "facts" are conveyed and how they are interpreted. The facts and their policy implications are seldom unambiguous or uncontested. True, an armed attack on Americans like the Japanese bombing of Pearl Harbor—once it comes—will be taken by almost every American as a strong argument for declaring war. But did North Korea's attack on South Korea, in a context of a civil struggle, call for a similar U.S. reaction? What about the Tonkin Gulf incident offshore from Vietnam? Or Iraq's invasion of Kuwait? Did OPEC's oil boycott and price rises of the 1970s dictate price controls, or windfall profits taxes, or a breakup of big oil companies? Courting Arab oil producers, or using military force against them? Did civil rights demonstrations mean people should react with antidiscrimination laws or with political repression? Obviously much depends upon how such events are reported and understood.

Events seldom speak for themselves. To work out the implications of an event for the costs and benefits of alternative public policies requires complex reasoning, involving knowledge or beliefs about what actually happened, and also ideas about what it means in terms of a set of goals and objectives and a view of how the world works (a system of beliefs about background facts and causal connections). It requires *interpretation* of the event.

As we have indicated, we believe that ordinary citizens are capable of such political reasoning to a much greater extent than they are usually given credit for. Still, learning and thinking about politics costs time and effort and offers only limited rewards. Most people sensibly spend most of their time and energy on work and family and leisure activities rather than pondering the wisdom found in the *New York Times*. When it comes to political analysis, most people delegate most of the work to people they trust as like-minded agents.

There is reason to believe that many chosen agents of interpretation and analysis are respected individuals or groups whose words and behavior are reported in the mass media, especially on television. That is, particular *sources of news and commentary* speak to the public through the media, providing much of the factual and interpretative material that mediates the effects of objective events upon public opinion. Such sources may therefore have important effects on the policy preferences of the public. It is important to learn who they are and how much effect they have.

Media Impact Studies

Based upon recent research, including our own, we now have much more evidence than ever before about how messages communicated through the media influence public opinion. In particular, a series of studies relating the contents of TV news reports to the magnitude and direction of changes in public opinion have shown that news from various different *sources* can, over time, cause changes in the public's collective policy preferences.

In one study of the 1969–1983 period, for example, we selected eighty survey questions about public policy that were asked, in identical form, twice within a short period of time—mostly within three to six months. (The data and methods are described more fully in Page et al. 1987.) These questions were fielded by several different survey organizations and covered a variety of foreign ($n=32$) and domestic ($n=48$) policy issues. In about half the cases public opinion changed significantly within the period; in about half it did not. For each of these eighty cases we calculated the amount, if any, by which public opinion changed from the first to the second survey, noting the direction in which it changed—coding as a "positive" change an increase in the percentage of the public that favored the most prominent (the first-mentioned) policy alternative in the survey question. We then proceeded to predict the amount and direction of this opinion change (the number of positive or negative percentage points of change) as a function of independent variables drawn from TV news. (For methodological reasons, the preferred dependent variable is actually the proportion of the public favoring the most prominent policy alternative at t_2, and the level of opinion at t_1 is included as a predictor variable; the estimated news effects come out virtually the same with change scores as the dependent variable.)

For the independent variables taken from TV news, we and our research assistants coded the daily network television news from one or more randomly selected network *every day*, beginning two months before the first ("t_1") survey and going through to the time of the second ("t_2") survey, using the brief summaries found in the *Television News Index and Abstracts* of the Vanderbilt Television News Archive.[5]

We distinguished among ten different exhaustive and mutually exclusive categories of news sources—that is, particular actors or providers of information: the president, members of his administration and fellow partisans, members of the opposing party, interest groups and individuals not fitting into other categories, experts, network commentators or reporters themselves, friendly (or neutral) foreign nations or individuals, unfriendly foreign states or individuals, courts and judges, and objective conditions or events not attributable to identified human actors.

We analyzed each relevant statement or action from each kind of source on a given day. Each such "source-story" constituted a unit of analysis for measuring media content for a particular opinion case. For each source-story we coded its degree of relevance to the policy issue, its salience in the news broadcast, and—most important—the pro-con *direction* of intended impact of the reported statement or action in relation to the most prominent policy alternative mentioned in the opinion item. A president's advocacy of a big appropriation of money for federal aid to education, for example, was coded as a presidential source-story "pro" the policy alternative of having the government in Washington help build schools. It proved rather easy to code reported statements and actions on a five-point directional scale going from "clearly pro," through "probably pro," "uncertain or neutral," and "probably con," to "clearly con."

For each type of news source in each opinion case we summed all the numerical values of pro-con codes (ranging from $+2$ to -2, with 0 for neutral) over the appropriate period, in order to compute measures of total directional thrust of the news from each source. The sums of directional codes for all relevant news from each distinct source (keeping track of whether the report came before t_1 or between t_1 and t_2) constituted substantively appropriate independent variables to account for opinion changes.

TABLE 8.5 Effects of TV News from Various Sources

News Source	Impact of News between t_1 and t_2
President	0.30
	(1.34)
Party of president	−0.09
	(−0.73)
Opposition party	0.44
	(2.00)
Interest groups	−0.38
	(−1.93)
Events	0.54
	(1.27)
Commentary	4.34*
	(4.25)
Experts	3.37*
	(2.32)
Foreign-friendly, neutral	0.08
	(0.14)
Foreign-unfriendly	0.48
	(0.99)
Courts	−2.02*
	(−2.22)
Intercept	−1.34
	(−0.56)

R-squared $= .94$
Adjusted R-squared $= .91$
$N = 80$

Source: Page, Shapiro, and Dempsey (1987, p. 30).
Note: Entries are unstandardized coefficients from a regression of opinion at t_2 on opinion at t_1 and on 20 different sums of relevant pro vs. con news story scores, 10 pre-t_1 and 10 between t_1 and t_2. The t_1 opinion and pre-t_1 news variables are treated as controls and their coefficients are omitted here.
*Significant at the .05 level or better by a two-tailed test (t values in parentheses).

Results

Table 8.5 displays the main results from a regression analysis in which the magnitude and direction of opinion changes was predicted by the sums of news content we coded from the TV news.[6]

The first thing to notice in table 8.5 is that we had a great deal of success in predicting changes in public opinion. With the regression equation, which includes the level of opinion at t_1, news from various sources just before t_1, and news between t_1 and t_2, we were able to account for more than 90% of the variance (across issues) in the level of opinion at t_2. Of course, this partly just reflects the fact that public opinion tends to be very stable; opinion at t_1 is a very strong predictor of opinion on the same issue at t_2. But when we changed the form of the analysis and directly predicted opinion change scores by the news variables alone, we still accounted for nearly half the variance in opinion change ($R^2 = .57$; adj. $R^2 = .41$). That is to say, what appears on TV news accounts in large part for the relatively short-term (neither instantaneous nor glacial) changes in public opinion.

Table 8.5 also indicates that there are big differences in the effects of news from different sources. News commentary (from the anchor person, reporters in the field, or special commentators) has the most dramatic positive impact. A single "probably pro" commentary was associated with more than four percentage points of opinion change, a very large amount. Stories about experts or research studies, too, have a strong positive effect on public opinion: after a single story indicating that experts favor a particular policy, public support tended to rise by about three percentage points.

Certain other estimated effects are probably meaningful even though they did not meet our conservative criterion of statistical significance, because we have obtained similar results in other studies. Presidents, for example, were estimated to have a modest impact of about three-tenths of a percentage point per "probably pro" story. Such small effects would add up, because presidential stories are much more frequent than those of experts or commentary. (Moreover, as we will see below, *popular* presidents do better.)

Stories about opposition party statements and actions may also have positive effects. Their impact may go beyond the small (not quite significant) estimated coefficient in table 8.5, if, as we believe, the presence of an opposition voice can help immunize the public against persuasive efforts by the president and administration. Our results suggest that such opposition will be particularly effective if it is coordinated with similar stands by (ostensibly nonpartisan) commentators and experts, and perhaps critics within the president's own party. It is not easy for an opposition party, on its own, to mobilize public opinion.[7]

Interest groups and the courts, on the other hand, seem in recent years actually to have had slightly *negative* effects on public opinion. That is, when their statements and actions have pushed in one direction—when corporations demanded subsidies, for example, or protestors (coded as an interest group) demonstrated against the Vietnam War, or when a federal court ordered school integration through busing—public opinion has tended, at least initially, to move in the opposite direction. This is presumably because the courts have little public support as policymakers (Adamany and Grossman 1983), and most interest groups are held in low esteem. (We are not certain about these negative effects, however, because special interests and groups may speak out most clearly when they are already losing public ground, and because of instability in the courts' coefficients across data sets.) As suggested below, some kinds of groups probably have negative effects, while others have positive.

Certain other kinds of news appear on the average to have less impact than might be expected, or to have no direct effect at all upon opinion. The president's administration and fellow partisans, when acting independently of the president himself, do not appreciably affect public opinion. It is also striking that events, which we have emphasized as fundamentally important in understanding opinion changes, do not generally have very strong direct effects. As we have said, events usually do not speak for themselves; they have most of their impact through the interpretations and reactions of other news sources. (The bivariate coefficient for events drops by more than 50% when other news sources are controlled.) Much the same applies to statements and actions from foreign countries or individuals, whether friends or foes. Americans usually do not listen to foreigners directly but only through interpretations by U.S. opinion leaders. This confirms our view of the importance of the media.

One factor in the markedly different effects of different types of news is undoubtedly source *credibility*. The public apparently tends to place great trust in the positions taken by television network commentators and by ostensibly nonpartisan experts. By contrast, interest groups that are presumed to pursue narrowly selfish aims may serve as negative reference points. Others may be seen as noncredible or irrelevant and, therefore, have no effect.[8] But there are also some further complications, beyond questions of credibility, in understanding exactly how various news sources influence public opinion.

News Commentary

We have been surprised by the remarkably strong estimated impact of news commentary, which has appeared in analyses of three separate sets of cases. We found a large effect of editorial columns in our earlier analysis of fifty-six opinion cases using news content data from the *New York Times* (Page and Shapiro 1984). And big commentary effects were also found in the first forty TV news cases we studied (Page, Shapiro, and Dempsey 1984), and in the forty new television cases that we analyzed separately before putting all eighty TV cases together. Moreover, other studies have subsequently found substantial commentary effects on support for presidents and presidential candidates (Brody and Shapiro 1989a, 1989b; West 1991; Shapiro et al. 1990a, 1990b). These studies echo laboratory findings that messages from trusted TV newscasters or editorials clearly affect attitudes (Cundy 1989; Freeman, Weeks, and Wertheimer 1955; Andreoli and Worchel 1978; for evidence on the perceived credibility of newscasters and commentators, see Robinson and Kohut 1988).

Examining specific cases in our data, there are a number of particularly noteworthy instances in which the statements of news commentators and reporters clearly paralleled opinion changes. These include Howard K. Smith's praise for Nixon's policies and his criticism of calls for unilateral withdrawal from Vietnam in 1969; various newsmen's support for continued slow withdrawal in 1969–1970; commentary favoring conservation and increased petroleum production rather than stopping military aid to Israel in order to get cheap oil in 1974–1975; Smith's and others' support for more attention to the Arabs in 1974–1975 and 1977–1978; Eric Severeid's, David Brinkley's, and Smith's advocacy of campaign contribution limits in 1973; Brinkley's and Smith's backing of stricter wage and price controls in 1972–1973; John Chancellor's editorializing on the importance of fighting unemployment rather than inflation in 1976; Smith's support for federal work projects in 1976; and commentaries in the spring of 1981 that Reagan's proposed tax cuts would benefit the wealthy.

Our regression estimates of very large commentary effects, controlling for news from all other sources, indicate that something substantial was going on. We cannot entirely rule out a reciprocal effect of public opinion upon audience-seeking reporters and media (which would inflate the estimates of commentary effects), but in many cases the timing of news commentary shortly after t_1 polls indicates a genuine influence upon opinion at t_2.

The exact nature of this influence, however, is harder to judge. We cannot quite believe that individual news commentators like Walter Cronkite and Howard K. Smith—for all the esteem in which they were held—had such potency in bringing about opinion change. Effects in natural settings, on aggregate public opinion, are not likely to be so simple as in the laboratory experiments alluded to above: see Shapiro et al. (1990a, 1990b). Instead, TV news commentary may serve as an indicator for other influences on public opinion that send similar messages at the same time, through channels other than TV news: print journalism, for example, or a widespread elite consensus, or even a "climate of opinion" in the country as a whole (see Noelle-Neumann 1984). (Remember, however, that our analysis controlled for many other kinds of televised elite sources when estimating the commentator effect.)

A slightly different, and perhaps more plausible, possibility is that commentators' positions are indicators of more general slants or biases in TV and newspaper coverage that are transmitted to citizens through the selection of news sources and quotations (see Nacos 1990) and through choices of visual footage, questions asked in interviews, camera angles used, and so forth. If TV commentaries are in basic agreement with official network sentiment and with the attitudes of reporters—perhaps providing cues for reporters who want to get ahead—our estimates of commentary effects could actually stand for broader kinds of effects on opinion by the media themselves and perhaps by their owners and managers.

We cannot, by means of our data, distinguish among these possibilities. We must be content to conclude that news commentators either constitute, or stand for, major influences upon public opinion, most or all of which operate through the mass media—though not necessarily TV alone.

Experts

The large estimated impact of those we have categorized as "experts" is perhaps less ambiguous, at least in terms of direct effects. The credibility of experts is presumably high because of their actual or portrayed objectivity, experience, expertise and nonpartisan status. (In fact, experts should be even more influential than commentators, since the latter explicitly express personal opinions.) It is not surprising that members of the public give great weight to expertise. Complex technical questions often bear upon the merits of policy alternatives.

Some reciprocal influences by anticipated public opinion upon reported expert statements cannot be ruled out; audience-seeking media, for example, may decide which experts to feature partly based on the popularity of their policy views. But reciprocal effects are probably limited in the short run because experts do not face immediate electoral pressures. That is, public attitudes may ultimately influence who are considered "experts" and what their basic values are, but, once established, experts are presumably less likely than presidents or other elected officials to bend quickly with the winds of opinion.

One important example of the influence of expert views as reported in the media concerns the Senate vote on the SALT II arms limitation treaty. Public support for such a treaty dropped by 5.5% from early February to late March 1979 (according to an NBC question), and by 19% from June to early November (according to a different CBS/*NYT* question). During both periods many retired generals and arms experts spoke out or testified against the treaty, citing difficulties of verification and an allegedly unequal balance of forces favoring the Soviets.

Experts seem also to have been important in building support for the 1981 AWACS (radar warning and control aircraft) sale to Saudi Arabia; in increasing skepticism about Reagan's proposed tax cuts between May and June 1981; cooling off enthusiasm for a tax on large cars in 1974; and encouraging support for public financing of political campaigns (1973) and banning handguns (1981).

Our estimate of the impact of experts is not, however, completely free of causal ambiguity; the direct effects of experts may reflect indirect influence by various others in society. Experts may be selected by the media in such a way as to promote the media's own biases or an elite consensus. Also, the expertise that is broadcast at a given historical moment seems to vary with the political tides of the day and especially with which party holds power in Washington (see Soley 1989 and Cooper and Soley 1990 on how the AEI and other sources of conservative expertise dominated the airwaves during the late Reagan administration). Moreover, corporations and organized interest groups are important in funding and publicizing expert studies favorable to their own interests (see Dye 1986, chap. 9; Saloma 1984). So the fundamental forces behind the influence of experts on public opinion may sometimes be the desires and efforts of the media, or a consensus of elites, or particular political parties, corporations, or organized groups.

Later we will discuss to what extent experts and other news sources educate or manipulate the public: to what extent the information and analysis they convey is correct and helpful, or false, misleading, or deceptive. But clearly it would be a mistake to assume at this point that experts' positions are always unbiased and accurate.

Presidents

Our finding in table 8.5 of only a relatively small impact by presidents requires qualification. It resulted from lumping all presidents together, during a period when most presidents, most of the time, were rather unpopular and presumably not very credible. In a further analysis, we separated our cases into two groups: those in which the president was popular (had a Gallup approval rating of 50% or more), and those in which he was unpopular at the time of the surveys. We analyzed each set of cases separately.

The result was that *popular presidents* were estimated to have nearly twice as much effect on opinion as was indicated in table 8.4: .58 percentage points per "probably pro" speech compared to .30.[9] Unpopular presidents were found to have essentially no effect at all (.05 percentage points per speech). This makes sense: when a president is popular we would expect people to put more faith in what he says and does and to be more apt to change their opinions accordingly.

Part of the estimated impact of popular presidents probably reflects a reciprocal relationship, in which popularity-seeking presidents take a stand in response to public opinion or in anticipation of it. It is also true that talkative presidents cannot hope to multiply their impact indefinitely through multiple speeches because of eventual saturation and overexposure. Still, our finding constitutes some evidence that a popular president does stand at a reasonably bully pulpit. On an issue he cares about, a president can hammer away with repeated speeches and statements and can expect to achieve a five or ten percentage point change in public opinion over the course of several months (see Page and Shapiro 1984, pp. 653–654; Page et al. 1987). Moreover, he can probably exert additional (indirect) influence upon the public by persuading other opinion leaders to take similar stands.

There is evidence in our data analysis that the effects of certain other news sources may interact with presidential popularity. Commentaries, for example, seem to have their strongest effect when presidents are unpopular. Perhaps news commentators gain credibility to substitute for an executive who is out of favor. In addition, administration officials and the president's fellow partisans in Congress and elsewhere, when acting independently of a popular president, appear to have a slightly negative impact on opinion, whereas they tend to have positive effects when presidents are unpopular.

In scrutinizing specific cases, we have found some indications that the relationship between presidents and public opinion is, indeed, reciprocal, with each influencing the other (see Page and Petracca 1983). But numerous cases support the inference that popular presidents' actions and statements, as reported in the media, do affect public opinion. These include President Nixon's persistent opposition to accelerating U.S. troop withdrawals from Vietnam during 1969, 1970, and 1971; Reagan's 1981 argument for AWACS airplane sales to Saudi Arabia; Carter's increased attention to Arab countries in 1977–1978; Carter's early 1980 shift (during a temporary peak in popularity) toward toughness in the Iranian hostage crisis; Reagan's 1982 bellicose posturing toward the Soviet Union; Ford's 1974–1975 defense of military spending; and, perhaps, Nixon's 1972–1973 support for wage and price controls.

On the other hand, unpopular presidents definitely do not have much success at opinion leadership. In a number of cases, unpopular presidents have made serious efforts to advocate policies but failed to persuade the public. This was true of Ford's attempts to increase military spending in

1976 and his resistance to jobs programs and health and education spending in the same year. Jimmy Carter in early 1979, with his popularity rating at 43% and falling, failed to rally support for SALT II. Carter was also unsuccessful at gaining significant ground on gasoline rationing, the military draft, or the Equal Rights Amendment in 1979 and 1980. Even Ronald Reagan, when near a low point of popularity (44% approval) in mid-1982, failed to move opinion toward more approval for a school prayer amendment to the Constitution.

Interest Groups

The finding that interest groups may tend to have a negative effect on public opinion holds only on the average, and only for direct effects. A closer examination of specific cases suggests that the public tends to be uninfluenced—or negatively influenced—by the statements of certain groups, namely, those whose interests are perceived to be selfish or narrow or antisocial, while it responds more favorably to groups and individuals thought to be concerned with broadly defined public interests. Moreover, even groups with negative direct effects in the short term may sway the public over time, or indirectly, through behind-the-scenes use of their money and organizational resources.

We found many cases—more than twenty—in which public opinion unequivocally moved *away* from positions advocated by groups and individuals representing special interests. In some cases the groups may have belatedly spoken up after public opinion had already started moving against their positions, producing a spurious negative relationship. But in many cases they seem actually to have antagonized the public and created a genuinely adverse effect.

Such cases include Vietnam War protestors in 1969–1970, protestors against draft registration in 1980, and perhaps the nuclear freeze movement in 1982. Americans have a long history of distaste for demonstrators and protestors, even peaceful ones, a distaste accentuated by official efforts to discredit and red-bait (see Parenti 1986, chap. 6). Most people apparently tend not to accept protestors as credible or legitimate sources of opinion leadership. (This is not to deny, however, that protestors may indirectly play a role in moving policymakers and the public, as when they raised the domestic costs of the war in Vietnam and expanded its visibility. And early civil rights demonstrations may have elicited unusually positive responses, perhaps because of the violent reactions by Southern whites: see Burstein and Freudenburg 1978; Burstein 1979.) Some examples of the public's aversion to protests and social movements are shown in table 8.6.

Similarly, many business groups and corporations are apparently per-

TABLE 8.6 Public Opposition to Protest and Social Movements

Protest in General	
"Suppose all other methods have failed and the person decides to try to stop the government from going about its usual activities with sit-ins, mass meetings, demonstrations and things like that? Would you approve of that, disapprove, or would it depend on the circumstances?" (SRC/CPS)	% Disapprove: 11/68 74 11/70 65 9/72 59 11/74 52
"Most people seem to agree that there is a great deal more dissent and protest in our society than there used to be. Do you feel the level of today's dissent and protest is generally a healthy thing for the country, or do you think it is dangerous and destructive?" (Harris)	% Dangerous: 8/70 70
"Do you tend to agree or disagree that protests in this country by students, blacks and antiwar demonstrators will lead to positive change and should be continued?" (Harris)	% Disagree: 1969/72

The Civil Rights Movement	
"Have you heard or read anything about the 'freedom rides' taking place in the South?" (Asked to the 63% responding "yes" to the first question) Do you approve or disapprove of what the 'freedom riders' are doing?" (Gallup)	% Disapprove: 5–6/61 64
"Do you feel demonstrations by Negroes have helped more or hurt more the advancement of Negro rights?" (Harris)	% "Hurt More": 1963 45 1965 58 9/66 80 10/66 86
"America has many different types of people in it. But we would like to know whether you think each of these people is more helpful or more harmful to American life, or don't they help or harm things one way or the other? . . . Civil rights demonstrators." (Harris)	% Harm: 9/69 69
"Let me ask you about different types of people in this country. For each, tell me if you feel they do more good than harm, more harm than good, or are neither helpful nor harmful to the country . . . Blacks who demonstrate for civil rights" (Harris)	% More Harm: 8/73 40

(continued)

TABLE 8.6 (*Continued*)

Antiwar and Student Protest	
"Do you approve or disapprove of the way the Chicago police dealt with the young people who were registering their protest against the Vietnam War at the time of the Democratic convention?" (Gallup)	% Approve: 9/68 56
"Did you happen to hear anything about what went on between the police and the demonstrators in Chicago at the Democratic convention? (IF YES) Do you think the police used too much force, the right amount of force, or not enough force with the demonstrators?" (SRC/CPS)	% Right Amount: 1968 43 % Not Enough: 1968 33
"America has many different types of people in it. But we would like to know whether you think each of these different types of people is more helpful or more harmful to American life, or don't they help or harm things one way or the other? . . . People who picket against the war in Vietnam." (Harris)	% Harmful: 9/69 59
"Some people are pretty upset about rioting and disturbances on college campuses and in high schools. Some feel sympathetic with the students and faculty who take part in these disturbances. Others think the schools should use police and the National Guard to prevent or stop these disturbances. And others fall somewhere in between these extremes. Where would you place yourself on this scale, or haven't you thought much about this?" (SRC/CPS)	% Use Force (5–7): 11/70 66 11/72 55
"Do you agree, or disagree, that college student protests and demonstrations in general have gone too far, and should be stopped?" (CBS)	% Agree: 10/70 81

The Women's Movement	
"Women who picket and participate in protests are setting a bad example for children. Their behavior is undignified and unwomanly." (Harris)	% Agree: 10/71 (women) 60 10/71 (men) 57
"Women are right to be unhappy with their role in American society, but wrong in the way they're protesting."	% Agree: 10/71 (women) 51 10/71 (men) 44

ceived as narrow and selfish, and have negligible or negative effects on opinion, whereas the public has responded more favorably to environmental groups and perhaps also to general "public interest" groups like Common Cause. In 1973–1974, for example, support for leasing federal land to oil companies declined, as TV news reported conservationists challenging the positions of the profit-seeking and presumably less credible oil companies. During the same period, support for a freeze on gasoline, heating, and power prices increased a bit despite opposition by gas station owners and oil companies.

Not only business corporations but also some mass-membership groups representing blacks, women, the poor, Jews, and organized labor were apparently (judging by our cases) not held in high repute during the 1970s and early 1980s; they were attacked politically as "special interests," and seem to have had null or negative effects on opinion about issues of direct concern to them, including social welfare policies and some Middle East issues.

What our analysis indicates is that protestors and business firms and certain other organized interests do not have direct, positive short-term effects on public opinion when they speak out in their own names. It would be a mistake to conclude from this, however, that organized groups are not major factors affecting opinion in the long run. The messages of protests and demonstrations may sink in over time. Our findings are also quite consistent with the idea that organized groups—especially those with a lot of talent and money, like business corporations—are able to encourage and publicize the work of chosen experts and quite possibly influence news commentators as well, which in turn affect the opinions of the general public. By these indirect methods, and by other means including institutional advertising and influence upon school textbooks and curricula, interest groups may have an extremely important impact on public opinion.

A Schematic Model

The causes of opinion change discussed in this chapter are neither few nor simple; they range from macrolevel historical processes, through specific events, to more micro-level ways in which events are reported and interpreted to the public. We have summarized this complex process with the schematic diagram displayed in figure 8.3. In the diagram, the boxes represent the major factors we have discussed, and arrows represent primary directions of causal influence.

We believe that the principal influences upon the collective policy preferences of Americans are gradual social and economic trends, and world and national events—which have some unmediated impact but are often filtered through interpretations by experts, commentators, and public officials, as reported in the mass media. Those mediators, in turn, may be influenced by various actors in society, including organized interests, corporations, and mass movements. And public policy, affected in part by

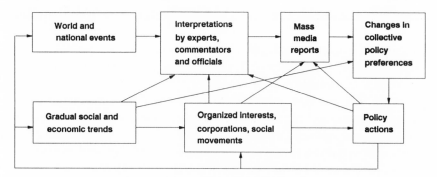

FIG. 8.3   Causes of changes in public opinion.

public opinion, has feedback effects upon events and trends and ultimately on policy preferences.

We cannot offer any precise estimates of how important each path of influence is, but we have tried in this chapter to assess the general tendencies and to suggest conditions under which influences vary. Gradual social and economic trends, for example, have a particularly important impact on domestic policy opinions; Americans' views on foreign policy are more subject to abrupt influence by world events, which are usually mediated through elite interpretations. Indeed, international events themselves can sometimes be controlled by the president and other U.S. officials.

We have seen that many changes in public opinion—especially those in the domestic realm, but also quite a few concerning foreign policy— have occurred in a more or less autonomous fashion: people seem to have reacted directly to events themselves, sometimes going against elite interpretations. But we have also noted that many influences on opinion— including most international events—work only through interpretations transmitted by the mass media and affected by various elites, interest groups, and the government itself. In those cases the *quality of information* conveyed in the media is of utmost importance.

Democratic theory can most comfortably deal with citizens' preferences that are autonomous, uninfluenced by others' wills, and thus a bedrock for social choice. It can also accommodate public opinion that is led, educated, or persuaded by elites, so long as the information and interpretations provided to the citizenry are correct and helpful. But the workings of democracy are deeply undermined if elites regularly influence the public's preferences through deception, misleading interpretations, or outright falsehoods. In the next chapter, therefore, we offer a brief summary of what we think we now know about the nature and quality of political ideas and information that are presented to the American public.

9 Education and Manipulation of Public Opinion

☑ Our findings that media-reported statements and actions strongly affect Americans' policy preferences, and that government officials can influence public opinion by controlling certain international events, raise important questions about democratic theory. If citizens' policy preferences are not always a completely autonomous force, welling up from objective needs and circumstances, the attractiveness (and even the meaningfulness) of the democratic ideal—that governments should do what their citizens want—is thrown into serious question.

If for example, the public's policy preferences sometimes reflect the wishes and interests of government officials, corporations, or organized groups, or the biased workings of the mass media, then there is reason for concern. In particular, if the public is systematically manipulated, deceived, or misled, one should draw little normative satisfaction from the translation of its mistaken wishes into policy. (Lindblom 1977 discusses this problem in terms of the "circularity of preferences"; Lukes 1975 refers to the "third face of power.")

The possibility that the public is systematically misled in its policy preferences also threatens the main thrust of our argument about the rationality of public opinion. The stability and coherent patterning of public opinion that we have found, and the public's capacity to react sensibly and responsibly to new information, are of little consequence if that information is regularly deceptive or false. Why should we pay any attention to public opinion, let alone urge governmental responsiveness to it, if citizens' policy preferences amount to no more than a blank slate upon which various elites can write whatever they wish?

If, on the other hand, leaders help the public to understand politics; if there exists an information system that regularly provides correct, useful information and interpretations, then there should arise an informed, authentic public opinion well worth heeding.

Thus it makes a great deal of difference precisely how and to what ends influences upon public opinion are exerted. We need to know for what purposes and in whose interests events are controlled, and especially *what quality of information and interpretations* are conveyed to the citizenry.

355

To the extent that the public receives useful interpretations, and correct and helpful information—information and interpretations that help it move toward the policy choices it would make if it were fully and completely informed—the policy preferences it expresses can be considered more "authentic," or "enlightened": better adapted to achieve people's basic values and goals. (Following Connolly [1972], Mansbridge [1980], Bartels [1990], and others, we define true, authentic or enlightened interests in terms of fully informed preferences.) Individuals or institutions that influence public opinion by providing correct, helpful political information, can be said to *educate* the public.

On the other hand, to the extent that the public is given erroneous interpretations or false, misleading, or biased information, people may make mistaken evaluations of policy alternatives and may express support for policies harmful to their own interests or to values they cherish. An extreme result of such mistaken evaluations could be the systematic "false consciousness" or "hegemony" about which some Marxists and other theorists speak (Gramsci 1971 [1929–1935]), or the widespread domination of "propaganda" as described by Ellul (1965).

Those who influence public opinion by providing incorrect, biased, or selective information, or erroneous interpretations, may be said to *mislead* the public. We will also sometimes refer to institutions, processes, or patterns of behavior (organizational and technical features of the media, for example) as misleading the public, if they systematically provide citizens with false or misleading information and interpretations.

If government officials or others mislead the public consciously and deliberately, by means of lies, falsehoods, deception, or concealment, we say (using the term in a particular way) that they *manipulate* public opinion. The concept of manipulation implies conscious, intentional human action. It can include the purposeful taking of action or creation of events (while misrepresenting their character) in order to influence opinion.

It is difficult to identify instances or patterns of education or manipulation with any certainty. In particular, the crucial distinctions between correct and incorrect information, and between helpful and misleading interpretations, are not easy to apply. Reasonable people disagree about what the facts are and how the world works. Scientists and scholars and others often differ among themselves, and indeed their very livelihoods are based on the premise that much remains unknown or uncertain. Given this inherent uncertainty, judgments about truth and falsehood (as well as judgments about awareness and motivation) are often subject to dispute. It is even more difficult to know whether or not the effect of particular information or actions is to lead citizens astray from what they would (hypothetically) believe if fully informed.

Thus one who tries to study education and manipulation of public opinion can easily wander into minefields of confusion and controversy. All observers (including the present authors) are inevitably influenced by their own beliefs and values in judging what is true and what is false; others, with contrasting beliefs and values, will often disagree. Still, the subject is so important to any serious discussion of public opinion and democracy that the attempt is worth making. Accordingly, we have done our best in this chapter to assess the extent to which the public appears to have been educated, misled, or manipulated, and to uncover systematic ways in which helpful or misleading information and interpretations may be conveyed. We begin with education and then proceed to discuss manipulation and patterns of misleading information.

Educating the Public

Our concept of education is a broad one, encompassing any and all means by which citizens receive information and interpretations that help them form the kind of policy preferences they would hold if they were fully and completely informed. These include not only formal schooling but also *leadership* by public officials, through both rhetoric and action; experiences undergone by citizens themselves; and the provision of information by experts, scholars, organized groups, social movements, and the mass media.

Formal Schooling

We have seen that formal education often makes a difference in citizens' policy preferences. It tends to provide people with basic political information, to teach them ways of interpreting political reality, and to give them motivation and cognitive skills for further learning (see, e.g., Dewey 1916; Hyman et al. 1975; Hyman and Wright 1979).

Very likely, then, the spread of formal education in the United States, the great increase of schooling at the elementary and secondary and college and postgraduate levels, has taught the citizenry more about politics. In fact, the rational public revealed by recent survey data may be partly a creation of the twentieth-century system of public and private formal education together with the modern media of mass communications.

It is hard to say, however, exactly to what extent schools in America actually "educate" citizens in the sense in which we are using the term, that is, to what extent they provide correct information and useful interpretations of politics. Plainly, much of what the schools teach is factually correct, noncontroversial, and tremendously useful: basic facts about other countries, for example, and about American history, society, and politics; and methods of reasoning and evaluating evidence, which are crucial for reaching judgments about policy alternatives and for resisting misleading rhetoric.

On the other hand, by many standards the schools fall short. The weakness of Americans' knowledge of world history and geography is notorious. Some of what the schools do teach is not so helpful; they may propagate certain kinds of systematic misconceptions and incorrect interpretations, flowing from society-wide information biases of the sorts explored below. But we cannot undertake here to judge the overall quality of political education provided by American schools, because we have no direct evidence on the subject.

Instead, we will focus our attention on information made available to citizens through the *mass media,* which, as the previous chapter made clear, has large, direct impacts on the public's formation of policy preferences. Television, in particular, pervades practically all American homes; large and increasing proportions of Americans (65% in 1988 compared with 51% in 1959, according to Roper surveys) say they rely on TV for most of their "news about what's going on in the world today"—more than on newspapers, magazines, or any other source.

It is clear that the American public has learned a great deal about the United States and the world through the mass media, especially television. Facts about foreign countries and international events, about U.S. social problems and resources and policy alternatives, have been conveyed through the media. The mass media, in fact, are the chief means by which most other major sources of political information actually reach the public.

Experts

Much of what people learn about politics, through popular books and articles and discussions with friends as well as through media reports, originates in scholarly research or expert commentary. In many cases, experts and research studies have provided accurate and useful new information that has helped the public better to understand problems facing the country and better to estimate the costs and benefits of policy alternatives. Thus scholars, researchers, and experts, and those publicizing their work (for example, the experts appearing on TV who can so strongly affect public opinion), have helped educate the public.

To recall an example from Chapter 3, anthropologists and sociologists who studied the cultural bases of human characteristics laid the basis for a new public understanding of racial differences as environmental rather than genetic, and undermined much of the rationale for racism (Myrdal 1944; Young 1979). Together with later studies of the detrimental effects of segregation upon minorities, they helped lead the public to accept civil rights policies aimed against discrimination and segregation. Similarly, research in the late 1950s and early 1960s, and publications like Michael Harrington's *The Other America* (1962), described widespread poverty in America and introduced many Americans to information about the formerly "invisible" poor. This knowledge helped increase public backing for various antipoverty programs.

Again, the writings of Rachel Carson (1962) and others revealed the environmental effects of heavy pesticide use and led the public to perceive the existence of problems that might be solved through environmental legislation. Ralph Nader (e.g., 1972 [1966]) and his associates did much the same for automobile safety and other consumer issues.

George Stigler (1971) and other economists pointed out the inefficiency (and the proproducer bias) of many licensing and regulatory policies, and thus gave impetus to sentiment for deregulation. Over the years, neoclassical economic analyses of tax loopholes and incentives, the negative impacts of wage and price controls, and the counterproductive effects of protective tariffs, minimum wages, and agricultural price supports have clearly contributed to public understanding of government policies.

Likewise, natural and social scientists have helped the public with studies of such matters as the workings of Head Start and other social welfare programs, the problem of welfare dependency, safety and environmental hazards of nuclear power, the consequences of nuclear war, the workings or nonworkings of strategic missile defenses, processes of global warming and ozone-layer depletion, and many other subjects.

In many cases, scientific or scholarly studies appear to have led to an altered expert consensus and then to relatively widespread elite agreement, with the conclusions subsequently entering the public's consciousness. Often publicizers and media commentators (particularly strong influences on the public, according to our media impact studies) have played important parts in the dissemination process. The questionable side of all this, however (discussed below), concerns possible partisan and ideological biases in exactly what sorts of experts are encouraged and publicized.

Politicians and Public Officials

These probably have made fewer unequivocal contributions to political education. The rhetoric of presidents, for example, rarely lives up to the ideal Woodrow Wilson propounded of informing and responding to public opinion (Wilson 1952 [1890]). Presidents often draw attention to the existence of problems and the merits of possible solutions. They rarely, however, rise to the level of what we have called education, because so much of what they say emphasizes values or goals rather than facts or analysis—politicians have incentives to be vague about conflictual issues—and because they frequently encapsulate their substantive arguments in symbols or slogans that are misleading. Oversimplification or misrepresentation should not necessarily be forgiven merely because it is used in what the observer considers a good cause.

Thus we saw that the educational impact of Franklin Roosevelt's warnings about the threat from Hitler and the need for aiding Britain and France was marred by his crafty maneuverings with Japan, his false characterizations of incidents in the Atlantic, and his denial that American troops would be needed when he knew they ultimately would be. Likewise, Harry Truman's warnings of Soviet expansionism, and his plea for a Marshall Plan to help rebuild Europe (surely a noble aim), involved an excessively strident and misleading indictment of the Soviets, which neglected historical context. John Kennedy's urging of an activist foreign policy and aid to developing countries also relied too heavily on exaggerated portrayals of a Soviet threat (and an illusory "missile gap") for it to constitute an unambiguous case of education. These examples remind us how strong is the temptation to mislead the public for "good" ends, and how difficult are the ethical questions thereby raised.

We find more evidence of education in Dwight Eisenhower's embrace of peaceful coexistence, Richard Nixon's late-blooming attentions to mainland China, and Jimmy Carter's efforts in the Middle East and his discussions of human rights in other countries, though none of these examples is entirely unequivocal.

Presidents probably tend to indulge less often in misleading rhetoric about domestic policies than foreign affairs. One could cite as educational certain major presidential efforts to lead public opinion on domestic issues like Roosevelt's espousal of certain New Deal programs, Eisenhower's advocacy of sound and efficient management, Kennedy's urging that the country "get moving again," Johnson's arguments for civil rights and antipoverty programs, and Reagan's advocacy of smaller, more efficient government.

But even in the domestic realm the quality of information conveyed by presidents is often open to suspicion. To the extent that politicians lead public opinion, it is more often by articulating widely held values and pointing toward their application in some policy area, or by shaping events, than by educating the public about specific facts or causal connections related to policy. (True, some have urged acceptance of minitheories—ideas about falling dominoes abroad or welfare programs causing dependency at home, for example—but these have tended toward the simplistic.)

Public officials below the presidential level usually have less visibility; their speeches and position papers and studies and testimony are filtered through other officials and experts and commentators, ordinarily reaching and educating the public only indirectly. Moreover, politicians at all levels are subject to incentives to be vague about conflictual issues (in order to avoid offending constituents) and to oversimplify or mislead (in order to sway them). The chief exceptions involve officials acting in their policy-making roles: executive branch officials studying problems and formulating policy solutions, legislators investigating and deliberating policies. A few highly visible legislators develop public reputations and become important communicators of inside information (see Carmines and Kuklinski 1989).

In some cases, televised congressional hearings have become serious occasions for direct public education: Senator Estes Kefauver's hearings on pharmaceuticals and on organized crime, for example; McClellan's on labor corruption; the Senate hearings on China in the 1950s; McGovern's on hunger; Fulbright's on Vietnam and foreign policy; Erwin's on Watergate; Church's on covert intelligence operations; and (despite their limited scope and lack of assertiveness) the joint hearings on the Iran-Contra scandal. The statements of officials and experts and other witnesses at these hearings helped inform many Americans about major policy issues.

Other Influences

Social movements, like politicians, lead opinion mainly by drawing attention to problems and articulating goals, whether equal treatment for blacks and women and Hispanics; peace in Vietnam, disarmament, a nuclear freeze; help for the poor; permission for or prevention of abortions; or any of a myriad of objectives. The civil rights movement, for example, dramatized the plight of blacks in the South by expressing black demands for equality and by exposing violent white reactions—church bombings, beatings of demonstrators, even murder.

But attention pointing and dramatizing can have educational effects by stimulating interest and getting people to think and seek new information. Social movements also tend to stimulate research and encourage the writing of books, articles, and commentary. In the long run, when demonstrations occur, better public analysis and understanding of policy may tend to follow. (Alternatively, however, protest activity—and press coverage of it—can produce a distorted sense of importance and urgency, distracting the public from other matters.)

Corporations and other organized interests often fund research and generate expertise and commentary, which (on occasion, at least) may help the public better to understand public policy. Even partisan and self-interested position taking is not necessarily without value, particularly when it forms part of a dialogue between contending views.

Experience is said to be a good teacher. To some extent, individuals are shaped by occurrences in their own lives: gains or losses of income, migration from country to city, entrance into or exit from the work force, and the like. Such changes in life circumstances can contribute to political education by affecting what people see as their own and others' interests, and by exposing them to new information. Political learning can also occur when people bump up against objective facts about the world: changes in the power of the United States or other nations, alterations in the terms of trade, or changes in the economy or society which affect both personal circumstances and more collective interests.

To a large extent, however, education of the public occurs in a mediated fashion, through purveyors of news and information—especially scholarship and research, the mass media, and the schools—and through analysis and interpretations by opinion leaders, which work together in ways that may facilitate collective deliberation.

Collective Deliberation

In accounting for the rationality of collective public opinion, we have tended to emphasize its basis in the behavior of individual citizens. In Chapter 1, for example, we suggested that rational individuals take account of new circumstances and new information, changing their calculations about costs and benefits and altering their policy preferences; when many individuals do so at once, collective public opinion changes in sensible and responsible ways. We have also emphasized that collective wisdom can emerge despite considerable individual ignorance or uncertainty, through the simple statistical aggregation of individuals' opinions. That is, when individuals' preferences are summed or averaged into measures of collective opinion, much random error or fluctuation in individuals' opinions may cancel out, leaving a stable and reasonable collective public opinion.

It should be evident from our discussion of the causes of opinion change, however, that collective public opinion does not arise solely through the action of external stimuli upon atomistic, isolated individuals. Not at all. Political information and interpretations are produced and disseminated through a complex social system which involves organizations, division of labor, and transmission through social networks. At its best, this information system contributes to *collective deliberation*, in which the public as a collectivity reasons about policy, and collective public opinion becomes something more than a sum of its individual parts. This social process, above and beyond the merely statistical aggregation of individuals' preferences, contributes significantly to the rationality of collective public opinion.

Federalist Paper no. 63 (apparently written by Madison) argues persuasively that the "cool and deliberate sense of the community"—as opposed to any temporary errors or delusions—ought ultimately to prevail in government (A. Hamilton et al. 1961 [1787–1788], p. 384; Bessette 1980 elaborates on this theme). Although the Founders tended to take the idea of deliberation in an elitist direction, disdaining public opinion and attempting to insulate leaders from it, we do not consider deliberation to be at all incompatible with majoritarian democracy. In fact, we see public or collective deliberation as essential to the realization of democratic ideals.

The point of democracy is not merely responsiveness of government policy to citizens' preferences but responsiveness to *well-informed* preferences, which accurately reflect the basic needs and values of the citizenry. Given the limited effort and resources that any one individual can—or would want to—devote to politics, a system of collective deliberation is needed so that people arrive at preferences reflecting the relevant facts and the realities of political causation: that is, preferences for policies that are appropriate means to achieve the ends they seek. Robert Dahl (1956, pp. 56–59), like other democratic theorists, has noted the necessity of time for public reflection, debate, and discussion. We would add the need for a system of research and expertise, the fruits of which are communicated to the general public.

John Dewey saw inquiry and communication as the keys to the functioning of democracy, as ways to make consequences known and to create an "organized, articulate Public." He forcefully argued for social inquiry that is effective, organized, continuous, and contemporaneous, and for communication of the results in artful ways so that they are published, shared, socially accessible, a common possession; so that their meaning and import and social consequences are known (Dewey 1954 [1927], pp. 176–184):

> We have but touched lightly and in passing upon the conditions
> which must be fulfilled if the Great Society is to become a Great
> Community: a society in which the ever-expanding and intricately
> ramifying consequences of associated activities shall be known in the

full sense of that word, so that an organized, articulate Public comes into being. The highest and most difficult kind of inquiry and a subtle, delicate, vivid and responsive art of communication must take possession of the physical machinery of transmission and circulation and breathe life into it. When the machine age has thus perfected its machinery it will be a means of life and not its despotic master. Democracy will come into its own, for democracy is a name for a life of free and enriching communion. (P. 184)

The "Great Community" that Dewey sought appears to be much the same thing that Habermas (e.g., 1989) has in mind when he speaks of the creation of a "public sphere," in which all citizens may confer in an unrestricted fashion about matters of general interest, with specific means for transmitting information.

Without question, an elaborate system for collective deliberation exists in the contemporary United States. It consists of many specialized elements (some of them discussed earlier in this chapter), organized in a complex fashion, communicating—through a number of direct and indirect links—with each other and with individual citizens.

For example, institutions for research and inquiry located in universities, think tanks, government bureaus, and private industry produce information and analyses relevant to public policy. There are also individuals and organizations engaged in publicizing these results and integrating and interpreting them: experts, commentators, officials, teachers, advocacy groups, policy studies centers. The media of communications transmit much of this information and interpretation to specialized and to broad mass audiences, through scientific and technical journals, books, magazines of analysis and opinion, newspapers, radio, and especially television. Social networks further help transmit political information to individual citizens; these involve political associations and groups, opinion leaders, coworkers, friends, families.

Collective deliberation entails dissemination of the results of inquiry to the general public, but not wholesale diffusion, because only a small part of what is said and thought can (or need) find its way to the citizenry: only certain summary information that emerges from an elaborate process of study and discussion in which ideas are tested and filtered. Scientists report findings, argue with each other, and are judged by peers and experts and commentators; major points are transmitted by the media to the public. Legislators, whose specialty is deliberation (see Bessette 1979; Maass 1983), question witnesses and debate the merits of policy proposals. Some of this reaches the public directly (through televised hearings of the sort we have mentioned), but more often the results are presented in capsule form by the media. Commentators, policy advocates, public officials, and others judge and distill contending views and communicate the highlights to citizens.

The result of this process of collective deliberation, when all works well, is that the general public receives accurate information and helpful interpretations that enable it to form policy preferences in accord with its needs and values. That is, Dewey's "organized, articulate Public," a truly public opinion, is formed. Or, as the Founders put it in Federalist Paper no. 10, public opinion is "refine(d) and enlarge(d)" (A. Hamilton et al. 1961 [1787–1788], p. 82)—not, however, by being passed through a (possibly unrepresentative) chosen body for decision making but through public debate that creates a public opinion worthy of democratic responsiveness.

Two important features of this process of collective deliberation should be emphasized: it involves extensive *division of labor,* and it is highly *decentralized.* Division of labor means that not everyone does the same thing. The system does not require a set of identical, "omnicompetent" citizens, as one brand of democratic mythology seems to prescribe. Instead, some people specialize in policy. Researchers apply special knowledge and techniques to produce policy-relevant information. Others—policy analysts, experts, and commentators—gather and examine and test those results, put them together into coherent solutions to policy problems, and communicate them to each other and to the public. Thus ordinary citizens need not master the intricacies of policy analysis, but can learn enough to form intelligent preferences simply by knowing whom to trust for a reliable conclusion—assuming, of course, that trustworthy cue givers are available and that the information provided by them is sufficiently unbiased. (These are crucial assumptions. If the public lacks like-minded and trustworthy cue givers, or if the available information is monolithic and distorted, collective deliberation breaks down.)

The process is highly decentralized. No central coordination is required, and very likely none is desirable. That is, problems are solved piece by piece, with specialists working independently. Researchers go off in their own directions; commentators offer diverse reactions; communicators present contending views. The outcome is determined not by a central authority but by public debate, and by a multitude of individual decisions about who and what is right.

In its reliance upon division of labor and decentralization, collective deliberation in a large society somewhat resembles the "parallel distributed processing" of information that has increasingly been found effective and efficient by designers of computer systems and analysts of organizational decision making.[1] The idea is that specialization permits depth of analysis and inquiry, soundness of judgment, and skill of interpretation beyond what interchangeable citizens could achieve; and that coordination through debate and discussion among diverse independent actors requires less cumbersome communication (and promises more hope of uncovering truths) than does coordination through a central authority.

The crucial question, then, is: Just how well does collective deliberation work in the United States? We will not offer any summary judgment until after we have discussed the evidence of manipulation and biased information which indicates that there are defects in the system of public discourse, that Dewey's "Great Community" is not yet fully achieved. Already, however, it should be obvious that collective deliberation does function sufficiently well to help produce the rationality we have found in collective public opinion. The public as a whole responds sensibly to events, not only as a result of statistical aggregation of individual preferences but also because social processes of collective reasoning often produce and communicate high-quality information and interpretations.

Misleading and Manipulating the Public

Still, there are many indications that collective deliberation does not always work perfectly. First, deliberation about policy alternatives can only occur after problems and issues are recognized and debated publicly: that is, after they are on the *agenda*. Schattschneider (1960), Bachrach and Baratz (1962, 1963), and others have suggested that manipulation can occur in agenda setting. Many important issues (perhaps including redistribution in the United States and human rights abroad) simply may not receive much attention.

Research has indicated that the amount of coverage given to an issue in the media has a powerful effect on how important the public considers that issue to be (McCombs and Shaw 1972; MacKuen 1981; Iyengar and Kinder 1987; Rogers and Dearing 1988). Moreover, press attention to a problem does not always correspond with objective indicators of its importance (Funkhauser 1973a, 1973b). Recent studies suggest there may be closer correspondence on some issues—for example, economic—than on others, like civil rights, urban unrest, wars, crime, drugs, education, the environment, and international terrorism (Behr and Iyengar 1985; Delli Carpini and Williams 1987; Tom Smith 1980a; MacKuen 1981; Downs 1972).

Second, and most important for our purposes, with respect to salient issues (some of them on the agenda for decades or longer) there are important instances in which the mass media contain misleading, biased, and even intentionally manipulative information and interpretations. By "framing" the public's understanding (Entman 1989; Iyengar 1990b; Krosnick and Kinder 1990 on "priming" effects) in misleading ways, such material may distort the public's policy preferences. In this section we will recall some examples we have already mentioned and recount some new ones, moving on to general patterns in the next section.

Many of the most conspicuous cases are found in foreign affairs. In matters of foreign policy, the executive branch of government often controls access to information, and it can sometimes conceal or misrepresent reality without being challenged. The political opposition is often intimidated or co-opted. Journalists, even when they are aware of what is going on, sometimes willingly hold back awkward truths in the name of "national security."

The "Missile Gap," Tonkin, and the Soviet Scare

One important incident that was mentioned in Chapter 6 and is worth further attention here was the flap about a "missile gap." During the late 1950s various conservative journalists and senators, followed by presidential candidate (and later president) John Kennedy—together with his campaign staff and then his administration—warned that the Soviet Union was in the process of gaining a huge advantage over the United States in numbers of intercontinental ballistic missiles. The Soviets were predicted to have 500 ICBMs by 1960 when the United States was expected to have only thirty. This gap was supposed to widen to a *2,000 : 30* Soviet advantage by 1963 unless the United States rushed to build up its forces. In fact, however, the Soviets fielded no operational ICBMs at all until 1961, when they had only four. The United States enjoyed a 6 : 1 ICBM advantage in 1961 and an 8 : 1 advantage in 1963, in addition to the enormous U.S. lead in nuclear-armed bombers and submarines (Kaplan 1983; Bottome 1971; Ball 1980).

Kennedy and others may perhaps have believed the "gap" prediction (based on Air Force- and RAND-inspired worst-case scenarios) during the campaign, despite President Eisenhower's protestations and offers of briefings; if so, they only misled the public inadvertently. By early 1961, however, the truth was clear to Defense Secretary MacNamara and others (who then had access to the secret U-2 photographs of Soviet installations), yet they suppressed it until a program to build 1,000 ICBMs had been approved by Congress (Stone 1970). Public acceptance of this huge escalation in the arms race—which caused a great deal of expense and danger and may have led to the Soviet gamble of installing missiles in Cuba—seems definitely to have been manipulated.

Another important case was the Tonkin Gulf incident off North Vietnam in August 1964. President Johnson's outraged condemnation of "un-provoked" aggression against two U.S. destroyers was doubly deceptive. The first North Vietnamese PT boat attack—which caused no damage—was provoked by the destroyer *Maddox*'s electronic stimulation of North Vietnamese coastal radar, which created the impression of U.S. armed attacks not far from where South Vietnamese commandos (in a long-standing U.S.-organized operation) were actually raiding the North. And the second alleged North Vietnamese attack, on the *Turner Joy,* apparently never occurred: an inexperienced sonar man got confused in stormy seas. President Johnson and his staff knew of doubts about the second attack and were fully aware of the United States and South Vietnamese provocations for the first. Indeed, it is possible that the very purpose of missions like that of the destroyers was to create an incident that would justify U.S. retaliation and convince the public and the Congress (for whom a draft of the Tonkin Resolution had been prepared in advance) that the United States should escalate its military involvement in Vietnam (Goulden 1969; Windchy 1971; Wise 1973; see Gravel 1971, vol. 3).

The Tonkin case is notable for its blend of executive branch control (and manipulation) of information, with official control of events. The Johnson administration in Vietnam, like the Roosevelt administration with Germany and Japan, appears to have decided that war was necessary to its policy objectives, and to have maneuvered so that war seemed to be thrust upon it. Varying combinations of control over both events and information also characterized incidents in the 1980s involving Libya, Grenada, Panama, and (perhaps) KAL007.

A third case of special importance, also cited in Chapter 6, is the Soviet arms scare of the 1970s and early 1980s, in which the Committee on the Present Danger and various politicians and experts portrayed the USSR as engaged in a massive buildup of strategic nuclear weapons that threatened to open a "window of vulnerability" to a first-strike attack on the United States (Sanders 1983). Like the "missile gap" and the "bomber gap" before it, the window of vulnerability never materialized. It did not take long before U.S. intelligence concluded that the Soviet buildup had been vastly exaggerated. Here, too, the initial misleading of the public may possibly have been accidental (though the accounting methods used to produce the false estimates seem hopelessly biased on their face), but the Reagan administration continued to repeat its rhetoric of vulnerability long after the revised estimates were widely known (Gervasi 1986; Halloran and Gelb 1983). The public, in its support for more military spending, was clearly misled and probably manipulated.

These three cases are especially important because each played a part in a major shift in U.S. foreign policy, with far-reaching consequences. They are also unusually well documented, despite the inevitable difficulty of penetrating the fog of secrecy and self-serving memoirs. But these cases do not by any means stand alone. The origins of the Cold War, for example, another critical turning point in U.S. foreign policy, involved several important instances of misleading the public. As we pointed out in Chapter 5, administration rhetoric repeatedly portrayed the Soviets as less reasonable and more threatening than they were. The Truman Doctrine speech misconstrued the situation in Greece. Truman and Acheson glossed over the civil war aspects of the Korean conflict. They and others depicted mainland China as far more a tool of the Soviet Union, and far more aggressive, than she was.

Covert Operations

The Cold War also involved many U.S. covert actions, which by their nature tended to mislead the public; sometimes almost everyone in the world except Americans seemed to know what the U.S. government was doing. For example, the United States (while making noises about Communist threats) did its best to prevent public knowledge of the CIA operations that overturned the nationalist Mussadiq government of Iran in 1953 (Roosevelt 1979; official denials continue: Cohen 1990) and the leftist Arbenz of Guatemala in 1954 (Immerman 1982), and that attempted to overthrow Sukarno of Indonesia in 1958. The government concealed U.S. organization of the Bay of Pigs invasion of Cuba in 1961. It hid multiple attempts to assassinate Fidel Castro, efforts to overthrow or assassinate Patrice Lumumba in the Congo, U.S. support for the 1965 military coup in the Dominican Republic, and many other covert operations (Wise and Ross 1964; Wise 1973; Marchetti and Marks 1984, chap. 4; U.S. Senate 1975.)

Of course, we cannot be sure whether or not the public would have opposed these covert operations if it had been fully informed about them. But the point is that the public had no chance to decide. Secrecy can manipulate public opinion in the sense of preventing any opinion from forming.

Vietnam

The Tonkin Gulf incident was not the only aspect of the Vietnam War in which public opinion was manipulated or misled. From the beginning of the Vietminh struggle against French colonialism, U.S. officials provided half-truths and untruths. They understated the broad nationalist appeal of the rebellion against the French; claimed (after 1954) that the North, rather than the United States and the South (fearing an electoral victory by Ho Chi

Minh), broke the Geneva accords; maintained that the repressive Diem regime stood for freedom and enjoyed popular support; ignored the artificiality of the temporary North-South boundary; asserted that the NLF insurgency was wholly imported from the North; and predicted that allowing South Vietnam to "fall to the communists" would topple a chain of dominoes that might extend as far as Hawaii (Kahin 1986; Herring 1979).

As we saw, the systematic bombing of North Vietnam was begun (in 1965) on a pretext of temporary retaliation for guerrilla attacks on U.S. air bases in the South. The buildup of U.S. ground forces and their use in combat were concealed; battlefield successes and enemy "body counts" were exaggerated; the devastation of civilian lives in the North and South, and the Americans' use of napalm and toxic gases, were minimized; phony U.S. "peace feelers" were given much publicity; the heavy bombing of Cambodia and the U.S. sabotage of its neutralist government were kept secret; and the invasion of Cambodia was launched on a spurious pretext. Even the inglorious U.S. defeat was cloaked in a pretense of "peace with honor" (Gravel 1971; Hersch 1983; Shawcross 1979; Snepp 1977).

When U.S. officials gave their misleading briefings, many reporters, "experts," and commentators went along. Only belatedly did the reporting and TV news footage turn critical (Hallin 1986). But gradually, and only partly as a result of this media turnaround (well before Tet), the public began to distrust official accounts and grew disillusioned with the war. Thus Vietnam constitutes an extreme case of opinion manipulation, but it also indicates that there are limits to manipulation, at least when reality is accessible and sharply discordant with the official line, when the issue is pressing enough to compel widespread attention, and when enough time passes for official misinformation to be exposed.

During the 1970s, the program to "destabilize" the Allende government of Chile was concealed (Hersh 1983, chaps. 21– 22), as was the covert operation to overthrow the Marxist government of Angola (Stockwell 1978). For the most part, however, the post-Vietnam retrenchment brought some respite from covert operations and from official opinion manipulation—indeed, it led to extensive revelations and criticisms of past operations—until the allegations of a Soviet arms buildup gathered steam.

At the end of the 1970s, massive media attention (magnified, to his later regret, by President Carter) transformed the Iranian hostage incident from a minor diplomatic affront—not unlike the North Korean seizure of the spy ship *Pueblo* and its crew in 1968—into a major international crisis which (as we have seen) helped turn the public further against Islamic fundamentalism and in favor of a U.S. arms buildup. The administration's and the media's portrayal of Soviet intervention in Afghanistan as an invasion aimed ultimately at the Persian Gulf (ignoring internal Afghan politics and Soviet security interests) also scared more Americans into favoring increased military spending and assertiveness abroad. These cases—more like the missile gap or the Soviet scare than the official manipulations of Tonkin—involved mixtures of officials, unofficial groups, and media misleading the public.

The Reagan Years

President Reagan, renowned for his communications skills, attempted to mislead or manipulate the public on a variety of foreign policy matters, with some—but not complete—success. Calling the Soviet Union an "evil empire," with leaders willing to "lie, cheat, and steal" for their ends, he exaggerated Soviet breaches of the SALT arms control treaties and portrayed the United States as advocating arms control while, in fact, resisting agreement (Talbott 1984; Gelb 1985). Reagan and Secretary of State Schultz vigorously condemned the Soviets' deliberate "act of barbarism" in shooting down the KAL007 commercial airliner in 1983, when they knew with reasonable certainty that the Russians had mistaken it for a spy plane—as well they might, since the airliner had passed close to a Soviet-watching U.S. RB-135, had flown far off course over sensitive Soviet defense installations during a Soviet missile test, and had ignored warnings to land (D. Pearson 1987; Hersh 1986). (Indeed, an outside observer cannot easily rule out the possibility that KAL007 *was* on an espionage mission, as some investigators including Pearson have suggested.) The Korean airliner incident, as interpreted by U.S. officials and reported in the U.S. media, inflamed public opinion against the Soviet Union just when sentiment for a nuclear freeze and other cooperative actions had been high and when European resistance threatened the basing of Pershing missiles.

The Reagan administration in the 1980s did its best to conceal renewed CIA military operations in Afghanistan, Ethiopia, Cambodia, and Angola. The administration also offered deceptive accounts of the invasion of Grenada and the bombing of Libya, but its biggest effort concerned Nicaragua.

Reagan exaggerated the failures and defects of the leftist Sandinista government (many of Nicaragua's ills stemmed from the U.S.-imposed guerrilla war and trade embargo) and misleadingly warned of a strategic Soviet "beachhead" in Central America within reach of Harlingen, Texas. The administration attempted to hide the U.S. actions of organizing and training the Contra rebels, supplying them with arms, laying mines in harbors, and blowing up fuel dumps (Chamorro 1987). When negative publicity nonetheless led to congressional restrictions, Reagan repeatedly praised the Contras as "freedom fighters" or "the moral equivalent of the Founding Fathers," ignoring their ties with the former dictator Somoza, their atrocities in the field, their involvement in drug dealing, and their corrupt misuses of U.S. funds. He also red-baited congressional opponents and tried to "marginalize"—that is, ignore or deny or discredit—the American public's opposition to Contra aid (W. Bennett 1989).

No doubt some Americans were misled; Reagan moved the public a bit in his direction on Nicaragua. Yet the remarkable thing, as we saw in Chapter 6, is how resistant the public was. A solid majority of about two-thirds of Americans persistently opposed U.S. aid to the Contras, and even more opposed direct U.S. intervention. The Nicaragua case, like Vietnam, suggests that there are limits to the efficacy of official opinion manipulation, at least when elites are divided and some raise voices in opposition.

Still, concerning a number of foreign policy matters over the last five or six decades, presidents, government officials, and others have attempted to mislead the public—often (as best we can tell) deliberately, and often with considerable success. In many cases misinformation from official sources has been accepted by experts and commentators (who are largely dependent on the official word) and then transmitted more or less intact through mass media reports of what the experts, commentators, and officials have to say. (Herman and Chomsky 1988 analyze this in terms of a "propaganda model" of the media.) In other cases, powerful groups (hawkish Democrats on the "missile gap"; the Committee on the Present Danger and others on the Soviet scare) have performed much the same function from outside the executive branch, using inside contacts and information and continuing their efforts when they got into office.

Furthermore, as we have noted, in foreign affairs the president and executive branch have been able to manipulate opinion by controlling events. A president can sometimes create a "rally 'round the flag" (at least temporarily), and gain policy support, by maneuvering the United States into war or crisis, or simply by taking unilateral action. Relatively minor examples include the Reagan administration's repeated naval maneuvers in and just outside the Gulf of Sidra, apparently designed to provoke Libya into a reaction so as to justify attacking the Qaddafi government (Hersh 1987), the Reagan invasion of Grenada, and the Bush administration invasion of Panama. Much more important were President Roosevelt's nudging of Germany and Japan into belligerency, and President Johnson's provocation of the North Vietnamese. To the extent that fully informed Americans would not have approved of the U.S. actions, or to the extent that the events as interpreted entailed misleading implications, they can be called manipulative.

Domestic Policy

In the domestic policy realm, sources of information are usually more diffuse and competitive, so that outright manipulation of opinion is probably much less common than in foreign policy. Nonetheless, the government, organized interests, or both are sometimes able to dominate public discourse and provide the public with misleading information over long periods of time.

Murray Edelman (1964) has pointed out how merely setting up and publicizing a regulatory agency can mislead the public into thinking that a particular problem has been "solved." The Interstate Commerce Commission was widely assumed to take care of abuses by railroads and truckers, and the Federal Communications Commission to do likewise with broadcasters, even though those agencies actually tended to create legal cartels and thereby further the anticompetitive interests of the regulated industries. The structuring of the Social Security Act might be considered to fall in the same category: some occupations heavily filled by blacks were initially excluded, contrary to the image of universality (Hamilton and Hamilton 1990); and the connection between contributions and benefits was exaggerated as a ploy for support.

Agencies also sometimes suppress information critical of their clients, as the Atomic Energy Commission did when it withheld reports questioning the safety of commercial nuclear reactors (Ford 1984). On the domestic edge of national security policy, government officials are particularly able to control what information is made available. In addition to the atomic energy example, they have concealed many domestic covert operations, thereby manipulating the public into unawareness of and/or acquiescence in actions against dissident groups (including some groups with substantial popular support), like the FBI's harassment of Martin Luther King and other civil rights leaders; the "COINTELPRO" operations of the Nixon years, in which antiwar groups were infiltrated and harassed and their files and offices destroyed (Goldstein 1978; Donner 1981); and the Reagan administration's harassment of opponents of its Central America policies.

Although presidents have probably misled the public less often—or at least less blatantly—on domestic than on foreign policy, domestic cases can be found. Lyndon Johnson, for example, oversold his "war on poverty," building support for policies of limited scope by implying that they could end poverty at low cost while the United States fought another war in Southeast Asia (Tulis 1987). Richard Nixon did just the opposite, overstating the defects of Great Society programs and suggesting that poverty and racism could be overcome by benign neglect. Ronald Reagan's talk of massive government waste, and his colorful anecdotes about welfare queens driving Cadillacs and cheaters spending their food stamps on gin, misled the public about the workings of social welfare programs (Green and McColl 1987).

More broadly, as we noted in Chapter 4, the 1970s and early 1980s were a time of much misleading rhetoric about domestic programs from corporate America as well as political and governmental figures. Politicians and commentators defined the price rises that followed the OPEC oil boycott as "inflation," to be cured with monetarist medicine of tight money and budget cuts—which led to sharp recessions and might well have been opposed by a fully informed public (see Greider 1987). A strong public relations offensive against social and regulatory programs was conducted by experts and publicists (and politicians) financed by conservative corporate interests (Saloma 1984; Edsall 1984; Ferguson and Rogers 1986). Many studies purported to show that Great Society programs like Head Start and the Job Corps had "failed" (Aaron 1978), that Social Security was going bankrupt, and that vast amounts of tax money (allegedly extracted from business to the detriment of investment and economic growth) were being wasted on ineffective domestic programs (Schwarz 1988 [1983]).

Here too, however, we saw the limits of opinion manipulation, which is generally more difficult on domestic policies than foreign. Even as elite politics turned rightward, the propaganda barrage largely failed to convince the public, which remained firmly committed to social welfare programs (see our Chap. 4, above; and Ferguson and Rogers 1986, chap. 1).

But the sheer volume of misleading rhetoric in the 1970s and early 1980s was great. Businessmen's worries about the cost of health and safety and antipollution regulations helped energize economists' studies and media commentary, and this fueled general public support for "deregulation." The consumer movement to abolish anticompetitive regulation of transportation and communications was thus deflected into opposition to any government regulation at all, including that of the environment and health and civil rights (and savings and loans institutions, deregulation's most spectacular failure)—though again public opinion did not change as much as elite politics did.

At the end of the 1970s a miraculous vision of "supply side" economics was used to befuddle many Americans. The idea—proposed by certain economists and political scientists on the fringes of academia, and taken up by businessmen and others who wanted to pay lower taxes—was that federal income tax rates could be cut sharply without hurting government programs because productive forces would be unshackled, taxable incomes would grow, and government revenues would actually rise (Blustein 1981). This alluring but wholly speculative and implausible idea captured the popular imagination and helped win public support for the deep tax cuts of 1981, which proved to be a bonanza for corporations and the wealthy, and which created huge budget deficits and pressure on government spending. Some, if not all, government officials were aware of the likelihood of these effects from the start (Greider 1981; Stockman 1986).

Over the years, misleading rhetoric has entered into many domestic policy debates, often provided or financed by organized interests, but it has seldom so thoroughly dominated discussion as it did in the late 1970s and the Reagan era, when Democratic party opposition wilted—as it often does on foreign policy matters. Usually domestic issues draw more diverse sources of argument and information, more political competition, and (for those reasons as well as access to direct personal experience) more public resistance to being misled.

There may, however, be certain patterns of pervasive, long-term slants or bias in information—encompassing many of the above examples but also going beyond them—which may tend to mislead or manipulate public opinion on both foreign and domestic policy issues.

Patterns of Misleading or Biased Information

Many of the instances of misleading information we have discussed, and others as well, seem to fit into consistent patterns. That is, they appear to represent not just isolated incidents of deception by particular individuals or groups, but general tendencies in the whole body of political information that is provided to the American public.

Such patterns are perhaps even harder to pin down than are particular cases of opinion manipulation. True, identifying them does not require difficult judgments about consciousness and motivation, nor even about absolute truth or falsehood. But it does require a clear conception of what is "misleading." (Again, we take that term to refer to messages that tend to lead average Americans away from the policy preferences they would hold if fully and accurately informed—a definition that is theoretically appealing, though difficult to apply in practice.) Moreover, identification of an information pattern requires some sort of quantitative assessment: a judgment, for example, that a given sort of misleading information is common or prevalent (perhaps as compared with errors in the opposite direction), or that the information reaching the public represents some sort of biased sample from the universe of potentially relevant information. The concept of "bias" is quite problematic in this context, since the universe from which a counterfactual unbiased sample would be drawn is hard to define.[2] Nor is it easy to judge how well the information and interpretations conveyed to the American public live up, or fail to live up, to such a hypothetical standard.

Given these conceptual and methodological difficulties, there is much to be said for the course followed by Herbert Gans (1979), who speaks of patterns of "values" conveyed by the media, leaving the reader to apply his or her own normative standards in assessing the nature and extent of bias. Those disagreeing with our standards will, no doubt, do the same. In any case, our suggestions about patterns of misleading or biased information and interpretations should be taken as tentative. They are based upon our current evaluations of the mass media and the historical record, supported in some measure by others' research.

We believe that the American public may be regularly exposed to certain kinds of misleading or biased information and interpretations that affect preferences concerning a wide range of foreign and domestic policies. These patterns very likely result from normal market forces, together with government control of certain types of information; from the nation-state system and the loyalties and interests it generates; from our predominately capitalist economy; and from the disproportionate resources with which business and other organized interests produce and disseminate political information.

The most pronounced pattern in information about foreign affairs is a *nationalistic* and *ethnocentric* bias. This means, for one thing, an agenda-setting effect: heavy attention to U.S. policies and activities and to those nations closest to the United States in culture and language and geography—or most closely tied to U.S. interests. The death of one American abroad often gets more media coverage than the deaths of thousands of foreigners, especially Asians or Africans. News from the Third World is generally neglected, except for sensational crises or events with clear impact on Americans.

Such an allocation of attention largely follows from the economics of the mass media and the concerns of American audiences: people care most about matters close to home and tend to like countries similar to or linked with the United States (Nincic and Russett 1979). Stories about poverty and repression in small, strange, faraway countries would not sell many newspapers or persuade many TV viewers to buy deodorant or toothpaste. Still, whatever its causes, lack of information about the world tends to encourage public stinginess with foreign developmental aid, acquiescence in U.S. support of repressive dictators, concern with military alliances rather than the well-being of other peoples, and a number of other opinions that a fully informed public probably would not hold.

The content as well as the coverage of information about foreign affairs is slanted in a nationalistic direction, where the nature of the national interest is largely defined by public officials. Since few correspondents are normally stationed abroad and since much relevant information is controlled by the U.S. government in any case, the media must rely heavily on government sources (Sigal 1973; Gans 1979). Those sources can focus attention on particular events or alleged events (a Soviet arms shipment to Nicaragua, Soviet "combat troops" in Cuba) and offer official U.S.-centered interpretations (a Soviet beachhead in the Western Hemisphere, a threat to U.S. security) that often go uncontradicted. Regimes and movements that are defined as "enemies" of the United States at a given moment are generally portrayed in a very negative light, and "friends" in a highly favorable light, even if they are hated and feared by their own people—as Batista, Somoza, Shah Pahlevi, and Marcos were (G. Black 1988; Dorman and Farhang 1987; Bonner 1987). Saddam Hussein of Iraq was tolerated as an ally when he invaded Iran in 1980 but portrayed as an evil madman when he invaded Kuwait in 1990. Media treatment of Stalin underwent similar transformations.

The flow of misleading information about foreign affairs is probably furthered by multinational corporations which invest abroad and want stable, friendly governments that will guarantee docile workers and good profits. The extent of business influence upon what officials define as the "national interest," though unclear, is no doubt substantial. But a nationalistic bias pervades the news in most other countries of the world, too, whether capitalist or Socialist or other; it follows from the self-interest of individuals and from their organization into competing nation states. (Ordinary Americans, as well as the United Fruit Company, have gained by obtaining cheap bananas from Central America. Our argument is that they might be willing to pay a few pennies more if informed about the exploitation of local workers.) Thus we take the fundamental source of the nationalistic bias to be the nation state system, not the nature of the U.S. economy.

A closely related pattern in information about foreign affairs has been an *anti-Communist* bias. Especially after World War II, when the United States and USSR emerged as the chief rivals on the world stage, ideological anti-Communism as well as a nationalistic focus on American security interests and markets and investments abroad often led U.S. government officials and other media news sources to exaggerate the evils of the Soviet

Union and its allied governments and movements. The Russian people were said to be oppressed by a hated, monolithic dictatorship that was starving them and that clung to power only by crushing dissent. National liberation movements and revolutionaries around the globe, even those with little or no Russian connection, were portrayed as tools in a Soviet scheme to conquer the world (Aronson 1973 [1970]; Parenti 1986, chaps. 8, 9). For many decades, the average American could not easily learn about day-to-day life in the USSR, or about the actual strengths and weaknesses of the Soviet system or those of revolutionary movements. Only in the early 1970s (briefly) and then in the late 1980s did coverage become fuller and less hostile, responding to détente and to Gorbachev's "glasnost" and "perestroika."

One need not reject the important elements of truth in anti-Soviet rhetoric—a colleague has likened the anti-Communist bias to a bias against earthquakes—in order to conclude that the public's anti-Communist sentiments were inflamed, and its support for military spending and alliances and sending troops abroad inflated, by systematic misinformation. The very rapidity with which détente was promoted in the early 1970s, then switched off rather abruptly and resumed in the late 1980s, suggests the extent of official control over relevant information. By the same token, however, as we saw in Chap. 6, the persistence of popular desires for cooperative relations with the Soviets even in the early Reagan years, and the spontaneous public warming to Gorbachev's reforms and peace initiatives, suggest again the limits to opinion manipulation.

In the information Americans receive about both foreign and domestic issues, we believe there is a pervasive *procapitalist* slant. American schools, besides training manageable workers, teach the virtues of free enterprise (Bowles and Gintis 1976; Miliband 1969). Corporate advertising trumpets the capitalist gospel; by the 1980s some $3 billion per year was spent in advocacy and promotion of corporations and capitalism. Big advertisers exert pressures on editorial content. Most news organizations are themselves owned by large corporations; more than half the newspaper and TV media were owned by just twenty-nine corporations in 1986 (down from fifty in 1981, according to Bagdikian 1987, chaps. 1–3). The media take the superiority of capitalism for granted, even while investigating and publicizing malfeasance by particular firms. (Media exposés of business scandals and the mild liberalism of a few elite reporters are sometimes mistaken for signs of opposition to capitalism, as in Lichter and Rothman 1981; see the telling critique in Entman 1989, chap. 2.)

The average American is bombarded throughout his or her life by messages about the productive power and efficiency of "free enterprise," the high standard of living it has provided, and the personal liberties it promotes. Rare is the voice that seriously questions the fairness of the system (for example, its relation to poverty and inequality) or explores economic and social alternatives.

Of course, one might argue that this reflects reality: facts and experience, not propaganda, have convinced a once-skeptical U.S. working class that capitalism is good. Quite possibly so. By the end of the 1980s, many efforts at socialism abroad had led to disillusionment, and capitalism (at least the German and Japanese variants) seemed to be riding high. But our point, without insisting on any particular vision of the counterfactual consequences should the American public have complete information, is simply that the information the public has actually had has been one-sided. Americans are heavily exposed—in what is sometimes called a "hegemonic" fashion—to a single pervasive worldview, with teachers and experts and commentators and advertisers and officials all taking for granted that a capitalist system is best (Miliband 1969, chaps. 8, 9; Gramsci 1971 [1929–1935]).

One offshoot of the anti-Communist and procapitalist biases is a tendency to ignore, malign, or degrade movements and individuals on the "extremes," especially the left. Their voices are seldom heard, except through sensational strikes or demonstrations, which are generally portrayed as bizarre, violent, and deviant (Gitlin 1980; Shoemaker 1982). Together with official repression (as in the Palmer raids of the 1920s, McCarthyism and the "security" investigations of the late 1940s and early 1950s, the infiltration and harassment of the civil rights and antiwar movements and the underground press—not to mention the Black Panthers and the Socialist Workers Party—in the 1960s and 1970s, and the harassment of Central America peace groups in the 1980s), this has limited the scope of political discourse in the United States (Freeland 1972; Goldstein 1978; Donner 1981; Rips 1981).

Applied to foreign policy, the procapitalist thrust of information fosters public support for regimes that welcome trade and investment from U.S. companies on terms that do not necessarily benefit their own people, and for regimes that claim to embrace a free enterprise ideology, as opposed to Communist or socialist or nationalist ones. Applied to domestic affairs, the slant toward capitalism feeds into a *minimal government* bias. If the free market promotes productivity, efficiency, and personal freedoms—the argument goes—what need is there for government, beyond bare essentials like national defense, law and order, enforcement of contracts, and maintenance of a sound monetary system? Anything more tends to be viewed with suspicion as potentially wasteful and dangerous to liberty.

This tendency is not all-embracing, of course; some enthusiasts of capitalism want government to deal with imperfect markets, public goods, and distributional equity. The minimal government bias coexists uneasily with an ambivalent but firmly rooted acceptance of the welfare state, and it seems to pass through cycles (related to partisan control of government) of ascendancy and descendancy, in which the 1970s and 1980s saw the most recent revolt against government. Year in and year out, however, Americans, compared to citizens in other countries, are exposed to a deluge of half-truths and misinformation about government waste and inefficiency. Those who have the most to lose from progressive taxation and redistributive spending—especially wealthy individuals and corporations that want government "off their backs"—have abundant resources to subsidize and publicize research, affect school curricula, place advertisements, and otherwise influence the media and politicians and other communicators to complain about governmental waste and inefficiency and to promote the minimal government line.

A pattern of biased information that sometimes partly, but only partly, counteracts the minimal government slant (by supporting the actions of current officials) is a ***pro-incumbent and pro–status quo*** bias. True, scandals and exposés make good press. If a prominent congressman is caught frolicking drunk in a Washington pool (or even, in relatively puritanical periods like the late 1980s, if he is observed chasing women or drinking heavily), he may make the news. More serious derelictions like financial corruption and abuse of power are sometimes pursued as well, and this has led some observers to mistakenly perceive an "anti-authority" bias in the media. Over the long haul, however, government officials and the order they represent tend to be treated well.

Presidents, who regularly complain about negative media, receive overwhelmingly positive coverage (Grossman and Kumar 1981; Gans 1979). Officials are the prime sources of political news and can control much of what is made public. Reporters have to cultivate friendly ties. Moreover, the large corporations that own most U.S. communications media depend upon the government for TV licenses and for help with labor relations, taxes, and other matters; it would not be wise for them to be too hostile. The result is a flow of information that tends to reflect official points of view, to emphasize the merits and accomplishments of incumbent officials, and to neglect the opposition (Sigal 1973).

A strong ***partisan*** bias also results from the deference paid to incumbents. The party that holds power in Washington (especially the party of the president) can shape much of the debate over public policy, both directly through the president's and his subordinates' speeches and remarks and testimony, and indirectly through the reporters and commentators who enjoy access and sing in tune with the administration's chorus. (Administrations bring experts, linked to networks of other experts, along with them when they take office: see Heclo, 1978). In addition, research money and media attention tend to flow to the visible and "effective" scholars and think tanks that generally agree with the administration, so that the tide of expert opinion generally seems to support the policies of those in power.

This partisan bias means that at different times the public is exposed to quite different views of the political world, even though underlying realities may remain much the same. Information conveyed about the nature and causes of poverty in America, for example, seemed to differ radically between the Johnson and Reagan (or even Nixon) administrations (see Aaron 1978), as epitomized by the relative prominence of the liberal Institute for Research on Poverty and then the conservative Hoover Institution and Heritage Foundation. The Johnson period's depiction of the poor (eager to work, but disabled or severely deprived, lacking access to jobs and education and medical care) gave way to the Reagan years' picture of the poor (when they were mentioned at all) as able-bodied but lazy and self-indulgent miscreants, who would rather breed babies on welfare than do an honest day's work. Given the somewhat different worldviews of Republicans and Democrats, the partisan bias and the alternation of parties in power produces cycles, or at least ebbs and flows, in the informational bias toward minimal government.

How Much Misleading Information?

For the reasons already noted, we cannot hope to offer a precise or definitive account of the extent (or, for that matter, the nature) of information biases in the United States. But if we are on track concerning important instances of opinion manipulation and general patterns of biased and misleading information, these pose troubling implications for the workings of democracy.

On the one hand, we see the American public as substantially capable of rational calculations about the merits of alternative public policies, based on the information that is made available to it. Moreover, that information is often good, useful, and educational; collective deliberation often works well. Even when it does not, even when public debate consists largely of outrageous nonsense, the public is surprisingly resistant to being fooled—so long as competing elites provide at least some alternative voices. The public mind is not simply a blank slate; it is not always easy to write upon.

On the other hand, we have suggested that the information available to the public may sometimes be overwhelmingly false, misleading, or biased. When it is, and especially when virtually no dissenting elite voices are heard—in some foreign policy situations, for example, where the executive branch controls information and events or where "bipartisan" foreign policy holds sway—the public may be led astray. The rational public can be deceived. It is important to learn more about how often this happens, exactly how it occurs, and what can be done to prevent it.

But in no event do we see the possibility of manipulation as a reason to reject democracy. It would be odd, indeed, to give officials more independence from ordinary citizens on the grounds that they had been fooling those citizens. Rather it is a reason to strengthen the education of the public, in a broad sense; to improve the information system; and to increase knowledge about and control of public officials.

10 Democracy, Information, and the Rational Public

☑ Democracy means that the people—the public—have power. It involves a connection between the policy preferences of citizens, on the one hand, and what their governments do, on the other. Our findings concerning the public's policy preferences, therefore, have some implications concerning the feasibility and desirability of democracy in the United States, and perhaps elsewhere as well.

Many influential critiques of the idea of majoritarian democracy, for example, and many arguments for restraining or ignoring the views of the general public, are based on alleged incapacities of ordinary citizens. Some critics say that ordinary people lack political information and lack the motivation or the cognitive skills to receive and process such information. They maintain that citizens may, therefore, hold policy preferences that do not correspond to their true values or to the public good, or, indeed, that citizens may have no policy preferences at all. It follows that democracy is unattainable or undesirable.

The evidence of this book indicates that these critics are wrong. The public, as a collectivity, has the capacity to govern. Any major defects of American democracy are more likely to be found at the elite level.

In this chapter, we will summarize our major findings and discuss what they imply for democratic theory, organizing the discussion around a set of nine propositions. The first four propositions concern the collective capacities of the public. The next five deal with the political information and experience that are provided (or not provided) to citizens in the United States.

The Political Capacity of the Public

1. *Americans' collective policy preferences are real, knowable, differentiated, patterned, and coherent.* An extreme version of the "nonattitudes" argument holds that ordinary citizens' policy preferences are unreal, meaningless, or at least unknowable through survey research, which is said to elicit nothing more than random responses or "doorstep opinions." If this were so, then to seek a correspondence between government policies

and citizens' preferences would be to seek a will-o'-the-wisp. Policy cannot respond to what does not exist or cannot be known.

Milder versions of this argument hold that public opinion offers no guidance on specific policy questions, or that it is incoherent or inconsistent. If public opinion had nothing to say about the concrete issues of the day, or if it were incoherent or self-contradictory, it might comfortably be ignored.

We have seen, however, that these indictments of public opinion are not well founded. Despite the evidence that most individual Americans have only limited knowledge of politics (especially of proper names and numbers and acronyms), and that individuals' expressions of policy preferences vary markedly and somewhat randomly from one survey to the next, *collective* policy preferences have very different properties.

The data we have presented in this book—the result of our analysis of thousands of questions asked in national surveys covering a period of more than fifty years—reveal that collective responses make sense; that they draw fine distinctions among different policies; and that they form meaningful patterns consistent with a set of underlying beliefs and values. Again and again, in Chapters 2 through 6, we saw that the public makes definite distinctions among policy alternatives: which spending programs to cut and which to increase, under what conditions to permit legal abortions, when to use U.S. military force abroad, what civil liberties to ensure for which groups, what kinds of assistance to provide which allies, and many others. The public's choices among policies were generally consistent with each other and with broader values, and were usually maintained over periods of years.[1]

This reasonable and coherent patterning of collective public opinion was revealed not only in well-known current academic surveys like the NORC General Social Survey and the SRC/CPS National Election Studies, but also—indeed more fully—by the early NORC and OPOR surveys and by the commercial polls and surveys that scholars sometimes scorn: polls conducted by Gallup, Harris, Roper, and many others, including all the major TV networks and several leading newspapers. That is, collective public opinion is not only measurable, it is in fact *measured* rather well, by many ongoing polls whose current results are easily available to analysts and political leaders and anyone else who cares to look.

The apparent paradox that collective opinion is solid and meaningful, while the measured opinions of many or most individuals seem to be shaky or nonexistent, can probably be explained by a combination of three factors. First, random measurement errors cancel out across large numbers of respondents, so that surveys yield much more accurate information about the collectivity than about any particular individual. Second, temporary opinion changes by different individuals occur in offsetting directions, so that they, too, cancel out and allow collective measurements to reflect the more enduring tendencies of opinion. Third, processes of collective deliberation, and reliance upon trusted cue givers, enable people to arrive at reasonable policy preferences without an extensive informational base.

For us, however, the most important point involves not the causes but the consequences of this collective phenomenon. Democracy is not made impossible by default, by public opinion being nonexistent or unknowable or irrelevant.[2] An attentive reader of polls and surveys can get a good deal of coherent guidance about policy.

2. *Collective policy preferences are generally stable; they change in understandable, predictable ways.* As we have seen, some of the reasons that the authors of the Federalist gave for restraining the popular will—shackling it with a powerful, indirectly elected president, an independent Senate protected by long terms in office, an appointed judiciary, and the like—had to do with alleged "temporary errors and delusions," or "fluctuations," or "transient impulse(s)," or "violent passions" in opinion. Similarly, Almond's (1960 [1950]) "mood theory" suggested that the public's opinions on foreign policy move erratically, responding impulsively to crises and then snapping back to their old state of apathy and ignorance.

After closely examining hundreds of repeated survey questions, however, we can be sure that Americans' policy preferences do not in fact change in a capricious, whimsical, or evanescent fashion. Chapter 2 and the graphs throughout the book show that collective public opinion about policy is generally quite stable. It rarely fluctuates. Despite the fact that many of our graphs were chosen to illustrate exceptionally large and important opinion trends, the overwhelming impression even from them is one of incremental change. What the public thinks about a given policy now is a very strong indicator of what it will think later.

Our analysis of historical context has shown that when collective preferences have changed, during the last fifty years, they have generally done so in predictable and understandable ways. As the domestic and foreign policy chapters made clear, and as Chapter 8 summarized, there have been regular patterns of responses to social and economic trends, events, and new information. Even abrupt changes in foreign policy preferences nearly always represent understandable reactions to sudden events: militant and activist responses to foreign threats, for example, and more peaceful reactions when conditions improve. Opinion does not tend to "snap back" to its earlier state. Any capriciousness of opinion that may have existed in the Founders' time is certainly not common now.[3]

For the most part, the public reacts consistently, in similar ways to similar stimuli. Particularly impressive are the systematic time series results which show regular shifts in policy preferences responding to changes in such objective indicators as rates of unemployment, inflation, and crime.

Short-term movements in public opinion, in fact, can largely be accounted for (and predicted) by quantitative analyses of what news, from what sources, appears in the mass media. The public's reactions are so consistent that more than half the variance in opinion changes can be accounted for in this way.

Again, the reason for these findings may have to do with the offsetting effects of random measurement errors or opinion movements by individuals, and with collective deliberation, so that collective public opinion can remain stable or respond coherently, even while many individuals' responses shift randomly. Once more, however, the consequence is more important for present purposes than the cause. There is little reason to fear collective public opinion or to denigrate it as capricious.[4]

3. *Citizens are not incapable of knowing their own interests or the public good.* The suggestion that ordinary citizens are simply too ignorant to know their own or their country's interests lies at the heart of many objections to majoritarian democracy. The authors of the Federalist Papers, for example, worried not merely that public opinion vacillated but that it erred. John Stuart Mill, considered a father of democratic theory, nonetheless advocated a severely limited suffrage and favored public rather than secret ballots, extra votes for the prosperous and the educated, "merit" appointment rather than election of most officials, no pledges by representatives to their constituents, and very limited functions for the elected body—all on the grounds that common people, especially the working class, were not competent to rule and were likely to demand class legislation (Mill 1958 [1861]).

In more recent times, as we have noted, Walter Lippmann (1922 and esp. 1925) issued scathing denunciations of the public's capabilities, maintaining that reality differs sharply from the "stereotypes" or "pictures" in people's heads. Joseph Schumpeter (1975 [1942]) declared that individuals' opinions are not "definite" or "independent" or "rational" and that on most political matters individual volition, command of fact, and method of inference are defective (chap. 21, esp. p. 261).

Early survey research (as we saw in Chap. 1) seemed to bear out these low estimates of public capacity. Surveys indicated that most Americans knew little about politics, cared little, and apparently made their voting decisions on the basis of demographic characteristics or party loyalties, which scholars (perhaps too quickly) took to indicate lack of rational deliberation. Converse's (1964) demonstration of weak ideological structure and unstable individual survey responses seemed, for a while, to close the case.

The result was a wholesale revision of democratic theory. Schumpeter's weak procedural definition of democracy, in which elite leadership competes for voters' acquiescence but does not necessarily respond to their policy preferences (1975 [1942], chap. 22), influenced more than a generation of scholars. Dahl (1956, chap. 2) cast doubt on the desirability of "populistic" democracy. Berelson et al. (1954) speculated that citizens' passivity might function as a useful buffer for system stability. Most of the leaders of the political science and sociology professions rejected majoritarian democracy, embracing some form of pluralistic or "polyarchical" system in which organized interest groups play an important part and in which participation by, and responsiveness to, the general public is limited.

We agree with Walker (1966), Kariel (1970, pt. 2), Pateman (1970), Barber (1984), and others that this revisionism mistakenly blamed the citizen victims, ignoring system-level influences upon peoples' behavior (apathy about elections, for example, may result from legal restrictions, repression, or lack of attractive candidates and parties rather than from defects of the citizenry); that it abandoned a worthy normative ideal and turned democratic theory into little more than a conservative ratifier of the status quo; and that it neglected the possibility that broader participation could promote political education and human development.

In particular, we believe that the revisionists misinterpreted survey research results and gave up too quickly on the public. This should have been clear even before research contrasting the 1960s with the 1950s cast a more favorable light on citizens' capacities by showing that people displayed more interest, knowledge, and ideological thinking when the political environment was more lively. The original findings that most Americans did not live up to "classical democratic theory"—a construct of dubious provenance, which called for citizens to have unrealistically and unnecessarily high levels of political knowledge and sophistication—never really had much relevance to the desirability or feasibility of majoritarian democracy.

People probably do not need large amounts of information to make rational voting choices. Cues from like-minded citizens and groups (including cues related to demographic characteristics and party labels) may be sufficient, in an environment where accurate information is available, to permit voters to act as if they had all the available information (McKelvey and Ordeshook 1986; Wittman 1989).

Much the same reasoning applies to our own topic, policy preferences. (We have had nothing new to say about voting, though we suspect that similar principles apply.) Using their underlying beliefs and values, together with cues from leaders and like-minded citizens they trust, people can come up with reasonable opinions (i.e., opinions consonant with their basic beliefs and values) about a wide variety of issues—even, as we saw in Chapter 1, on highly technical issues like the MX missile.

Moreover, our work indicates that *collective* public opinion reflects a considerably higher level of information and sophistication than is apparent at the individual level. In part, this results from the same aggregating processes we have previously alluded to, which average out measurement errors, uncertainties, and individuals' random opinion changes. In part, it reflects the logic of "information pooling": if each individual has a reasonably good (but very imperfect) chance of judging whether a particular assertion is true—or whether a particular policy will satisfy his or her interests or the common good—then, by simple operation of the laws of probability, a majority of independently judging individuals has a much higher probability of being right (N. Miller 1986; Grofman and Feld 1988). And, in substantial part, collective wisdom results from collective deliberation based on a division of labor. For all these reasons, collective public opinion far outshines the opinion of the average individual. It is both an aggregation of many individual opinions and the result of a process in which many individuals interact.

The role of collective deliberation also helps explain why (as discussed in Chap. 7) citizens' preferences reflect not only personal and group self-interest but also concerns for the common good at a national level.

Our research has led us to a view of collective public opinion that justifies the use of terms like "reasonable," "responsible," and "rational." Without claiming that we have any unique knowledge of what people's true interests are, we are convinced by the general stability, differentiation, and coherent patterning of collective policy preferences, and by their responsiveness to new situations and new information, that characterizations of public opinion as ignorant fall very wide of the mark. We do not know who is better able to judge the public interest than the public itself. Any alternative invites minority tyranny.

4. *The public generally reacts to new situations and new information in sensible, reasonable ways.* (Note that this refers to something more than the "predictable," "understandable" responses of proposition 2.) Some

critiques of democracies as "ungovernable" (e.g., Crozier et al. 1975) have suggested that the public cannot keep up with the complexity of an ever-changing world. Much the same theme animated Walter Lippmann's final (1956) fulmination against the public, in which he argued that the liberal democracies were paralyzed with regard to the great questions of war and peace because of the "derangement" of pressure from public opinion, which not only compulsively made mistakes and was easily deceived but was too slow to react (p. 24).

Our data provide little or no evidence that the American public has failed in this fashion, during Lippmann's 1950s or Crozier's 1970s or any other time. Collective opinion has responded rapidly and in sensible ways (given the information provided) to international events, wars, and crises as well as to more subtle gradual trends in technology, the economy, and society. When there has been less money to spend, the public has been less eager to spend, and when more, more. The *consistent* responses mentioned in connection with proposition 2 have also been *reasonable:* seeking harsher court treatment of criminals when crime is a more severe problem, wanting to try wage and price controls when inflation is rampant, favoring more spending on employment policies when unemployment is high. This book is full of examples.

Taking our first four propositions together, then, we see the public—at least the twentieth-century U.S. public—as considerably more *capable* and *competent* than critics of majoritarian democracy would have us believe. Most of the excuses for why public opinion can be ignored, why government ought not to respond to it, have little merit.

Whether or not the public's capacities are completely realized, however—and, therefore, whether or not majoritarian democracy fully lives up to its potential—depends in part upon the political environment in which citizens find themselves, especially upon what opportunities for political learning and what quality of political information are provided to them by what we can call the "information system."

If a society provides accurate, helpful information about public policy; if it offers moral leadership, encourages participation, and in a broad sense educates its citizenry, then there is every reason to expect that citizens will rise to the occasion and democracy will flourish. If, on the other hand, the system minimizes public participation, or obscures policy-making processes so that unpopular government actions go undetected, then democratic control will be diminished, no matter how competent the public. If politicians or others regularly deceive and mislead the public, if they manipulate citizens' policy preferences so as to betray their interests and values, democracy may be a sham. Responsiveness to manipulated preferences is nothing to celebrate. Our next set of propositions, therefore, concerns how well the information system serves the public.

The Information System and Democracy

Our findings about political education and about the nature and quality of information conveyed to the public through the mass media are less definite than the findings concerning public opinion itself, and the picture is a mixed one. But the evidence from Chapters 3–6 and Chapter 9 suggests that there is more reason to worry about the quality of the information system—that is, about the institutions and structures and activities at the elite level that produce and disseminate political information—than about the capacity of ordinary citizens. That is, defects in American democracy may be more the fault of elites than the public.

5. *Collective deliberation often works well.* The Federalist Papers argued that the "cool and deliberate sense of the community" ought ultimately to prevail in government. We agree. Democracy is most appealing if the majority's preferences are informed through public reflection, debate, and discussion, making use of a system of research and expertise. Ideally, this would amount to John Dewey's (1954 [1927]) effective system of social inquiry, which would produce a "Great Community" with an organized, articulate public.

Does there exist in the United States a system of deliberation sufficient to ensure that the public's policy preferences embody the "cool and deliberate sense of the community?" We think the answer, generally speaking, is "yes." Certainly an elaborate system exists by which policy-relevant research is conducted and then publicized through testimony, books, articles, and debates by experts, commentators, and political leaders. The thrust of such debates tends eventually to reach the public through the media of mass communications, especially (as we saw in Chapter 8) by means of editorial commentary and the reporting of experts' statements. Political conversations among ordinary citizens and their friends, family members, and coworkers further refine, interpret, and disseminate political information.

As noted in Chapter 9, the process of collective deliberation has some of the virtues of parallel distributed processing. It takes advantage of a division of labor among experts, commentators, communicators, cue givers, and attentive citizens. It is also, for the most part, pluralistic and decentralized (though this is less true of foreign policy matters than domestic). Ordinary citizens need not master the intricacies of policy analysis but can get the general drift by knowing whom to trust for a reliable conclusion—assuming, of course, that trustworthy cue givers are available.

Thus, by the time national polls are taken, public opinion has often been "refined and enlarged" through public debate. The system of collective deliberation could certainly be improved upon, as we will argue below. But it already works well enough to produce generally well-informed collective public opinion that responds to changing realities and new information, as our survey data reveal.

6. *Political education in the United States could be improved.* A judgment concerning whether political education in the United States is adequate must depend heavily upon evidence outside our scope, and upon choice of a standard of adequacy, but undoubtedly there is much room for improvement.

A number of democratic theorists have taken education of one sort or another—if not the acquisition of large amounts of information, then at least the sharpening of cognitive skills and the ability to evaluate public debate, or the development of good moral character—as a crucial prerequisite, concomitant, and/or consequence of popular rule.

Rousseau, for example, saw participation in a civil state as itself a source of education concerning duty, a sense of what is right, regard for others, and the consultation of reason (1957 [1762], pp. 18–19). People can be deceived (hence the difference between the will of all and the general will: p. 26); therefore, it is necessary to "make people see things as they are," to "point out to them the right path which they are seeking," to provide guidance and increase public knowledge (p. 35), to transform each individual into part of a much greater whole (p. 36).

John Stuart Mill (1958 [1861]) also attributed high importance to education and agreed with Rousseau that participation by the whole people in representative government promotes energetic character and sound moral instruction (chap. 3), though (curiously) he went on to favor severely limiting such participation on the very grounds that people lacked formal education: "[U]niversal teaching must precede universal enfranchisement" (p. 132). Extra votes might be allowed to persons engaged in occupations evidencing a high level of education (p. 138).

Thomas Jefferson, America's quintessential democrat, put a heavy emphasis on the need for universal public schooling, which he actively promoted, and for informative political debate through free and diverse newspapers.

Perhaps the most important recent voice on this subject is that of John Dewey, whose own philosophy of formal education, advocating active experience to develop capacities for thinking and reflection, was aimed at training citizens for democracy (Dewey 1916). As noted in Chapter 9, Dewey saw inquiry and communication as the keys to the functioning of democracy, as ways to make consequences known, and to create an "organized, articulate Public" (1954 [1927], pp. 176–184). Dewey also wrote of democracy as the "truly human way of living," saying that the participation of all is necessary not only for the social welfare but to develop human beings as individuals. Human intelligence, together with pooled and cooperative experience (with all people having equal rights to express judgments), produces the knowledge and wisdom needed for collective action (Dewey 1939, pp. 400–404).

Education involves learning and instruction of many sorts, having to do with facts, causal connections and interpretations, cognitive skills, moral reasoning; it involves many individuals and institutions—families, schools, workplaces, associations, political leadership, the mass media, and direct participation in politics. It would not be easy for us to evaluate the American system of political education as a whole, particularly those parts of it we have not studied directly.

What is most apparent from our work is that education does not fail completely; in fact, it has been quite successful, in the sense that collective public opinion does display considerable sophistication. In Chapter 9, we mentioned a good many examples in which the public debates of experts and others have informed and educated the citizenry.

At the same time, however, one can imagine a much higher level of political teaching. The schools' treatment of public policy tends to be skimpy and bland. Political figures, facing electoral incentives to be ambiguous, seldom offer serious analyses of policy; they often rely on images and so-called sound bites. Political parties fall short of the "responsible party" ideal (Ranney 1962), especially when they are engaged in collusive ("bipartisan") policy-making or are both financed by the same special interests. Journalism often fails to probe beneath the surface of events and does not cover some issues at all. On many issues, neither experts nor would-be leaders of mass movements speak clearly to the public.

Perhaps the most conspicuous deficiency is the lack of opportunity for political learning through direct participation. In a country where only about half the eligible citizens vote in presidential elections, where town meetings are rare, where most workplaces are hierarchical, and where most citizens are not mobilized by a congenial issue-oriented party or political group, the educational potential of participation is not fully realized. Pateman (1970), Mansbridge (1980), Greenberg (1986), and Barber (1984), among others, have offered useful ideas about how this situation could be remedied. Some of their suggestions go beyond the individualistic utilitarian stream of democratic thinking (which tends to legitimize narrowly self-interested behavior), seeking transformations of character and the fulfillment of humankind's communitarian potential.

In short, we see considerable room for more and better political information, more moral leadership, and more mobilization and organization of the public for participation.[5]

7. *Lack of available information may permit government nonresponsiveness to public opinion.* Research by ourselves and others indicates that governmental responsiveness to public opinion is substantial but imperfect; policy tends to be out of harmony with what the public wants roughly one-third of the time (A. Monroe 1979; Page and Shapiro 1983), a significant proportion. Though evidence on the matter is limited, there are indications that government responsiveness is weaker when public information, and hence salience and attention, are low. (We found, for example (Page and Shapiro 1983, pp. 181–182), that policy moves in harmony with opinion changes more often when "don't know" survey responses are few. The general findings of rather high congruence between opinion and policy, of course, are based on issues of high enough salience to ask survey questions about.) The level of information, then, may be an important determinant of how well the public can control government.

The point is not merely that the public doesn't care about some issues or is inattentive. Rather the *availability* of key facts about certain public policies may be low, for reasons of chance or design; the public may have no way (no helpful cue givers, no free information on TV) to know what is going on—to know whether or not the government is doing what the citizenry wants, for example—and may, therefore, have no way to enforce its will and ensure responsiveness.

A number of scholars and observers have concluded that lack of available information does often give elites leeway to act in unpopular ways. Schattschneider (1960), for example, argues that when visibility is low, when the "scope of conflict" is narrow, organized groups (e.g., corporations seeking tax loopholes in midnight meetings of the House Ways and Means Committee) have a good chance of prevailing over an unaware public. McConnell (1966) makes a similar point with respect to small constituencies and interest groups' capture of administrators. Bachrach and Baratz (1962) suggest that elites may often be able to mute the public's voice by controlling what is on the agenda—what is discussed, what is viewed as a public problem, and what are seen as possible solutions. Edelman (e.g., 1964) argues persuasively that symbols frequently work to conceal government actions and inactions.

We do not know exactly how often these sorts of concealment or deception occur. But there does seem to be substantial slippage in democratic responsiveness, a substantial discrepancy between what citizens want and what the government does, which may result from a dim spotlight that does not direct public attention to unpopular policies—especially when there is bipartisan collusion of the sorts we have already alluded to, and when few or no dissenting elite voices speak up. (The savings and loan debacle of the 1980s comes to mind.)

8. *Elites sometimes mislead the public or manipulate its policy preferences.* Opinion manipulation, as we have said, is a crucial matter for democratic theory. If power has a "third face" (Lukes 1975), and elites create or influence the very wants of the public; if, as Lindblom (1977, chap. 15) suggests, preferences are "circular," with businessmen and politicians and others strongly affecting what the public wants; and if elite influence is exerted in such a way as to lead people astray from their own true interests and values,[6] then the most responsive political machinery in the world will not produce democratic outcomes.

To be sure, this subject is full of difficulties, and our own work on it is neither complete nor conclusive. But some of the instances and patterns examined in this book have disturbing implications. The historical record indicates that government officials often mislead and sometimes lie, particularly in foreign affairs, where government control of information is great. Opposing countries and movements are commonly portrayed as aggressive and evil (and U.S. government actions as benevolent), for example, regardless of the facts, in order to mobilize public support for official policies. This tendency is not unique to the United States; it may result from the nation-state system, which gives every country's officials both the tools and the incentives to mislead their citizenry for the sake of their own power and the projection of national influence. That is, the nation-state system enables elites to create "national interests" that may diverge from what national populations would want if fully informed.

We have suggested that the information presented to the public through the mass media has certain persistent biases, slants, or value tendencies that may distort the public's picture of the world and lead its policy preferences astray. These tendencies may result from the nation-state system and official control of information, as described above. They may also reflect such factors as the capitalist character of the economy, which ensures that many powerful voices will support capitalism and oppose communism or socialism in the United States and abroad; the weakness of the American labor movement; journalists' perennial need to rely on official sources; and the tendency for expertise and commentary to change with shifts in party control of government. Hence we find anti-Communist, pro-capitalist, minimal government, pro-incumbent, and partisan biases as well as the pervasive ethnocentric or nationalistic slant.

These informational biases can arise without any government monopoly power or any conspiracy among elites; some of them probably result from the normal operation of a competitive free enterprise system and a free press. Political information is often a public or social good. Information which is of significant but small use to many different people cannot be sold efficiently: people cannot easily be excluded from consumption in order to force them to pay for it, and even when exclusion is possible there are increasing returns to scale (i.e., a degree of nonrivalness in consumption) that upset market pricing. Political information of value to millions of citizens, therefore, probably tends to be underproduced, whereas large, organized political actors can find out what they need to know. A large corporation, for example, with extensive resources and a big stake in political action, has a much better chance of learning how a tax bill will affect it than do many unorganized taxpayers with small, diffuse interests that (in the aggregate) add up to a great deal.

Moreover, the producers and transmitters of political information often have corporate or other interests of their own which may influence what they put out to the public. Their financial returns are affected not only by their sales of books and airtime and the like but also by the political impact of the information they disseminate. Corporations fund foundations and think tanks that produce research studies and support the "experts" seen on TV, often, presumably (if businessmen behave in a rational fashion), serving corporate purposes. The mass media are mostly owned by large corporations that are distinctly uninterested in undermining the capitalist system, upsetting their own labor relations, or stirring populist tendencies among the citizenry (see Bagdikian 1987).

Patterns of biases or tendencies similar to those we have found have been reported in a number of studies of political communications. But judgments about political truth and falsehood are subject to disagreement. Any assessment of bias must struggle with difficulties of conceptualization and measurement, so that we cannot be absolutely sure how widespread misinformation and misleading interpretations are.

The good news, in any case, is that misinformation does not always succeed in actually affecting the public's policy preferences in the intended ways. Public opinion is quite resistant to being led astray, particularly when at least a few elite voices dissent, or when policy preferences are based on personal experience, or when events are inherently easy to understand. We have given several striking examples, including the failure of barrages of publicity in the late 1970s and early 1980s to dislodge Americans from their advocacy of social welfare programs and arms control, or to persuade them to aid the Nicaraguan Contras. (See Chaps. 4 and 6. To be sure, in some cases unpopular policies went forward despite citizens' opposition.)

Still, there is reason for concern that democracy in the United States may be undermined to some extent by systematic distortions in the information that is provided to the public.

9. *The "marketplace of ideas" cannot always be counted upon to reveal political truth.* It is a prime tenet of liberal faith that, if all views are permitted free expression, truth will overcome falsehood through a vigorous competition of ideas. Long ago John Milton (1918 [1644]) declared: "Let her and Falsehood grapple; who ever knew Truth put to the worse, in a free and open encounter?" (p. 58). Thomas Jefferson in his first inaugural address (1801) referred to "the safety with which error of opinion may be tolerated where reason is left free to combat it." John Stuart Mill (1947 [1859]) wrote: "Wrong opinions and practices gradually yield to fact and argument" (p. 19); to silence the expression of an opinion robs the human race, either of the opportunity of changing error for truth, or of "the clearer perception and livelier impression of truth, produced by its collision with error" (p. 16). And Justice Holmes (1919) put it in terms of an economic metaphor: "[T]he best test of truth is the power of the thought to get itself accepted in the competition of the market."

Milton, Jefferson, Mill, and Holmes were all concerned chiefly with tolerating dissent and avoiding excessive government *restraints* on speech through licensing, censorship, punishment, or the like. Their arguments seem altogether persuasive on that point: society has little to lose from hearing the odd dissenter when he or she is wrong, and much to gain when the dissenter happens to be right. The more general point also has some force: in the long run, no doubt, even under inauspicious circumstances, the truth does tend to win out.

But does it follow that a laissez-faire market in information will provide accurate, unbiased, and accessible political information to ordinary citizens? Our empirical material suggests that, in fact, it does not. There are theoretical reasons for doubt, as well, even beyond the obvious points that the long run can be very long, and that as old lies are exposed new ones can be invented.

In the first place, the logic of a competitive market does not work well in the presence of monopoly or collusion. The market fails, for example, when the government holds centralized control of national security information and uses its control to propagate untruths, or when financial interests convince both parties not to compete with each other and not to reveal uncomfortable political truths.

But the problem goes deeper than that. Even in a perfectly function-ing market, production and consumption are, in a sense, dominated by the consumer power of those with the most money and other resources. Thus market forces lead available political information to reflect the needs of the wealthier individuals and organizations. Economic inequality tends to over-come political equality in the information sphere, just as unequal resources to make campaign contributions may offset equal rights to vote. Further-more, as we mentioned in the previous section, markets for political infor-mation may be imperfect even absent government monopoly, because of public goods problems which advantage concentrated interests and disad-vantage small, diffuse consumers of information. And information produc-ers can reap indirect (political) gains at the expense of the citizenry. For all these reasons, ordinary citizens cannot necessarily count on the market to provide easy access to the useful and correct political information they need.[7]

When it comes to political applications, the "marketplace of ideas" remains little more than an unexamined metaphor. The natural working of free enterprise economics may lead to patterns of misleading political in-formation that distort citizens' policy preferences and political choices.

Traditional defenses of free speech—with their emphasis upon free-dom from government restraints—tend to neglect the issue of what sorts of institutional arrangements and allocations of economic resources would be necessary for *effective* expression of varying points of view and for a bal-anced or unbiased political discourse.[8] To provide incentives and opportu-nities for such discourse might well require active policy interventions.

Improving American Democracy

It is not unusual to hear complaints from both Left and Right that de-mocracy does not work well in the United States. If it does not, our research suggests that the American public should not be blamed. The fault is more likely to lie with officials and elites who fail to respond to the citizenry, and with defects in the system by which the public is provided with political information.

It is simply not the case that the collective policy preferences of the U.S. public are nonexistent, unknowable, capricious, inconsistent, or ig-norant. Instead, they are real, meaningful, well measured by polls, differentiated, coherent, and stable. They react understandably and pre-dictably to events and new information. The classic justifications for ignoring public opinion do not hold up.

Moreover, the information system works well enough so that public opinion does not merely respond sensibly to available information; it has generally reacted directly and responsibly to objective realities. Collective deliberation does occur, and substantial political education takes place.

Thus our research provides little reason for anyone to fear or oppose majoritarian democracy in the United States. There is no need to sneer at politicians who "read the Gallup polls," so long as they do so correctly. In our view, in fact, government should pay more attention to what the public wants. More democratic responsiveness, rather than less, would be all to the good, and institutional changes to that end (reducing the role of money in politics, easing voter registration, strengthening political competition,[9] broadening electoral accountability) should be encouraged.

At the same time, we have suggested that political education—in the broad sense of providing useful political experience and information and moral guidance to the citizenry—is not what it could be; that concealment of (or failure to provide) relevant information sometimes permits government to pursue unpopular policies, outside of public view; and that the public's policy preferences may sometimes be manipulated by deceptive leaders and by flows of information subject to various biases or distortions.

There is some truth to the epigram (1966, p. 2) of V. O. Key, Jr., that "(t)he voice of the people is but an echo." The public has a remarkable collective capacity for reasonable political thought, even in the face of misleading or downright false counsel from its leaders. But information inputs do matter; they can have substantial effects on policy preferences, bending them away from citizens' true interests or conceptions of the common good.

A chief focus for improvement, we believe, should be the political information system. The public deserves better political education, more opportunities for participation, and access to better information about public policy. Thomas Jefferson expressed the point neatly, in a famous passage from his letter of September 28, 1820, to William C. Jarvis:

> I know of no safe depository of the ultimate powers of the society but the people themselves, and if we think them not enlightened enough to exercise their control with a wholesome discretion, the remedy is not to take it from them but to inform their discretion by education. (Jefferson 1955, p. 93)

Or, as V. O. Key, Jr., pointedly put it:

> [T]hose political leaders who shirk the task of popular education are misfits who do not understand the responsibilities of their jobs. And those leaders who act as if they thought the people to be fools responsive only to the meanest appeals deserve only scorn. (Key 1961, p. 555)

Appendix to Figures

Questions for Figures in Chapter One

Figure 1.1. QUESTION (CBS/*NYT* News Polls): "Is your opinion of Michael Dukakis (. . . Dan Quayle . . . Lloyd Bentsen) favorable, not favorable, undecided, or haven't you heard enough about Michael Dukakis (Dan Quayle, Lloyd Bentsen) yet to have an opinion?" Survey dates (Dukakis): 5/87, 10/87A, 10/87B, 3/88, 11/88B; (Probable Electorate): 8/88, 9/88A, 9/88B, 10/88A, average of 10/88B and 10/88C, 11/88B; (Registered Voters): 3/88, 5/88, 7/88, 8/88A, 8/88B, 9/88A, 9/88B, 10/88A, average of 10/88B and 10/88C, 11/88A. (Quayle, Registered Voters): 8/88B, 9/88A, 9/88B, 10/88A, average of 10/88B, and 10/88C, 11/88A. (Bentsen, Registered Voters): 8/88A, 8/88B, 9/88A, 9/88B, 10/88A, average of 10/88B and 10/88C, 11/88A.

The "Probable Electorate" refers to percentages for the estimated electorate based upon responses to questions on voter registration, past voting history, and likelihood of voting in 1988 as a measure of the probability of a particular respondent's voting in November. "Registered" refers to percentages of survey respondents who say they are registered to vote. "A," "B," and "C" refer, respectively, to the first, second, and third surveys in a given month.

Questions for Figures in Chapter Two

Figure 2.1. QUESTION (Gallup, NORC-GSS): "Do you think it will (would) best for the future of this country if we take an active part in world affairs or if we stay(ed) out of world affairs?" Survey dates: (Gallup) 10/45, 2/46, 11/46, 8/46, 11/50; (NORC) 3/47, 6/47, 3/48, 6/48, 9/49, 1/50, 12/50, 10/52, 2/53, 9/53, 4/54, 3/55, 11/56. QUESTION (Gallup): Reported as the above (*Public Opinion Quarterly,* "The Quarterly Polls"), but we are suspect. Survey dates: 3/43, 5/44; QUESTION (OPOR): "Which of these two things do you think the United States should try to do when the war is over—stay out of world affairs (as much as we can) or take an active part in world affairs?" Survey dates: 1/42, 5/43, 11/43, 4/44, 6/44, 3/45.

Figure 2.2. QUESTION (Roper, NORC-GSS): "We are faced with many problems in this country, none of which can be solved easily or inexpensively. I'm going to name some of these problems, and for each one I'd like you to tell me whether you think we're spending too much money on it, too little money, or about the right amount . . . Are we spending too much, too little, or about the right amount on . . . Halting the rising crime rate? . . . Improving the nation's education system? . . . Mass transportation? . . . Highways and bridges? . . . Space exploration program? . . . Foreign aid?" Survey dates (Roper): 10/71, 12/73, 12/74, 12/75, 12/76, 12/77, 12/78, 12/79, 12/80, 12/81, 12/82, 12/83, 12/84, 12/85, 12/86; (NORC-GSS): 3/73, 3/74, 3/75, 3/76, 3/77, 3/78, 3/80, 3/82, 3/83, 3/84, 3/85, 3/86, 3/87, 3/88, 3/89, 3/90.

Figure 2.3. QUESTION (Gallup): "People are called 'hawks' if they want to step up our military effort in Vietnam. They are called 'doves' if they want to reduce our military effort in Vietnam. How would you describe yourself—as a 'hawk' or as a 'dove'?" Survey dates: 12/67, 1/68, 2/1–6/68 and 2/22–27/68 (averaged), 3/68, 4/68, 9/68, 11/69.

Figure 2.4. QUESTION (NORC): "Do you approve or disapprove of continuing to send economic aid to Western Europe under the Marshall Plan?" Survey dates: 3/49, 4/49, early 6/49, 6–7/49, 8/49, 9/49, 1/50, 4/50, 7/50, 12/50. QUESTION (NORC): "Do you approve or disapprove of continuing to send economic aid to Western Europe like we have been doing under the Marshall Plan?" Survey dates: 11/51, 6/52.

Figure 2.5. QUESTION (NORC, NORC-GSS; based on responses of *whites,* since this question was asked by NORC only of whites in some years): "Do you think white students and (Negro/black) students should go to the same schools or to separate schools?" Survey dates (NORC): 6/42, 4/56, 6/56, 9/56, 5/63, 11–12/63, 5–6/64, 6/65, 10/65, 4/70, 11/72; (NORC-GSS): 3/72, 3/76, 3/77, 3/80, 3/82, 3/84, 3/85. QUESTION (Gallup): "The U.S. (United States) Supreme Court has ruled that racial segregation in (all) the public schools is illegal. This means that children, no matter what their race, must be allowed to go to the same schools. Do you approve or disapprove of this decision?" Survey dates: 5/54, 6/54, 12/54, 4/55, 11/55, 12/56, 4/57, 7/57, 9/57, 3/59, 5/59, 5/61.

Figure 2.6. QUESTION (NORC, NORC-GSS): "Please tell me whether or not *you* think it should be possible for a pregnant woman to obtain a legal abortion if . . . If there is a strong chance of serious defect in the baby? . . . If she is married and does not want any more children? . . . If the woman's own health is seriously endangered by the pregnancy? . . . If the family has a very low income and cannot afford any more children?" Survey dates (NORC): 12/65, 11/72; (NORC-GSS): 3/72, 3/73, 3/74, 3/75, 3/76, 3/77, 3/78, 3/80, 3/82, 3/83, 3/84, 3/85, 3/87, 3/88, 3/89, 3/90. QUESTION (Gallup): "Do you think abortion operations should or should not be legal in the following cases: . . . When the child may be born deformed? . . . Where the parents simply have all the children they want although there would be no major health or financial problems involved in having another child? (5/68 11% and 12/68 14%, not shown) . . . Where the health of the mother is in danger? . . . Where the family does not have enough money to support another child?" Survey dates: 8/62, 12/65, 5/68 and 12/68 (averaged), 9/69.

Questions for Figures in Chapter Three

Figure 3.1. *NORC and NORC-GSS* surveys are data for **white respondents** only, unless otherwise noted. QUESTION (NORC, NORC-GSS): "Do you think there should be laws against marriage between (Negroes/blacks) and whites?" Survey dates (NORC): 12/63, 10/64, 4/68, 4/70; (NORC-GSS): 3/72, 3/73, 3/74, 3/75, 3/76, 3/77, 3/80, 3/82, 3/84, 3/85, 3/87, 3/88, 3/89, 3/90. QUESTION (Gallup): "Some states have laws making it a crime for a white person to marry a Negro. Do you approve or disapprove of such laws?" Survey dates: 1/65, 8/70. QUESTION (NORC, NORC-GSS): "Here are some opinions other people have expressed in connection with (Negro/black)-white relations. Which statement on the card comes closest to how you, yourself, feel? [Hand Card Z] . . . (Negroes/blacks) shouldn't push themselves where they're not wanted." (Agree/Disagree) Survey dates (NORC): 12/63, 1/66, 4/68; (NORC-GSS): 3/72, 3/73, 3/75, 3/76, 3/77, 3/80, 3/82, 3/84, 3/85. QUESTION (NORC-GSS, **all respondents**): "In general, do you favor or oppose the busing of (Negro/black) and white school children from one district to another?" Survey dates: 3/72, 3/74, 3/75, 3/76, 3/77, 3/78, 3/82, 3/83, 3/85, 3/86, 3/88, 3/89, 3/90. QUESTION (Gallup, asked of all respondents who "heard or read about the busing of Negro and white children from one school district to another"): "In general, do you . . . one school district to another?" Survey dates: 3/70, 8/71 and 10/71 (averaged). QUESTION (NORC-GSS): "Suppose there is a community-wide vote on the general housing issue. There are two possible laws to vote on (A. One law says that a homeowner decide for himself whom to sell his house to, even if he prefers not to sell it to (Negroes/blacks). B. The second law says that a homeowner cannot refuse to sell to someone because of their race or color.) Which law would you vote for?" Survey dates: 3/73, 3/75, 3/76, 3/78, 3/80, 3/83, 3/84, 3/86, 3/87, 3/88, 3/89, 3/90. QUESTION (NORC, NORC-GSS): "Here are some opinions other people have expressed in connection with (Negro/black)-white relations. Which statement on the card comes closest to how you, yourself, feel? [Hand Card Z] . . . White people have a right to keep (Negroes/blacks) out of their neighborhoods if they want to, and (Negroes/blacks) should respect that right." (Agree/Disagree) Survey dates (NORC): 12/63, 4/68, 4/70; (NORC-GSS): 3/72, 3/76, 3/77, 3/80, 3/82, 3/84, 3/85, 3/87, 3/88, 3/89, 3/90.

Figure 3.2. QUESTION (Gallup): "Some Southern states require every voter to pay a poll tax amounting to about a dollar a year before they can vote. Do you think these poll taxes should be abolished (done away with)?" Survey dates: 12/40, 3/48, 3/49, 11/49. QUESTION (Gallup): "Do you favor or oppose a law in this state which would require employers to hire a person if he is qualified for the job, regardless of his race or color?" Survey dates: 6/45, 7/47. QUESTION (NORC, whites only): "Do you think Negroes should have as good a chance as white people to get any kind of job, or do you think white people should have the first chance at any kind of job?" Survey dates: 5/44, 5/46, 12/63. QUESTION (NORC, whites only): "In general, do you think Negroes are as intelligent as white people—that is, can they learn things just as well if they are given the same education and training?" Survey dates: 6/42, 5/44, 5/46, 1/56, 4/56, 5/63, 12/63. QUESTION (NORC): "As far as you know, is Negro blood the same as white blood, or is it different in some way?" Survey dates: 5/44, 5/46. QUESTION (Gallup): "Would you favor or oppose a state law that would require employees to work alongside persons of any race or color?" Survey dates: 6/45, 7/47.

Figure 3.3. QUESTION (NORC, NORC-GSS): See figure 2.5. We thank Lawrence Bobo for providing the data from Schuman et al. (1985, figure 3.1, p. 78).

Figure 3.4. QUESTION (NORC-Gallup, NORC-GSS): "There are always some people whose ideas are considered bad or dangerous by other people. ("Atheist" or "Anti-Religionist") For instance, somebody who is against all churches and religion . . . Should such a person be allowed to teach in a college or university, or not?" ("Socialist") "Or consider a person who favored government ownership of all railroads and all big industries . . . " ("Racist") "Or consider a person who believes that blacks are genetically inferior . . . " ("Communist") "Now I would like to ask you some questions about a man who admits he is a Communist . . . Suppose he is teaching in college. Should he be fired, or not?" ("Militarist") "Consider a person who advocates doing away with elections and letting the military run the country . . . Should such a person be allowed to teach in a college or university, or not?" ("Homosexual") "And what about a man who admits he is a homosexual? . . . Should such a person be allowed to teach in a college or university, or not?" Survey dates (NORC-Gallup): 6/54; (NORC-GSS): 3/72, 3/73, 3/74, 3/76, 3/77, 3/78, 3/80, 3/82, 3/84, 3/85, 3/87, 3/88, 3/89, 3/90.

Figure 3.5. QUESTION (NORC): "Do you think members of the Communist party in this country should be allowed to speak on the radio?" Survey dates: 3/46, 11/53, 1/54, 1/56, 12/56, 4/57, 11/63. QUESTION (NORC var.): "In peacetime, do you think members of the Communist party should be allowed to speak on the radio?" Survey dates: 11/43, 11/45, 4/48. QUESTION (Gallup): "Do you believe in freedom of speech?" The ninety-six percent of the sample who said they believed in free speech were asked: "Do you believe in it (free speech) to the extent of allowing radicals to hold meetings and express their views in this community?" Survey date: 5/38; (ΘPOR): "Do you believe in free speech to the extent of allowing radicals to hold meetings and express their views in this community?" Survey dates: 7/42, 11/43, 4/44, 2/45. QUESTION (Gallup): "Do you think membership in the Communist party in this country should be forbidden by law?" Survey dates: 5/41, 3/46, 6/46, 3/47, 10/47, 3/49, 11/49, 12/50. QUESTION (Gallup): "Do you think there should be a law to prevent people in this country from belonging to the Communist party?" Survey dates: 7/40, 5/41, 6/42. QUESTION (NORC-Gallup, NORC-GSS): "Now, I should like to ask you some questions about a man who admits he is a Communist. Suppose this admitted Communist wanted to make a speech in your community. Should he be allowed to speak, or not?" Survey dates (Gallup-NORC): 6/54; (NORC-GSS): 3/72, 3/73, 3/74, 3/76, 3/77, 3/78, 3/80, 3/82, 3/84, 3/85, 3/87, 3/88, 3/89, 3/90.

Figure 3.6. QUESTION (Gallup, NORC-GSS): "Are you in favor of the death penalty for persons convicted of murder?" Var. in 1936 and 1937: ". . . death penalty for murder?" Survey dates (Gallup): 4/36, 11/36, 11/37, 11/53, 3–4/56, 8–9/57, 3/60, 1/65, 5/66, 6/67, 1/69, 10–11/71, 11/72, 4/76 (ave. with 3/76 NORC), 3/78 (ave. with NORC), 1/81, 1/85 (ave. with 3/85 NORC), 11/85, 1/86 (ave. with 3/86 NORC), 9/88; (NORC-GSS): 3/72, 3/73. QUESTION (NORC-GSS): "Do you favor or oppose the death penalty for persons convicted of murder?" Survey dates: 3/74, 3/75, 3/76, 3/77, 3/78, 3/80, 3/82, 3/83, 3/84, 3/85, 3/86, 3/87, 3/88, 3/89, 3/90. QUESTION (Gallup, NORC-GSS, *LAT*): "In general, do you think the courts in this area deal too harshly or not harshly enough with criminals?" Survey dates (Gallup): 4/65, 8–9/65, 2/68, 1/69, 12/72, 6/89 (". . . in your area . . ."); (NORC-GSS): 3/72, 3/73, 3/74, 3/75, 3/76, 3/77, 3/78, 3/80, 3/82, 3/83, 3/84, 3/85, 3/86, 3/87, 3/88, 3/89, 3/90; (*LAT*): 1/81. The violent crime figures are rates per 100,000 inhabitants and are taken from Stanley and Niemi (1990, p. 372; for definitions of crimes, see their original source: *Statistical Abstract of the U.S.* 1976, p. 153; 1987, p. 155; 1989, p. 166).

Figure 3.7. QUESTION (Gallup, NORC-GSS): "Would you favor or oppose a law which would require a person to obtain a police permit before he or she could buy a gun?" Survey dates (Gallup): 7/59, 12/63, 1/65, 9/65, 8/66, 8/67, 10/71, 5/72; (NORC-GSS): 3/72, 3/73, 3/74, 3/75, 3/76, 3/77, 3/80, 3/82, 3/84, 3/85, 3/87, 3/88, 3/89, 3/90. QUESTION (Gallup): "Do you think there should or should not be a law that would ban the possession of handguns except by the police and other authorized persons?" Survey dates: 12/80, 4/81, 6/81, 10/87, 7/88, 9/90. QUESTION (Gallup, var. of previous question): "Now here is a question about pistols and revolvers. Do you think . . . would forbid the possession of this type of gun except by . . . ?" Survey dates: 7/59, 1/65, 3/75, 11/79. QUESTION (Gallup): In general, do you feel that the laws covering the sale of handguns should be made more strict, less strict, or kept as they are now?" Survey dates: 10/75, 1/80, 12/80, 4/81, 5/83, 4/86, 1987, 7/88; ". . . sale of firearms . . . ?" Survey dates: 2–3/89, 9/90.

Figure 3.8. QUESTION (Gallup): "Do you think epileptics should or should not be employed in jobs like other people?" Survey dates: 4/49, 2/54, 6/59, 6/64, 6/69, 1/74, 10/79. QUESTION (Gallup): "Do you think epilepsy is a form of insanity or not?" Survey dates: 4/49, 2/54, 6/59, 6/64, 6/69, 1/74, 10/79.

Figure 3.9. QUESTION (NORC-GSS): "What about sexual relations between two adults of the same sex—do you think it is always wrong, almost always wrong, wrong only sometimes, or not wrong at all?" Survey dates: 3/73, 3/74, 3/76, 3/77, 3/80, 3/82, 3/84, 3/85, 3/87, 3/88, 3/89, 3/90. QUESTION (Gallup): "Do you think homosexual relations between consenting adults should or should not be legal?" Survey dates: 6/77, 6/82, 11/85, 9/86, 3/87, 10/89. QUESTION (Gallup): "Do you think homosexuals should or should not be hired for each of the following occupations . . . Salespersons? . . . Armed forces? . . . Doctors? . . . Elementary school teachers?" Survey dates: 6/77, 6/82, 11/85, 3/87, 10/89.

Figure 3.10. QUESTION (Gallup, NORC-GSS): "Do you approve or disapprove of a married woman earning money in business or industry if she has a husband capable of supporting her?" or "Do you approve of . . ." Survey dates (Gallup): 8/36 ("Should a married woman earn money if . . ."), 6/37 (omits "or disapprove"), 10/38 (registered voters; omits "or disapprove"), 10/45 ("Do you approve of . . . holding a job in . . . if her husband is able to support her?"), 9/69, 6/70 (omits "or disapprove"), 9/75 (omits "or disapprove"); (NORC-GSS): 3/72, 3/74, 3/75, 3/77, 3/78, 3/82, 3/83, 3/85, 3/86, 3/88, 3/89, 3/90. QUESTION (NORC-GSS): "Do you agree or disagree with this statement: Women should take care of running their homes and leave running the country up to men?" Survey dates: 3/74, 3/75, 3/77, 3/78, 3/82, 3/83, 3/85, 3/86, 3/88, 3/89, 3/90.

Figure 3.11. QUESTION (Roper): "Here are some of the amendments to the Constitution that are currently being talked about. [Card shown respondent.] Would you read down the list, and for each one tell me whether you would favor or oppose such an amendment? First . . . an amendment to assure equal rights for women." Survey dates: 3/79, 8/80, 8/82. QUESTION (CBS/*NYT*): "Do you favor or oppose the Equal Rights Amendment—also known as E.R.A.—the constitutional amendment concerning women?" Survey dates: 2/80, 3/80, 6/80, 8/80, early 9/80, mid 9/80, late 9/80, 10/80, 11/80, 4/81, 1/82, 6/82, 5/87, 7/88. QUESTION (Gallup, NBC, asked of respondents who had "heard or read about the Equal Rights Amendment"): "Do you favor or oppose this amendment?" Survey dates (Gallup): 3/75, 3/76, 6/78, 7/80, 7/81, 6/82; (NBC): 12/75, 1/77, 5/77, 3/78, 6/78 (averaged with Gallup results for 6/78), 8/78, 12/79 (see Mansbridge 1986, pp. 206–11). QUESTION (ABC/*WP*): "I am going to read you a few statements. After each, please tell me if you agree or disagree with it, or if, perhaps, you have no opinion about that statement . . . The Equal Rights Amendment should be ratified." Survey dates: 7/84, 7/88. QUESTION (*LAT*): "Generally speaking, are you in favor of the equal rights amendment, the ERA, are you opposed to it—or haven't you heard enough about it yet to say?" Survey dates: 7/86, 7/87.

Figure 3.12. QUESTION (Gallup, NORC-GSS): "In some places in the United States, it is not legal to supply birth control *information*. How do you feel about this—do you think birth control information should be available to anyone who wants it, or not?" Survey dates (Gallup): 12/59, 3/61, 8/62, 4/63, 12/64, 1/65; (NORC-GSS): 3/74, 3/75, 3/77, 3/82, 3/83. QUESTION (NORC-GSS): "Do you think birth control *information* should be made available to teenagers who want it, or not?" Survey dates: 3/74, 3/75, 3/77, 3/82, 3/83. QUESTION (NORC-GSS): "Would you be for or against sex education in the public schools?" Survey dates: 3/74, 3/75, 3/77, 3/82, 3/83, 3/85, 3/86, 3/88, 3/89, 3/90. QUESTION (Harris): "Do you favor or oppose a federal law prohibiting family planning clinics from giving birth control assistance to teenagers unless they have received permission from their parents?" Survey dates: 2/82, 7/82, 3/84, 9/85.

Figure 3.13. QUESTION (Gallup, MAP, NORC-GSS): "When a person has a disease that cannot be cured, do you think doctors should be allowed by law to end the patient's life by some painless means if the patient and his family request it?" Survey dates (Gallup): 6/47, 1/50, 7/73; (MAP): 4/75, 6/77; (NORC-GSS): 3/77 (ave.

with 6/77 MAP), 3/78, 3/82, 3/83, 3/85, 3/86, 3/88, 3/89, 3/90. Note: MAP refers to "Monitoring Attitudes of the Public" surveys commissioned by the Institute of Life Insurance. QUESTION (Harris): "All doctors take an oath saying they will maintain, restore, and prolong human life in their treatment of patients. It is now argued by some people that in many cases people with terminal diseases (those which can only end in death) have their lives prolonged unnecessarily, making them endure much pain and suffering for no real reason. Do you think a patient with a terminal disease ought to be able to tell his doctor to let him die rather than to extend his life when no cure is in sight, or do you think this is wrong?" Survey dates: 2/73, 1/77, 5/81, 1/85. QUESTION (NORC-GSS): "Do you think a person has a right to end his or her own life if this person . . . has an incurable disease?" Survey dates: 3/77, 3/78, 3/82, 3/83, 3/85, 3/86, 3/88, 3/89, 3/90.

Figure 3.14. QUESTION (SRC/CPS): "Some people think it is all right for the public schools to start each day with a prayer. Others feel that religion does not belong in the public schools but should be taken care of by the family and the church. Have you been interested enough in this to favor one side over the other?" (If YES) "Which do you think?" Survey dates: November 1964, 1966, 1968, 1980, 1984. QUESTION (NORC-GSS): "The United States Supreme Court has ruled that no state or local government may *require* the reading of the Lord's Prayer or Bible verses in public schools. What are your view on this—do you approve or disapprove of the court ruling?" (Gallup): ". . . do you approve or disapprove of this?" Survey dates (Gallup): 10/71; (NORC-GSS): 3/74, 3/75, 3/77, 3/82, 3/83, 3/85, 3/86, 3/88, 3/89, 3/90. QUESTION (NORC-GSS): "Which of these statements comes closest to your feelings about pornography laws? There should be laws against the distribution of pornography whatever the age. There should be laws against the distribution of pornography to persons under 18. There should be no laws forbidding the distribution of pornography." Survey dates: 3/73, 3/75, 3/76, 3/78, 3/80, 3/83, 3/84, 3/86, 3/87, 3/88, 3/89, 3/90.

Figure 3.15. QUESTION (Gallup): "Would you favor or oppose a law forbidding the sale of all beer, wine(s), and liquor throughout the nation?" Survey dates: 2/42, 8/55, 1/56, 3/57, 8/58, early 5/61, late 5/61 12/61, 1/66, 1/77, 5/79, 1/81, 7/84, 7/87. QUESTION (Gallup, NORC-GSS): "Do you think the use of marijuana should be made legal or not?" Survey dates (Gallup): 10/69, 2/72, 1/73, 3/77, 5/79, 6/80, 10/82, 5/85 ("or not" was left off); (NORC-GSS): 3/73 (ave. with 1/73 Gallup), 3/75, 3/76, 3/78, 3/80 (ave. with 6/80 Gallup), 3/83, 3/84, 3/86, 3/87, 3/88, 3/89, 3/90.

Questions for Figures in Chapter Four

Figure 4.1. QUESTION (Trendex): "I would like to get your opinion on several areas of important government activities. As I read each one, please tell me if you would like the government to do more, do less, or do about the same as they have been on . . . improving Social Security benefits." Note: Trendex surveys were not based on random digit dialing (RDD) sampling methods but on sampling from telephone directories. Survey dates: 5/78, 11/78, 2/79, 5/79, 8/79, 2/80,

5/80, 8/80, 2/81, 5/81, 8/81, 11/81, 2/82, 5/82, 8/82, 11/82. QUESTION (NORC-GSS): See figure 2.2. ". . . Social Security?" Survey dates: 3/84, 3/85, 3/86, 3/87, 3/88, 3/89, 3/90.

Figure 4.2. QUESTION (Trendex): See figure 4.1. ". . . expanding employment?" Survey dates: 2/66, 1/68, 5/68, 2/69, 4/70, 8/70, 5/71, 11/71, 5/72, 8/72, 11/72, 2/73, 8/73, 1/74, 5/74, 7/74, 10/74, 2/75, 4/75, 7/75, 11/75, 5/76, 8/76, 11/76, 2/77, 5/77, 8/77, 11/77, 2/78, 5/78, 11/78, 2/79, 5/79, 8/79, 11/79, 2/80, 5/80, 8/80, 11/80, 2/81, 5/81, 8/81, 2/82, 5/82, 8/82, 11/82. QUESTION (NBC): "What do you think is the most important economic problem for the government to help control during the next three years—high unemployment, high inflation, or high interest rates?" Survey dates: 10/81, 11/81, 12/81, 1/82 ("high" omitted 8/81, 9/81, 3/82, 5/82, 6/82). QUESTION (NBC): "In your opinion which is the most important problem facing the country today— finding jobs for people who are unemployed or holding down inflation?" Survey dates: 3/77, 4/77, 8/77, 3/78, 5/78, 6/78, 8/78, 9/78, 11/78, 12/78, 3/79, 9/79, 10/79, 3/80, 5/80, 7/80, 8/80, 9/80.

Figure 4.3. QUESTION (Roper, NORC-GSS): See figure 2.2. ". . . welfare?" Survey dates (Roper): 10/71, 12/73, 12/74, 12/75, 12/76, 12/78, 12/79, 12/80, 12/81 12/82, 12/83, 12/84, 12/85, 12/86; (NORC-GSS): 3/73, 3/74, 3/75, 3/76, 3/77, 3/78, 3/80, 3/82, 3/83, 3/84, 3/85, 3/86, 3/87, 3/88, 3/89, 3/90.

Figure 4.4. QUESTION (NORC, NORC-GSS): "Some people think that the government in Washington ought to reduce the income differences between the rich and the poor, perhaps by raising taxes of wealthy families or by giving income assistance to the poor. Others think that the government should not concern itself with reducing income difference between the rich and the poor. Here is a card with a scale from 1 to 7. Think of a score of 1 as meaning that the government ought to reduce the income differences between rich and poor, and a score of 7 meaning that the government should not concern itself with reducing income differences. What score between 1 and 7 come closest to the way you feel?" combined categories 1– 3 are graphed. Survey dates (NORC): 12/73; (NORC-GSS): 3/78, 3/80, 3/82, 3/83, 3/84, 3/86, 3/87, 3/88, 3/89, 3/90. QUESTION (ORC): "In all industries where there is competition, do you think companies should be allowed to make all the profit they can, or should the government put a limit on the profits companies can make?" Survey dates: 1946, 1948, 1953, 1955, 1962, 1971, 1973, 1975, 1976, 1979, 1981, 1983, 1986. QUESTION (ORC): "Do you think business as a whole is making too much profit, a reasonable profit, or not enough profit?" Survey dates: 1965, 1967, 1969, 1971, 1973, 1975, 1977, 1979, 1981, 1983, 1986.

Figure 4.5. QUESTION (Trendex): See figure 4.1. ". . . health measures?" Survey dates: 1/68, 4/68, 10/68, 1/69, 7/69, 4/70, 4/71, 10/71, 4/72, 7/72, 10/72, 1/73, 7/73, 1/74, 7/74, 10/74, 1/75, 4/75, 7/75, 10/75, 4/76, 7/76, 10/76, 1/77, 4/77, 7/77, 10/77, 1/78, 4/78, 10/78, 1/79, 4/79, 7/79, 10/79, 1/80, 4/80, 7/80, 10/80, 1/81, 4/81, 7/81, 10/81, 1/82, 4/82, 7/82, 10/82. QUESTION (Trendex var.): "I would like to get your opinion on several areas of important expenditures, first, on the part of the government. As I read each one, please tell me if you would like to see the government spend more, spend less or spend about the same amount as they have been on . . . health measures?" Survey dates: 1/65, 1/66. QUESTION (Roper, NORC-GSS): See figure 2.2. ". . . improving and protecting the nation's health?" Survey dates (Roper): 10/71, 12/73, 12/74, 12/75, 12/76, 12/77, 12/78, 12/79, 12/80, 12/81, 12/82, 12/83, 12/84, 12/85, 12/86; (NORC-GSS): 3/73, 3/74, 3/75, 3/76, 3/77, 3/78, 3/80, 3/82, 3/83, 3/84, 3/85, 3/86, 3/87, 3/88, 3/89, 3/90.

Figure 4.6. QUESTION (Roper, NORC-GSS): See figure 2.2. ". . . improving the nation's education system?" Survey dates (Roper): 10/71, 12/73, 12/74, 12/75, 12/76, 12/77, 12/78, 12/79, 12/80, 12/81, 12/82, 12/83, 12/84, 12/85, 12/86; (NORC-GSS): 3/73, 3/74, 3/75, 3/76, 3/77, 3/78, 3/80, 3/82, 3/83, 3/84, 3/85, 3/86, 3/87, 3/88, 3/89, 3/90. QUESTION (Trendex): See figure 4.1. ". . . education?" Survey dates: 1/68, 5/68, 11/68, 2/69, 7/69, 4/70, 8/70, 5/71, 11/71, 5/72, 8/72, 11/72, 2/73, 8/73, 1/74, 7/74, 10/74, 2/75, 4/75, 7/75, 11/75, 5/76, 8/76, 11/76, 2/77, 8/77, 11/77, 2/78, 5/78, 11/78, 2/79, 5/79, 8/79, 11/79, 2/80, 5/80, 8/80, 11/80, 2/81, 5/81, 8/81, 11/81, 2/82, 5/82, 8/82, 11/82. QUESTION (Gallup): "Some people say that the federal government in Washington should give financial help to build new public schools, especially in the poorer states. Others say that this will mean higher taxes for everyone and that states and local communities should build their own schools. How do you, yourself, feel—do you favor or oppose federal aid to build new public schools?" Survey dates: 12/55, 1/57, 6/57, 1/60, 2/61.

Figure 4.7. QUESTION (Roper, NORC-GSS): See figure 2.2. ". . . solving the problems of the big cities?" Survey dates (Roper): 10/71, 12/73, 12/74, 12/75, 12/76, 12/77, 12/78, 12/79, 12/80, 12/81, 12/82, 12/83, 12/84, 12/85, 12/86; (NORC-GSS): 3/73, 3/74, 3/75, 3/76, 3/77, 3/78, 3/80, 3/82, 3/83, 3/84, 3/85, 3/86, 3/87, 3/88, 3/89, 3/90. QUESTION (NORC-GSS): ". . . improving the conditions of blacks?" Survey dates: 3/73, 3/74, 3/75, 3/76, 3/77, 3/78, 3/80, 3/82, 3/83, 3/84, 3/85, 3/86, 3/87, 3/88, 3/89, 3/90. QUESTION (Trendex): "I would like to get your opinion on several areas of important expenditures, first on the part of the government. As I read each one, please tell me if you would like to see the government spend more, spend less or spend about the same amount as they have been on . . . urban renewal?" Survey dates: 1–2/65, 1–2/66. QUESTION (Trendex): See figure 4.1. ". . . urban renewal?" Survey dates: 1–2/68, 4–5/68, 10–11/68, 1–2/69, 7–8/69, 4–5/70, 7–8/70, 4–5/71, 10–11/71, 4–5/72, 7–8/72, 10–11/72, 1–2/73, 7–8/73, 1–2/74, 7–8/74, 10–11/74, 1–2/75, 4–5/75, 7–8/75, 10–11/75, 4–5/76, 7–8/76, 10–11/76, 1–2/77, 4–5/77, 7–8/77, 10–11/77, 1–2/78, 4–5/78, 10–11/78, 1–2/79, 4–5/79, 7–8/79, 10–11/79, 1–2/80, 4–5/80, 7–8/80, 10–11/80, 1–2/81, 4–5/81, 7–8/81, 10–11/81, 1–2/82, 4–5/82, 7–8/82, 10–11/82. QUESTION (Roper): "There are many problems facing our nation today. But at certain times some things are more important than others, and need more attention from our federal government than others. [Card shown respondent] I'd like to know for each of the things on this list whether you think it is something the government should be making a major effort on now, or something the government should be making some effort on now, or something not needing any particular effort now . . . Trying to solve the problems caused by ghettos, race, and poverty?" Survey dates: 6/74, 6/75, 6/76, 6/77, 6/78, 6/79, 6/80, 6/81, 6/82, 6/83, 6/84, 6/85, 6/86, 5/87.

Figure 4.8. QUESTION (Gallup): "Are you in favor of labor unions?" Survey dates: 7/36, 6/37, 10/38, 5/39, 8/39, 11/39, early and late 5/40 (averaged), 5–6/41, 10/41, 5/43, 2/46. QUESTION (Gallup), ABC/*WP*, NBC/*Wall Street Journal*, *LAT*): "In general, do you approve or disapprove of labor unions?" Survey dates: (Gallup): 7/47, 12/48, 10/53, 1/57, 4/57, 8/57, 10/58, 1/59, 8/59, 1/61, 5/61, 9/61, 6–7/62, 1/63, 2/65, 5/65, 9/67, 3/72, 12/72, 1/78, 5/79, 8/81, 4/85 and 7/86 (omits "In general"); (ABC/*WP*): 1/82, 9/86; (*LAT*): 3/81, 8/82; (NBC/*WSJ*): 8/86. QUESTION (NORC): "Do you think the government's attitude toward labor unions is too strict, about right, or not strict enough?" Survey dates: 5/42, 11/42, 6/43, 9/43, 10/45. QUESTION (Gallup): "Do you think the laws regulating labor unions are too strict or not strict enough?" Survey dates: 1/59, 5/61, 9/61, 6–7/62, 12/64, 1/66.

Figure 4.9. QUESTION (Gallup): "Should public school teachers be permitted to strike or not?" Survey date: 10/65, 2/68, 12/68, 9/75, 1/78 ("teachers"), 8/78 ("teachers"), 5/79 ("teachers"), 5/80. QUESTION (NBC): "Should public school teachers be permitted to (go on) strike, or don't you think so?" Survey dates: 8/81, 6/82. QUESTION (Gallup): "Should firemen be permitted to strike, or not?" Survey dates: 9/75, 1/78, 8/78, 5/79, 8/81. QUESTION (Gallup): "Should policemen be permitted to strike, or not?" Survey dates: 10/65, 9/75, 1/78, 8/78, 5/79, 8/81. QUESTION (Gallup): "Should sanitation workers be permitted to strike, or not?" Survey dates: 9/75, 8/78, 8/81.

Figure 4.10. QUESTION (Roper): "Now I'm going to name some things. And for each one would you tell me whether you think there is too much government regulation of it now, or not enough government regulation now, or about the right amount of government regulation now? . . . the honesty and accuracy of claims that are made by advertisers." Survey dates: 2/74, 2/75, 2/77, 2/79, 2/80, 1/82, 2/84. QUESTION (Harris): "Some people have suggested that the federal government should develop more extensive standards for safety. Do you favor or oppose the federal government developing more extensive standards for product safety?" Survey dates: 1971, 2/74, 3/75, 1/77. QUESTION (Harris): "If eliminating the antitrust laws in this country meant . . . In some industries, it would be found more efficient to have only a few big companies instead of a lot of small ones . . . would you favor or oppose eliminating those antitrust laws?" Survey dates: 7/74, 3/76, 5/77. QUESTION (ORC): "I am going to read you some statements that have been made about large companies. On each one, please tell me whether you agree or disagree . . . For the good of the country, many of our largest companies ought to be broken up into smaller companies." (The percentages graphed do not exclude "don't knows.") Survey dates: 1959, 1961, 1963, 1965, 1967, 1969, 1971, 1973, 1975, 1977, 1979, 1981, 1983, 1985.

Figure 4.11. QUESTION (NORC): "Do you think gasoline rationing through-out the nation is necessary?" Survey dates: 6/42, 7/42, 7/42, 9/42, 11/42 (2 surveys), 12/42, 7/43, 12/43, 4/44. QUESTION (NORC): "Do you think there should be any limit on how high wages and salaries should go during the war?" Survey dates: 7/42, 8/42, 9/42, 11/42, 5/43, 6/43, 9/43, 1/44. QUESTION (NORC): "Would you be willing to have the government freeze your income where it is now?" Survey dates: 5/43, 9/43, 1/44, 6/44.

Figure 4.12. QUESTION (Gallup): "It has been suggested that prices and wages (salaries) be 'frozen'—that is, kept at their present level, as long as the war in Vietnam lasts. Do you think this is a good idea or a poor idea?" Survey dates: 12/65–1/66, 4/66, 10/66, 10/67, 1/68; QUESTION (Gallup, var.): "It has been suggested that . . . as the Vietnam War lasts. Do you . . . ?" Survey dates: 6/69, 5/70, 9/70, 2/71, 6/71. QUESTION (Gallup): "Would you favor or oppose having the government bring back wage and price controls?" Survey dates: 8/74, 12/76, 2/78, 4/78, 5/78, 7/78, 9/78, 5/79, 8/79, 2/80, 5/80, 9/80, 1/81, 6/81. QUESTION (Gallup): "Do you think the wage-price (price-wage) controls should be more strict, less strict, or kept about the same as they are (now)?" Survey dates: 11/71, 1/72, 3/72, 8/72, 4/73.

Figure 4.13. QUESTION (Roper): "There are so many problems facing our nation today. But at certain times some things are more important than others and need attention from our federal government. I'd like to know for each of the things on this list whether you think it is something the government should be making a major effort on now, or something the government should be making some effort on now, or something not needing any particular government effort now . . . try-ing to develop new energy sources and find better ways to conserve fuel?" Survey dates: 6/75, 6/76, 6/77, 6/78, 6/79, 6/80, 6/81, 6/82, 6/83, 5–6/84. QUESTION (Roper): See figure 2.2. ". . . increasing the nation's energy supply?" Survey dates: 12/73, 12/74, 12/75, 12/76, 12/77, 12/78, 12/79, 12/80, 12/81, 12/82, 12/83, 12/84, 12/85, 12/86. QUESTION (Harris): "Would you favor or oppose de-regulation of the price of all oil produced in the United States if this would encourage development of more oil production here at home?" Survey dates: 7/74, 4/75, 6/75, 7/75, 12/78.

Figure 4.14. QUESTION (Harris): "In general, do you favor or oppose the building of more nuclear power plants in the United States?" Survey dates: 3/75, 7/76, 4/77 (". . . oppose building more . . . "), 3/78, 9–10/78, 4/79, 5/79, 11/80, 2/83, 12/88 ("On the question of nuclear power . . . "); QUESTION (Roper): "(There are differences in opinion about how safe atomic energy plants are. Some people say they are completely safe, while others say that they present dangers and hazards. How do you feel—that it would be safe to have an atomic energy plant someplace near here, or that it would present dangers?" Survey dates: 9–10/73, 9–10/74, 9–10/75, 10/76, 9/77, 9/79, 9–10/80, 9/81, 9/82, 9/83. QUESTION (NBC): "Do you think more nuclear power plants should be built in the United States, or do you think they should not be built?" Survey dates: 6/77, 11/81, 1/82, 11/82, 4/86. QUESTION (Yankelovich): "In general, do you feel we should continue to build nuclear power plants or do you feel it's too dangerous to continue to build these plants?" Survey dates: 9/85, 5/86.

Figure 4.15. QUESTION (Harris): "Do you favor or oppose . . . strict enforcement of air and water pollution controls as now required by the Clean Air and Water Acts?" Survey dates: 2/82, 7/82, 12/83, 5/84, 7/84 (voters). QUESTION (Harris): "This year Congress will reconsider the Clean Air Act which is now ten years old. Given the costs involved in cleaning up the environment, do you think Congress should make the Clean Air Act stricter than it is now, keep it about the same, or make it less strict?" Survey dates: 2/81, 5/81, 9/81 ("Congress will soon reconsider . . . "), 12/82–1/83 and 11/83 (". . . This next year Congress will reconsider the Clean Air and Clean Water Acts. Given . . . ") QUESTION (Harris): "Next year Congress will reconsider the Clean Water Act. Given the costs involved in cleaning up the environment, do you think Congress should make the Clean Water Act stricter than it is now, keep it about the same, or make it less strict?" Survey dates: 5/81, 12/82–1/83 and 11/83 (". . . This next year Congress will reconsider the Clean Air and Clean Water Acts. Given . . . "). QUESTION (Trendex): "Would you like to see something done in your community or part of the country on the following issues . . . controlling air pollution? . . . controlling water pollution? . . . increase national parks and wilderness areas?" Survey dates: 1–2/66, later 1966, 1/67, 7–8/67, 1–2/68, 7–8/68, 2/69, 1–2/72, 1–2/73, 11/75, 10–11/76, 10–11/77, 10–11/78, 10–11/79, 11/80, 11/81. QUESTION (Roper, NORC-GSS): See figure 2.2. ". . . improving and protecting the environment?" Survey dates (Roper): 10/71, 12/73, 12/74, 12/75, 12/76, 12/77, 12/78, 12/79, 12/80, 12/81, 12/82, 12/83, 12/84, 12/85, 12/86; (NORC-GSS): 3/73, 3/74, 3/75, 3/76, 3/77, 3/78, 3/80, 3/82, 3/83, 3/84, 3/85, 3/86, 3/87, 3/88, 3/89, 3/90.

Figure 4.16. QUESTION (Gallup, NORC-GSS): "Do you consider the amount of federal income tax which you have to pay as too high, about right, or too low?" Survey dates (Gallup, asked of those who said they had to file and pay federal income tax): 3/47, 11/47, 3/48, 3/49, 3/50, 2/51, 2/52, 1/53; (Gallup, all respondents): 2/56, 4/57, 3/59, 2/61, 2/62, 6/62, 1/63, 2/64, 2/66, 3/67, 3/69, 2/73, 6/85, 3/90; (NORC-GSS): 3/76, 3/77, 3/80, 3/82, 3/84, 3/85, 3/87, 3/88, 3/89, 3/90. Correlation with inflation rate remains after controlling for variant sample.

Questions for Figures in Chapter Five

Figure 5.1. QUESTION (Gallup, NORC, NORC-GSS): "Do you think it will be best for the future of this country if we take an active part in world affairs, or if we stay out of world affairs?" Survey dates: 10/45, 2/46, 11/46, 3/47, 6/47, 8/47, 3/48, 6/48, 9/49, 1/50, 11/50, 12/50, 10/52, 2/53, 9/53, 4/54, 3/55, 11/56, 6/65, 3/75, 3/76, 3/78, 11/78, 3/82, 11/82, 3/83, 3/84, 3/85, 3/86, 11/86, 3/88, 3/89, 3/90. QUESTION (SRC/CPS): "I am going to read you a statement about U.S. foreign policy and I would like you to tell me whether you agree or disagree. This country would be better off if we just stayed home and did not concern ourselves with the problems of the world." (Agree/Disagree) Survey dates: 9/56, 11/58, 9/60, 11/68, 9/72, 11/76, 11/80, 11/85, 9/88. QUESTION (Gallup): "The United States should mind its own business internationally and let other countries get along as best they can on their own." Survey dates: 1964, 1968, 1972, 1974, 1976, 1980, 1983, 1985. QUESTION (Gallup): "Would it be better for the United States to keep independent in world affairs—or would it be better for the United States to work closely with other nations?" Survey dates: 1953, 1963, 1967, 1969.

Figure 5.2. QUESTION (NORC, NORC-GSS): See the first question listed for figure 5.1.

Figure 5.3. QUESTION (OPOR): "Which of these two things do you think is the more important—that this country keep out of war, or that Germany be defeated?" Survey dates: early 12/40, mid 12/40, later 12/40, 7/41, early 11/41, later 11/41. QUESTION (OPOR): "Which of these two things do you think is more important—that this country keep out of war, or that Germany be defeated, even at the risk of our getting into the war?" Survey dates: early–mid 3/41, late 3/41. QUESTION (Roper): "Which one of the following sentences most nearly represents your attitude toward the present war? . . . Those who think this is our war are wrong, and the people of this country should resist to the last ditch any move that would lead us any further toward war . . . ?" The percentages graphed are those rejecting this view (favoring "support in full" for "the government's program" or an even more belligerent position). Survey dates: 6/41, 9/41, 10/41, 12/41. QUESTION (Gallup): "Which of these two things do you think is the more important for the United States to try to do—to keep out of war ourselves, or to help England win even at the risk of getting into the war?" Survey dates: 6/40, 9/40, 11/40, 12/40, 1/41, 3/41, 9/41. (Gallup, var. no. 2): same as previous question except "win" omitted and "more important" instead of "the more important." Survey dates: 4/41, 5/41. (Gallup, var. no. 3): same as var. no. 2 except "Britain" instead of "England." Survey dates: 4/41, 5/41 (responses averaged for the 4/41 and 5/41 variants). QUESTION (Gallup): "At the present time, which of the following should the United States do about helping England and France: (1) Do less than we are doing now; (2) do no more or no less than we are doing now; (3) do everything possible to help England and France except go to war; (4) declare war on Germany and send our army and navy to Europe?" Survey dates: mid 5/40, late 5/40, mid 6/40, late 6/40, 9/40. QUESTION (OPOR, var. of previous Gallup question): "At the present . . . England: (1) Do nothing or less than we are doing now; (2) . . . (3) . . . England except . . . (4) . . . on Germany and Italy and send . . . ?" Survey dates: 12/40, 4/41, 5/41. QUESTION (Gallup): "Should the Neutrality Act be changed to permit American merchant ships with American crews to carry war materials to Britain?" Survey dates: 9/41, first week 10/41, second week 10/41, late 10/41.

Figure 5.4. QUESTION (OPOR): "If the German army overthrew Hitler and then offered to stop the war and discuss peace terms with the allies, would you favor or oppose accepting the offer of the German army?" Survey dates: 1/42, 6/42, 3/43, 6/43, 8/43, 1/44, 4/44, 6/44, 8/44, 2/45, 4/45. QUESTION (OPOR):

"If Hitler offered to discuss peace terms now, should the allies accept this offer and discuss peace terms with Hitler?" Survey date: 1/44, 3/44, 4/44, 6/44, 8/44, 3/45; (OPOR): "If Hitler offered to stop the war now and discuss peace terms with the allies, would you favor or oppose accepting Hitler's offer?" Survey date: 1/42. QUESTION (OPOR): "When the war is over, should the peace treaty be less severe, or more severe, than the treaty at the end of the last war?" Survey dates: 1/44, 4/44, early 6/44, late 6/44, 8/44, 3/45.

Figure 5.5. QUESTION (Gallup): "Do you think the United States is being too soft or too tough in its policy toward Russia?" Survey dates: 3/46, 10/47, 3/48, 6/48, 1/49. QUESTION (NORC): "How do you feel about our dealings with Russia—do you think the United States should be more willing to compromise with Russia, or is our present policy about right, or should we be even firmer than we are today?" Survey dates: 4/48, 6/48, 11/48, 1/49, 6/49, 3/50. For the other trend items graphed there is occasional confusion in reports by others (Caspary 1968; Walsh 1947, see esp. pp. 186, 190). Distinguishing OPOR from Gallup is especially difficult (and we have yet to sort this out fully) since at least some early OPOR surveys apparently used Gallup's field staff; and they and NORC used several slightly different question wordings. QUESTION (NORC): "Do you think that Russia can be depended on to cooperate with us after the war?" Survey dates: Average of 3/42 and Gallup/OPOR point of same date, 5/42, average of two 7/42 points, 8/42, 9/42, average of two 11/42 points, 6/43, 11/43 and average of Gallup point of same date, 6/46. (NORC): "(How about) during the next few years? Do you think Russia can be trusted to cooperate with us?" 10/46, 12/46; (NORC): "Do you think that Russia can be trusted to meet us half-way in working out world problems?" 2/47; (NORC): "Do you think we can count on Russia to meet us half-way in working out problems together?" 6/47, 10/47, 12/47, 6/48, 8/48, 10/48, 1/49, 6/49, 7/49, 8/49, 9/49, 10/49. (Gallup): "Do you think Russia can be trusted to cooperate with us after the war?" average of 3/42 and NORC point of same date, average of 11/43 and NORC point of same date, 7/44, 12/44, 3/45, 6/45, 9/45; (Gallup): "Do you think Russia will cooperate with us in world affairs?" 10/45, 5/46, 10/46 and average of NORC point of same date, 1/47 (cf. Caspary 1968, pp. 26–28, 43–44).

Figure 5.6. QUESTION (NORC): ". . . Well (as you say/as you probably know), under this pact the countries of western Europe, Canada and the United States would agree to defend each other against attack. Now it's up to the United States Senate to vote for or against the treaty. How do you feel about it—are you in favor of the North Atlantic treaty, or against it?" Survey dates: ("under this treaty") 4/49, early 6/49, 6–7/49. QUESTION (NORC): "As you may recall, the United States signed an agreement with Canada and the countries of western Europe last year, to defend each other against any attack. How do you feel about this treaty now—do you think it's a good idea or a bad idea to have this agreement?" Survey dates: 3/50, 7/50, 12/50. QUESTION (NORC): "As you know, the United States has an agreement with the countries of western Europe, to defend each other against any attack. How do you feel about this treaty—is it a good idea or a bad idea?" Survey dates: 6/53, 5/54, 10/55, 11/55, 11/56. QUESTION (NORC): "How do you feel about the number of American troops stationed in Europe—in general, do you feel we have too many troops there now, about the right number, or should we send more?" Survey dates: 12/51, 11/53, 9/54, 10/56, 11/56. QUESTION (NORC): "Would you approve or disapprove of sending military supplies to the countries of western Europe now, in order to strengthen them against any future attack?" Survey dates: 3/49, 4/49, early 6/49, 6–7/49, 8/49, 9/49. (NORC, var. of previous question): "Do you approve or . . . ?" Survey dates: 1/50, 3/50, 4/50, 6/50, 7/50, 10/50, 11/50, 12/50, 1/51, 3/51. QUESTION (NORC): "Do you approve or disapprove of sending military supplies to the countries of western Europe?" Survey dates: 5/51, 11/51, 6/52, 10/55, 11/55, 11/56. QUESTION (NORC): (Var. intro.) "Do you approve or disapprove of . . . sending military supplies to strengthen the countries of western Europe?" Survey dates: 11/48, 1/49, 10/49. QUESTION (NORC): "Would you approve or disapprove of the United States sending military supplies to these countries (of western Europe) now, in order to strengthen them against any future attack?" Survey dates: 4/48, 6/48, 10/48.

Figure 5.7. See figure 5.5 and Caspary (1968) for question wordings and documentation. The data plotted do not average any survey results as in figure 5.5, and the "don't know" responses have not been excluded (as they were not reported in Caspary [1968, p. 29], nor were otherwise available to us), so that the percentages graphed, when combined into a national total, are lower than those shown in figure 5.5.

Figure 5.8. QUESTION (Gallup): "In view of the developments since we entered the fighting in Korea, do you think the United States made a mistake in deciding to defend Korea (South Korea) or not?" Survey dates: 8/50, 12/50. QUESTION (Gallup): "Do you think the United States made a mistake in going into the war in Korea or not?" Survey dates: 2/51, 3/51, 4/51, 6/51, 8/51, 3/52, early 10/52, late 10/52, 1/53. QUESTION (NORC): "Do you think the United States was right or wrong in sending American troops to stop the Communist invasion of South Korea?" Survey dates: 9/50, 12/50, 1/51, 3/51, 4/51, 5/51, 8/51, 11/51, 12/51, 3/52. QUESTION (NORC): "As things stand now, do you feel that the war in Korea has been worth fighting, or not?" Survey dates: 10/52, 11/52, 12/52, 4/53, 6/53, 8/53. QUESTION (NORC): "As things stand now, do you feel that the war in Korea was worth fighting, or not?" Survey dates: 11/53, 11/54, 9/56. (Combined trend) QUESTION (NORC): "Do you think the people in this country have been asked to make too many sacrifices to support the defense program, not enough sacrifices, or about the right amount?" Survey dates: 3/51, 4/51, 8/51, 11/51, 12/51, 2/52, 4/52, 5/52, 6/52, 8/52, 11/52. QUESTION (NORC): "Do you think the people in this country have been asked to make too many sacrifices, or not enough sacrifices, to support the defense program?" Survey dates: 10/50, 11/50, 12/50, 1/51, 5/51. QUESTION (NORC): "Do you think the people in this country are being asked to make too many sacrifices to support the defense program, not enough sacrifices, or about the right amount?" Survey dates: 2/53, 6/53. QUES-

TION (NORC): "If Communist armies attack any other countries in the world, do you think the United States should stay out of it, or should we help defend these countries like we did in Korea?" Survey dates: 9/50, 12/50, 8/51, 12/51, 6/52, 10/52, 8/53, 11/53, 10/55, 11/56. QUESTION (NORC): "Do you think our government is doing (has done) all it should to try to stop the spread of Communism in the world?" Survey dates: 6/51, 2/52, 8/52, 4/53. QUESTION (NORC): "Do you think our government is doing all it should to try to stop Communism from spreading to other countries in the world?" Survey dates: 9/53, 5/54, 11/55.

Figure 5.9. QUESTION (Gallup): "Do you think the United States should give up its membership in the United Nations?" Survey date: 1/51, 5/51, 11/51, 1/62, 11/63, 7/67, 2/75, 11/75, 6/82, 10/83, 8/85, 10/90. QUESTION (NORC, NORC-GSS): "Do you think our government should continue to belong to the United Nations, or should we pull out of it now?" Survey dates (NORC): 8/55, 4/56, 11/56, 6/65 ("United Nations Organization" replaces "United Nations" 1/51, 5/52, 2/53, 6/53, 11/53). (NORC-GSS): 3/73, 3/75, 3/76, 3/78, 3/82, 3/83, 3/85, 3/86, 3/88, 3/89, 3/90. QUESTION (Gallup): "The United States should cooperate fully with the United Nations?" Survey dates: 1964, 1968, 1972, 1974, 1976, 1980, 1983.

Questions for Figures in Chapter Six

Figure 6.1. QUESTION (Gallup): "In view of the developments since we entered the fighting in Vietnam, do you think the U.S. made a mistake sending troops to fight in Vietnam?" Survey dates: 8/65, 3/66, 5/66, 9/66, 11/66, 2/67, 5/67, 7/67, 10/67, 12/67, 2/68, 3/68, 4/68, 8/68, 10/68, 2/69, 9/69, 1/70, 3/70, 4/70, 5/70, 1/71, 5/71. QUESTION (Gallup): "Some people think we should not have become involved with our military forces in Southeast Asia, while others think we should have. What is your opinion?" Survey dates: 1/65, 5/65, 11/65. QUESTION (Gallup, asked of those who reported paying attention to events): "Do you think we did the right thing in getting into the fighting in Vietnam or should we have stayed out?" Survey dates: 11/64, 11/66, 11/68 (all respondents), 5/70 (all respondents). QUESTION (Gallup): "Here are four different plans the United States could follow in dealing with the war in Vietnam. Which one do you prefer: withdraw all troops from Vietnam immediately, withdraw all troops by end of 1970, withdraw troops but take as many years to do this as are needed to turn the war over to the South Vietnamese, send more troops to Vietnam and step up the fighting?" Survey dates: 12/69, 2/70, 5/70, 7/70. QUESTION (CBS): "As of today do you favor or oppose immediate withdrawal of all American troops from Vietnam?" Survey dates: 10/69, 11/69, 5/70. QUESTION (Harris): "If the reductions of U.S. troops continued at the present rate and the South Vietnamese government collapsed, would you favor or oppose continuing the withdrawal of troops?" Survey dates: 10/69, 4/70, 4/71, 7/71.

Figure 6.2. QUESTION (Harris): (Version A) "In general, do you feel the pace at which the President is withdrawing troops from Vietnam is too fast, too slow, or about right?" Survey dates: 10/69, 12/69. (Version B) adds "Nixon."

Survey date: 8/70. (Version C) omits "from Vietnam." Survey date: 10/69. (Version D) adds "U.S." Survey date: 4/70. (Version E) puts "slow" first. Survey date: 1/71. (Version G) substitutes "think." Survey dates: 5/70, 7/70. (Version H) adds "Nixon" and "slow" first. Survey dates: 3/71, 4/71. (Version I) omits "in general," "slow" first. Survey date: 10/71. (Version J) long prologue on RN plan, substitutes "more rapid rate," "slower rate," "satisfactory." Survey date: 10/71. (Version K) "Do you feel the pace of withdrawal of U.S. troops from . . . ?" Survey dates: 2/72, 5/72. Source for U.S. troop data: SS-2 Unclassified Statistics on Southeast Asia, Comptroller, Office of the Secretary of Defense, table 6. Reported in Littauer and Uphoff (1972, pp. 265–272, table 6).

Figure 6.3. QUESTION (Gallup): "Do you think Communist China should or should not be admitted as a member of the United Nations (U.N.)?" Survey dates: 7/54, 7/54, 5/55, 8/55, 7/56, 12/56, 2/57, 1/58, 8/58, 3/61, 9/61, 2/64, 11/64, 2/65, 3/66, 9/66, 1/69, 9/70, 5/71. QUESTION (NORC): "Would you approve or disapprove of letting Communist China become a member of the United Nations." Survey dates: 11/53, 3/54, 9/56. QUESTION (Gallup): "Suppose a majority of the members of the United Nations decides to admit Communist China to the United Nations. Do you think the United States should go along with the UN decision, or not?" Survey dates: 8/55, 7/56, 2/61, 9/61, 1/64, 2/65, 12/65, 3/66, 9/66, 1/69, 5/71. QUESTION (Harris): "Do you think Communist China should or should not be admitted as a member of the United Nations?" Survey dates: 6/64, 11/64.

Figure 6.4. QUESTION (Harris): "It has been argued that we could deal with the People's Republic of China (Communist China) better if we officially recognized them. This would allow us to have an ambassador in China as we have in other communist countries. Do you favor or oppose official recognition of Communist China?" Survey dates: 1966, 1967, 1968, 5/71, 8/71, 10/71, 9/77, 7/78. QUESTION (Harris): "In general, do you approve or disapprove of President Nixon accepting the invitation of the Communist Chinese to visit their country?" Survey dates: 8/71, 10/71, 2/72, 5/72. QUESTION (Harris): "Should we continue or should we end our defensive alliance with the Nationalist Chinese government on Taiwan?" Survey dates: 1976, 1977, 1978. QUESTION (Roper): "The United States has formed ties of varying degrees with different nations in the world. Here is a list of a few countries. Would you read down the list and tell me for each country what you think would be best for us in the long run—to strengthen our ties with them, or to continue things about as they are, or to lessen our commitments to them?" Survey dates: 1/74, 1/75, 1/77, 2/80 ("Mainland China"), 1/81. QUESTION (Harris): "Would you like to see friendlier relations between the United States and the People's Republic of China (Communist China) or would you rather not see that happen?" Survey dates: 5/71, 10/77, 9/78.

Figure 6.5. QUESTION (Roper): "With regard to (turning for a minute to [Roper/AJC var.]) the situation in the Middle East at the present time do you find yourself more in sympathy with Israel, or more in sympathy with the Arab nations?" Survey dates: 11/73, 12/73, 6/74, 12/74, 2/75, 4/75, 6/75, 1/77, 3/77, 1/78, 4/78, 3/79, 3/80, 7/81, 8/81, 6/82, 9/82, 10/82, 7/83, 1/84 (Roper/AJC),

3/84, 10/84, 4–5/85 (Roper/AJC), 8/85, 6/86 (Roper/AJC), 2/87 (Roper/AJC), 2/88, 4/88 (Roper/AJC), 2/89, 4/89 (Roper/AJC), 2/90; (CBS/*NYT*, same question): 6/90. Note: Response categories (vol.) of "Neither" and "Both" are included, so that the Roper question yields lower levels of sympathy for Israel; the other survey organizations reported here only code "Neither." Responses of "depends" have been excluded. QUESTION (Gallup, asked of those who had heard or read about the situation in the Middle East; ABC, all respondents): "In the Middle East situation, are your sympathies more with Israel or more with the Arab nations?" Survey dates (Gallup): 6/67, 1/69, 3/70, 10/73, 12/73, 1/75, 4/75, 6/77, 10/77, 12/77, 2/78, 3/78, 4–5/78, 8/78, early 9/78, late 9/78, 11/78, 1/79, 3/79, 7–8/81, 1/82, 4–5/82, 6/82, 7/82, 1/83, 3/83, 7/83; Survey dates (ABC/*WP*): 3/82, 8/82, 9/82, 1/83, 2/83, 9/83, 6–7/85, 6/86. QUESTION (Gallup, var. of previous question): ". . . Palestinian Arabs . . . ?" Survey dates: 5/86, 12/88, 8/89, 10/90.

Figure 6.6. QUESTION (Trendex): See figure 4.1. ". . . defense?" Survey dates: 2/68, 5/68, 11/68, 2/69, 8/69, 5/70, 8/70, 5/71, 11/71, 5/72, 8/72, 11/72, 2/73, 5/73, 8/73, 2/74, 8/74, 11/74, 2/75, 5/75, 8/75, 11/75, 5/76, 11/76, 2/77, 5/77, 8/77, 11/77, 2/78, 5/78, 8/78, 11/78, 2/79, 5/79, 8/79, 11/79, 2/80, 5/80, 8/80, 11/80, 2/81, 5/81, 8/81, 11/81, 2/82, 5/82, 8/82, 11/82. QUESTION (Gallup): "There is much discussion as to the amount of money the government in Washington should spend for national defense and military purposes. How do you feel about this? Do you think we are spending too little, too much, or about the right amount?" Survey dates: 7/69, 11/69, 3/71, 2/73, 9/73, 9/74, 1–2/76, 7/77, 12/79, 1/80, 1/81, 3/82, 11/82, 1/83, 8/83, 9/83, 2/84, 7/84, 1/85, 3/86, 5/87, 1/90, 8/90. QUESTION (Roper, NORC-GSS): See figure 2.2. ". . . the military, armaments and national defense?"

Figure 6.7. QUESTION (Gallup): "The United States should come to the defense of major European allies with military force if necessary if any of them are attacked by the Soviet Union." Survey dates: 1972, 1974, 1975, 1976, 1978, 1979, 1980, 1983, 1985. QUESTION (Gallup): "The United States should come to the defense of Japan with military force if necessary if it is attacked by Soviet Russia or Communist China." Survey dates: 1972, 1974, 1975, 1976, 1978, 1979, 1980, 1983, 1985. QUESTION (Roper): "There has been some discussion about the circumstances that might justify using U.S. troops in other parts of the world. I'd like to ask your opinion about several different situations. First, would you favor or oppose the use of U.S. troops, if the Soviet Union invaded . . . Western Europe, . . . West Berlin, . . . (Cuban troops involved in a communist takeover of a Central American country), . . . Poland, . . . Yugoslavia." Survey dates: 7/78, 2/80, 2/81, 1/82, 10–11/83.

Figure 6.8. QUESTION (Roper): "You may have differing opinions about selling arms and weapons to certain specific countries. Here is a list of some different countries. Would you go down the list, and for each one tell me whether you think the United States should or should not sell them arms? . . . England . . . West Germany . . . Turkey . . . Greece . . . South Korea . . . Japan . . . Iran?" (Includes (vol.) responses of having mixed feeling about) Survey dates: 8/75, 11/76, 3/78, 8/80, 8/81, 8/83, 10/85.

Figure 6.9. QUESTION (CBS/*NYT*): "Do you think the military strength of the United States should be superior to the Soviet Union, should be about equal in strength, or doesn't the United States need to be exactly as strong as the Soviet Union?" Survey dates: (var., omits "exactly") 6/78, 6/79, 8/80, 2/81, 1/85; (registered voters): early and later 9/80, 10/80. QUESTION (ABC/*WP*): "Do you favor or oppose a new agreement between the United States and Russia which would limit nuclear weapons?" Survey dates: 1/78, 6/78, 8/78, 10/78, 11/78 (voters), 2/79, 3/79, 5/79, 7/79, 9/79, 10/80. QUESTION (Roper): "There are many problems facing our nation today. But at certain times some things are more important than others, and need more attention from our Federal Government than others. I'd like to know for each of the things on this list whether you think it is something the government should be making a major effort on now, or something the government should be making some effort on now, or something not needing any particular government effort now . . . Trying to improve relations between the United States and Russia." Survey dates: 6/74, 6/75, 6/76, 6/77, 6/78, 6/79, 6/80, 6/81, 6/82, 6/83, 5–6/84, 6/85, 6/86, 5/87. QUESTION (Roper): Same as previous question: ". . . trying to seek agreements with other nations to limit nuclear weapons." Survey dates: 6/74, 6/75, 6/76, 6/77, 6/78, 6/79, 6/80, 6/81, 6/82, 6/83, 5–6/84, 6/85, 6/86, 5/87. QUESTION (CBS/*NYT*): "What do you think the United States should do (now)—should the United States try harder to reduce tensions with the Russians or instead should (the U.S.) get tougher in its dealings with the Russians?" Graph excludes "both/neither." Survey dates: 1/80, 5/82, 9/82, 2/84 (2 pts. ave.), 9/85, 11/85 (2 ave.). QUESTION (ABC): "There have been proposals that the United States and the Soviet Union both agree to halt, or freeze, the testing, production and installation of nuclear weapons. Would you approve or disapprove of a freeze on nuclear weapons by both the United States and the Soviet Union?" Survey dates: 4/82, 4/83, 9/83, 11/83.

Figure 6.10. QUESTION (ABC/*WP*): "Would you approve or disapprove of the United States sending troops to fight in El Salvador?" Survey dates: 3/82, 5/83. QUESTION (Roper): ". . . Here is a list of possible steps the U.S. could take to protect its interest in El Salvador and other parts of Central America and the Caribbean. [Card shown respondent] For each one, would you tell me if you favor it strongly, generally favor it, generally oppose it, or oppose it strongly? 'First, . . . keep U.S. military advisors in El Salvador to help train the El Salvador government troops in their fight against leftist guerrillas there." Survey dates: 2/82, 2/83, 9/83, 2/84, 1/85. QUESTION (ABC/*WP*): "The Reagan administration wants to send an increased amount of military equipment and weapons to the government of El Salvador. Do you approve or disapprove of that?" Survey dates: 3/82, 5/83. QUESTION (ABC/*WP*): "Which side should the United States help: the government in El Salvador, the rebels in El Salvador, or should the United States stay out of the situation?" Survey dates: 3/82, 5/83. QUESTION (Roper): (Same as previous Roper question on El Salvador) ". . . send increased military aid to El

Salvador to help its government fight against the leftist guerillas?" Survey dates: 9/83, 2/84, 1/85. QUESTION (Roper): (Same) ". . . use U.S. air and naval forces to stop Cuban ships and planes carrying military supplies to the leftist guerillas in El Salvador?" Survey dates: 2/82, 2/83, 2/84. QUESTION (Roper): (Same) ". . . send increased economic aid to El Salvador to help its government cope with the damage caused by the conflict with the leftist guerillas?" Survey dates: 2/82, 2/83, 2/84, 1/85. QUESTION (Roper): (Same) ". . . send U.S. troops to El Salvador if this is the only way to prevent the government of El Salvador from being overthrown by the leftist guerillas?" Survey dates: 2/82, 2/83, 2/84, 1/85.

Figure 6.11. QUESTION (CBS/*NYT*): "The Reagan administration says the U.S. should help people in Nicaragua who are trying to overthrow the pro-Soviet government there. Other people say that even if our country doesn't like the government in Nicaragua, we should not help overthrow it. Do you think we should help overthrow the government of Nicaragua, or not?" Survey dates: 6/83, 10/83, 4/84, 10/84 (registered voters), 5/85. QUESTION (ABC/*WP*): "As you may know, the United States through the CIA is supporting the rebels. Would you say you approve or disapprove of the United States being involved in trying to overthrow the government in Nicaragua?" Survey dates: 7/83, 11/83, 1/84, 3/86. QUESTION (ABC/*WP*): "Should the U.S. be involved in trying to overthrow the government of Nicaragua, or not?" Survey dates: 2/85, 3/85, 6/85, 3/86, 1/87, 5/87, 8/87. QUESTION (Harris): "If it came to it, would you favor or oppose the U.S. invading Nicaragua to overthrow the Sandinista government?" Survey dates: 5/85, 4/86; 3/85, 6/87 and 7/87 (var.: "Would you favor or oppose . . ."). QUESTION (ABC/*WP*): "Do you generally favor or oppose the U.S. Congress granting military aid to the Nicaraguan rebels known as the 'Contras'?" Survey dates: 3/87, 5/87, 7/87 (average from 2 surveys), 8/87 (average from 2 surveys), 9/87, 10/87, 6/86 and 1/87 (variant: "military and other aid"). QUESTION (NBC/*WSJ*): "Do you approve or disapprove of the Reagan administration's support of the rebels in Nicaragua?" Survey dates: 11/86, 12/86, 1/87, 3/87, 5/87, 7/87, 9/87.

Questions for Figures in Chapter Seven

In several cases below we have reported the linear regression slopes (*b*'s) of the trend lines for subgroups over the time periods indicated:

Figure 7.1. QUESTION (NORC-GSS): see figure 3.7.

Figure 7.2. QUESTION (NORC-GSS): see figure 3.1. *b*'s, 1975–1990: white = 1.12, black = .78.

Figure 7.3. QUESTION (NORC-GSS): see figure 4.3. *b*'s, 1976–1990: lowest = $-.91$, middle = $-.96$, upper middle = -2.00, high = -2.11. *b*'s, 1974–1977: lowest = 7.13, middle = 6.82, upper middle = 7.67, high = 8.31.

Figure 7.4. QUESTION (Gallup): see figure 5.8. *b*'s, 1950–1952: young = $-.51$, middle = $-.67$, oldest = $-.70$ (data from Mueller 1973, pp. 138, 274).

Figure 7.5. QUESTION (NORC-GSS): see figure 2.6.

Figure 7.6. QUESTION (NORC-GSS): see figure 2.2. ". . . improving the conditions of blacks?" *b*'s, 1977–1990: Democrats = 1.43, Independents = .97,

Republicans = 1.06; *b*'s, 1973–1978: Democrats = −2.51, Independents = −1.16, Republicans = −1.27.

Figure 7.7. QUESTION (Gallup): see figure 6.1. *b*'s, 8/65–1/70: Republicans = −.59, Democrats = −.74, Independents = −.76 (data from Mueller 1973, pp. 119, 271).

Figure 7.8. QUESTION (NORC-GSS): see figure 2.2. ". . . the military, armaments, and defense." *b*'s, 1972–1980: Northeast = 5.29, North Central = 6.24, South = 6.24, West = 5.73; *b*'s, 1980–1985: Northeast = −7.93, North Central = −9.96, South = −9.93, West = −8.72; *b*'s, 1985–1990: Northeast = −.91, North Central = .13, South = −1.07, West = −.84.

Figure 7.9. QUESTION (NORC-GSS): see figure 3.15. *b*'s, 1973–1978: non–h.s. grads = −2.43, h.s. grad = −2.58, some coll. = −1.88, coll. grad = −2.72; *b*'s, 1976–1990: non–h.s. grad = .31, h.s. grad = 1.12, some coll. = 1.68, coll. grad = 2.07.

Figure 7.10 QUESTION (NORC-GSS): see figure 2.6.

Questions for Figures in Chapter Eight

Figure 8.1. QUESTION Fertility rate: *n* live births per 1,000 women, aged 15–44. U.S. Department of Commerce, Bureau of the Census, *Statistical Abstract 1990*, table 84; *Historical Statistics of the U.S. to 1970*, series B 5–10. Marital instability rate: *n* divorces/annulments per marriage. U.S. Department of Commerce, Bureau of the Census, *Statistical Abstract 1990*, tables 126,133; *Historical Statistics of the U.S. to 1970*, series B 1–4. Labor force participation rate: see table 8.4. Feminist activity index: adapted from figure 1.1, "Feminist activism and legislative success, 1899–1980," reported in Klein (1984, pp. 10, 12)—measured by numbers of events aimed at changing women's traditional status, per year; the index graphed is the number of events divided by 3.5.

Figure 8.2. QUESTION (Gallup): "So you think President Nixon should be impeached and compelled to leave office, or not?" Survey dates: 3/73, 6/73, 7/73, 8/73, 8/73, 10/73, 10/73, 11/73, 11/73, 1/74, 2/74, 5/74. QUESTION (Gallup): "Impeachment, as you probably know . . . Now, let me ask you first of all if you think there is enough evidence of possible wrongdoing in the case of President Nixon to bring him to trial before the Senate, or not?" Survey dates: 4/74, 5/74, 5/74, 7/74, 8/74. QUESTION (Harris): "In view of what has happened in the Watergate affair, do you think President Nixon should resign (as President), or not?" Survey dates: 5/73, 6/73, 7/73, 8/73, 9/73, 10/73, 11/73. QUESTION (Harris): "If it is proven that President Nixon ordered or knew about the cover-up of White House involvement in Watergate (after Republican agents were caught there), do you think he should resign, or not?" Survey dates: 8/73, 9/73, 10/73, 11/73, 12/73, 2/74, 5/74. QUESTION (Gallup): "Just from the way you feel now, do you think his actions are serious enough to warrant his being removed from the presidency or not?" Survey dates: 4/74, 5/74, 6/74, 7/74, 8/74. QUESTION (Roper): "Actually, impeachment begins with an investigation of charges made against him by the House of Representatives and if they think the charges have sufficient basis, a later trial by the Senate. Because of the various charges that have recently been made against President Nixon, do you think impeachment proceedings should be brought against him or not?" Survey dates: 11/73, 4/74, 5/74. QUESTION (Harris): "If the Congress decides that President Nixon was involved in the Watergate cover-up, do you think Congress should impeach him and remove him from office?" Survey dates: 5/74, 5/74, 6/74; ("U.S. Senate Watergate Committee" was substituted for "Congress," and "or not" replaced "and remove him from office"): 8/73, 9/73, 10/73, 11/73, 12/73, 2/74.

Notes

1. Sullivan, Piereson, and Marcus (1978), however, showed that part of the apparent difference was an artifact of changes in question wording, indicating that Americans all along had somewhat better organized belief systems than earlier researchers thought. In an even more iconoclastic spirit, E. R. A. N. Smith (1989) has provided evidence that the "levels of conceptualization" and attitude consistency measures that were used had questionable validity and reliability and that better measures revealed no change in the public's sophistication or knowledge.

2. The rational ignorance argument provides a useful warning against the hope (entertained in certain democratic theories) that political seminars will spring up in every citizen's living room. At the same time, if not properly understood, the argument encourages unnecessary defeatism about the possibilities of public education. Rational self-interested citizens, and the polity as a whole, can certainly profit from the provision of low-cost, high-quality political information, and from opportunities to participate in politics. We return to these topics in Chapters 9 and 10.

3. Implicit in this list of characteristics are a number of counterhypotheses, or "null models," against which our argument of public rationality can be tested. We are asserting that collective policy preferences are *not* unstable, immovable, random, meaningless, mutually inconsistent, or incoherent; that they do *not* change in erratic, unpredictable, or inconsistent ways, or without relation to objective circumstances. Each of these hypotheses is testable, and evidence bearing on each will be found at various points in the book.

Our use of the term "rationality," of course, differs from the usage by most economists, who refer to maximizing behavior (often restricted to pursuit of individual material self-interest). We insist, like Humpty Dumpty, upon our right to make the word mean exactly what we say it means. "Rationality" is too fine a concept to become the private property of one discipline.

An economics-style model of rational individual behavior (e.g., McCubbins and Page 1984) is, in fact, consistent with our view of collective public opinion but is not required for it. Our argument about individuals and the collectivity also has some kinship with Becker (1962). Even for economists, the treatment of rationality as optimization can be problematic in explaining economic change (see Nelson and Winter 1982).

4. The early attitude measurement literature outlines various models in which survey responses reflect true underlying preferences but are also subject to random variation. In recent years, there seems to have emerged a virtual consensus on this general point, though with important variations. See, e.g., Achen 1975; Erikson 1979; Jackson 1979, 1983; Enelow and Hinich 1984; McCubbins and Page 1984; Feldman 1990; Zaller and Feldman 1988; Bartels 1988.

5. Our view on this matter is akin to that of Achen (1975), Erikson (1979), Jackson (1979), Zaller and Feldman (1988), Bartels (1988), Brady and Ansolabehere (1989), Inglehart (1985, 1990), and others, who argue that individuals have meaningful long-term preferences which can be measured accurately by taking account of measurement error. We differ in also allowing for true short-term fluctuations in individuals' opinions due to new information. The distinction becomes important when we think about changes in collective public opinion, which sometimes occur as a result of society-wide short-term inputs of information (affecting many respondents at once) even when survey instrumentation and other sources of measurement error remain constant.

6. We have been addressing issues of measurement *reliability*. *Validity* of collective preference measurement depends also upon such factors as how balanced the question wording is, and how accurately it matches both the actual policy alternatives and the respondent's conception of the alternatives.

7. Granted, the explicit mention of presidential and congressional cues in these questions made responses easier (no doubt partly accounting for the paucity of "don't knows"), but this also may have made the measurement of preferences more accurate by providing helpful contexts or "frames" (see Iyengar 1991; Zaller and Feldman 1989).

In November 1985, in response to a *Los Angeles Times* question, 61% of those with opinions said it was a good idea for the United States to "proceed with further development of weapons systems like the MX nuclear missile and the B-1 bomber, if the main intention is to use them as bargaining chips in disarmament negotiations." This support for development and negotiation is not at all inconsistent with delaying funds and "cutting back" on the MX and, indeed, seems to be the reason Reagan ultimately got his missiles.

Chapter Two

1. A related pitfall is that the sampling and interviewing and callback practices of different survey organizations may differ in ways that affect responses. This suggests that it may be best, when possible, to compare only identical questions asked by the *same survey organization,* which is our general practice.

But the evidence indicates that "house effects" are mostly limited to one specific area: "don't knows." The degree of insistence with which interviewers are trained to probe for answers can markedly affect the frequency of "don't know" and "no opinion" responses (Tom Smith 1978). Thus it is generally safe to compare identical questions across survey organizations, so long as one excludes "don't knows"—as we regularly do. Still, we make a point of referring to the survey organization that fielded each survey item we report, indicating when we have bridged across organizations.

There remains the possibility that responses to identical questions may differ because the questions are embedded in different survey contexts. We are alert to this danger and will point out context effects when we are aware of them. Fortunately, however, contextual artifacts do not seem to be at all widespread in our data. Most reputable survey organizations try to avoid them, often by the administratively easy expedient of making the fewest possible changes in previously used questionnaires.

A final issue that requires attention is some survey organizations' use of "weights" to bring their samples into line with the population's distribution of various characteristics. In reporting percentage point changes of opinion we have made every effort to compare only weighted or only unweighted marginal frequencies. It rarely matters which. But because of this insistence on consistency, some of our Gallup and Harris percentages may differ slightly from those published elsewhere.

2. The "most important problem" question seems to ask, in effect, "What have newspapers and radio and television treated as most important during the last few weeks?" Answers very often fluctuate according to what has appeared in the media, not necessarily corresponding to objective conditions (see Funkhauser 1973a, 1973b; MacKuen 1981; Behr and Iyengar 1985; Delli Carpini and Williams 1987).

3. The on-line Public Opinion Location Library ("POLL") data base of the Roper Center for Public Opinion Research (University of Connecticut, Storrs) has greatly helped to alleviate the problem of data availability, although—at the time we write—the user must still piece together trends from single items, and many early polls are not yet included in the data base.

4. The collection in our survey archive is virtually complete through 1986 or 1987, depending on the survey organization. For the later period, up to 1990 (when we were going to press), it includes only some of the most important and readily available data.

In addition to marginal frequencies, in many cases we have also gathered data on responses by different subgroups of the population: the young and old, women and men, blacks and whites, people of high and low income or education, and the like. These data are used at various points in the book and especially in Chapter 7.

5. Our archive is currently housed at the Center for the Social Sciences, Columbia University, and is available for use by other scholars who contact the authors. It is especially useful for early survey data. The Roper Center's POLL data base, which we ourselves now use, is much more comprehensive for the most recent surveys.

We are grateful to the National Science Foundation (grant no. SES-7912969) and NORC for support in the early stages of data collection, and to Columbia University for its continued support.

6. The one-thousand figure is based upon our last full count of items, done in 1986 (see Shapiro and Page 1988). An early tally and analysis was completed in 1979 (see Page and Shapiro 1982). This book describes a number of trends through 1989 and 1990, but the opinion change data analyzed systematically in this chapter and reported in the tables carry only through 1982.

7. The data used in this chapter are updated and considerably expanded (from 613 items to 1,128) compared with those reported in Page and Shapiro (1982). (The treatment of "don't knows" has also been made fully consistent.) The mix of policies has changed somewhat—now including significantly more domestic than foreign items, for example—largely because of the addition of the predominately domestic Harris data. But the findings remain substantially the same as before, except where noted.

8. "Don't know" responses are excluded in this chapter, and throughout the book, in order to track the *balance* of opinion among those people who express opinions. Changes in proportions of "don't knows" occasionally (though only occasionally) play an important part in altering the balance of opinion, as we will note in particular cases. But if "don't knows" were not generally excluded, they would confuse the presentation and interpretation of percentages favoring or opposing a given policy. A change in responses from 20% "favor," 40% "oppose," and 40% "no opinion," for example, to 30% "favor," 60% "oppose," and only 10% "no opinion," might seem—if only the percentages "favor" or the percentages "oppose" at the two time points were cited—to represent either a big jump in support or a big jump in opposition. By excluding "don't know" responses, we can see that in this example there is no change at all in the *balance of opinion:* a steady 33% of those with opinions favored the policy, and 67% opposed it.

Excluding "don't knows" makes it possible to report trends in a compact fashion by simply citing percentages over time for a single category of response (e.g., "33% favored it in both years," or "the 33% in favor rose to 42% in just one year"), since response frequencies for other substantive categories are simply mirror images of those that are given—100% minus the reported percentages. We will note occasional cases when "don't knows" may constitute a substantively important middle response, or when focusing on a single percentage figure would conceal complex patterns of change among multiple categories of responses.

9. The 6% criterion is appealing for two reasons. First, it allows for survey designs that entail bigger errors than a simple random sample (SRS), for which a 3% criterion would be appropriate; none of the surveys in our collection are actually based on simple random samples (see Lee, Forthofer, and Lorimer 1989). Second, it substitutes, in a rough fashion, for macrotests: we are studying enormous numbers of observed differences in survey responses, among which a good many would be expected to occur by chance under the 3% ($p < .05$ for SRS) criterion. The 6% criterion virtually eliminates chance observations of change ($p < .001$ for SRS). Even within a long time series for a single survey item, the chance of some pair of observations yielding a 3% or 4% difference by chance is quite substantial.

10. In the case of multiply repeated survey questions, instances of change are computed from peaks to troughs and from troughs to peaks of opinion. That is, they are calculated to maximize the amount of measured opinion change. This makes our finding of few large changes all the more impressive.

11. Since we required roughly 95% certainty that a given change was not produced by sampling error before calling it significant, a number of our "insignificant" 3% and 4% changes probably represent real—though slight—movements of opinion. There is no way to avoid uncertainty about the exact number and identity of genuine opinion changes; faced with inevitable sampling error in surveys, one must either count some random deviations as significant changes, or else dismiss some real (but small) cases of opinion change as insignificant. The important point is that any real changes we missed were very small.

12. The findings reported here and in Shapiro and Page (1988) differ from our earlier report (Page and Shapiro 1982) of a nearly equal, roughly 50%, proportion of significant changes for both foreign and domestic issues. As we will see, foreign policy opinions tend to change more quickly than domestic, when they change at all. Thus when we added to our data set many Harris and OPOR surveys with questions repeated at shorter time intervals than other organizations (and with foreign policy questions often repeated right after major international events), they apparently captured about as high a proportion of foreign policy opinion changes as in our preliminary data set, but a lower proportion of the gradual, time-consuming domestic changes. Hence the indication of somewhat higher domestic than foreign opinion stability. This is but one example of how variations in the behavior of survey researchers and pollsters must be taken into account in interpreting their data.

13. Here and elsewhere, we report some statistical tests that treat our aggregate opinion change cases as a random sample from a hypothetical population of survey measures that would be produced by repeatedly conducting surveys under the same technical, economic, and political conditions that affect what kinds of questions are asked, and when.

14. As we will see in Chapter 5, after the 1950s opinion on the "active part" question did, in fact, change somewhat.

15. By the same token, the time intervals on horizontal axes should ideally be presented in standardized ways so that rates of opinion change are portrayed without distortion: that is, slow changes should look gradual and rapid changes should be more steeply sloped. This is hard to accomplish, however, when graphing, on pages of constant width, time series that vary in duration from a few weeks to several decades, and when working with available technology. Readers should be alert to variations from one graph to another in the length of time covered.

16. A further technical problem is that a straight-line, connect-the-dot graph implies a perfectly linear movement of opinion between observed points, but, of course, we cannot be sure what went on between surveys while no survey researcher was watching. Still, the linear assumption is the most parsimonious that can be made and is generally plausible. Often our graphs will connect far-apart dots with straight but broken or fuzzy lines, which give a good estimate of movement between points but also acknowledge a degree of uncertainty.

17. We can speculate that opinion may have been *less* volatile before pervasive mass media exposed millions of people, with higher levels of education, simultaneously to new preference-changing information. De Tocqueville, for one, rejected the idea that Americans of the 1830s were "constantly changing their opinions and feelings"—though he thought that might be true of small democracies in which the whole community could be assembled in a public place and "excited at will" (just as some might claim the media affect the modern global village). What struck him was "the difficulty of shaking the majority in an opinion once conceived" (de Tocqueville 1945 [1835, 1840], 2:271, 272).

On the other hand, the United States was still relatively small and homogeneous in the Founders' day. As Jeffrey Tulis, Joseph Bessette, and others have suggested to us, the present stability and rationality of American public opinion could well reflect the successful development of the "extensive commercial republic" that Madison and the other Founders established.

18. We examined more than 3,300 pairs of time points for our 473 change items, which averaged 3.5 time points per survey question; and more than 1,000 for the 655 no-change items, averaging about 2.5 time points per question.

19. When there are more than two observations that do not fall on a perfectly straight line, our technique generally gives a slightly higher estimated rate of change than does the method of regressing levels of opinion on a time variable (see Taylor 1980). The latter method is ordinarily preferable, but it would have been cumbersome to perform separate regressions for each of our hundreds of instances of change, and the difference is usually small. For two-point time series the results are identical.

The calculation of rates is sensitive to the frequency with which survey questions are asked; we take this into account in discussing fluctuations and gradual versus non-gradual changes. Of course, it is always possible that abrupt opinion changes may occur while no surveys are in the field, but, as we suggested, pollsters' incentives to detect change reduce the likelihood of this.

20. Even public opinion concerning support for presidents or presidential candidates, perceptions of economic conditions, and assessments of the nation's "most important problem," all of which fluctuate much more than collective policy preferences, tend to do so in understandable and predictable (indeed, reasonable) ways. Numerous studies (e.g.,

Mueller 1970; Brody and Page 1975; Kernell 1978; Shapiro and Conforto 1980; MacKuen 1983) have shown that economic conditions, wars, and good or bad news about other events can largely explain the ups and downs in presidential popularity. Reports and commentaries about campaign events and the words and deeds of presidential candidates affect levels of candidate support (e.g., Bartels 1988; Fan, 1988; Shapiro et al. 1990a, 1990b). Changes in inflation and unemployment are readily noticed and perceived as serious problems with broad consequences (Hibbs 1979; Shapiro and Conforto 1980). And, as we noted earlier, the public's response to the "most important problem" question can be predicted by media reports about real-world events and conditions.

21. We cannot be sure from these data alone that the change from 1942 to 1956 (while the question was not asked) was smooth and linear, but the trends on related items suggest that it was; see Chapter 3.

Chapter Three

1. Except where otherwise indicated, all the percentage figures in this book exclude "no opinion" and "don't know" responses so that we may easily compare the balance of opinion at different times among those with opinions.

2. For this and certain other civil rights issues, we deviate from our usual insistence on identical question wording, and infer trends from questions that switched from the early use of the term "Negro" to later use of "black." (Sometimes apparently interviewers were allowed to use whichever term seemed appropriate in a given interview.) We believe this to be a rare instance in which identity of meaning was best assured by changing wording rather than keeping it the same.

3. One reason the Gallup disapproval figures were somewhat higher than those of NORC is probably that making intermarriage a "crime" implies harsher sanctions than having "laws against" it. Opposition to laws against interracial marriage has now reached the same level as the public's support for federal antilynching laws in the 1940s (Gallup).

4. This SRC/CPS item suffers, however, from a long and complicated prologue— "As you may know, Congress passed a bill . . ."—that may have caused confusion and introduced extraneous factors; moreover, the 1964 phrase "white people" was later changed to "anybody else," which may have inflated support.

5. Northern whites have long been especially sensitive to large-scale neighborhood integration (see Hyman and Sheatsley 1956, p. 37), and feelings can run high, as the racial violence at the end of the 1980s in Bensonhurst and Howard Beach, New York, illustrated.

6. Schuman et al. (1985, p. 125), however, show that from 1942 to 1944 opinion already had begun to change in the *South,* with as yet no change in the North—where more than half the respondents already believed in equal intelligence of blacks and whites. Both these studies support our main point, that opinion change was already under way during World War II. The same point is indicated by Sheatsley's (1966, n. 7) assertion that the NORC question concerning whites and Negroes attending the "same schools" was asked in 1944 and 1946, showing a trend toward racial equality; but we have been unable to find any other record of such data.

7. The comparison is complicated by the fact that in 1954 Stouffer used a split-half sample, with surveys by both NORC and Gallup. Since the response frequencies for the two surveys were virtually identical, we have combined them, deviating from our usual practice of comparing only items fielded by the same organization. Some other comparisons involving items fielded first by Gallup or Roper and then by NORC-GSS are

made and noted elsewhere in the book. As we indicated in Chap. 2, our exclusion of "don't know" responses overcomes the main hazard of cross-organization comparisons.

8. The 1963 survey closely (and purposely) followed President Kennedy's assassination, which may have affected the results—perhaps increasing anti-Communist responses and obscuring an even stronger liberal trend up to that time.

9. This comparison across two different survey organizations appears to be sound; we compared other identical questions asked at approximately the same time by Gallup and OPOR, and found (once "don't knows" were excluded) that the percentages were within normal sampling error of each other.

10. In the early years, at least, Communists were probably the main referent of the term "radicals." When asked in a February 1939 Gallup survey whether Communists or Nazis living in this country were the greater danger, 54% of the respondents said Communists, 46% Nazis. A June 1938 survey found that communism was thought worse than fascism, 58%–42%. During the war, Nazis presumably aroused more concern.

11. In the same 1977 survey in which the GSS found 66% favoring a woman's right to work according to the Gallup wording, it found a dramatically lower 36% approval according to a variant question: "If there is a limited number of jobs, do you approve or disapprove of a married woman holding a job in business or industry when her husband is able to support her?" The effect of the reference to a limited number of jobs (and to the slightly more definite *ability*, rather than *capacity*, to support) may have been accentuated by a questionnaire context effect: having both questions in one survey emphasized the contrast between them.

12. A minor exception is the low point of 60% approval in June 1978, but this came in response to a special Gallup telephone survey, which apparently tended to tap a more Republican and conservative sample than face-to-face interviews did (Mansbridge 1986, p. 209).

13. We are indebted to Susan Sherman Karplus for research assistance on the abortion issue, which is drawn upon in this and the following paragraphs (see Karplus 1979).

14. Other NORC-GSS items reveal distinctions in support for ending a patient's life based on a decision by a board of doctors, or (by the patient's own decision) due to financial bankruptcy, dishonor, or simply being tired of living.

Chapter Four

1. It might be argued that the 1935 level of support is overstated because the word "pensions" was ambiguous at that time and the focus on the "needy" did not exactly correspond with the universalistic Social Security scheme, but other data largely overcome this objection.

2. The fact that these Trendex (General Electric–sponsored) surveys were based on telephone directory samples rather than random digit dialing does not seem seriously to have affected the trend results, though some caution is appropriate in drawing inferences about *levels* of opinion (see Black 1983).

3. See the *Philadelphia Inquirer*, August 7, 1967.

4. This range actually represented *stable* preferences. The curious fluctuations in responses can be attributed to a context effect: the "present system" consistently received more support when the question was asked after a series of inquiries about the respondent's own medical care and costs; NHI narrowly won when the question was asked with no medical questions preceding it (Roper 1990).

5. As we have noted before, shifting referents like those in these items ("more"

action is relative to current activity) mean that changing responses can be consistent with stable levels of policy preferences in the face of real or perceived changes in government activity.

6. The interpretation of this and other Roper/NORC-GSS spending items is complicated by the fact that they do not explicitly mention government; despite the prologue that "we" face many difficult problems, people might conceivably respond in terms of private spending. The largely similar results on Trendex surveys that do specify "government" spending, however, suggests that most respondents interpret ROPER/NORC-GSS items in the same way. There remains ambiguity about which *level* or levels of government—federal, state, or local—respondents have in mind. Even the best survey researchers sometimes neglect important political distinctions that the public may be quite capable of responding to.

7. Since these Trendex surveys were not based on random digit dialing, they may have overrepresented upper-SES, high-education citizens, who—as will be seen in Chapter 7—often change their aggregate preferences most because they are exposed to the most new information. The greater fluctuation in Trendex than Roper and NORC-GSS responses also may reflect sampling error from smaller Trendex samples.

8. When NORC-GSS asked in 1990 about "assistance to big cities" instead of "solving problems" in them, only 26% (vs. 58%) said "too little" was being spent, suggesting a mistrust of city governments (see Rasinski 1989).

9. Pollsters, like the mass media (Parenti 1986), have tended to show more concern with the faults of labor unions, and with proposed restrictions on them, than with positive aspects (see Kornhauser 1946). In Chapter 9 we will suggest that a tilt toward capital, as opposed to labor, is characteristic of the U.S. information system.

10. The reason for U.S. pollsters' perennial obsession with inflation rather than unemployment may have to do with a political climate more sympathetic to capital than to labor. In the case of the early years, part of the explanation is easy: NORC surveys on inflation and economic controls were sponsored by the U.S. Office of Price Administration.

11. Responses to the massive Harris energy and inflation surveys of the 1970s may be especially subject to question-wording and questionnaire-context effects. The sheer number of energy-related items, the long factual (or purportedly factual) prologues, and the many specific policy suggestions embedded in the questions may have affected citizens' answers, biasing estimates of the public's policy preferences. If such effects remained constant from one Harris survey to another, assessments of trends over time would still be valid; but we cannot rule out the possibility that some trend results are artifacts of the design of these particular surveys.

12. Other data from about the same time also show public willingness or eagerness to cut spending on space, agriculture, welfare, and certain other programs apparently not covered in this survey. Likewise, other surveys demonstrate public receptivity to various kinds of loophole closing, improved IRS enforcement, users' fees, and other revenue-raising measures.

13. The impression that the public is fiscally irresponsible is partly an artifact of pollsters asking about taxes and spending independently, without inquiring into trade-offs between the two (see Welch 1985; Ladd et al. 1979; Citrin 1979; Tuchfarber, Oldendick, and Bishop 1984). NORC-GSS experiments indicate that when trade-offs are implicitly suggested by questionnaire context (i.e., by asking about taxes after spending questions, or vice versa), responses are affected.

14. Most or all of these Harris changes may have resulted from the timing of the May 1974 survey, just after the cruel taxpaying month of April—when citizens are especially sensitive to their own tax burdens and amenable to shifting the weight to others. The January 1975 drops in objections to personal taxes and in zeal to raise companies' taxes and close loopholes may just reflect a return to normal attitudes. Only the rise in support for an income tax cut remains an anomaly, perhaps signaling a genuine long-term change.

15. Curiously, ABC surveys showed an extremely sharp 29% rise (from 45% to 74%) in the percentage who felt taxes were "too high" from January to May 1985, and then a drop to 61% by June. No other survey data are available to confirm or disconfirm this change (the time period did not overlap with NORC-GSS, for example), but we are aware of no sampling or other methodological problems to throw doubt on its reality. Very likely, ABC picked up a temporarily heightened consciousness of tax burdens immediately after the taxpaying month of April, just as happened with the 1974–1975 Harris surveys.

16. These apparent changes in preferences, however, may have resulted from the omission in the prologue to the 1951 question of any reference to being a member of Congress; respondents may have reported their (high) perceptions of actual current tax rates in that year rather than their preferred lower rates.

17. Attitudes about U.S. territories and statehood have had their own wrinkles as well as connections with foreign policy. Large majorities in Gallup polls have approved of independence or statehood for Puerto Rico (which, however, has seemed content with its commonwealth status). For more than a decade before the joint admission deal of 1959, Alaska and Hawaii both enjoyed very high public support for admission to statehood: about 85% and 80%, respectively (Gallup). Backing for Hawaiian statehood jumped up about 10% when the Korean War highlighted the islands' strategic importance.

Chapter Five

1. This may have changed. The fact is that the State Department tracks public opinion and puts considerable effort into analyzing it. As Graham (1989b) points out, the political advisers to presidents tend to be especially sensitive to public opinion.

2. For example, Graham (1988) shows that the public has had a good general understanding of nuclear weapons, lacking knowledge only of technical details and jargon. Comparable data for judging changes of policy knowledge over time are difficult to obtain. One piece of evidence is that percentages of "don't know" and "no opinion" responses have appeared to drop a bit since the late 1960s; this applies to both domestic and foreign policy issues (Shapiro 1982, pp. 80–81; Shapiro and Mahajan 1986, pp. 56–58; but see S. Bennett 1989 on certain domestic issues).

3. The interpretation of opinion data about internationalism depends partly upon the treatment of "don't know" and "no opinion" responses. Here, as throughout the book, we have computed percentages based on the number of respondents who gave definite answers—excluding "don't knows"—in order to reveal the balance of opinion among those with opinions. In certain cases, however, "don't know" responses may be substantively important, and some have argued that this is such a case: that anyone who is unsure whether the United States should take an active part thereby rejects internationalism.

If uncertain respondents are counted as isolationists, the internationalist majority shrinks somewhat, dropping about five percentage points, to the 61%–78% range, during most of the 1945–1990 period. But it is by no means clear that those saying "don't know" should be treated this way. Rather than rejecting internationalism or holding no opinions, they may be ambivalent about the relative importance of domestic versus foreign affairs, or unsure whether U.S. foreign policy has actually been beneficial—thus standing about halfway between the activist and anti-activist response options. (By the same token, anti-activist responses, scorned by foreign policy elites as backward and ignorant, may, of course, represent a reasoned position that domestic priorities should come first and/or that current U.S. foreign policies are doing the world more harm than good.) In any case, even when "don't knows" are treated as isolationists, the internationalists have constituted a substantial majority throughout virtually the entire period in which these questions have been asked.

4. NORC, for some reason, apparently substituted "will" for Gallup's "would," and "stay" for "stayed."

5. Caspary (1970, pp. 536–37), stating that he relies only on data "gathered by" NORC (and apparently including "don't knows"), reports virtually unchanging preferences during the 1942–1954 period. We are almost certain that his wartime data include polls conducted by at least one organization other than NORC, however (probably using differently worded Gallup or OPOR questions), since we have been unable to find any other traces of such questions in NORC surveys conducted before October 1945 (see also Graham 1989b, pp. 127–128; Niemi et al. 1989, p. 53).

6. Davies (1952, p. 788) similarly questions the "superior sensitivity" or ability of any class or group on the grounds that all tend to react to events in parallel fashion.

7. In many foreign policy cases, it is essential to know the precise dates of surveys and events in order to pin down what influenced public opinion. We have given in parentheses several exact interviewing periods so that the reader can be sure what preceded what.

8. A very minor example of Rooseveltian duplicity came to light with Robert Butow's 1979 discovery of the "Roosevelt tapes." Pressed at an October 4, 1940, news conference to react to the Japanese prime minister's remark that the United States should recognize the "new era" in the Far East and abandon its bases there, Roosevelt said he could not comment in any way because he hadn't seen the remark. Shortly afterward he was recorded telling Cordell Hull, "I saw the dispatch itself. . . . but I'm inclined to think that complete silence is the best thing—no comment. Don't you?" (Four days later he remarked, "This country is ready to pull the trigger if the Japs do anything. I mean we won't stand any nonsense, public opinion won't" [S. Roberts 1988].)

9. A split ballot variant item excluding the phrase "which they have destroyed" produced an 18% change in responses from July to April, with 61% rising to 79% favoring the policy. At each time point, inclusion of the phrase won 7%–10% more support. This does not just demonstrate the effect of providing one-sided information in a survey question; it probably reflects the public's greater support for city-specific restitution than for wholesale donation of German labor to Russia.

10. These are complex and sometimes confusing data. Even Cantril with Strunk (1951) misses some slight wording variations (e.g., "when" the war is over vs. "after" the war) in his own OPOR surveys, judging by our copies of the original OPOR questionnaires. Adding to the confusion, early OPOR surveys were apparently fielded by Gallup (see J. Converse 1987; Caspary 1968, pp. 26–27; Cantril with Strunk 1951, pp. 370–372; Walsh 1947, pp. 186, 190).

11. Caspary's figures include "don't knows" in the percentage base but do not report their frequency. Our own breakdowns of NORC data, excluding "don't knows," are not yet complete. The education gaps in opinion *levels* should be less when "don't knows" are excluded but this is less likely to affect *trends*.

12. Tom Graham points out that the role of opposition parties and political leaders is crucial. Henry Wallace, for example, never tailored his peace message to fit with preexisting ideas of the public. Graham (1989b) recounts a number of striking post–World War II cases in which elite advocates of arms control (including Presidents Kennedy and Carter as well as early backers of international control of atomic energy and of test bans) failed to understand public opinion well enough to frame appealing policy alternatives, thereby leaving the public open to persuasion by others.

13. These issues are further discussed in Leigh (1976), which emphasizes the beneficial effects of leadership in building public support for the Marshall Plan, and in Levering (1978) and Foster (1983), which take a similar tack. Contrast Kolko (1968) and LaFeber (1985). Yergin (1977) offers a balanced account that notes some important ways in which the public was misled. John Gaddis, though the father of cold war "postrevisionism," nonetheless acknowledges that manipulation of opinion about specific policies was widespread (1983, pp. 178, 181).

14. One caveat: Davies's postspeech sample was very small, including only 16% of the total 999 respondents.

Davies (1952) presents a concise and compelling—and, in the literature, quite unusual—argument that "the general public reacts rationally to its changing political and economic environment" (p. 777). In addition to the Malik truce talk example, he offers evidence from SRC interviews done just before and after the February 4, 1948, slump in the grain market: the 50% of respondents who before the slump had expected a general price rise dropped to 15% afterward, consistent with reasonable inferences from the event. Here, too, virtually all subgroups moved in the same way; "(t)he commodity market slump appears mediately or immediately to have caught the attention of, and had meaning for, the poor, unlettered, unskilled individual just as it did for the elite" (pp. 778–779).

15. Here and elsewhere, we have tried to flag all unexplained changes in order to make clear that the vast majority of opinion changes in our data are easily explicable and understandable. The exceptions are not very troubling; among our hundreds of cases one would expect a few large observed changes to reflect sampling error, and in some instances of real opinion change we may simply have overlooked the reasons.

16. Erskine (1964, p. 165) lists a January 1936 *release* date; Foster (1983, p. 19) reports this as a 1935 poll.

17. We infer a drop in U.N. support after October 1949, when 75% said the United Nations had done a good job "in trying to settle *world problems*" (our emphasis), because that former wording was more sweeping and should have produced *lower* percentages at a given level of support.

Chapter Six

1. It is also our impression that there were *fewer* cases of change relative to stable opinions in the 1953–1962 period, but there is no convenient way to count cases of stability in order to substantiate this. The relative paucity of survey data during this period might itself be taken as a sign of less opinion change, since pollsters tend to ask more questions when they are finding interesting changes. But extraneous factors also affect the

frequency of polling. The intensive government-sponsored NORC foreign policy surveys, for example, were discontinued in the 1950s when some members of Congress complained that they constituted interference in domestic politics.

2. We thank Eugene Wittkopf for reminding us of the December 1956 repetition, which we originally excluded because of a varying introduction to the question; the basic question wordings are identical.

3. For the sake of comparability between surveys, these data (and, as noted in Chap. 2, some data elsewhere in the book) are unweighted. Hence the percentage figures may differ slightly from those that others have published.

4. The 1960 NES codebook is ambiguous on precise question wording compared to 1956 and 1958; we assume that the questions were identical. Several NES questions have varied from one survey to another in minor ways that prevent firm inferences about changes over time, so that they have not been included in our discussions.

5. In early 1965, as throughout the war, large majorities of Americans favored negotiations. Gallup surveys in January and February revealed that fully 88% would like to see LBJ "try to arrange a conference with leaders of Southeast Asia and China to see if a peace agreement can be worked out." Desire for negotiated settlements (with certain exceptions during World War II) is a pervasive pattern in American public opinion. The question about "present policy" is another example of a shifting referent: current policy was changing rapidly, so that altered survey responses did not necessarily reflect any change in the public's preferences.

6. The lengthy interviewing periods for some SRC/CPS surveys make it difficult to ascertain the state of opinion at any one moment and relate it to specific events. It is possible to partition the data by interview date, but comparable samples cannot be guaranteed.

7. The estimated coefficients reported below for the impact of public opinion on policy are presumably depressed by measurement errors caused by these variant question wordings. That is, the true relationships are probably stronger than reported. Ideally, dummy variables would be used to take account of question wording effects, but in this case there are too many minor variations in wording (and no compelling way to group them) to permit this approach.

8. In six surveys between 1974 and 1983, Roper repeatedly found majorities (ranging from 51% to 66%) wanting to "strengthen our ties" with Canada—versus "continu(ing)" as things were or "lessen(ing)" commitments—in clear contrast to the much smaller fractions of the public wanting to strengthen ties with Japan, India, France, West Germany, or England. These data, like others, show increasing support for international involvement by 1980.

9. Harris, in May 1971, recorded an even larger 64% in favor of admission, with only 36% opposed. The Harris question began with a possibly biasing (though factually accurate) prologue: "Each year, the United Nations has considered admitting Communist China to membership."

10. We cannot be sure of the exact magnitude or timing of the above opinion changes because of irritating ambiguities and/or errors in Harris releases concerning interview dates and question wordings.

11. Copies of the original NORC questionnaires and codebooks, however, reveal several slight variations in the wording of this question.

In accord with our usual practice, the above discussion excludes "don't knows" and respondents who were filtered out (had not "heard or read . . .") in the base for percentages, but we have included "both" and "neither" as substantive responses. The exclusion of "don't knows" is especially important because of variations (apparently not noticed by Gilboa) in the use of filter questions here.

12. See Gilboa 1987, pp. 47–48. Here again we have excluded "don't know," "no opinion," and "not sure" responses but included "both" and "neither" as being clearly substantive responses.

13. Changing responses to such "screener" items, like variations in proportions of "don't knows," complicate the tracking of collective opinion changes over time. We can do no better than to compare the opinions of "aware" opinion-holding groups at different times, even though those populations may differ from one survey to another. We are chiefly interested in the balance of opinion among those with opinions.

14. Initially belligerent reactions to reports of foreign aggression are not uncommon in our data, in connection with World War II, the wars in Korea and Vietnam, and various international crises. We take it as consistent with collective rationality that, after further deliberation, the public has sometimes (e.g., in the case of Pearl Harbor) kept on favoring forceful responses, but other times (e.g., after the Tet offensive or the marine bombing in Lebanon or the taking of hostages in Iran) has moved toward favoring peaceful resolution of disputes. Circumstances vary. To sort them out can take time.

15. Fan (1988) used an innovative automated content analysis method to explore the impact of mass media upon public opinion changes in the Lebanon troops case, and offered a general model of media influences that is broadly consistent with our own account—not, however, distinguishing among different news *sources* as is done in Chapter 8, below.

16. The 1987 survey that reported 56% pro-Israel sympathy is listed as conducted by Roper and the American Jewish Committee (AJC). An April 1988 survey that yielded a 44% sympathy figure was also done by Roper/AJC, indicating a real drop from 1987 to 1988 regardless of any possible inflation in measured pro-Israel sentiment due to AJC participation.

17. Harris reported in 1973 and 1974 that 60% and 61% favored recognition of Cuba, but these results were marred by a slanted prologue (. . . "with the war in Vietnam over and with relations with communist Russia and China getting better . . .").

18. Tom Graham has pointed out to us that the CPD may have deliberately exaggerated its influence upon the public in order to intimidate political opponents, and, furthermore, that the opinion movement in a hawkish direction was facilitated by the ineptness of the Carter administration's political strategy.

19. The higher level of approval for a SALT II in Harris data (80%) than in Roper (63%) probably reflects two differences between the survey questions: Roper specified "with Russia," a less attractive option than the possibly multilateral agreement evoked by Harris; and Harris specified an "arms control" agreement, more attractive than the still unfamiliar "SALT" acronym used by Roper. Question wording affects the meaning of questions and the nature of answers. Note, however, the similarity of *trends*.

20. The "*SALT II*" acronym undoubtedly confused the public. Still, NBC tracked an enormous rise in the salience of the treaty between March 1979, when only 19% said they had enough information to have an opinion about it, and October, when 51% did. This and the CBS/*NYT* figures of 36% for June and 45% for November are consistent with a steep and more or less linear increase in public attention and knowledge as President Carter signed the treaty and the issue became prominent in the media. See Graham 1988 and our discussion of information levels in Chapter 1.

21. We exclude "not sures." The figure of 36% favoring defense cutbacks fell to 25% (still a bit more than the 22% for expansion) when the same question was repeated outside the domestic spending context and after a series of foreign policy questions (see Rielly 1983, pp. 28–29).

22. We are indebted to Andrew Rojecki for use of his careful study of freeze coverage by *Time* magazine.

23. Brody (1984) and Brody and Shapiro (1989a and 1989b) discuss this in the context of crisis-based "rallies" in presidential popularity.

24. Similarly, little media attention or public opinion polling (hence, little space in this book) has been devoted to human rights abroad, especially in places where that subject would be inconvenient to U.S. foreign policy. Abuses by such friendly dictators as Chiang, Franco, Rhee, Batista, Trujillo, Somoza, Shah Pahlevi, Duvalier, Marcos, and Doe—and, while he was still a CIA asset, Noriega—have tended to go unremarked except in retrospect. When the issue of human rights is raised, it has often been directed at Communist or Third-World nationalist countries for political purposes (see Geyer and Shapiro 1988).

Chapter Seven

1. For partial exceptions see Miller et al. 1980, and Miller and Traugott 1989, but the wordings of some of their items vary over time. Thorough and impressive analyses of subgroup trends on particular large sets of issues include Tom Graham (1989b) and Weil (1985, 1989).

2. The very numerous pairs of survey observations were laboriously compared by hand, since the time and expense required to make all 3,000 subgroup time trends machine readable and to design a specialized computer program to analyze them would have been prohibitive. This means, however, that some minor human errors occurred in the results reported in Shapiro and Page (1984). Upon rechecking, we have determined that the only serious error was that regarding occupational categories, which is noted below and corrected in table 7.1. The NORC-GSS data analyzed in table 7.2, of course, are all computerized, and the analysis is replicable from the original raw data using the latest GSS Cumulative File (1972–present), available from the ICPSR or the Roper Center.

3. For many of the categories of subgroupings we are comparing, a ten percentage point difference would be statistically significant at slightly better than the .05 confidence level, assuming subgroup n's of 500, 50%–50% opinion splits, and simple random sampling (SRS). Although the surveys examined are not based strictly upon SRS, most of the opinion splits are not fifty-fifty and, therefore, require smaller differences to reach significance.

4. By the definition of the .05 confidence level, nearly 95% of the cases that just fail to reach that level would nonetheless be expected to represent real differences. Moreover, for some of the larger subgroupings, 8% differences are in fact statistically significant at the .05 level, assuming SRS and even opinion splits.

5. Eight percent subgroup differences generally approximate a .10 level of statistical significance, though in some cases (e.g., with subgroups including only about 100 survey respondents) the level is closer to .20.

6. In some cases of small subgroup categories, the cut-off point for significant differences was set at higher levels: as high as 13%, for example, in the case of small racial groupings.

7. The higher figure of 11.8% for occupational groups, reported in Shapiro and Page (1984, p. 36), is erroneous. It resulted from the use of Gallup occupational breakdowns for which subgroup n's were not reported; we assumed that the "clerical and sales" category included approximately 300 respondents, but Gallup's more recent publications indicate that it often includes barely over 100 people. Application of the 10% criterion (rather than a more appropriate 13% or so) to such a small group led to the inclusion of many random opinion differences as being significant, and nearly doubled the observed frequency of differences in occupational subgroup trends.

The relatively high (8.4%) frequency of divergent trends between Protestants and Catholics may reflect Gallup's tendency to report religious breakdowns only on issues where religion is most relevant.

8. Other considerations bolster this point further. Precise statistical corrections for cluster sampling, especially in conjunction with the small subgroup N's for the variables with four or more categories (and for some with relatively large proportions of missing data, like occupation and income), would almost certainly require that a number of these differences be excluded from our table as not actually statistically significant. (For the same reason, we must be cautious in interpreting differences among groupings in table 7.1.) Also, our method separates the up-and-down movements in fluctuations of opinion, so that if two parallel subgroup trends diverged for a single time period only but then returned to normal—as often happened in our data—then two divergent movements were counted, even though the long-term parallelism was arguably more important. Finally, some subgroup differences in trends are artifacts of floor or ceiling effects, in which one or more subgroups simply could not change opinion any further in the direction in which others were doing so.

9. True, offsetting opinion changes by different subgroups can occur (see Franklin and Kosaki 1989 for an interesting example), but we have found that such movements are uncommon and generally temporary. Most differential subgroup changes occur when there is also change in overall collective public opinion.

10. In order to check for newly emerging or disappearing subgroup differences, we also did our multivariate analyses of the group bases of individuals' opinions on the various issues separately for the periods before and after 1981. There were no differences of importance.

11. For each survey item we did a multivariate analysis of individuals' opinions, controlling for race (black, white), gender, region (Northeast, South, North Central, West), education (less than high school, high school graduate, some college, college graduate), income (quartiles), community of residence (urban, suburban, town, rural), and age (four groups).

12. The small sample size for blacks at each time point introduces some randomness.

13. The small estimated differences on noneconomic issues that remain after controlling for education may be artifacts of measurement errors (including imperfect categorization of the length of schooling and failure to distinguish among types of schools) in the education variable.

14. With our data and resources, we could not fully explore opinion differences among different Protestant sects and denominations, such as the distinctive views of fundamentalists. See Jelen (1989).

15. To more confidently sort out the role of party in these opinion trends would require panel data and/or a simultaneous equation analysis in which party identification

was specified as endogenous (see Brody and Page 1972; Markus and Converse 1979; Page and Jones 1979; Fiorina 1981).

16. The South looks less clearly conservative when compared with a "non-South" that lumps together the rather conservative Midwest or North Central region with the West and Northeast, as in Cotter and Stovall 1990. See E. Black and Black 1987; Key 1949, 1961.

17. Conversely, income and status effects diminish substantially once education is controlled.

18. This may be a slight underestimate, however, since only three educational groups were compared in this analysis; when college graduates are examined separately from those with some college, more distinctive trends appear.

19. The ongoing investigations of exposure and acceptance effects by Zaller (1987, 1990b) and others are quite valuable. We cannot undertake a comparable analysis here, because crucial data on information and exposure levels are often unavailable. (Even if they were available, it would be a mind-boggling task to use them to analyze trends over time in scores or hundreds of survey items.) In any case, such an analysis does not appear to be necessary for our purposes.

20. Hence our special interest in the partisan flip-flops on civil rights and foreign policy attitudes. One particularly striking case of opinion divergence occurred between 1977 and 1988: nonsmokers strongly increased their support for a "complete ban on cigarette advertising" (from 47% to 67% in favor), while smokers firmly resisted the trend, going only from 30% to 36% in favor (Gallup). For a further discussion of this apparent manifestation of self-interest, see Green and Gerken (1989).

Chapter Eight

1. In order to present a full and accurate picture of opinion change, we have attempted to mention as many significant changes as possible (explicable or not), in all the policy areas we discussed. The abbreviated treatment in Chapter 4 of political institutions and domestic aspects of foreign policy required us to omit full descriptions of some instances of opinion change, but those instances did not differ in nature or dynamics from the others.

2. On broad societal and economic changes and their consequences, see Ginsberg 1972, 1973; Jacobs and Shapiro 1989; Mayer 1990.

3. This assumes that the way in which citizens evaluate their needs is not itself manipulated. See Bartels's (1990) intriguing analysis of public opinion, enlightened ical interests, and "false consciousness."

4. The overtime Pearson correlation between percentage of the public favoring capital punishment and the violent crime rate was just over .8 ($p < .05$; for the murder rate, $r = .5, p < .07$.) Similarly, the proportion of the public saying court treatment of criminals was "not harsh enough" correlated highly with the violent crime rate ($r = .8, p < .05$) and with the murder rate ($r = .7, p < .05$). See Chapter 3, figure 3.6. Crime rates were taken from Stanley and Niemi (1990, p. 372) table 12–20, which relied on the *Statistical Abstract of the United States*.

5. This coding required an enormous effort—more than 10,000 hours of work. We hope that computer-assisted coding will make such essential data collection easier in the future, but current technology has not yet reached that point (see Nacos et al. 1991).

6. In this table, for the sake of clarity, we have omitted the estimates of effects for pre-t_1 news, which mostly show a negative impact. That is, when news is very favorable to a

particular policy just before the first survey and then turns neutral before the second survey, public support tends to drop, indicating that part of the effect of news is temporary. The results presented here should be read as estimates of the effects of current news, controlling for past news.

7. On related issues, see Brody and Shapiro (1989a, 1989b) and Graham (1989b). Carmines and Stimson (1989) demonstrate another kind of party influence on opinion: beginning in the 1950s the congressional parties (and, ultimately, presidential candidates) turned race into an issue dividing Republicans and Democrats. No doubt, parties also help "frame" issues.

8. Despite the fact that *source credibility* has long been found important in experimental research on communications, only recently has it been examined in terms of real-world influences on public opinion. See the works cited below in the section on news commentary, and Hovland and Weiss (1951), Hovland (1954), McGuire (1986), Sternthal, Phillips, and Dholakia (1978), and Wu and Shaffer (1987).

9. This estimate still did not quite reach statistical significance at the .05 level by a two-tailed test, but our finding of strong popular-president effects in the newspaper study (Page and Shapiro 1984), and our interpretive analysis of individual cases in both studies, convince us that this is a meaningful result.

Chapter Nine

1. This analogy was suggested by Philip Shrodt in a personal communication, September 1988.

2. A standard of equal representation of *all possible* information and interpretations would make little sense, even if one could enumerate all possible views; it would dictate that Nazi and astrological interpretations of events should be given equal time with those of contemporary liberals and conservatives. By contrast, representative sampling from a universe of *all existing* facts and ideas would mean that unbiased news would consist mostly of reports of ordinary people eating and sleeping and working, and that currently conventional ideas (and therefore the status quo) would have a big advantage.

A fully worked out concept of unbiased news would probably have to include criteria of *relevance,* specifying what kinds of information are useful for making political decisions—no simple matter; and also criteria of interpretations' *correctness*—an even harder matter. Thus our own assessment of biases (like those of other observers) necessarily depends upon what we see as true and what we see as useful, based on our own systems of beliefs and values—which are certainly not independent of the twentieth-century American society in which we live.

Chapter Ten

1. One further challenge to the reality and measurability of public opinion comes from the fact that some survey respondents can be persuaded to offer opinions about nonexistent, fictitious congressional policies. In these cases, we believe that people use available cues from the survey question (along with their background knowledge) to guess what Congress has done and then react to it. It is not at all clear that collective responses to such questions are totally meaningless; they may actually provide some information about the public's evaluation of whatever legislation exists on the topic in question. But in any case, these results tell us little about the public's responses to real policy alternatives—where much more information is available, "don't know" answers are far fewer, and collective responses are stable and fit into coherent patterns with other issues.

2. A different reason that democracy might be impossible or undefined is related to Arrow's (1963) (im)possibility theorem (see Barry and Hardin 1982). Since most of our survey questions elicited only "favor" or "oppose" responses to stated policies, or choices between two policies—rather than preference rankings among several policies, let alone rankings of alternative social states—we can tell little or nothing about whether or not Americans' preference profiles have generally been such that there have existed Condorcet winners (packages of policies that could defeat all other packages by majority vote in pairwise comparisons), or whether there have been cyclical majorities. This is an important question worth investigating through surveys designed for the purpose.

Our conjecture is similar to that of Thomas Schwartz (1986): even if Condorcet winners do not generally exist, cycles may be restricted to a relatively small set of alternatives (e.g., a "top cycle set"), so that it is reasonable to speak of any member of that set—perhaps reached through a structure-induced equilibrium—as constituting a democratic outcome. Given the nature of our data, we have had to proceed issue by issue, implicitly treating preferences as separable.

3. As we noted earlier, the present condition of public opinion may reflect the success of the Founders' experiment: the great increase in prosperity, the spread of public education, the development of mass media of communications, and other changes during the past 200 years of American history. Lacking representative national survey data from the eighteenth and nineteenth centuries, we cannot tell for sure. The best historical research, however, reveals nothing at odds with our present-day conclusions concerning the public's collective capacities. (For a review, see Jacobs and Shapiro 1989.)

4. The fact that public opinion is generally stable and changes in predictable and reasonable ways does not, of course, dispose of the Founders' concern that majority opinion might be dangerous to "rights," especially property rights: that ordinary citizens might come up with "improper or wicked" projects like the printing of paper money (Madison, Federalist Paper no. 10, in A. Hamilton et al. 1961 [1787–1788], p. 84). Nor does it dispose of de Tocqueville's (1945 [1835, 1840]) fear of "tyranny of the majority," which amounts to much the same thing. But in our secular times, skeptical of absolutes and sensitive to trade-offs, it is not easy to specify rights that deserve complete protection against majority rule. If one focuses on the constitutional provisions in highest repute among libertarians (freedom of speech, assembly, the press, religious observance, privacy and the like), the aggregate survey data and other evidence leave it far from clear that the general public has been markedly less supportive of such rights than have decision-making elites and courts. (See Gibson 1988 on the crucial policy role of elites in the McCarthy period.)

5. It does not follow that we favor instant popular referenda on issues. The rational public opinion we have studied, as revealed in surveys, generally reflects the results of debate and deliberation that take time. For a thorough review and critique of the politics of referenda, see Cronin (1989).

6. Again, we define interests in terms of fully informed preferences. Although such hypothetical preferences are difficult to ascertain (see Bartels 1990 for an important effort), inferences about deviations from them can sometimes be drawn from the prevalence of false information.

7. McKelvey and Ordeshook (1986) convincingly show how, in the electoral setting, voters can (without excessive effort or investment) make use of all *available* information by relying upon cue givers. But they do not address the possibility that the available information and the cue-giving processes are contaminated by bias or falsehood.

8. Graber (1990) points out that the Chafee/Holmes/Brandeis line of argument about the First Amendment, in avoiding the links with economic arrangements that were inherent in earlier nineteenth-century libertarian views, tended to obscure the relevance of economic resources to effective expression of ideas.

9. Tom Graham (e.g., 1989b) argues forcefully that vigorous party competition, with the parties closely attentive to surveys, aware of what the public wants, and capable of formulating sound political strategies, is essential—both to ensure policy responsiveness and to check opinion manipulation.

Bibliography

Aaron, Henry J. 1978. *Politics and the Professors*. Washington, D.C.: Brookings.

Abramson, Paul R. 1983. *Political Attitudes in America: Formation and Change*. San Francisco: Freeman.

Achen, Christopher H. 1975. Mass Political Attitudes and the Survey Response. *American Political Science Review* 69:1218–1231.

———. 1978. Measuring Representation. *American Journal of Political Science* 22:475–510.

———. 1983. Toward Theories of Political Data. In *Political Science: The State of the Discipline*, ed. Ada Finifter, 69–93. Washington, D.C.: American Political Science Association.

Adamany, David, and Joel B. Grossman. 1983. Support for the Supreme Court as a National Policy Maker. *Law & Policy Quarterly* 5 (October): 405–437.

Advisory Commission on Intergovernmental Relations (ACIR). 1975–1977; 1980–1985. *Changing Public Attitudes on Government and Taxes*. Washington, D.C.: ACIR.

Ahrari, M. E. 1987. Congress, Public Opinion, and Synfuels Policy. *Political Science Quarterly* 102:589–606.

Aldrich, John H., John L. Sullivan, and Eugene Borgida. 1989. Foreign Affairs and Issue Voting: Do Presidential Candidates "Waltz before a Blind Audience?" *American Political Science Review* 63:123–141.

Almond, Gabriel A. 1960 [1950]. *The American People and Foreign Policy*. New York: Praeger.

Andreoli, Virginia, and Stephen Worchel. 1978. Effects of Media, Communicator, and Message Position on Attitude Change. *Public Opinion Quarterly* 42:59–70.

Apple, R. W. 1989. Limits on Abortion Seem Less Likely. *New York Times*, September 29, pp. 1, 8.

Aronson, James. 1973 [1970]. *The Press and the Cold War*. Boston: Beacon.

Arrow, Kenneth J. 1963 [1951]. *Social Choice and Individual Values*. 2d ed. New York: Wiley.

Axelrod, Robert. 1972. Where the Votes Come From: An Analysis of Electoral Coalitions. *American Political Science Review* 66:11–20. Also Communications, in *APSR* 68 (1974): 17–20; *APSR* 72 (1978): 622–624; *APSR* 76 (1982): 394–395; and *APSR* 80 (1986): 281—284.

Bachrach, Peter, and Morton S. Baratz. 1962. Two Faces of Power. *American Political Science Review* 56:947–952.

———. 1963. Decisions and Nondecisions: An Analytical Framework. *American Political Science Review* 57:632–642.

Bachrack, Stanley D. 1976. *The Committee of One Million: "China Lobby" Politics, 1953–1971*. New York: Columbia University Press.

Bagdikian, Ben H. 1987 [1983]. *The Media Monopoly*. 2d ed. Boston: Beacon.

Ball, Desmond. 1980. *Politics and Force Levels*. Berkeley: University of California Press.

Barber, Benjamin R. 1984. *Strong Democracy: Participatory Politics for a New Age*. Berkeley: University of California Press.

Barnet, Richard J. 1990. *The Rockets' Red Glare: When America Goes to War—the Presidents and the People.* New York: Simon and Schuster.

Barry, Brian, and Russell Hardin, eds. 1982. *Rational Man and Irrational Society?* Beverly Hills, Calif.: Sage Publications.

Bartels, Larry. 1988. *Presidential Primaries and the Dynamics of Public Choice.* Princeton: Princeton University Press.

———. 1990. Public Opinion and Political Interests. Paper presented at the annual meeting of the Midwest Political Science Association, Chicago.

Barton, Allen. 1968. The Columbia Crisis: Campus, Vietnam, and the Ghetto. *Public Opinion Quarterly* 32:333–351.

Bayley, Edwin R. 1981. *Joe McCarthy and the Press.* Madison: University of Wisconsin Press.

Beard, Charles A. 1946. *American Foreign Policy in the Making, 1932–1940: A Study in Responsibilities.* New Haven: Yale University Press.

———. 1948. *President Roosevelt and the Coming of the War 1941: A Study in Appearances and Realities.* New Haven: Yale University Press.

Becker, Gary S. 1962. Irrational Behavior and Economic Theory. *Journal of Political Economy* 70 (February): 1–13.

Behr, Roy L., and Shanto Iyengar. 1985. Television News, Real-World Cues, and Changes in the Public Agenda. *Public Opinion Quarterly* 49:38–57.

Belkaoui, Janice Monti. 1978. Images of Arabs and Israelis in the Prestige Press, 1966–1974. *Journalism Quarterly* 55:732–738, 799.

Belknap, George, and Angus Campbell. 1951–1952. Political Party Identification and Attitudes toward Foreign Policy. *Public Opinion Quarterly* 15:601–623.

Bennett, Stephen Earl. 1989. Trends in Americans' Political Information, 1967–1987. *American Politics Quarterly* 17:422–435.

Bennett, W. Lance. 1988. *News: The Politics of Illusion.* 2d ed. New York: Longman.

———. 1989. Marginalizing the Majority: Conditioning Public Opinion to Accept Managerial Democracy. In *Manipulating Public Opinion,* ed. Michael Margolis and Gary Mauser, 322–361. Pacific Grove, Calif.: Brooks/Cole.

———. 1990. Toward a Theory of Press–State Relations in the United States. *Journal of Communication* 40(2): 103–125.

Bensel, Richard F. 1984. *Sectionalism and American Political Development: 1880–1980.* Madison: University of Wisconsin Press.

Berelson, Bernard R., Paul F. Lazarsfeld, and William N. McPhee. 1954. *Voting: A Study of Opinion Formation in a Presidential Campaign.* Chicago: University of Chicago Press.

Berkman, Ronald, and Laura W. Kitch. 1986. *Politics in the Media Age.* New York: McGraw-Hill.

Bessette, Joseph M. 1979. Deliberation in Congress. Paper presented to the annual meeting of the American Political Science Association, Washington, D.C.

———. 1980. Deliberative Democracy: The Majority Principle in Republican Government. In *How Democratic Is the Constitution?* ed. Robert A. Goldwin and William A. Schambra, 102–116. Washington, D.C.: American Enterprise Institute.

Bill, James A. 1988. *The Eagle and the Lion: The Tragedy of American-Iranian Relations.* New Haven: Yale University Press.

Black, Earl, and Merle Black. 1987. *Politics and Society in the South.* Cambridge, Mass.: Harvard University Press.

Black, George. 1988. *The Good Neighbor: How the United States Wrote the History of Central American and the Caribbean.* New York: Pantheon.

Black, Joan S. 1983. General Electric Brings the Polls to Life. *Public Opinion* 6 (June/July): 27.

Black, Merle, David M. Kovenock, and William C. Reynolds. 1974. *Political Attitudes in the Nation and the States.* Chapel Hill, N.C.: Institute for Research in Social Science.

Blumenthal, Sidney. 1986. *The Rise of the Counter-Establishment: From Conservative Ideology to Political Power.* New York: Random House.

Blustein, Paul. 1981. Supply-Side Theories Became Federal Policy with Unusual Speed: Politicians and Journalists, Rather than Academics, Played a Crucial Role. *Wall Street Journal,* October 8, pp. 1, 20.

Bobo, Lawrence. 1988. Attitudes toward the Black Political Movement: Trends, Meaning, and Effects on Racial Policy Preferences. *Social Psychology Quarterly* 51 (4): 287–302.

———. 1991. Societal Obligation, Individualism, and Redistributive Policies. *Sociological Forum* 6, forthcoming.

Bobo, Lawrence, and Frederick C. Licari. 1989. Education and Political Tolerance: Testing the Effects of Cognitive Sophistication and Target Group Affect. *Public Opinion Quarterly* 53:285–308.

Bonner, Raymond. 1987. *Waltzing with a Dictator: The Marcoses and the Making of American Policy.* New York: Times Books.

Bottome, Edgar M. 1971. *The Missile Gap.* Rutherford, N.J.: Fairleigh Dickinson University Press.

Bowles, Samuel, and Herbert Gintis. 1976. *Schooling in Capitalist America.* New York: Basic.

Bradburn, Norman M., and Seymour Sudman. 1979. *Improving Interview Method and Questionnaire Design.* San Francisco: Jossey-Bass.

———. 1988. *Polls and Surveys: Understanding What They Tell Us.* San Francisco: Jossey-Bass.

Brady, Henry, and Stephen Ansolabehere. 1989. The Nature of Utility Functions in Mass Publics. *American Political Science Review* 83:143–163.

Braestrup, Peter. 1976. *Big Story: How the American Press and Television Reported and Interpreted the Crisis of Tet 1968 in Vietnam and Washington.* 2 vols. Boulder, Colo.: Westview.

Branch, Taylor. 1988. *Parting the Waters: America in the King Years.* New York: Simon and Schuster.

Brody, Richard A. 1984. International Crises: A Rallying Point for the President. *Public Opinion* 6 (December/January): 41–43, 60.

Brody, Richard A., and Benjamin I. Page. 1972. Comment: The Assessment of Policy Voting. *American Political Science Review* 66:450–458.

———. 1975. The Impact of Events on Presidential Popularity. In *Perspectives on the Presidency,* ed. Aaron Wildavsky, 136–148. New York: Little, Brown.

Brody, Richard A., Benjamin I. Page, Sidney Verba, and Jerome Laulicht. 1969. Vietnam, the Urban Crisis, and the 1968 Presidential Election: A Preliminary Analysis, Paper presented at the annual meeting of the American Sociological Association, San Francisco.

Brody, Richard A., and Catherine R. Shapiro. 1989a. Policy Failure and Public Support: The Iran-Contra Affair and Public Assessment of President Reagan. *Political Behavior* 11:353–369.

———. 1989b. A Reconsideration of the Rally Phenomenon in Public Opinion. In *Political Behavior Annual,* ed. Samuel Long. Vol. 2. Boulder, Colo.: Westview.

Brown, Thad A. 1988. *Migration and Politics: The Impact of Population Mobility on American Voting Behavior.* Chapel Hill: University of North Carolina Press.

Bryce, James. 1897 [1893]. *The American Commonwealth.* 2 vols. 3d ed. New York: Macmillan.

Burstein, Paul. 1979. Public Opinion, Demonstrations, and the Passage of Anti-Discrimination Legislation. *Public Opinion Quarterly* 43:157–172.

Burstein, Paul, and William Freudenburg. 1978. Changing Public Policy: The Impact of Public Opinion, Antiwar Demonstrations and War Costs on Senate Voting on Vietnam War Motions. *American Journal of Sociology* 84:99–122.

Caldeira, Gregory A. 1987. Public Opinion and the U.S. Supreme Court: FDR's Court-Packing Plan. *American Political Science Review* 81:1139–1153.

Cambridge Reports, Inc. 1985. *America Looks Ahead.* Cambridge, Mass.: Cambridge Reports.

Campbell, Angus, Philip E. Converse, Warren E. Miller, and Donald E. Stokes. 1960. *The American Voter.* New York: Wiley.

Campbell, Angus, and Homer C. Cooper. 1956. *Group Differences in Attitudes and Votes.* Ann Arbor, Mich.: Survey Research Center.

Cantril, Hadley. 1940. America Faces the War: A Study in Public Opinion. *Public Opinion Quarterly* 4:387–407.

———. 1967. *The Human Dimension: Experiences in Policy Research.* New Brunswick, N.J.: Rutgers University Press.

Cantril, Hadley, and Research Associates in the Office of Public Opinion Research (Princeton University). 1947. *Gauging Public Opinion.* Princeton: Princeton University Press.

Cantril, Hadley, with Mildred Strunk. 1951. *Public Opinion, 1935–1946.* Princeton: Princeton University Press.

Caraley, Demetrios. 1986. Changing Conceptions of Federalism. *Political Science Quarterly* 101:289–306.

———. 1991. *America Abandons Its Cities: From Carter to Reagan,* forthcoming.

Carmines, Edward G., and James H. Kuklinski. 1990. Incentives, Opportunities, and the Logic of Public Opinion in American Political Representation. In *Information and Democratic Processes,* ed. John A. Ferejohn and James H. Kuklinski, 240–268. Urbana: University of Illinois Press.

Carmines, Edward G., and James A. Stimson. 1989. *Issue Evolution: Race and the Transformation of American Politics.* Princeton: Princeton University Press.

Carson, Rachel. 1962. *Silent Spring.* Greenwich, Conn.: Fawcett Publications.

Caspary, William R. 1968. United States Public Opinion during the Onset of the Cold War. *Peace Research Society (International) Papers,* pp. 25–46.

———. 1970. The "Mood Theory": A Study of Public Opinion and Foreign Policy. *American Political Science Review* 64:536–547.

Casper, Jonathan. 1972. *The Politics of Civil Liberties.* New York: Harper and Row.

Chafetz, Ze'ev. 1985. *Double Vision: How the Press Distorts America's View of the Middle East.* New York: Morrow.

Chamorro, Edgar. 1987. *Packaging the Contras: A Case of CIA Disinformation.* New York: Institute for Media Analysis.

Childs, Harwood L. 1965. *Public Opinion: Nature, Formation, and Role.* Princeton, N.J.: Van Nostrand.

Chomsky, Noam. 1978. The U.S. Media and the Tet Offensive. *Race and Class* 20:21–39.

———. 1982. *Fateful Triangle.* Boston: South End.

———. 1986. *Pirates and Emperors: International Terrorism in the Real World.* New York: Claremont Research and Publications.

Chong, Dennis. 1991. *Collective Action and the Civil Rights Movement.* Chicago: University of Chicago Press.

Chong, Dennis, Herbert McClosky, and John Zaller. 1983. Patterns of Support for Democratic and Capitalist Values in the United States. *British Journal of Political Science* 13:401–440.

Citrin, Jack. 1979. Do People Want Something for Nothing: Public Opinion on Taxes and Government Spending. *National Tax Journal* 32 (Supplement): 112–128.

Citrin, Jack, and Donald Philip Green. 1990. The Self-Interest Motive in American Public

Opinion. In *Research in Micropolitics: A Research Annual. Public Opinion*, ed. Samuel Long, 1–27. Greenwich, Conn.: JAI.

Cohen, Bernard C. 1973. *The Public's Impact on Foreign Policy*. Boston: Little, Brown.

Cohen, Warren I. 1990. At the State Dept., Historygate. *New York Times*, May 8, p. A29.

Condorcet, Nicolas Caritat de. 1785. Essai sur l'application de l'analyse a la probabilité des decisions rendues a la pluralite des voix. Paris.

Connolly, William E. 1972. On "Interests" in Politics. *Politics and Society* 2:459–477.

Converse, Jean M. 1987. *Survey Research in the United States: Roots and Emergence 1890–1960*. Berkeley: University of California Press.

Converse, Philip E. 1962. Information Flows and the Stability of Partisan Attitudes. *Public Opinion Quarterly* 26:578–599.

———. 1964. The Nature of Belief Systems in Mass Publics. In *Ideology and Discontent*, ed. David E. Apter, 206–261. New York: Free Press.

———. 1970. Attitudes and Non-Attitudes: Continuation of a Dialogue. In *The Quantitative Analysis of Social Problems*, ed. Edward R. Tufte, 168–189. Reading, Mass.: Addison-Wesley.

Converse, Philip E., and Gregory B. Markus. 1979. Plus ca change . . . : The New CPS Election Study Panel. *American Political Science Review* 73:32–49.

Cook, Fay Lomax. 1979. *Who Should be Helped*. Beverly Hills, Calif.: Sage Publications.

Cook, Fay Lomax, and Edith J. Barrett. 1988. Public Support for Social Security. *Journal of Aging Studies* 2:339–356.

Cooper, Marc, and Lawrence C. Soley. 1990. All the Right Sources. *Mother Jones* (February/March): 20–27, 45–48.

Cotter, Patrick R., and James Glen Stovall. 1990. The Conservative South. *American Politics Quarterly* 18:103–119.

Cottrell, Leonard S., Jr., and Sylvia Eberhart. 1969 [1948]. *American Opinion on World Affairs in the Atomic Age*. New York: Greenwood.

Cronin, Thomas E. 1989. *Direct Democracy: The Politics of Initiative, Referendum, and Recall*. Cambridge, Mass.: Harvard University Press.

Crozier, Michael, Samuel P. Huntington, and Joji Watanuki. 1975. *The Crisis of Democracy: Report on the Governability of the Democracies to the Trilateral Commission*. New York: New York University Press.

Cumings, Bruce. 1981a. Chinatown: Foreign Policy and Elite Realignment. In *The Hidden Election*, ed. Thomas Ferguson and Joel Rogers, 196–231. New York: Random House.

———. 1981b. *The Origins of the Korean War: Liberation and the Emergence of Separate Regimes, 1945–1947*. Princeton: Princeton University Press.

———. 1990. *The Origins of the Korean War: Vol. 2, The Roaring of the Cataract, 1947–1950*. Princeton: Princeton University Press.

Cundy, Donald T. 1989. Televised Political Editorials and the Low-Involvement Viewer. *Social Science Quarterly* 70:911–922.

Dahl, Robert A. 1956. *A Preface to Democratic Theory*. Chicago: University of Chicago Press.

Dallek, Robert. 1979. *Franklin D. Roosevelt and American Foreign Policy, 1932–1945*. New York: Oxford University Press.

Daugherty, David, and Michael Warden. 1979. Prestige Press Editorial Treatment of the Mideast during 11 Crisis Years. *Journalism Quarterly*, 776–782.

Davies, James C. 1952. Some Relations between Events and Attitudes. *American Political Science Review* 46:777–789.

Davis, James A. 1975. Communism, Conformity, Cohorts, and Categories: American Tolerance in 1954 and 1972–73. *American Journal of Sociology* 81:491–513.

———. 1980. Conservative Weather in a Liberalizing Climate: Changes in Selected NORC General Social Survey Items, 1972–1978. *Social Forces* 58:1129–1156.

———. 1987. *Social Differences in Contemporary America*. San Diego: Harcourt Brace Jovanovich.

———. 1988. Communism and Cohorts Continued: American Tolerance in 1954 and 1972–1987. Unpublished paper, NORC and Harvard University.

Davis, James A., and Tom W. Smith. 1982; 1987; 1989. *General Social Survey Cumulative Codebook(s), 1972–82, 1972–1987, 1972–1989*. Chicago: NORC/The Roper Center.

———. 1990. *General Social Surveys, 1972–90: Cumulative Codebook*. Chicago: NORC.

Davis, Otto A., Melvin J. Hinich, and Peter C. Ordeshook. 1970. An Expository Development of a Mathematical Model of the Electoral Process. *American Political Science Review* 64:426–448.

Delli Carpini, Michael. 1986. *Stability and Change in American Politics: The Coming of Age of the Generation of the 1960s*. New York: New York University Press.

Delli Carpini, Michael X., and Scott Keeter. 1991. Stability and Change in the U.S. Public's Knowledge of Politics. *Public Opinion Quarterly* 55, forthcoming.

Delli Carpini, Michael X., and Lee Sigelman. 1986. Do Yuppies Matter? Competing Explanations of Their Political Distinctiveness. *Public Opinion Quarterly* 50:502–518.

Delli Carpini, Michael X., and Bruce A. Williams. 1987. Television and Terrorism: Patterns of Presentation and Occurrence, 1969 to 1980. *Western Political Quarterly* 40:45–64.

de Tocqueville, Alexis. 1945 [1835, 1840]. *Democracy in America*. 2 vols. New York: Vintage Books. (The Henry Reeve text, as revised by Francis Bowen and edited by Phillips Bradley.)

Devine, Donald J. 1970. *The Attentive Public: Polyarchical Democracy*. Chicago: Rand McNally.

Dewey, John. 1916. *Democracy and Education: An Introduction to the Philosophy of Education*. New York: Macmillan.

———. 1939. Democracy and Educational Administration. In *Intelligence in the Modern World,* ed. Joseph Ratner, 13–16. New York: Random House. (Excerpt in Kariel 1970.)

———. 1954 [1927]. *The Public and Its Problems*. Athens, Ohio: Swallow Press.

Dionne, E. J., Jr. 1989. Poll on Abortion Finds the Nation is Sharply Divided. *New York Times,* April 26, pp. 1, 13.

Donner, Frank J. 1981. *The Age of Surveillance: The Aims and Methods of America's Political Intelligence System*. New York: Random House.

Dorman, William A., and Mansour Farhang. 1987. *The U.S. Press and Iran: Foreign Policy and the Journalism of Deference*. Berkeley: University of California Press.

Downs, Anthony. 1957. *An Economic Theory of Democracy*. New York: Harper.

———. 1972. Up and Down with Ecology—the "Issue-Attention Cycle." *Public Interest* 28:28–50.

Dunlap, Riley E. 1985. Public Opinion: Behind the Transformation. *EPA Journal* 11:15–17.

Dye, Thomas R. 1986. *Who's Running America: The Conservative Years*. 4th ed. Englewood Cliffs, N.J.: Prentice-Hall.

Edelman, Murray. 1964. *The Symbolic Uses of Politics*. Urbana: University of Illinois Press.

———. 1988. *Constructing the Political Spectacle*. Chicago: University of Chicago Press.

Edsall, Thomas Byrne. 1984. *The New Politics of Inequality*. New York: Norton.

Eichenberg, Richard C. 1989. *Public Opinion and National Security in Western Europe*. Ithaca: Cornell University Press.

Elam, Stanley M., ed. 1978. *A Decade of Gallup Polls of Attitudes toward Education, 1969–1978*. Bloomington, Ind.: Phi Delta Kappa.

Ellul, Jacques. 1965. *Propaganda: The Formation of Men's Attitudes*. Translated by Konrad Kellen and Jean Lerner. New York: Farrar, Strauss and Giroux.

Emerson, Steven. 1985. *The American House of Saud: The Secret Petrodollar Connection*. New York: Franklin Watts.

Enelow, James M., and Melvin J. Hinich. 1984. *The Spatial Theory of Voting: An Introduction*. New York: Cambridge University Press.

Entman, Robert M. 1989. *Democracy without Citizens: Media and the Decay of American Politics*. New York: Oxford University Press.

Erbring, Lutz, Edie N. Goldenberg, and Arthur H. Miller. 1980. Front-Page News and Real-World Cues. *American Journal of Political Science* 24:16–49.

Erikson, Robert S. 1979. The SRC Panel Data and Mass Political Attitudes. *British Journal of Political Science* 9:89–114.

Erikson, Robert S., Thomas D. Lancaster, and David W. Romero. 1989. Group Components of the Presidential Vote, 1952–84. *Journal of Politics* 51:337–346.

Erikson, Robert S., and Norman R. Luttbeg. 1973. *American Public Opinion: Its Origins, Content, and Impact*. New York: Wiley.

Erikson, Robert S., Norman R. Luttbeg, and Kent L. Tedin. 1988. *American Public Opinion: Its Origins and Impact*. 3d ed. New York: Macmillan. (Also editions of 1980, 1984.)

Erikson, Robert S., Gerald C. Wright, Jr., and John P. McIver. 1989. Political Parties, Public Opinion, and State Policy in the United States. *American Political Science Review* 83:729–750.

Erskine, Hazel Gaudet. 1963. The Polls: Atomic Weapons and Nuclear Energy. *Public Opinion Quarterly* 24:155–190.

———. 1964. The Polls: Some Gauges of Conservatism. *Public Opinion Quarterly* 28: 154–168.

———. 1975a. The Polls: Government Role in Welfare. *Public Opinion Quarterly* 39:257–274.

———. 1975b. The Polls: Health Insurance. *Public Opinion Quarterly* 39:128–241.

Fallows, James. 1986. The New Celebrities of Washington. *New York Review of Books* 33, June 12, pp. 41–49.

Fan, David. 1988. *Predictions of Public Opinion from the Mass Media: Content Analysis and Mathematical Modeling*. Westport, Conn.: Greenwood.

Farkas, Steve, Robert Y. Shapiro, and Benjamin I. Page. 1990. The Dynamics of Public Opinion and Policy. Paper presented at the annual meeting of the American Association for Public Opinion Research, Lancaster, Pa.

Feld, Scott L., and Bernard Grofman. 1988. Ideological Consistency as a Collective Phenomenon. *American Political Science Review* 82:773–788.

Feldman, Stanley. 1988. Structure and Consistency in Public Opinion: The Role of Core Beliefs and Values. *American Journal of Political Science*. 32:416–438.

———. 1990. Measuring Issue Preferences: The Problem of Response Instability. In *Political Analysis*, ed. James A. Stimson, 1:25–60. Ann Arbor: University of Michigan Press.

Feller, William. 1950. *An Introduction to Probability Theory and Its Applications. Volume One*. New York: Wiley.

Ferguson, Thomas. 1983. Party Realignment and American Industrial Structure: The Investment Theory of Political Parties in Historical Perspective. In *Research in Political Economy*, ed. P. Zarembka, 6:1–82. Greenwich, Conn.: JAI.

———. 1984. From Normalcy to New Deal: Industrial Structure, Party Competition, and American Public Policy in the Great Depression. *International Organization* 38:41–94.

Ferguson, Thomas, and Joel Rogers. 1981. *The Hidden Election: Politics and Economics in the 1980 Presidential Campaign*. New York: Random House.

———. 1986. *Right Turn: The Decline of the Democrats and the Future of American Politics*. New York: Farrar, Strauss and Giroux.

Findley, Paul. 1985. *They Dare to Speak Out: People and Institutions Confront Israel's Lobby*. Westport, Conn.: Lawrence Hill.

Fiorina, Morris P. 1981. *Retrospective Voting in American National Elections*. New Haven: Yale University Press.

Firebaugh, Glenn, and Kenneth E. Davis. 1988. Trends in Antiblack Prejudice, 1972–1984: Region and Cohort Effects. *American Journal of Sociology* 94:251–272.

Ford, Daniel. 1984. *The Cult of the Atom: The Secret Papers of the Atomic Energy Commission*. New York: Simon and Schuster.

Foster, H. Schuyler. 1983. *Activism Replaces Isolationism: U.S. Public Attitudes, 1940–1975*. Washington, D.C.: Foxhall.

Franklin, Charles H., and Liane C. Kosaki. 1989. The Republican Schoolmaster: The Supreme Court, Public Opinion, and Abortion. *American Political Science Review* 83:751–771.

Franklin, John Hope, and Alfred A. Moss, Jr. 1988. *From Slavery to Freedom: A History of Negro Americans*. 6th ed. New York: Knopf.

Freeland, Richard M. 1972. *The Truman Doctrine and the Origins of McCarthyism: Foreign Policy, Domestic Politics, and Internal Security*. New York: Knopf.

Freeman, Howard E., H. Ashley Weeks, and Walter J. Wertheimer. 1955. News Commentator Effect: A Study in Knowledge and Opinion Change. *Public Opinion Quarterly* 19:209–215.

Freudenburg, William R., and Eugene A. Rosa, eds. 1984. *Public Reaction to Nuclear Power: Are There Critical Masses?* Boulder, Colo.: Westview.

Fuchs, Ester Rachel. 1991. *Mayors and Money: Fiscal Policy in New York and Chicago*. Chicago: University of Chicago Press.

Funkhauser, G. Ray. 1973a. The Issues of the Sixties: An Exploratory Study in the Dynamics of Public Opinion. *Public Opinion Quarterly* 37:62–75.

———. 1973b. Trends in Media Coverage of the Issues of the Sixties. *Journalism Quarterly* 50:533–558.

Gaddis, John Lewis. 1972. *The United States and the Origins of the Cold War, 1941–1947*. New York: Columbia University Press.

———. 1982. *Strategies of Containment: A Critical Appraisal of Postwar American National Security Policy*. New York: Oxford University Press.

———. 1983. The Emerging Post-Revisionist Synthesis on the Origins of the Cold War. *Diplomatic History* 7:171–190; Comments 191–204.

Gallup, George H. 1972. *The Gallup Poll: Public Opinion 1935–1971*. Vol. 1. New York: Random House.

Gallup, George, and Claude Robinson. 1938. American Institute of Public Opinion—Surveys, 1935–1938. *Public Opinion Quarterly* 2:373–398.

Galtung, Johann. 1965. Foreign Policy as a Function of Social Position. *Peace Research Society Papers* 2:206–231.

Gamson, William A., and Andre Modigliani. 1966. Knowledge and Foreign Policy Opinions: Some Models for Consideration. *Public Opinion Quarterly* 30:187–99.

Gans, Herbert J. 1979. *Deciding What's News*. New York: Random House.

Garrow, David J. 1978. *Protest at Selma: Martin Luther King, Jr., and the Voting Rights Act of 1965*. New Haven: Yale University Press.

Geddes, Barbara, and John Zaller. 1989. Sources of Support for Authoritarian Regimes. *American Journal of Political Science* 33:319–347.

Gelb, Leslie H. 1985. Arms Control and the Russians: Battle on Compliance Heats Up. *New York Times*, June 7, pp. 1, 4.

Gervasi, Tom. 1986. *The Myth of Soviet Military Supremacy*. New York: Harper.

Geyer, Anne E., and Robert Y. Shapiro. 1988. The Polls—a Report: Human Rights. *Public Opinion Quarterly* 52: 386–398.

Gibbs, David. 1991. *Private Interests and International Conflict: The Political Economy of Intervention in the Congo Crisis*. Chicago: University of Chicago Press.

Gibson, James L. 1988. Political Intolerance and Political Repression during the McCarthy Red Scare. *American Political Science Review* 82:511–529.

———. 1989. The Policy Consequences of Political Intolerance: Political Repression during the Vietnam War Era. *Journal of Politics* 51:13–35.

Gibson, James L., and Richard D. Bingham. 1985. *Civil Liberties and Nazis: the Skokie Free-Speech Controversy*. New York: Praeger.

Gilboa, Eytan. 1987. *American Public Opinion toward Israel and the Arab-Israeli Conflict*. Lexington, Mass.: D. C. Heath.

Gilligan, Carol. 1982. *In a Different Voice*. Cambridge, Mass.: Harvard University Press.

Gillroy, John M. 1980. United States Foreign Policy and American Public Opinion toward Russia, 1945–1949: An Analysis of Democratic Responsiveness. Master's thesis, University of Chicago.

Gillroy, John M., and Robert Y. Shapiro. 1986. The Polls: Environmental Protection. *Public Opinion Quarterly* 50:270–279.

Ginsberg, Benjamin. 1972. Critical Elections and the Substance of Party Conflict: 1844 to 1968. *Midwest Journal of Political Science* 16:603–625.

———. 1973. Critical Elections and American Public Policy. Ph.D. dissertation, University of Chicago.

———. 1986. *The Captive Public: How Mass Opinion Promotes State Power*. New York: Basic.

Gitlin, Todd. 1980. *The Whole World Is Watching: Mass Media in the Making and Unmaking of the New Left*. Berkeley: University of California Press.

Glenn, Norval. 1977. *Cohort Analysis*. Beverly Hills, Calif.: Sage Publications.

———. 1989. A Caution about Mechanical Solutions to the Identification Problem in Cohort Analysis: Comment on Sasaki and Suzuki. *American Journal of Sociology* 95:754–761.

Goldfield, Michael. 1988. *The Decline of Organized Labor in the United States*. Chicago: University of Chicago Press.

Goldstein, Robert Justin. 1978. *Political Repression in Modern America*. Cambridge, Mass.: Schenkman.

Goulden, Joseph C. 1969. *Truth is the First Casualty: The Gulf of Tonkin Affair—Illusion and Reality*. Chicago: Rand McNally.

Graber, Mark Aaron. 1990. *The Transformation of the Modern Constitutional Defense of Free Speech*. Berkeley: University of California Press.

Graham, Thomas W. 1988. The Pattern and Importance of Public Knowledge in the Nuclear Age. *Journal of Conflict Resolution* 32:319–334.

———. 1989a. *American Public Opinion on NATO, Extended Deterrence, and Use of Nuclear Weapons*. SIA Occasional Paper no. 4. Lanham, Md.: University Press of America.

———. 1989b. The Politics of Failure: Strategic Nuclear Arms Control, Public Opinion, and Domestic Politics in the United States, 1945–1985. Ph.D. dissertation, Massachusetts Institute of Technology.

Gramsci, Antonio. 1971 [1929–1935]. *Selections from the Prison Notebooks*. Edited and translated by Quintin Hoare and Geoffrey Nowell Smith. New York: International Publishers.

Gravel, Mike, ed. 1971. *The Pentagon Papers: The Defense Department History of the United States Decisionmaking on Vietnam*. 4 vols. Boston: Beacon.

Greeley, Andrew. 1989. Protestant and Catholic: Is the Analogical Imagination Extinct? *American Sociological Review* 54:485–502.

———. 1990. *The Catholic Myth: The Behavior and Beliefs of American Catholics.* New York: Scribners.

Greeley, Andrew M., and Paul B. Sheatsley. 1971. Attitudes toward Racial Integration. *Scientific American* 225:13–19.

Green, Donald Philip. 1990. The Price Elasticity of Mass Preferences. Unpublished paper, Yale University, Department of Political Science.

Green, Donald Philip, and Ann Elizabeth Gerken. 1989. Self-Interest and Public Opinion toward Smoking Restrictions and Cigarette Taxes. *Public Opinion Quarterly* 53:1–16.

Green, Mark, and Gail McColl. 1987. *Ronald Reagan's Reign of Error: An Instant Nostalgia Collector's Guide.* New York: Pantheon.

Greenberg, Edward S. 1986. *Workplace Democracy: The Political Effects of Participation.* Ithaca: Cornell University Press.

Greider, William. 1981. The Education of David Stockman. *The Atlantic* (December): 27–54.

———. 1987. *Secrets of the Temple: How the Federal Reserve Runs the Country.* New York: Simon and Schuster.

Grofman, Bernard, and Scott L. Feld. 1988. Rousseau's General Will: A Condorcetian Perspective. *American Political Science Review* 82:567–576.

Grofman, Bernard, and Guillermo Owen, eds. 1986. *Information Pooling and Group Decision Making.* Greenwich, Conn.: JAI.

Grose, Peter. 1983. *Israel in the Mind of America.* New York: Knopf.

Grossman, Michael Baruch, and Martha Joynt Kumar. 1981. *Portraying the President: The White House and the News Media.* Baltimore: Johns Hopkins University Press.

Habermas, Jurgen. 1989. *The Structural Transformation of the Public Sphere: An Inquiry into a Category of Bourgeois Society.* Translated by Thomas Burger. Cambridge, Mass.: MIT Press.

Hall, E. J., and M. M. Ferree. 1986. Race Differences in Abortion Attitudes. *Public Opinion Quarterly* 50:193–207.

Hall, Robert L., Mark Rodeghier, and Bert Useem. 1986. Effects of Education on Attitude to Protest. *American Sociological Review* 51:564–573.

Halliday, Fred. 1986. *The Making of the Second Cold War.* 2d ed. London: Routledge Chapman and Hall.

Hallin, Daniel C. 1986. *The "Uncensored War": The Media and Vietnam.* New York: Oxford University Press.

Halloran, Richard, and Leslie Gelb. 1983. CIA Analysts Now Said to Find U.S. Overstated Soviet Arms Rise. *New York Times* March 3, p. 1.

Hamilton, Alexander, James Madison, and John Jay. 1961 [1787–1788]. *The Federalist Papers.* Edited by Clinton Rossiter. New York: New American Library.

Hamilton, Charles V., and Dona L. Hamilton. 1990. The Dual Agenda: Social Policies and Civil Rights Organizations, New Deal to the Present. Unpublished paper, Columbia University and Lehman College.

Hamilton, Richard F. 1972. *Class Politics in the United States.* New York: Wiley.

Hansen, Susan B. 1983. *The Politics of Taxation: Revenue without Representation.* New York: Praeger.

Harrington, Michael. 1962. *The Other America: Poverty in the United States.* New York: Macmillan.

Harris, Louis, and Associates, Inc. 1971; 1973; 1976; 1976. *The Harris Survey Yearbook of Public Opinion.* 4 vols. (reporting data for 1970, 1971, 1972, 1973.) New York: Louis Harris and Associates, Inc.

Harris, Louis and Associates, Inc., and Alan F. Westin. 1990. *Equifax Report on Consumers in the Information Age*. Atlanta: Equifax, Inc.

Harris, Richard. 1970. *Justice: The Crisis of Law, Order, and Freedom in America*. New York: Avon.

Hartz, Louis. 1955. *The Liberal Tradition in America: An Interpretation of American Political Thought since the Revolution*. New York: Harcourt, Brace.

Hastings, Philip K., and Jessie C. Southwick, eds. 1975. *Survey Data for Trend Analysis*. Storrs, Conn.: The Roper Public Opinion Research Center in cooperation with the Social Science Research Council.

Heclo, Hugh. 1978. Issue Networks and the Executive Establishment. In *The New American Political System*, ed. Anthony King, 87–124. Washington, D.C.: American Enterprise Institute.

Heinrichs, Waldo. 1988. *Threshold of War: Franklin D. Roosevelt and American Entry into World War II*. New York: Oxford University Press.

Herman, Edward S. 1982. *The Real Terror Network: Terrorism in Fact and Propaganda*. Boston: South End.

Herman, Edward S., and Frank Brodhead. 1986. *The Rise and Fall of the Bulgarian Connection*. New York: Sheridan Square.

Herman, Edward S., and Noam Chomsky. 1988. *Manufacturing Consent: The Political Economy of the Mass Media*. New York: Pantheon.

Hero, Alfred O., Jr. 1965. *The Southerner and World Affairs*. Baton Rouge: Louisiana State University Press.

———. 1966. The American Public and the UN, 1954–1966. *Journal of Conflict Resolution* 10:436–475.

———. 1973. *American Religious Groups View Foreign Policy: Trends in Rank-and-File Opinion, 1937–1969*. Durham, N.C.: Duke University Press.

Herring, George C. 1979. *America's Longest War: The United States and Vietnam, 1950–1975*. New York: Knopf.

Hersh, Seymour M. 1983. *The Price of Power: Kissinger in the Nixon White House*. New York: Summit.

———. 1986. *The Target is Destroyed: What Really Happened to Flight 007 and What America Knew about It*. New York: Random House.

———. 1987. Target Quaddafi. *New York Times Magazine*, February 22, p. 17.

Hibbs, Douglas A., Jr. 1979. The Mass Public and Macroeconomic Performance: Dynamics of Public Opinion toward Unemployment and Inflation. *American Journal of Political Science* 23:705–731.

Himmelstein, Jerome L., and James A. McRae, Jr. 1988. Social Issues and Socioeconomic Status. *Public Opinion Quarterly* 52:492–512.

Hochschild, Jennifer. 1981. *What's Fair? Americans' Attitudes toward Distributive Justice*. Cambridge, Mass.: Harvard University Press.

———. 1984. *The New American Dilemma: Liberal Democracy and School Desegregation*. New Haven: Yale University Press.

Hodge, Robert W., and Donald J. Treeman. 1968. Class Identification in the United States. *American Journal of Sociology* 73:535–547.

Holmes, Oliver Wendell, Jr. 1919. Opinion in *Abrams v. U.S.* 250 U.S. 616, 630.

Holsti, Ole R. 1987. Public Opinion and Containment. In *Containing the Soviet Union: A Critique of U.S. Policy*, ed. Terry L. Deibel and John Lewis Gaddis, 20–58. Washington, D.C.: Pergamon.

Hovland, Carl I. 1954. Effects of the Mass Media of Communication. In *Handbook of Social Psychology*, ed. Gardner Lindzey, 2:1062–1103. Reading, Mass.: Addison–Wesley.

Hovland, Carl I., and Walter Weiss. 1951. The Influence of Source Credibility on Communication Effectiveness. *Public Opinion Quarterly* 16:635–650.

Huff, Darrell. 1954. *How to Lie with Statistics*. New York: Norton.

Hughes, Barry B. 1978. *The Domestic Context of American Foreign Policy*. San Francisco: W. H. Freeman.

Hyman, Herbert H., and Paul B. Sheatsley. 1953. Trends in Public Opinion on Civil Liberties. *Journal of Social Issues* 9:6–16.

———. 1956. Attitudes toward Desegregation. *Scientific American* 195:35–39.

Hyman, Herbert H., and Charles R. Wright. 1979. *Education's Lasting Influence on Values*. Chicago: University of Chicago Press.

Hyman, Herbert H., Charles R. Wright, and John Shelton Reed. 1975. *The Enduring Effects of Education*. Chicago: University of Chicago Press.

Immerman, Richard H. 1982. *The CIA in Guatemala: The Foreign Policy of Intervention*. Austin: University of Texas.

Inglehart, Ronald. 1985. Aggregate Stability and Individual Level Flux in Mass Belief Systems: The Level of Analysis Paradox. *American Political Science Review* 79:97–116.

———. 1990. *Culture Shift in Advanced Industrial Society*. Princeton: Princeton University Press.

Iyengar, Shanto. 1987. Television News and Citizens' Explanations of National Issues. *American Political Science Review* 81:815–832.

———. 1990a. The Accessibility Bias in Politics: Television News and Public Opinion. *International Journal of Public Opinion Research* 2:1–15.

———. 1990b. Framing Responsibility for Political Issues: The Case of Poverty. *Political Behavior* 12:19–40.

———. 1991. *Is Anyone Responsible? How Television News Frames Political Issues*. Chicago: University of Chicago Press.

Iyengar, Shanto, and Donald Kinder R. 1987. *News That Matters*. Chicago: University of Chicago Press.

Jackman, Mary R. 1978. General and Applied Tolerance: Does Education Increase Commitment to Racial Integration? *American Journal of Political Science* 22:302–324.

Jackman, Mary R., and Robert W. Jackman. 1983. *Class Awareness in the United States*. Berkeley: University of California Press.

Jackson, John E. 1979. Statistical Estimation of Possible Response Bias in Close-ended Issue Questions. *Political Methodology* 6:393–424.

———. 1983. The Systematic Beliefs of the Mass Public: Estimating Policy Preferences from Survey Data. *Journal of Politics* 45:840–865.

Jacobs, Lawrence R. 1991. The Recoil Effect: Public Opinion and Policy Making in the United States and Britain. *Comparative Politics,* forthcoming.

Jacobs, Lawrence R., and Robert Y. Shapiro. 1989. Public Opinion and the New Social History: Some Lessons for the Study of Public Opinion and Democratic Policy-making. *Social Science History* 13:1–24.

Jefferson, Thomas. 1955. *The Political Writings of Thomas Jefferson: Representative Selections*. Edited by Edward Dumbauld. New York: Liberal Arts Press.

Jelen, Ted, ed. 1989. *Religion and Political Behavior in the United States*. New York: Praeger.

Jencks, Christopher, and Kathryn Edin. 1990. The Real Welfare Problem. *The American Prospect* (Spring): 31–50.

Jennings, M. Kent, and Richard D. Niemi. 1981. *Generations and Politics: A Panel Study of Young Adults and Their Parents*. Princeton: Princeton University Press.

Johnson, Walter. 1944. *The Battle against Isolation*. Chicago: University of Chicago Press.

Kagay, Michael R. 1989. Homosexuals Gain More Acceptance. *New York Times*, October 25, p. 13.

Kahin, George McT. 1986. *Intervention: How America Became Involved in Vietnam.* New York: Knopf.

Kaplan, Fred. 1983. *The Wizards of Armageddon.* New York: Simon and Schuster.

Karetzky, Stephen, ed. 1986. *The Media's War against Israel.* New York: Shapolsky.

Kariel, Henry S., ed. 1970. *Frontiers of Democratic Theory.* New York: Random House.

Karplus, Susan Sherman. 1979. Public Opinion Change and Policy Change: The Legalization of Abortion in the United States. Unpublished paper, University of Chicago.

Katz, Elihu, and Paul F. Lazarsfeld. 1965. *Personal Influence.* Glencoe: Free Press.

Katz, James E., and Annette R. Tassone. 1990. The Polls—a Report: Public Opinion Trends: Privacy and Information Technology. *Public Opinion Quarterly* 54:125–143.

Keeter, Scott, and Cliff Zukin. 1983. *Uninformed Choice: Failure of the New Presidential Nominating System.* New York: Praeger.

Kennan, George F. ("X.") 1947. The Sources of Soviet Conduct. *Foreign Affairs* 25:566–582.

Kernell, Samuel. 1976. The Truman Doctrine Speech: A Case Study of the Dynamics of Presidential Opinion Leadership. *Social Science History* (Fall): 20–44.

———. 1978. Explaining Presidential Popularity. *American Political Science Review* 72:506–522.

———. 1986. *Going Public: New Strategies of Presidential Leadership.* Washington, D.C.: Congressional Quarterly.

Key, V. O., Jr. 1949. *Southern Politics.* New York: Knopf.

———. 1961. *Public Opinion and American Democracy.* New York: Knopf.

Key, V. O., Jr., with the assistance of Milton C. Cummings, Jr. 1966. *The Responsible Electorate: Rationality in Presidential Voting, 1936–1960.* Cambridge, Mass.: Harvard University Press.

Kinder, Donald R., and D. Roderick Kiewiet. 1979. Economic Discontent and Political Behavior: The Role of Personal Grievances and Collective Economic Judgments in Congressional Voting. *American Journal of Political Science* 23:495–527.

———. 1981. Sociotropic Politics: The American Case. *British Journal of Political Science* 11:129–161.

Kinder, Donald R., and David O. Sears. 1985. Public Opinion and Political Action. In *Handbook of Social Psychology,* ed. Gardner Lindzey and Elliot Aronson, 2:659–741. 3d ed. New York: Random House.

Klein, Ethel. 1984. *Gender Politics: From Consciousness to Mass Politics.* Cambridge, Mass.: Harvard University Press.

Knoke, David. 1979. Stratification and the Dimensions of American Political Orientations. *American Journal of Political Science* 23:772–791.

Koen, Ross Y. 1974. [1960] *The China Lobby in American Politics.* New York: Harper.

Kolko, Gabriel. 1968. *The Politics of War: The World and United States Foreign Policy, 1943–1945.* New York: Random House.

Kornhauser, Arthur. 1946. Are Public Opinion Polls Fair to Organized Labor? *Public Opinion Quarterly* 10:484–500.

Kriesberg, Martin. 1946–1947. Soviet News in the "New York Times." *Public Opinion Quarterly* 10:540–564.

Krosnick, Jon A., and Donald R. Kinder. 1990. Altering the Foundations of Support of the President through Priming. *American Political Science Review* 84:497–512.

Kuniholm, Bruce Robellet. 1980. *The Origins of the Cold War in the Near East: Great Power Conflict and Diplomacy in Iran, Turkey, and Greece.* Princeton: Princeton University Press.

Kusnitz, Leonard A. 1984. *Public Opinion and Foreign Policy: America's China Policy, 1949–1979.* Westport, Conn.: Greenwood.

Ladd, Everett Carll. 1983. Public Opinion: Questions at the Quinquennial. *Public Opinion* 6 (April/May): 20, 41.

Ladd, Everett C., and Charles D. Hadley. 1973. *Political Parties and Political Issues: Patterns in Differentiation since the New Deal.* Beverly Hills, Calif.: Sage Publications.

Ladd, Everett C., with Charles D. Hadley. 1978. *Transformations of the American Party System.* 2d ed. New York: Norton.

Ladd, Everett Carll, with M. Potter, L. Basilick, S. Daniels, and D. Suszkiw. 1979. The Polls: Taxing and Spending. *Public Opinion Quarterly* 43:126–135.

LaFeber, Walter. 1980. *America, Russia, and the Cold War 1945–1980.* 4th ed. New York: Wiley.

———. 1985. *America, Russia, and the Cold War 1945–1984.* 5th ed. New York: Knopf.

Lane, Robert E. 1959. The Fear of Equality. *American Political Science Review* 53:35–51.

———. 1962. *Political Ideology.* New York: Free Press.

Lang, Gladys Engel and Kurt Lang. 1983. *The Battle for Public Opinion: The President, the Press, and the Polls during Watergate.* New York: Columbia University Press.

Larson, Deborah Welch. 1985. *Origins of Containment: A Psychological Explanation.* Princeton: Princeton University Press.

Lazarsfeld, Paul F., Bernard Berelson, and Hazel Gaudet. 1968 [1944]. *The People's Choice: How the Voter Makes Up His Mind in a Presidential Campaign.* 3d ed. New York: Columbia University Press.

Lee, Eun Sul, Ronald N. Forthofer, and Ronald J. Lorimor. 1989. *Analyzing Complex Survey Data.* Newbury Park, Calif.: Sage Publications.

Lee, R. Alson. 1980 [1966]. *Truman and Taft-Hartley.* Westport, Conn.: Greenwood.

Lefler, Melvin. 1984. The American Conception of National Security and the Beginnings of the Cold War, 1945–48. *American Historical Review* 89:346–381.

Leigh, Michael. 1976. *Mobilizing Consent: Public Opinion and American Foreign Policy, 1937–1947.* Westport, Conn.: Greenwood.

Levering, Ralph B. 1976. *American Opinion and the Russian Alliance, 1939–1945.* Chapel Hill: University of North Carolina Press.

———. 1978. *The Public and American Foreign Policy, 1918–1978.* New York: Morrow.

Lichter, S. Robert, and Stanley Rothman. 1981. Media and Business Elites. *Public Opinion* 4 (October/November): 42–46, 59–60.

Lichter, S. Robert, Stanley Rothman, and L. S. Lichter. 1986. *The Media Elite.* Bethesda, Md.: Adler and Adler.

Lichty, Lawrence W. 1973. The War We Watched on Television. *AFI Report* 4 (Winter): 29–37.

Lindblom, Charles E. 1977. *Politics and Markets.* New York: Basic.

Lippmann, Walter. 1922. *Public Opinion.* New York: Macmillan.

———. 1925. *The Phantom Public.* New York: Macmillan.

———. 1956. *Essays in the Public Philosophy.* New York: New American Library.

Lipset, Seymour Martin. 1976. The Wavering Polls. *Public Interest* 43:70–89.

Lipset, Seymour Martin, and William Schneider. 1983. *The Confidence Gap: Business, Labor, and Government in the Public Mind.* New York: Free Press.

Littauer, Raphael, and Norman Uphoff, eds. 1972. *The Air War in Indochina.* Boston: Beacon.

Luke, Timothy W. 1990. Chernobyl: The Packaging of Transnational Ecological Disaster. In *Media Power in Politics,* ed. Doris A. Graber, 379–389. 2d ed. Washington, D.C.: Congressional Quarterly.

Luker, Kristin. 1984. *Abortion and the Politics of Motherhood.* Berkeley: University of California Press.

Lukes, Steven. 1975. *Power: A Radical View.* New York: Humanities Press.

Maass, Arthur. 1983. *Congress and the Common Good.* New York: Basic.

McClosky, Herbert. 1964. Consensus and Ideology in American Politics. *American Political Science Review* 58:361–382.

McClosky, Herbert, and Alida Brill. 1983. *Dimensions of Tolerance: What Americans Believe about Civil Liberties.* New York: Russell Sage Foundation.

McClosky, Herbert, P. J. Hoffman, and Rosemary O'Hara. 1960. Issue Conflict and Consensus among Party Leaders and Followers. *American Political Science Review* 54:406–427.

McClosky, Herbert, and John Zaller. 1984. *The American Ethos: Public Attitudes toward Capitalism and Democracy.* Cambridge, Mass.: Harvard University Press.

McCombs, Maxwell E., and Donald L. Shaw. 1972. The Agenda-setting Function of the Mass Media. *Public Opinion Quarterly* 36:176–187.

McConnell, Grant. 1966. *Private Power and American Democracy.* New York: Knopf.

McCubbins, Mathew D., and Benjamin I. Page. 1984. Rational Public Opinion: Its Nature and Measurement. Paper delivered at the annual meeting of the Midwest Political Science Association, Chicago.

McCutcheon, Allan L. 1985. A Latent Class Analysis of Tolerance for Nonconformity in the American Public. *Public Opinion Quarterly* 49:474–488.

McGuire, William J. 1986. The Myth of Massive Media Impact: Savagings and Salvagings. In *Public Communication and Behavior, Volume I,* ed. George Comstock, 175–257. New York: Academic Press.

McKelvey, Richard D., and Peter C. Ordeshook. 1986. Information, Electoral Equilibria, and the Democratic Ideal. *Journal of Politics* 48:909–937.

MacKuen, Michael B. 1981. Social Communication and the Mass Policy Agenda. In *More Than News: Two Studies of Media Power,* ed. MacKuen and Steven L. Coombs, 19–144. Beverly Hills, Calif.: Sage Publications.

———. 1983. Political Drama, Economic Conditions, and the Dynamics of Presidential Popularity. *American Journal of Political Science* 27:165–192.

———. 1984. Exposure to Information, Belief Integration, and Individual Responsiveness to Agenda Change. *American Political Science Review* 78:372–81.

McNichol, Elizabeth. 1980. School Busing for Integration: A Case Study in Opinion Change and Policy Change. Master's thesis, University of Chicago.

Mansbridge, Jane J. 1980. *Beyond Adversary Democracy.* New York: Basic.

———. 1986. *Why We Lost the ERA.* Chicago: University of Chicago Press.

———. 1990. *Beyond Self Interest.* Chicago: University of Chicago Press.

Marchetti, Victor, and John D. Marks. 1984. *The CIA and the Cult of Intelligence.* Rev. ed. New York: Dell.

Margolis, Michael. 1977. From Confusion to Confusion: Issues and the American Voter, 1956–1972. *American Political Science Review* 71:31–43.

Markus, Gregory, and Philip E. Converse. 1979. A Dynamic Simultaneous Equation Model of Electoral Choice. *American Political Science Review* 73:1055–1070.

Marshall, George C. 1947. The Marshall Plan. Address delivered at Harvard University, June 5, 1947. In *Documents in American History,* ed. Henry Steele Commager, 532–534. New York: Appleton-Century-Crofts, 1973.

Martin, Cathie Jo. 1991. *Shifting the Burden: The Politics of Corporate Income Taxation.* Chicago: University of Chicago Press.

Martin, Elizabeth, Diana McDuffee, and Stanley Presser. 1981. *Sourcebook of Harris National Surveys: Repeated Questions 1963–1976.* Chapel Hill: Institute for Research in Social Science, University of North Carolina at Chapel Hill.

Mayer, William. 1990. Public Opinion and the Liberal Malaise: How and Why American Public Opinion Changed between 1960 and 1988. Unpublished ms.

Miliband, Ralph. 1969. *The State in Capitalist Society.* New York: Basic.

Mill, John Stuart. 1947 [1859]. *On Liberty.* Edited by Alburey Castell. New York: Appleton-Century-Crofts.

————. 1958 [1861]. *Considerations on Representative Government*. Edited by Currin V. Shields. Indianapolis: Bobbs-Merrill.

Miller, Jon D. 1983. *The American People and Science Policy*. New York: Pergamon Press.

————. 1987. The Challenger Accident and Public Opinion: Attitudes towards the Space Programme in the USA. *Space Policy* (May): 122–140.

Miller, Nicholas R. 1986. Information, Electorates, and Democracy: Some Extensions and Interpretations of the Condorcet Jury Theorem. In *Information Pooling and Group Decision Making*, ed. Bernard Grofman and Guillermo Owen. Greenwich, Conn.: JAI.

Miller, Warren E., Arthur H. Miller, and Edward J. Schneider. 1980. *American National Election Studies Data Sourcebook, 1952–1978*. Cambridge, Mass.: Harvard University Press.

Miller, Warren E., and Santa A. Traugott. 1989. *American National Election Studies Data Sourcebook, 1952–1986*. Cambridge, Mass.: Harvard University Press.

Milton, John. 1918 [1644]. *Areopagitica, with a Commentary by Sir Richard C. Jebb*. Cambridge: Cambridge University Press.

Monroe, Alan D. 1975. *Public Opinion in America*. New York: Dodd, Mead.

————. 1979. Consistency between Public Preferences and National Policy Decisions. *American Politics Quarterly* 7:3–19.

————. 1983. American Party Platforms and Public Opinion. *American Journal of Political Science* 27:27–42.

Monroe, Kristen Renwick. 1984. *Presidential Popularity and the Economy*. New York: Praeger.

Morin, Richard. 1987. The Best of the Worst of the Summertime Surveys: 'Tis the Season for Baring American Ignorance. *Washington Post National Weekly Edition*, September 21, p. 37.

Mueller, John E. 1970. Presidential Popularity from Truman to Johnson. *American Political Science Review* 64:18–34.

————. 1971. Trends in Popular Support for the Wars in Korea and Vietnam. *American Political Science Review* 65:358–375.

————. 1973. *War, Presidents and Public Opinion*. New York: Wiley.

————. 1979. Public Expectations of War during the Cold War. *American Journal of Political Science* 23:301–329.

———. 1988. Trends in Political Tolerance. *Public Opinion Quarterly* 52:1–25.

Myrdal, Gunnar. 1944. *An American Dilemma*. 2 vols. New York: Random House.

Nacos, Brigitte L. 1990. *The Press, Presidents, and Crises*. New York: Columbia University Press.

Nacos, Brigitte L., Robert Y. Shapiro, John T. Young, David P. Fan, Torsten Kjellstrand, and Craig McCaa. 1991. Content Analysis of News Reports: Comparing Human Coding and a Computer–Assisted Method. *Communication*, forthcoming.

Nader, Ralph. 1972 [1966]. *Unsafe at Any Speed: The Designed-in Dangers of the American Car*. New York: Grossman.

Nelson, Richard R., and Sidney G. Winter. 1982. *An Evolutionary Theory of Economic Change*. Cambridge, Mass.: Belknap Press of Harvard University Press.

Nelson, Thomas E., and Donald R. Kinder. 1989. Experimental Investigations of Opinion Frames and Survey Responses: A Proposal to the National Election Study Board. University of Michigan.

Neuman, W. Russell. 1986. *The Paradox of Mass Politics: Knowledge and Opinion in the American Electorate*. Cambridge, Mass.: Harvard University Press.

————. 1990. The Threshold of Public Attention. *Public Opinion Quarterly* 54:159–176.

New York Times. 1971. *The Pentagon Papers as Published by the New York Times*. New York: Bantam.

New York Times. 1990. The People Dissent, June 12, p. A15.

Nie, Norman H., Sidney Verba, and John Petrocik. 1979 [1976]. *The Changing American Voter.* Enlarged ed. Cambridge, Mass.: Harvard University Press.

Niemi, Richard G., John Mueller, and Tom W. Smith. 1989. *Trends in Public Opinion: A Compendium of Survey Data.* New York: Greenwood.

Nincic, Miroslav, and Bruce Russett. 1979. The Effect of Similarity and Interest on Attitudes toward Foreign Countries. *Public Opinion Quarterly* 43:68–78.

Noelle-Neumann, Elisabeth. 1979. Public Opinion and the Classical Tradition: A Re-evaluation. *Public Opinion Quarterly* 43:143–156.

———. 1984. *The Spiral of Silence: Public Opinion—Our Social Skin.* Chicago: University of Chicago Press.

Nunn, Clyde A., Harry J. Crockett, Jr., and J. Allen Williams. 1978. *Tolerance for Nonconformity: A National Survey of Changing Commitment to Civil Liberties.* San Francisco: Jossey-Bass.

O'Connell, Martin, and Maurice J. Moore. 1980. The Legitimacy Status of First Births to U.S. Women Aged 15–24, 1939–1978. *Family Planning Perspectives* 12 (no. 1), (January/February): 16–25.

Opinion Roundup. 1988. Ten Years of Public Opinion: An Ambivalent Public. *Public Opinion* 11 (September/October): 21–40.

Oreskes, Michael. 1990. Grudging Public Thinks Tax Rise Now Must Come. *New York Times,* May 27, pp. 1, 13.

Organski, A. F. K. 1990. *The $36 Billion Bargain: Why Does the U.S. Give Aid to Israel?* New York: Columbia University Press.

Page, Benjamin I. 1978. *Choices and Echoes in Presidential Elections: Rational Man and Electoral Democracy.* Chicago: University of Chicago Press.

———. 1979. Taxes and Inequality: Do the Voters Get What They Want? Discussion paper no. 432-77, Institute for Research on Poverty, University of Wisconsin, Madison.

———. 1983. *Who Gets What from Government.* Berkeley: University of California Press.

Page, Benjamin I., and Richard A. Brody. 1972. Policy Voting and the Electoral Process: The Vietnam War Issue. *American Political Science Review* 66:979–995.

Page, Benjamin I., and Calvin C. Jones. 1979. Reciprocal Effects of Policy Preferences, Party Loyalties, and the Vote. *American Political Science Review* 73:1071–1089.

Page, Benjamin I., and Mark P. Petracca. 1983. *The American Presidency.* New York: McGraw-Hill.

Page, Benjamin I., and Robert Y. Shapiro. 1982. Changes in Americans' Policy Preferences, 1935–1979. *Public Opinion Quarterly* 46:24–42.

———. 1983. Effects of Public Opinion on Policy. *American Political Science Review* 77:175–190.

———. 1984. Presidents as Opinion Leaders: Some New Evidence. *Policy Studies Journal* 12:649–661.

———. 1989a. Educating and Manipulating the Public. In *Manipulating Public Opinion: Essays on Public Opinion as a Dependent Variable,* ed. Michael Margolis and Gary A. Mauser, 294–320. Pacific Grove: Brooks/Cole.

———. 1989b. Restraining the Whims and Passions of the Public. In *The Federalist Papers and the New Institutionalism,* ed. Bernard Grofman and Donald Wittman, 53–70. New York: Agathon.

Page, Benjamin I., Robert Y. Shapiro, and Glenn R. Dempsey. 1984. Television News and Changes in Americans' Policy Preferences. Paper presented at the annual meeting of the Midwest Political Science Association, Chicago.

———. 1987. What Moves Public Opinion? *American Political Science Review* 81:23–43.

Parenti, Michael. 1986. *Inventing Reality: The Politics of the Mass Media.* New York: St. Martin's.

Pateman, Carole. 1970. *Participation and Democratic Theory.* New York: Cambridge University Press.

Paterson, Thomas G. 1988. *Meeting the Communist Threat: Truman to Reagan.* New York: Oxford University Press.

Payne, Stanley L. 1946. Some Opinion Research Principles Developed through Studies of Social Medicine. *Public Opinion Quarterly* 10:93–98.

———. 1951. *The Art of Asking Questions.* Princeton: Princeton University Press.

Pearson, David E. 1987. *KAL007: The Cover-Up.* New York: Summit.

Pearson, Robert. 1980. Elections and Congress: An Empirical Assessment of the Electoral Accountability Thesis. Ph.D. dissertation, University of Chicago.

Pechman, Joseph A., and Benjamin A. Okner. 1970. *Who Bears the Tax Burden?* Washington, D.C.: Brookings.

Penner, Rudolph. 1982. Spooking the Public: The Social Security Specter. *Public Opinion* 5 (October/November): 16–18.

Peterson, Paul E. 1985. The New Politics of Deficits. In *The New Direction in American Politics,* ed. John E. Chubb and Paul E. Peterson, 365–397. Washington, D.C.: Brookings.

Petrocik, John R. 1981. *Party Coalitions, Realignment, and the Decline of the New Deal Party System.* Chicago: University of Chicago Press.

Pomper, Gerald M. 1972. From Confusion to Clarity: Issues and American Voters, 1956–1968. *American Political Science Review* 66:415–428.

Ponza, Michael, Greg J. Duncan, Mary Corcoran, and Fred Groskind. 1988. The Guns of Autumn: Age Differences in Support for Income Transfers to the Young and Old. *Public Opinion Quarterly* 52:441–466.

Popkin, Samuel L. 1991. *The Reasoning Voter: Communication and Persuasion in Presidential Campaigns.* Chicago: University of Chicago Press.

Popkin, Samuel, John W. Gorman, Charles Phillips, and Jeffrey A. Smith. 1976. Comment: What Have You Done for Me Lately? Toward an Investment Theory of Voting. *American Political Science Review* 70:779–805.

Prothro, James W., and Charles M. Grigg. 1960. Fundamental Principles of Democracy: Bases of Agreement and Disagreement. *Journal of Politics* 22:276–294.

Public Opinion Report. 1990. *Public Perspective* 1 (July/August): 81–104.

Ranney, Austin. 1962. *The Doctrine of Responsible Party Government: Its Origins and Present State.* Urbana: University of Illinois.

Rasinski, Kenneth A. 1989. The Effect of Question Wording on Public Support for Government Spending. *Public Opinion Quarterly* 53:388–394.

Rees, David. 1964. *Korea: The Limited War.* New York: St. Martin's.

Reich, Charles. 1971. *The Greening of America.* New York: Random House.

Richman, Alvin. 1972. Public Opinion and Foreign Policy: The Mediating Influence of Educational Level. In *Communications in International Politics,* ed. Richard L. Merritt, 232–251. Urbana: University of Illinois Press.

———. 1989. The Polls—a Report: American Attitudes toward Israeli-Palestinian Relations in the Wake of the Uprising. *Public Opinion Quarterly* 53:415–430.

———. 1991. The Polls—Poll Trends: Changing American Attitudes toward the Soviet Union. *Public Opinion Quarterly,* 55:133–148.

Rielly, John E., ed. 1975. *American Public Opinion and U.S. Foreign Policy, 1975.* Chicago: Chicago Council on Foreign Relations. (Also editions of 1979, 1983, 1987, and 1991.)

Rips, Geoffrey. 1981. *The Campaign against the Underground Press.* San Francisco: City Lights.

Roberts, Chalmers. 1954. The Day We Didn't Go to War. *The Reporter* 11, September 14, pp. 31–35.

Roberts, Steven V. 1988. Tapes Offer a Rare Glimpse of the Private FDR. *New York Times,* March 2, p. A18.

Robinson, John P. 1970. Public Reaction to Political Protest: Chicago, 1968. *Public Opinion Quarterly* 34:1–9.

Robinson, Michael J., and Andrew Kohut. 1988. Believability and the Press. *Public Opinion Quarterly* 52:174–189.

Rogers, Everett M., and James W. Dearing. 1988. Agenda-setting Research: Where Has It Been, Where Is It Going. In *Communication Yearbook 11*, ed. James A. Anderson, 555–594. Newbury Park, Calif.: Sage Publications.

Rogers, W. C., B. Stuhler, and D. A. Koenig. 1967. Comparisons of Informed and General Public Opinion on U.S. Foreign Policy. *Public Opinion Quarterly* 31:242—252.

Roosevelt, Franklin D. 1940. There Can Be no Appeasement with Ruthlessness. . . . We Must Be the Great Arsenal of Democracy. Fireside Chat on National Security. White House, Washington, D.C. December 29, 1940. In *The Public Papers and Addresses of Franklin D. Roosevelt*, 633–644. New York: Macmillan, 1941.

Roosevelt, Kermit. 1979. *Countercoup: The Struggle for the Control of Iran*. New York: McGraw-Hill.

Roper, Burns W. 1990. The Subtle Effects of Context. *Public Perspective* 1 (January/February): 25.

Rosenau, James N. 1961. *Public Opinion and Foreign Policy*. New York: Random House.

Rosenberg, Gerald N. 1991. *The Hollow Hope: Can Courts Bring About Social Change?* Chicago: University of Chicago Press.

Rosenberg, Milton J., Sidney Verba, and Philip E. Converse. 1970. *Vietnam and the Silent Majority: The Dove's Guide*. New York: Harper and Row.

Roshco, Bernard. 1978. The Polls: Polling on Panama—si; don't know; hell, no! *Public Opinion Quarterly* 42:551–562.

Rosi, E. J. 1965. Mass and Attentive Opinion on Nuclear Weapons Tests and Fallout, 1954–1963. *Public Opinion Quarterly* 29:280–297.

Ross, Irwin. 1968. *The Loneliest Campaign: The Truman Victory of 1948*. New York: New American Library.

Roth, Byron M. 1990. Social Psychology's "Racism." *The Public Interest* 98 (Winter): 26–36.

Rothman, Stanley, and S. Robert Lichter. 1982. The Nuclear Energy Debate: Scientists, the Media and the Public. *Public Opinion* 5 (August/September): 47–52.

———. 1987. Elite Ideology and Risk Perception in Nuclear Energy Policy. *American Political Science Review* 81:383–404.

Rousseau, Jean Jacques. 1957 [1762]. *The Social Contract*. Edited and translated by Charles Frankel. New York: Hafner.

Rovner, Mark. 1987. *Trouble at Our Doorstep: Public Attitudes and Public Policy on Central America*. Washington, D.C.: Roosevelt Center for American Policy Studies.

Russett, Bruce. 1974. The Revolt of the Masses: Public Opinion toward Military Expenditures. In *The New Civil-Military Relations*, ed. J. Lowell and P. Kronenberg. New Brunswick, N.J.: Transaction Books.

———. 1990. *Controlling the Sword: The Democratic Governance of National Security*. Cambridge, Mass.: Harvard University Press.

Russett, Bruce, and Donald R. Deluca. 1981. "Don't Tread on Me": Public Opinion and Foreign Policy in the 1980s. *Political Science Quarterly* 96:381–399.

Russett, Bruce, and Thomas W. Graham. 1989. Public Opinion and National Security Policy: Relationships and Impacts. In *Handbook of War Studies*, ed. Manus J. Midlarsky. Boston: Unwin Hyman.

Said, Edward. 1981. *Covering Islam: How the Media and the Experts Determine How We See the Rest of the World*. New York: Pantheon.

Saloma, John S., III. 1984. *Ominous Politics: The New Conservative Labyrinth*. New York: Farrar, Straus.

Sanders, Jerry W. 1983. *Peddlers of Crisis: The Committee on the Present Danger and the Politics of Containment*. Boston: South End.

Sapiro, Virginia. 1984. *The Political Integration of Women: Roles, Socialization, and Politics*. Urbana: University of Illinois Press.

Savage, James D. 1988. *Balanced Budgets and American Politics*. Ithaca: Cornell University Press.

Schattschneider, E. E. 1960. *The Semisovereign People: A Realist's View of Democracy in America*. New York: Holt.

Schelling, Thomas C. 1978. *Micromotives and Macrobehavior*. New York: Norton.

Schiller, Herbert J. 1969. *Mass Communications and American Empire*. New York: Augustus M. Kelley.

Schiltz, Michael E. 1970. *Public Attitudes toward Social Security 1935–1965*. Washington, D.C.: Government Printing Office.

Schirmer, Daniel. 1972. *Republic or Empire? American Resistance to the Philippine War*. Cambridge, Mass.: Schenkman.

Schuman, Howard, and Stanley Presser. 1977. Question Wording as an Independent Variable in Survey Analysis. *Sociological Methods and Research* 6:151–176.

———. 1981. *Questions and Answers in Attitude Surveys: Experiments on Question Form, Wording, and Context*. New York: Academic Press.

Schuman, Howard, and Jacqueline Scott. 1989. Response Effects over Time: Two Experiments. *Sociological Methods and Research* 17:398–408.

Schuman, Howard, Charlotte Steeh, and Lawrence Bobo. 1985. *Racial Attitudes in America: Trends and Interpretations*. Cambridge, Mass.: Harvard University Press.

Schumpeter, Joseph A. 1975 [1942]. *Capitalism, Socialism and Democracy*. 3d ed. New York: Harper and Row.

Schwartz, Mildred A. 1967. *Trends in White Attitudes toward Negroes*. Chicago: National Opinion Research Center.

Schwartz, Thomas. 1986. *The Logic of Collective Choice*. New York: Columbia University Press.

Schwarz, John E. 1988 [1983]. *America's Hidden Success: A Reassessment of Public Policy from Kennedy to Reagan*. Rev. ed. New York: Norton.

Scott, Jacqueline, and Howard Schuman. 1988. Attitude Strength and Social Action in the Abortion Dispute. *American Sociological Review* 53:785–793.

Scott, William A., and Stephen B. Withey. 1958. *The United States and the United Nations: The Public View*. New York: Carnegie Endowment for International Peace.

Sears, David O., and Jack Citrin. 1982. *Tax Revolt: Something for Nothing in California*. Cambridge, Mass.: Harvard University Press.

Sears, David O., Carl P. Hensler, and Leslie K. Speer. 1979. Whites' Opposition to "Busing": Self-Interest or Symbolic Politics? *American Political Science Review* 73:369–384.

Sears, David O., Richard R. Lau, Tom R. Tyler, and H. M. Allen, Jr. 1980. Self–interest vs. Symbolic Politics in Policy Attitudes and 1976 Presidential Voting. *American Political Science Review* 74:670–684.

Shapiro, Robert Y. 1982. *The Dynamics of Public Opinion and Public Policy*. Ph.D. dissertation, University of Chicago.

Shapiro, Robert Y., and Bruce M. Conforto. 1980. Presidential Performance, the Economy, and the Public's Evaluation of Economic Conditions. *Journal of Politics* 42:49–67.

Shapiro, Robert Y., and Glenn R. Dempsey. 1982. Polling the Pollsters: The Less Famous National Opinion Surveys. Unpublished paper, NORC, Chicago.

Shapiro, Robert Y., and John M. Gillroy. 1984a. The Polls: Regulation—Part I. *Public Opinion Quarterly* 48:531–542.

———. 1984b. The Polls: Regulation—Part II. *Public Opinion Quarterly* 48:666–677.

Shapiro, Robert Y., and Lawrence R. Jacobs. 1989. The Relationship between Public Opinion and Public Policy: A Review. In *Political Behavior Annual*, ed. Samuel Long, 149–179. Boulder, Colo.: Westview.

Shapiro, Robert Y., and Harpreet Mahajan. 1986. Gender Differences in Policy Preferences: A Summary of Trends from the 1960s to the 1980s. *Public Opinion Quarterly* 50:42–61.

Shapiro, Robert Y., and Benjamin I. Page. 1984. Subgroup Trends in Policy Choices: A Preliminary Report on Some Theories and Findings. Paper presented at the annual meeting of the Midwest Political Science Association, Chicago.

———. 1988. Foreign Policy and the Rational Public. *Journal of Conflict Resolution* 32:211–247.

Shapiro, Robert Y., and Kelly D. Patterson. 1986. The Dynamics of Public Opinion toward Social Welfare Policy. Paper presented at the annual meeting of the American Political Science Association, Washington, D.C.

Shapiro, Robert Y., Kelly D. Patterson, Judith Russell, and John M. Young. 1987a. The Polls: Public Assistance. *Public Opinion Quarterly* 51:120–130.

———. 1987b. The Polls: Employment and Social Welfare. *Public Opinion Quarterly* 51:268–281.

Shapiro, Robert Y., and Tom W. Smith. 1985. The Polls: Social Security. *Public Opinion Quarterly* 49:561–572.

Shapiro, Robert Y., and John M. Young. 1986. The Polls: Medical Care in the United States. *Public Opinion Quarterly* 50:418–428.

———. 1989. Public Opinion and the Welfare State: The United States in Comparative Perspective. *Political Science Quarterly* 104:59–89.

Shapiro, Robert Y., John T. Young, Kelly D. Patterson, Jill E. Blumenfeld, Sara M. Offenhartz, and Ted. E. Tsekerides. 1990a. Media Influences on Candidate Support in Primary Elections. Paper presented at the 1990 annual meeting of the World Association for Public Opinion Research, Lancaster, Pa.

Shapiro, Robert Y., John T. Young, Kelly D. Patterson, Jill E. Blumenthal, Steve Farkas, Sara Offenhartz, and Ted E. Tsekerides. 1990b. The Impact of the Media on Candidate Support in Presidential Primary and General Elections. Paper presented at the annual meeting of the American Political Science Association, San Francisco.

Shawcross, William. 1979. *Sideshow: Kissinger, Nixon, and the Destruction of Cambodia*. New York: Simon and Schuster.

Sheatsley, Paul. 1966. White Attitudes toward the Negro. *Daedalus* 95:217–237.

Shoemaker, Pamela J. 1982. The Perceived Legitimacy of Deviant Political Groups: Two Experiments on Media Effects. *Communications Research* 9:249–286.

Shoup, Laurence H. 1980. *The Carter Presidency and Beyond: Power and Politics in the 1980s*. Palo Alto, Calif.: Ramparts.

Shoup, Laurence H., and William Minter. 1977. *Imperial Brain Trust: The Council on Foreign Relations and United States Foreign Policy*. New York: Monthly Review Press.

Sigal, Leon V. 1973. *Reporters and Officials: The Organization and Politics of Newsmaking*. Lexington, Mass.: D. C. Heath.

Sigelman, Lee, and Pamela Johnston Conover. 1981. The Dynamics of Presidential Support during International Conflict Situations: The Iranian Hostage Crisis. *Political Behavior* 3:303–318.

Simon, Rita James. 1974. *Public Opinion in America: 1936–1970*. Chicago: Rand McNally.

Simon, Rita J., and Jean M. Landis. 1989. The Polls—a Report: Women's and Men's Attitudes about a Woman's Place and Role. *Public Opinion Quarterly* 53:265–276.

Singer, Eleanor, Theresa F. Rogers, and Mary Corcoran. 1987. The Polls—a Report: AIDS. *Public Opinion Quarterly* 51:580–595.

Sklar, Holly, ed. 1980. *Trilateralism: The Trilateral Commission and Elite Planning for World Management.* Boston: South End.

Small, Melvin. 1974. How We Learned to Love the Russians: American Media and the Soviet Union during World War II. *The Historian* 36 (May): 455–478.

Smith, A. Wade. 1982. White Attitudes toward School Desegregation, 1954–1980: An Update on Continuing Trends. *Pacific Sociological Review* 25:3–25.

Smith, Eric R. A. N. 1989. *The Unchanging American Voter.* Berkeley: University of California Press.

Smith, Paul A. 1961. Opinion Publics and World Affairs in the United States. *Western Political Quarterly* 14:698–714.

Smith, Ted J., III, and J. Michael Hogan. 1985. Public Opinion and the Panama Canal Treaties of 1977: A Critical Analysis. Paper presented at the annual meeting of the American Association for Public Opinion Research, McAfee, N.J.

———. 1987. Public Opinion and the Panama Canal Treaties of 1977. *Public Opinion Quarterly* 51:5–30.

Smith, Tom W. 1978. In Search of House Effects: A Comparison of Responses to Various Questions by Different Survey Organizations. *Public Opinion Quarterly* 42:443–463.

———. 1980a. America's Most Important Problem: A Trend Analysis 1946–1976. *Public Opinion Quarterly* 44:164–180.

———. 1980b. The 75% Solution: An Analysis of the Structure of Attitudes on Gun Control, 1959–1977. *Journal of Criminal Law and Criminology* 71:300–316.

———. 1982a. Educated Don't Knows: An Analysis of the Relationship between Education and Item Nonresponse. *Political Methodology* 8:47–57.

———. 1982b. General Liberalism and Social Change in Post World War II America: A Summary of Trends. *Social Indicators Research* 10:1–28.

———. 1984. The Polls: Gender and Attitudes toward Violence. *Public Opinion Quarterly* 48:384–96.

———. 1987. That which We Call Welfare by Any Other Name Would Smell Sweeter: An Analysis of the Impact of Question Wording on Response Patterns. *Public Opinion Quarterly* 51:75–83.

———. 1989. Liberal and Conservative Trends in the United States since World War II. GSS Social Change Report no. 29. Chicago: NORC.

———. 1990a. Jewish Attitudes toward Blacks and Race Relations. *Jewish Sociology Papers.* New York: American Jewish Committee.

———. 1990b. The Polls—a Report: National Service. *Public Opinion Quarterly* 54:273–285.

———. 1990c. The Polls—a Report: The Sexual Revolution? *Public Opinion Quarterly* 54:415–435.

Smith, Tom W., and Bradley J. Arnold. 1990. *Annotated Bibliography of Papers Using the General Social Surveys.* 8th ed. Chicago: NORC.

Smith, Tom W., with Guy J. Rich. 1980. *A Compendium of Trends on General Social Survey Questions.* NORC Report no. 129. Chicago: NORC.

Smith, Tom W., and Paul B. Sheatsley. 1984. American Attitudes toward Race Relations. *Public Opinion* 7 (October/November): 14–15, 50–53.

Snepp, Frank. 1977. *Decent Interval: An Insider's Account of Saigon's Indecent End Told by the CIA's Chief Strategy Analyst in Vietnam.* New York: Random House.

Sniderman, Paul M. 1975. *Personality and Democratic Politics.* Berkeley: University of California Press.

Sniderman, Paul M., and Richard A. Brody. 1977. Coping: The Ethics of Self-Reliance. *American Journal of Political Science* 21:501–521.

Sniderman, Paul M., and Michael Gray Hagen. 1985. *Race and Inequality: A Study in American Values.* Chatham, N.J.: Chatham House.

Sniderman, Paul M., and Philip E. Tetlock. 1986. Interrelationships of Political Ideology and Public Opinion. In *Political Psychology*, ed. Margaret E. Hermann, 62–96. San Francisco: Jossey-Bass.

Sobel, Richard. 1989. The Polls—a Report: Public Opinion about United States Intervention in El Salvador and Nicaragua. *Public Opinion Quarterly* 53:114–128.

Soley, Lawrence C. 1989. The News Shapers: The Individuals Who Explain the News. Unpublished paper, School of Journalism, University of Minnesota.

Stanley, Harold W., and Richard G. Niemi. 1990. *Vital Statistics on American Politics*. 2d ed. Washington, D.C.: Congressional Quarterly Press.

Steel, Ronald. 1980. *Walter Lippmann and the American Century*. Boston: Little, Brown.

Steele, A. J. 1966. *The American People and China*. New York: McGraw-Hill.

Steele, Richard W. 1985a. News of the "Good War": World War II News Management. *Journalism Quarterly* (Winter): 707–716, 783.

———. 1985b. *Propaganda in an Open Society: The Roosevelt Administration and the Media, 1933–1941*. Westport, Conn.: Greenwood.

Steiner, Gilbert V. 1985. *Constitutional Inequality: The Political Fortunes of the Equal Rights Amendment*. Washington, D.C.: Brookings.

Stember, Charles H. 1961. *Education and Attitude Change*. New York: Institute of Human Relations Press.

Sternthal, Brian, Lynn W. Phillips, and Ruby Dholakia. 1978. The Persuasive Effects of Source Credibility: A Situational Analysis. *Public Opinion Quarterly* 42:285–314.

Stigler, George. 1971. The Theory of Economic Regulation. *Bell Journal of Economics and Management Science* 2:3–21.

Stinchcombe, Arthur L., Rebecca Adams, Carol A. Heimer, Kim Lane Scheppele, Tom W. Smith, and D. Garth Taylor. 1980. *Crime and Punishment: Changing Attitudes in America*. San Francisco: Jossey-Bass.

Stipp, Horst, and Dennis Kerr. 1989. Determinants of Public Opinion about AIDS. *Public Opinion Quarterly* 53:98–106.

Stockman, David A. 1986. *The Triumph of Politics: How the Reagan Revolution Failed*. New York: Harper.

Stockwell, John. 1978. *In Search of Enemies: A CIA Story*. New York: Norton.

Stone, I. F. 1970. Theater of Delusion. *New York Review of Books*, April 23, pp. 15–24.

Stouffer, Samuel A. 1955. *Communism, Conformity, and Civil Liberties*. New York: Doubleday.

Sullivan, John L., James E. Piereson, and George E. Marcus. 1978. Ideological Constraints in the Mass Public: A Methodological Critique and Some New Findings. *American Journal of Political Science* 22:234–49.

———. 1982. *Political Tolerance and American Democracy*. Chicago: University of Chicago Press.

Sullivan, John L., Michael Shamir, Patrick Walsh, and Nigel S. Walsh. 1985. *Political Tolerance in Context: Support for Unpopular Minorities in Israel, New Zealand, and the United States*. Boulder, Colo.: Westview.

Sussman, Barry. 1988. *What Americans Really Think and Why Our Politicians Pay No Attention*. New York: Pantheon.

Talbott, Strobe. 1984. *Deadly Gambits: The Reagan Administration and the Stalemate in Nuclear Arms Control*. New York: Random House.

Tatalovich, Raymond. 1988. Abortion: Prochoice versus Prolife. In Tatalovich and Daynes 1988, pp. 177–209.

Tatalovich, Raymond, and Byron W. Daynes. 1981. *The Politics of Abortion: A Study of Community Conflict in Public Policymaking*. New York: Praeger.

———. 1988. *Social Regulatory Policy: Moral Controversies in American Politics*. Boulder, Colo.: Westview.

Taylor, D. Garth. 1978. *The Diffusion and Change of Public Attitudes toward Some Social Issues in Recent American History*. Ph.D. dissertation, University of Chicago.

———. 1980. Procedures for Evaluating Trends in Public Opinion. *Public Opinion Quarterly* 44:86–100.

———. 1981. American Politics, Public Opinion, and Social Security Financing. In *Social Security Financing*, ed. Felicity Skidmore. Cambridge, Mass.: M.I.T. Press.

Taylor, D. Garth, Paul B. Sheatsley, and Andrew Greeley. 1978. Attitudes toward Racial Integration. *Scientific American* 238:42–51.

Terchek, Ronald J. 1970. *The Making of the Test Ban Treaty*. The Hague, Netherlands: Martinus Nijhoff.

Tichenor, P. J., G. A. Donahue, and C. N. Olien. 1970. Mass Media Flow and Differential Growth in Knowledge. *Public Opinion Quarterly* 34:159–170.

Truman, David B. 1971. *The Governmental Process*. 2d ed. New York: Knopf.

Truman, Harry S. 1947. The Truman Doctrine. Message to Congress, March 12, 1947. In *Documents of American History*, ed. Henry Steele Commager. New York: Appleton-Century-Crofts.

Tuchfarber, A. J., Oldendick, R. W., and Bishop, G. F. 1984. Citizen Attitudes toward Taxation and Spending: Inconsistent Answers or the Wrong Questions? Paper presented at the annual meeting of the American Political Science Association.

Tuchman, Gaye. 1978. *Making News: A Study in the Construction of Reality*. New York: Free Press.

Tufte, Edward R. 1983. *The Visual Display of Quantitative Information*. Cheshire, Conn.: Graphics Press.

Tulis, Jeffrey. 1987. *The Rhetorical Presidency*. Princeton: Princeton University Press.

Turner, Kathleen. 1985. *Johnson's Dual War: Vietnam and the Press*. Chicago: University of Chicago Press.

U.S. 1987. *Report of the President's Special Review Board*. (The "Tower Commission" report). Washington, D.C.: Government Printing Office.

U.S. Congress. 1961. *Freedom of Communications*. Final Report of the Committee on Commerce, United States Senate, 87th Congress, 1st Sess. Part I.

U.S. Congress. 1987. *Report of the Congressional Committees Investigating the Iran-Contra Affair*. Washington, D.C.: Government Printing Office.

U.S. Department of Defense, Comptroller. 1972. Unclassified Statistics on Southeast Asia. In *The Air War in Indochina*, ed. Raphael Littauer and Norman Uphoff. Rev. ed. 267–272. Boston: Beacon.

U.S. President. 1989. *Economic Report of the President*. Washington, D.C.: Government Printing Office.

U.S. Senate. Select Committee to Study Government Operations with Respect to Intelligence Activities. 1975. *Alleged Assassination Plots Involving Foreign Leaders*. (The "Church Committee" interim report). Washington, D.C.: Government Printing Office.

Verba, Sidney, and Gary Orren. 1985. *Equality in America: The View from the Top*. Cambridge, Mass.: Harvard University Press.

Wade, Nicholas. 1983. Editorial Notebook: The Embarrassment of "Yellow Rain." *New York Times*, November 27, p. 22.

Walker, Jack L. 1966. A Critique of the Elitist Theory of Democracy. *American Political Science Review* 60:285–295.

Walsh, Warren B. 1944–1945. What the American People Think of Russia. *Public Opinion Quarterly* 8:513–522.

———. 1947. American Attitudes toward Russia. *Antioch Review* 7:183–190.

Weil, Frederick L. 1985. The Variable Effects of Education on Liberal Attitudes: A Comparative-Historical Analysis of Antisemitism Using Public Opinion Data. *American Sociological Review* 50:458–474.

————. 1989. The Sources and Structure of Legitimation in Western Democracies: A Consolidated Model Tested with Time-Series Data in Six Countries since World War II. *American Sociological Review* 54:682–706.

Weissberg, Robert. 1976. *Public Opinion and Popular Government*. Englewood Cliffs, N.J.: Prentice-Hall.

Welch, Susan. 1972. The American Press and Indochina, 1950–1956. In *Communication in International Politics*, ed. Richard L. Merritt. Urbana: University of Illinois Press.

————. 1985. The "More for Less" Paradox: Public Attitudes on Taxes and Spending. *Public Opinion Quarterly* 49:310–316.

Wells, Samuel. 1979. Sounding the Tocsin: NSC 68 and the Soviet Threat. *International Security* (Fall): 116–158.

West, Darrell M. 1991. Television and Presidential Popularity in America. *British Journal of Political Science*, 21:199–214.

Wheeler, Michael. 1976. *Lies, Damn Lies, and Statistics: The Manipulation of Public Opinion in America*. New York: Liveright.

White, Graham J. 1979. *FDR and the Press*. Chicago: University of Chicago Press.

Wilcox, Clyde. 1990. Race Differences in Abortion Attitudes: Some Additional Evidence. *Public Opinion Quarterly* 54:248–55.

Wilensky, Harold L. 1975. *The Welfare State and Equality: Structure and Ideological Roots of Public Expenditures*. Berkeley: University of California Press.

Williams, William A. 1959. *The Tragedy of American Diplomacy*. Cleveland: World.

Wilson, Woodrow. 1952 [1890]. *Leaders of Men*, ed. T. H. Vail Motter. Princeton: Princeton University Press.

Windchy, Eugene G. 1971. *Tonkin Gulf*. New York: Doubleday.

Winfield, Betty Houchen. 1984. The New Deal Publicity Operation: Foundation for the Modern Presidency. *Journalism Quarterly* 61 (Spring): 40–48.

Wirls, Donald. 1986. Reinterpreting the Gender Gap. *Public Opinion Quarterly* 50:316–30.

Wise, David. 1973. *The Politics of Lying: Government Deception, Secrecy, and Power*. New York: Random House.

Wise, David and Thomas B. Ross. 1964. *The Invisible Government*. New York: Random House.

Wittkopf, Eugene R. 1990. *Faces of Internationalism: American Public Opinion and Foreign Policy*. Durham, N.C.: Duke University Press.

Wittman, Donald A. 1973. Parties as Utility Maximizers. *American Political Science Review* 67:490–498.

————. 1989. Why Democracies Produce Efficient Results. *Journal of Political Economy* 97 (6): 1395–1424.

Wittner, Lawrence S. 1982. *American Intervention in Greece, 1943–1949*. New York: Columbia University Press.

Wright, Erik Olin, and Luca Perrone. 1977. Marxist Class Categories and Income Inequality. *American Sociological Review* 42:32–55.

Wright, Gerald, Jr. 1977. Race and Welfare Policy in America. *Social Science Quarterly* 57 (March): 718–730.

Wright, Gerald C., Jr., Robert S. Erikson, and John P. McIver. 1987. Public Opinion and Policy Liberalism in the American States. *American Journal of Political Science* 31:980–1001.

Wu, Chenghuan, and David R. Shaffer. 1987. Susceptibility to Persuasive Appeals as a Function of Source Credibility and Prior Experience With the Attitude Object. *Journal of Personality and Social Psychology* 52:677–688.

Wyden, Peter. 1979. *Bay of Pigs: The Untold Story*. New York: Simon and Schuster.

Yankelovich, Skelly, and White, Inc. 1985. *A Fifty-year Report Card on the Social Security System: The Attitudes of the American Public*.

Yergin, Daniel. 1977. *Shattered Peace: The Origins of the Cold War and the National Security State*. Boston: Houghton Mifflin.

Young, Richard P. 1979. *Societal Change and the Evolution of American Race Relations*. Ph.D. dissertation, Stanford University.

Zaller, John. 1987. The Diffusion of Political Attitudes. *Journal of Personality and Social Psychology* 53:821–833.

———. 1990a. Bringing Converse Back In: Modifying Information Flow in Political Campaigns. In *Political Analysis*, ed. James A. Stimson, 1:181–234. Ann Arbor: University of Michigan Press.

———. 1990b. Political Awareness, Elite Opinion Leadership, and the Mass Survey Response. *Social Cognition*, 8(1): 125–153.

Zaller, John, and Stanley Feldman. 1988. Answering Questions vs. Revealing Preferences: A Simple Theory of the Survey Response. Paper presented at the annual meeting of the Political Methodology Society.

———. 1989. An Experimental Attempt to Reduce Measurement Error. Memo to Members of the National Election Studies Board of Overseers. University of California, Los Angeles.

Index

Political Science

Drawing on an enormous body of research, Benjamin I. Page and Robert Y. Shapiro provide the richest available portrait of the political views of Americans, from the 1930s to 1990. Their comprehensive critical survey of the policy preferences of the American public covers all types of domestic and foreign policy issues, and considers how opinions vary by age, gender, race, region, and other factors.

"The Rational Public seeks definitive answers to questions which have troubled a generation of scholars concerning the rationality of the American electorate. This substantial volume, the work of years of research and reflection, offers the most persuasive resolution to the controversy that we are likely to see in our time. In the process, Page and Shapiro provide a detailed, carefully charted, and elegantly executed history of American public opinion over more than half a century.

"There is a longstanding argument that it is rational for individuals to invest little time in acquiring political knowledge; Page and Shapiro nevertheless overwhelmingly demonstrate that at the *collective* level, public opinion displays impressive characteristics of stability, rational responsiveness to concrete political situations, and the capacity to adapt as new issues become available and change the contours of these situations.

"The Rational Public is required reading for any scholar or journalist who deals with American public opinion."
—Walter Dean Burnham, University of Texas, Austin

"The Rational Public is especially noteworthy in its efforts to link the opinions of the citizenry with the real world of politics that acts upon and is acted upon by those opinions. This book will rank with The American Voter and The Changing American Voter as milestones in the study of American public opinion."
—Morris Fiorina, Harvard University

Benjamin I. Page, the Gordon Scott Fulcher Professor of Decision Making at Northwestern University, is the author of several books, including Who Gets What From Government. Robert Y. Shapiro is associate professor of political science at Columbia University.

American Politics and Political Economy series

The University of Chicago Press

ISBN 0-226-64478-2

9 780226 644783

90000>

Cover photo: Ted Lacey